ULTIMATE SPIDER-MAN

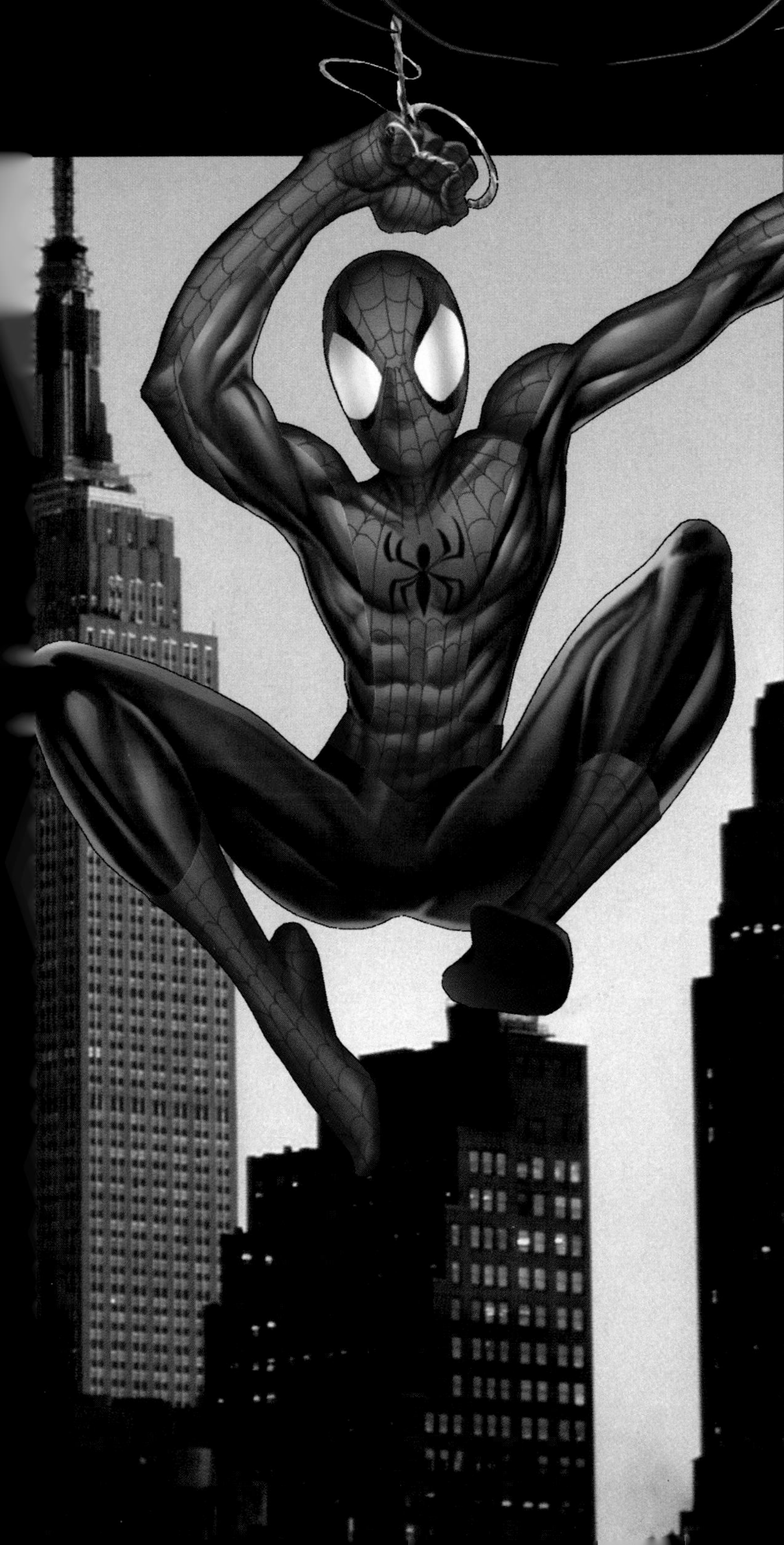

STORY
BILL JEMAS &
BRIAN MICHAEL
BENDIS

SCRIPT
BRIAN MICHAEL
BENDIS

PENCILS
MARK BAGLEY

INKS
ART THIBERT

COVER ART
JOE QUESADA

COLORS
TRANSPARENCY DIGITAL,
STEVE BUCCELLATO,
MARIE JAVINS &
COLORGRAPHIX

LETTERS
RICHARD STARKINGS &
COMICRAFT

ASSOCIATE EDITOR
BRIAN SMITH

COLLECTIONS EDITOR
MATTY RYAN

EDITOR
RALPH MACCHIO

EDITOR IN CHIEF
JOE QUESADA

PRESIDENT & INSPIRATION
BILL JEMAS

SPECIAL THANKS TO
MIKE FARAH, PATRICK
MCGRATH, CAMILLE
MURPHY, CORY PETIT, CORY
SEDLMEIER & JEOF VITA

MASTHEAD

MANAGING EDITOR
David Bogart
PRODUCTION DIRECTOR
Dan Carr
SENIOR MANUFACTURING MANAGER
Fred Pagan
PUBLISHING BUSINESS MANAGER
Chet Krayewski
MARKETING COMMUNICATIONS MANAGER
Bill Rosemann

ADVERTISING—PROMOTION—RETAIL SALES

SR. VICE PRESIDENT/ CONSUMER PRODUCTS, PROMOTIONS, AND MEDIA SALES
Russell A. Brown
VICE PRESIDENT/RETAIL SALES
Matt Ragone
DIRECT SALES/MASS MARKET SALES MANAGER
Fletcher Chu-Fong
DIRECT RESPONSE MANAGER
Tina Christman
ADVERTISING SALES
Sara Beth Schrager

MARVEL ENTERPRISES, INC.

CHIEF EXECUTIVE OFFICER
Peter Cuneo
CHIEF CREATIVE OFFICER
Avi Arad
CHIEF INFORMATION OFFICER
Gui Karyo
PRESIDENT CEO, TOY BIZ
Alan Fine
EXECUTIVE V.P.-BUSINESS & LEGAL AFFAIRS
Allen Lipson
EXECUTIVE SALES V.P.-TOY BIZ
Ralph Lancelotti
VICE PRESIDENT-PURCHASING
Avi Katoni
V.P.-HUMAN RESOURCES
Mary Sprowls

CONTENTS

CHAPTERS

1 POWERLESS

2 GROWING PAINS

3 WANNABE

4 WITH GREAT RESPONSIBILITY

5 LIFE LESSONS

6 BIG TIME SUPERHERO

7 REVELATIONS

8 WORKING STIFF

9 MEET THE ENFORCERS

10 THE WORST THING

11 DISCOVERY

12 BATTLE ROYAL

13 CONFESSIONS

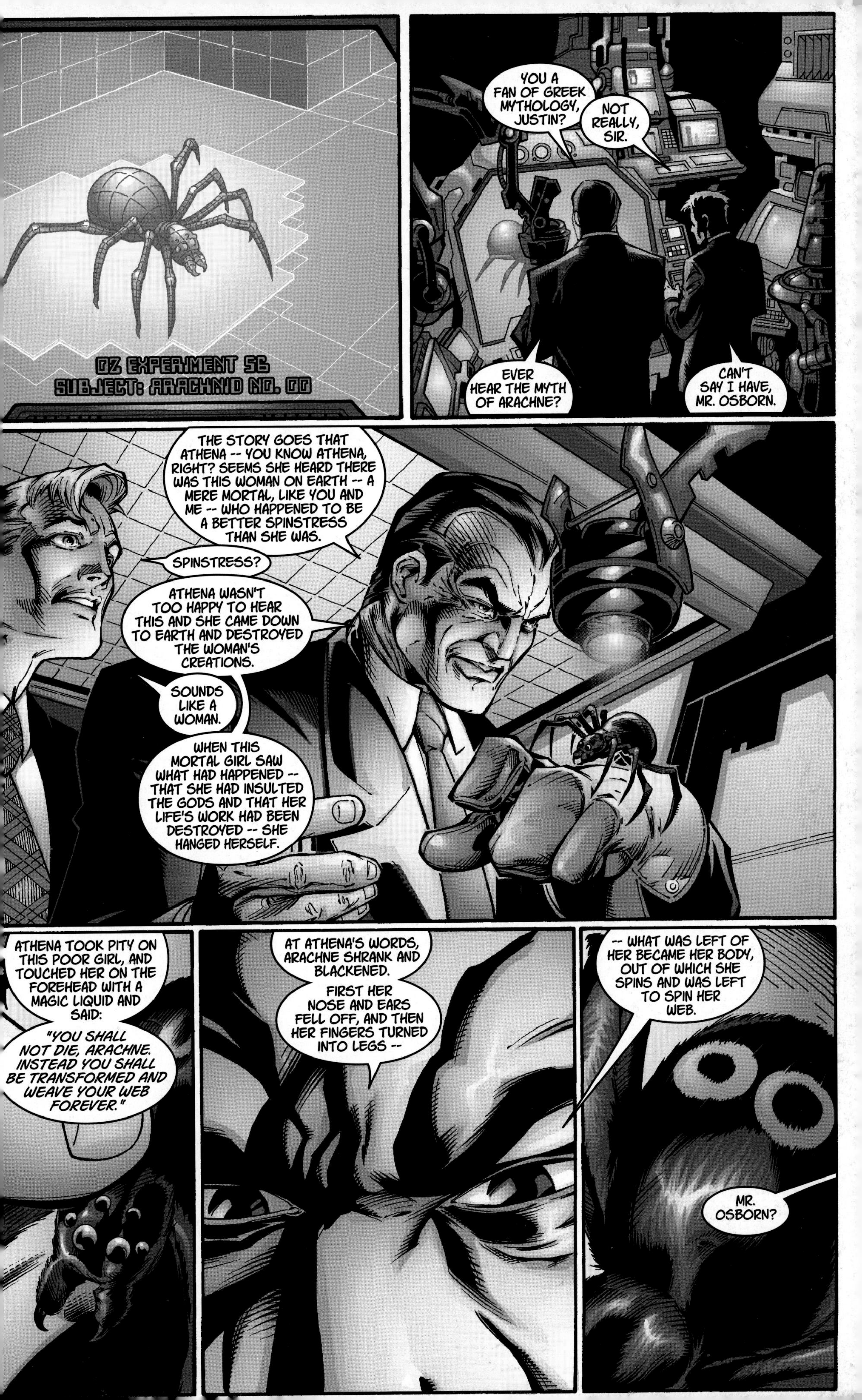
OZ EXPERIMENT 56
SUBJECT: ARACHNID NO. 00
YOU A FAN OF GREEK MYTHOLOGY, JUSTIN?
NOT REALLY, SIR.
EVER HEAR THE MYTH OF ARACHNE?
CAN'T SAY I HAVE, MR. OSBORN.
THE STORY GOES THAT ATHENA -- YOU KNOW ATHENA, RIGHT? SEEMS SHE HEARD THERE WAS THIS WOMAN ON EARTH -- A MERE MORTAL, LIKE YOU AND ME -- WHO HAPPENED TO BE A BETTER SPINSTRESS THAN SHE WAS.
SPINSTRESS?
ATHENA WASN'T TOO HAPPY TO HEAR THIS AND SHE CAME DOWN TO EARTH AND DESTROYED THE WOMAN'S CREATIONS.
SOUNDS LIKE A WOMAN.
WHEN THIS MORTAL GIRL SAW WHAT HAD HAPPENED -- THAT SHE HAD INSULTED THE GODS AND THAT HER LIFE'S WORK HAD BEEN DESTROYED -- SHE HANGED HERSELF.
ATHENA TOOK PITY ON THIS POOR GIRL, AND TOUCHED HER ON THE FOREHEAD WITH A MAGIC LIQUID AND SAID:
"YOU SHALL NOT DIE, ARACHNE. INSTEAD YOU SHALL BE TRANSFORMED AND WEAVE YOUR WEB FOREVER."
AT ATHENA'S WORDS, ARACHNE SHRANK AND BLACKENED.
FIRST HER NOSE AND EARS FELL OFF, AND THEN HER FINGERS TURNED INTO LEGS --
-- WHAT WAS LEFT OF HER BECAME HER BODY, OUT OF WHICH SHE SPINS AND WAS LEFT TO SPIN HER WEB.
MR. OSBORN?

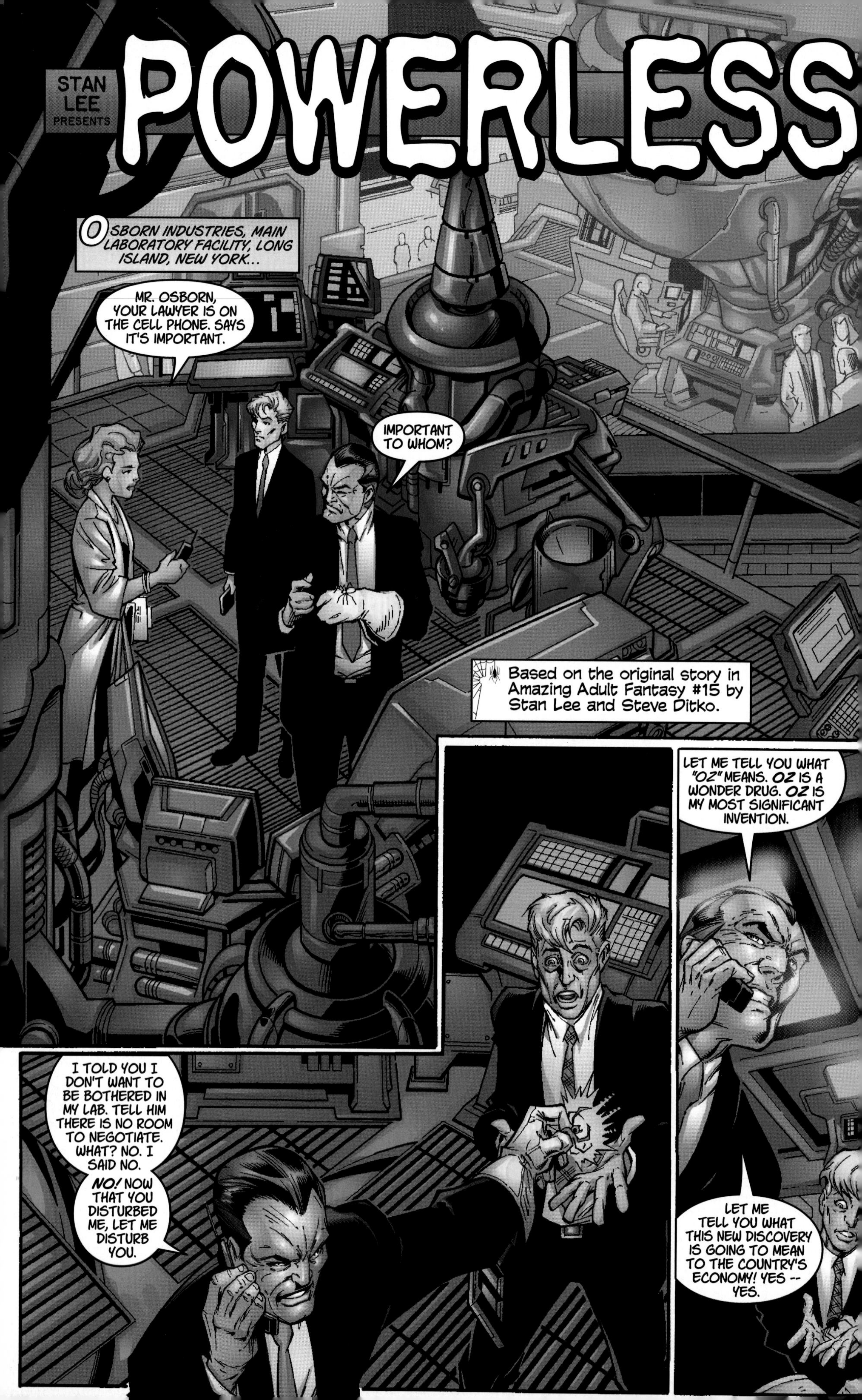
STAN LEE PRESENTS
POWERLESS
OSBORN INDUSTRIES, MAIN LABORATORY FACILITY, LONG ISLAND, NEW YORK...
MR. OSBORN, YOUR LAWYER IS ON THE CELL PHONE. SAYS IT'S IMPORTANT.
IMPORTANT TO WHOM?
Based on the original story in Amazing Adult Fantasy #15 by Stan Lee and Steve Ditko.
LET ME TELL YOU WHAT "OZ" MEANS. OZ IS A WONDER DRUG. OZ IS MY MOST SIGNIFICANT INVENTION.
I TOLD YOU I DON'T WANT TO BE BOTHERED IN MY LAB. TELL HIM THERE IS NO ROOM TO NEGOTIATE. WHAT? NO. I SAID NO.
NO! NOW THAT YOU DISTURBED ME, LET ME DISTURB YOU.
LET ME TELL YOU WHAT THIS NEW DISCOVERY IS GOING TO MEAN TO THE COUNTRY'S ECONOMY! YES -- YES.

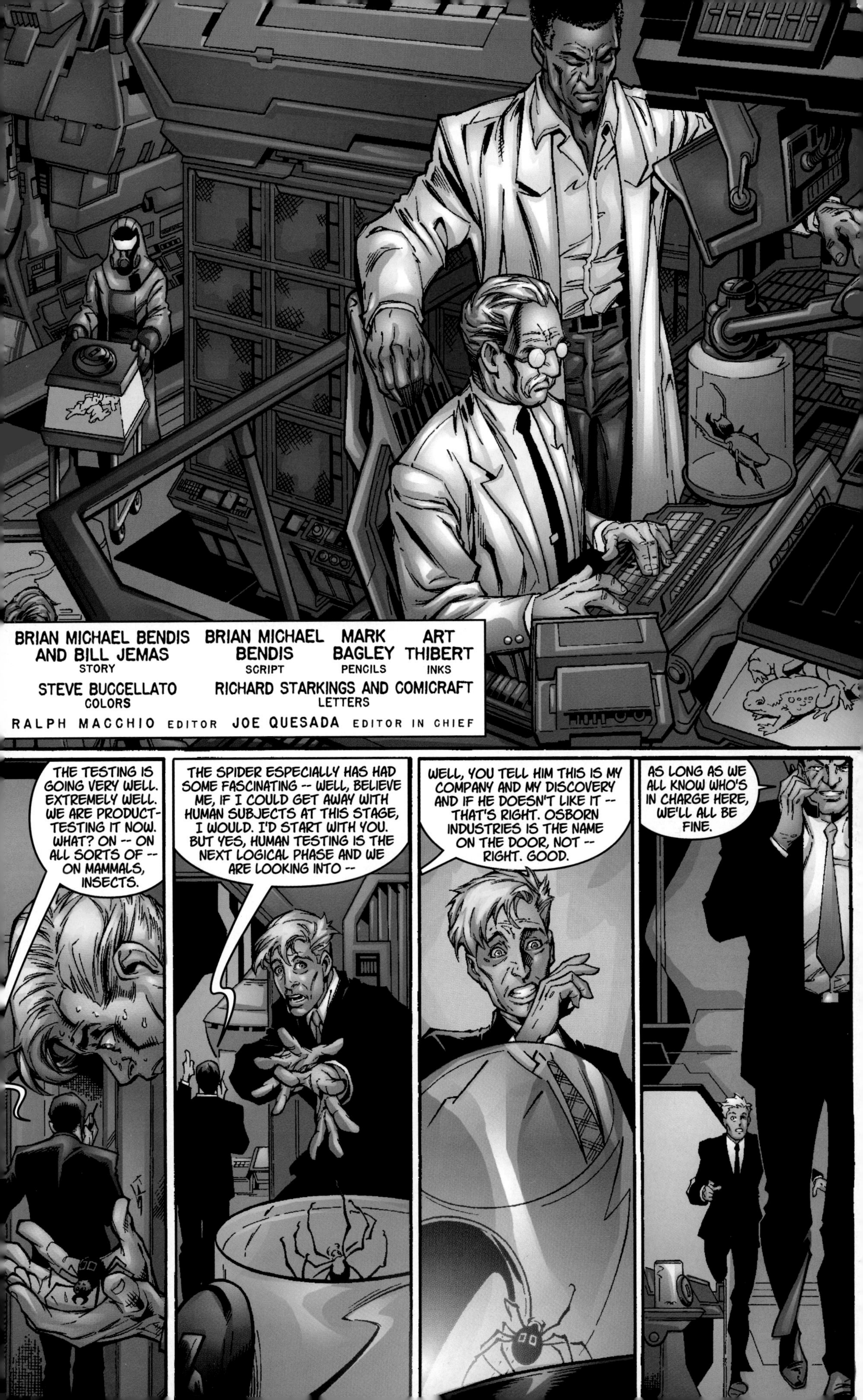
BRIAN MICHAEL BENDIS AND BILL JEMAS
STORY
BRIAN MICHAEL BENDIS
SCRIPT
MARK BAGLEY
PENCILS
ART THIBERT
INKS
STEVE BUCCELLATO
COLORS
RICHARD STARKINGS AND COMICRAFT
LETTERS
RALPH MACCHIO EDITOR JOE QUESADA EDITOR IN CHIEF
THE TESTING IS GOING VERY WELL. EXTREMELY WELL. WE ARE PRODUCT-TESTING IT NOW. WHAT? ON -- ON ALL SORTS OF -- ON MAMMALS, INSECTS.
THE SPIDER ESPECIALLY HAS HAD SOME FASCINATING -- WELL, BELIEVE ME, IF I COULD GET AWAY WITH HUMAN SUBJECTS AT THIS STAGE, I WOULD. I'D START WITH YOU. BUT YES, HUMAN TESTING IS THE NEXT LOGICAL PHASE AND WE ARE LOOKING INTO --
WELL, YOU TELL HIM THIS IS MY COMPANY AND MY DISCOVERY AND IF HE DOESN'T LIKE IT -- THAT'S RIGHT. OSBORN INDUSTRIES IS THE NAME ON THE DOOR, NOT -- RIGHT. GOOD.
AS LONG AS WE ALL KNOW WHO'S IN CHARGE HERE, WE'LL ALL BE FINE.

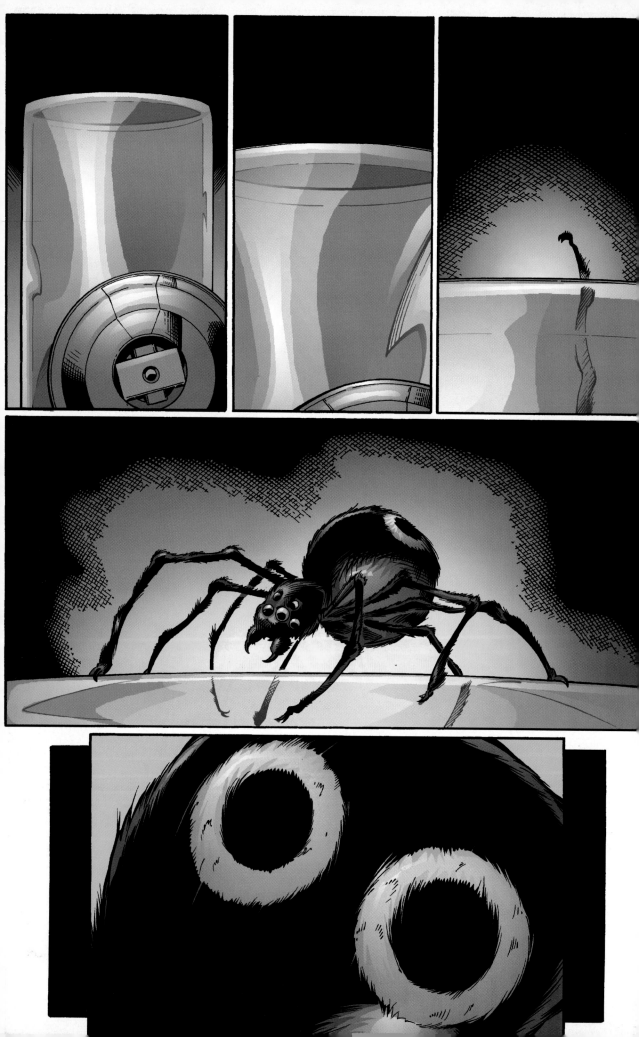

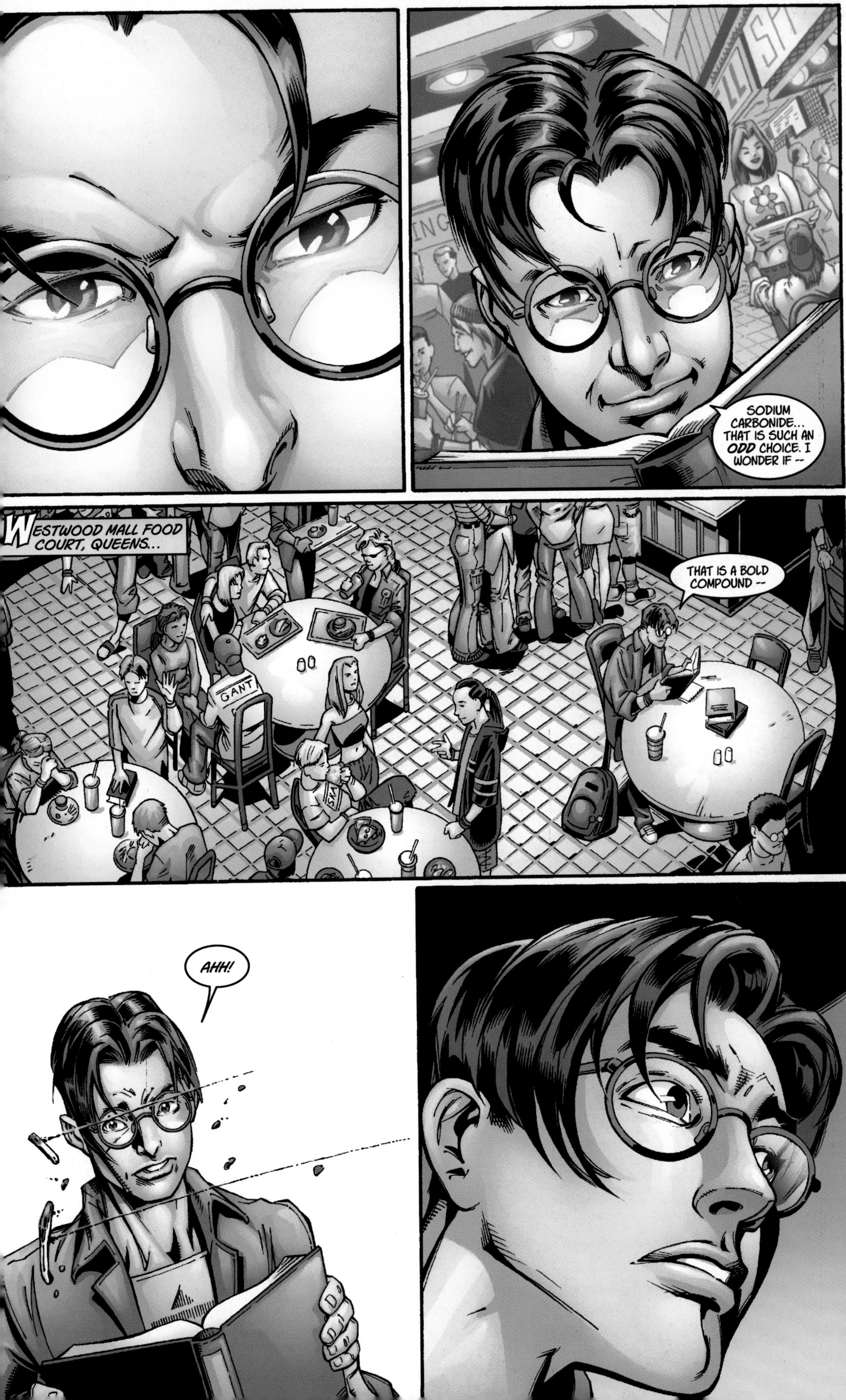
SODIUM CARBONIDE... THAT IS SUCH AN ODD CHOICE. I WONDER IF --
WESTWOOD MALL FOOD COURT, QUEENS...
THAT IS A BOLD COMPOUND --
AHH!

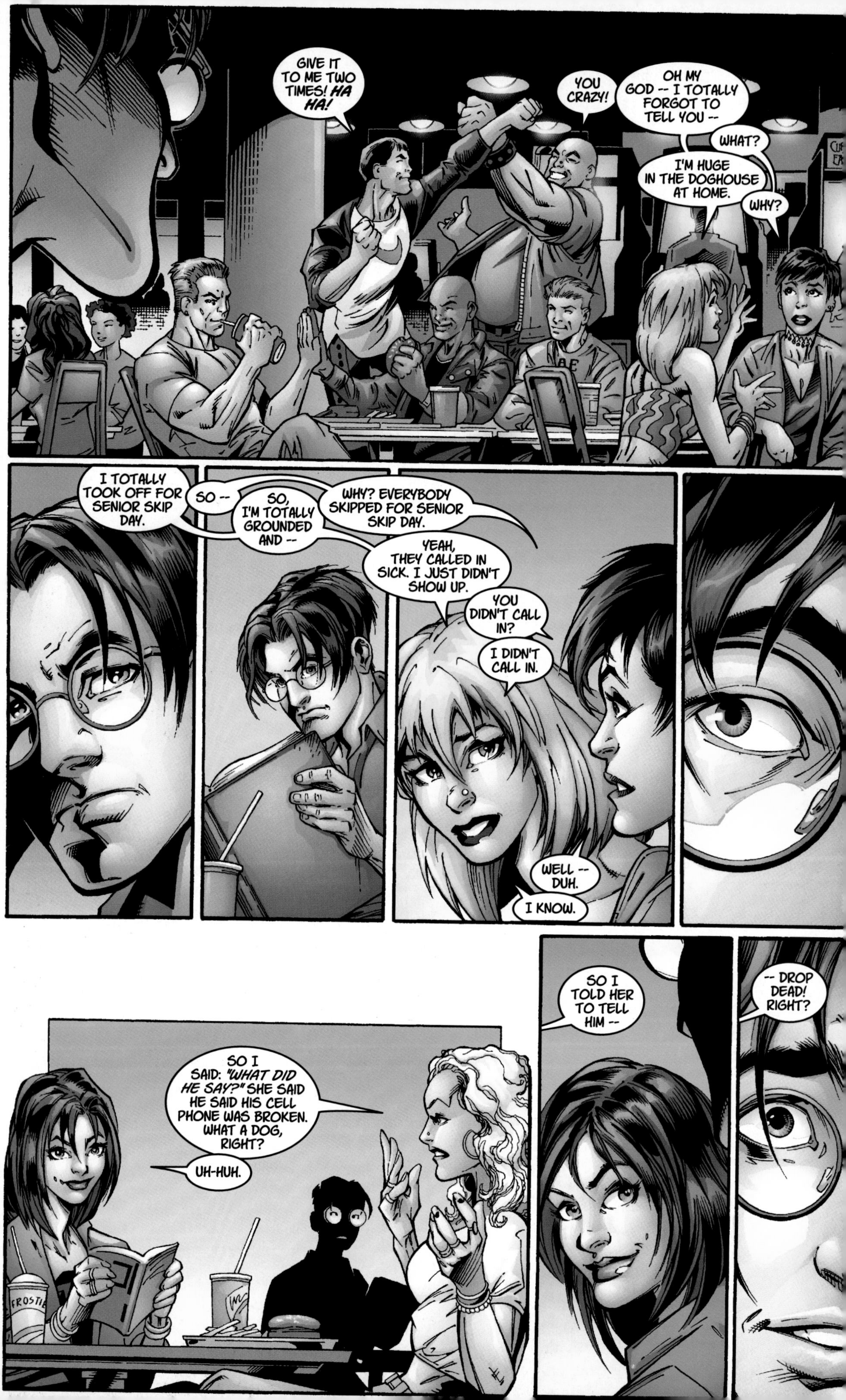
GIVE IT TO ME TWO TIMES! HA HA!
YOU CRAZY!
OH MY GOD -- I TOTALLY FORGOT TO TELL YOU --
WHAT?
I'M HUGE IN THE DOGHOUSE AT HOME.
WHY?
I TOTALLY TOOK OFF FOR SENIOR SKIP DAY.
SO --
SO, I'M TOTALLY GROUNDED AND --
WHY? EVERYBODY SKIPPED FOR SENIOR SKIP DAY.
YEAH, THEY CALLED IN SICK. I JUST DIDN'T SHOW UP.
YOU DIDN'T CALL IN?
I DIDN'T CALL IN.
WELL -- DUH.
I KNOW.
SO I SAID: "WHAT DID HE SAY?" SHE SAID HE SAID HIS CELL PHONE WAS BROKEN. WHAT A DOG, RIGHT?
UH-HUH.
SO I TOLD HER TO TELL HIM --
-- DROP DEAD! RIGHT?

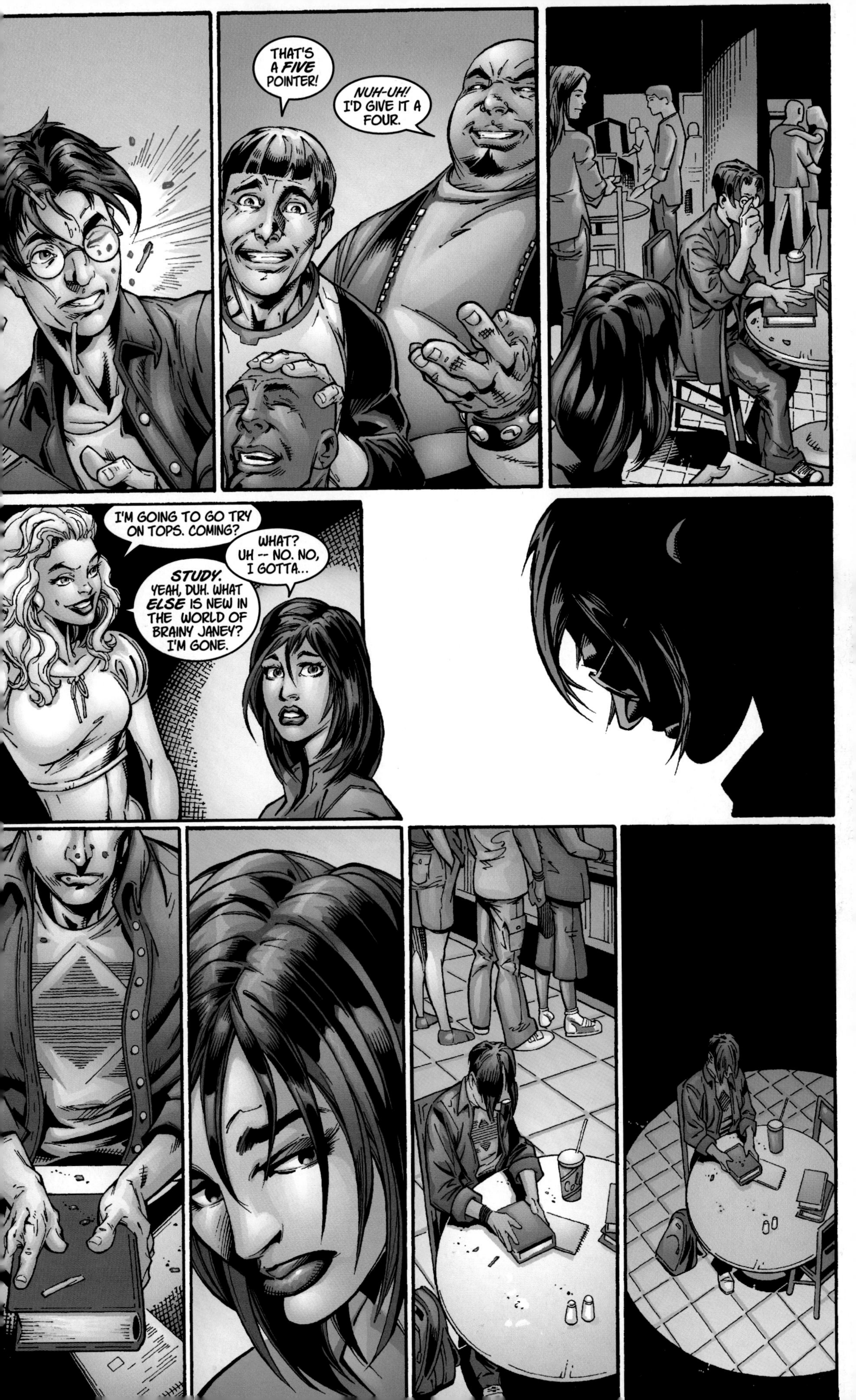
THAT'S A *FIVE* POINTER!
NUH-UH! I'D GIVE IT A FOUR.
I'M GOING TO GO TRY ON TOPS. COMING?
WHAT? UH -- NO. NO, I GOTTA...
STUDY. YEAH, DUH. WHAT *ELSE* IS NEW IN THE WORLD OF BRAINY JANEY? I'M GONE.

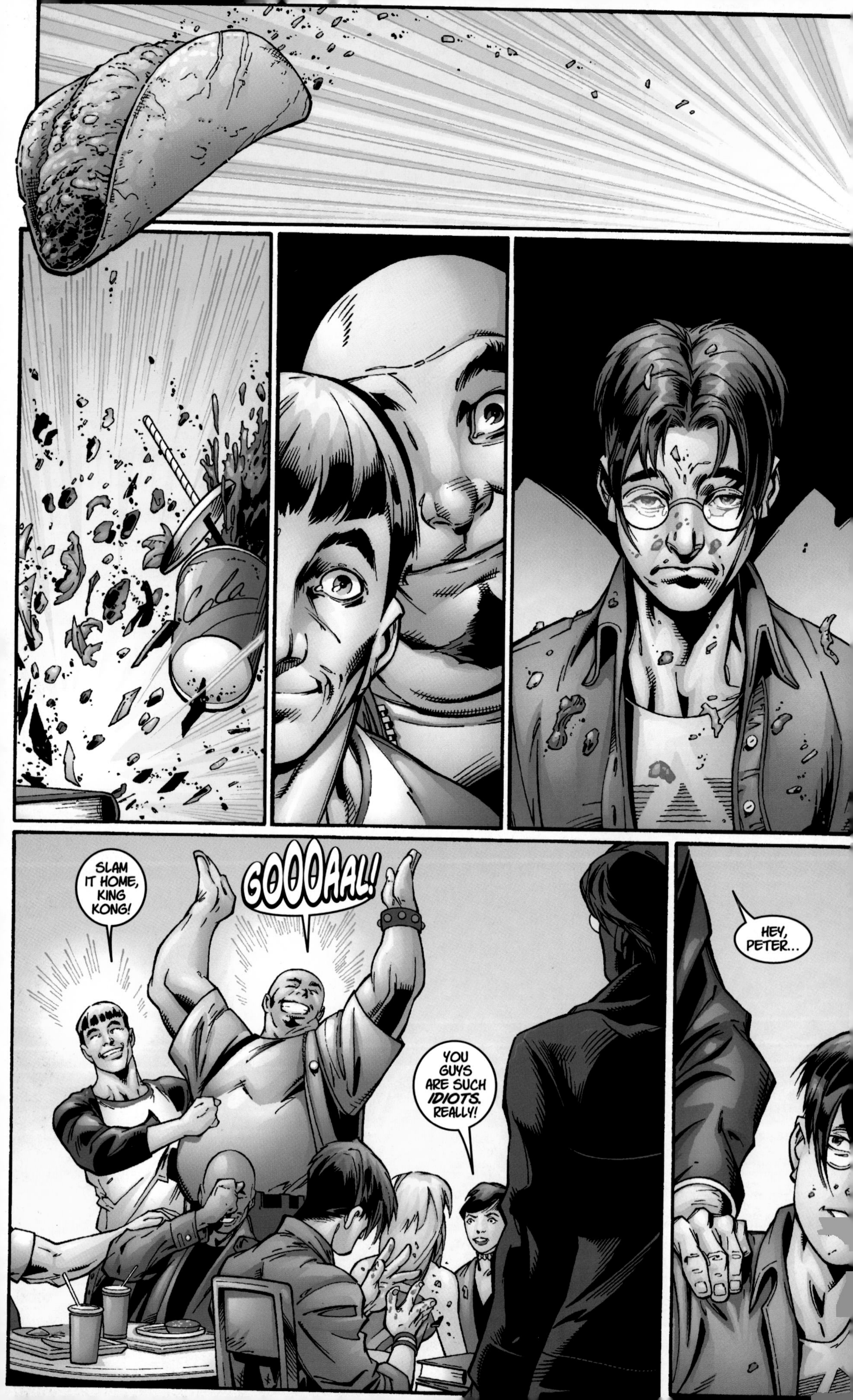

SLAM IT HOME, KING KONG!
GOOOAAL!
YOU GUYS ARE SUCH *IDIOTS*. REALLY!
HEY, PETER...

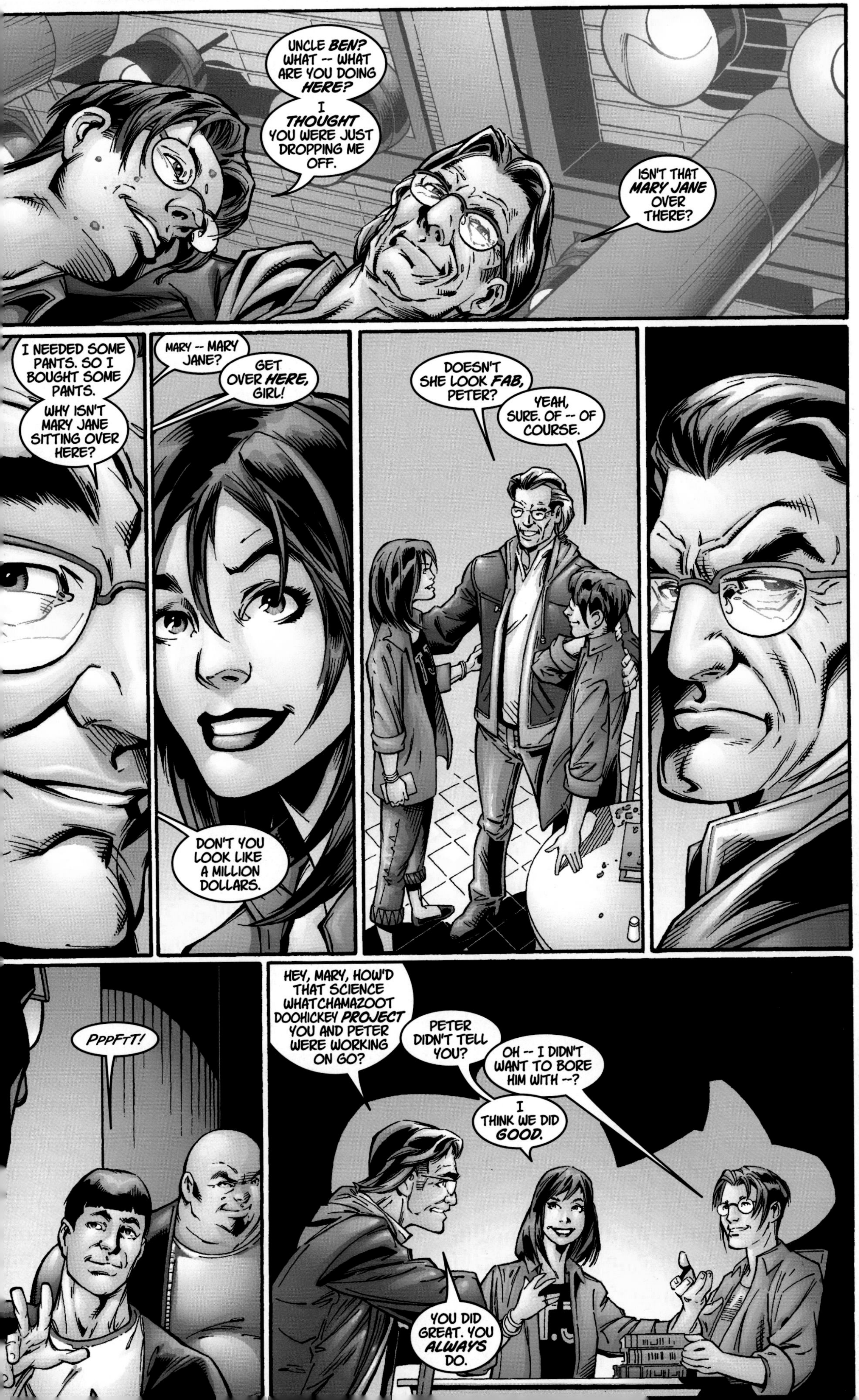
UNCLE BEN? WHAT -- WHAT ARE YOU DOING HERE?
I THOUGHT YOU WERE JUST DROPPING ME OFF.
ISN'T THAT MARY JANE OVER THERE?
I NEEDED SOME PANTS. SO I BOUGHT SOME PANTS.
WHY ISN'T MARY JANE SITTING OVER HERE?
MARY -- MARY JANE?
GET OVER HERE, GIRL!
DON'T YOU LOOK LIKE A MILLION DOLLARS.
DOESN'T SHE LOOK FAB, PETER?
YEAH, SURE. OF -- OF COURSE.
PPPFTT!
HEY, MARY, HOW'D THAT SCIENCE WHATCHAMAZOOT DOOHICKEY PROJECT YOU AND PETER WERE WORKING ON GO?
PETER DIDN'T TELL YOU?
OH -- I DIDN'T WANT TO BORE HIM WITH --?
I THINK WE DID GOOD.
YOU DID GREAT. YOU ALWAYS DO.

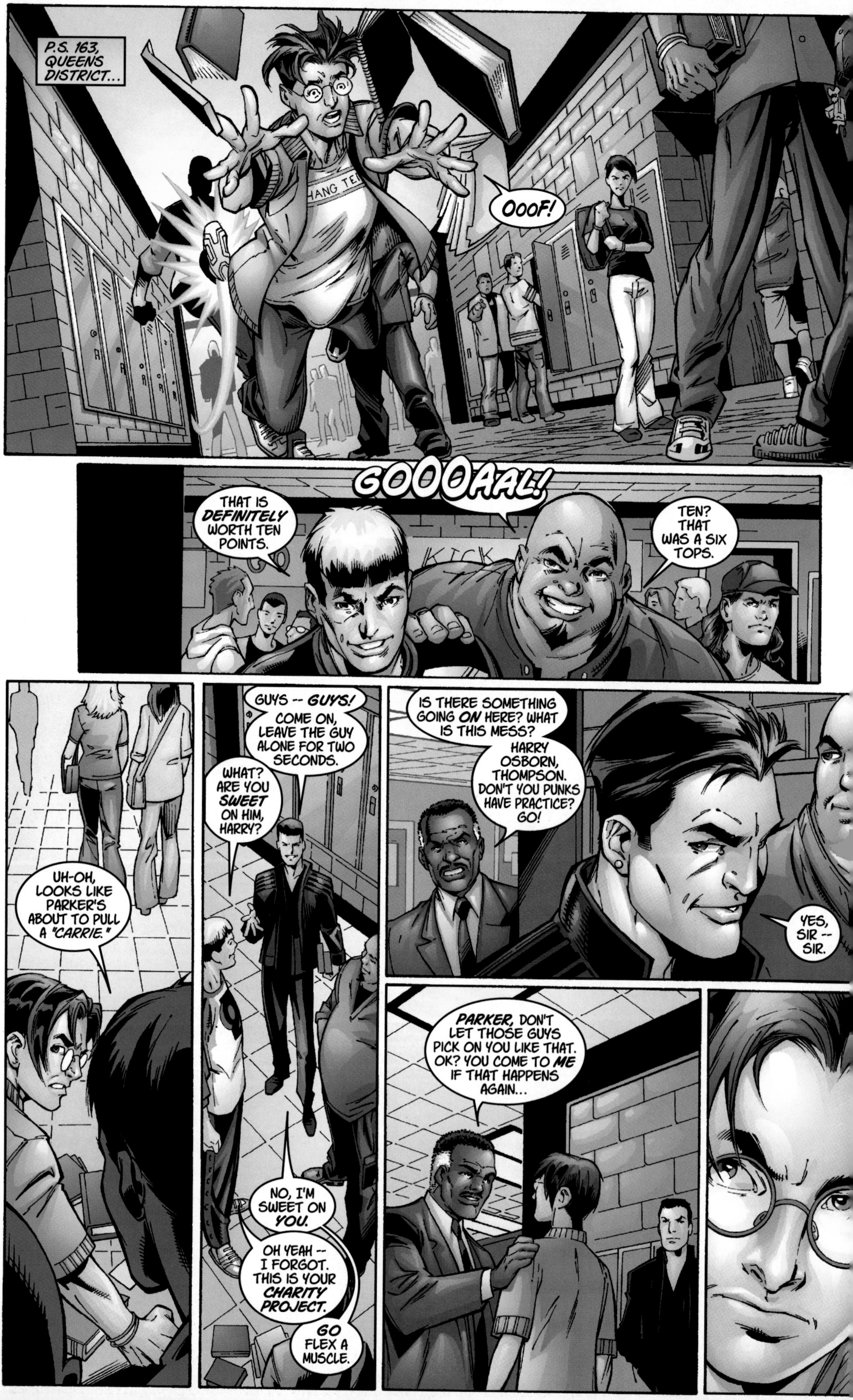
P.S. 163, QUEENS DISTRICT...
HANG TEN
OOOF!
GOOOAAL!
THAT IS DEFINITELY WORTH TEN POINTS.
TEN? THAT WAS A SIX TOPS.
KICK
UH-OH, LOOKS LIKE PARKER'S ABOUT TO PULL A "CARRIE."
GUYS -- GUYS! COME ON, LEAVE THE GUY ALONE FOR TWO SECONDS.
WHAT? ARE YOU SWEET ON HIM, HARRY?
NO, I'M SWEET ON YOU.
OH YEAH -- I FORGOT. THIS IS YOUR CHARITY PROJECT.
GO FLEX A MUSCLE.
IS THERE SOMETHING GOING ON HERE? WHAT IS THIS MESS?
HARRY OSBORN, THOMPSON. DON'T YOU PUNKS HAVE PRACTICE? GO!
YES, SIR -- SIR.
PARKER, DON'T LET THOSE GUYS PICK ON YOU LIKE THAT. OK? YOU COME TO ME IF THAT HAPPENS AGAIN...

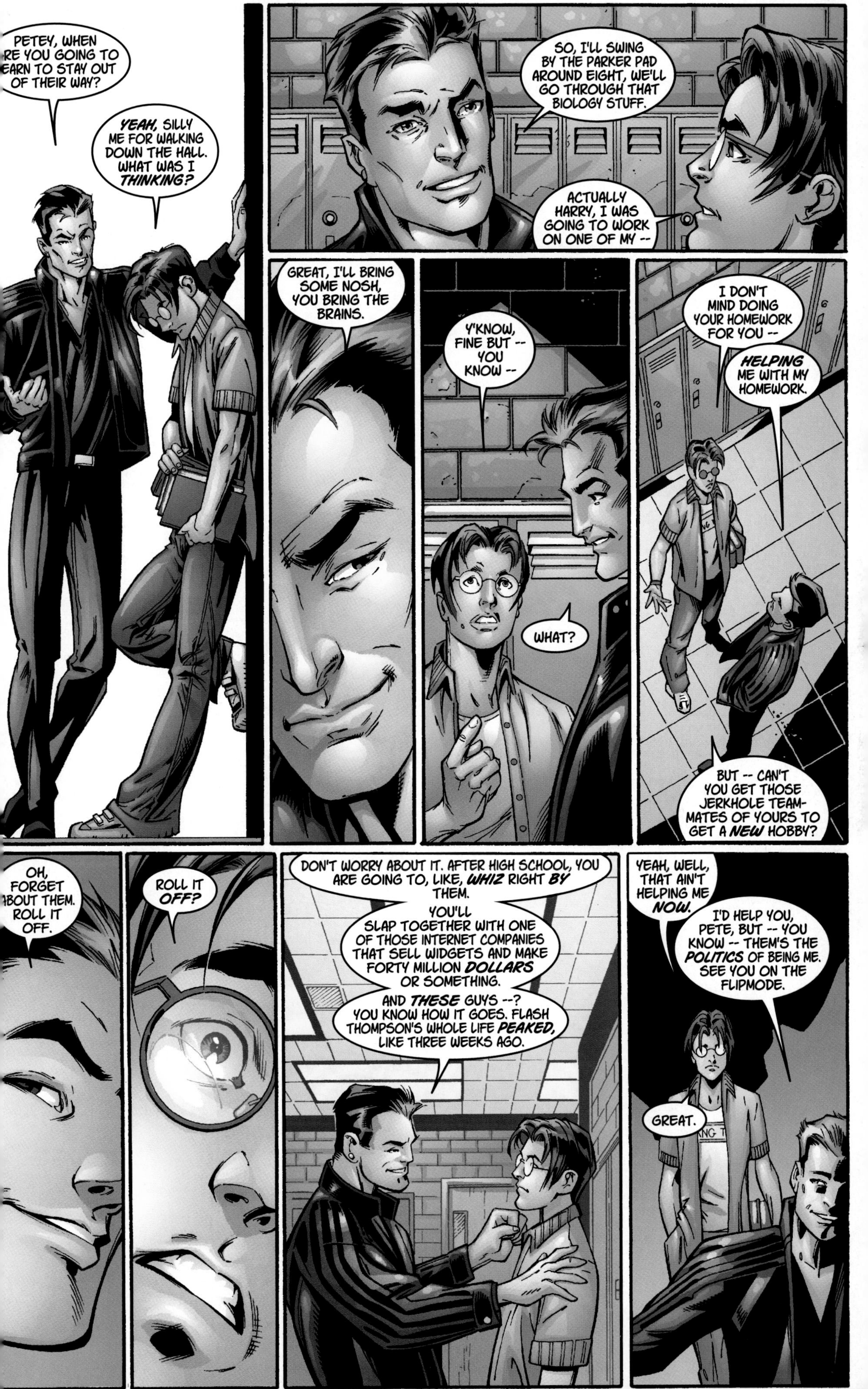
PETEY, WHEN ARE YOU GOING TO LEARN TO STAY OUT OF THEIR WAY?
YEAH, SILLY ME FOR WALKING DOWN THE HALL. WHAT WAS I THINKING?
SO, I'LL SWING BY THE PARKER PAD AROUND EIGHT, WE'LL GO THROUGH THAT BIOLOGY STUFF.
ACTUALLY HARRY, I WAS GOING TO WORK ON ONE OF MY --
GREAT, I'LL BRING SOME NOSH, YOU BRING THE BRAINS.
Y'KNOW, FINE BUT -- YOU KNOW --
WHAT?
I DON'T MIND DOING YOUR HOMEWORK FOR YOU --
HELPING ME WITH MY HOMEWORK.
BUT -- CAN'T YOU GET THOSE JERKHOLE TEAM-MATES OF YOURS TO GET A NEW HOBBY?
OH, FORGET ABOUT THEM. ROLL IT OFF.
ROLL IT OFF?
DON'T WORRY ABOUT IT. AFTER HIGH SCHOOL, YOU ARE GOING TO, LIKE, WHIZ RIGHT BY THEM.
YOU'LL SLAP TOGETHER WITH ONE OF THOSE INTERNET COMPANIES THAT SELL WIDGETS AND MAKE FORTY MILLION DOLLARS OR SOMETHING.
AND THESE GUYS --? YOU KNOW HOW IT GOES. FLASH THOMPSON'S WHOLE LIFE PEAKED, LIKE THREE WEEKS AGO.
YEAH, WELL, THAT AIN'T HELPING ME NOW.
I'D HELP YOU, PETE, BUT -- YOU KNOW -- THEM'S THE POLITICS OF BEING ME. SEE YOU ON THE FLIPMODE.
GREAT.

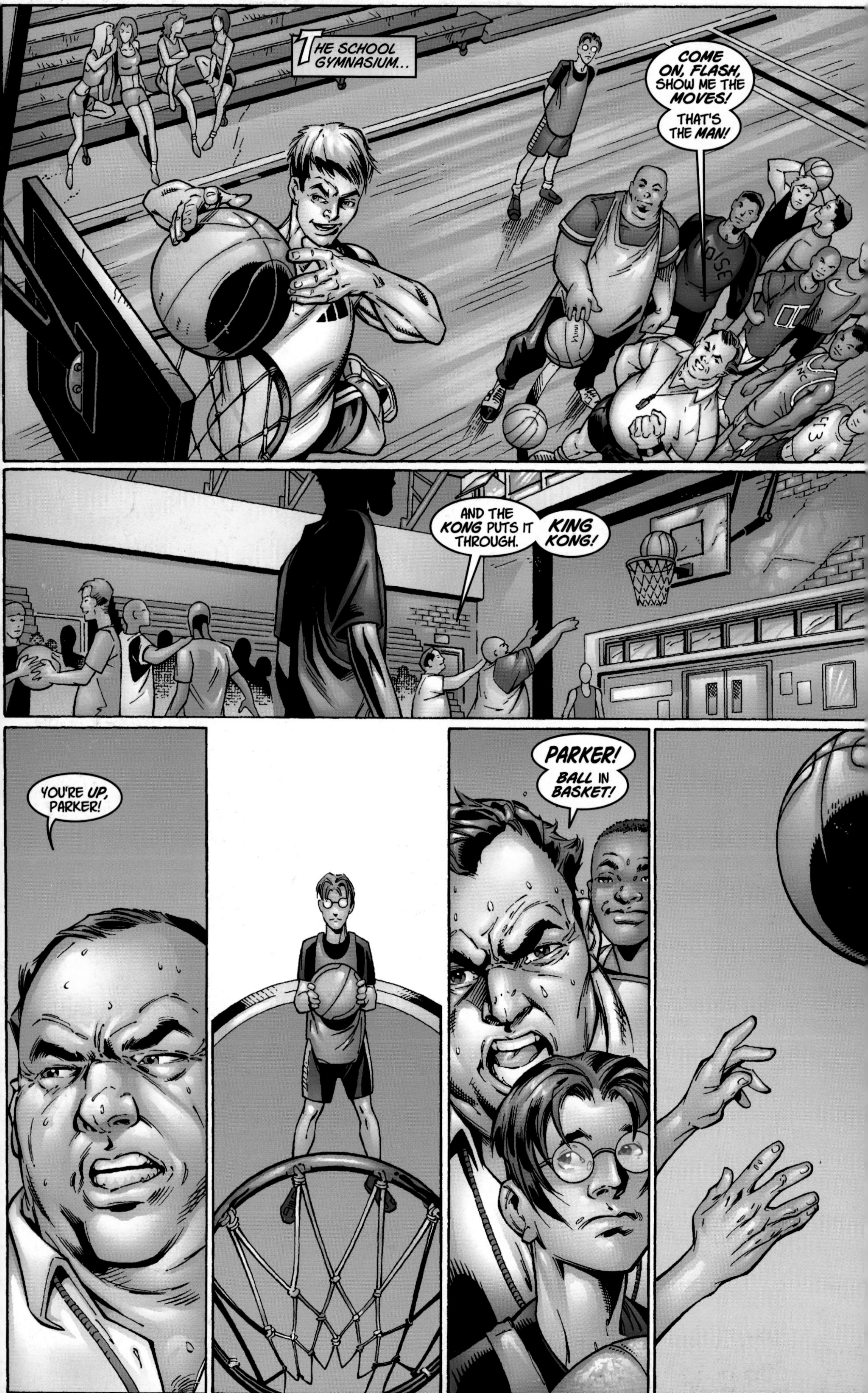
THE SCHOOL GYMNASIUM...
COME ON, FLASH, SHOW ME THE MOVES!
THAT'S THE MAN!
AND THE KONG PUTS IT THROUGH.
KING KONG!
YOU'RE UP, PARKER!
PARKER! BALL IN BASKET!

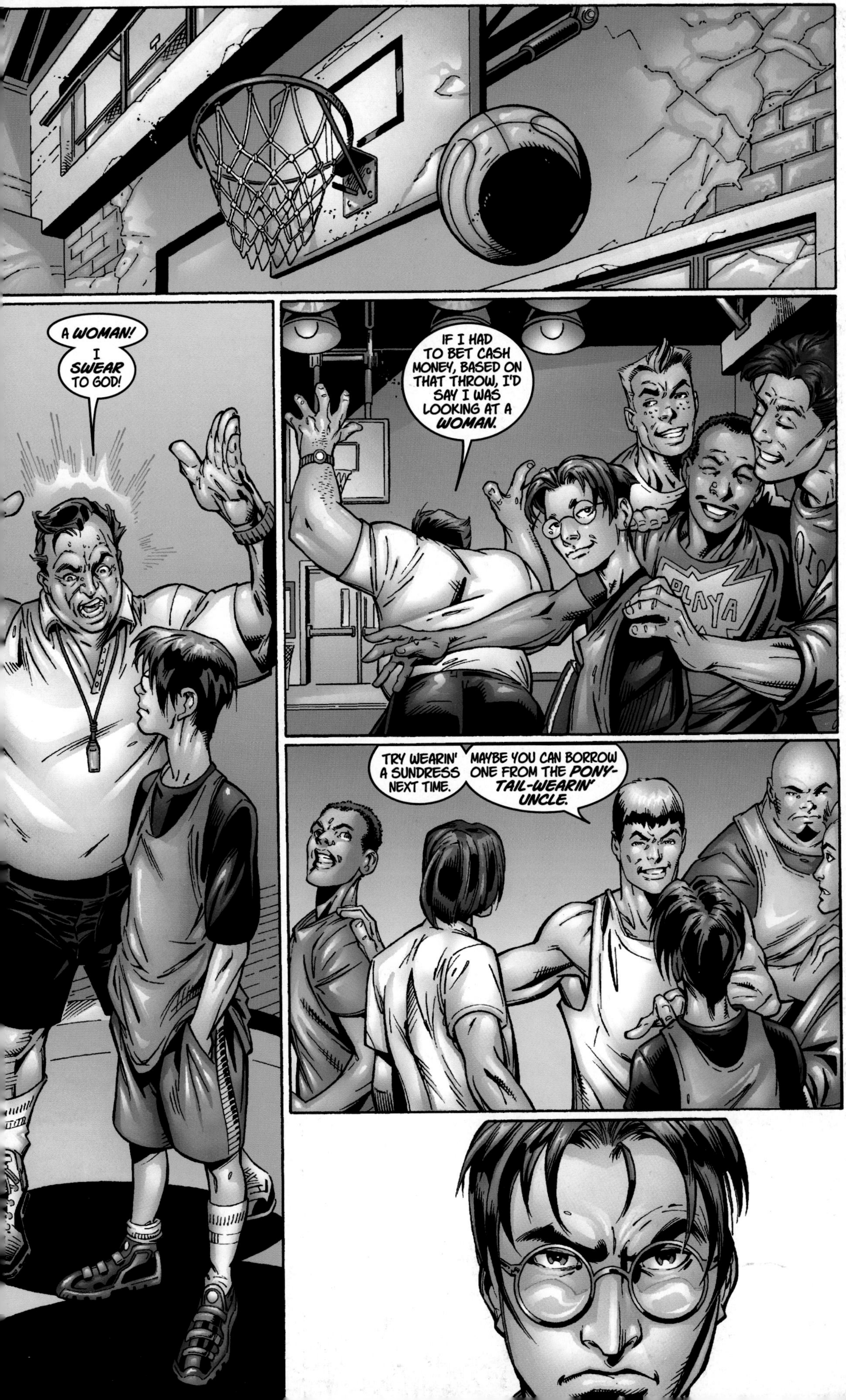
A WOMAN! I SWEAR TO GOD!
IF I HAD TO BET CASH MONEY, BASED ON THAT THROW, I'D SAY I WAS LOOKING AT A WOMAN.
PLAYA
TRY WEARIN' A SUNDRESS NEXT TIME.
MAYBE YOU CAN BORROW ONE FROM THE PONY-TAIL-WEARIN' UNCLE.

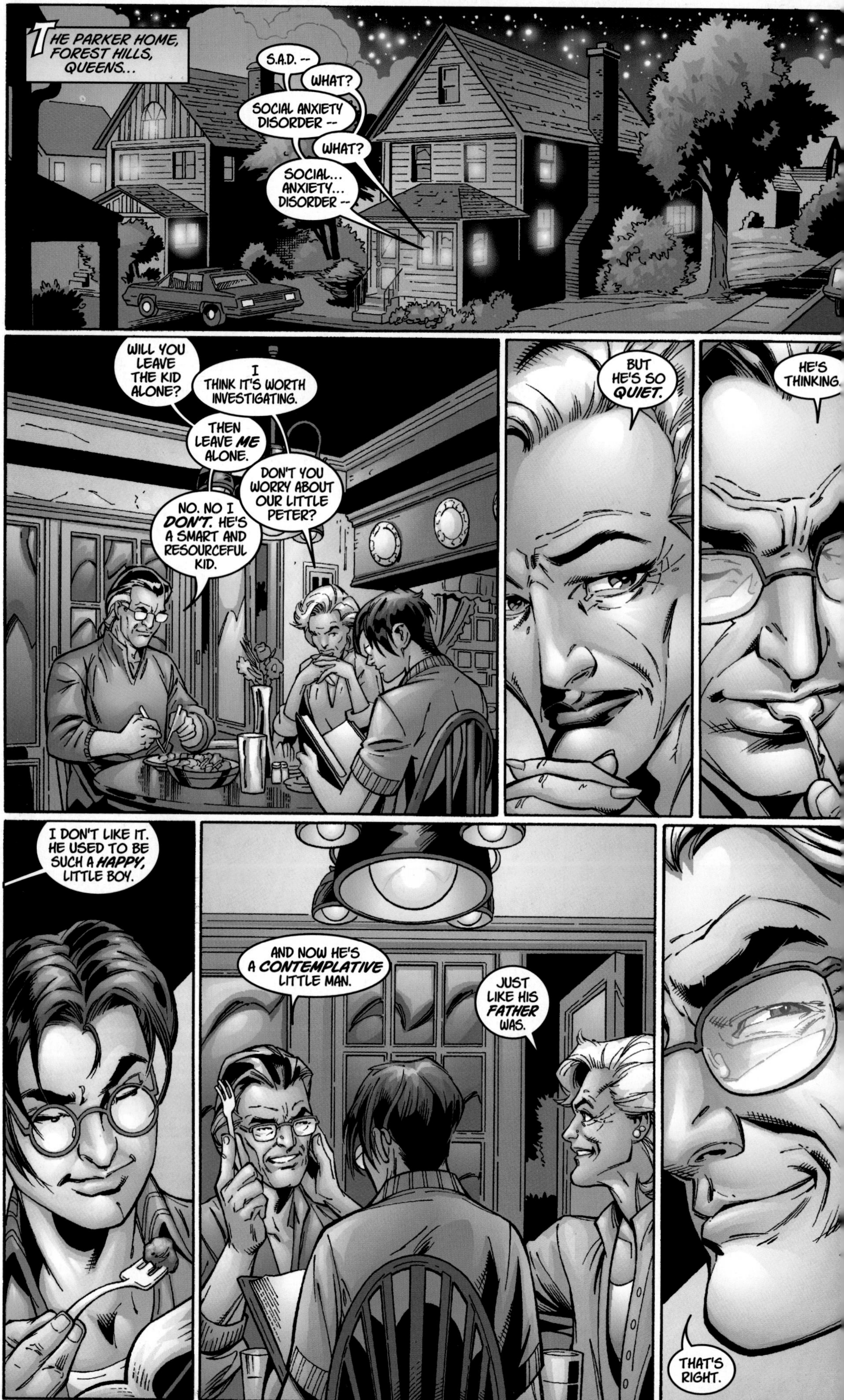
THE PARKER HOME, FOREST HILLS, QUEENS...
S.A.D. --
WHAT?
SOCIAL ANXIETY DISORDER --
WHAT?
SOCIAL... ANXIETY... DISORDER --
WILL YOU LEAVE THE KID ALONE?
I THINK IT'S WORTH INVESTIGATING.
THEN LEAVE ME ALONE.
DON'T YOU WORRY ABOUT OUR LITTLE PETER?
NO. NO I DON'T. HE'S A SMART AND RESOURCEFUL KID.
BUT HE'S SO QUIET.
HE'S THINKING.
I DON'T LIKE IT. HE USED TO BE SUCH A HAPPY, LITTLE BOY.
AND NOW HE'S A CONTEMPLATIVE LITTLE MAN.
JUST LIKE HIS FATHER WAS.
THAT'S RIGHT.

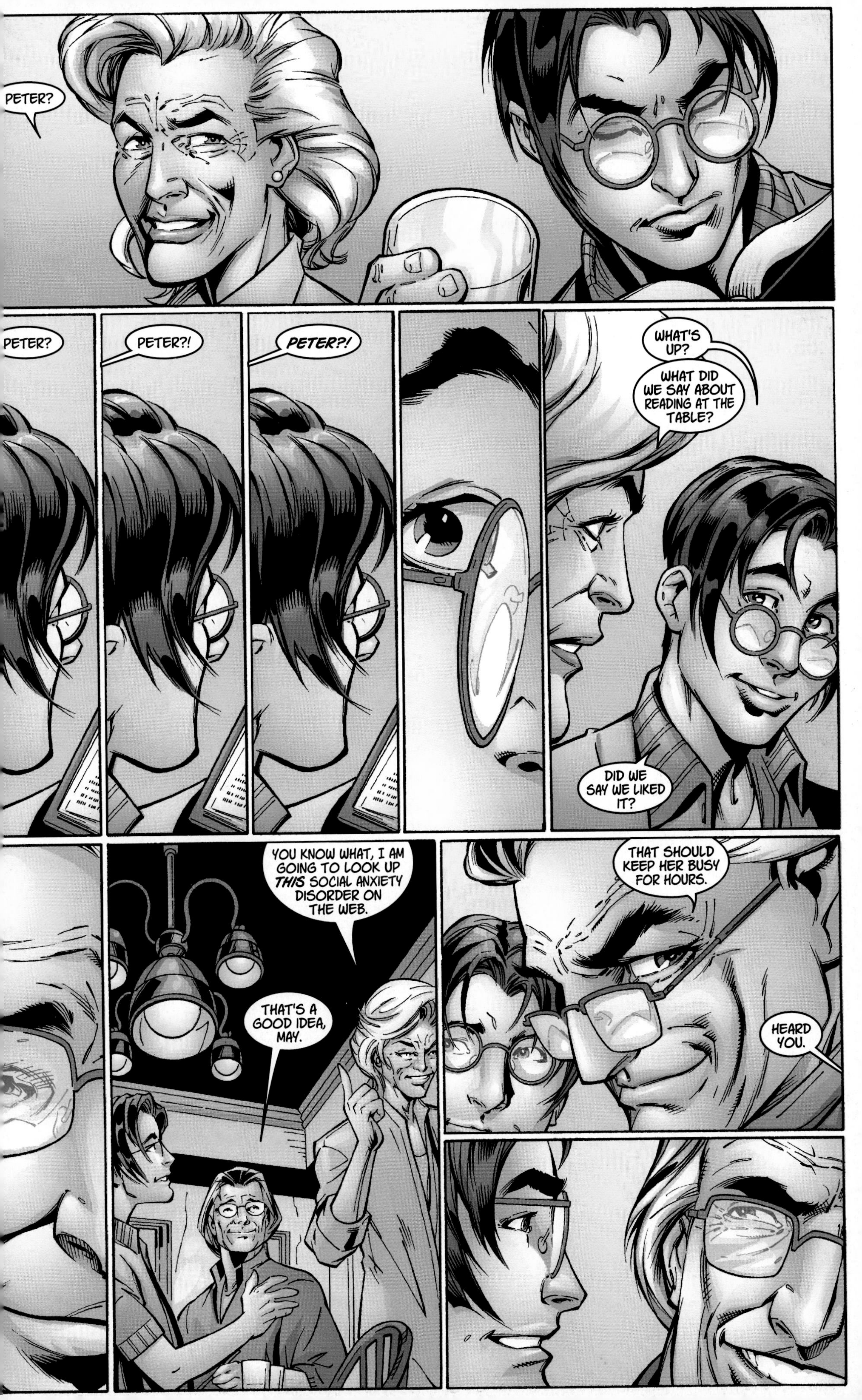
PETER?
PETER?
PETER?!
PETER?!
WHAT'S UP?
WHAT DID WE SAY ABOUT READING AT THE TABLE?
DID WE SAY WE LIKED IT?
YOU KNOW WHAT, I AM GOING TO LOOK UP THIS SOCIAL ANXIETY DISORDER ON THE WEB.
THAT'S A GOOD IDEA, MAY.
THAT SHOULD KEEP HER BUSY FOR HOURS.
HEARD YOU.

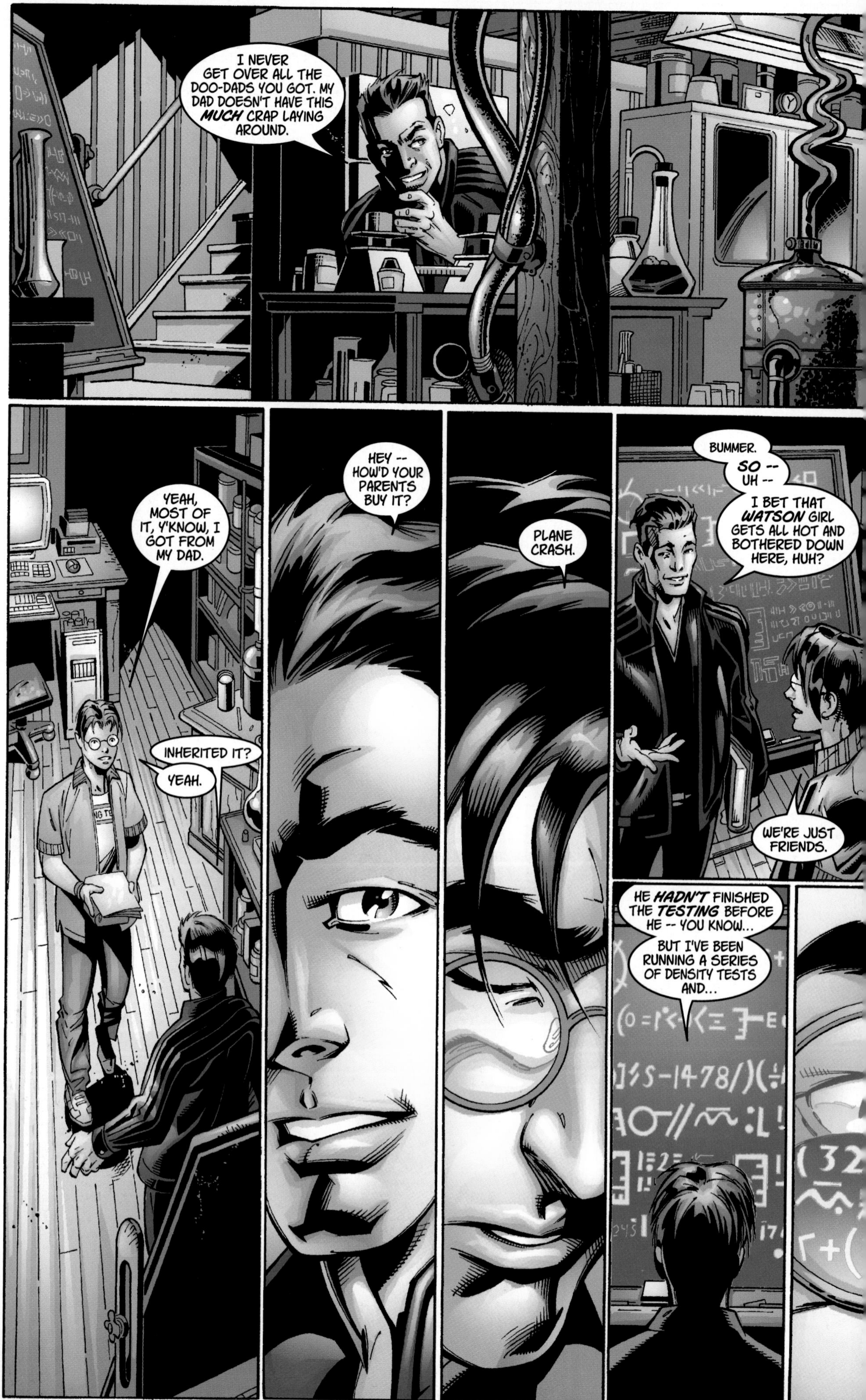
I NEVER GET OVER ALL THE DOO-DADS YOU GOT. MY DAD DOESN'T HAVE THIS MUCH CRAP LAYING AROUND.
YEAH, MOST OF IT, Y'KNOW, I GOT FROM MY DAD.
INHERITED IT?
YEAH.
HEY -- HOW'D YOUR PARENTS BUY IT?
PLANE CRASH.
BUMMER.
SO -- UH --
I BET THAT WATSON GIRL GETS ALL HOT AND BOTHERED DOWN HERE, HUH?
WE'RE JUST FRIENDS.
HE HADN'T FINISHED THE TESTING BEFORE HE -- YOU KNOW...
BUT I'VE BEEN RUNNING A SERIES OF DENSITY TESTS AND...

UH-*HUH.*

OH, NO. DON'T *DO* THAT.

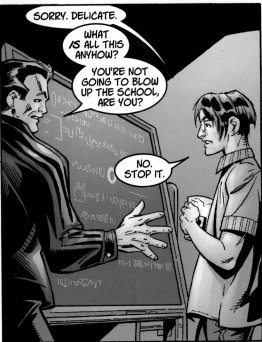

SORRY. DELICATE.

WHAT *IS* ALL THIS ANYHOW?

YOU'RE NOT GOING TO BLOW UP THE SCHOOL, ARE YOU?

NO. STOP IT.

THIS IS -- IT'S REALLY --

SEE, MY *FATHER* WAS WORKING ON A COUPLE OF PATENTS --

-- THIS ONE WAS FOR THIS INTERESTING MOLECULAR ADHESIVE.

I *CAN'T* -- I HAVEN'T WRAPPED MY HEAD AROUND SOME OF THE MORE COMPLEX COMPONENTS.

...AND...

YEAH -- SO, LISTEN.

I'M GOING TO BAIL OUT OF HERE.

SO --

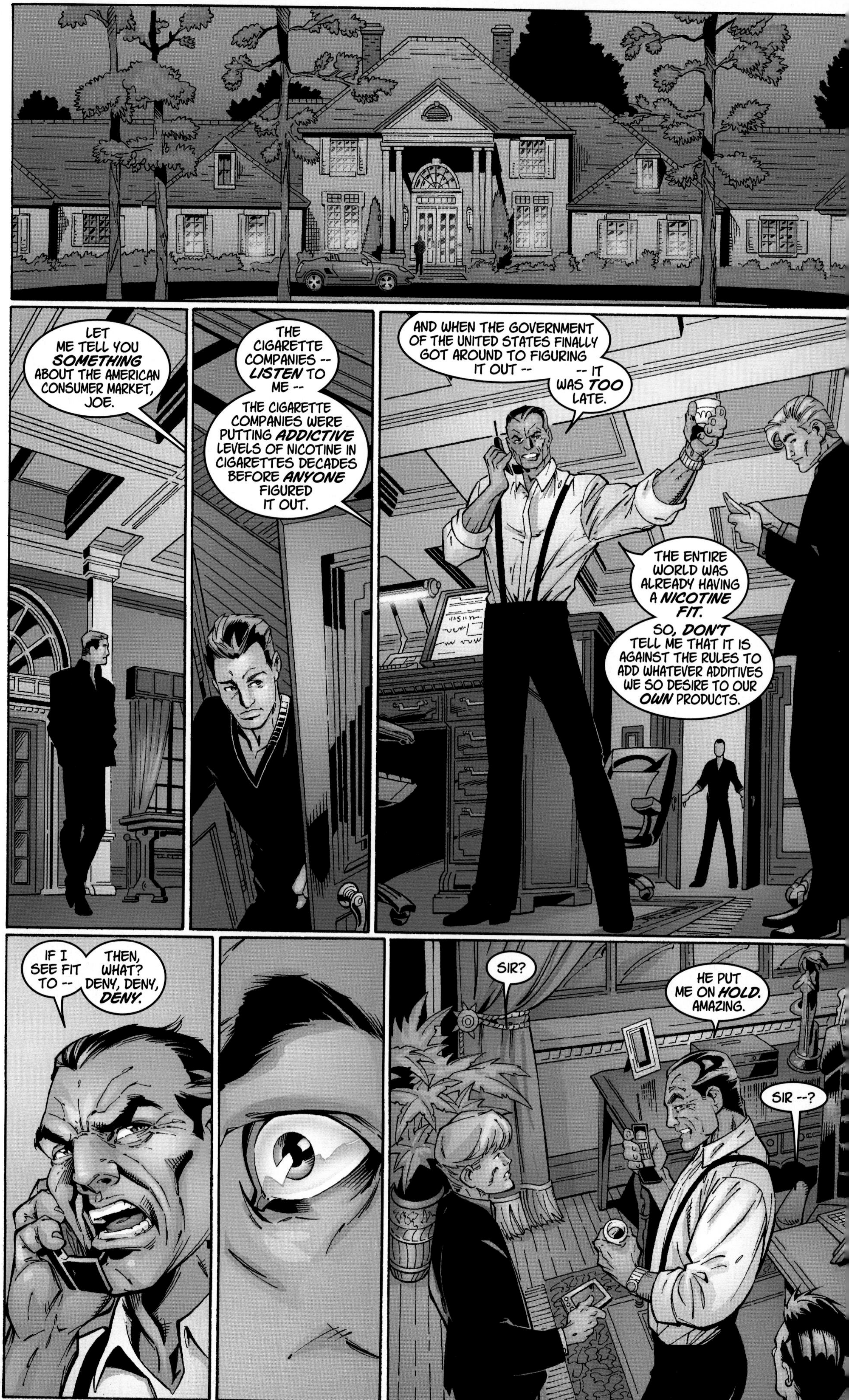
LET ME TELL YOU *SOMETHING* ABOUT THE AMERICAN CONSUMER MARKET, JOE.
THE CIGARETTE COMPANIES -- *LISTEN* TO ME --
THE CIGARETTE COMPANIES WERE PUTTING *ADDICTIVE* LEVELS OF NICOTINE IN CIGARETTES DECADES BEFORE *ANYONE* FIGURED IT OUT.
AND WHEN THE GOVERNMENT OF THE UNITED STATES FINALLY GOT AROUND TO FIGURING IT OUT --
-- IT WAS *TOO* LATE.
THE ENTIRE WORLD WAS ALREADY HAVING A *NICOTINE FIT.*
SO, *DON'T* TELL ME THAT IT IS AGAINST THE RULES TO ADD WHATEVER ADDITIVES WE SO DESIRE TO OUR *OWN* PRODUCTS.
IF I SEE FIT TO --
THEN, WHAT? DENY, DENY, *DENY.*
SIR?
HE PUT ME ON *HOLD.* AMAZING.
SIR --?

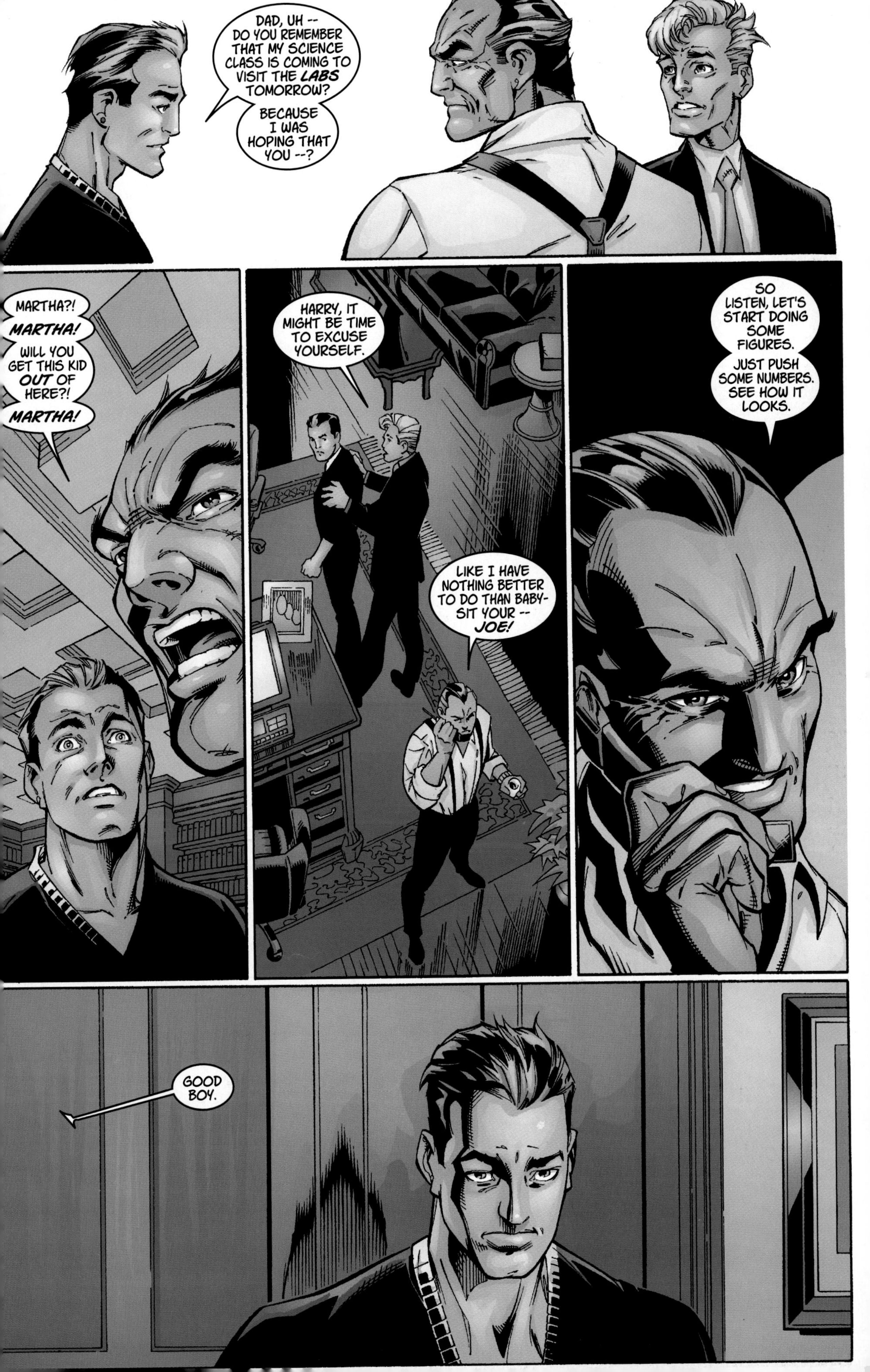
DAD, UH -- DO YOU REMEMBER THAT MY SCIENCE CLASS IS COMING TO VISIT THE *LABS* TOMORROW?
BECAUSE I WAS HOPING THAT YOU --?
MARTHA?!
MARTHA!
WILL YOU GET THIS KID *OUT* OF HERE?!
MARTHA!
HARRY, IT MIGHT BE TIME TO EXCUSE YOURSELF.
LIKE I HAVE NOTHING BETTER TO DO THAN BABY-SIT YOUR -- *JOE!*
SO LISTEN, LET'S START DOING SOME FIGURES.
JUST PUSH SOME NUMBERS. SEE HOW IT LOOKS.
GOOD BOY.

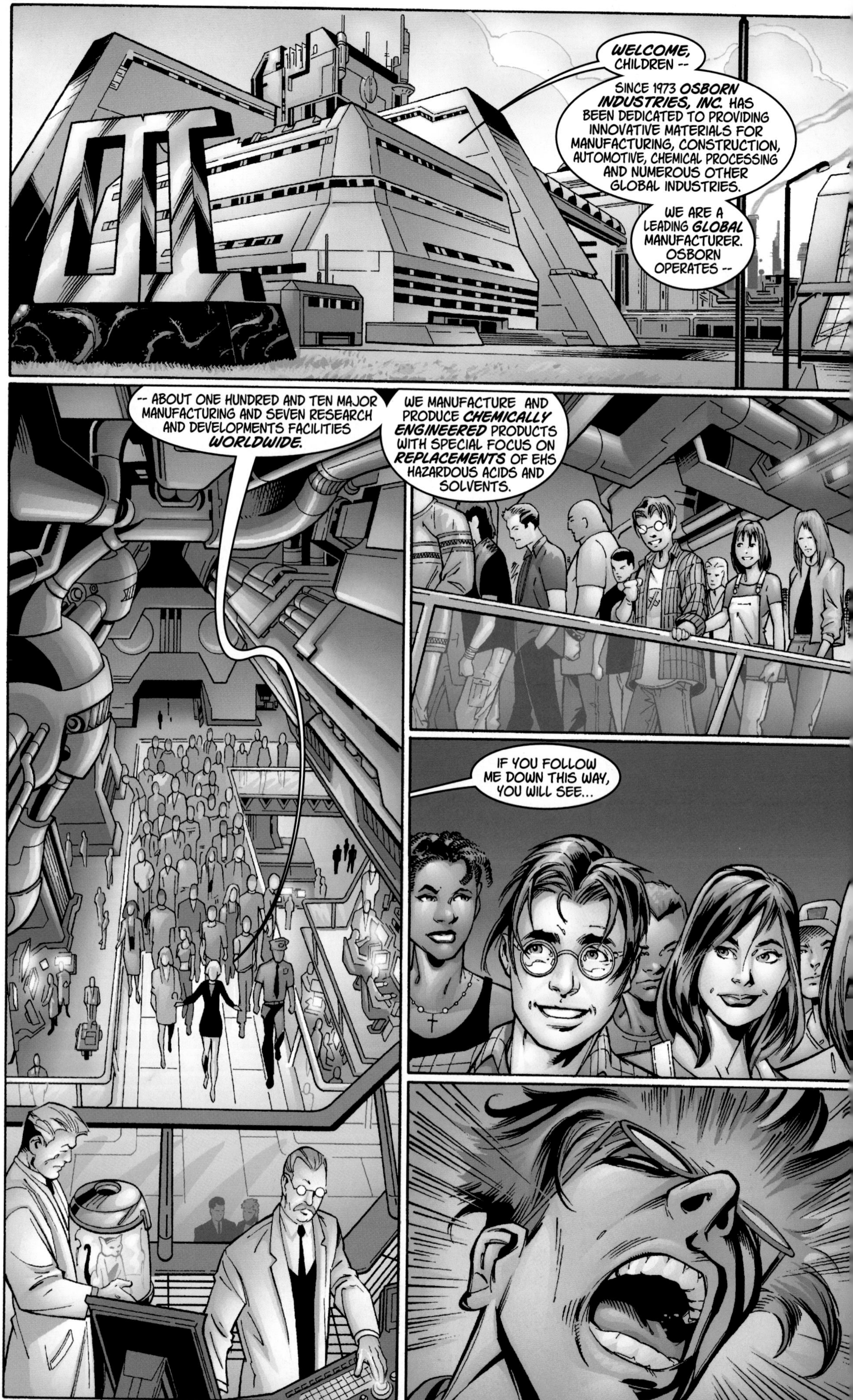
WELCOME, CHILDREN --
SINCE 1973 OSBORN INDUSTRIES, INC. HAS BEEN DEDICATED TO PROVIDING INNOVATIVE MATERIALS FOR MANUFACTURING, CONSTRUCTION, AUTOMOTIVE, CHEMICAL PROCESSING AND NUMEROUS OTHER GLOBAL INDUSTRIES.
WE ARE A LEADING GLOBAL MANUFACTURER. OSBORN OPERATES --
-- ABOUT ONE HUNDRED AND TEN MAJOR MANUFACTURING AND SEVEN RESEARCH AND DEVELOPMENTS FACILITIES WORLDWIDE.
WE MANUFACTURE AND PRODUCE CHEMICALLY ENGINEERED PRODUCTS WITH SPECIAL FOCUS ON REPLACEMENTS OF EHS HAZARDOUS ACIDS AND SOLVENTS.
IF YOU FOLLOW ME DOWN THIS WAY, YOU WILL SEE...

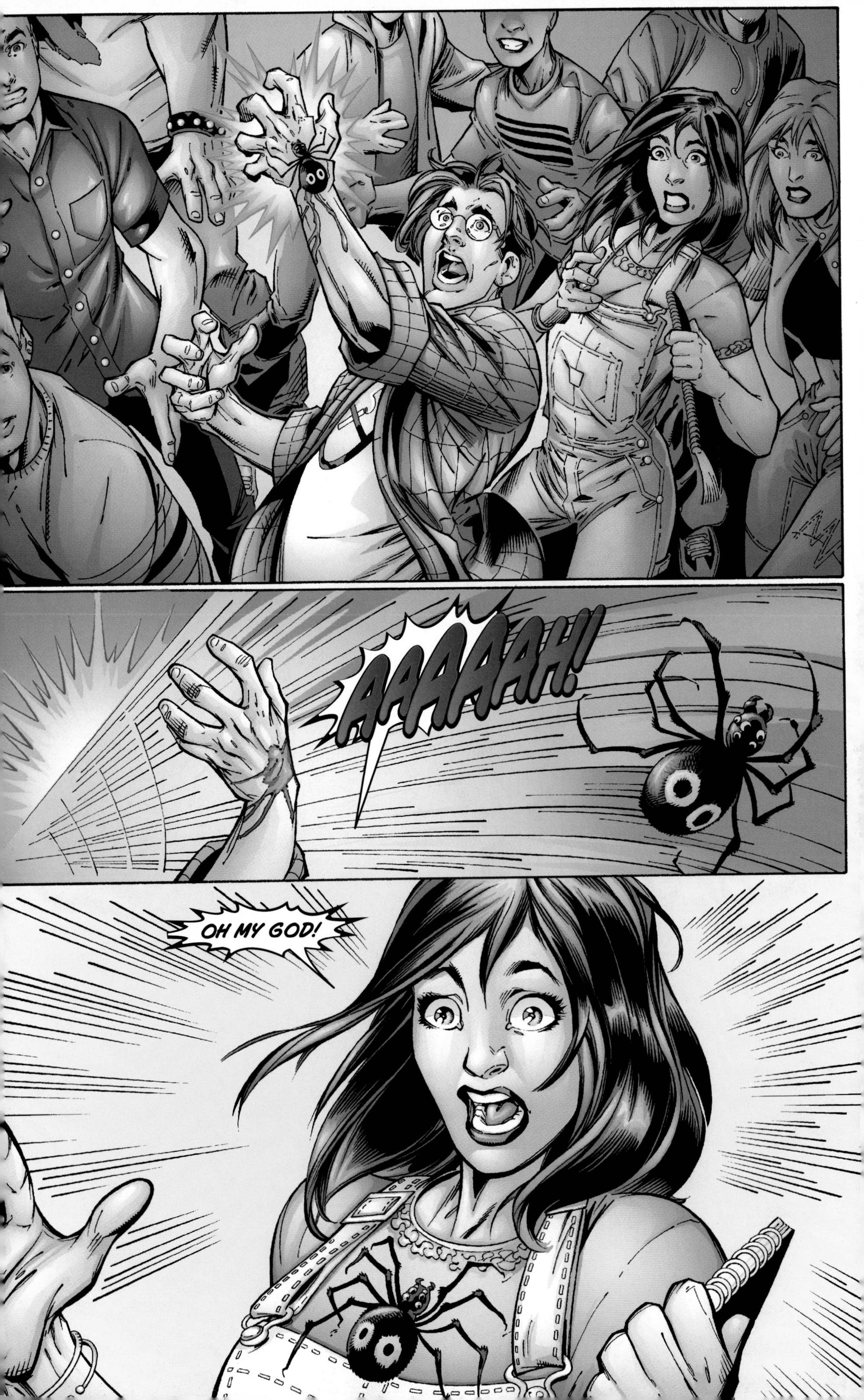
AAAAAH!
OH MY GOD!

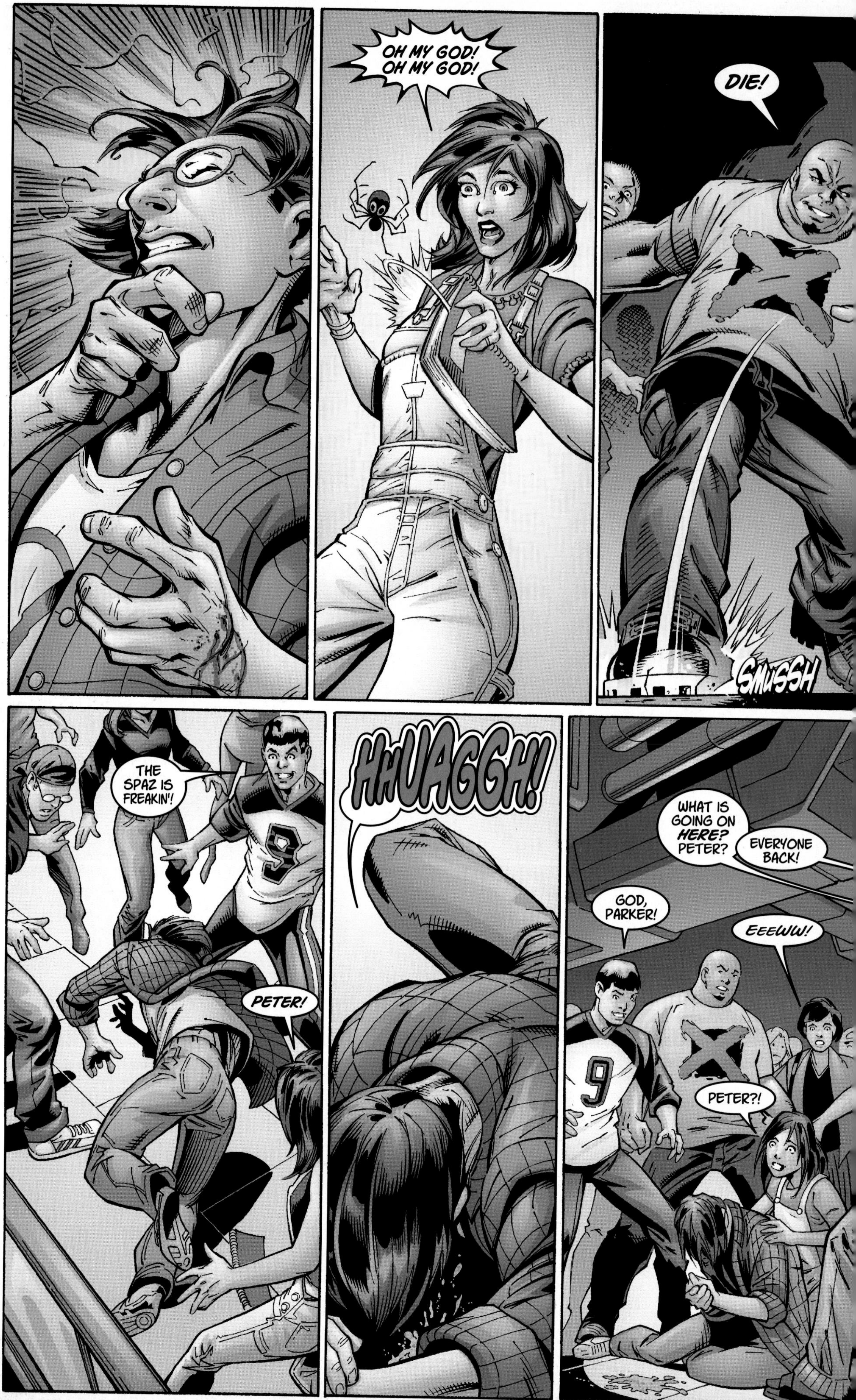

OH MY GOD! OH MY GOD!
DIE!
SMUSSH
THE SPAZ IS FREAKIN'!
PETER!
HHUAGGH!
WHAT IS GOING ON HERE? PETER?
EVERYONE BACK!
GOD, PARKER!
EEEWW!
PETER?!

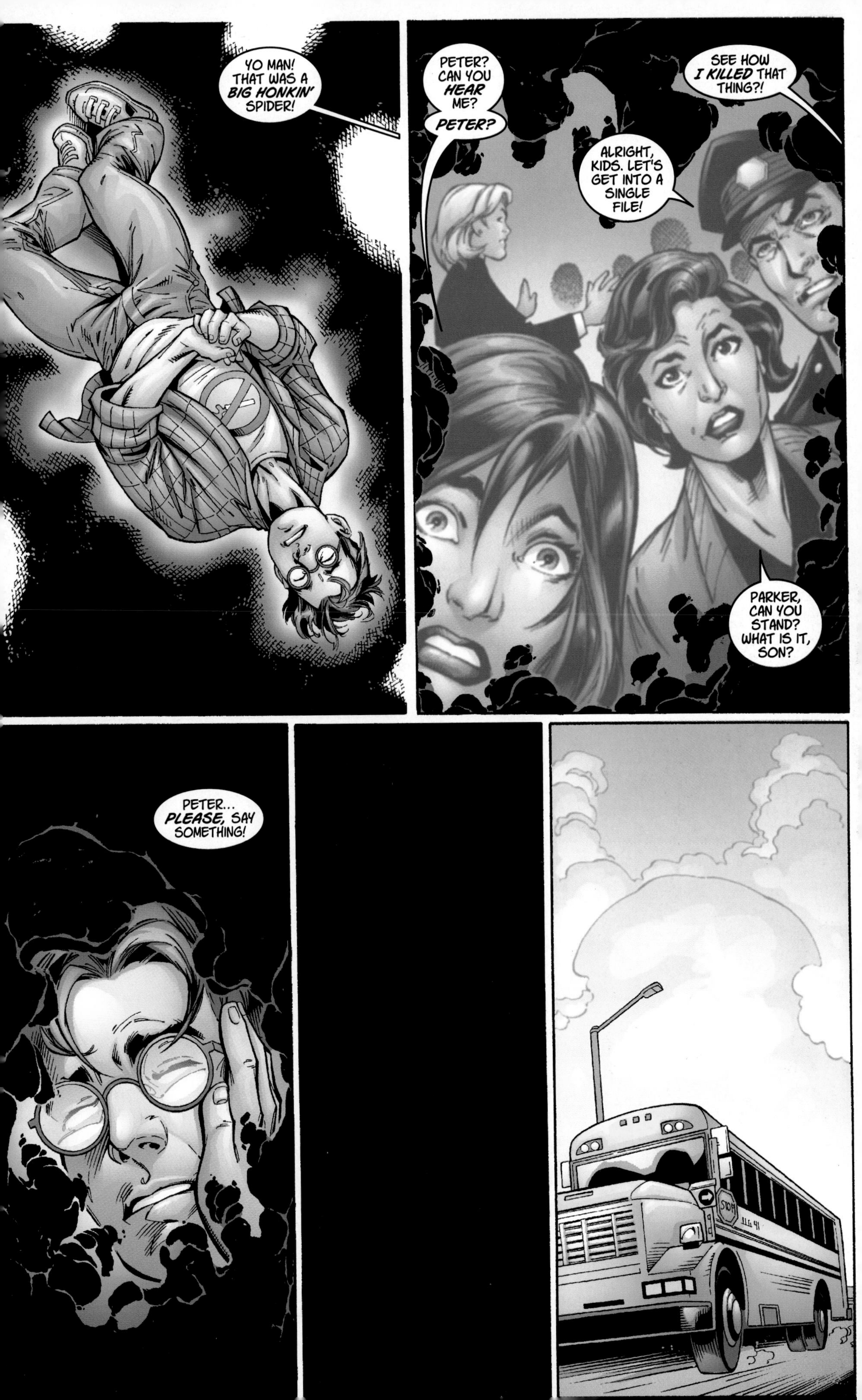
YO MAN! THAT WAS A BIG HONKIN' SPIDER!
PETER? CAN YOU HEAR ME? PETER?
SEE HOW I KILLED THAT THING?!
ALRIGHT, KIDS. LET'S GET INTO A SINGLE FILE!
PARKER, CAN YOU STAND? WHAT IS IT, SON?
PETER... PLEASE, SAY SOMETHING!

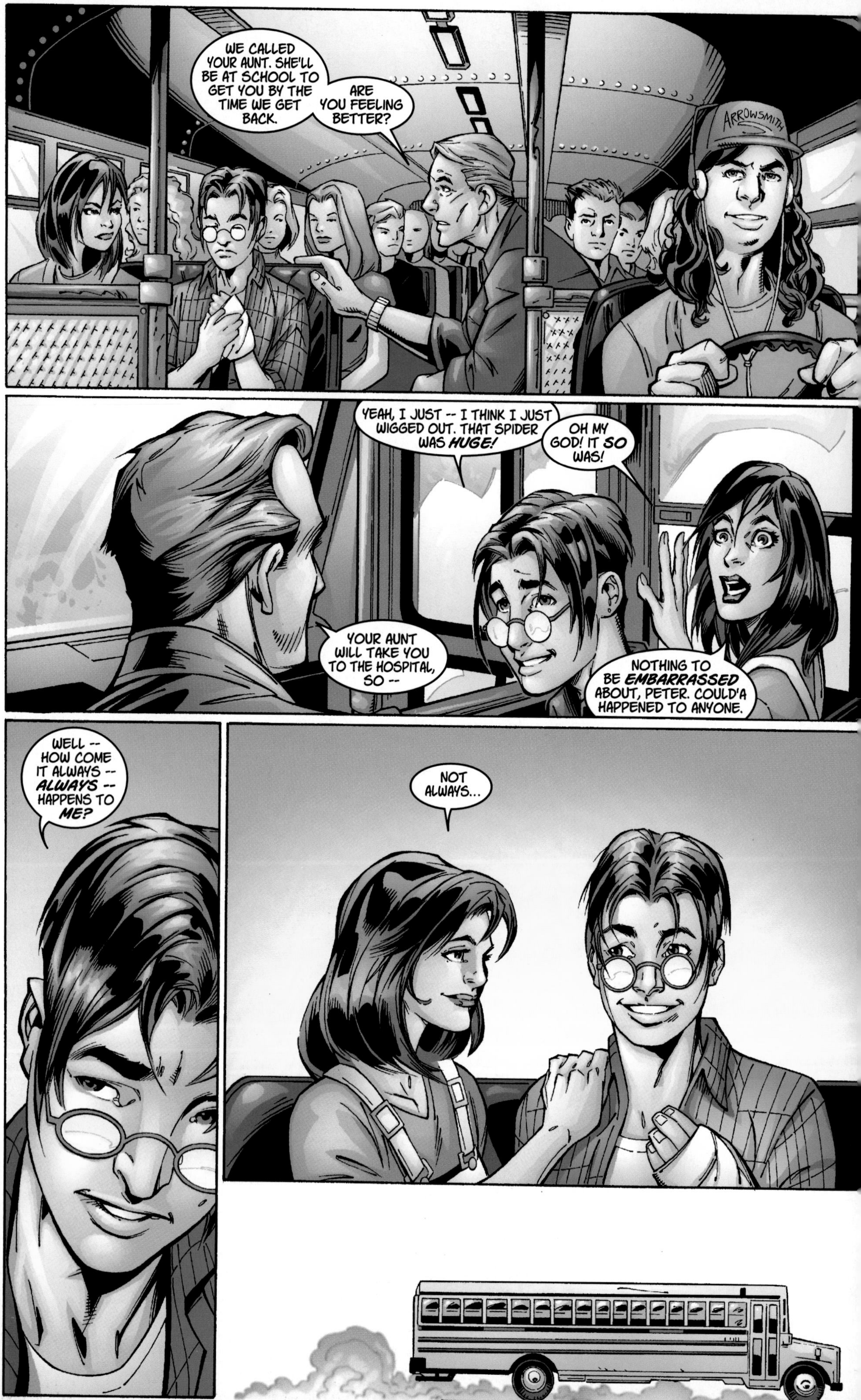

WE CALLED YOUR AUNT. SHE'LL BE AT SCHOOL TO GET YOU BY THE TIME WE GET BACK.
ARE YOU FEELING BETTER?
ARROWSMITH
YEAH, I JUST -- I THINK I JUST WIGGED OUT. THAT SPIDER WAS *HUGE!*
OH MY GOD! IT *SO* WAS!
YOUR AUNT WILL TAKE YOU TO THE HOSPITAL, SO --
NOTHING TO BE *EMBARRASSED* ABOUT, PETER. COULD'A HAPPENED TO ANYONE.
WELL -- HOW COME IT ALWAYS -- *ALWAYS* -- HAPPENS TO *ME?*
NOT ALWAYS...

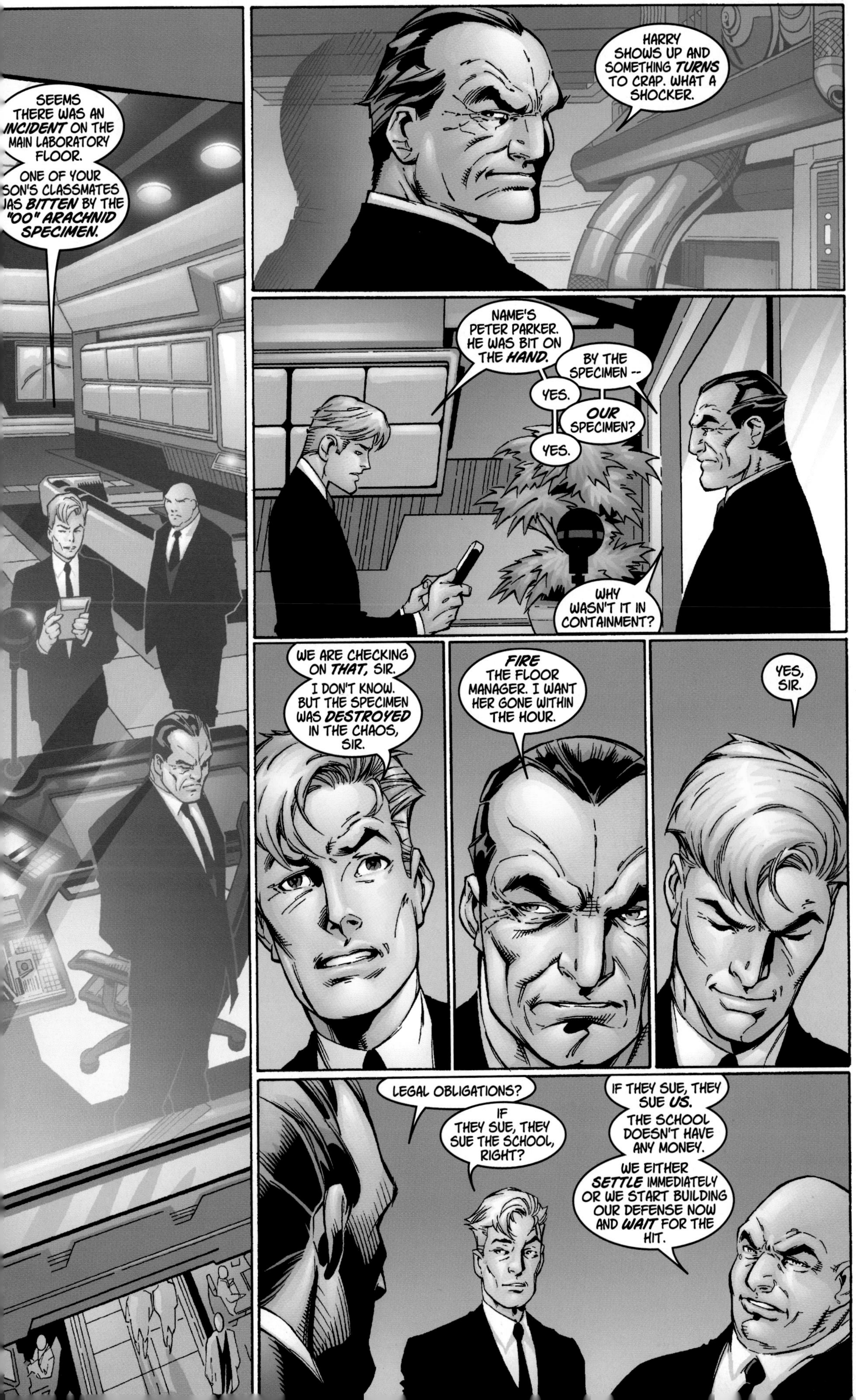
SEEMS THERE WAS AN INCIDENT ON THE MAIN LABORATORY FLOOR.
ONE OF YOUR SON'S CLASSMATES WAS BITTEN BY THE "OO" ARACHNID SPECIMEN.
HARRY SHOWS UP AND SOMETHING TURNS TO CRAP. WHAT A SHOCKER.
NAME'S PETER PARKER. HE WAS BIT ON THE HAND.
BY THE SPECIMEN --
YES.
OUR SPECIMEN?
YES.
WHY WASN'T IT IN CONTAINMENT?
WE ARE CHECKING ON THAT, SIR.
I DON'T KNOW. BUT THE SPECIMEN WAS DESTROYED IN THE CHAOS, SIR.
FIRE THE FLOOR MANAGER. I WANT HER GONE WITHIN THE HOUR.
YES, SIR.
LEGAL OBLIGATIONS?
IF THEY SUE, THEY SUE THE SCHOOL, RIGHT?
IF THEY SUE, THEY SUE US.
THE SCHOOL DOESN'T HAVE ANY MONEY.
WE EITHER SETTLE IMMEDIATELY OR WE START BUILDING OUR DEFENSE NOW AND WAIT FOR THE HIT.

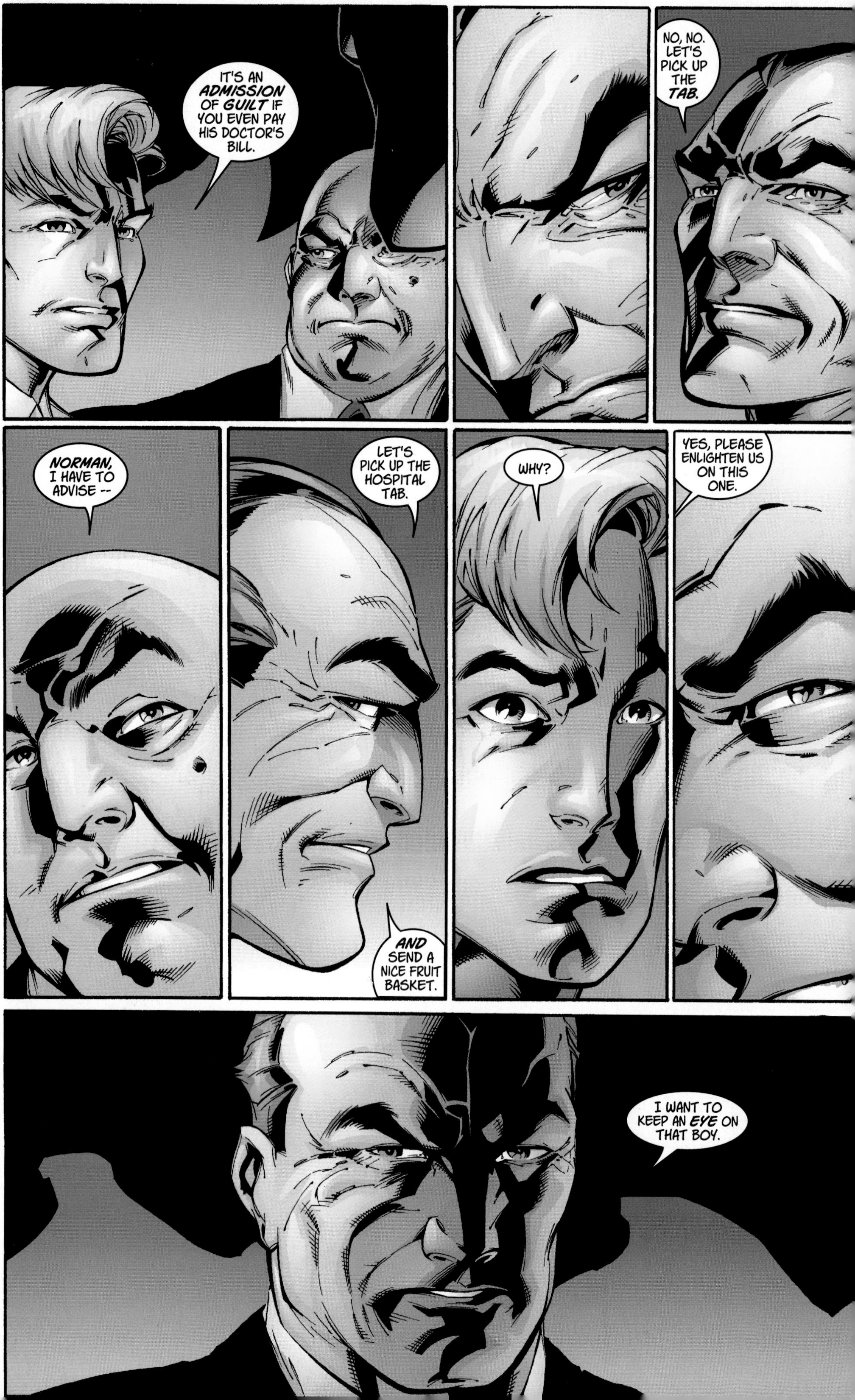
IT'S AN ADMISSION OF GUILT IF YOU EVEN PAY HIS DOCTOR'S BILL.
NO, NO. LET'S PICK UP THE TAB.
NORMAN, I HAVE TO ADVISE --
LET'S PICK UP THE HOSPITAL TAB.
AND SEND A NICE FRUIT BASKET.
WHY?
YES, PLEASE ENLIGHTEN US ON THIS ONE.
I WANT TO KEEP AN EYE ON THAT BOY.

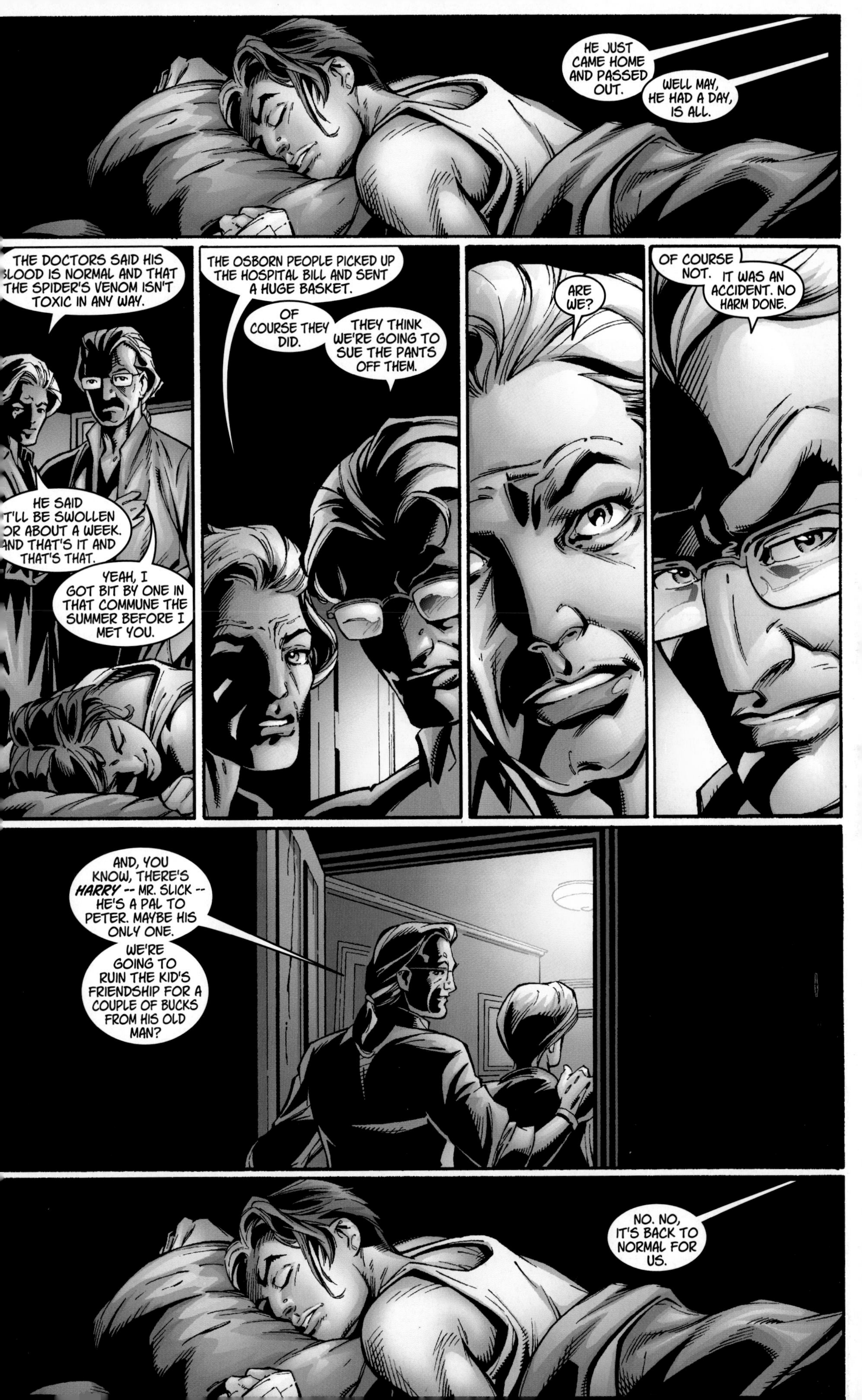

HE JUST CAME HOME AND PASSED OUT.
WELL MAY, HE HAD A DAY, IS ALL.
THE DOCTORS SAID HIS LOOD IS NORMAL AND THAT THE SPIDER'S VENOM ISN'T TOXIC IN ANY WAY.
HE SAID T'LL BE SWOLLEN OR ABOUT A WEEK. ND THAT'S IT AND THAT'S THAT.
YEAH, I GOT BIT BY ONE IN THAT COMMUNE THE SUMMER BEFORE I MET YOU.
THE OSBORN PEOPLE PICKED UP THE HOSPITAL BILL AND SENT A HUGE BASKET.
OF COURSE THEY DID.
THEY THINK WE'RE GOING TO SUE THE PANTS OFF THEM.
ARE WE?
OF COURSE NOT.
IT WAS AN ACCIDENT. NO HARM DONE.
AND, YOU KNOW, THERE'S HARRY -- MR. SLICK -- HE'S A PAL TO PETER. MAYBE HIS ONLY ONE.
WE'RE GOING TO RUIN THE KID'S FRIENDSHIP FOR A COUPLE OF BUCKS FROM HIS OLD MAN?
NO. NO, IT'S BACK TO NORMAL FOR US.

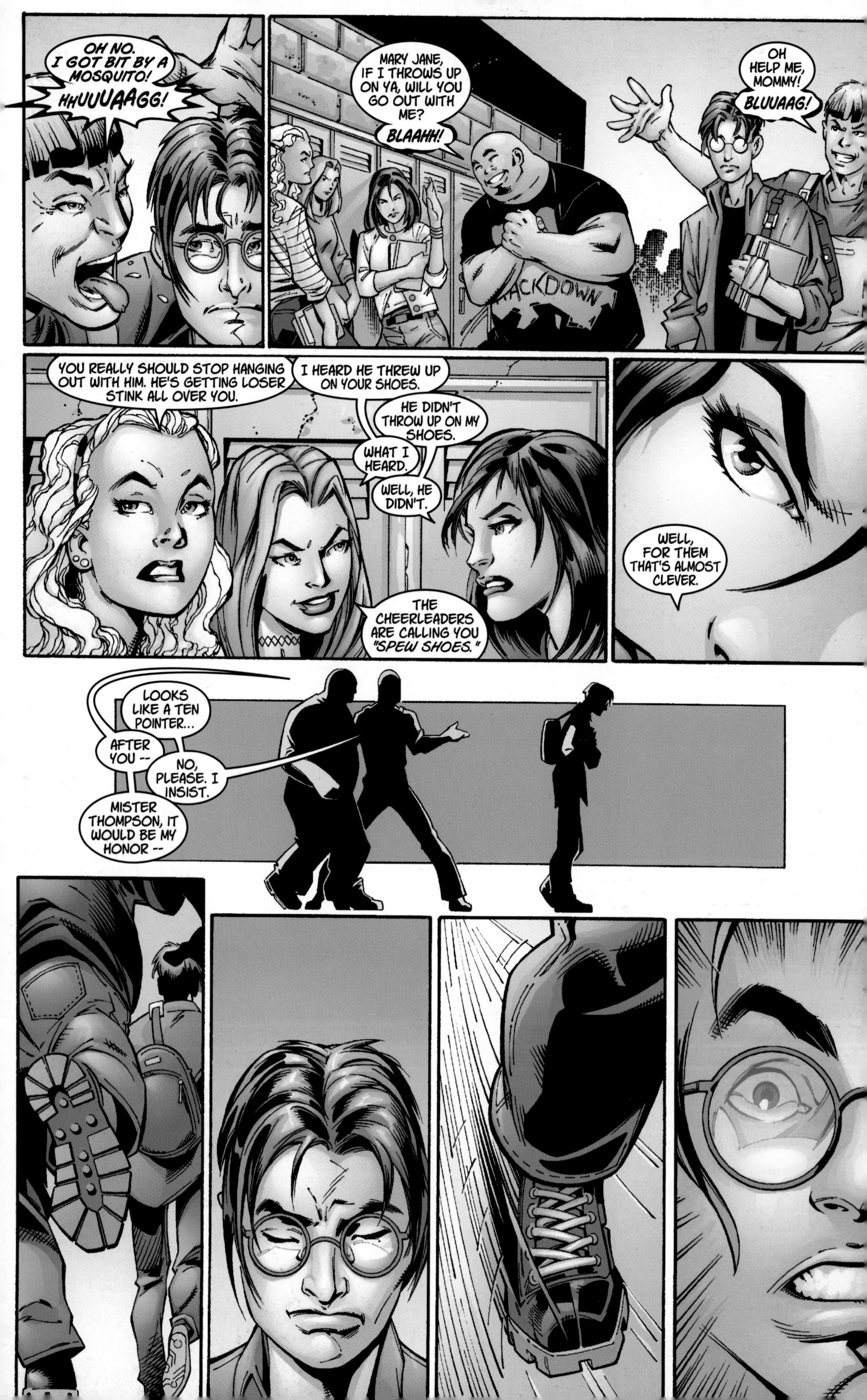
OH NO. I GOT BIT BY A MOSQUITO! HHUUUAAGG!
MARY JANE, IF I THROWS UP ON YA, WILL YOU GO OUT WITH ME? BLAAHH!
OH HELP ME, MOMMY! BLUUAAG!
YOU REALLY SHOULD STOP HANGING OUT WITH HIM. HE'S GETTING LOSER STINK ALL OVER YOU.
I HEARD HE THREW UP ON YOUR SHOES.
HE DIDN'T THROW UP ON MY SHOES.
WHAT I HEARD.
WELL, HE DIDN'T.
THE CHEERLEADERS ARE CALLING YOU "SPEW SHOES."
WELL, FOR THEM THAT'S ALMOST CLEVER.
LOOKS LIKE A TEN POINTER...
AFTER YOU --
NO, PLEASE. I INSIST.
MISTER THOMPSON, IT WOULD BE MY HONOR --
HACKDOWN

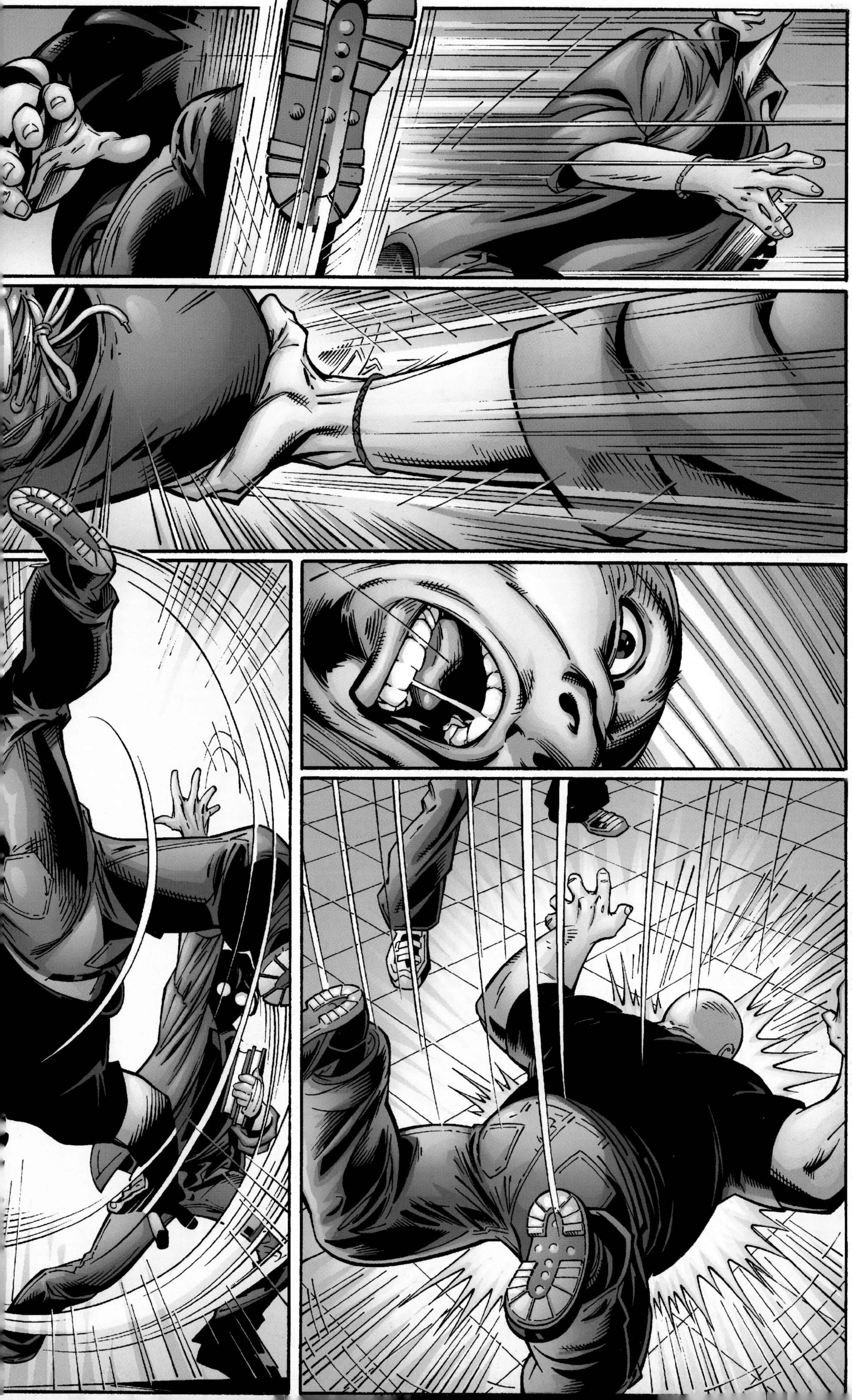

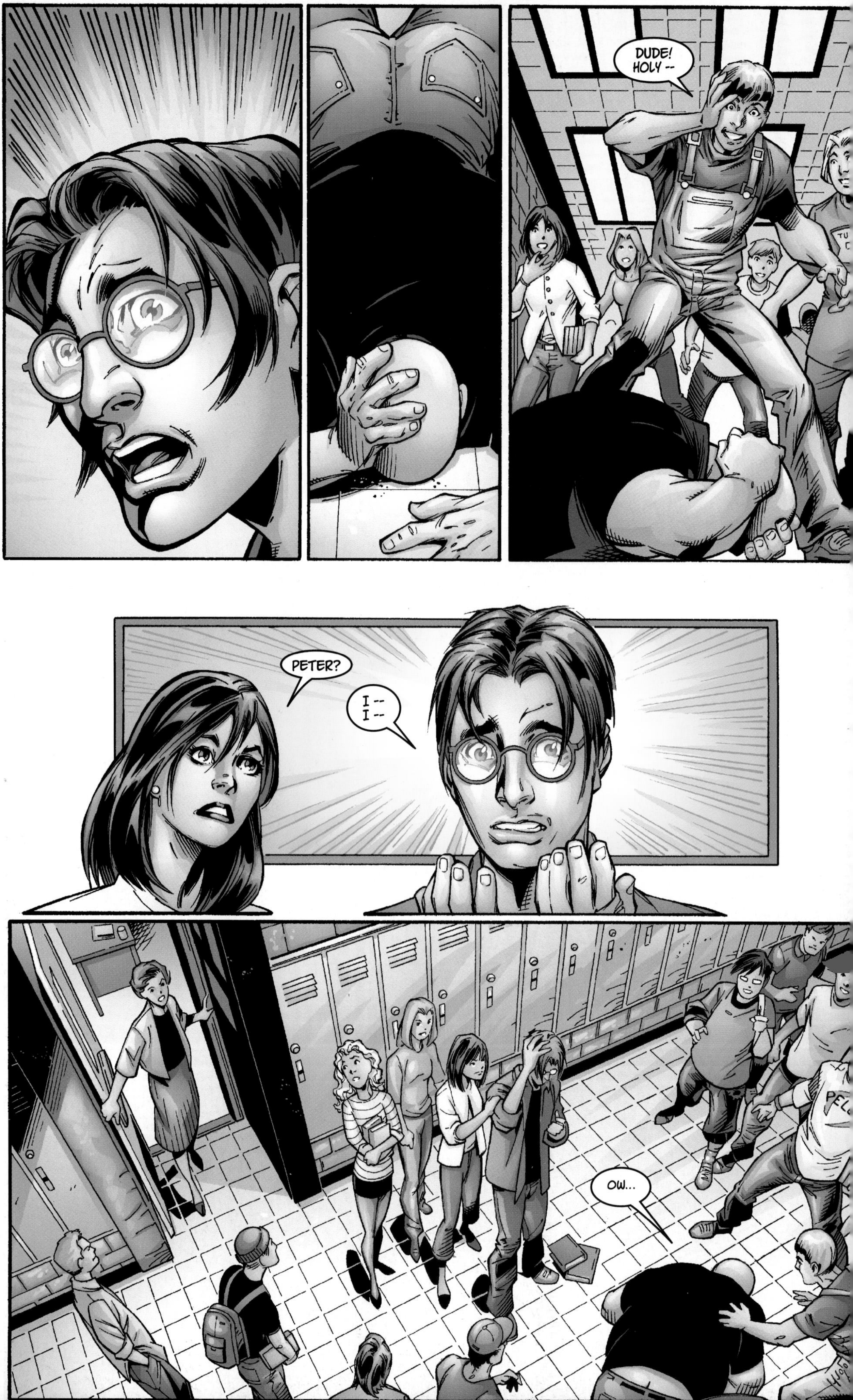
DUDE! HOLY --
PETER?
I --
I --
OW...

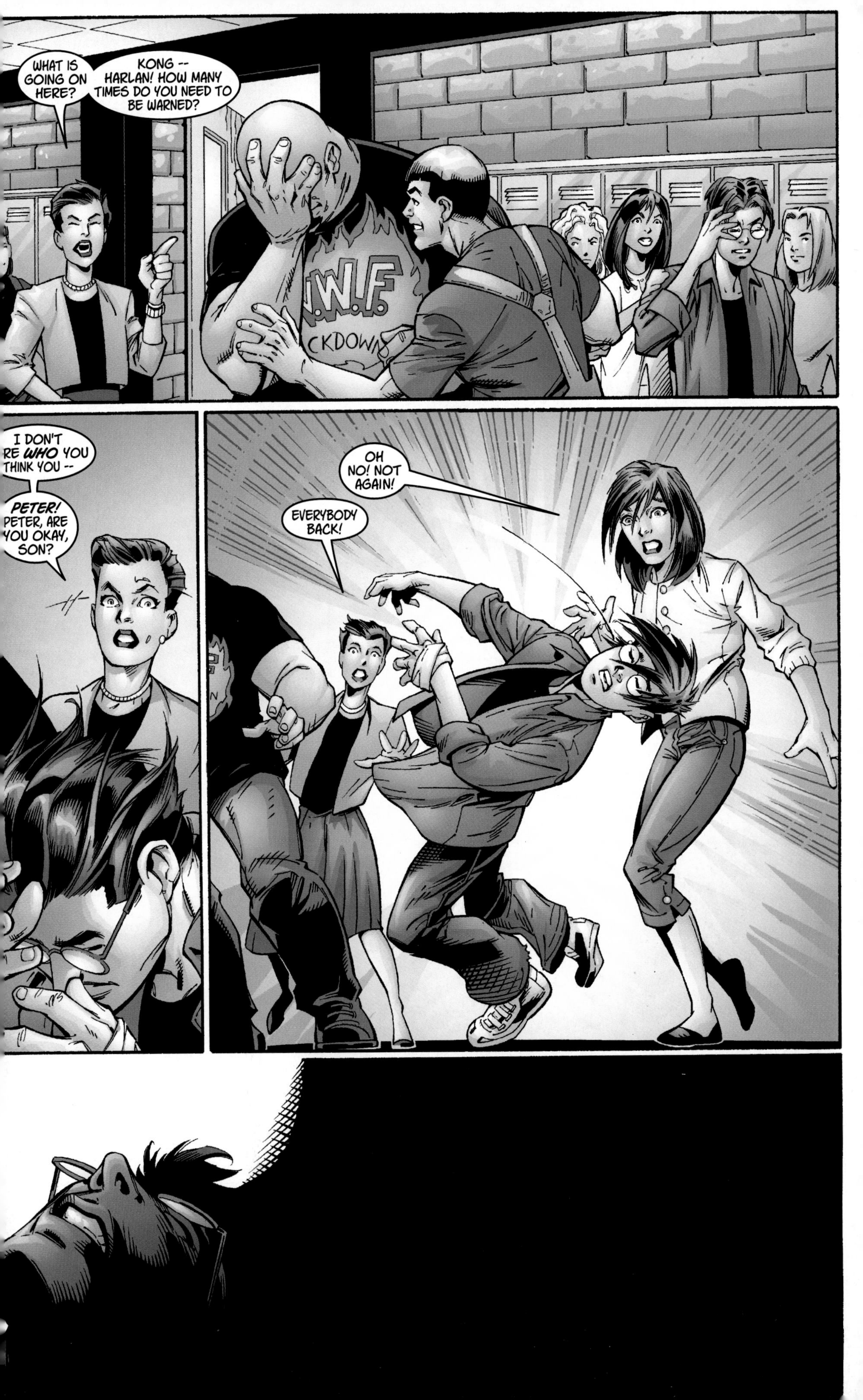
WHAT IS GOING ON HERE?
KONG -- HARLAN! HOW MANY TIMES DO YOU NEED TO BE WARNED?
N.W.F.
CKDOWN
I DON'T RE WHO YOU THINK YOU --
PETER! PETER, ARE YOU OKAY, SON?
OH NO! NOT AGAIN!
EVERYBODY BACK!

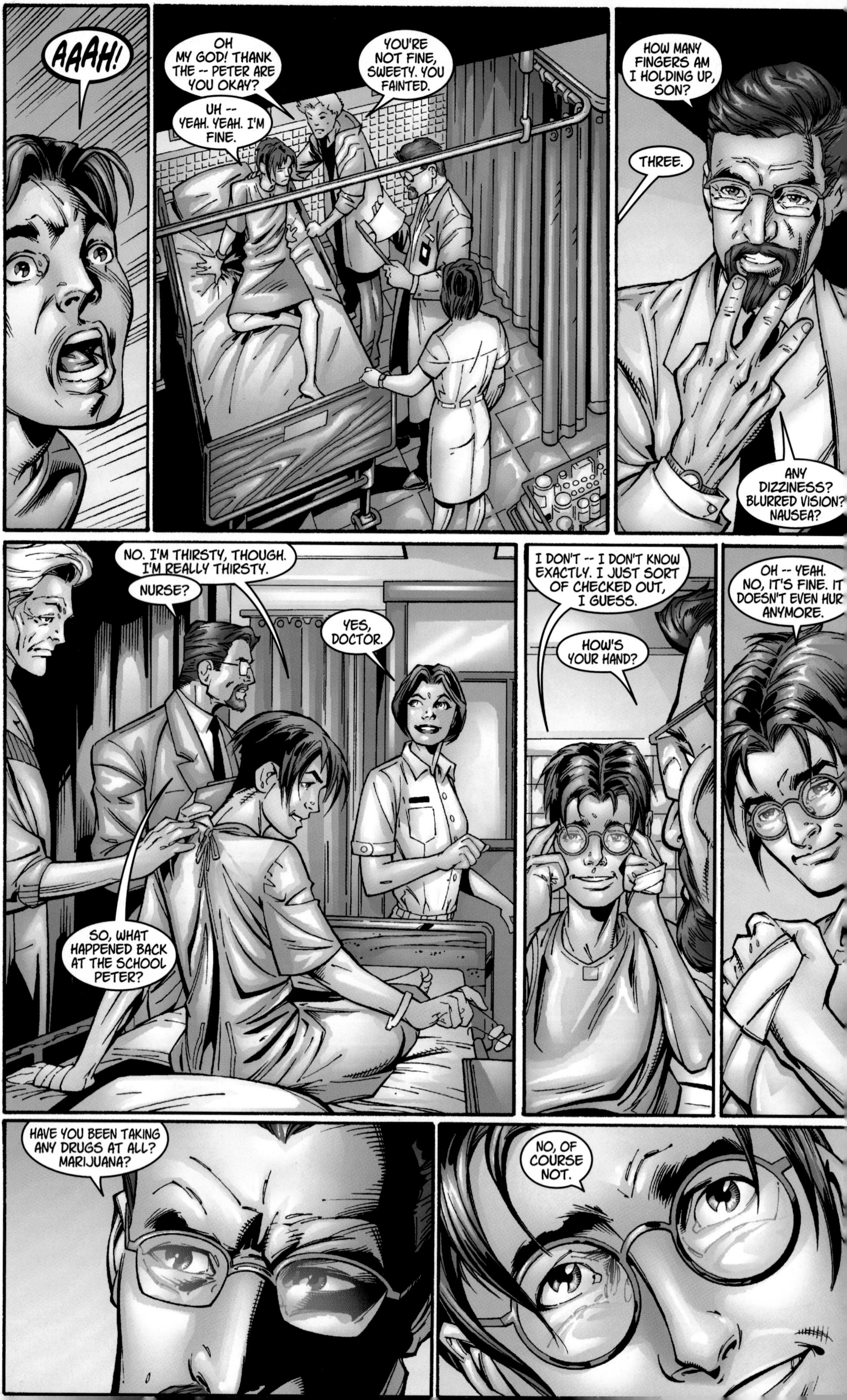
AAAH!
OH MY GOD! THANK THE -- PETER ARE YOU OKAY?
UH -- YEAH. YEAH. I'M FINE.
YOU'RE NOT FINE, SWEETY. YOU FAINTED.
HOW MANY FINGERS AM I HOLDING UP, SON?
THREE.
ANY DIZZINESS? BLURRED VISION? NAUSEA?
NO. I'M THIRSTY, THOUGH. I'M REALLY THIRSTY.
NURSE?
YES, DOCTOR.
SO, WHAT HAPPENED BACK AT THE SCHOOL PETER?
I DON'T -- I DON'T KNOW EXACTLY. I JUST SORT OF CHECKED OUT, I GUESS.
HOW'S YOUR HAND?
OH -- YEAH. NO, IT'S FINE. IT DOESN'T EVEN HUR ANYMORE.
HAVE YOU BEEN TAKING ANY DRUGS AT ALL? MARIJUANA?
NO, OF COURSE NOT.

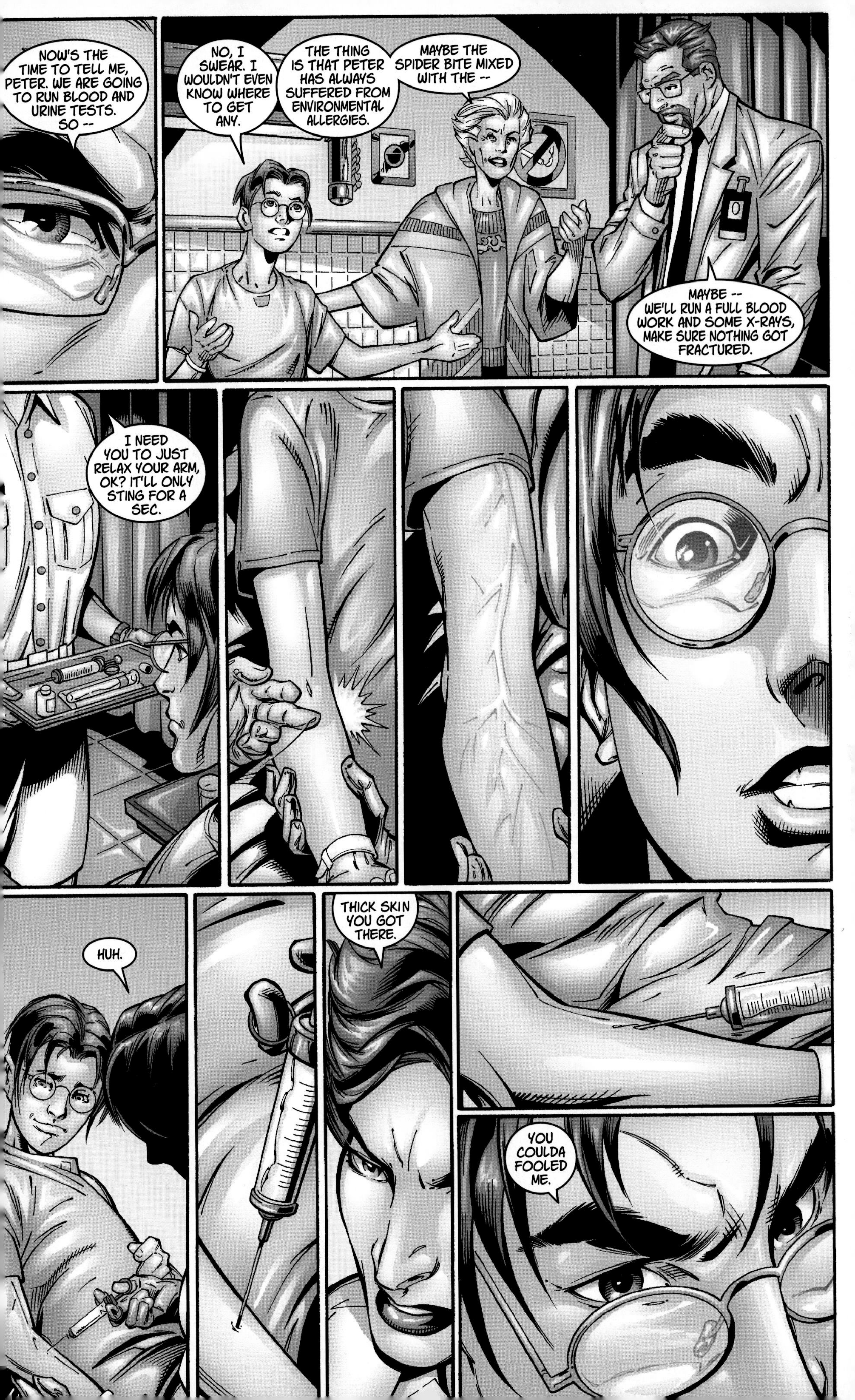
NOW'S THE TIME TO TELL ME, PETER. WE ARE GOING TO RUN BLOOD AND URINE TESTS. SO --
NO, I SWEAR. I WOULDN'T EVEN KNOW WHERE TO GET ANY.
THE THING IS THAT PETER HAS ALWAYS SUFFERED FROM ENVIRONMENTAL ALLERGIES.
MAYBE THE SPIDER BITE MIXED WITH THE --
MAYBE -- WE'LL RUN A FULL BLOOD WORK AND SOME X-RAYS, MAKE SURE NOTHING GOT FRACTURED.
I NEED YOU TO JUST RELAX YOUR ARM, OK? IT'LL ONLY STING FOR A SEC.
HUH.
THICK SKIN YOU GOT THERE.
YOU COULDA FOOLED ME.

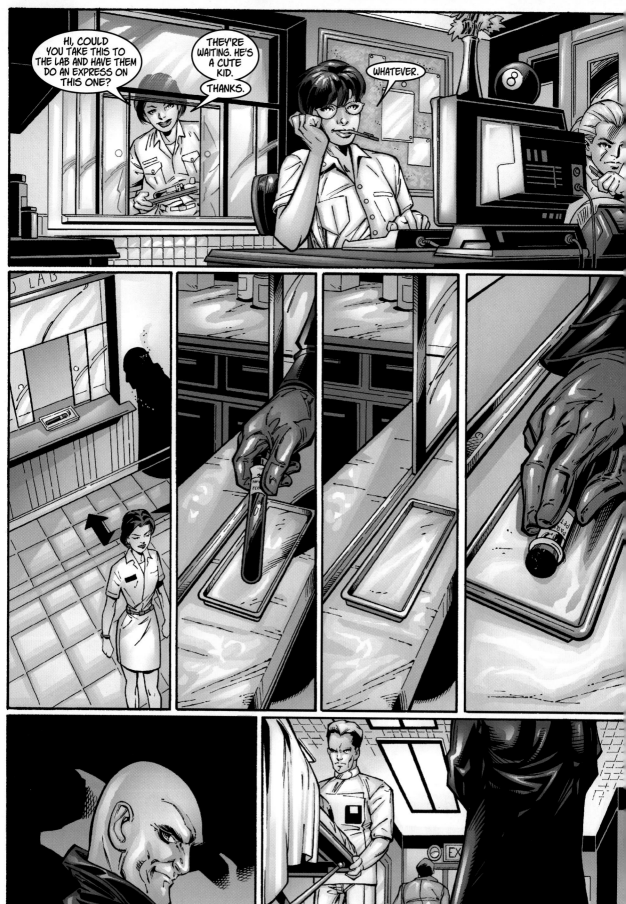

HI, COULD YOU TAKE THIS TO THE LAB AND HAVE THEM DO AN EXPRESS ON THIS ONE?

THANKS.

THEY'RE WAITING. HE'S A CUTE KID.

WHATEVER.

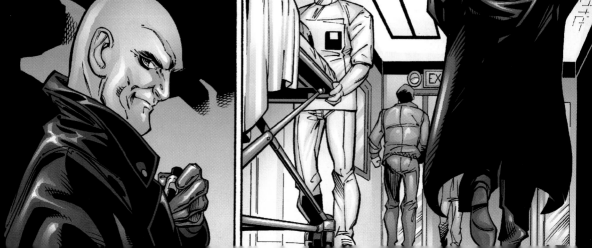

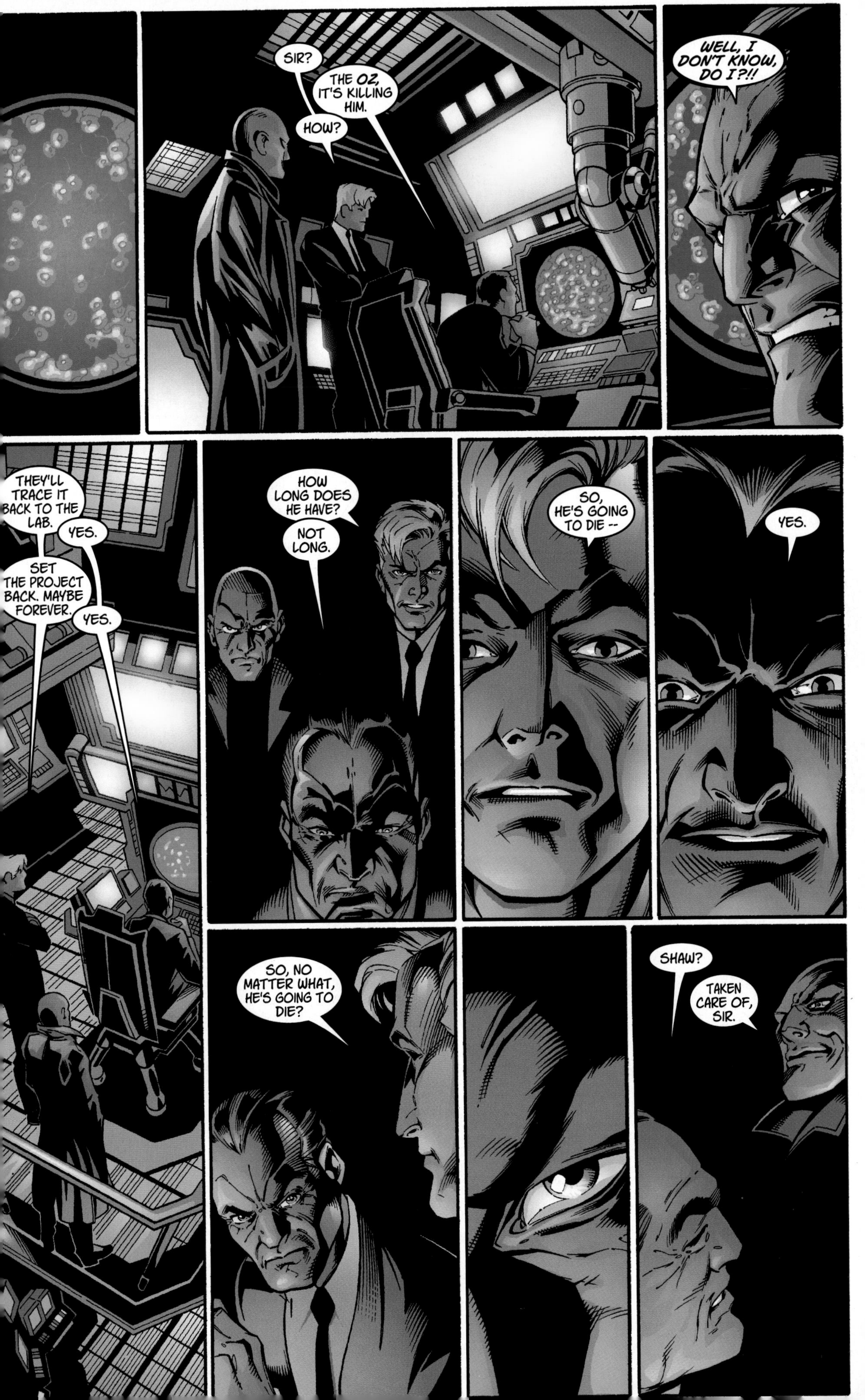
SIR?
THE OZ, IT'S KILLING HIM.
HOW?
WELL, I DON'T KNOW, DO I?!!
THEY'LL TRACE IT BACK TO THE LAB.
YES.
SET THE PROJECT BACK. MAYBE FOREVER.
YES.
HOW LONG DOES HE HAVE?
NOT LONG.
SO, HE'S GOING TO DIE --
YES.
SO, NO MATTER WHAT, HE'S GOING TO DIE?
SHAW?
TAKEN CARE OF, SIR.

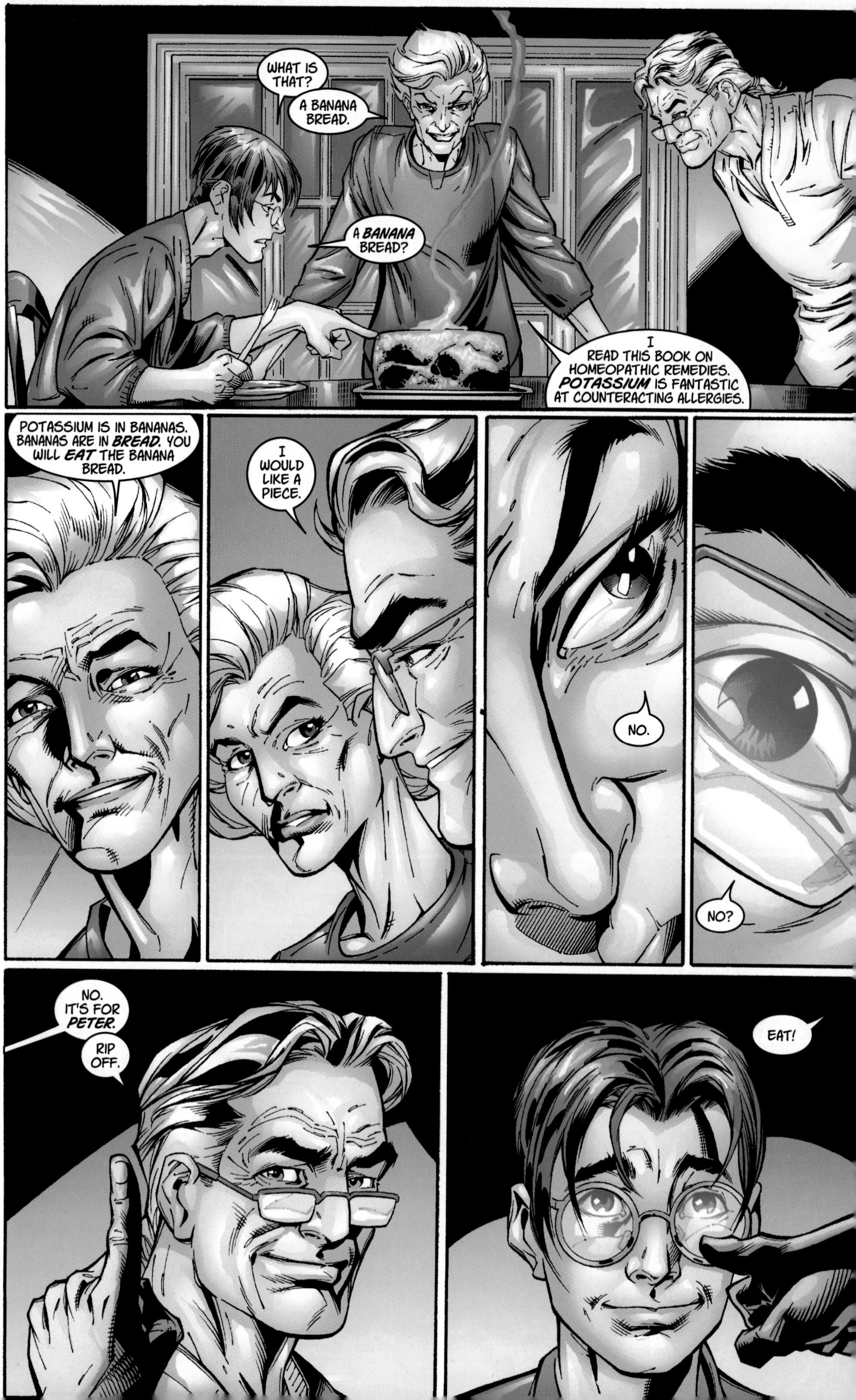
WHAT IS THAT?
A BANANA BREAD.
A *BANANA* BREAD?
I READ THIS BOOK ON HOMEOPATHIC REMEDIES. ***POTASSIUM*** IS FANTASTIC AT COUNTERACTING ALLERGIES.
POTASSIUM IS IN BANANAS. BANANAS ARE IN ***BREAD.*** YOU WILL ***EAT*** THE BANANA BREAD.
I WOULD LIKE A PIECE.
NO.
NO?
NO. IT'S FOR ***PETER.***
RIP OFF.
EAT!

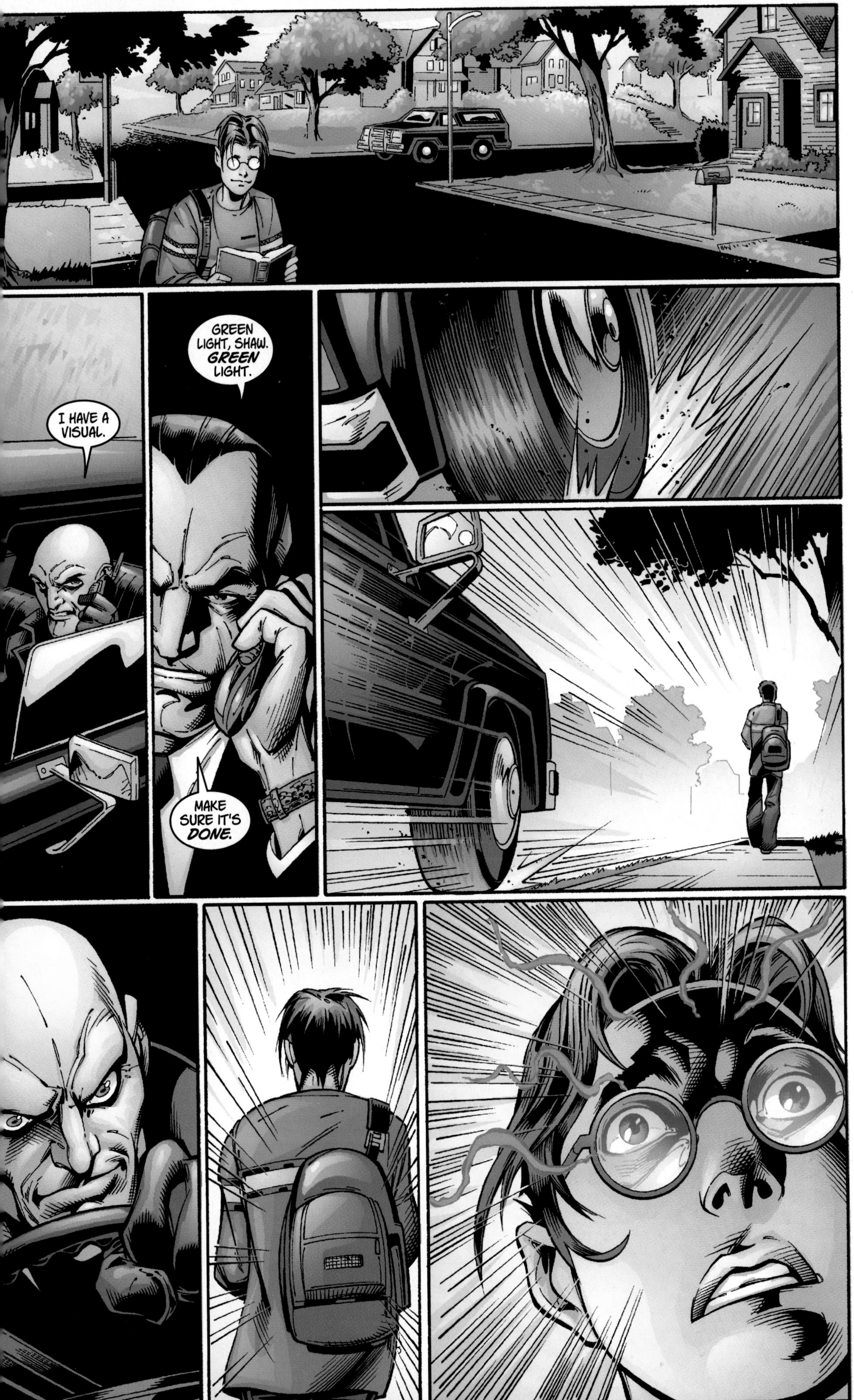
I HAVE A VISUAL.
GREEN LIGHT, SHAW. GREEN LIGHT.
MAKE SURE IT'S DONE.

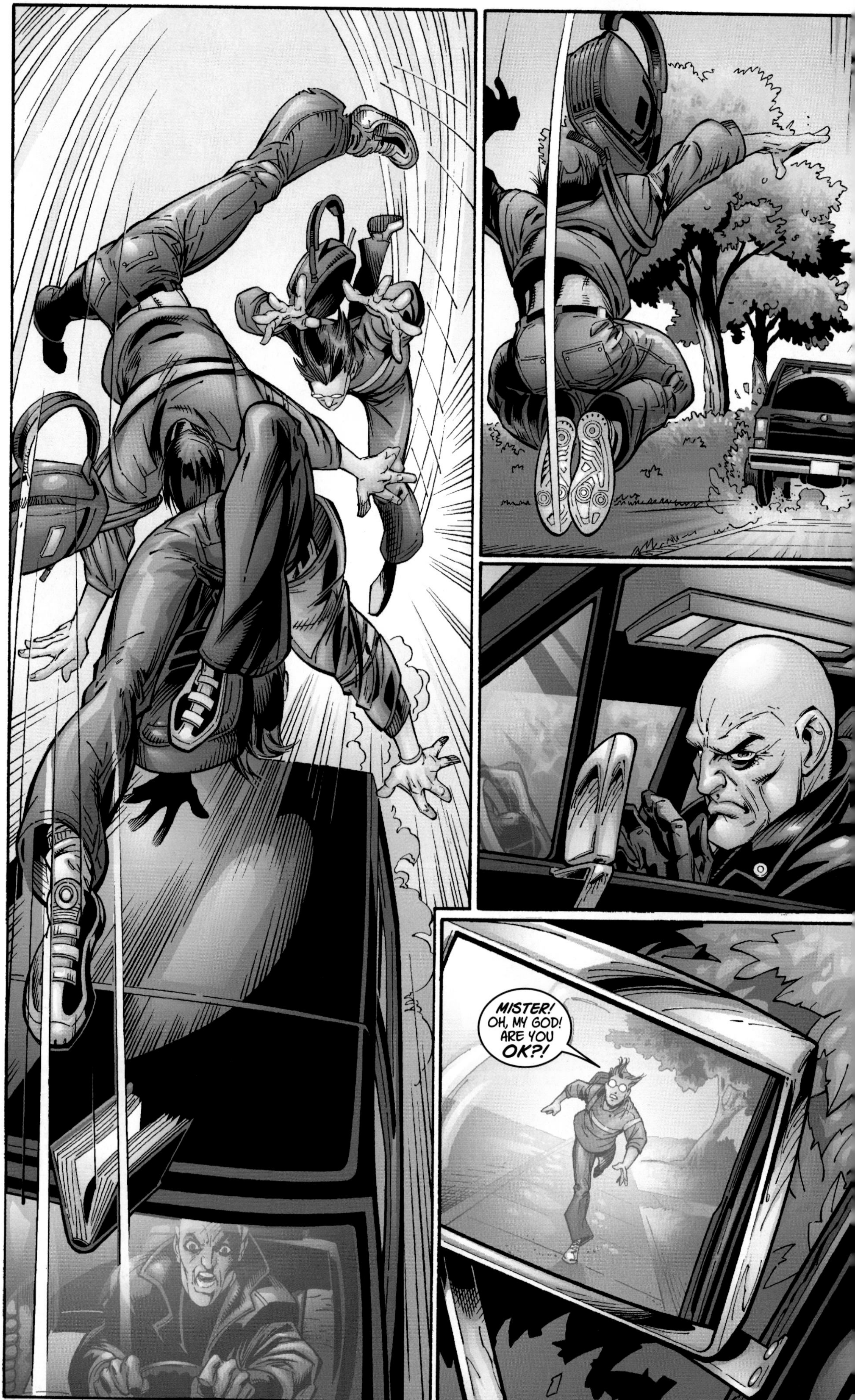
MISTER! OH, MY GOD! ARE YOU OK?!

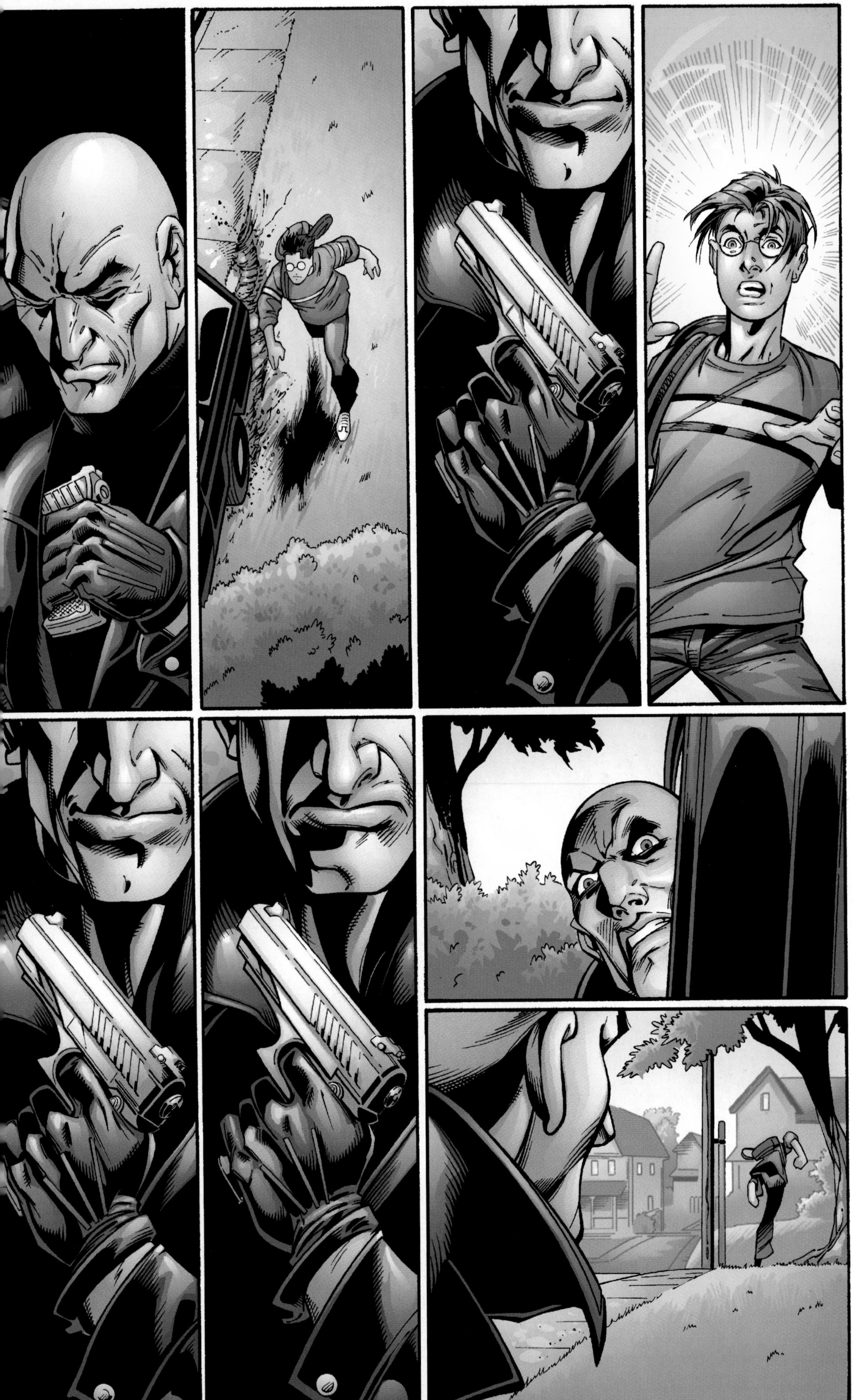

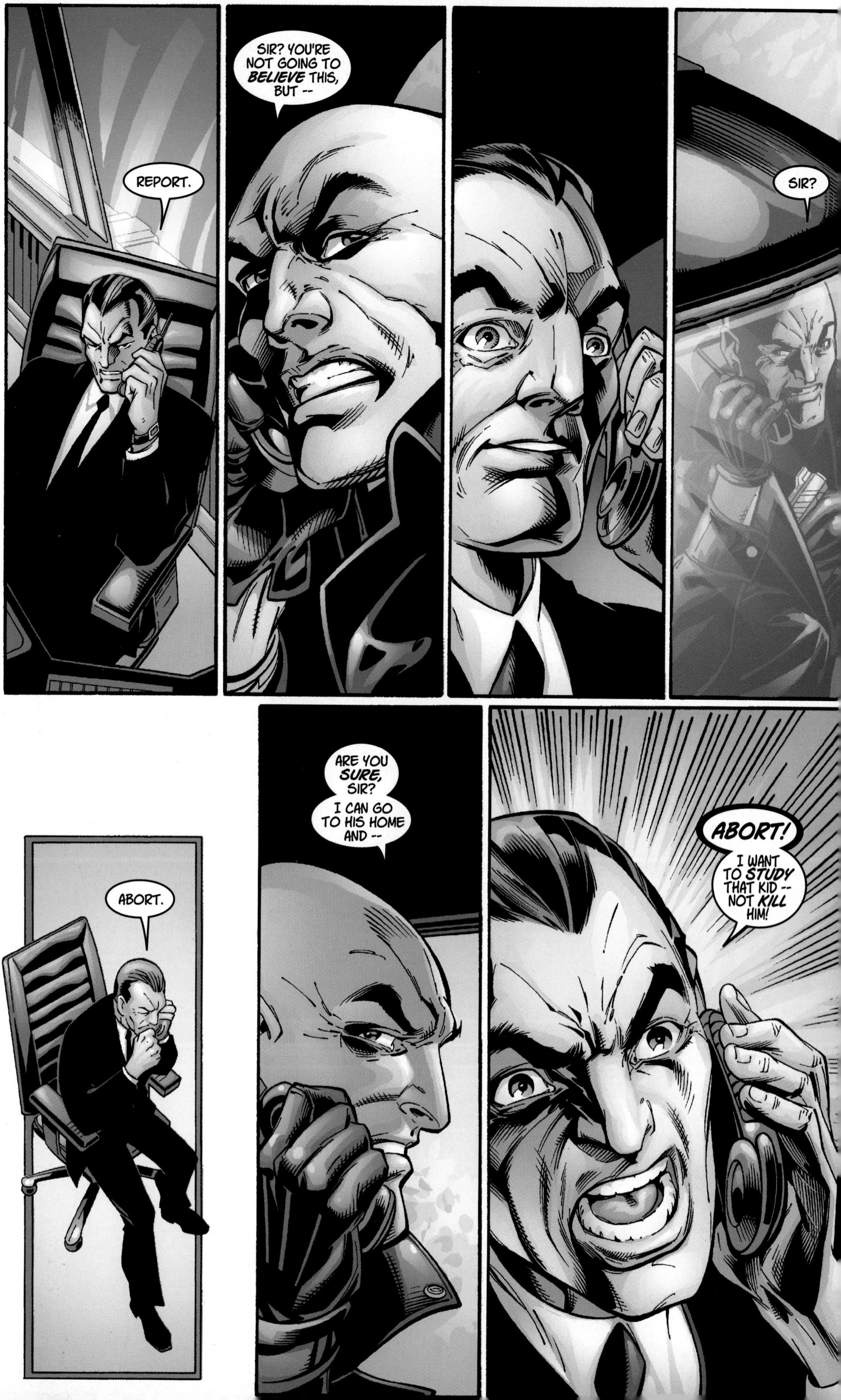
REPORT.
SIR? YOU'RE NOT GOING TO BELIEVE THIS, BUT --
SIR?
ABORT.
ARE YOU SURE, SIR?
I CAN GO TO HIS HOME AND --
ABORT!
I WANT TO STUDY THAT KID -- NOT KILL HIM!

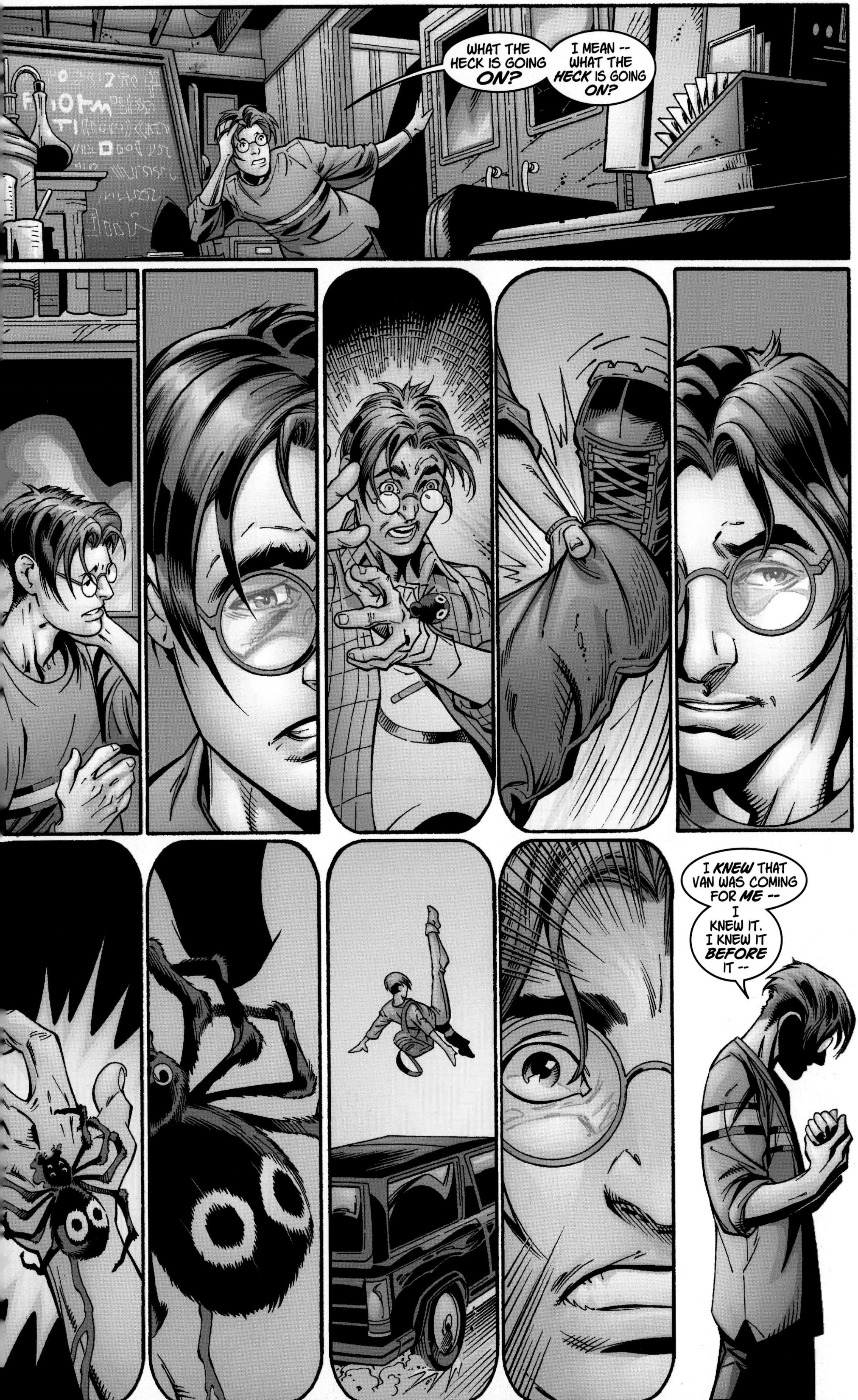
WHAT THE HECK IS GOING ON?
I MEAN -- WHAT THE HECK IS GOING ON?
I KNEW THAT VAN WAS COMING FOR ME --
I KNEW IT. I KNEW IT BEFORE IT --

SEARCH:

WWW.OSBORNINDUSTRIES.

SEARCH:

SPIDERS.

MANY PEOPLE
CONFUSE SPIDER
WITH INSECTS. B
BELONG TO THE
PHYLUM ARTHRO
IN THE ANIMAL
KINGDOM --

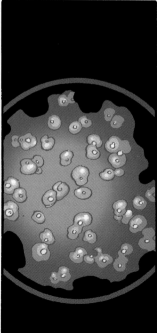

WELL,
WHADDAYA
THINK OF
THAT.

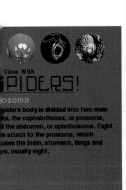

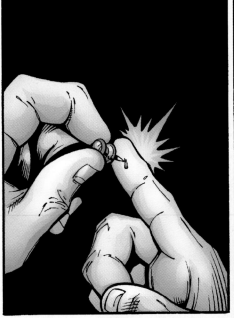

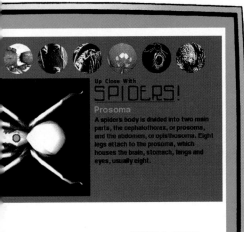

Up Close With
SPIDERS!
Prosoma
A spider's body is divided into two main parts, the cephalothorax, or prosoma, and the abdomen, or opisthosoma. Eight legs attach to the prosoma, which houses the brain, stomach, fangs and eyes, usually eight.
-- HAVE A GOOD DEVELOPED FEELING MECHANISM THAT MAKES THEM CAPABLE OF DETECTING MOVEMENTS OF --
NO WAY!

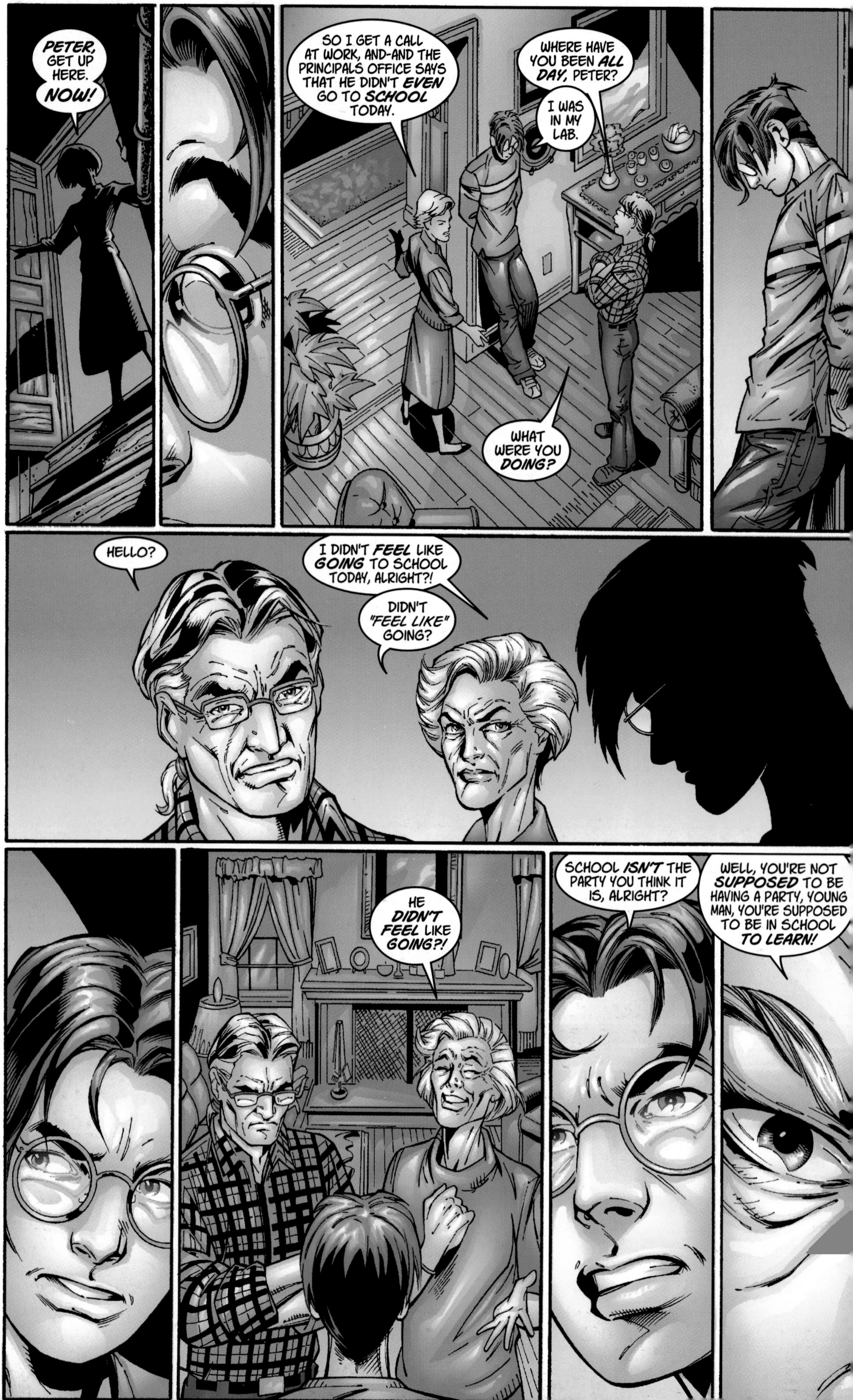
PETER, GET UP HERE. NOW!
SO I GET A CALL AT WORK, AND-AND THE PRINCIPALS OFFICE SAYS THAT HE DIDN'T EVEN GO TO SCHOOL TODAY.
WHERE HAVE YOU BEEN ALL DAY, PETER?
I WAS IN MY LAB.
WHAT WERE YOU DOING?
HELLO?
I DIDN'T FEEL LIKE GOING TO SCHOOL TODAY, ALRIGHT?!
DIDN'T "FEEL LIKE" GOING?
HE DIDN'T FEEL LIKE GOING?!
SCHOOL ISN'T THE PARTY YOU THINK IT IS, ALRIGHT?
WELL, YOU'RE NOT SUPPOSED TO BE HAVING A PARTY, YOUNG MAN, YOU'RE SUPPOSED TO BE IN SCHOOL TO LEARN!

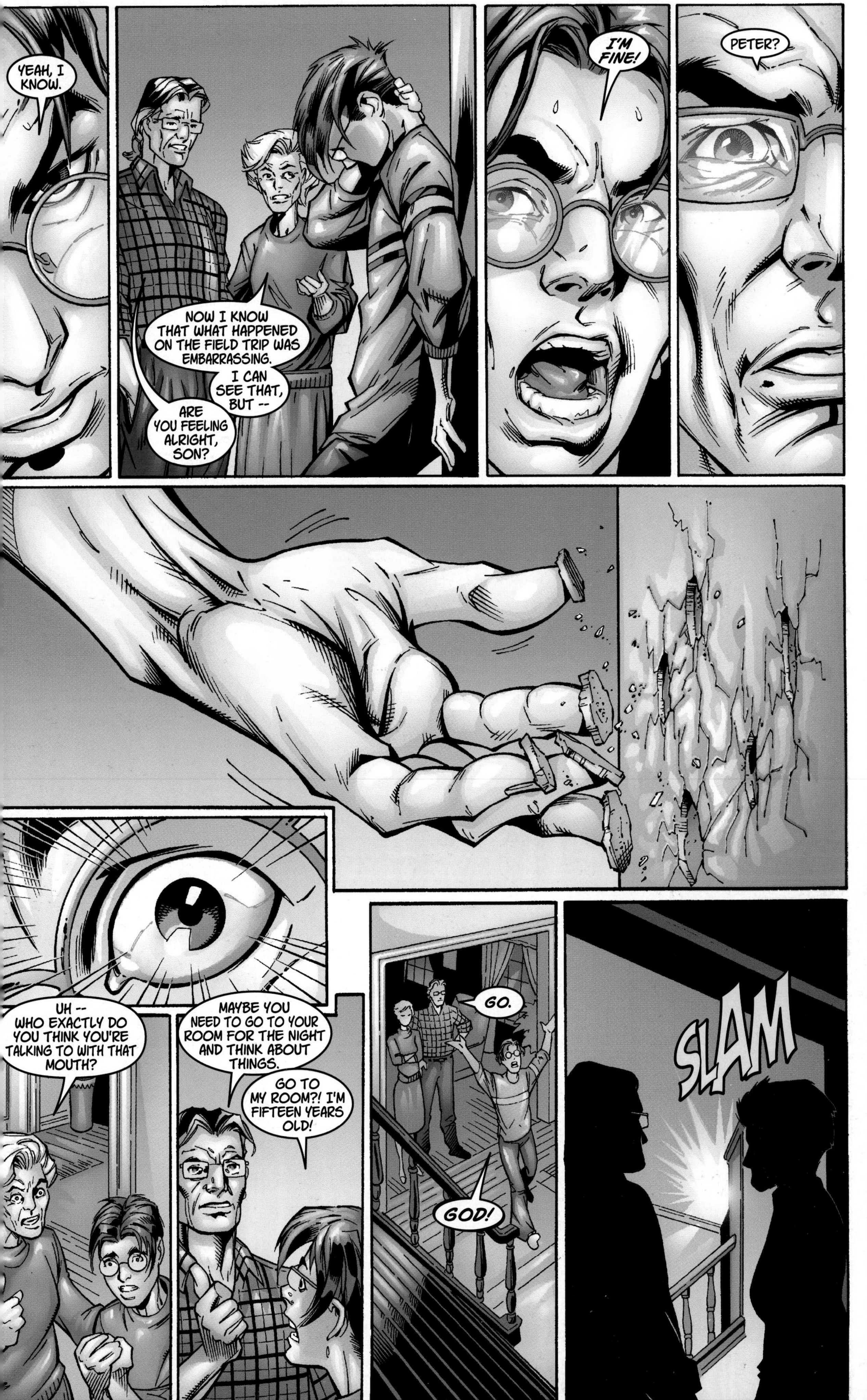
YEAH, I KNOW.
NOW I KNOW THAT WHAT HAPPENED ON THE FIELD TRIP WAS EMBARRASSING.
I CAN SEE THAT, BUT --
ARE YOU FEELING ALRIGHT, SON?
I'M FINE!
PETER?
UH -- WHO EXACTLY DO YOU THINK YOU'RE TALKING TO WITH THAT MOUTH?
MAYBE YOU NEED TO GO TO YOUR ROOM FOR THE NIGHT AND THINK ABOUT THINGS.
GO TO MY ROOM?! I'M FIFTEEN YEARS OLD!
GO.
GOD!
SLAM

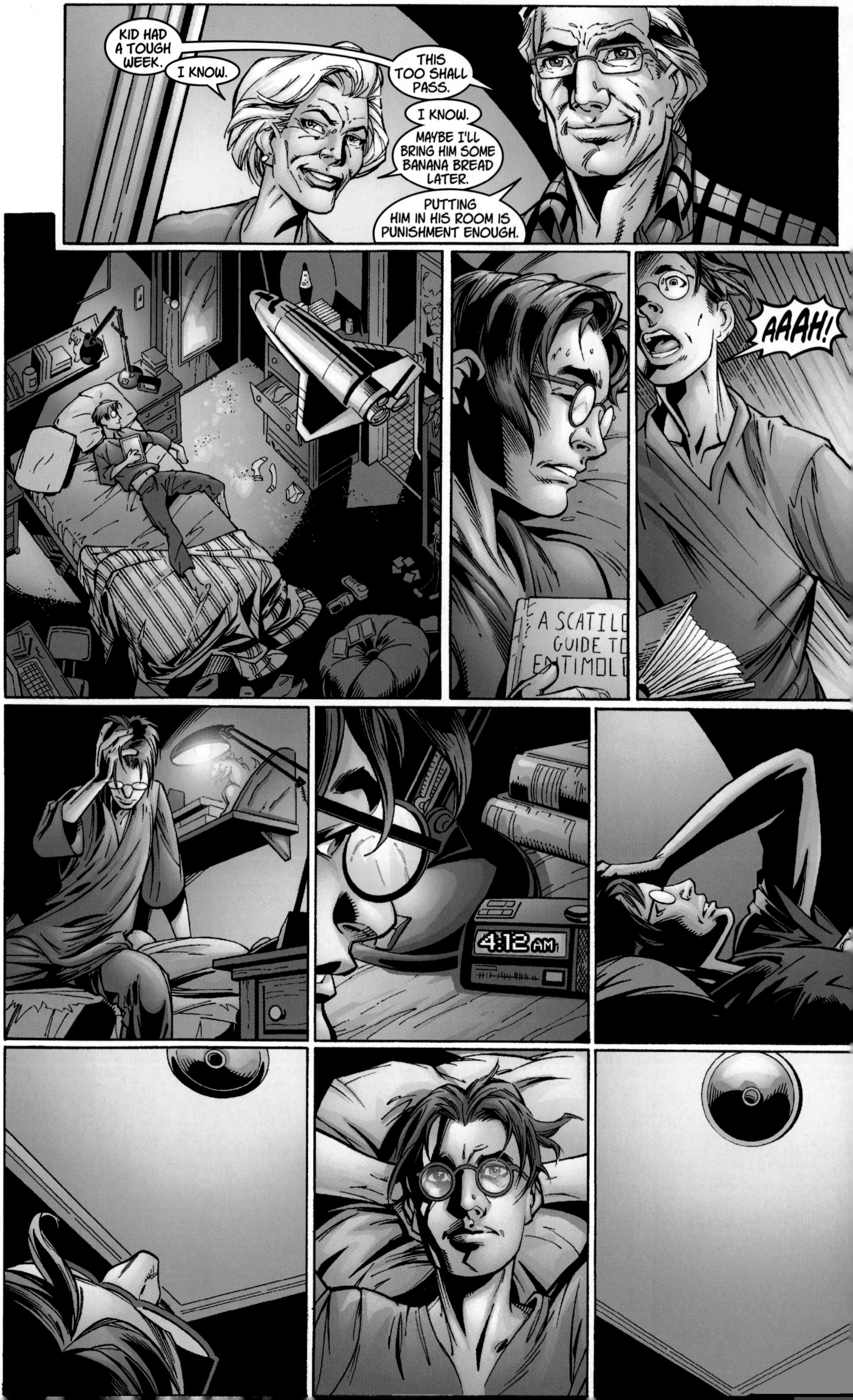
KID HAD A TOUGH WEEK.
I KNOW.
THIS TOO SHALL PASS.
I KNOW.
MAYBE I'LL BRING HIM SOME BANANA BREAD LATER.
PUTTING HIM IN HIS ROOM IS PUNISHMENT ENOUGH.
A SCATILO GUIDE TO ENTIMOL
AAAH!
4:12 AM

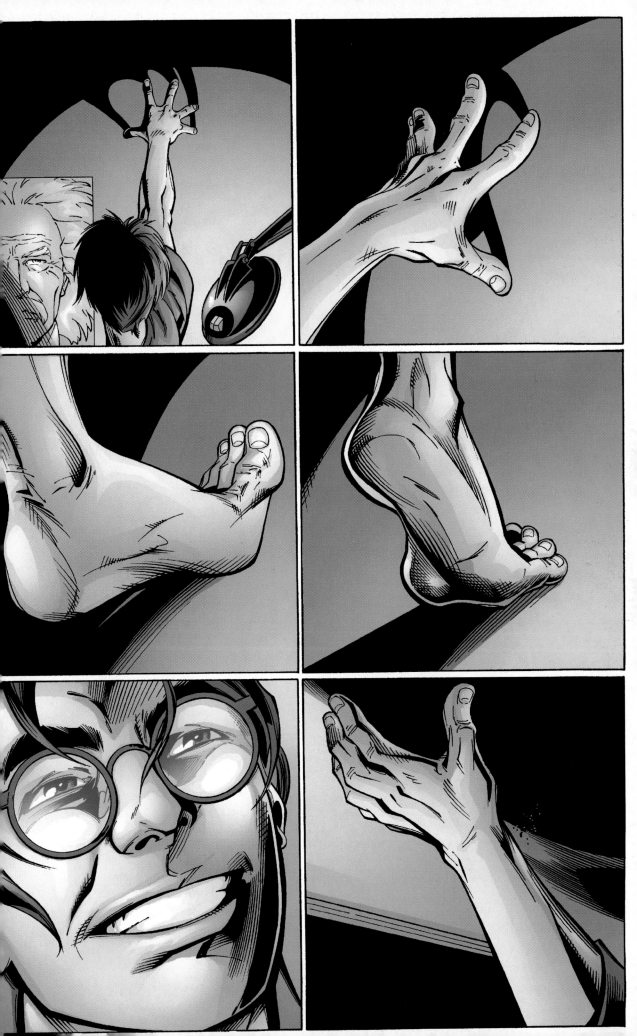

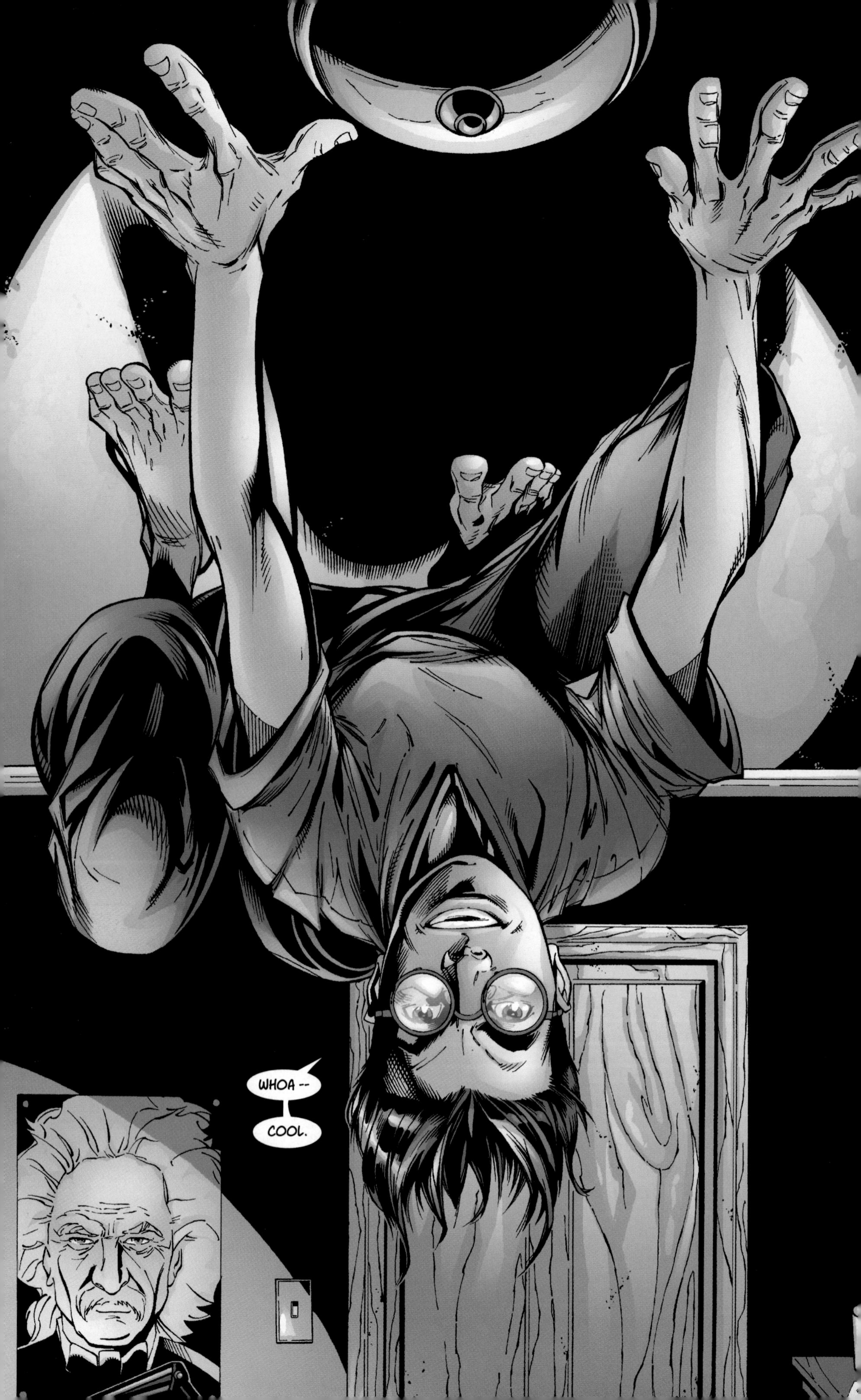
WHOA --
COOL.

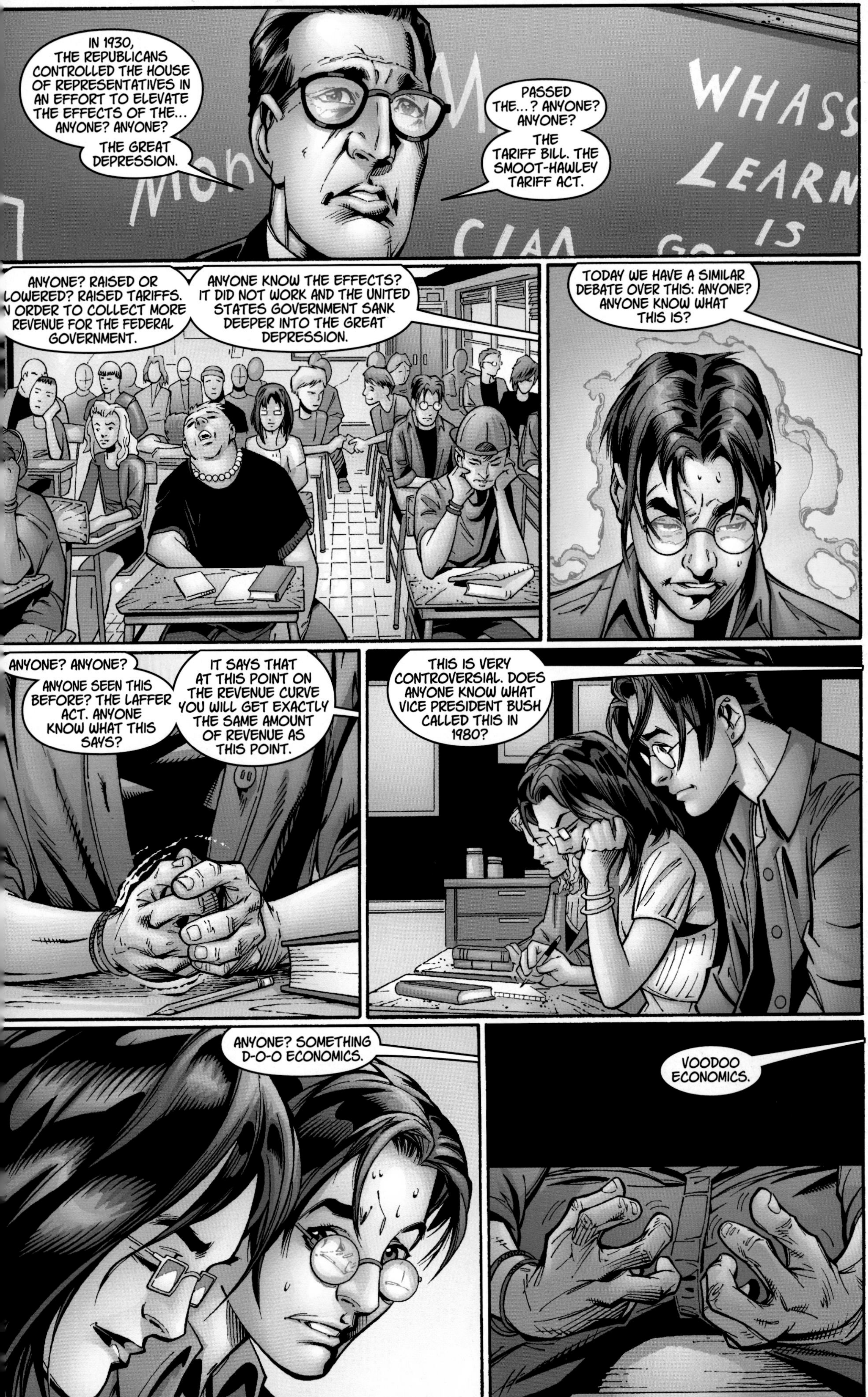

IN 1930, THE REPUBLICANS CONTROLLED THE HOUSE OF REPRESENTATIVES IN AN EFFORT TO ELEVATE THE EFFECTS OF THE... ANYONE? ANYONE?
THE GREAT DEPRESSION.
PASSED THE...? ANYONE? ANYONE?
THE TARIFF BILL. THE SMOOT-HAWLEY TARIFF ACT.
ANYONE? RAISED OR LOWERED? RAISED TARIFFS. N ORDER TO COLLECT MORE REVENUE FOR THE FEDERAL GOVERNMENT.
ANYONE KNOW THE EFFECTS? IT DID NOT WORK AND THE UNITED STATES GOVERNMENT SANK DEEPER INTO THE GREAT DEPRESSION.
TODAY WE HAVE A SIMILAR DEBATE OVER THIS: ANYONE? ANYONE KNOW WHAT THIS IS?
ANYONE? ANYONE?
ANYONE SEEN THIS BEFORE? THE LAFFER ACT. ANYONE KNOW WHAT THIS SAYS?
IT SAYS THAT AT THIS POINT ON THE REVENUE CURVE YOU WILL GET EXACTLY THE SAME AMOUNT OF REVENUE AS THIS POINT.
THIS IS VERY CONTROVERSIAL. DOES ANYONE KNOW WHAT VICE PRESIDENT BUSH CALLED THIS IN 1980?
ANYONE? SOMETHING D-O-O ECONOMICS.
VOODOO ECONOMICS.

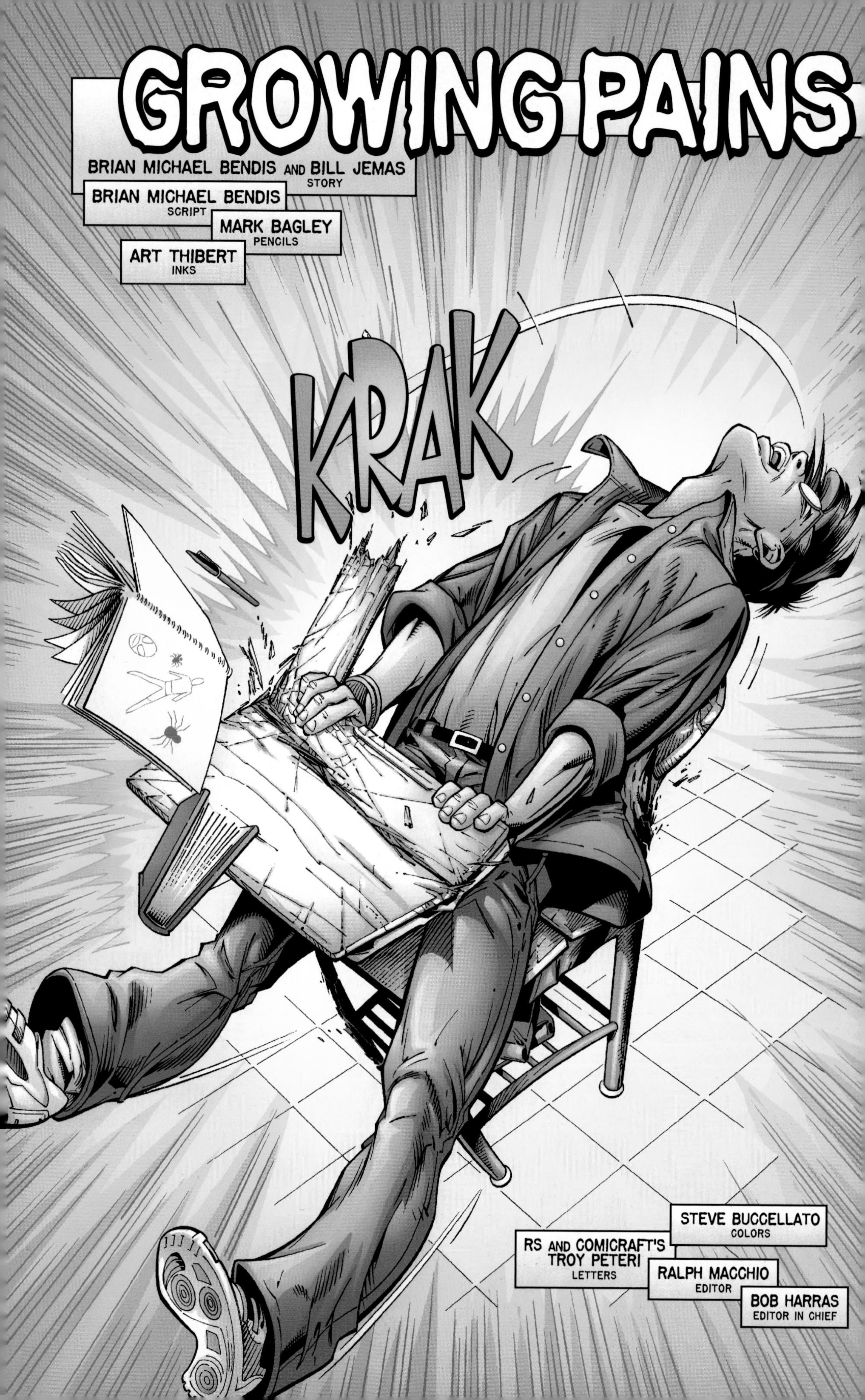
GROWING PAINS
BRIAN MICHAEL BENDIS AND BILL JEMAS
STORY
BRIAN MICHAEL BENDIS
SCRIPT
MARK BAGLEY
PENCILS
ART THIBERT
INKS
KRAK
STEVE BUCCELLATO
COLORS
RS AND COMICRAFT'S
TROY PETERI
LETTERS
RALPH MACCHIO
EDITOR
BOB HARRAS
EDITOR IN CHIEF

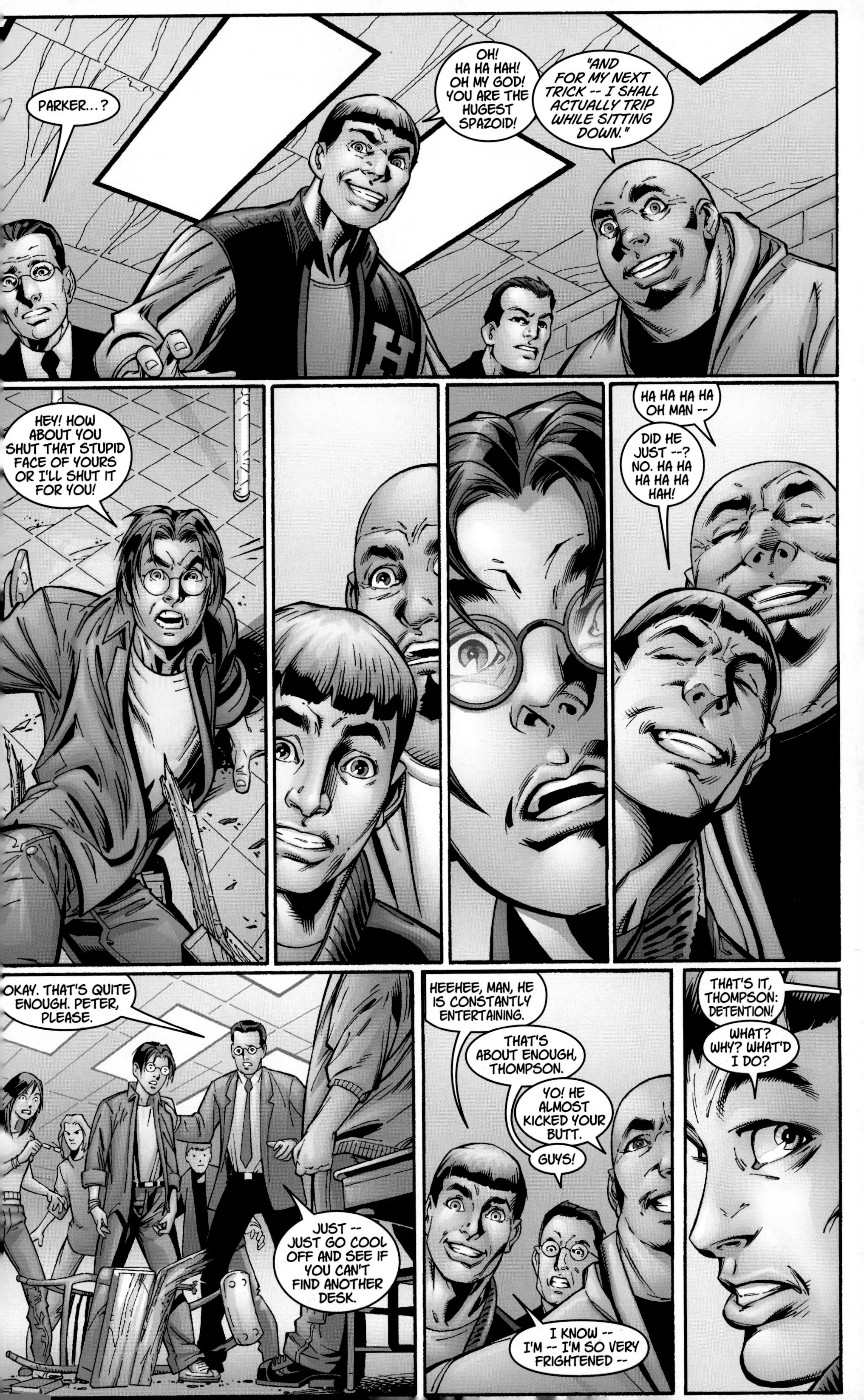
PARKER...?
OH! HA HA HAH! OH MY GOD! YOU ARE THE HUGEST SPAZOID!
"AND FOR MY NEXT TRICK -- I SHALL ACTUALLY TRIP WHILE SITTING DOWN."
HEY! HOW ABOUT YOU SHUT THAT STUPID FACE OF YOURS OR I'LL SHUT IT FOR YOU!
HA HA HA HA OH MAN --
DID HE JUST --? NO. HA HA HA HA HA HAH!
OKAY. THAT'S QUITE ENOUGH. PETER, PLEASE.
JUST -- JUST GO COOL OFF AND SEE IF YOU CAN'T FIND ANOTHER DESK.
HEEHEE, MAN, HE IS CONSTANTLY ENTERTAINING.
THAT'S ABOUT ENOUGH, THOMPSON.
YO! HE ALMOST KICKED YOUR BUTT.
GUYS!
I KNOW -- I'M -- I'M SO VERY FRIGHTENED --
THAT'S IT, THOMPSON: DETENTION!
WHAT? WHY? WHAT'D I DO?

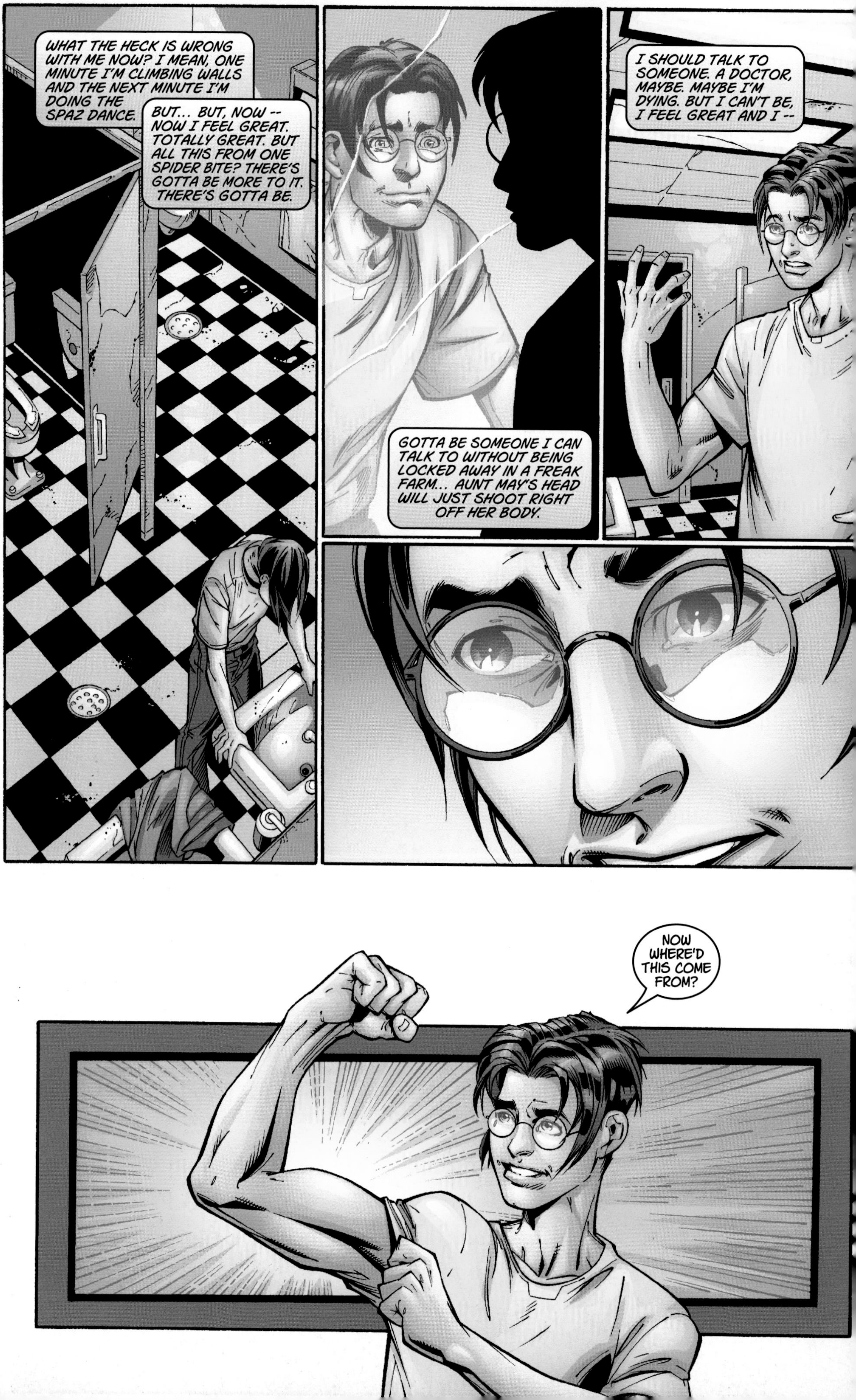
WHAT THE HECK IS WRONG WITH ME NOW? I MEAN, ONE MINUTE I'M CLIMBING WALLS AND THE NEXT MINUTE I'M DOING THE SPAZ DANCE.
BUT... BUT, NOW -- NOW I FEEL GREAT. TOTALLY GREAT. BUT ALL THIS FROM ONE SPIDER BITE? THERE'S GOTTA BE MORE TO IT. THERE'S GOTTA BE.
GOTTA BE SOMEONE I CAN TALK TO WITHOUT BEING LOCKED AWAY IN A FREAK FARM... AUNT MAY'S HEAD WILL JUST SHOOT RIGHT OFF HER BODY.
I SHOULD TALK TO SOMEONE. A DOCTOR, MAYBE. MAYBE I'M DYING. BUT I CAN'T BE, I FEEL GREAT AND I --
NOW WHERE'D THIS COME FROM?

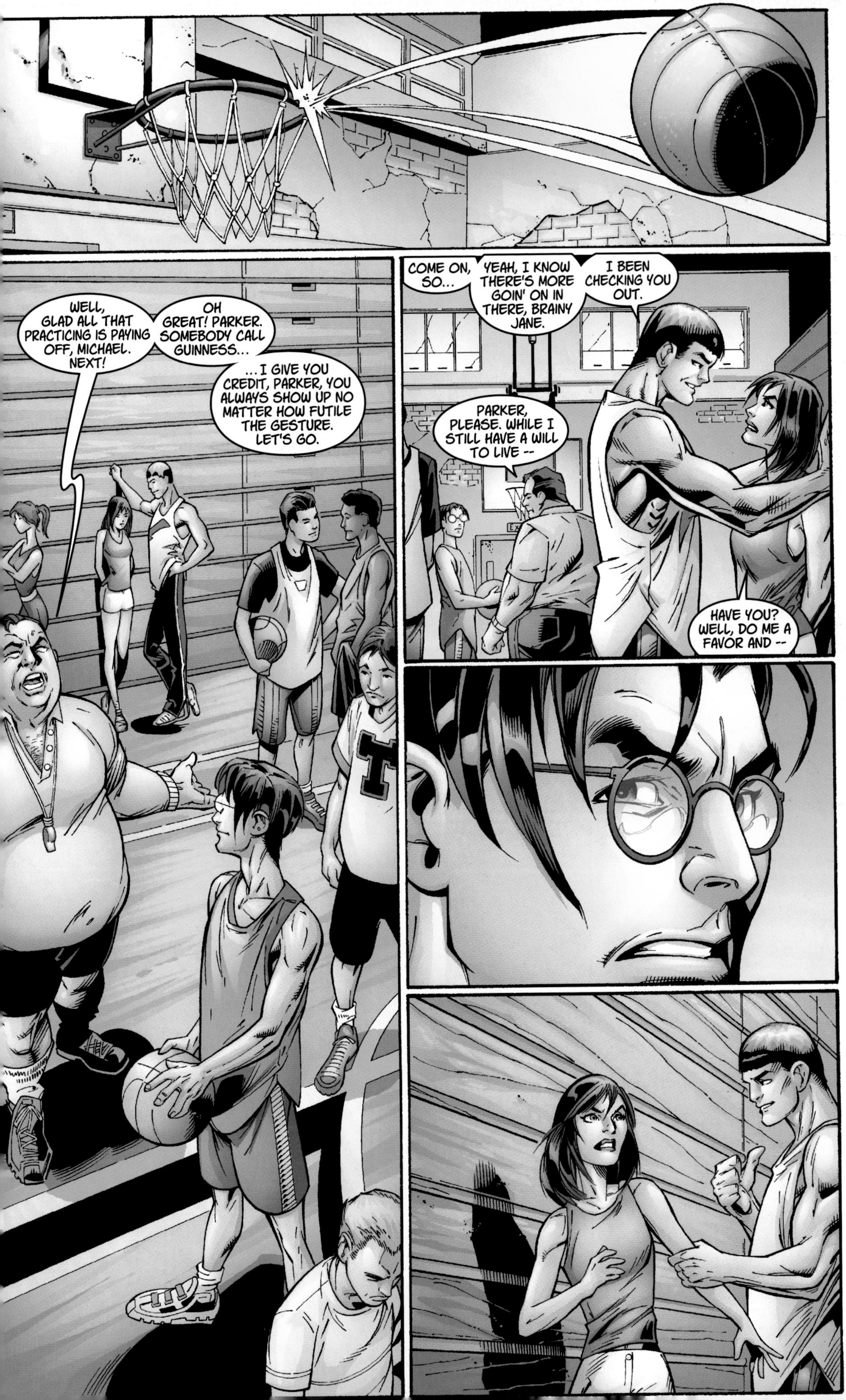
WELL, GLAD ALL THAT PRACTICING IS PAYING OFF, MICHAEL. NEXT!
OH GREAT! PARKER. SOMEBODY CALL GUINNESS...
...I GIVE YOU CREDIT, PARKER, YOU ALWAYS SHOW UP NO MATTER HOW FUTILE THE GESTURE. LET'S GO.
COME ON, SO...
YEAH, I KNOW THERE'S MORE GOIN' ON IN THERE, BRAINY JANE.
I BEEN CHECKING YOU OUT.
PARKER, PLEASE. WHILE I STILL HAVE A WILL TO LIVE --
HAVE YOU? WELL, DO ME A FAVOR AND --

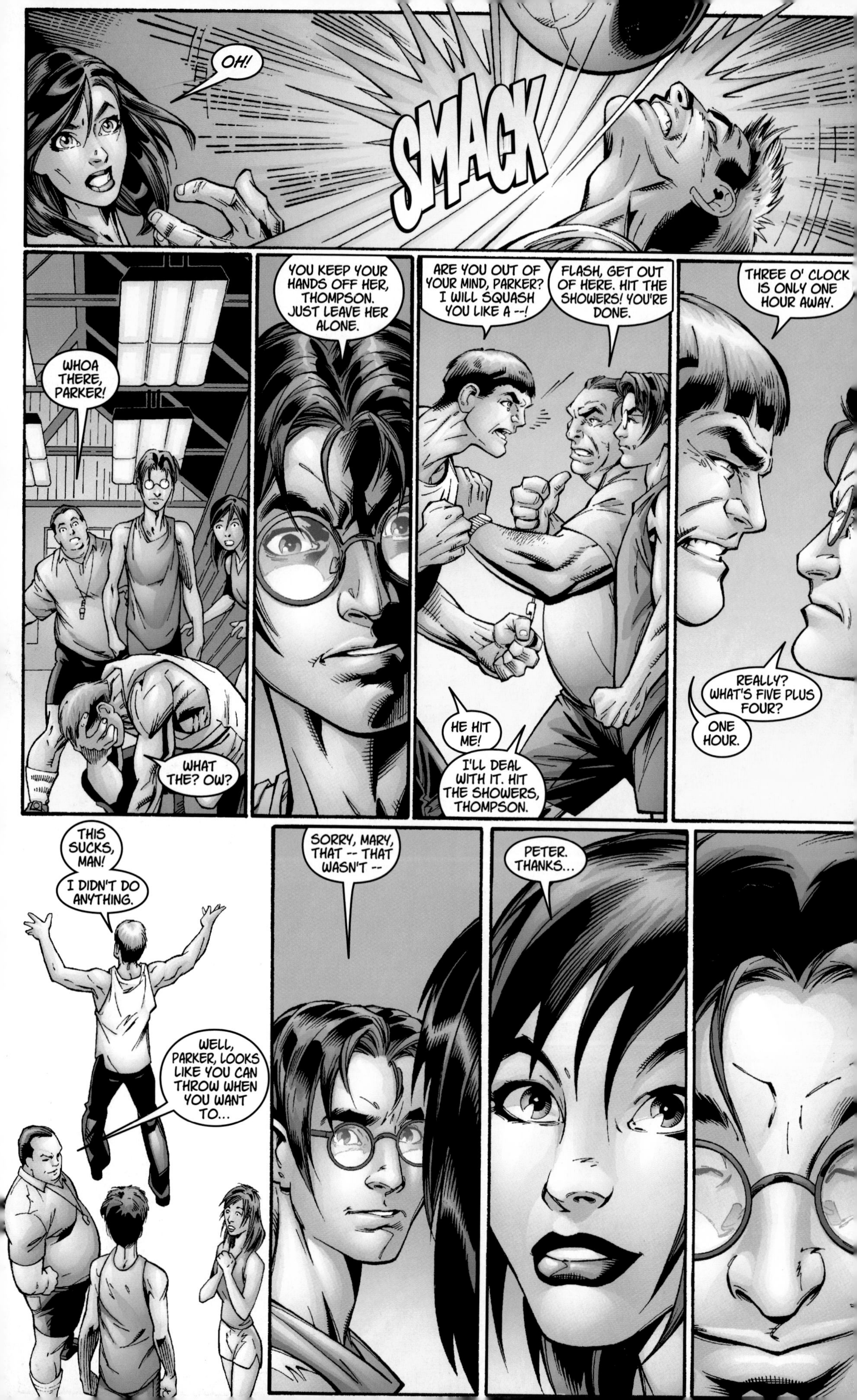
OH!
SMACK
WHOA THERE, PARKER!
WHAT THE? OW?
YOU KEEP YOUR HANDS OFF HER, THOMPSON. JUST LEAVE HER ALONE.
ARE YOU OUT OF YOUR MIND, PARKER? I WILL SQUASH YOU LIKE A --!
FLASH, GET OUT OF HERE. HIT THE SHOWERS! YOU'RE DONE.
HE HIT ME!
I'LL DEAL WITH IT. HIT THE SHOWERS, THOMPSON.
THREE O' CLOCK IS ONLY ONE HOUR AWAY.
REALLY? WHAT'S FIVE PLUS FOUR?
ONE HOUR.
THIS SUCKS, MAN!
I DIDN'T DO ANYTHING.
WELL, PARKER, LOOKS LIKE YOU CAN THROW WHEN YOU WANT TO...
SORRY, MARY, THAT -- THAT WASN'T --
PETER. THANKS...

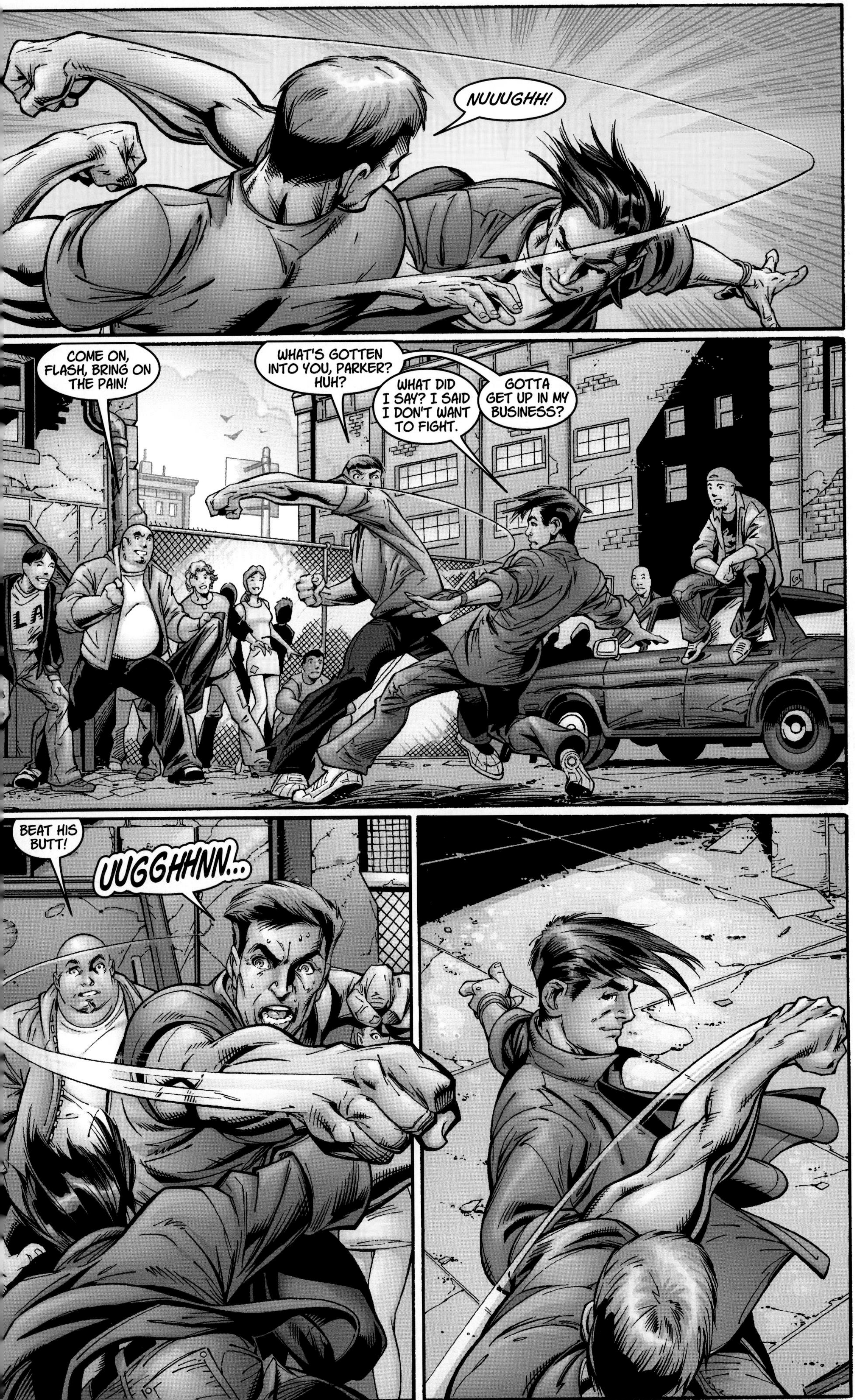
NUUUGHH!
COME ON, FLASH, BRING ON THE PAIN!
WHAT'S GOTTEN INTO YOU, PARKER? HUH?
WHAT DID I SAY? I SAID I DON'T WANT TO FIGHT.
GOTTA GET UP IN MY BUSINESS?
BEAT HIS BUTT!
UUGGHHNN...

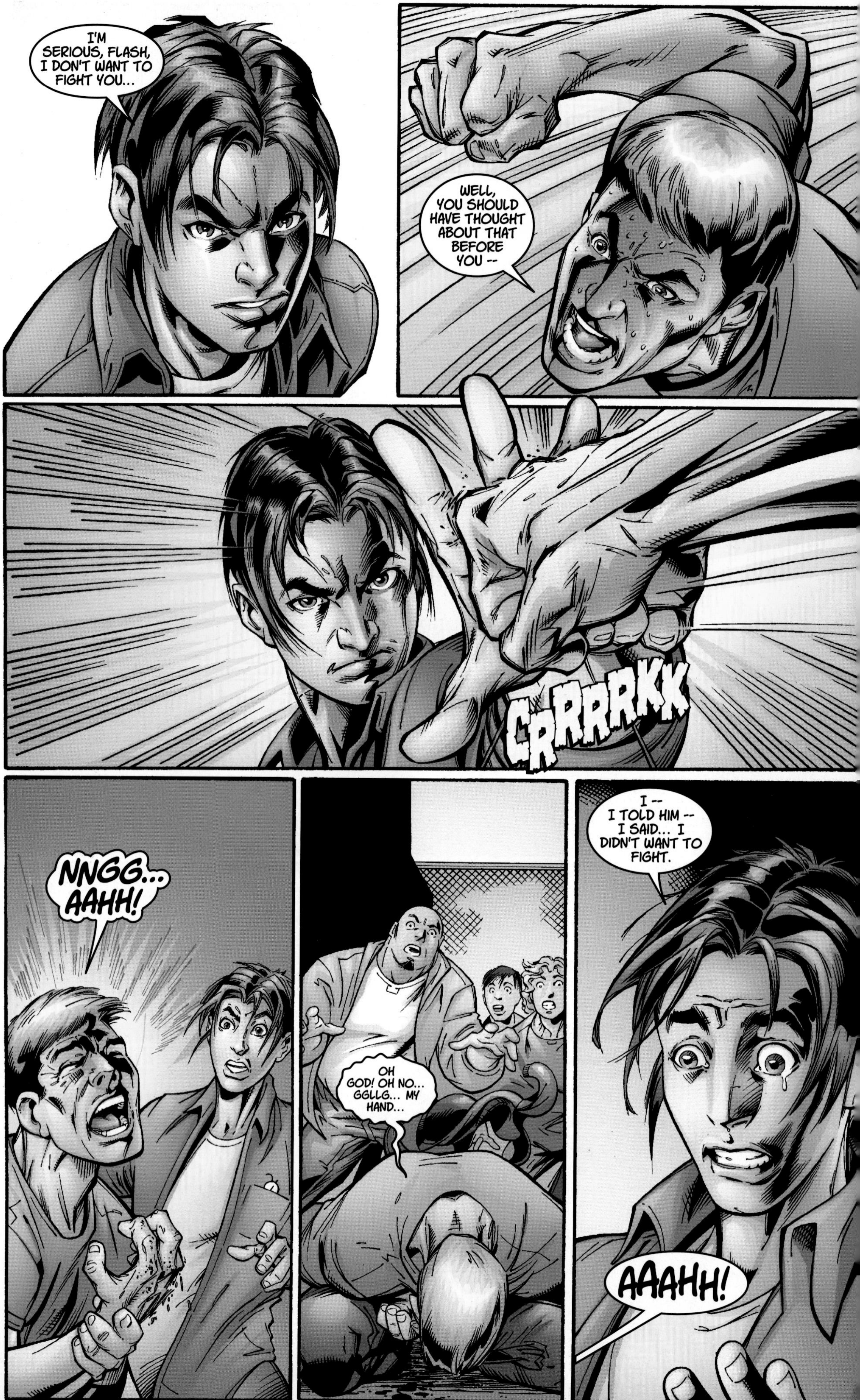
I'M SERIOUS, FLASH, I DON'T WANT TO FIGHT YOU...
WELL, YOU SHOULD HAVE THOUGHT ABOUT THAT BEFORE YOU --
CRRRRKK
NNGG... AAHH!
OH GOD! OH NO... GGLLG... MY HAND...
I -- I TOLD HIM -- I SAID... I DIDN'T WANT TO FIGHT.
AAAHH!

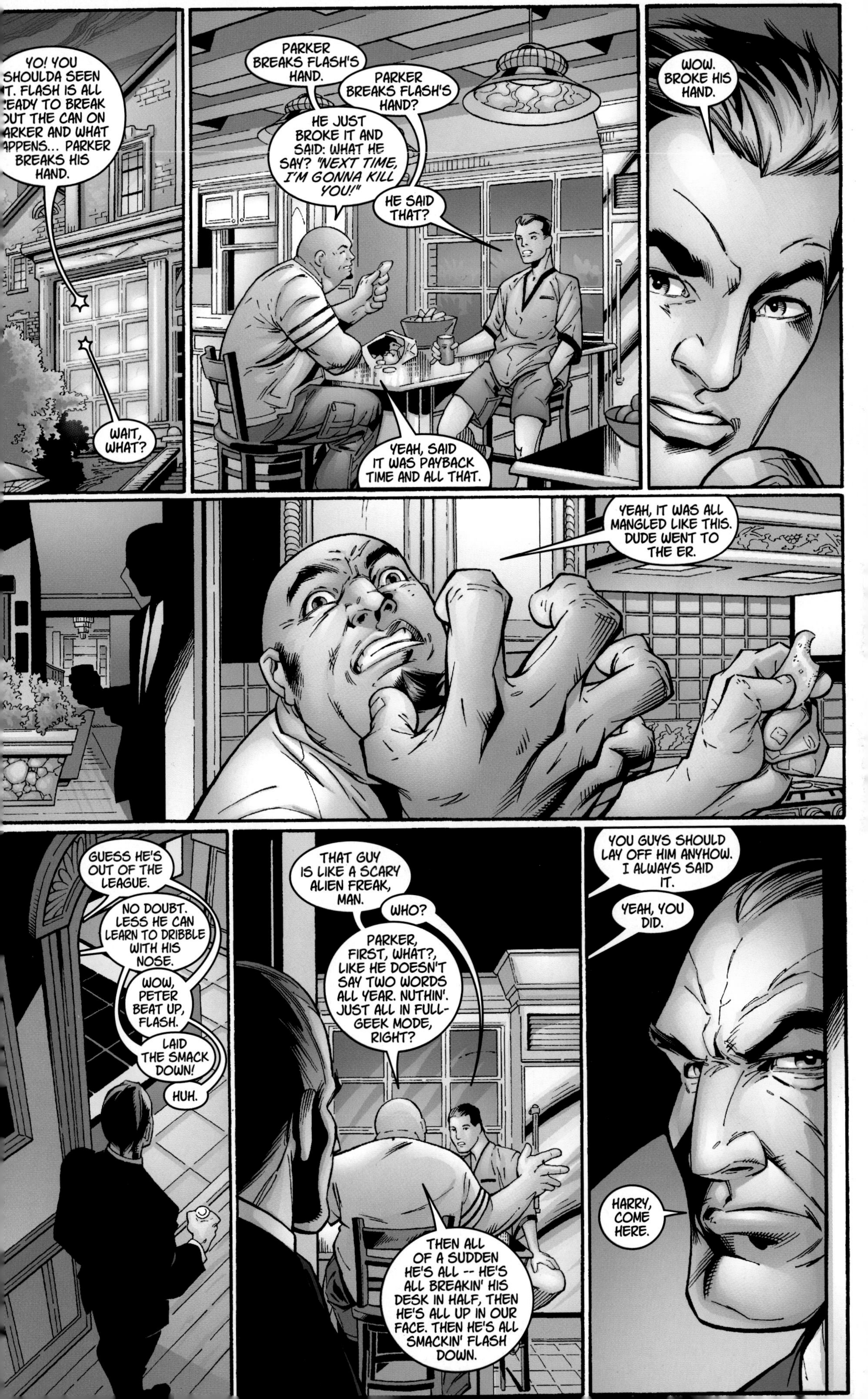

YO! YOU SHOULDA SEEN IT. FLASH IS ALL READY TO BREAK OUT THE CAN ON PARKER AND WHAT HAPPENS... PARKER BREAKS HIS HAND.
WAIT, WHAT?
PARKER BREAKS FLASH'S HAND.
PARKER BREAKS FLASH'S HAND?
HE JUST BROKE IT AND SAID: WHAT HE SAY? "NEXT TIME, I'M GONNA KILL YOU!"
HE SAID THAT?
YEAH, SAID IT WAS PAYBACK TIME AND ALL THAT.
WOW. BROKE HIS HAND.
YEAH, IT WAS ALL MANGLED LIKE THIS. DUDE WENT TO THE ER.
GUESS HE'S OUT OF THE LEAGUE.
NO DOUBT. LESS HE CAN LEARN TO DRIBBLE WITH HIS NOSE.
WOW, PETER BEAT UP, FLASH.
LAID THE SMACK DOWN!
HUH.
THAT GUY IS LIKE A SCARY ALIEN FREAK, MAN.
WHO?
PARKER, FIRST, WHAT?, LIKE HE DOESN'T SAY TWO WORDS ALL YEAR. NUTHIN'. JUST ALL IN FULL-GEEK MODE, RIGHT?
THEN ALL OF A SUDDEN HE'S ALL -- HE'S ALL BREAKIN' HIS DESK IN HALF, THEN HE'S ALL UP IN OUR FACE. THEN HE'S ALL SMACKIN' FLASH DOWN.
YOU GUYS SHOULD LAY OFF HIM ANYHOW. I ALWAYS SAID IT.
YEAH, YOU DID.
HARRY, COME HERE.

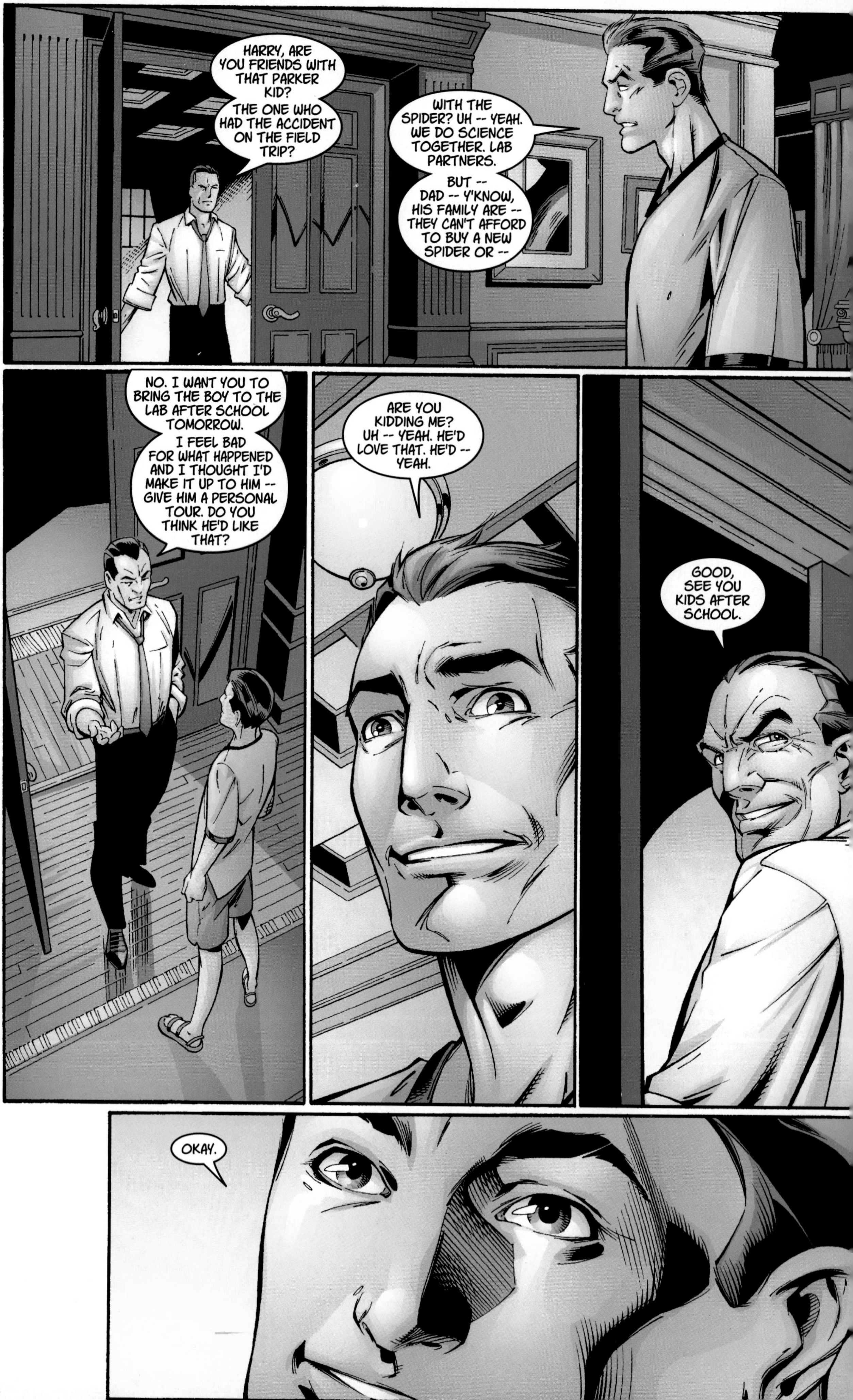
HARRY, ARE YOU FRIENDS WITH THAT PARKER KID?
THE ONE WHO HAD THE ACCIDENT ON THE FIELD TRIP?
WITH THE SPIDER? UH -- YEAH. WE DO SCIENCE TOGETHER. LAB PARTNERS.
BUT -- DAD -- Y'KNOW, HIS FAMILY ARE -- THEY CAN'T AFFORD TO BUY A NEW SPIDER OR --
NO. I WANT YOU TO BRING THE BOY TO THE LAB AFTER SCHOOL TOMORROW.
I FEEL BAD FOR WHAT HAPPENED AND I THOUGHT I'D MAKE IT UP TO HIM -- GIVE HIM A PERSONAL TOUR. DO YOU THINK HE'D LIKE THAT?
ARE YOU KIDDING ME? UH -- YEAH. HE'D LOVE THAT. HE'D -- YEAH.
GOOD, SEE YOU KIDS AFTER SCHOOL.
OKAY.

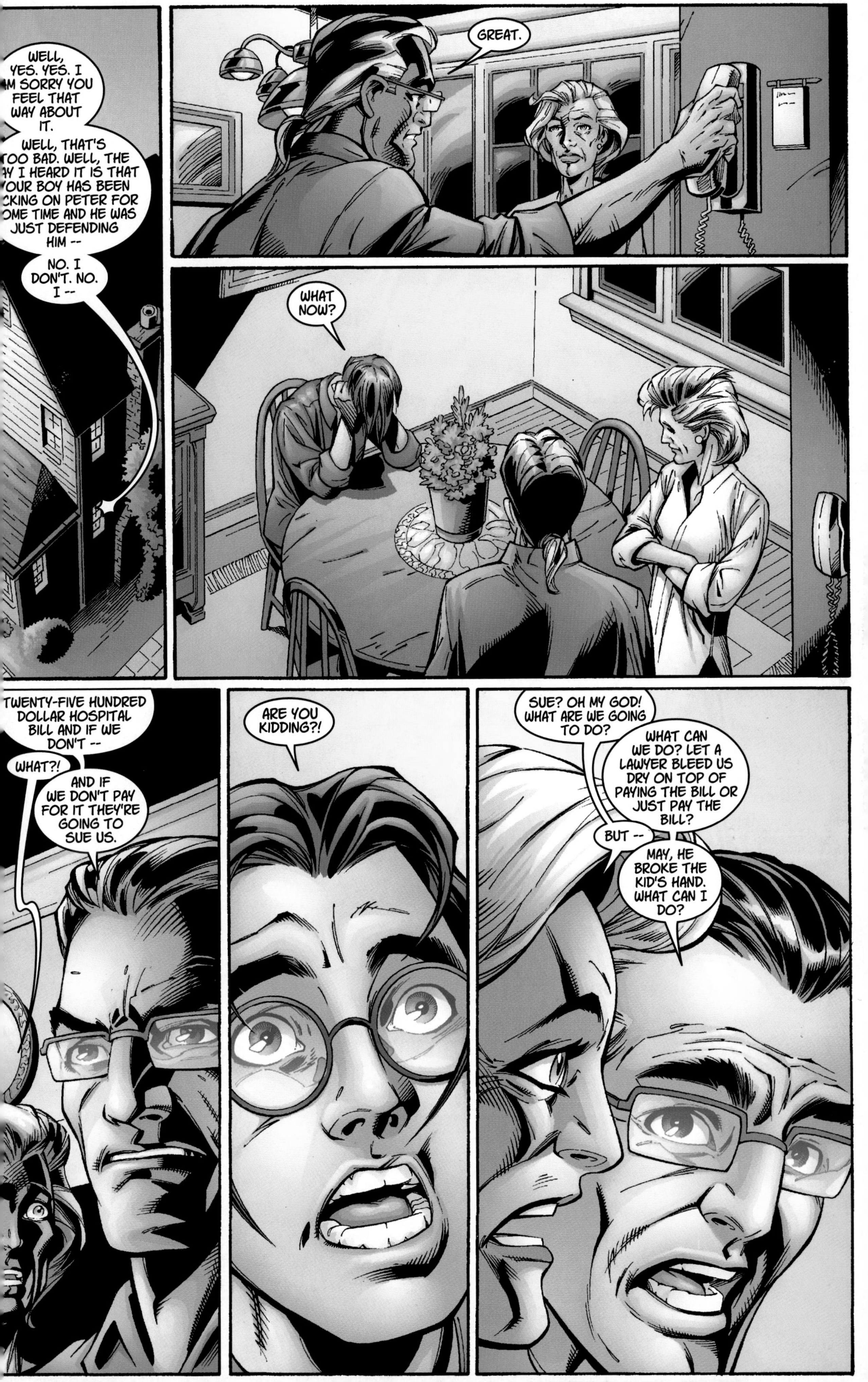
WELL, YES. YES. I AM SORRY YOU FEEL THAT WAY ABOUT IT.
WELL, THAT'S TOO BAD. WELL, THE WAY I HEARD IT IS THAT YOUR BOY HAS BEEN PICKING ON PETER FOR SOME TIME AND HE WAS JUST DEFENDING HIM --
GREAT.
NO. I DON'T. NO. I --
WHAT NOW?
TWENTY-FIVE HUNDRED DOLLAR HOSPITAL BILL AND IF WE DON'T --
WHAT?!
AND IF WE DON'T PAY FOR IT THEY'RE GOING TO SUE US.
ARE YOU KIDDING?!
SUE? OH MY GOD! WHAT ARE WE GOING TO DO?
WHAT CAN WE DO? LET A LAWYER BLEED US DRY ON TOP OF PAYING THE BILL OR JUST PAY THE BILL?
BUT --
MAY, HE BROKE THE KID'S HAND. WHAT CAN I DO?

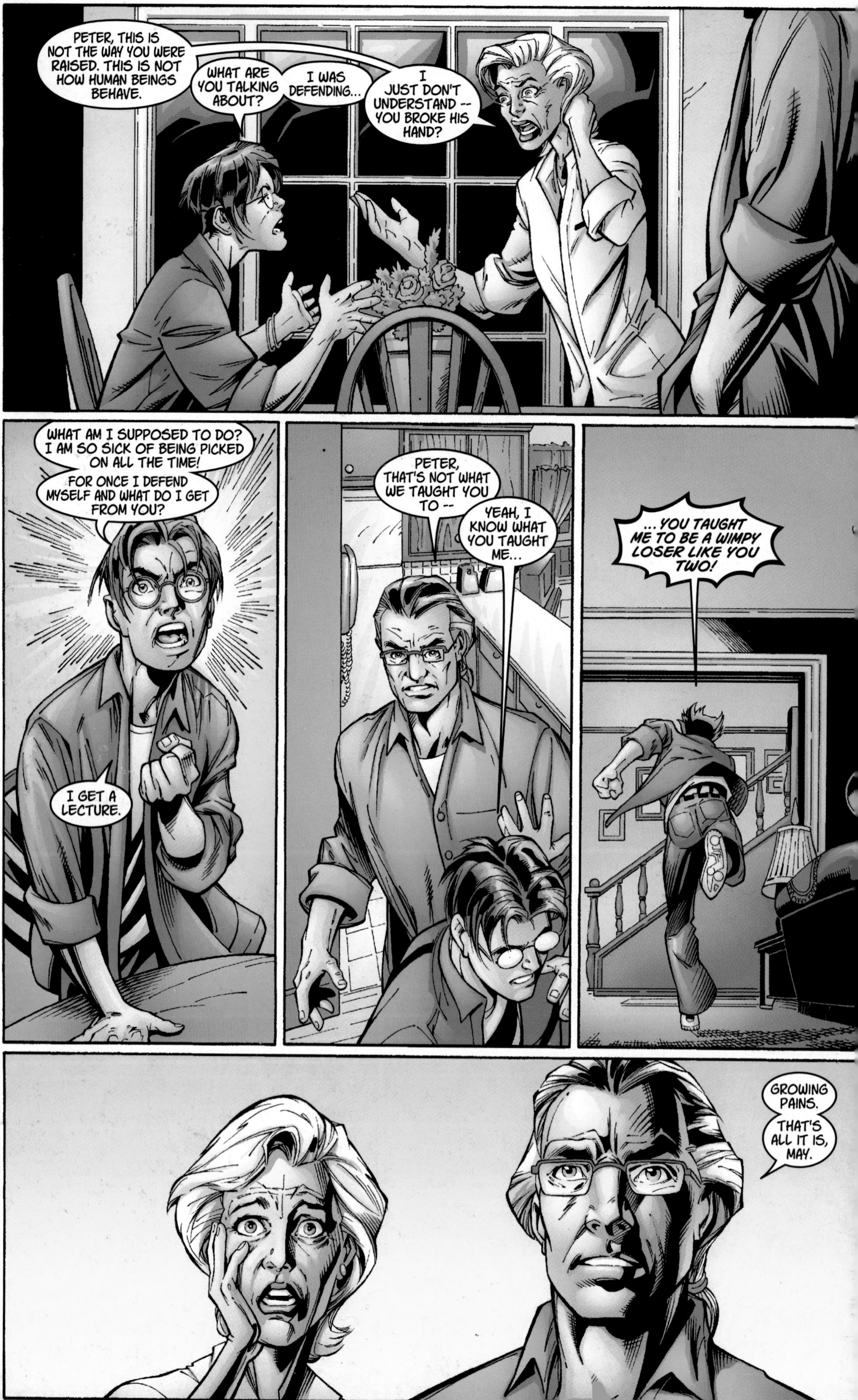
PETER, THIS IS NOT THE WAY YOU WERE RAISED. THIS IS NOT HOW HUMAN BEINGS BEHAVE.
WHAT ARE YOU TALKING ABOUT?
I WAS DEFENDING...
I JUST DON'T UNDERSTAND -- YOU BROKE HIS HAND?
WHAT AM I SUPPOSED TO DO? I AM SO SICK OF BEING PICKED ON ALL THE TIME!
FOR ONCE I DEFEND MYSELF AND WHAT DO I GET FROM YOU?
I GET A LECTURE.
PETER, THAT'S NOT WHAT WE TAUGHT YOU TO --
YEAH, I KNOW WHAT YOU TAUGHT ME...
...YOU TAUGHT ME TO BE A WIMPY LOSER LIKE YOU TWO!
GROWING PAINS.
THAT'S ALL IT IS, MAY.

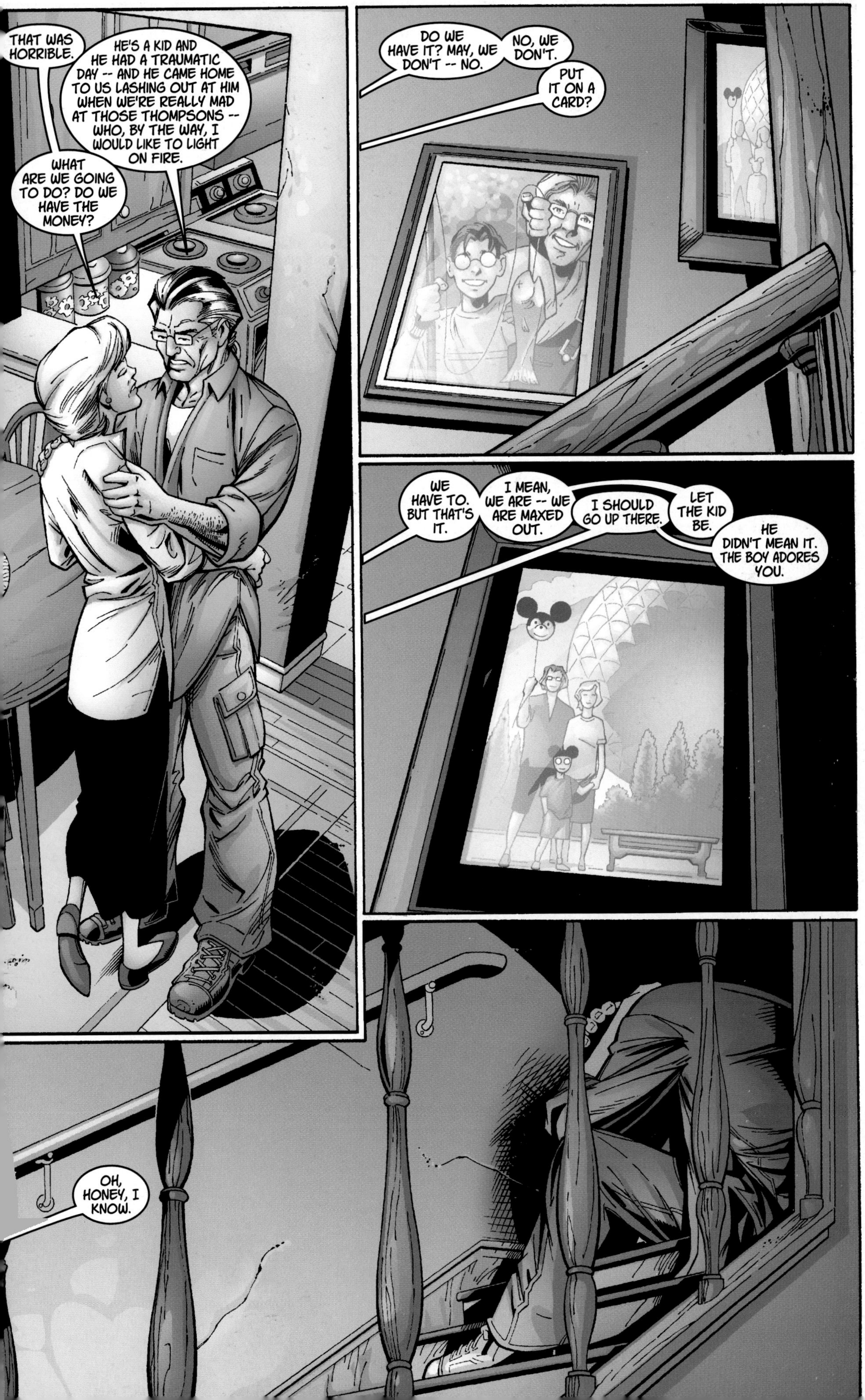

THAT WAS HORRIBLE.
HE'S A KID AND HE HAD A TRAUMATIC DAY -- AND HE CAME HOME TO US LASHING OUT AT HIM WHEN WE'RE REALLY MAD AT THOSE THOMPSONS -- WHO, BY THE WAY, I WOULD LIKE TO LIGHT ON FIRE.
WHAT ARE WE GOING TO DO? DO WE HAVE THE MONEY?
DO WE HAVE IT? MAY, WE DON'T -- NO.
NO, WE DON'T.
PUT IT ON A CARD?
WE HAVE TO. BUT THAT'S IT.
I MEAN, WE ARE -- WE ARE MAXED OUT.
I SHOULD GO UP THERE.
LET THE KID BE.
HE DIDN'T MEAN IT. THE BOY ADORES YOU.
OH, HONEY, I KNOW.

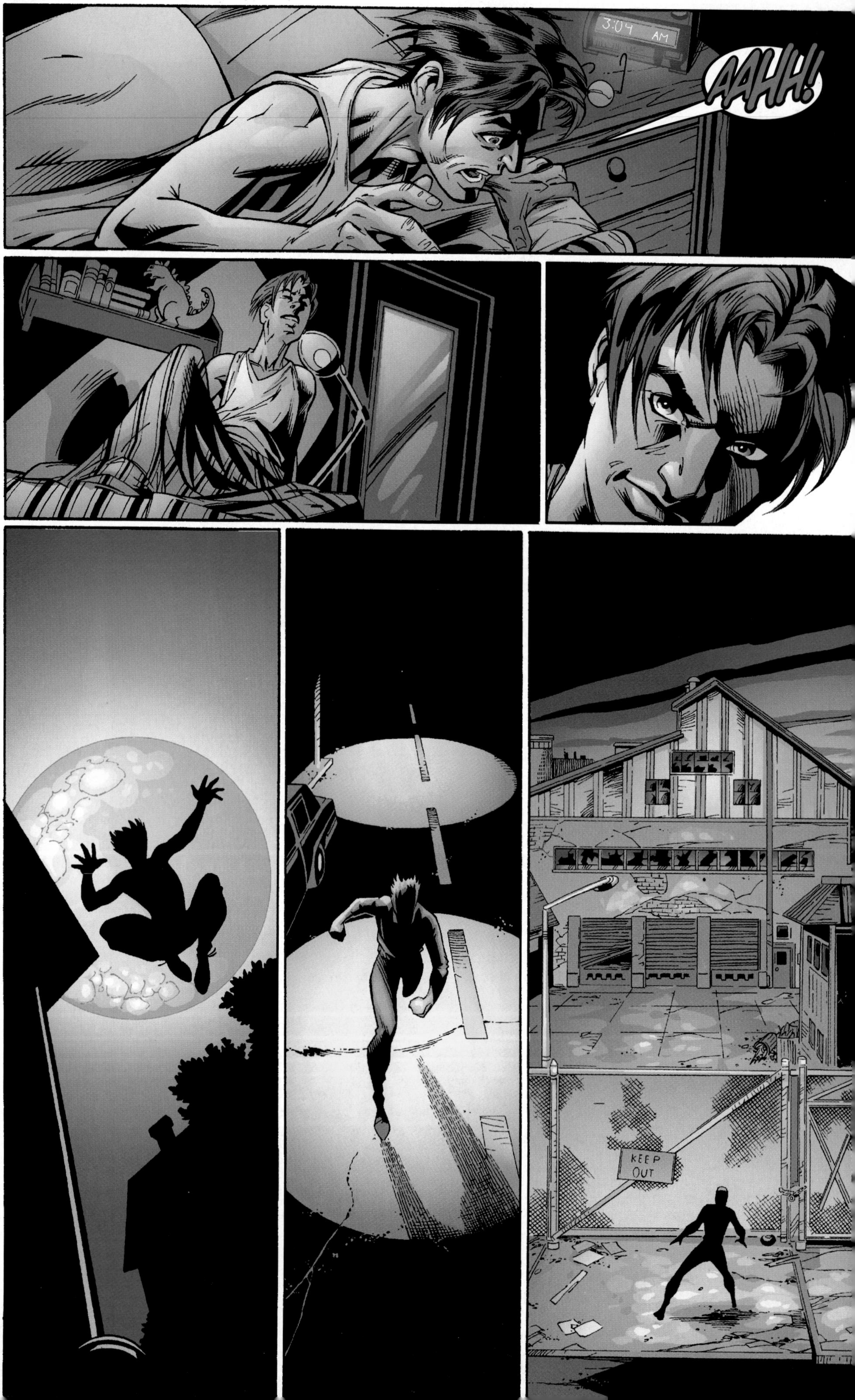
3:04 AM
AAHH!
KEEP OUT

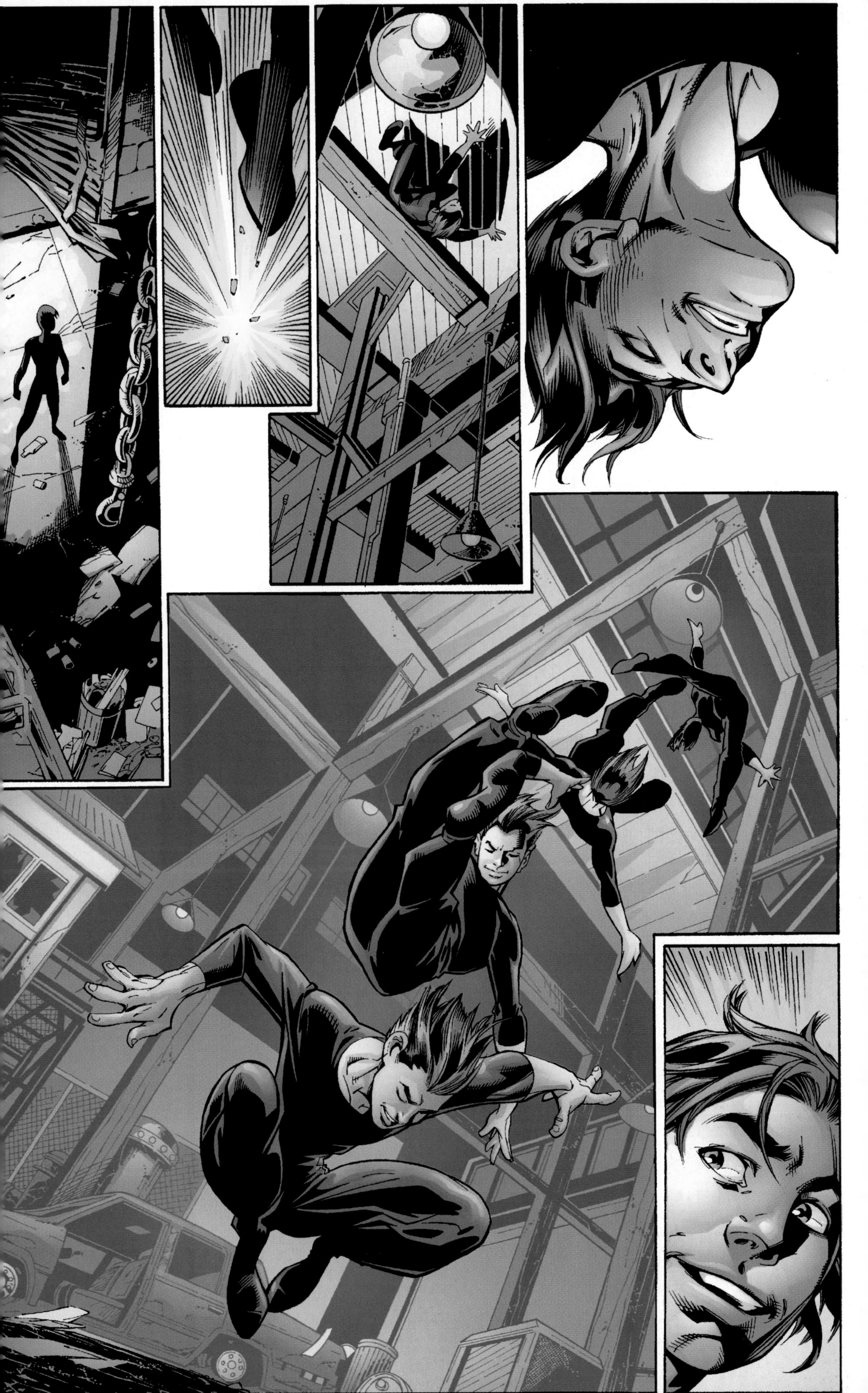

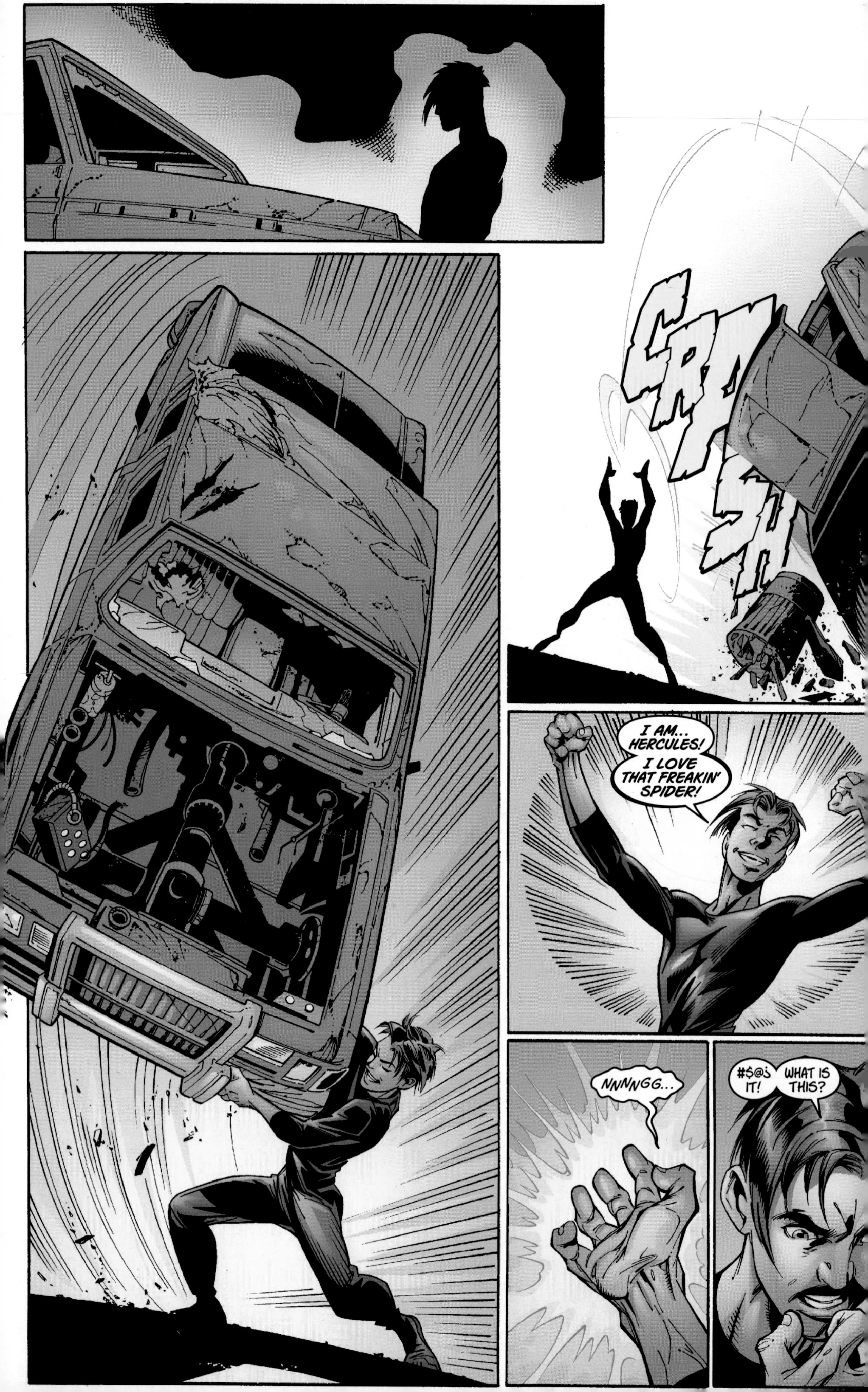
CRASH
I AM... HERCULES! I LOVE THAT FREAKIN' SPIDER!
NNNNGG...
#$@¿ IT!
WHAT IS THIS?

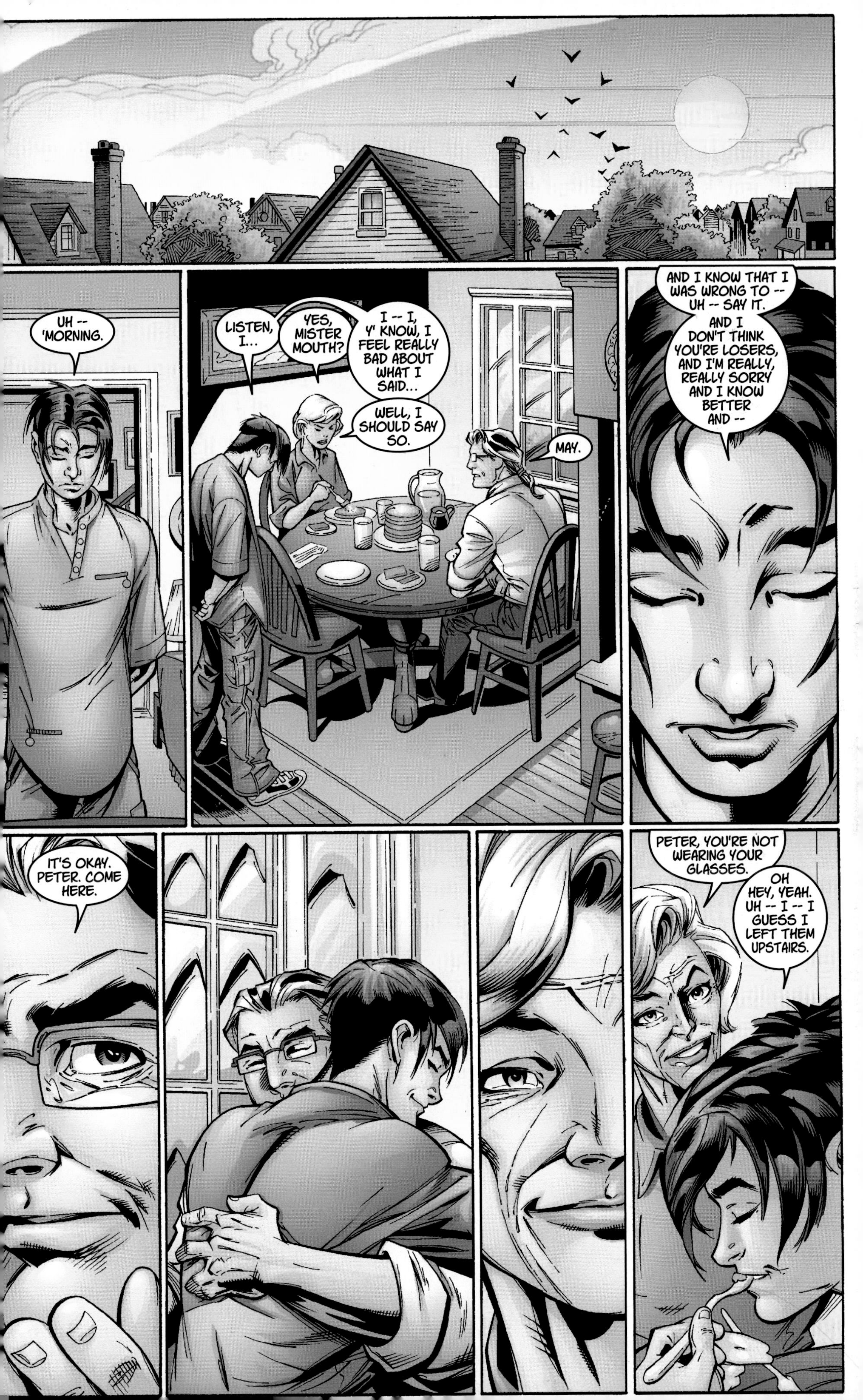
UH -- 'MORNING.
LISTEN, I...
YES, MISTER MOUTH?
I -- I, Y' KNOW, I FEEL REALLY BAD ABOUT WHAT I SAID...
WELL, I SHOULD SAY SO.
MAY.
AND I KNOW THAT I WAS WRONG TO -- UH -- SAY IT.
AND I DON'T THINK YOU'RE LOSERS, AND I'M REALLY, REALLY SORRY AND I KNOW BETTER AND --
IT'S OKAY. PETER. COME HERE.
PETER, YOU'RE NOT WEARING YOUR GLASSES.
OH HEY, YEAH. UH -- I -- I GUESS I LEFT THEM UPSTAIRS.

OSBORN INDUSTRIES
WORKING TOWARD YOUR FUTURE

I'M SERIOUS, HARRY. I TOTALLY WANT TO WORK IN A PLACE JUST LIKE THIS.

YOU WOULD.

I WOULD!

I KNOW.

SO, WHAT ARE WE DOING HERE?

LIKE I SAID, MY DAD FELT BAD ABOUT THE WHOLE SPIDER THING AND HE KNOWS YOU REALLY GET OFF ON THIS STUFF SO HE SAID: COME ON DOWN...

IT'S AMAZINGLY SOLID OF HIM. I MEAN, FOR HIM.

THAT'S PRETTY SOLID OF HIM.

YO, DOC OCK!

THIS HERE IS DOCTOR OTTO OCTAVIUS.

DOC OCK?

DOCTOR OCTAVIUS.

HE'S A BIG BRAIN AROUND HERE. VERY BIG BRAIN. SCARY BIG.

I HEAR YOU'RE QUITE THE TALENT IN THE SCIENCE ARTS.

OH, WELL, THAT'S -- HEY, I WOULDN'T MIND HAVING ONE OF THOSE 9-640'S.

OH, YOU DON'T WANT THAT. IT'S AN OLD ONE.

CAN I HAVE IT WHEN YOU THROW IT OUT?

HEY, DARLENE, WHERE YOU BEEN?

WAITING FOR YOU TO HIT PUBERTY, JUNIOR.

WHAT? HOW COULD YOU SAY THAT? I DID THAT EARLIER IN THE WEEK.

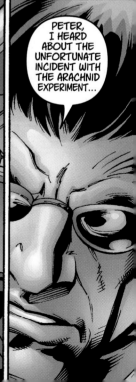

PETER, I HEARD ABOUT THE UNFORTUNATE INCIDENT WITH THE ARACHNID EXPERIMENT...

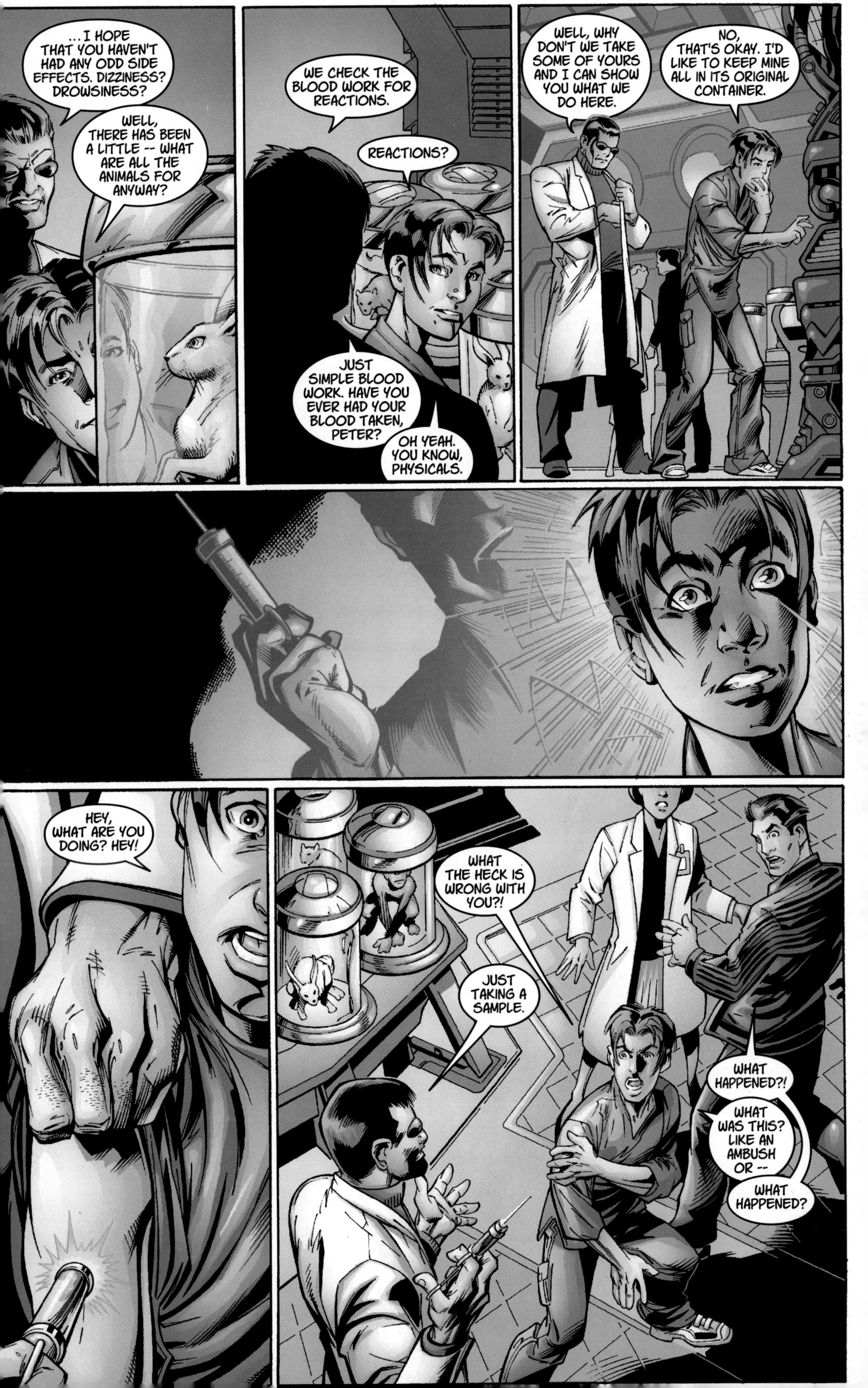
...I HOPE THAT YOU HAVEN'T HAD ANY ODD SIDE EFFECTS. DIZZINESS? DROWSINESS?
WELL, THERE HAS BEEN A LITTLE -- WHAT ARE ALL THE ANIMALS FOR ANYWAY?
WE CHECK THE BLOOD WORK FOR REACTIONS.
REACTIONS?
JUST SIMPLE BLOOD WORK. HAVE YOU EVER HAD YOUR BLOOD TAKEN, PETER?
OH YEAH. YOU KNOW, PHYSICALS.
WELL, WHY DON'T WE TAKE SOME OF YOURS AND I CAN SHOW YOU WHAT WE DO HERE.
NO, THAT'S OKAY. I'D LIKE TO KEEP MINE ALL IN ITS ORIGINAL CONTAINER.
HEY, WHAT ARE YOU DOING? HEY!
WHAT THE HECK IS WRONG WITH YOU?!
JUST TAKING A SAMPLE.
WHAT HAPPENED?!
WHAT WAS THIS? LIKE AN AMBUSH OR --
WHAT HAPPENED?

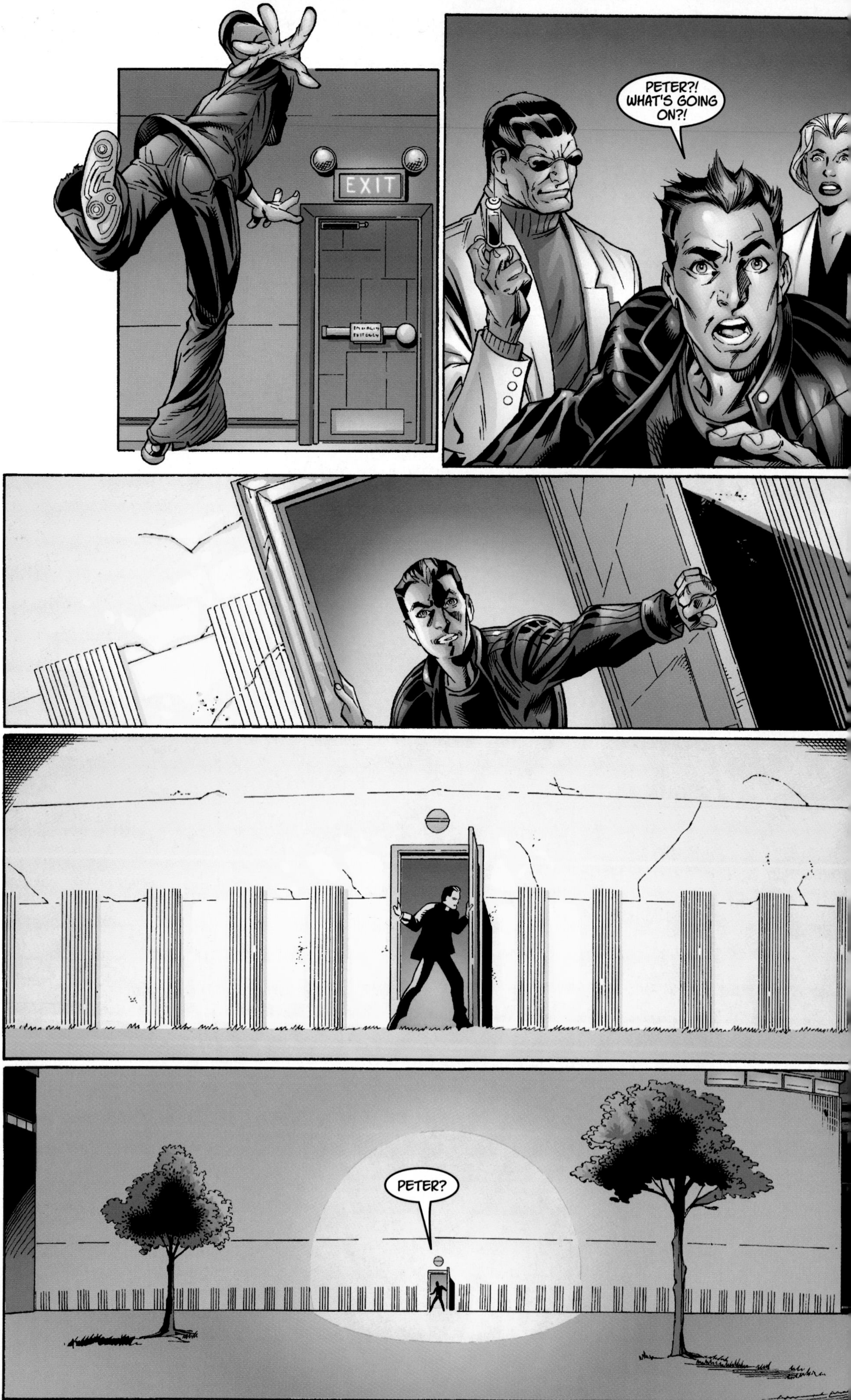
EXIT
PETER?! WHAT'S GOING ON?!
PETER?

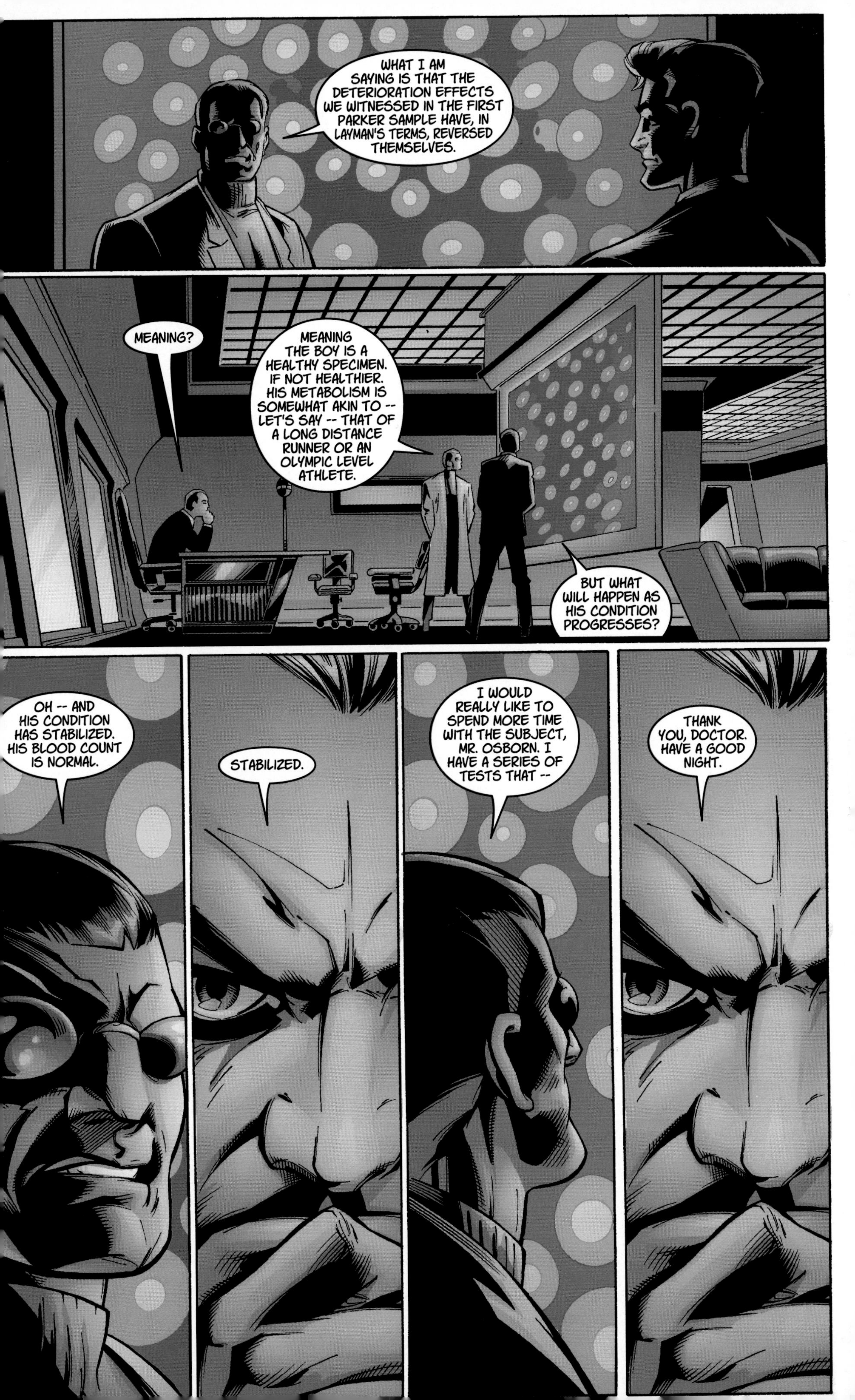
WHAT I AM SAYING IS THAT THE DETERIORATION EFFECTS WE WITNESSED IN THE FIRST PARKER SAMPLE HAVE, IN LAYMAN'S TERMS, REVERSED THEMSELVES.
MEANING?
MEANING THE BOY IS A HEALTHY SPECIMEN. IF NOT HEALTHIER. HIS METABOLISM IS SOMEWHAT AKIN TO -- LET'S SAY -- THAT OF A LONG DISTANCE RUNNER OR AN OLYMPIC LEVEL ATHLETE.
BUT WHAT WILL HAPPEN AS HIS CONDITION PROGRESSES?
OH -- AND HIS CONDITION HAS STABILIZED. HIS BLOOD COUNT IS NORMAL.
STABILIZED.
I WOULD REALLY LIKE TO SPEND MORE TIME WITH THE SUBJECT, MR. OSBORN. I HAVE A SERIES OF TESTS THAT --
THANK YOU, DOCTOR. HAVE A GOOD NIGHT.

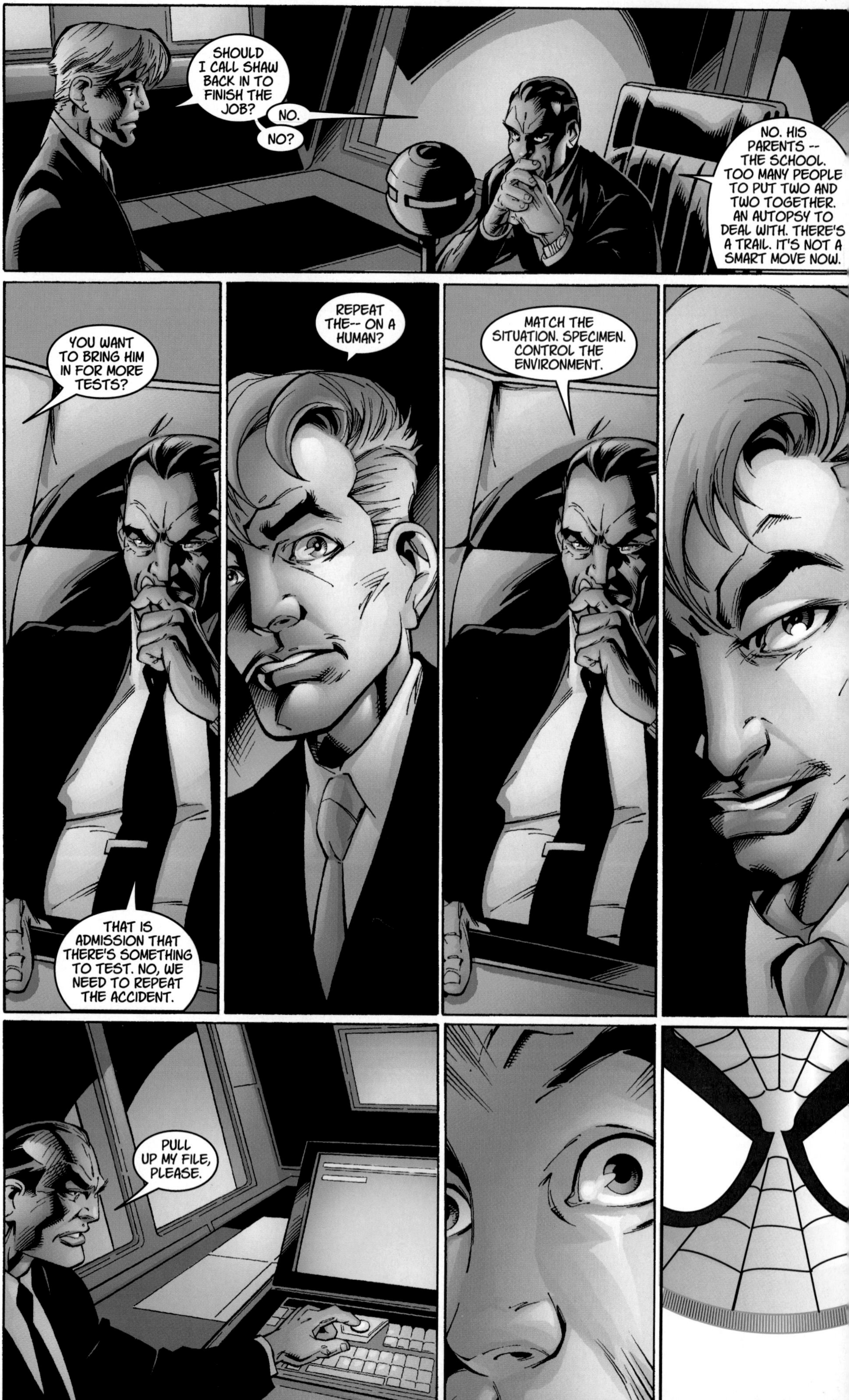

SHOULD I CALL SHAW BACK IN TO FINISH THE JOB?
NO.
NO?
NO. HIS PARENTS -- THE SCHOOL. TOO MANY PEOPLE TO PUT TWO AND TWO TOGETHER. AN AUTOPSY TO DEAL WITH. THERE'S A TRAIL. IT'S NOT A SMART MOVE NOW.
YOU WANT TO BRING HIM IN FOR MORE TESTS?
THAT IS ADMISSION THAT THERE'S SOMETHING TO TEST. NO, WE NEED TO REPEAT THE ACCIDENT.
REPEAT THE-- ON A HUMAN?
MATCH THE SITUATION. SPECIMEN. CONTROL THE ENVIRONMENT.
PULL UP MY FILE, PLEASE.

"RIGHT THERE -- YES.

"RIGHT THERE WE CAN SEE WHERE THE ARACHNID OZ EXPERIMENT NUMBER "OO" BIT THAT PARKER BOY.

"INITIALLY, THE BIOLOGICAL EFFECTS TO THE PARKER BOY WERE NEGATIVE. VERY NEGATIVE.

"AND HIS CHANCE FOR SURVIVAL WAS VERY SLIM. FATAL.

"BUT WE NOW BELIEVE THAT IT WAS THE MIXTURE OF SPIDER VENOM WITH THE OZ THAT CREATED THE ADVERSE EFFECTS TO THE BOY'S SYSTEM.

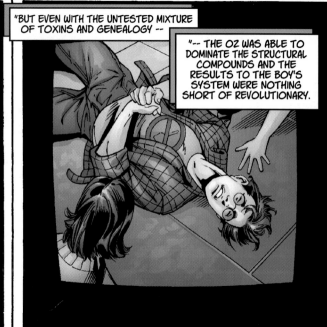

"BUT EVEN WITH THE UNTESTED MIXTURE OF TOXINS AND GENEALOGY --

"-- THE OZ WAS ABLE TO DOMINATE THE STRUCTURAL COMPOUNDS AND THE RESULTS TO THE BOY'S SYSTEM WERE NOTHING SHORT OF REVOLUTIONARY.

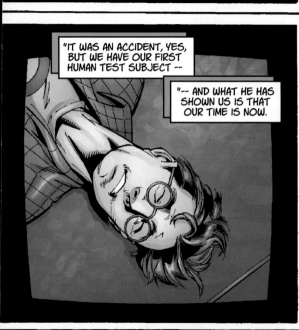

"IT WAS AN ACCIDENT, YES, BUT WE HAVE OUR FIRST HUMAN TEST SUBJECT --

"-- AND WHAT HE HAS SHOWN US IS THAT OUR TIME IS NOW.

"TURN IT OFF, PLEASE."

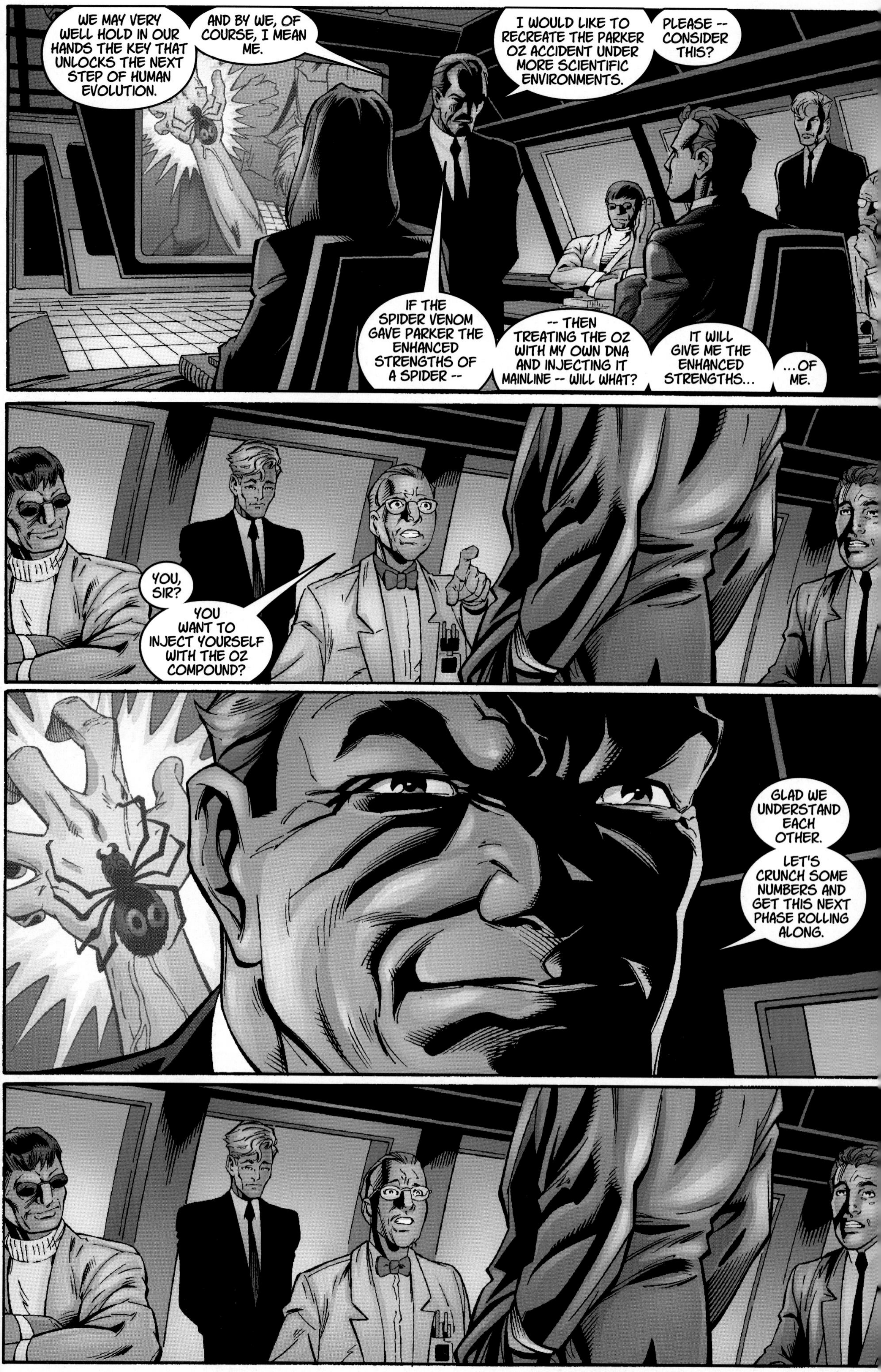
WE MAY VERY WELL HOLD IN OUR HANDS THE KEY THAT UNLOCKS THE NEXT STEP OF HUMAN EVOLUTION.
AND BY WE, OF COURSE, I MEAN ME.
I WOULD LIKE TO RECREATE THE PARKER OZ ACCIDENT UNDER MORE SCIENTIFIC ENVIRONMENTS.
PLEASE -- CONSIDER THIS?
IF THE SPIDER VENOM GAVE PARKER THE ENHANCED STRENGTHS OF A SPIDER --
-- THEN TREATING THE OZ WITH MY OWN DNA AND INJECTING IT MAINLINE -- WILL WHAT?
IT WILL GIVE ME THE ENHANCED STRENGTHS...
...OF ME.
YOU, SIR?
YOU WANT TO INJECT YOURSELF WITH THE OZ COMPOUND?
GLAD WE UNDERSTAND EACH OTHER.
LET'S CRUNCH SOME NUMBERS AND GET THIS NEXT PHASE ROLLING ALONG.

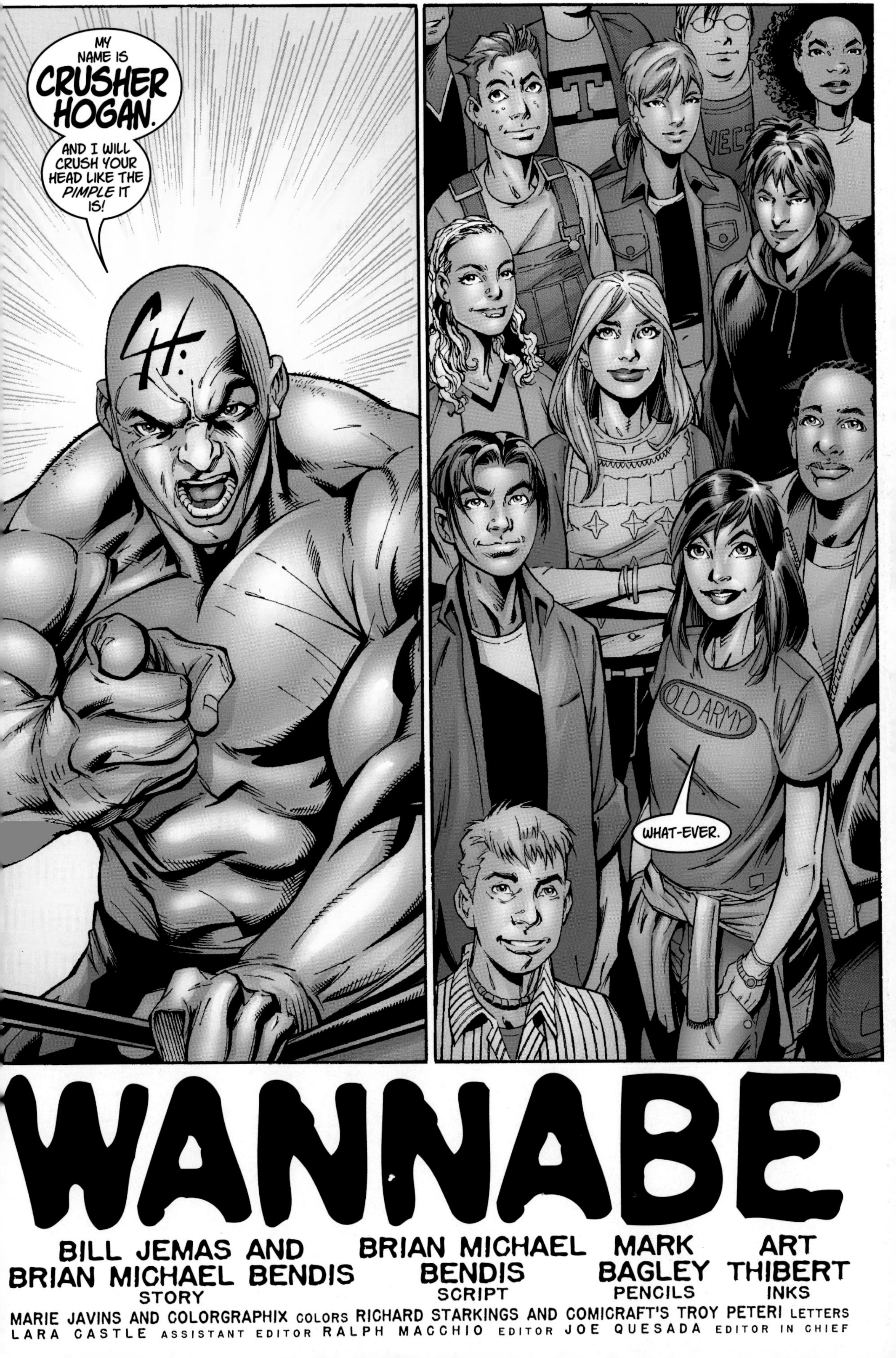
MY NAME IS CRUSHER HOGAN.
AND I WILL CRUSH YOUR HEAD LIKE THE *PIMPLE* IT IS!
OLD ARMY
WHAT-EVER.

WANNABE

BILL JEMAS AND BRIAN MICHAEL BENDIS STORY
BRIAN MICHAEL BENDIS SCRIPT
MARK BAGLEY PENCILS
ART THIBERT INKS
MARIE JAVINS AND COLORGRAPHIX COLORS RICHARD STARKINGS AND COMICRAFT'S TROY PETERI LETTERS
LARA CASTLE ASSISTANT EDITOR RALPH MACCHIO EDITOR JOE QUESADA EDITOR IN CHIEF

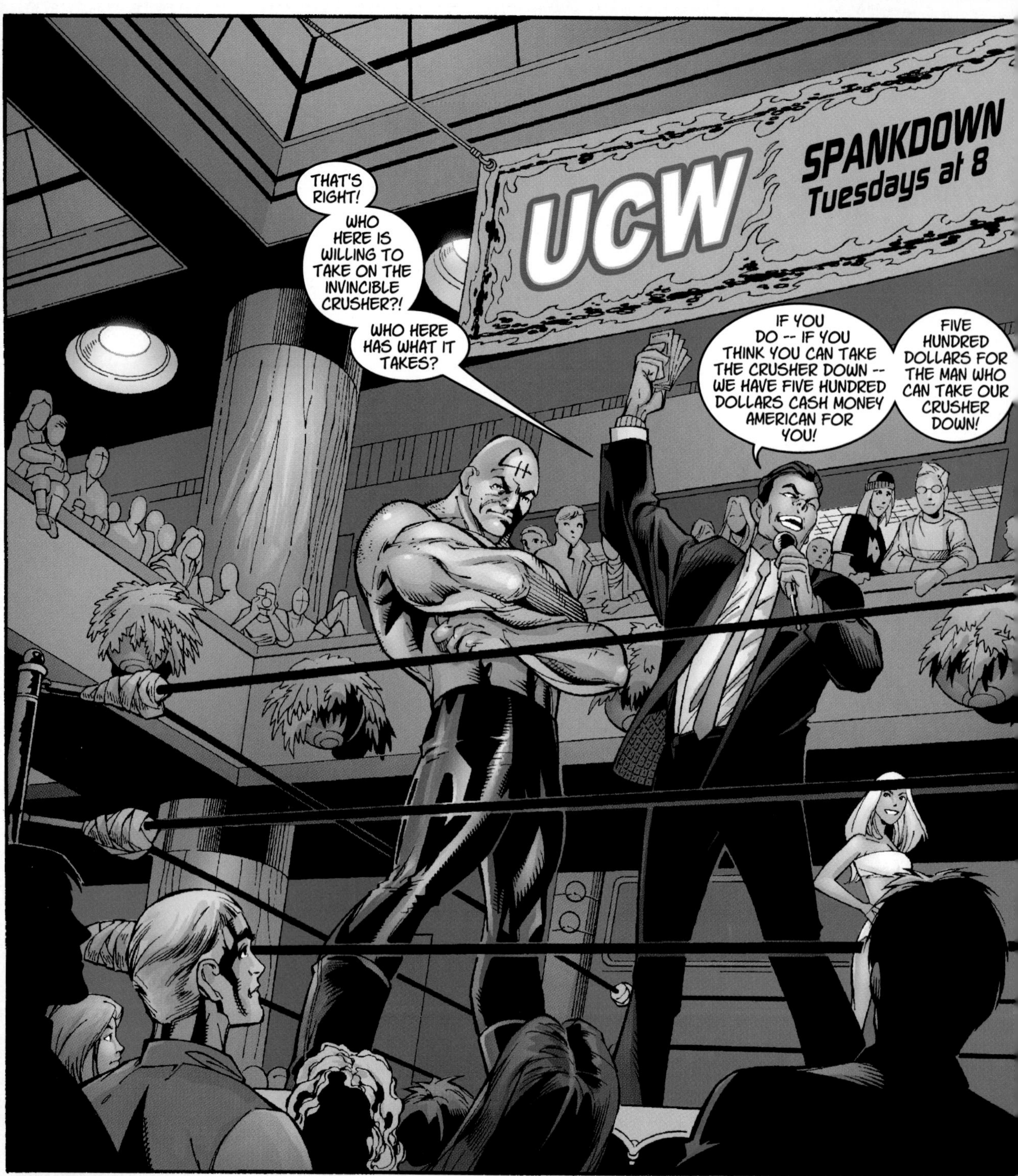
UCW
SPANKDOWN
Tuesdays at 8
THAT'S RIGHT!
WHO HERE IS WILLING TO TAKE ON THE INVINCIBLE CRUSHER?!
WHO HERE HAS WHAT IT TAKES?
IF YOU DO -- IF YOU THINK YOU CAN TAKE THE CRUSHER DOWN -- WE HAVE FIVE HUNDRED DOLLARS CASH MONEY AMERICAN FOR YOU!
FIVE HUNDRED DOLLARS FOR THE MAN WHO CAN TAKE OUR CRUSHER DOWN!
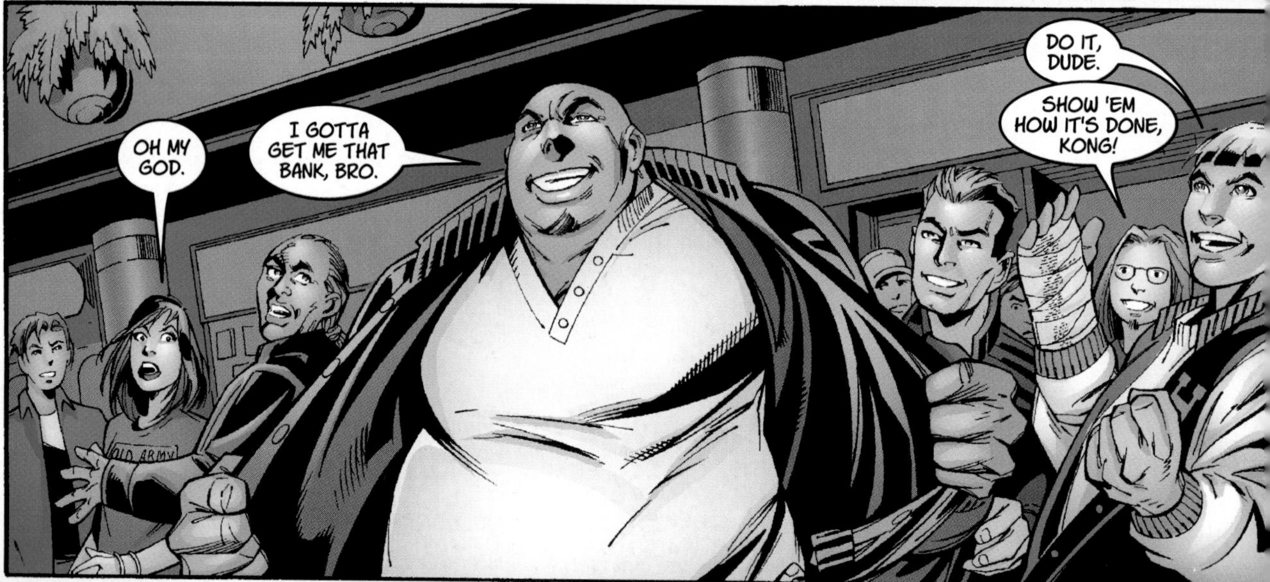
OH MY GOD.
I GOTTA GET ME THAT BANK, BRO.
DO IT, DUDE.
SHOW 'EM HOW IT'S DONE, KONG!
OLD ARMY

YO, I WANT IN! RIGHT HERE!

NO WAY, YOUNGSTER. 21 AND UP. SORRY.

NO WAY.

INSURANCE PURPOSES.

OH MY GOD! TOTAL RIP!

YOU SUCK, CRUSHER!

GET A DRIVER'S LICENSE AND WE'LL TALK.

TOTAL DIS!

PARKER, GO GET 'EM.

YOU KNOW WHAT, FLASH?

HOW ABOUT YOU HOP IN THE RING?

AND THEN WHEN YOU LOSE -- YOUR FAMILY CAN SUE HIS FAMILY.

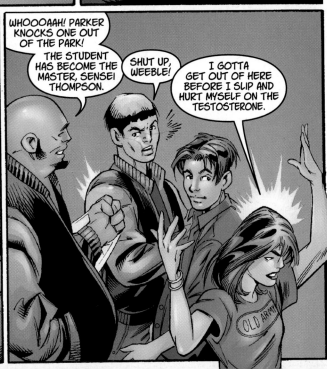

WHOOOAAH! PARKER KNOCKS ONE OUT OF THE PARK!

THE STUDENT HAS BECOME THE MASTER, SENSEI THOMPSON.

SHUT UP, WEEBLE!

I GOTTA GET OUT OF HERE BEFORE I SLIP AND HURT MYSELF ON THE TESTOSTERONE.

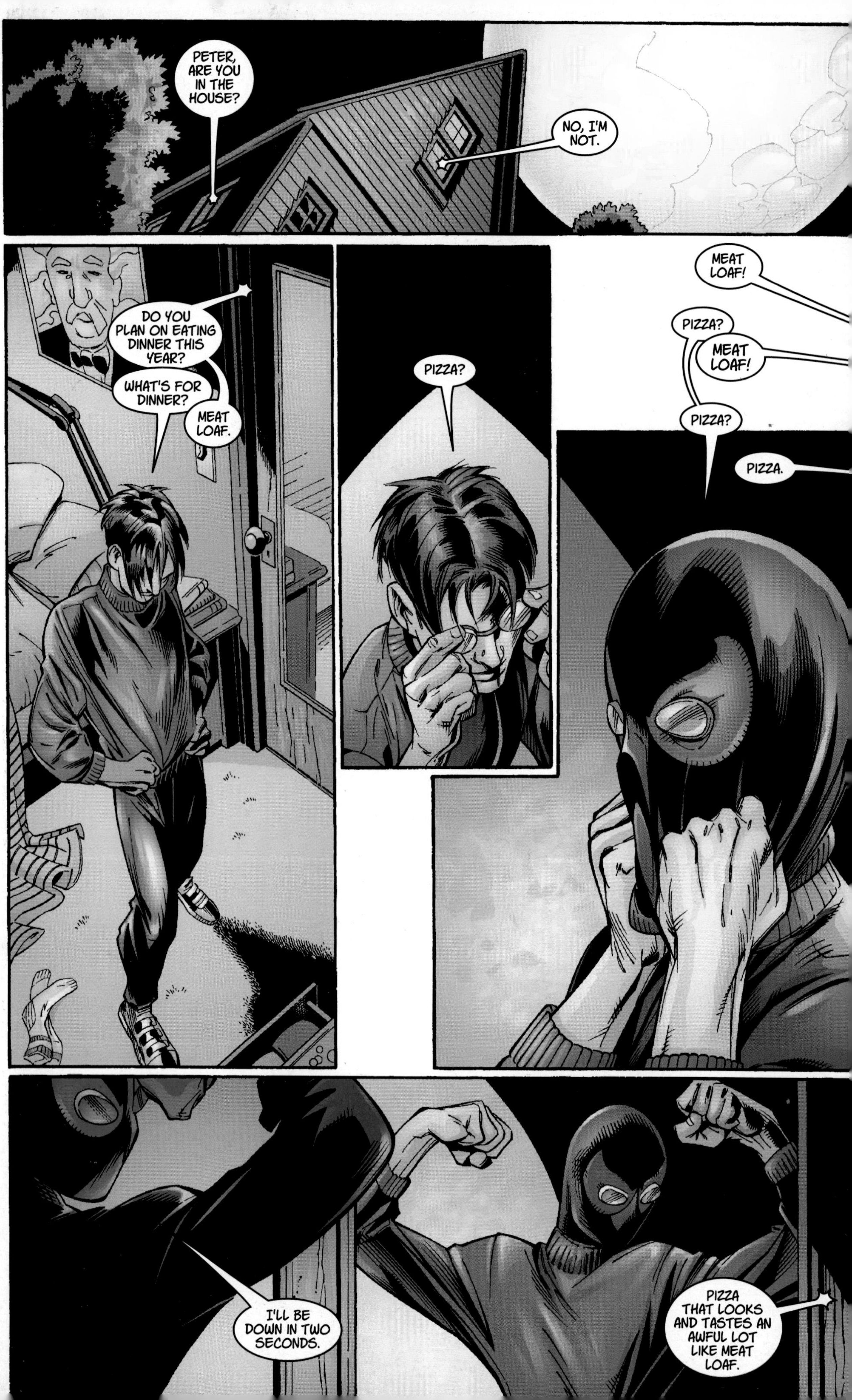

PETER, ARE YOU IN THE HOUSE?
NO, I'M NOT.
DO YOU PLAN ON EATING DINNER THIS YEAR?
WHAT'S FOR DINNER?
MEAT LOAF.
PIZZA?
MEAT LOAF!
PIZZA?
MEAT LOAF!
PIZZA?
PIZZA.
I'LL BE DOWN IN TWO SECONDS.
PIZZA THAT LOOKS AND TASTES AN AWFUL LOT LIKE MEAT LOAF.

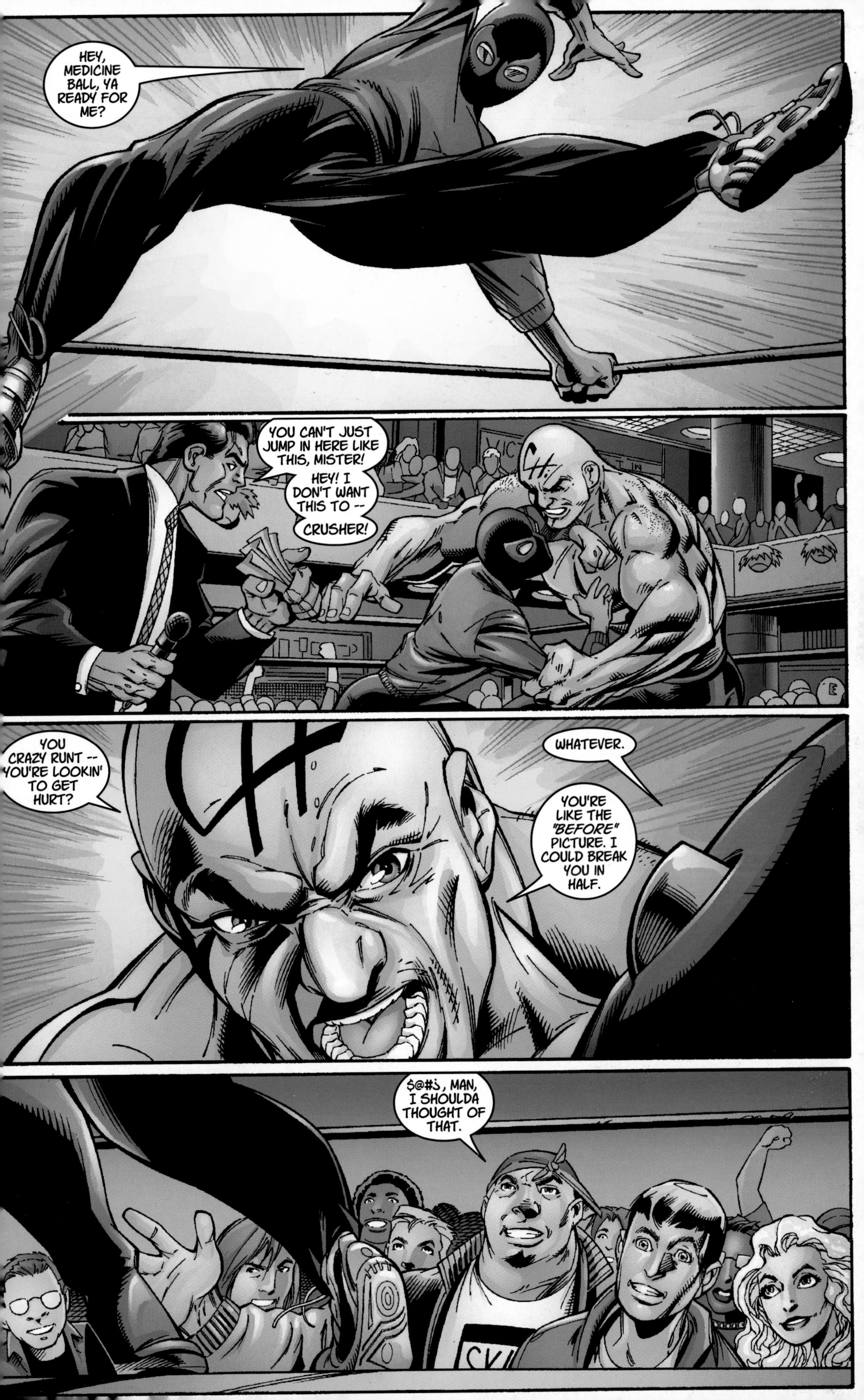
HEY, MEDICINE BALL, YA READY FOR ME?
YOU CAN'T JUST JUMP IN HERE LIKE THIS, MISTER!
HEY! I DON'T WANT THIS TO --
CRUSHER!
YOU CRAZY RUNT -- YOU'RE LOOKIN' TO GET HURT?
WHATEVER.
YOU'RE LIKE THE "BEFORE" PICTURE. I COULD BREAK YOU IN HALF.
$@#3, MAN, I SHOULDA THOUGHT OF THAT.

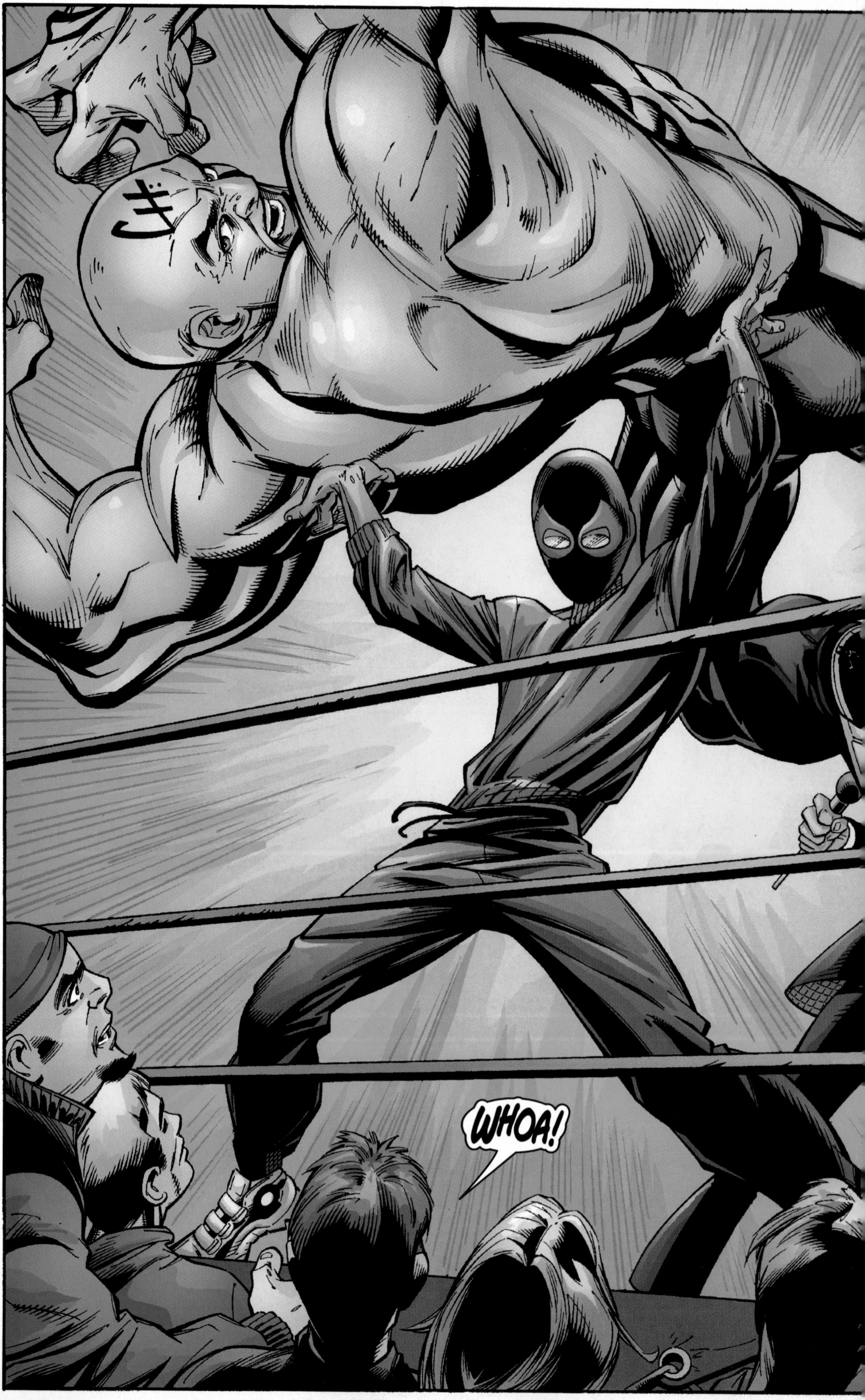
WHOA!

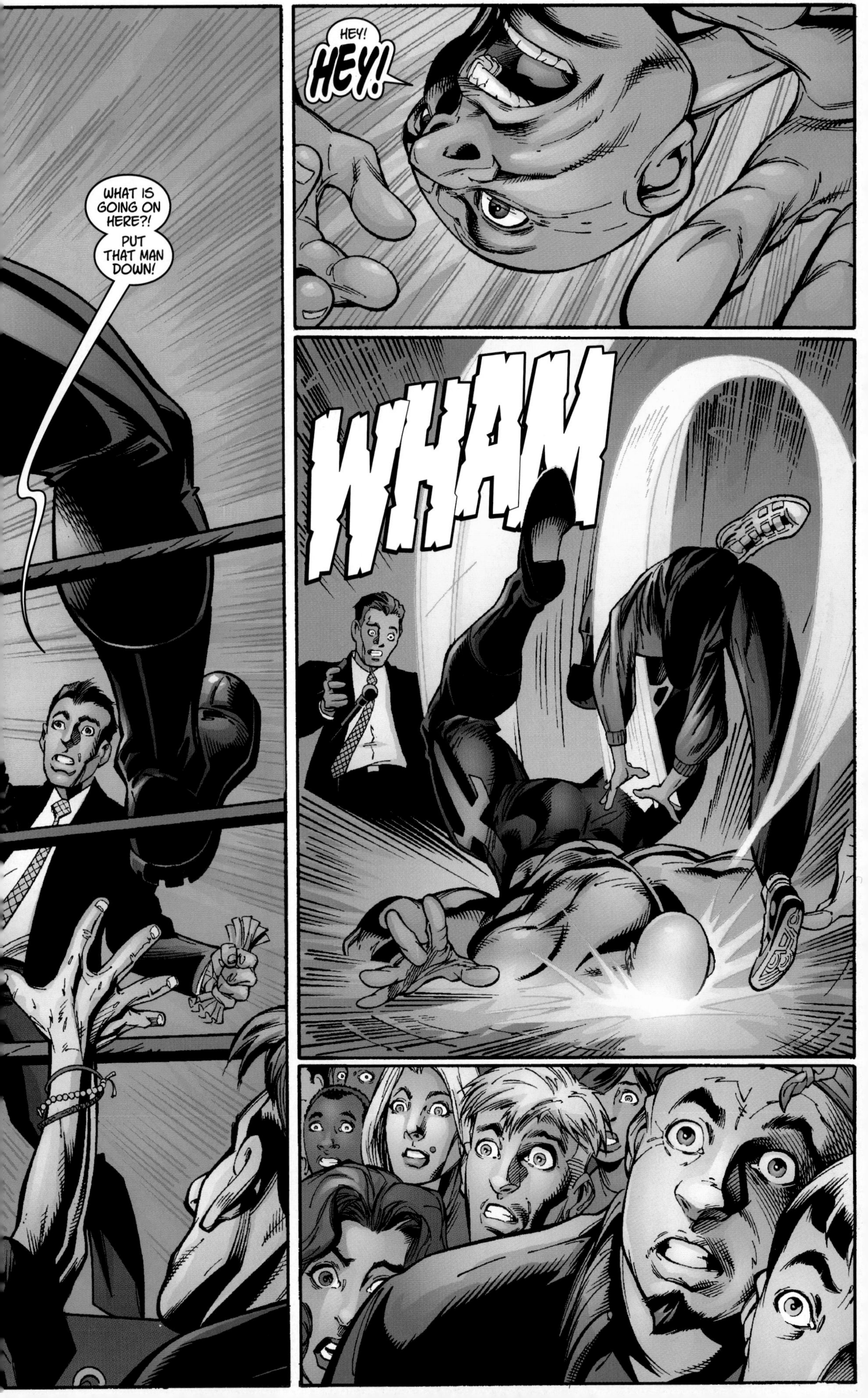

WHAT IS GOING ON HERE?!
PUT THAT MAN DOWN!
HEY! HEY!
WHAM

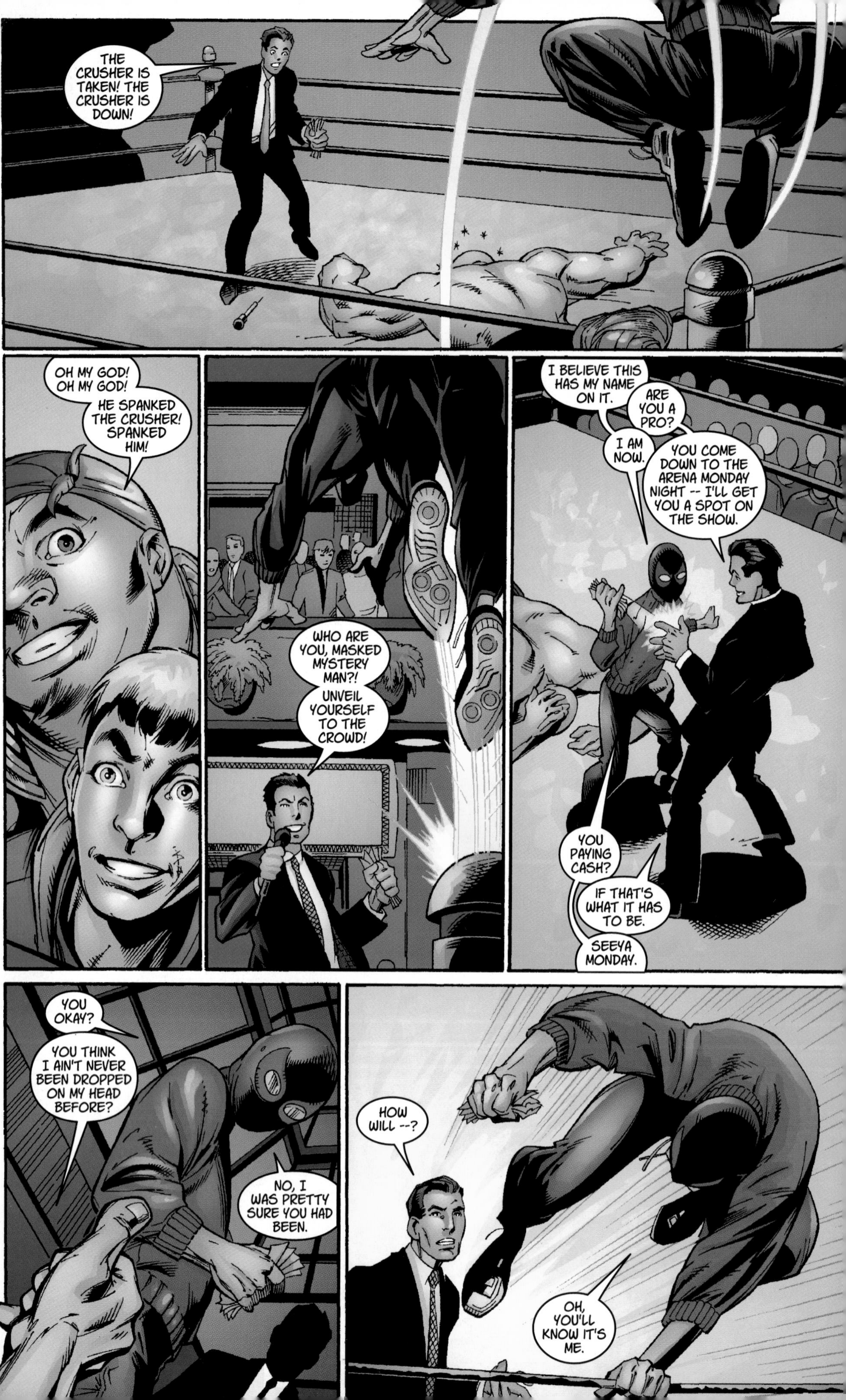
THE CRUSHER IS TAKEN! THE CRUSHER IS DOWN!
OH MY GOD! OH MY GOD!
HE SPANKED THE CRUSHER! SPANKED HIM!
WHO ARE YOU, MASKED MYSTERY MAN?! UNVEIL YOURSELF TO THE CROWD!
I BELIEVE THIS HAS MY NAME ON IT.
ARE YOU A PRO?
I AM NOW.
YOU COME DOWN TO THE ARENA MONDAY NIGHT -- I'LL GET YOU A SPOT ON THE SHOW.
YOU PAYING CASH?
IF THAT'S WHAT IT HAS TO BE.
SEEYA MONDAY.
YOU OKAY?
YOU THINK I AIN'T NEVER BEEN DROPPED ON MY HEAD BEFORE?
NO, I WAS PRETTY SURE YOU HAD BEEN.
HOW WILL --?
OH, YOU'LL KNOW IT'S ME.

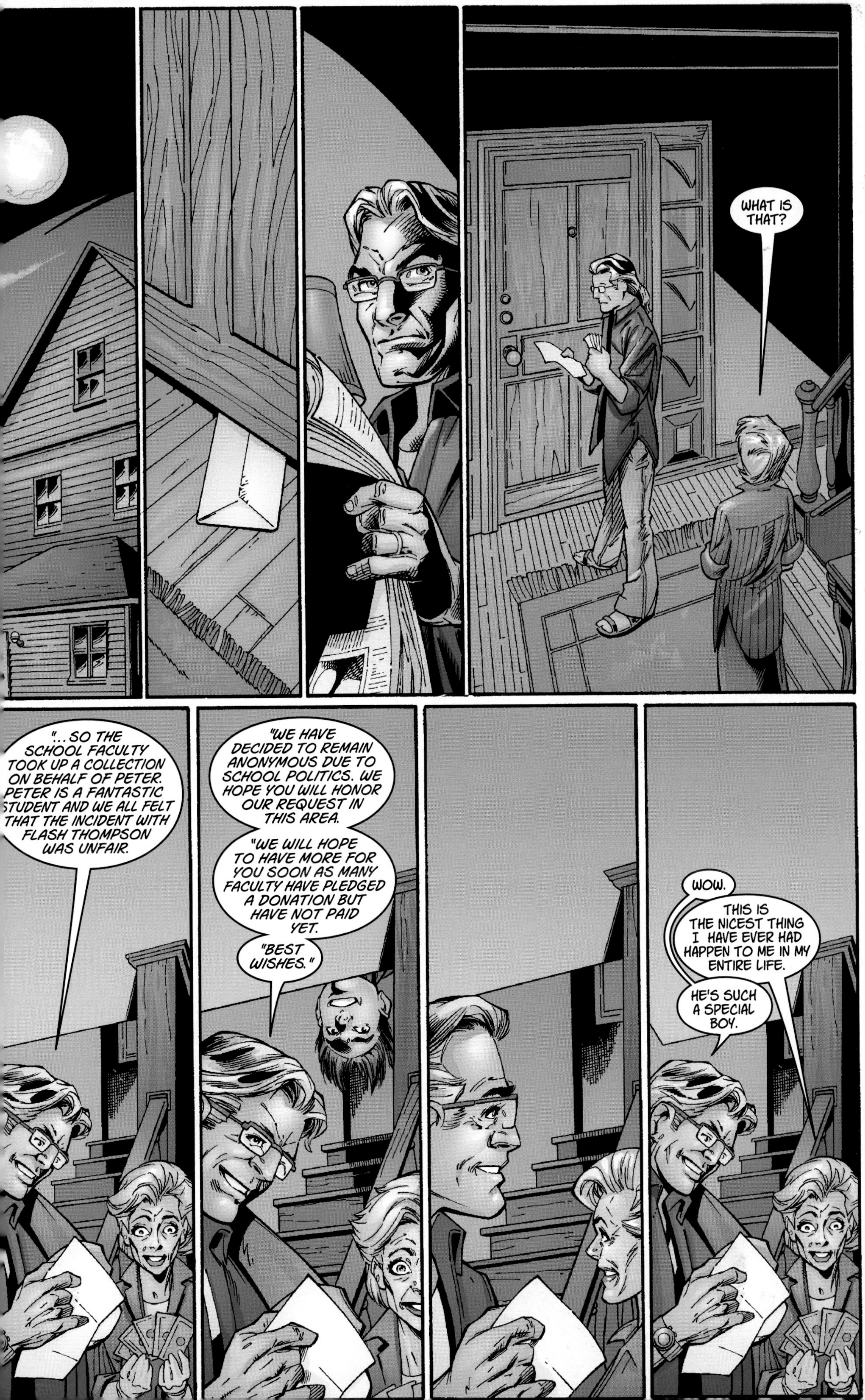
WHAT IS THAT?
"...SO THE SCHOOL FACULTY TOOK UP A COLLECTION ON BEHALF OF PETER. PETER IS A FANTASTIC STUDENT AND WE ALL FELT THAT THE INCIDENT WITH FLASH THOMPSON WAS UNFAIR.
"WE HAVE DECIDED TO REMAIN ANONYMOUS DUE TO SCHOOL POLITICS. WE HOPE YOU WILL HONOR OUR REQUEST IN THIS AREA.
"WE WILL HOPE TO HAVE MORE FOR YOU SOON AS MANY FACULTY HAVE PLEDGED A DONATION BUT HAVE NOT PAID YET.
"BEST WISHES."
WOW.
THIS IS THE NICEST THING I HAVE EVER HAD HAPPEN TO ME IN MY ENTIRE LIFE.
HE'S SUCH A SPECIAL BOY.

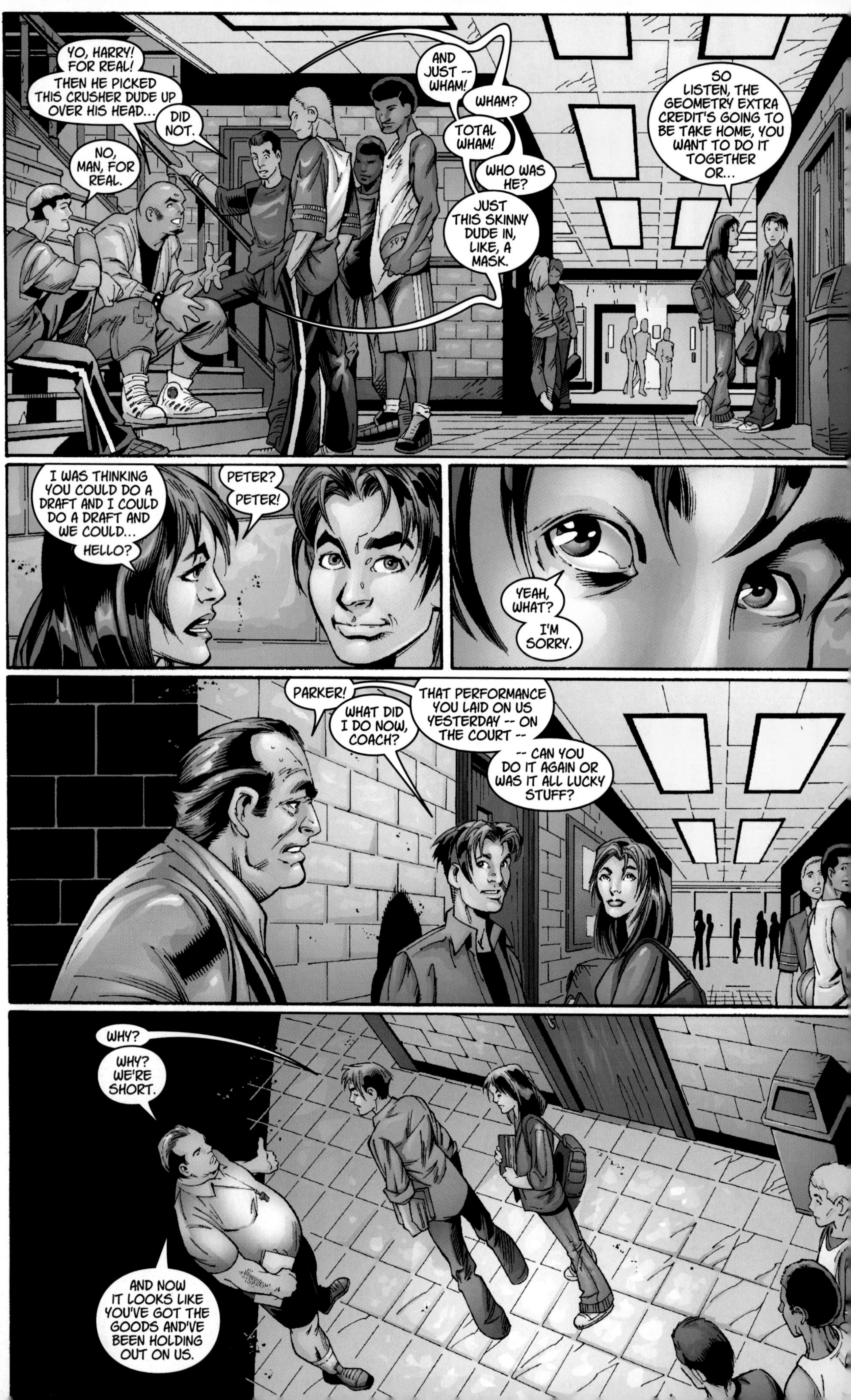
YO, HARRY! FOR REAL!
THEN HE PICKED THIS CRUSHER DUDE UP OVER HIS HEAD...
DID NOT.
NO, MAN, FOR REAL.
AND JUST -- WHAM!
WHAM?
TOTAL WHAM!
WHO WAS HE?
JUST THIS SKINNY DUDE IN, LIKE, A MASK.
SO LISTEN, THE GEOMETRY EXTRA CREDIT'S GOING TO BE TAKE HOME, YOU WANT TO DO IT TOGETHER OR...
I WAS THINKING YOU COULD DO A DRAFT AND I COULD DO A DRAFT AND WE COULD...
HELLO?
PETER?
PETER!
YEAH, WHAT?
I'M SORRY.
PARKER!
WHAT DID I DO NOW, COACH?
THAT PERFORMANCE YOU LAID ON US YESTERDAY -- ON THE COURT --
-- CAN YOU DO IT AGAIN OR WAS IT ALL LUCKY STUFF?
WHY?
WHY? WE'RE SHORT.
AND NOW IT LOOKS LIKE YOU'VE GOT THE GOODS AND'VE BEEN HOLDING OUT ON US.

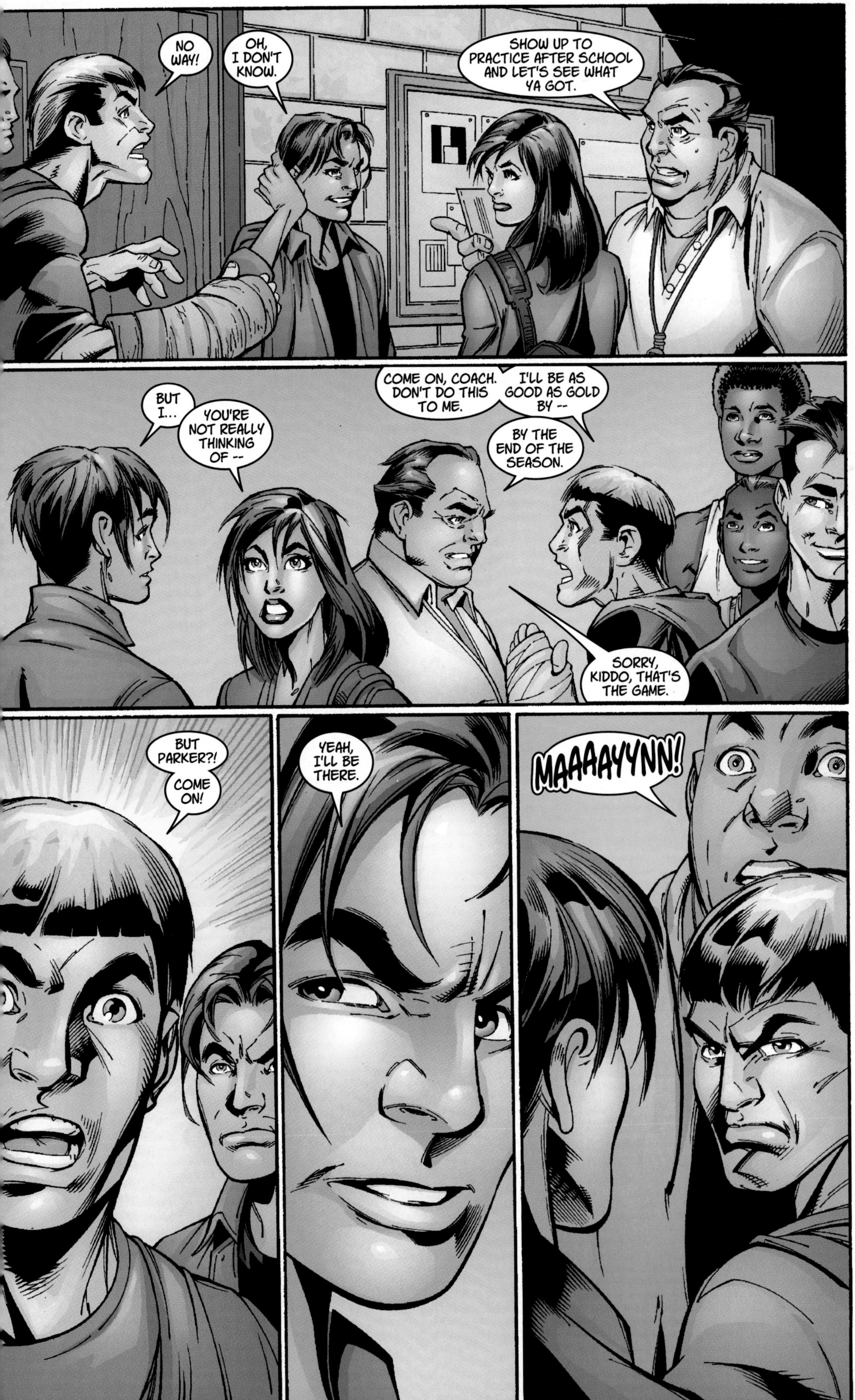
NO WAY!
OH, I DON'T KNOW.
SHOW UP TO PRACTICE AFTER SCHOOL AND LET'S SEE WHAT YA GOT.
BUT I...
YOU'RE NOT REALLY THINKING OF --
COME ON, COACH. DON'T DO THIS TO ME.
I'LL BE AS GOOD AS GOLD BY --
BY THE END OF THE SEASON.
SORRY, KIDDO, THAT'S THE GAME.
BUT PARKER?!
COME ON!
YEAH, I'LL BE THERE.
MAAAAYYNN!

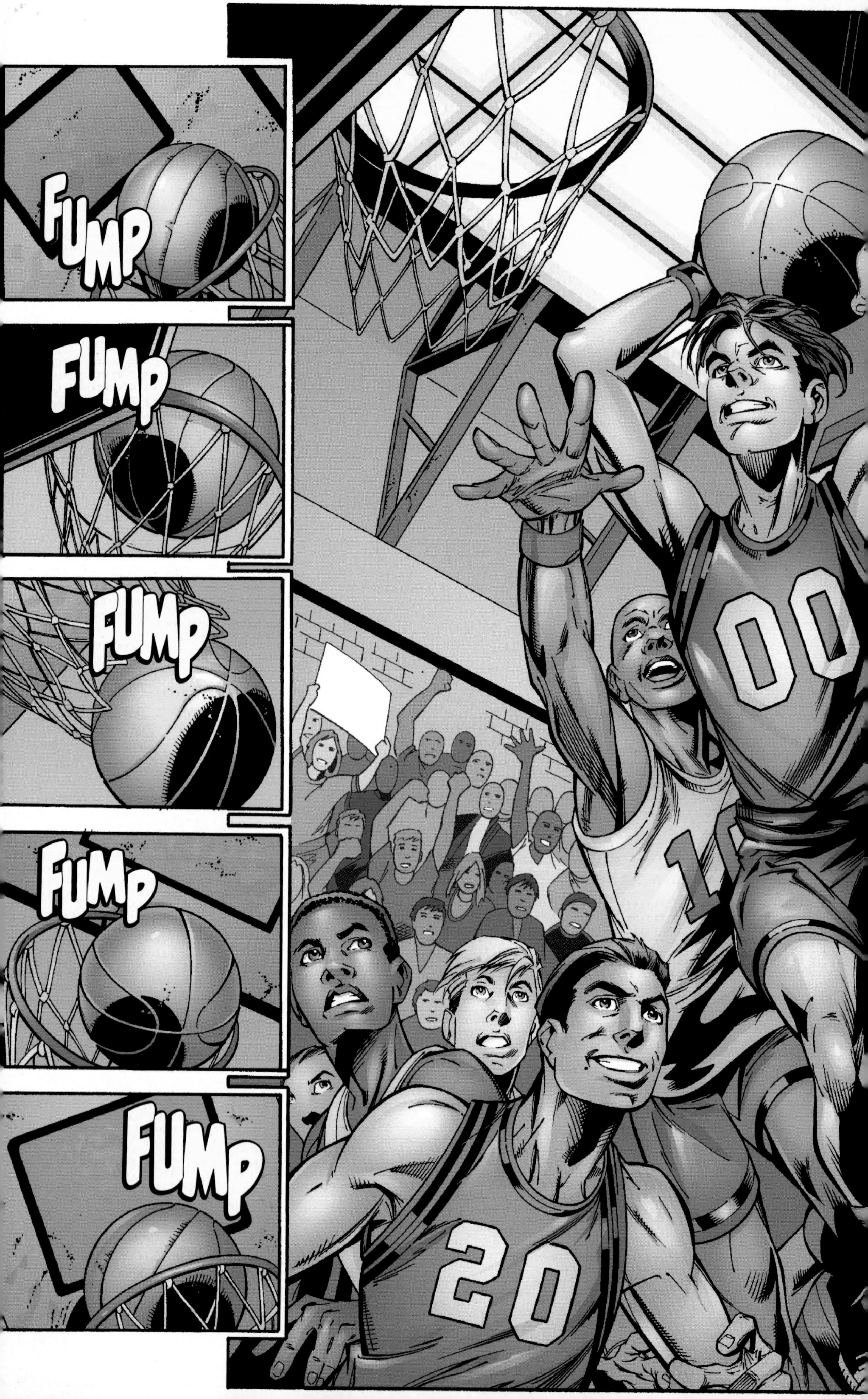
FUMP
FUMP
FUMP
FUMP
FUMP

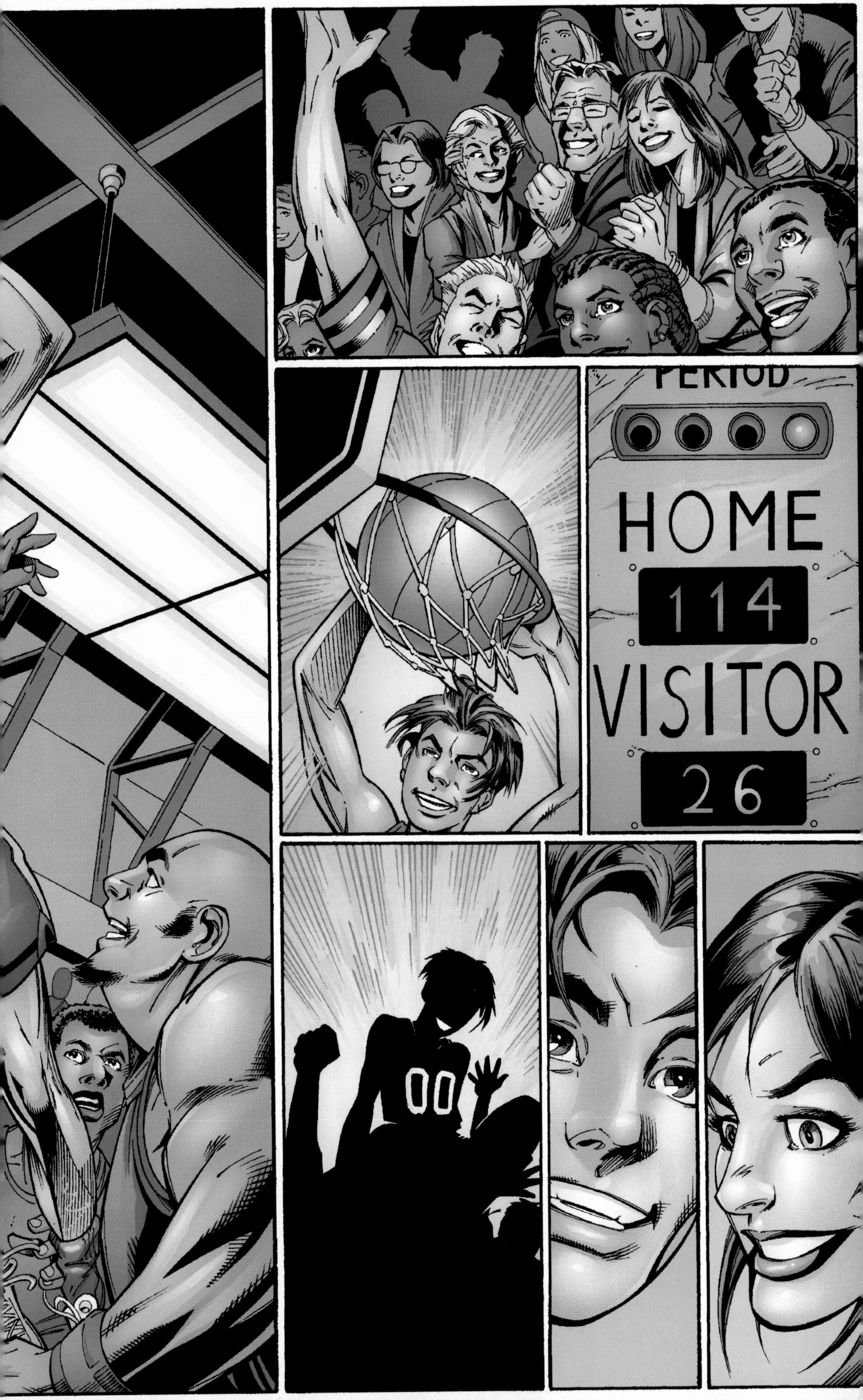
PERIOD
HOME
114
VISITOR
26
00

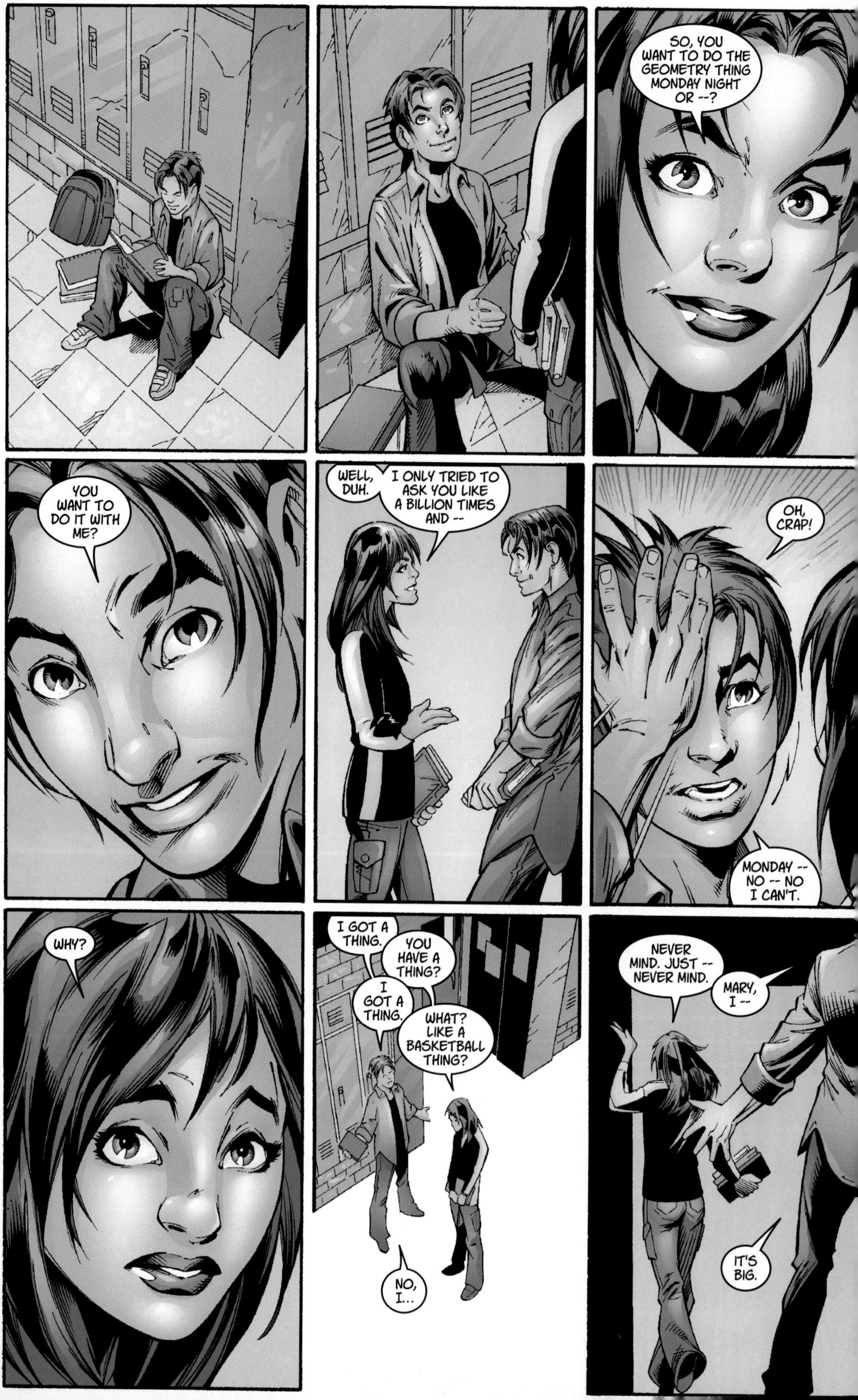
SO, YOU WANT TO DO THE GEOMETRY THING MONDAY NIGHT OR --?
YOU WANT TO DO IT WITH ME?
WELL, DUH.
I ONLY TRIED TO ASK YOU LIKE A BILLION TIMES AND --
OH, CRAP!
MONDAY -- NO -- NO I CAN'T.
WHY?
I GOT A THING.
YOU HAVE A THING?
I GOT A THING.
WHAT? LIKE A BASKETBALL THING?
NO, I...
NEVER MIND. JUST -- NEVER MIND.
MARY, I --
IT'S BIG.

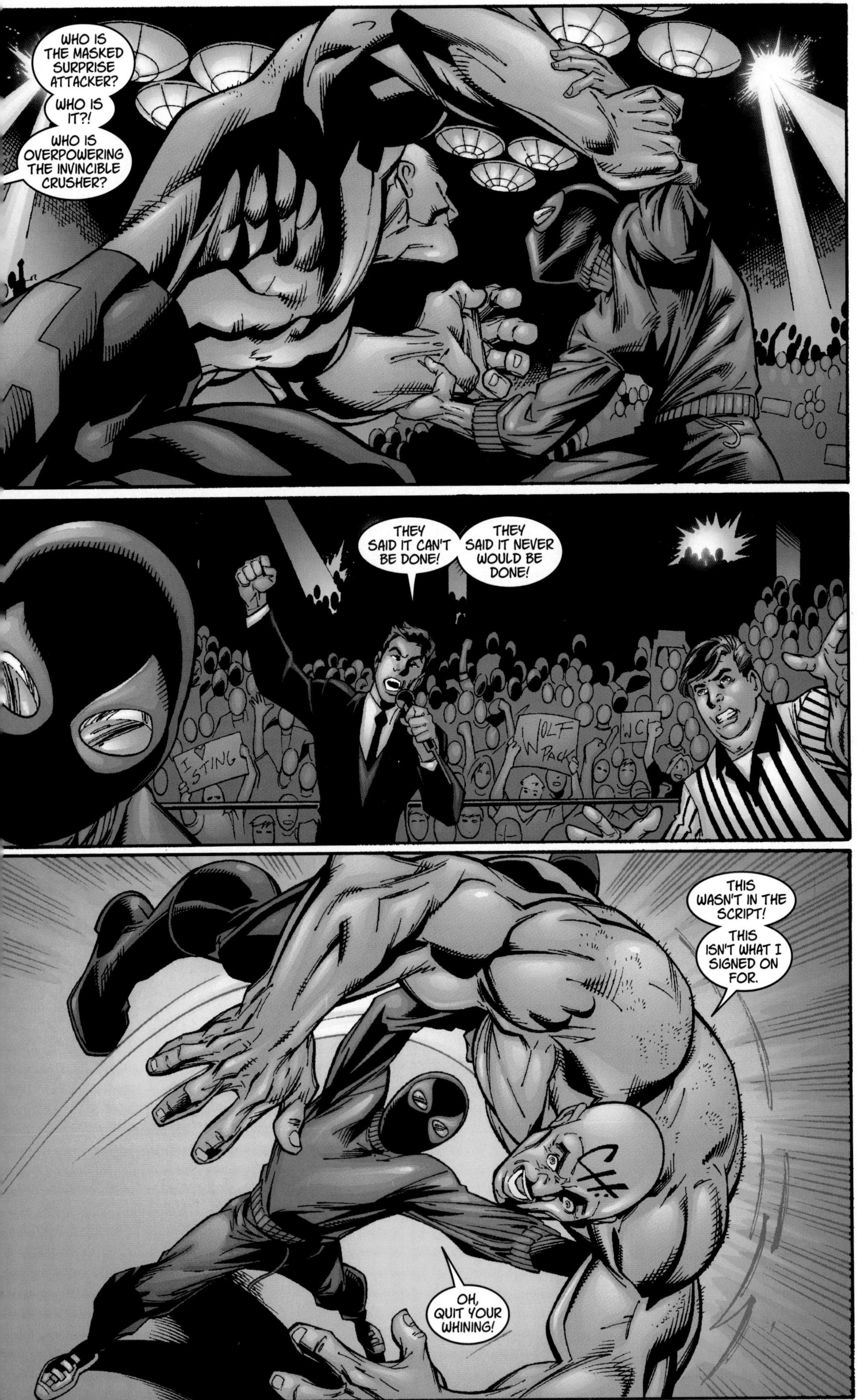
WHO IS THE MASKED SURPRISE ATTACKER?
WHO IS IT?!
WHO IS OVERPOWERING THE INVINCIBLE CRUSHER?
THEY SAID IT CAN'T BE DONE!
THEY SAID IT NEVER WOULD BE DONE!
I ♥ STING
WOLF PACK
WC
THIS WASN'T IN THE SCRIPT!
THIS ISN'T WHAT I SIGNED ON FOR.
OH, QUIT YOUR WHINING!

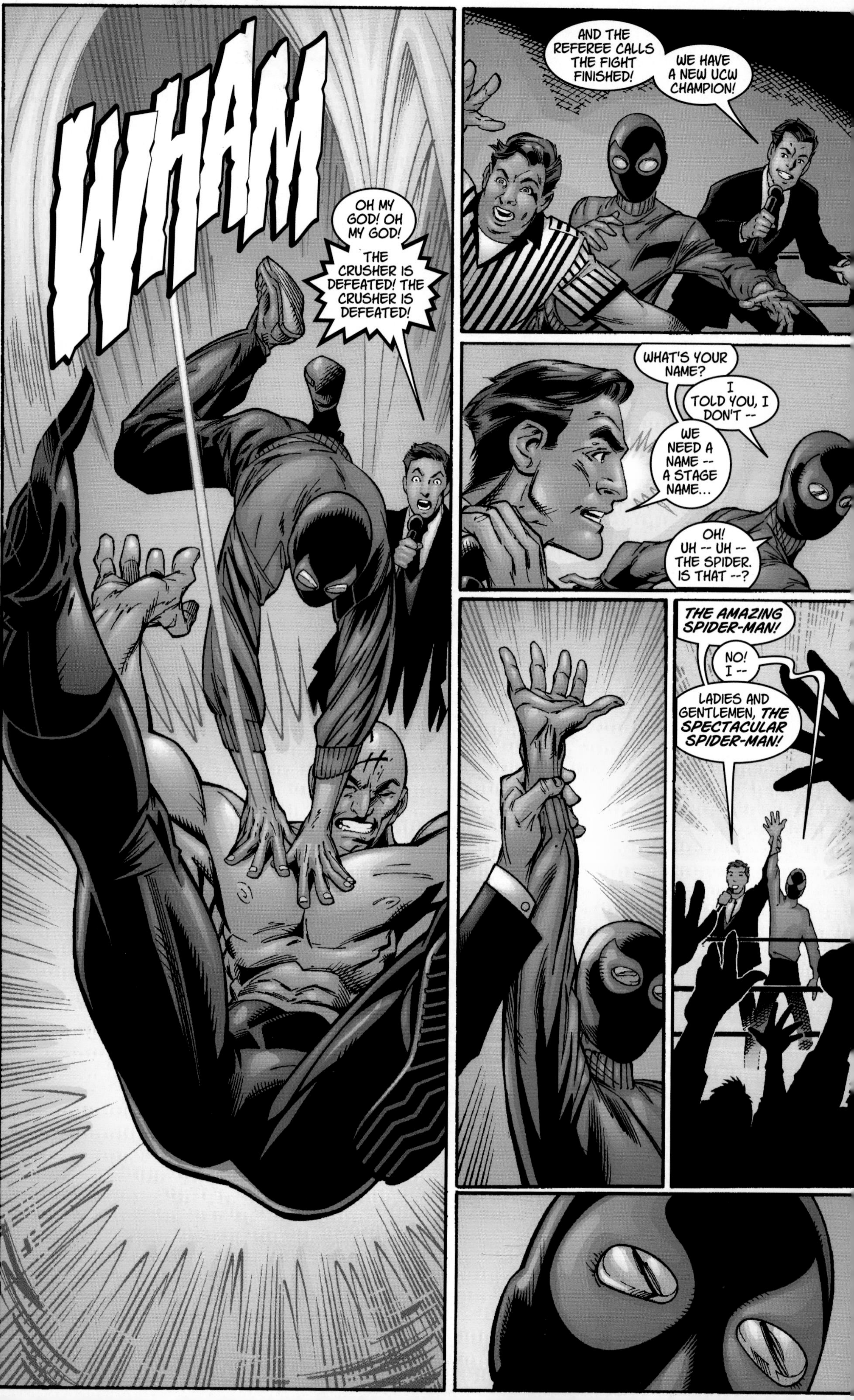
WHAM
OH MY GOD! OH MY GOD!
THE CRUSHER IS DEFEATED! THE CRUSHER IS DEFEATED!
AND THE REFEREE CALLS THE FIGHT FINISHED!
WE HAVE A NEW UCW CHAMPION!
WHAT'S YOUR NAME?
I TOLD YOU, I DON'T --
WE NEED A NAME -- A STAGE NAME...
OH! UH -- UH -- THE SPIDER. IS THAT --?
THE AMAZING SPIDER-MAN!
NO! I --
LADIES AND GENTLEMEN, THE SPECTACULAR SPIDER-MAN!

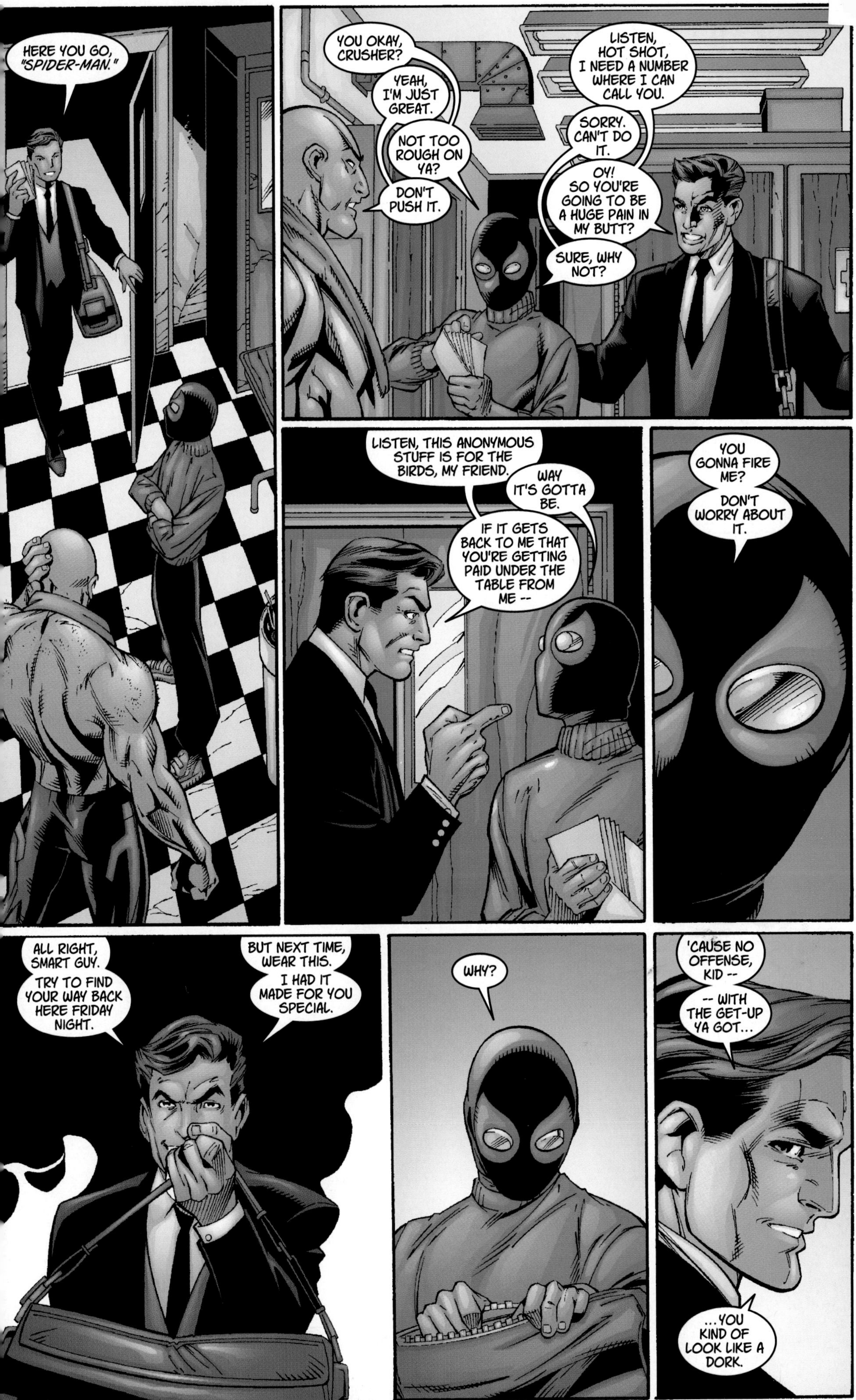
HERE YOU GO, "SPIDER-MAN."
YOU OKAY, CRUSHER?
YEAH, I'M JUST GREAT.
NOT TOO ROUGH ON YA?
DON'T PUSH IT.
LISTEN, HOT SHOT, I NEED A NUMBER WHERE I CAN CALL YOU.
SORRY. CAN'T DO IT.
OY! SO YOU'RE GOING TO BE A HUGE PAIN IN MY BUTT?
SURE, WHY NOT?
LISTEN, THIS ANONYMOUS STUFF IS FOR THE BIRDS, MY FRIEND.
WAY IT'S GOTTA BE.
IF IT GETS BACK TO ME THAT YOU'RE GETTING PAID UNDER THE TABLE FROM ME --
YOU GONNA FIRE ME?
DON'T WORRY ABOUT IT.
ALL RIGHT, SMART GUY.
TRY TO FIND YOUR WAY BACK HERE FRIDAY NIGHT.
BUT NEXT TIME, WEAR THIS.
I HAD IT MADE FOR YOU SPECIAL.
WHY?
'CAUSE NO OFFENSE, KID --
-- WITH THE GET-UP YA GOT...
...YOU KIND OF LOOK LIKE A DORK.

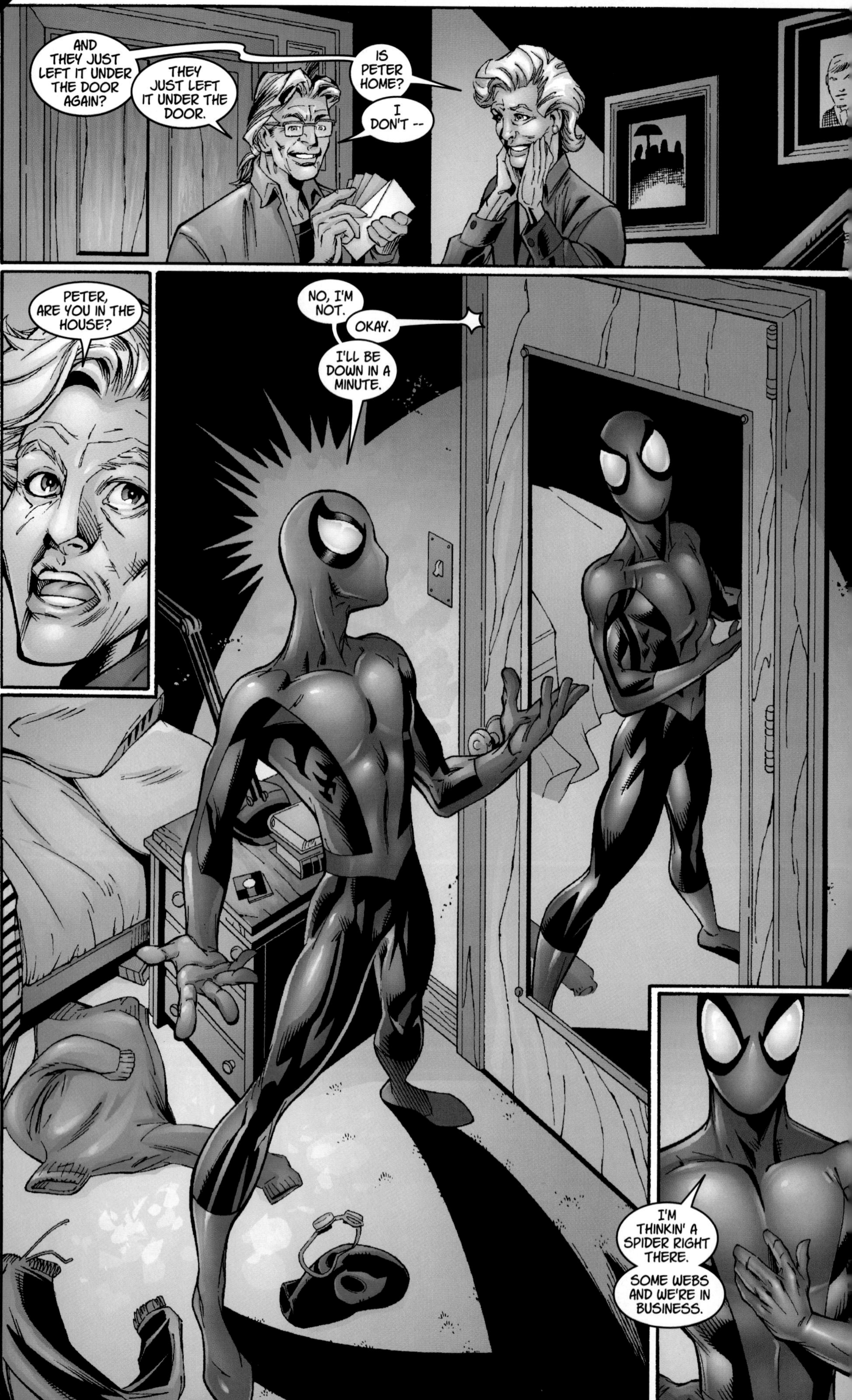
AND THEY JUST LEFT IT UNDER THE DOOR AGAIN?
THEY JUST LEFT IT UNDER THE DOOR.
IS PETER HOME?
I DON'T --
PETER, ARE YOU IN THE HOUSE?
NO, I'M NOT.
OKAY.
I'LL BE DOWN IN A MINUTE.
I'M THINKIN' A SPIDER RIGHT THERE.
SOME WEBS AND WE'RE IN BUSINESS.

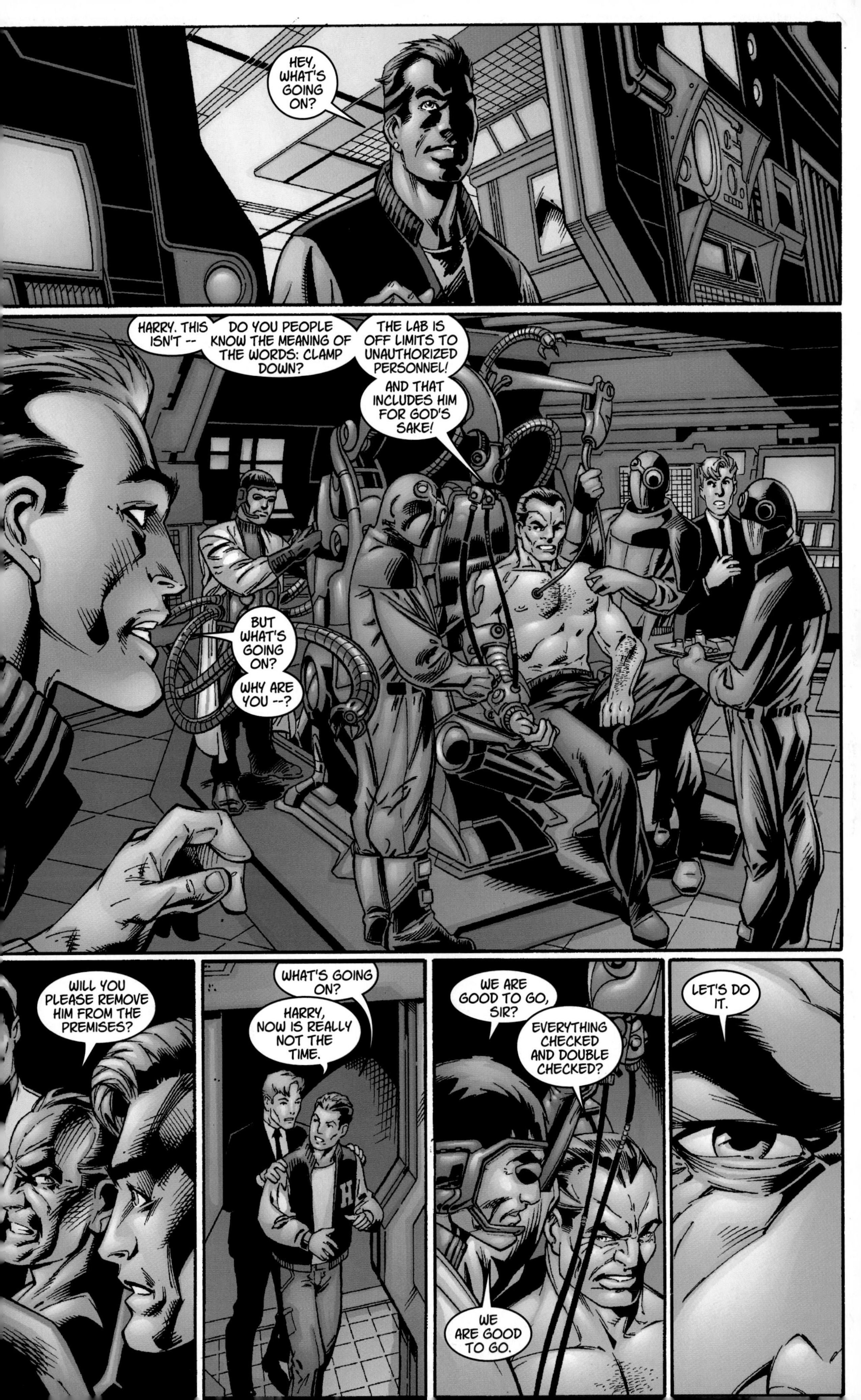
HEY, WHAT'S GOING ON?
HARRY. THIS ISN'T --
DO YOU PEOPLE KNOW THE MEANING OF THE WORDS: CLAMP DOWN?
THE LAB IS OFF LIMITS TO UNAUTHORIZED PERSONNEL!
AND THAT INCLUDES HIM FOR GOD'S SAKE!
BUT WHAT'S GOING ON?
WHY ARE YOU --?
WILL YOU PLEASE REMOVE HIM FROM THE PREMISES?
WHAT'S GOING ON?
HARRY, NOW IS REALLY NOT THE TIME.
WE ARE GOOD TO GO, SIR?
EVERYTHING CHECKED AND DOUBLE CHECKED?
WE ARE GOOD TO GO.
LET'S DO IT.

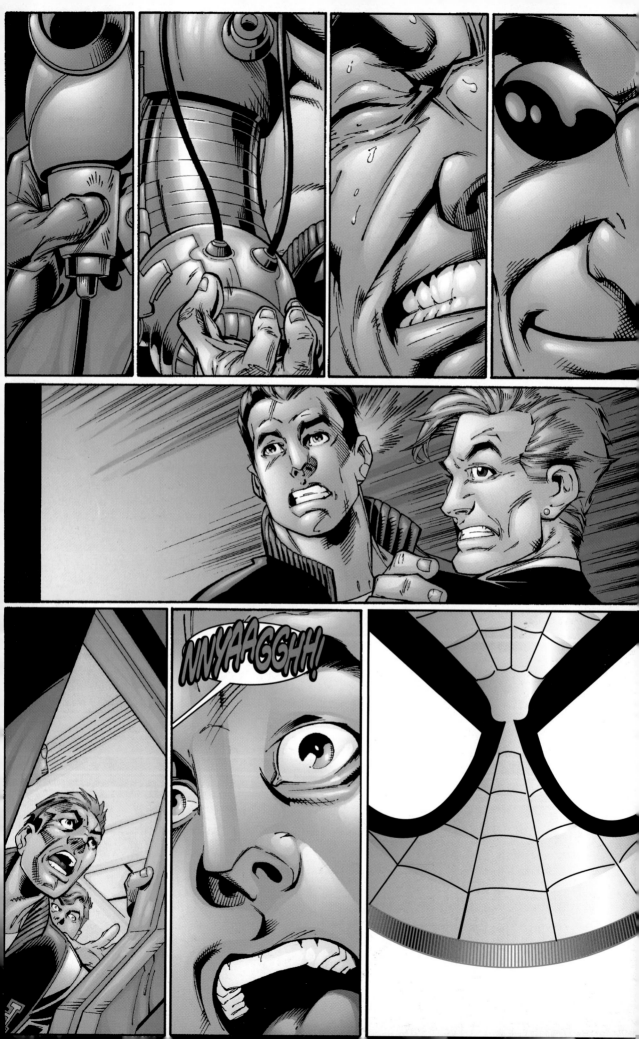

NNYAAGGHH!

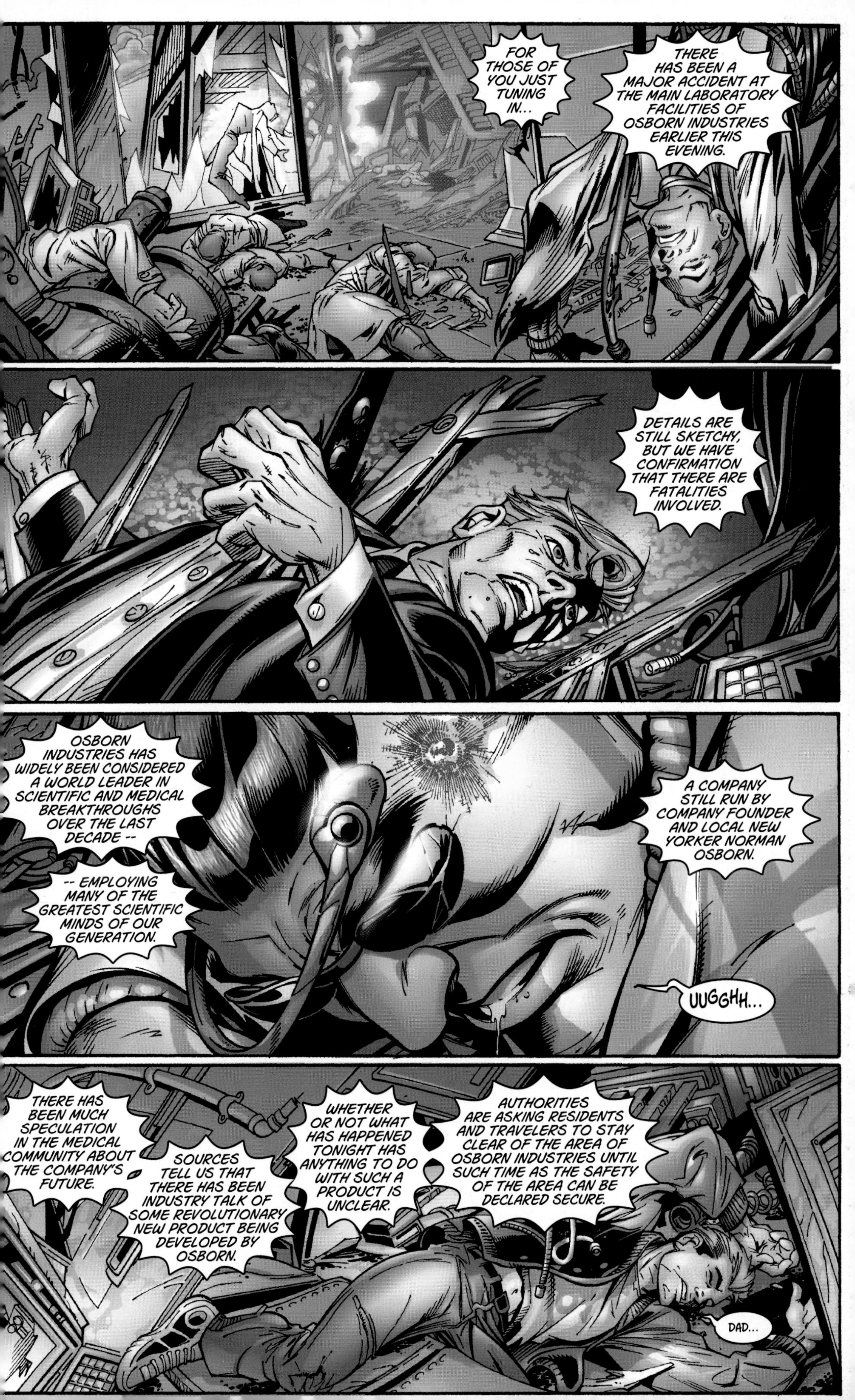
FOR THOSE OF YOU JUST TUNING IN...
THERE HAS BEEN A MAJOR ACCIDENT AT THE MAIN LABORATORY FACILITIES OF OSBORN INDUSTRIES EARLIER THIS EVENING.
DETAILS ARE STILL SKETCHY, BUT WE HAVE CONFIRMATION THAT THERE ARE FATALITIES INVOLVED.
OSBORN INDUSTRIES HAS WIDELY BEEN CONSIDERED A WORLD LEADER IN SCIENTIFIC AND MEDICAL BREAKTHROUGHS OVER THE LAST DECADE --
-- EMPLOYING MANY OF THE GREATEST SCIENTIFIC MINDS OF OUR GENERATION.
A COMPANY STILL RUN BY COMPANY FOUNDER AND LOCAL NEW YORKER NORMAN OSBORN.
UUGGHH...
THERE HAS BEEN MUCH SPECULATION IN THE MEDICAL COMMUNITY ABOUT THE COMPANY'S FUTURE.
SOURCES TELL US THAT THERE HAS BEEN INDUSTRY TALK OF SOME REVOLUTIONARY NEW PRODUCT BEING DEVELOPED BY OSBORN.
WHETHER OR NOT WHAT HAS HAPPENED TONIGHT HAS ANYTHING TO DO WITH SUCH A PRODUCT IS UNCLEAR.
AUTHORITIES ARE ASKING RESIDENTS AND TRAVELERS TO STAY CLEAR OF THE AREA OF OSBORN INDUSTRIES UNTIL SUCH TIME AS THE SAFETY OF THE AREA CAN BE DECLARED SECURE.
DAD...

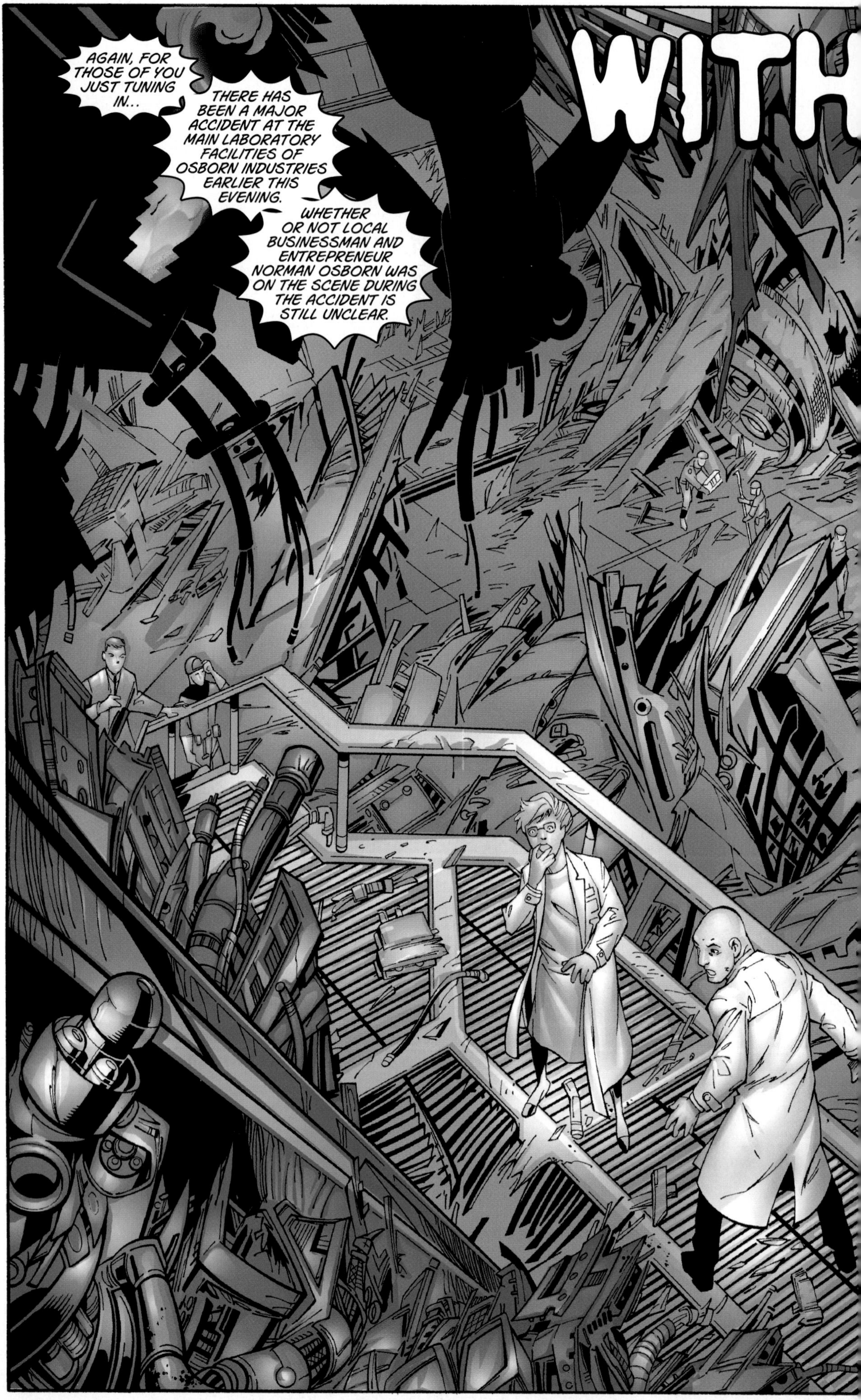
WITH
AGAIN, FOR THOSE OF YOU JUST TUNING IN...
THERE HAS BEEN A MAJOR ACCIDENT AT THE MAIN LABORATORY FACILITIES OF OSBORN INDUSTRIES EARLIER THIS EVENING.
WHETHER OR NOT LOCAL BUSINESSMAN AND ENTREPRENEUR NORMAN OSBORN WAS ON THE SCENE DURING THE ACCIDENT IS STILL UNCLEAR.

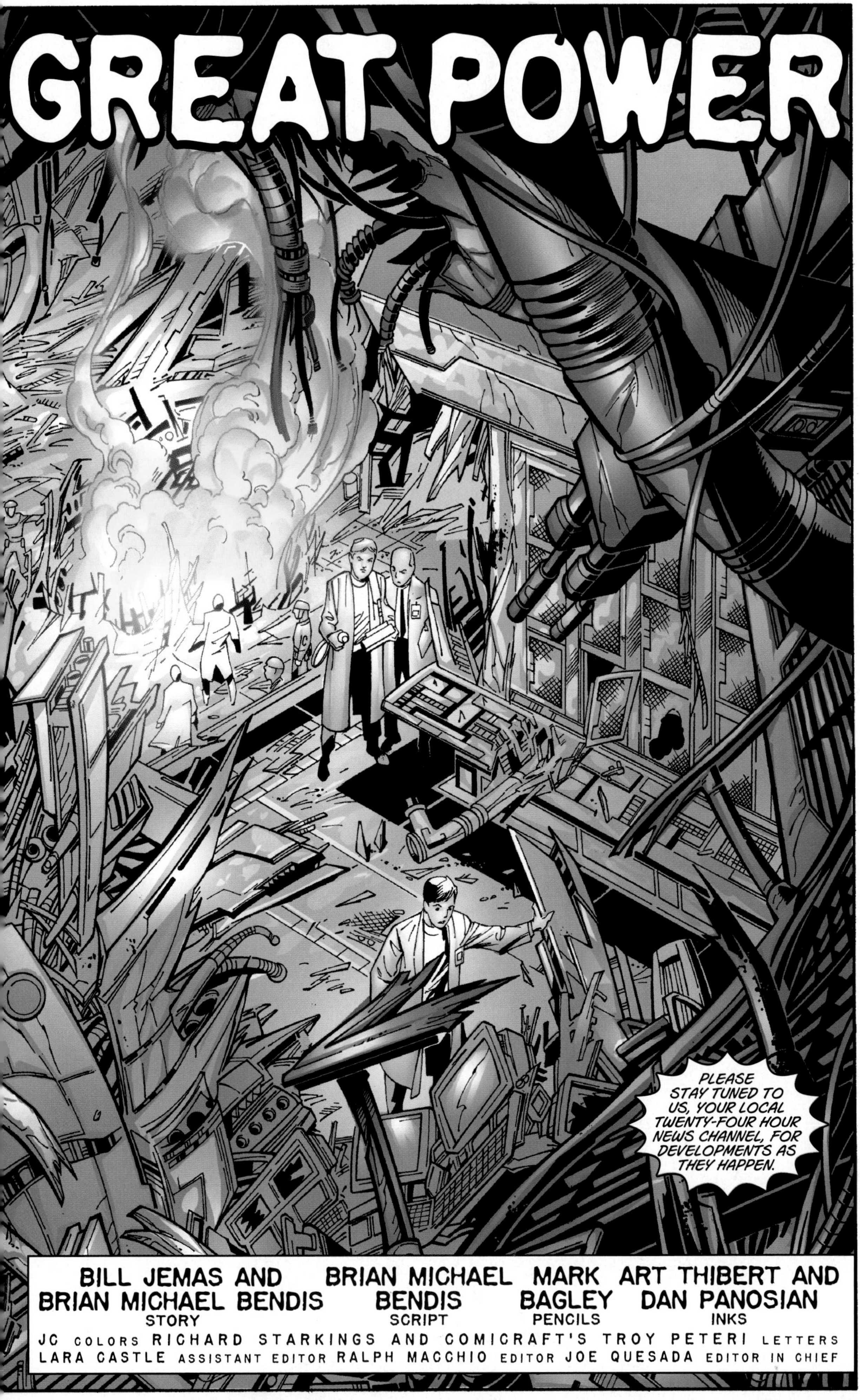
GREAT POWER
PLEASE STAY TUNED TO US, YOUR LOCAL TWENTY-FOUR HOUR NEWS CHANNEL, FOR DEVELOPMENTS AS THEY HAPPEN.
BILL JEMAS AND BRIAN MICHAEL BENDIS STORY
BRIAN MICHAEL BENDIS SCRIPT
MARK BAGLEY PENCILS
ART THIBERT AND DAN PANOSIAN INKS
JC COLORS RICHARD STARKINGS AND COMICRAFT'S TROY PETERI LETTERS
LARA CASTLE ASSISTANT EDITOR RALPH MACCHIO EDITOR JOE QUESADA EDITOR IN CHIEF

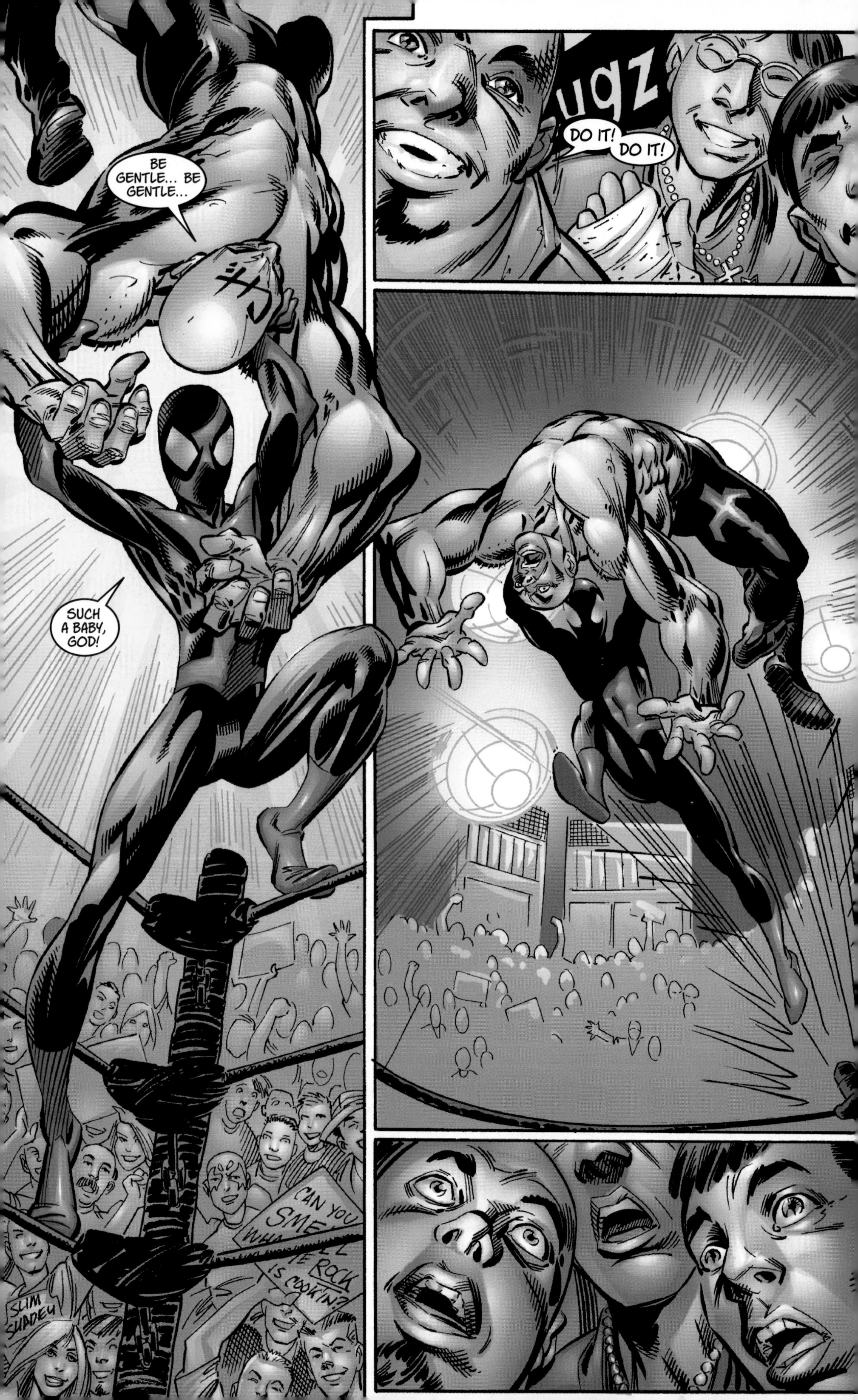
BE GENTLE... BE GENTLE...
SUCH A BABY, GOD!
SLIM SHADEY
DO IT!
DO IT!

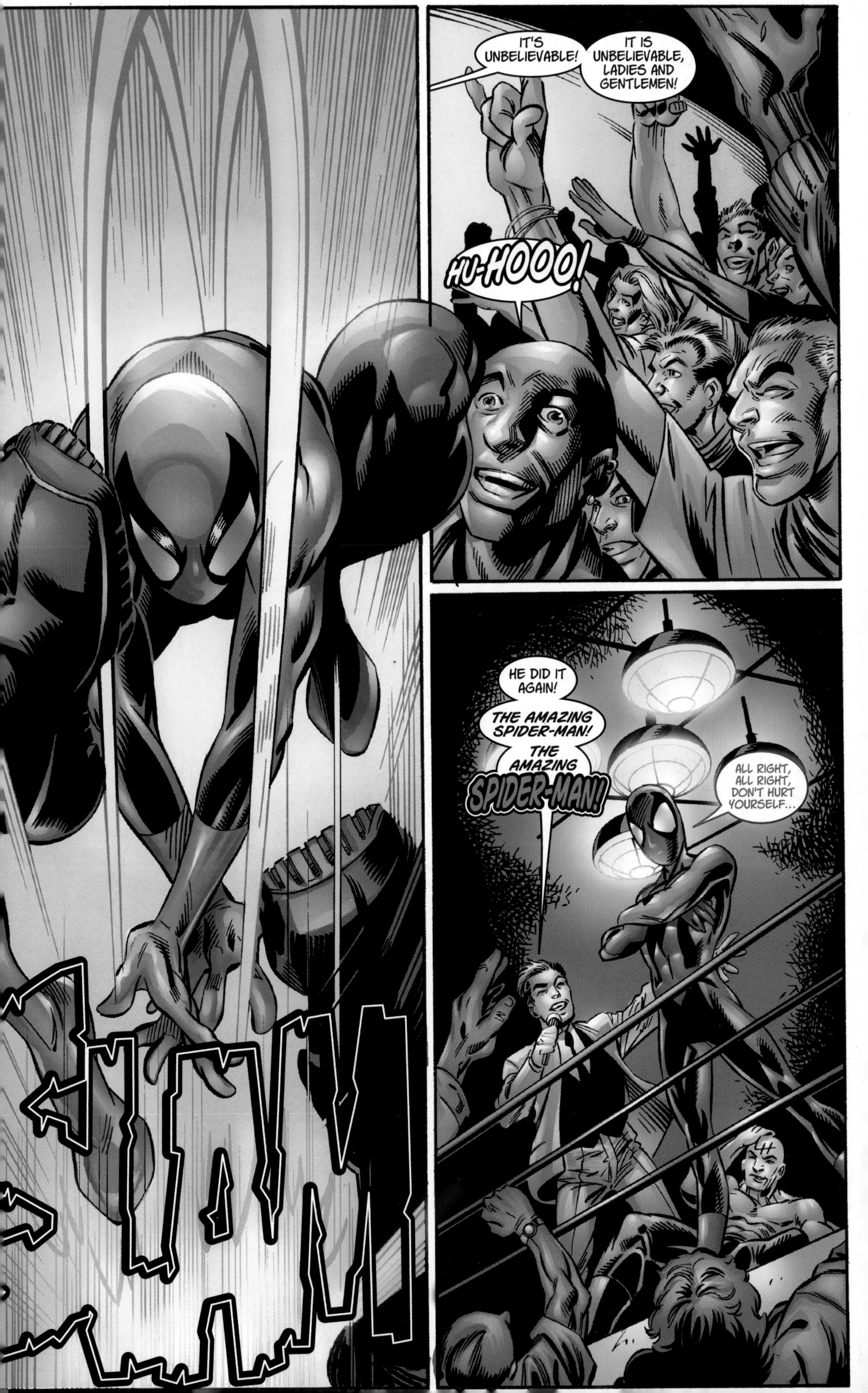

IT'S UNBELIEVABLE!
IT IS UNBELIEVABLE, LADIES AND GENTLEMEN!
HU-HOOO!
HE DID IT AGAIN!
THE AMAZING SPIDER-MAN!
THE AMAZING SPIDER-MAN!
ALL RIGHT, ALL RIGHT, DON'T HURT YOURSELF...

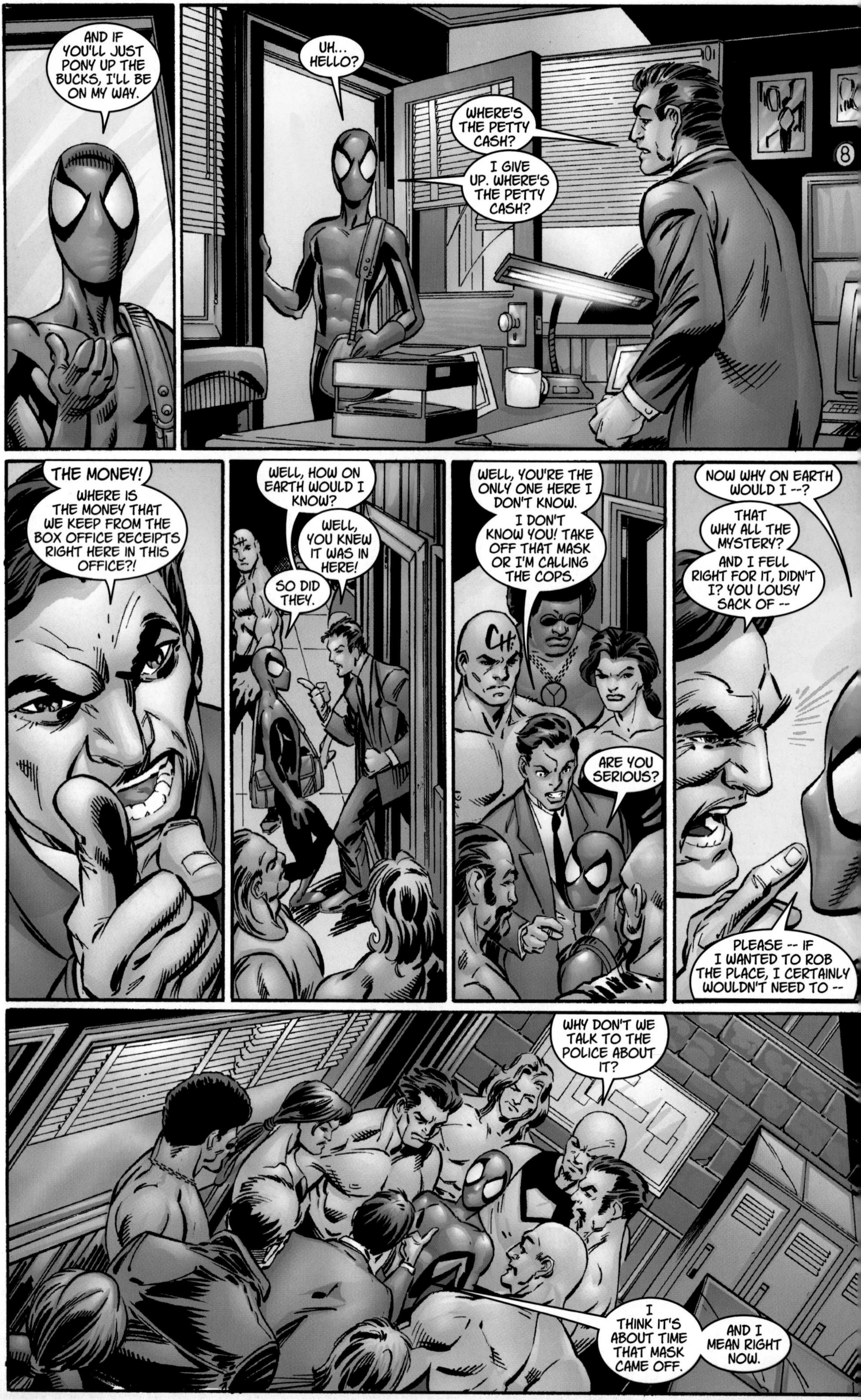
AND IF YOU'LL JUST PONY UP THE BUCKS, I'LL BE ON MY WAY.
UH... HELLO?
WHERE'S THE PETTY CASH?
I GIVE UP. WHERE'S THE PETTY CASH?
THE MONEY!
WHERE IS THE MONEY THAT WE KEEP FROM THE BOX OFFICE RECEIPTS RIGHT HERE IN THIS OFFICE?!
WELL, HOW ON EARTH WOULD I KNOW?
WELL, YOU KNEW IT WAS IN HERE!
SO DID THEY.
WELL, YOU'RE THE ONLY ONE HERE I DON'T KNOW.
I DON'T KNOW YOU! TAKE OFF THAT MASK OR I'M CALLING THE COPS.
ARE YOU SERIOUS?
NOW WHY ON EARTH WOULD I --?
THAT WHY ALL THE MYSTERY?
AND I FELL RIGHT FOR IT, DIDN'T I? YOU LOUSY SACK OF --
PLEASE -- IF I WANTED TO ROB THE PLACE, I CERTAINLY WOULDN'T NEED TO --
WHY DON'T WE TALK TO THE POLICE ABOUT IT?
I THINK IT'S ABOUT TIME THAT MASK CAME OFF.
AND I MEAN RIGHT NOW.

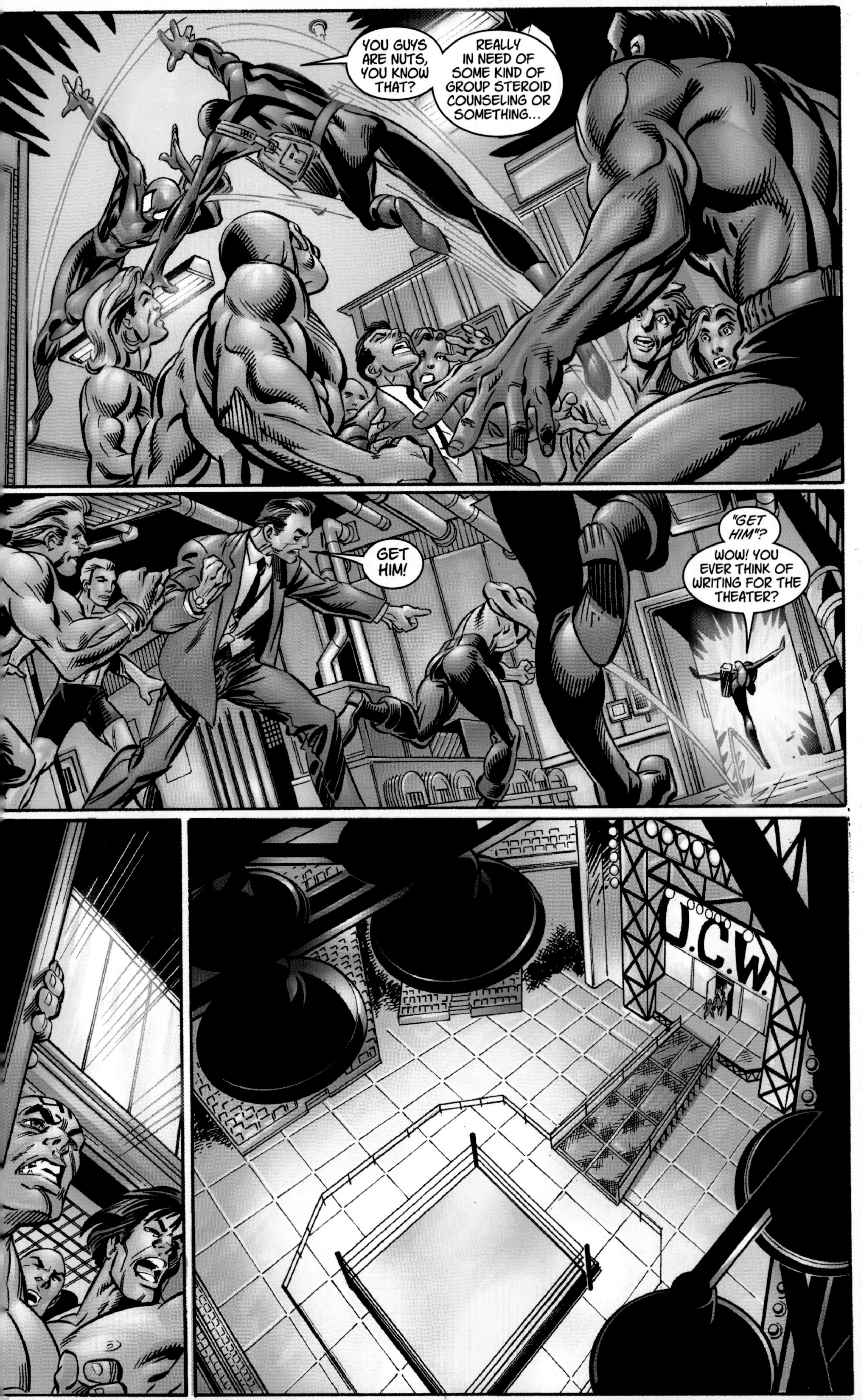
YOU GUYS ARE NUTS, YOU KNOW THAT?
REALLY IN NEED OF SOME KIND OF GROUP STEROID COUNSELING OR SOMETHING...
GET HIM!
"GET HIM"? WOW! YOU EVER THINK OF WRITING FOR THE THEATER?
U.C.W.

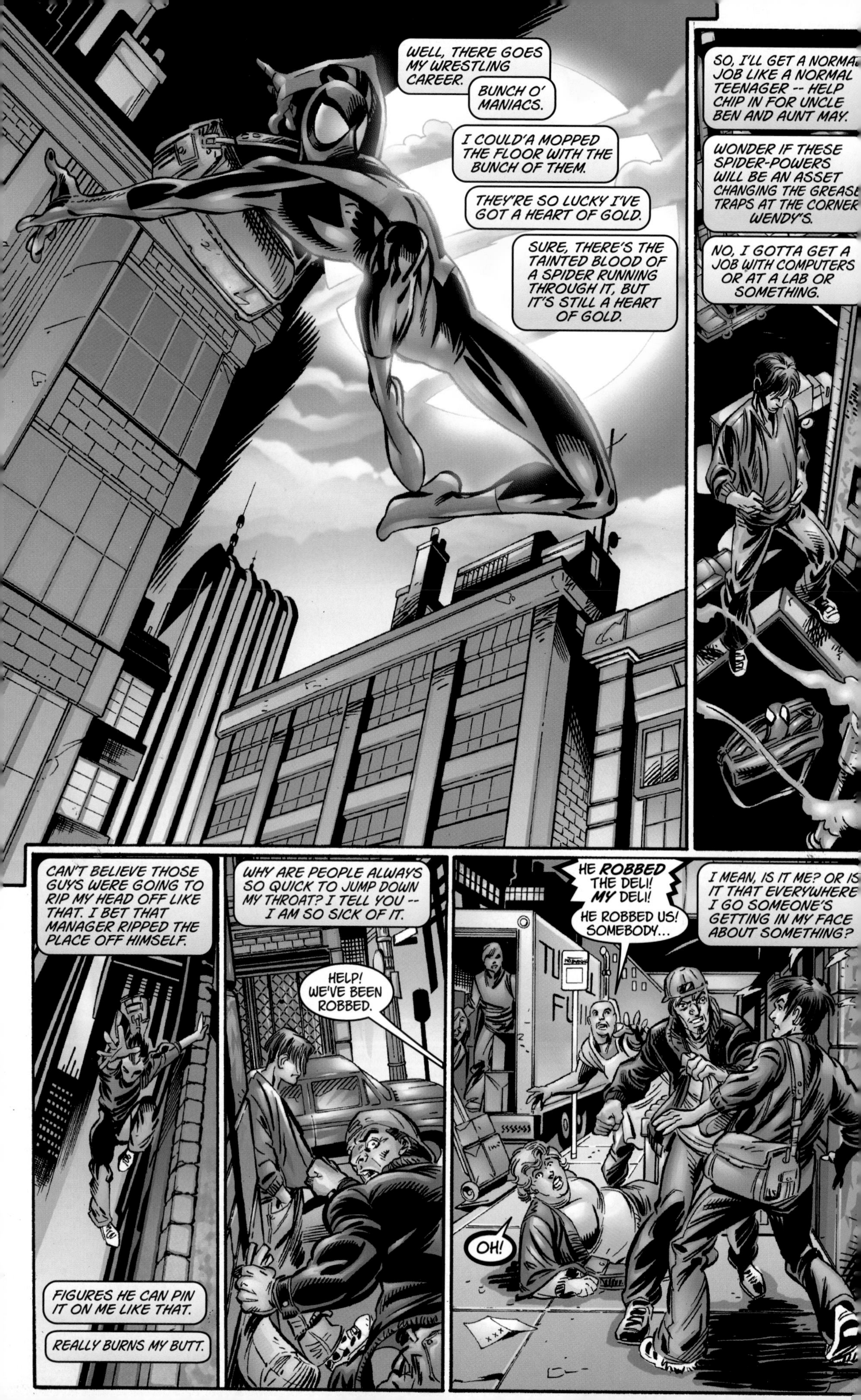
WELL, THERE GOES MY WRESTLING CAREER.
BUNCH O' MANIACS.
I COULD'A MOPPED THE FLOOR WITH THE BUNCH OF THEM.
THEY'RE SO LUCKY I'VE GOT A HEART OF GOLD.
SURE, THERE'S THE TAINTED BLOOD OF A SPIDER RUNNING THROUGH IT, BUT IT'S STILL A HEART OF GOLD.
SO, I'LL GET A NORMAL JOB LIKE A NORMAL TEENAGER -- HELP CHIP IN FOR UNCLE BEN AND AUNT MAY.
WONDER IF THESE SPIDER-POWERS WILL BE AN ASSET CHANGING THE GREASE TRAPS AT THE CORNER WENDY'S.
NO, I GOTTA GET A JOB WITH COMPUTERS OR AT A LAB OR SOMETHING.
CAN'T BELIEVE THOSE GUYS WERE GOING TO RIP MY HEAD OFF LIKE THAT. I BET THAT MANAGER RIPPED THE PLACE OFF HIMSELF.
FIGURES HE CAN PIN IT ON ME LIKE THAT.
REALLY BURNS MY BUTT.
WHY ARE PEOPLE ALWAYS SO QUICK TO JUMP DOWN MY THROAT? I TELL YOU -- I AM SO SICK OF IT.
HELP! WE'VE BEEN ROBBED.
HE ROBBED THE DELI! MY DELI!
HE ROBBED US! SOMEBODY...
I MEAN, IS IT ME? OR IS IT THAT EVERYWHERE I GO SOMEONE'S GETTING IN MY FACE ABOUT SOMETHING?
OH!

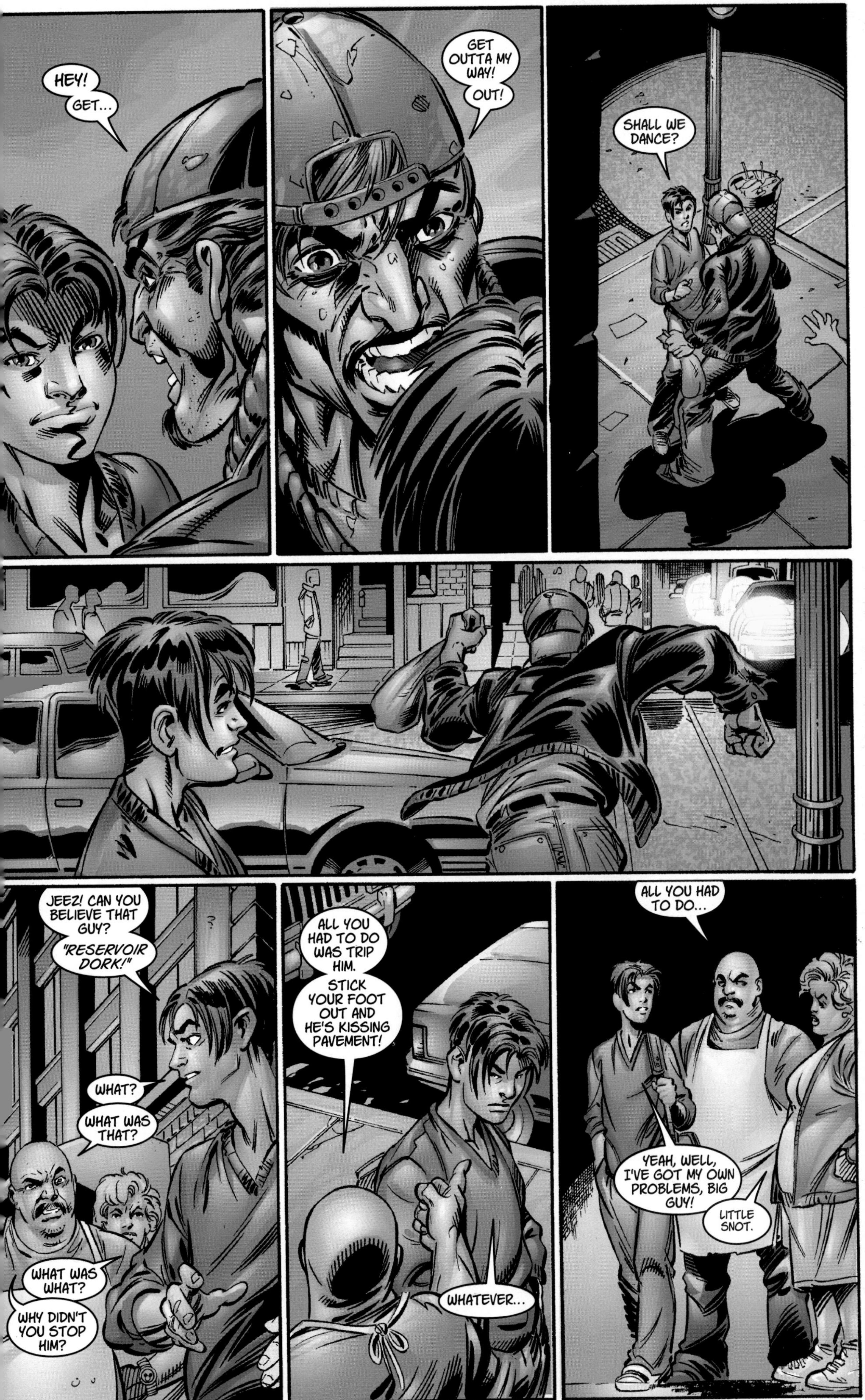
HEY!
GET...
GET OUTTA MY WAY!
OUT!
SHALL WE DANCE?
JEEZ! CAN YOU BELIEVE THAT GUY?
"RESERVOIR DORK!"
WHAT?
WHAT WAS THAT?
WHAT WAS WHAT?
WHY DIDN'T YOU STOP HIM?
ALL YOU HAD TO DO WAS TRIP HIM.
STICK YOUR FOOT OUT AND HE'S KISSING PAVEMENT!
WHATEVER...
ALL YOU HAD TO DO...
YEAH, WELL, I'VE GOT MY OWN PROBLEMS, BIG GUY!
LITTLE SNOT.

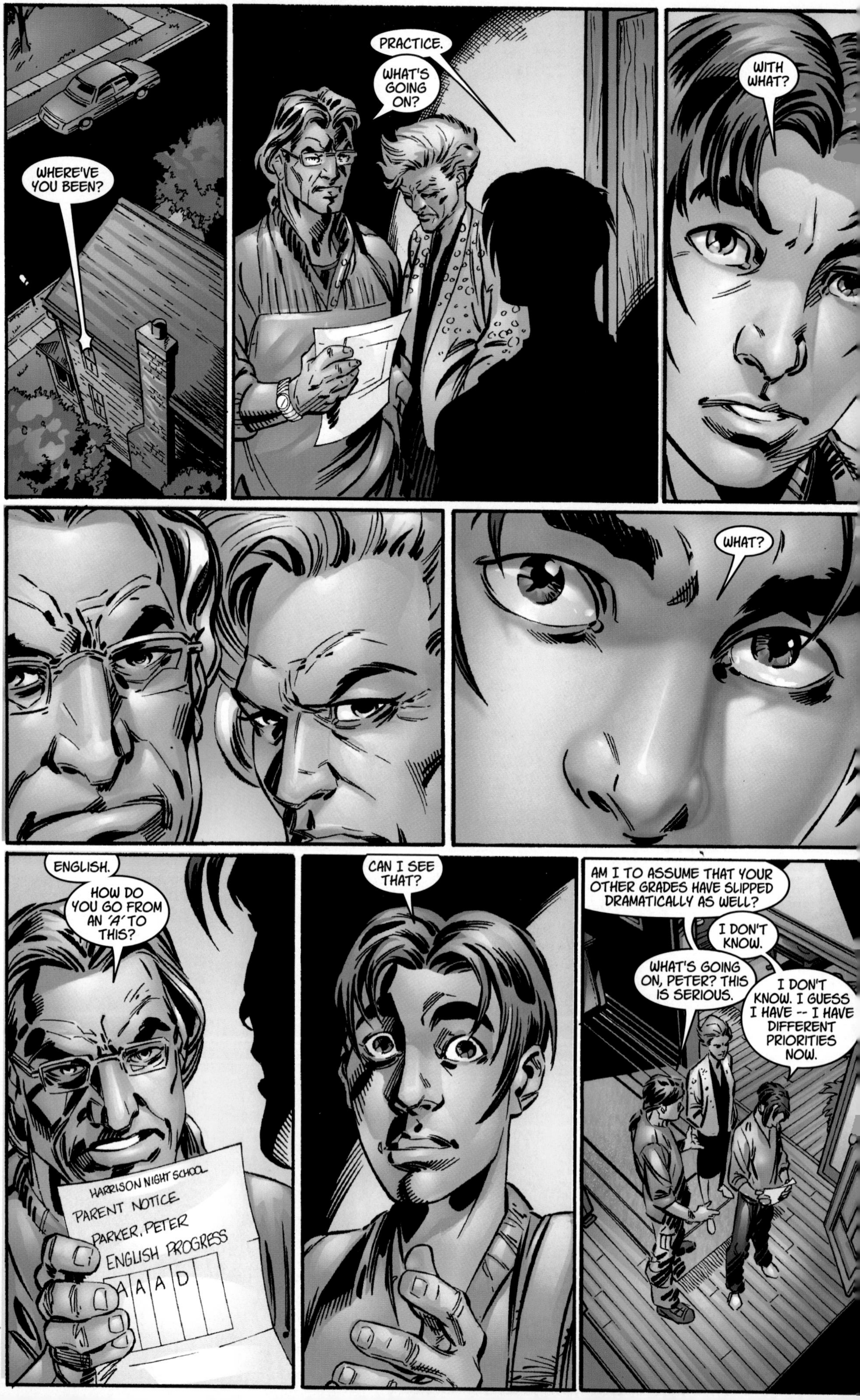
WHERE'VE YOU BEEN?
PRACTICE.
WHAT'S GOING ON?
WITH WHAT?
WHAT?
ENGLISH.
HOW DO YOU GO FROM AN 'A' TO THIS?
HARRISON NIGHT SCHOOL
PARENT NOTICE
PARKER, PETER
ENGLISH PROGRESS
A A A D
CAN I SEE THAT?
AM I TO ASSUME THAT YOUR OTHER GRADES HAVE SLIPPED DRAMATICALLY AS WELL?
I DON'T KNOW.
WHAT'S GOING ON, PETER? THIS IS SERIOUS.
I DON'T KNOW. I GUESS I HAVE -- I HAVE DIFFERENT PRIORITIES NOW.

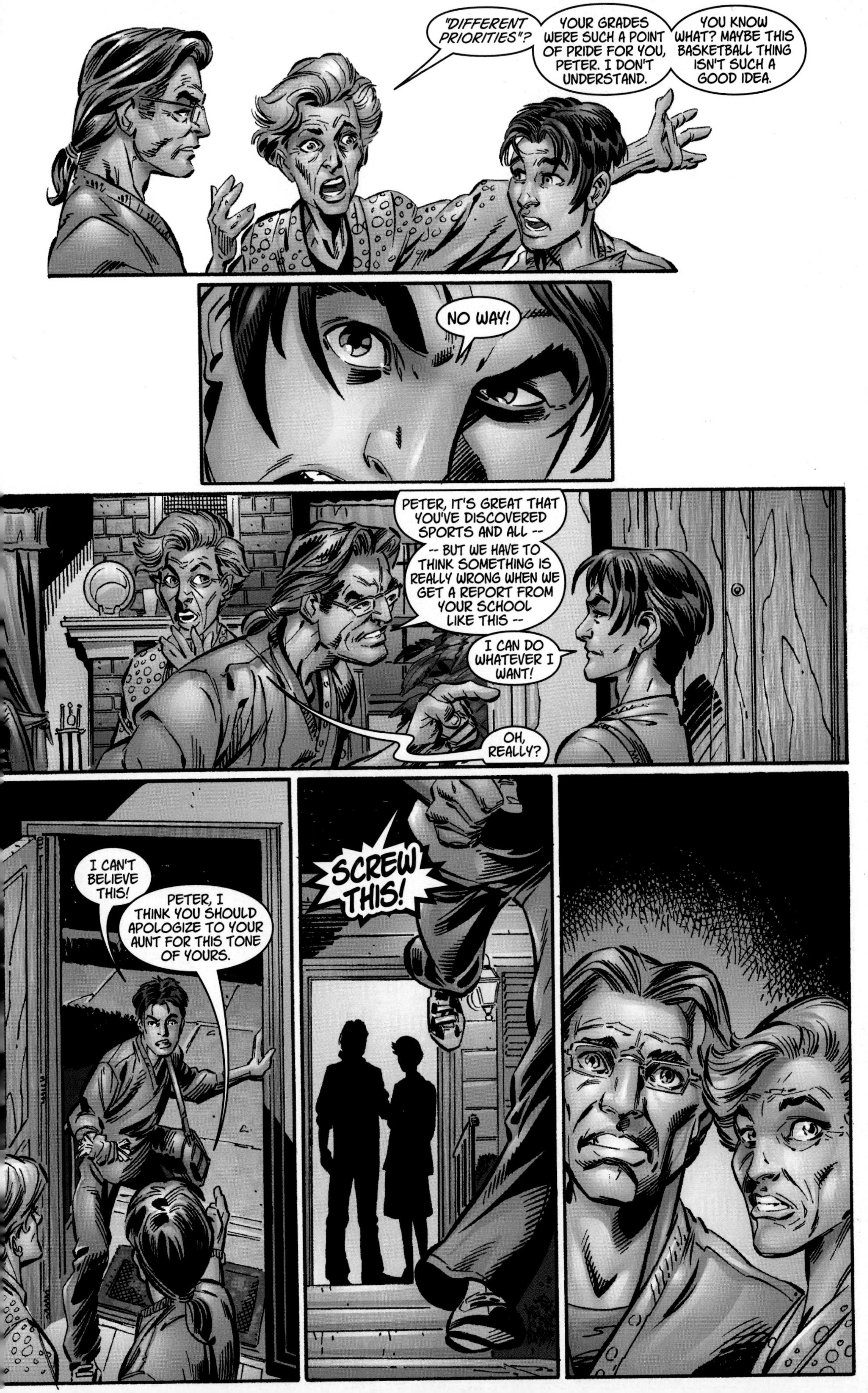
"DIFFERENT PRIORITIES"?
YOUR GRADES WERE SUCH A POINT OF PRIDE FOR YOU, PETER. I DON'T UNDERSTAND.
YOU KNOW WHAT? MAYBE THIS BASKETBALL THING ISN'T SUCH A GOOD IDEA.
NO WAY!
PETER, IT'S GREAT THAT YOU'VE DISCOVERED SPORTS AND ALL --
-- BUT WE HAVE TO THINK SOMETHING IS REALLY WRONG WHEN WE GET A REPORT FROM YOUR SCHOOL LIKE THIS --
I CAN DO WHATEVER I WANT!
OH, REALLY?
I CAN'T BELIEVE THIS!
PETER, I THINK YOU SHOULD APOLOGIZE TO YOUR AUNT FOR THIS TONE OF YOURS.
SCREW THIS!

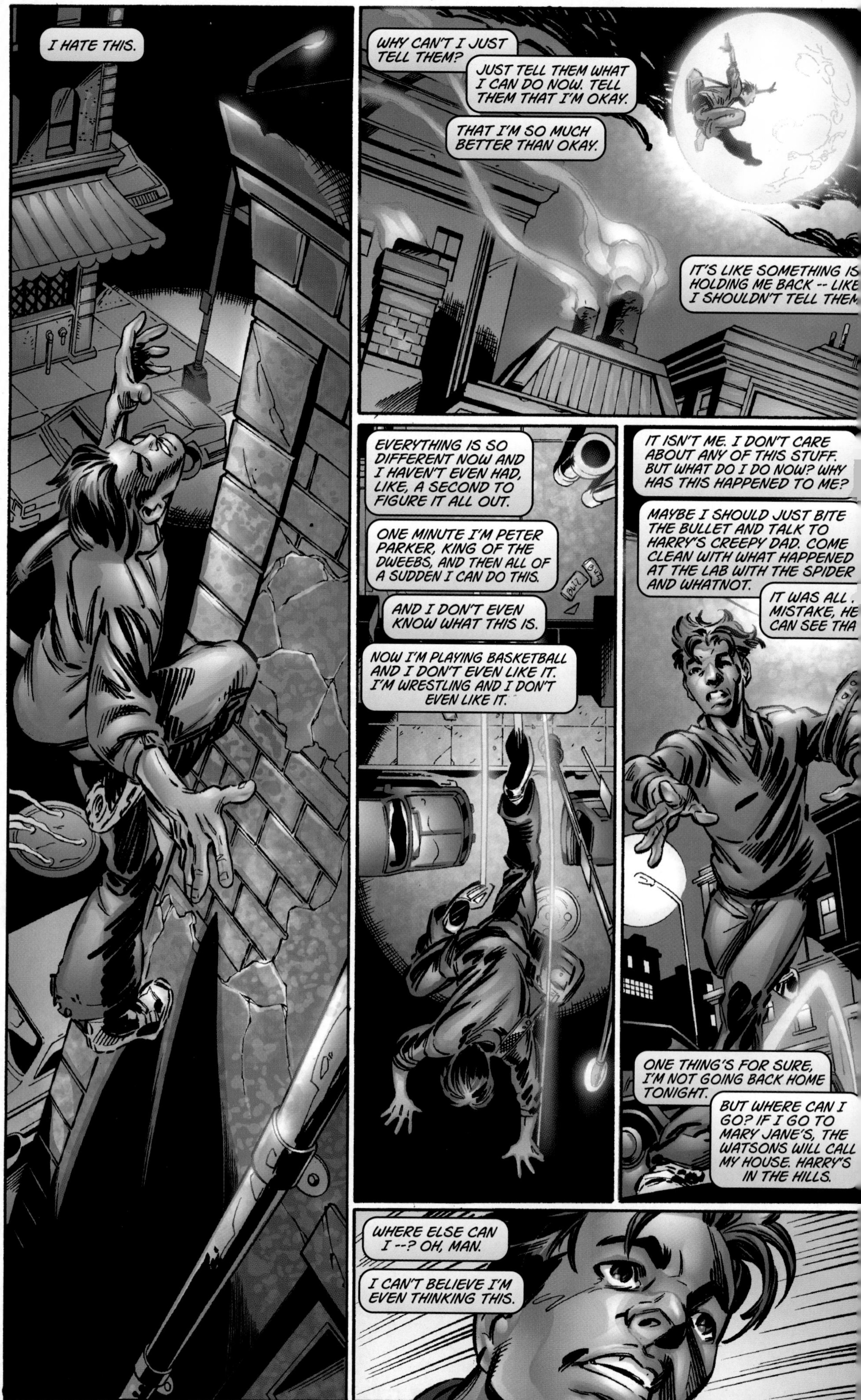
I HATE THIS.
WHY CAN'T I JUST TELL THEM?
JUST TELL THEM WHAT I CAN DO NOW. TELL THEM THAT I'M OKAY.
THAT I'M SO MUCH BETTER THAN OKAY.
IT'S LIKE SOMETHING IS HOLDING ME BACK -- LIKE I SHOULDN'T TELL THEM
EVERYTHING IS SO DIFFERENT NOW AND I HAVEN'T EVEN HAD, LIKE, A SECOND TO FIGURE IT ALL OUT.
ONE MINUTE I'M PETER PARKER, KING OF THE DWEEBS, AND THEN ALL OF A SUDDEN I CAN DO THIS.
AND I DON'T EVEN KNOW WHAT THIS IS.
NOW I'M PLAYING BASKETBALL AND I DON'T EVEN LIKE IT. I'M WRESTLING AND I DON'T EVEN LIKE IT.
IT ISN'T ME. I DON'T CARE ABOUT ANY OF THIS STUFF. BUT WHAT DO I DO NOW? WHY HAS THIS HAPPENED TO ME?
MAYBE I SHOULD JUST BITE THE BULLET AND TALK TO HARRY'S CREEPY DAD. COME CLEAN WITH WHAT HAPPENED AT THE LAB WITH THE SPIDER AND WHATNOT.
IT WAS ALL MISTAKE, HE CAN SEE THA
ONE THING'S FOR SURE, I'M NOT GOING BACK HOME TONIGHT.
BUT WHERE CAN I GO? IF I GO TO MARY JANE'S, THE WATSONS WILL CALL MY HOUSE. HARRY'S IN THE HILLS.
WHERE ELSE CAN I --? OH, MAN.
I CAN'T BELIEVE I'M EVEN THINKING THIS.

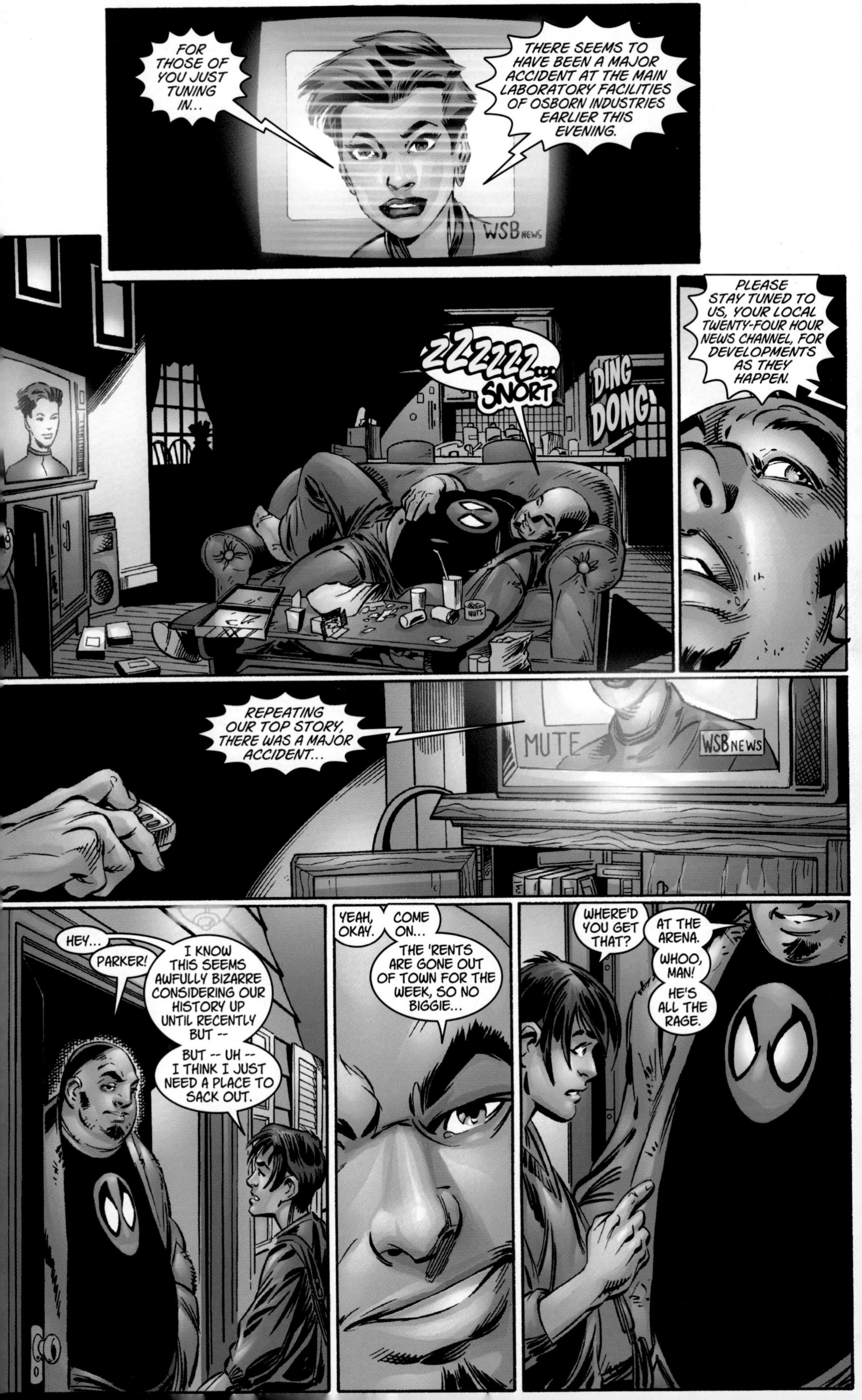
FOR THOSE OF YOU JUST TUNING IN...
THERE SEEMS TO HAVE BEEN A MAJOR ACCIDENT AT THE MAIN LABORATORY FACILITIES OF OSBORN INDUSTRIES EARLIER THIS EVENING.
WSB NEWS
ZZZZZZ... SNORT
DING DONG
PLEASE STAY TUNED TO US, YOUR LOCAL TWENTY-FOUR HOUR NEWS CHANNEL, FOR DEVELOPMENTS AS THEY HAPPEN.
REPEATING OUR TOP STORY, THERE WAS A MAJOR ACCIDENT...
MUTE
WSB NEWS
HEY...
PARKER!
I KNOW THIS SEEMS AWFULLY BIZARRE CONSIDERING OUR HISTORY UP UNTIL RECENTLY BUT --
BUT -- UH -- I THINK I JUST NEED A PLACE TO SACK OUT.
YEAH, OKAY.
COME ON...
THE 'RENTS ARE GONE OUT OF TOWN FOR THE WEEK, SO NO BIGGIE...
WHERE'D YOU GET THAT?
AT THE ARENA.
WHOO, MAN!
HE'S ALL THE RAGE.

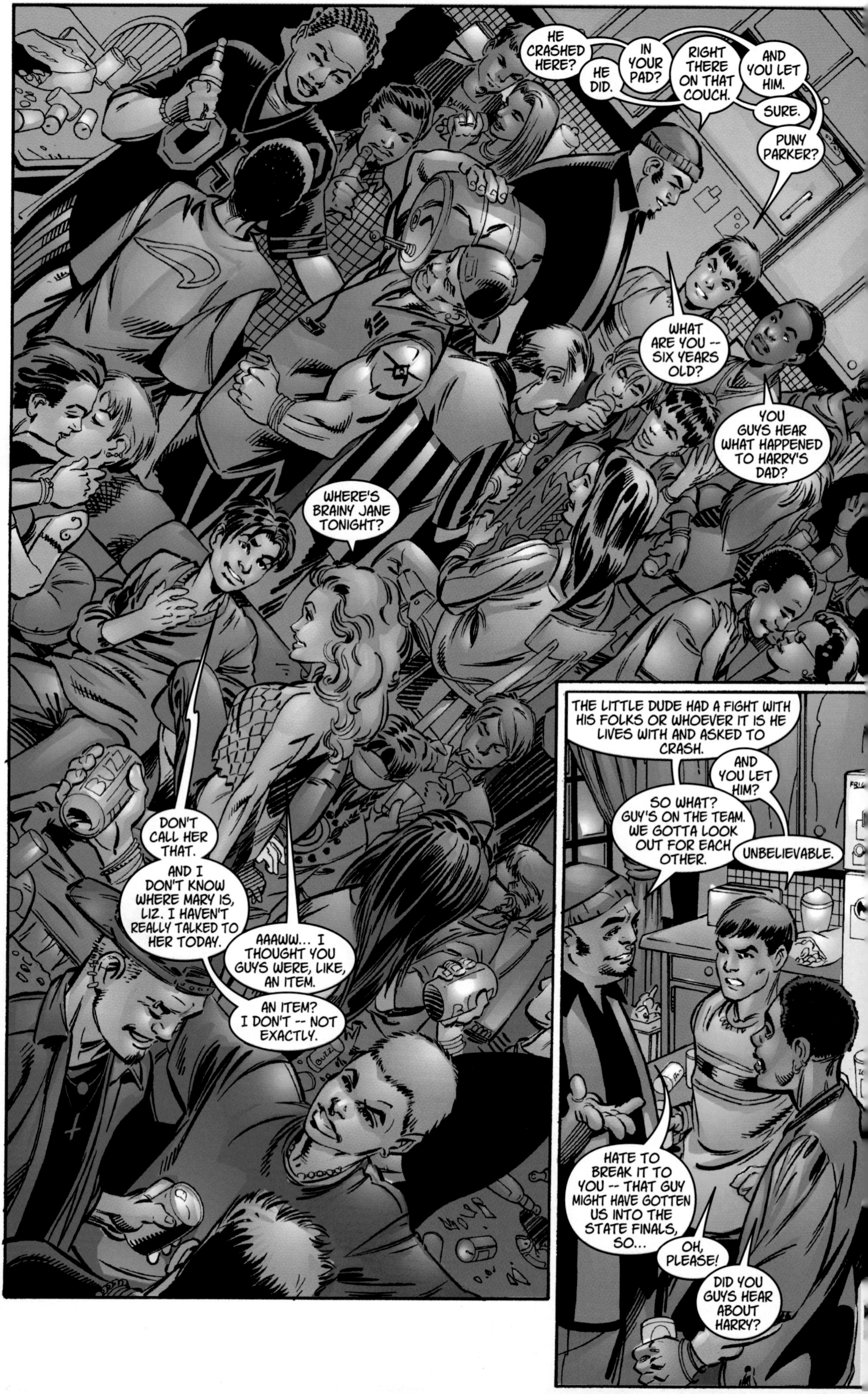
HE CRASHED HERE?
HE DID.
IN YOUR PAD?
RIGHT THERE ON THAT COUCH.
AND YOU LET HIM.
SURE.
PUNY PARKER?
WHAT ARE YOU -- SIX YEARS OLD?
YOU GUYS HEAR WHAT HAPPENED TO HARRY'S DAD?
WHERE'S BRAINY JANE TONIGHT?
DON'T CALL HER THAT.
AND I DON'T KNOW WHERE MARY IS, LIZ. I HAVEN'T REALLY TALKED TO HER TODAY.
AAAWW... I THOUGHT YOU GUYS WERE, LIKE, AN ITEM.
AN ITEM? I DON'T -- NOT EXACTLY.
BUZZ
THE LITTLE DUDE HAD A FIGHT WITH HIS FOLKS OR WHOEVER IT IS HE LIVES WITH AND ASKED TO CRASH.
AND YOU LET HIM?
SO WHAT? GUY'S ON THE TEAM. WE GOTTA LOOK OUT FOR EACH OTHER.
UNBELIEVABLE.
HATE TO BREAK IT TO YOU -- THAT GUY MIGHT HAVE GOTTEN US INTO THE STATE FINALS, SO...
OH, PLEASE!
DID YOU GUYS HEAR ABOUT HARRY?

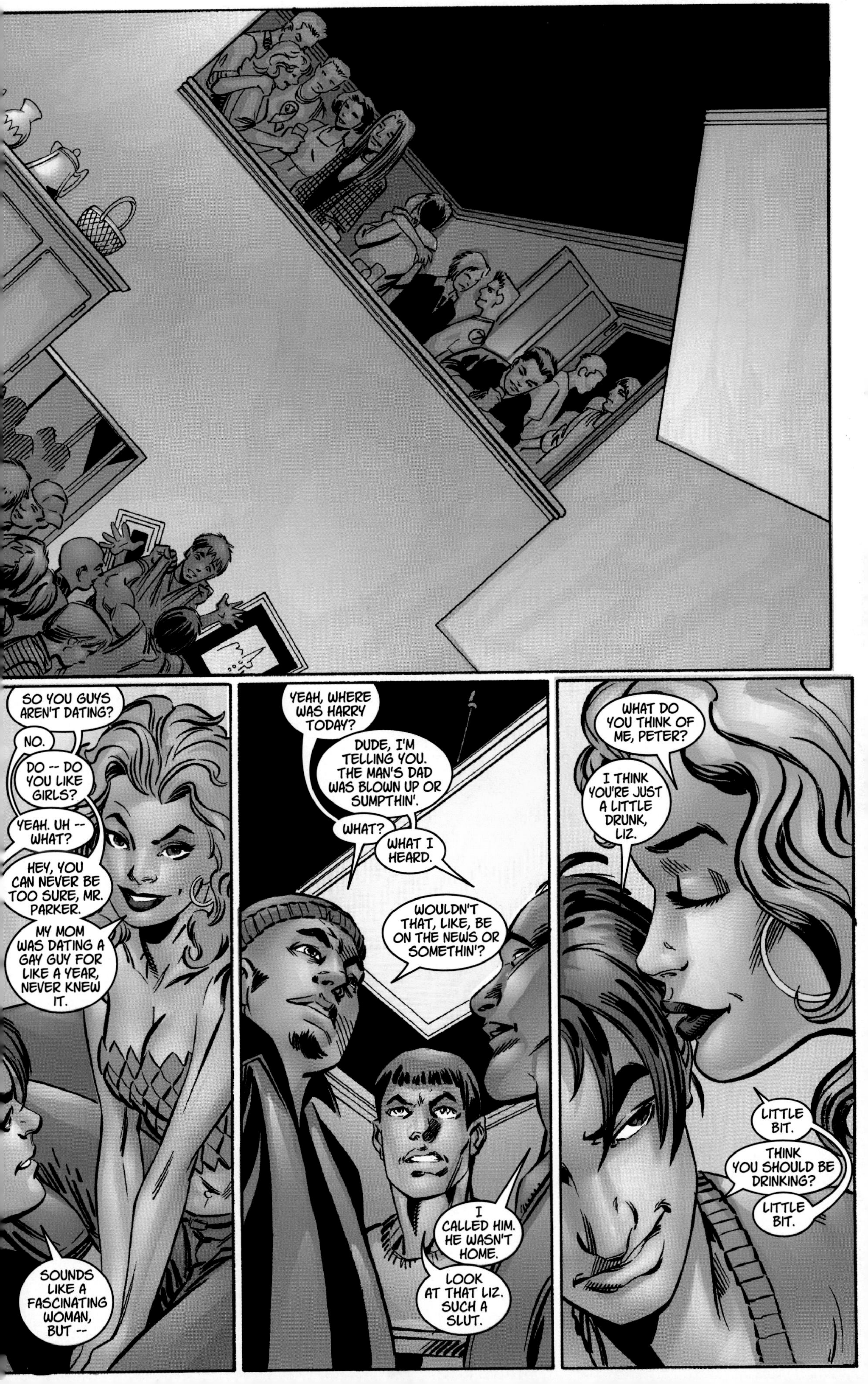
SO YOU GUYS AREN'T DATING?
NO.
DO -- DO YOU LIKE GIRLS?
YEAH. UH -- WHAT?
HEY, YOU CAN NEVER BE TOO SURE, MR. PARKER.
MY MOM WAS DATING A GAY GUY FOR LIKE A YEAR, NEVER KNEW IT.
SOUNDS LIKE A FASCINATING WOMAN, BUT --
YEAH, WHERE WAS HARRY TODAY?
DUDE, I'M TELLING YOU. THE MAN'S DAD WAS BLOWN UP OR SUMPTHIN'.
WHAT?
WHAT I HEARD.
WOULDN'T THAT, LIKE, BE ON THE NEWS OR SOMETHIN'?
I CALLED HIM. HE WASN'T HOME.
LOOK AT THAT LIZ. SUCH A SLUT.
WHAT DO YOU THINK OF ME, PETER?
I THINK YOU'RE JUST A LITTLE DRUNK, LIZ.
LITTLE BIT.
THINK YOU SHOULD BE DRINKING?
LITTLE BIT.

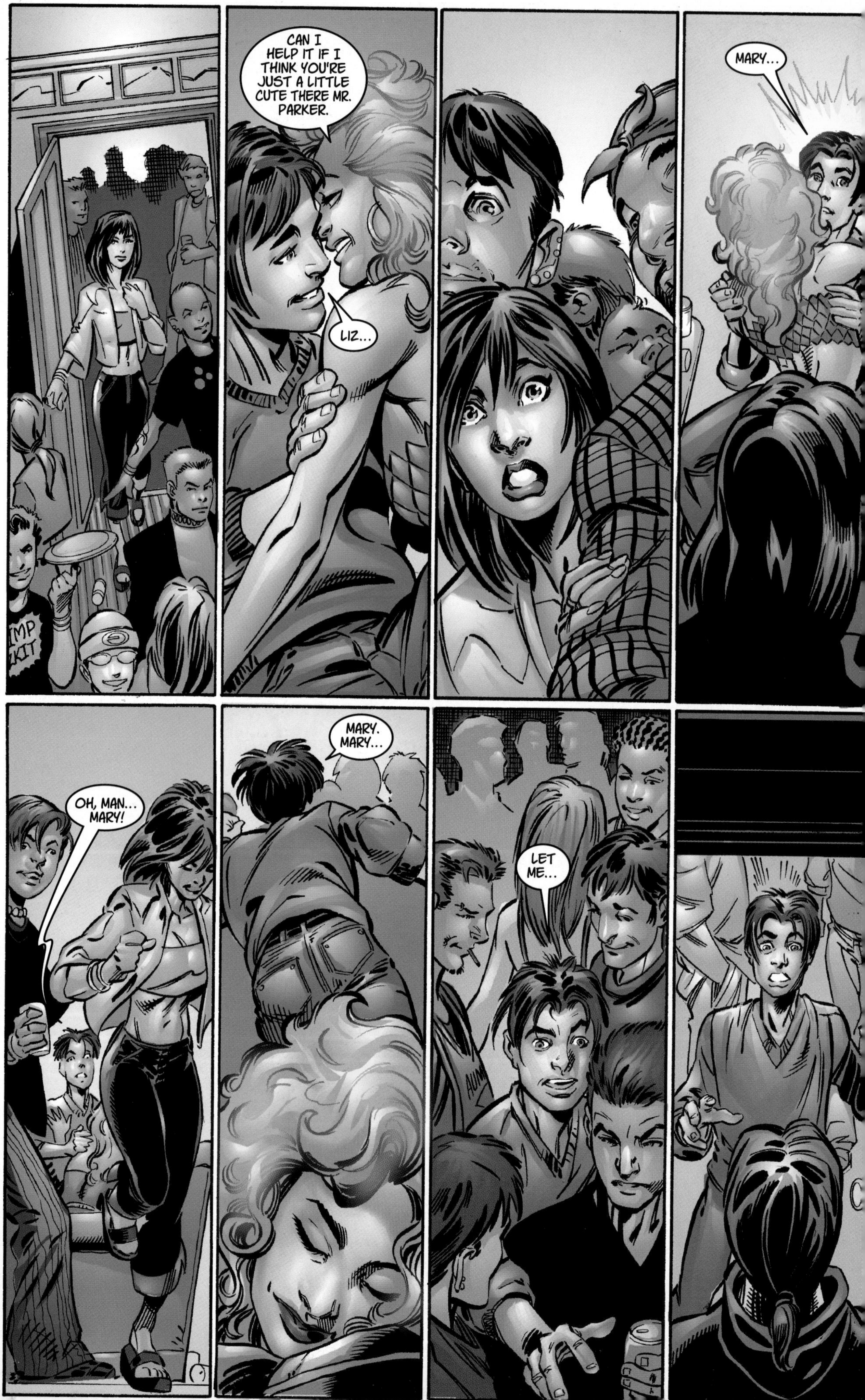
CAN I HELP IT IF I THINK YOU'RE JUST A LITTLE CUTE THERE MR. PARKER.
LIZ...
MARY...
OH, MAN... MARY!
MARY. MARY...
LET ME...

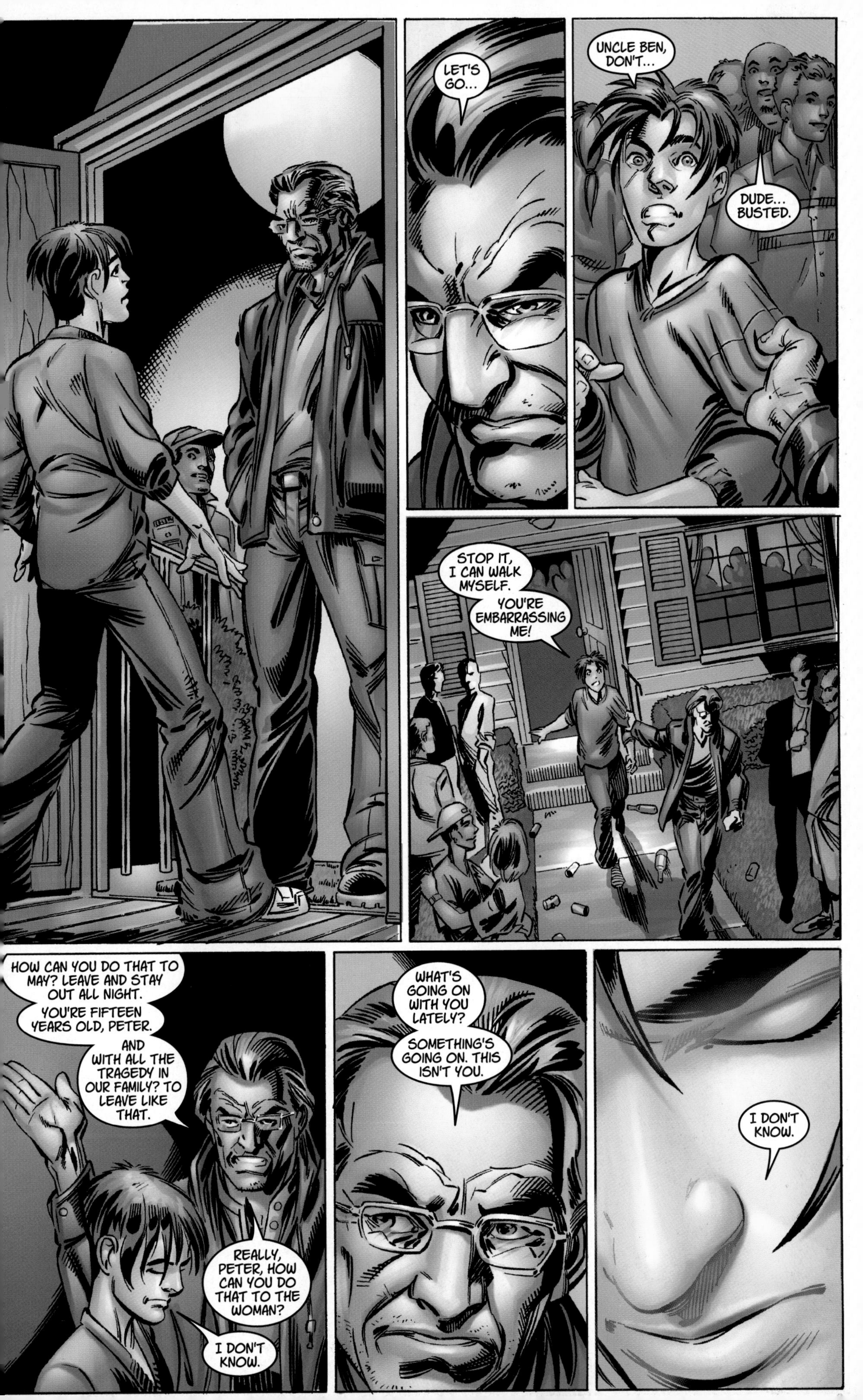
LET'S GO...
UNCLE BEN, DON'T...
DUDE... BUSTED.
STOP IT, I CAN WALK MYSELF.
YOU'RE EMBARRASSING ME!
HOW CAN YOU DO THAT TO MAY? LEAVE AND STAY OUT ALL NIGHT.
YOU'RE FIFTEEN YEARS OLD, PETER.
AND WITH ALL THE TRAGEDY IN OUR FAMILY? TO LEAVE LIKE THAT.
REALLY, PETER, HOW CAN YOU DO THAT TO THE WOMAN?
I DON'T KNOW.
WHAT'S GOING ON WITH YOU LATELY?
SOMETHING'S GOING ON. THIS ISN'T YOU.
I DON'T KNOW.

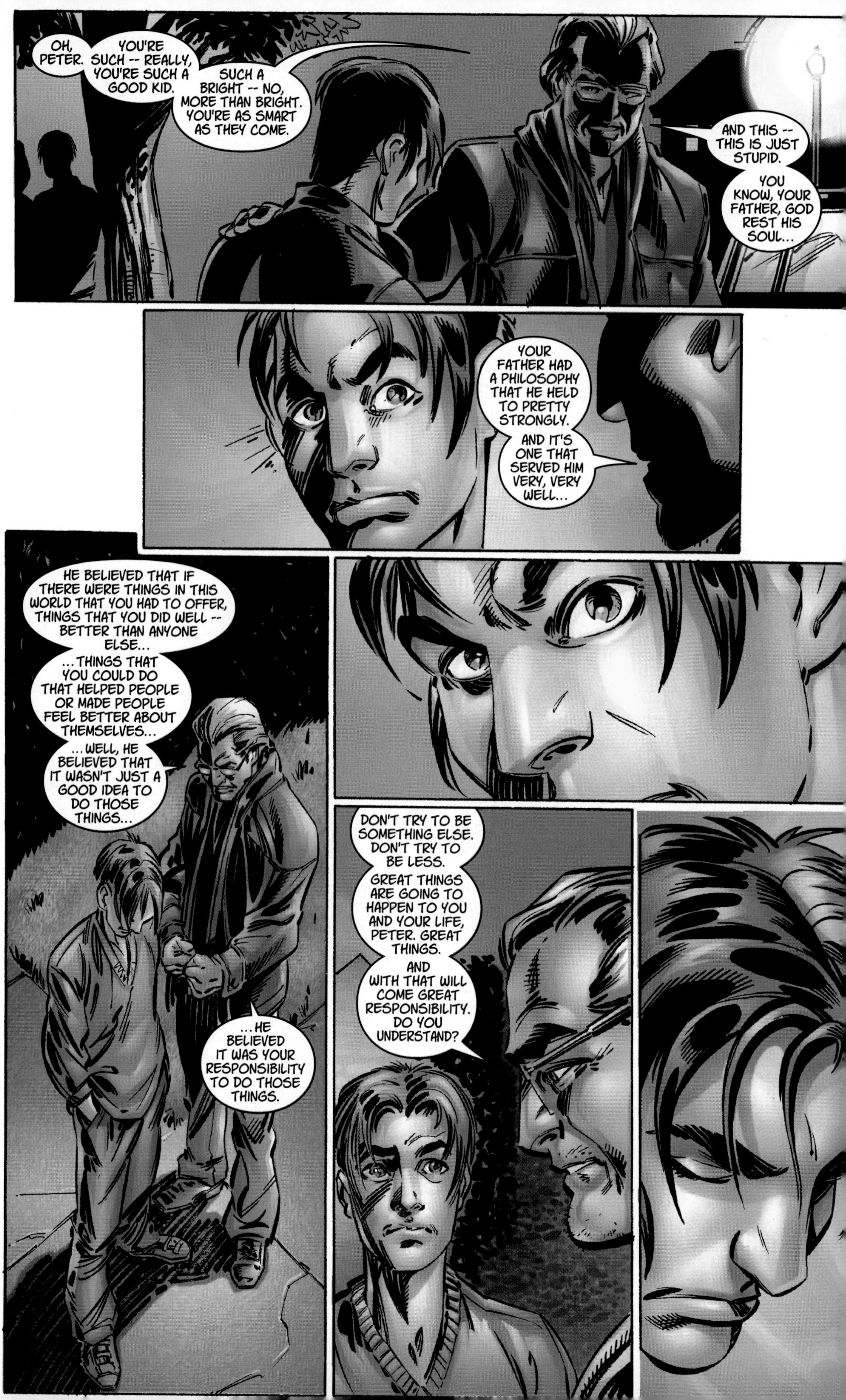

OH, PETER.
YOU'RE SUCH -- REALLY, YOU'RE SUCH A GOOD KID.
SUCH A BRIGHT -- NO, MORE THAN BRIGHT. YOU'RE AS SMART AS THEY COME.
AND THIS -- THIS IS JUST STUPID.
YOU KNOW, YOUR FATHER, GOD REST HIS SOUL...
YOUR FATHER HAD A PHILOSOPHY THAT HE HELD TO PRETTY STRONGLY.
AND IT'S ONE THAT SERVED HIM VERY, VERY WELL...
HE BELIEVED THAT IF THERE WERE THINGS IN THIS WORLD THAT YOU HAD TO OFFER, THINGS THAT YOU DID WELL -- BETTER THAN ANYONE ELSE...
...THINGS THAT YOU COULD DO THAT HELPED PEOPLE OR MADE PEOPLE FEEL BETTER ABOUT THEMSELVES...
...WELL, HE BELIEVED THAT IT WASN'T JUST A GOOD IDEA TO DO THOSE THINGS...
...HE BELIEVED IT WAS YOUR RESPONSIBILITY TO DO THOSE THINGS.
DON'T TRY TO BE SOMETHING ELSE. DON'T TRY TO BE LESS.
GREAT THINGS ARE GOING TO HAPPEN TO YOU AND YOUR LIFE, PETER. GREAT THINGS.
AND WITH THAT WILL COME GREAT RESPONSIBILITY. DO YOU UNDERSTAND?

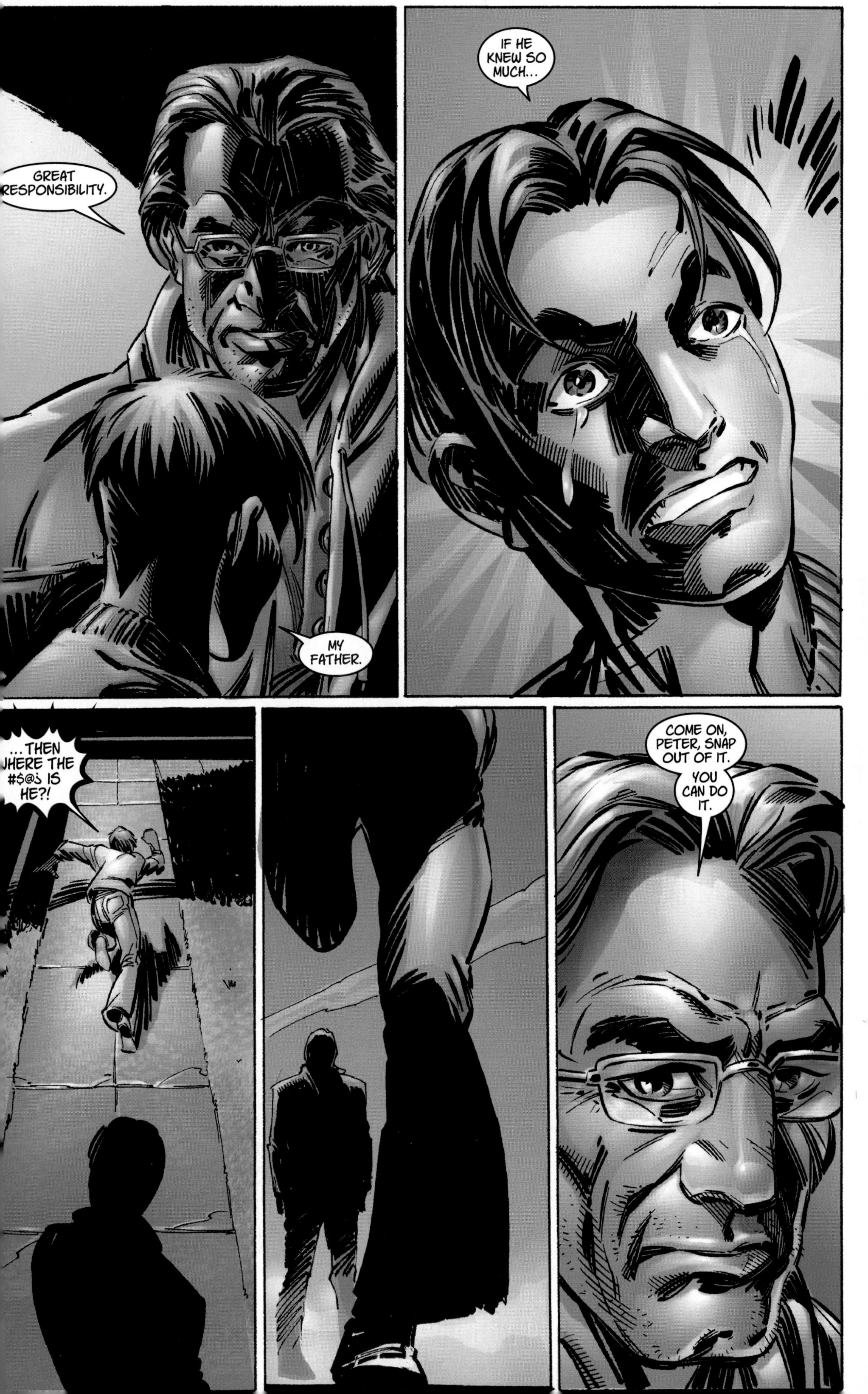
GREAT RESPONSIBILITY.
MY FATHER.
IF HE KNEW SO MUCH...
...THEN WHERE THE #$@¿ IS HE?!
COME ON, PETER, SNAP OUT OF IT.
YOU CAN DO IT.

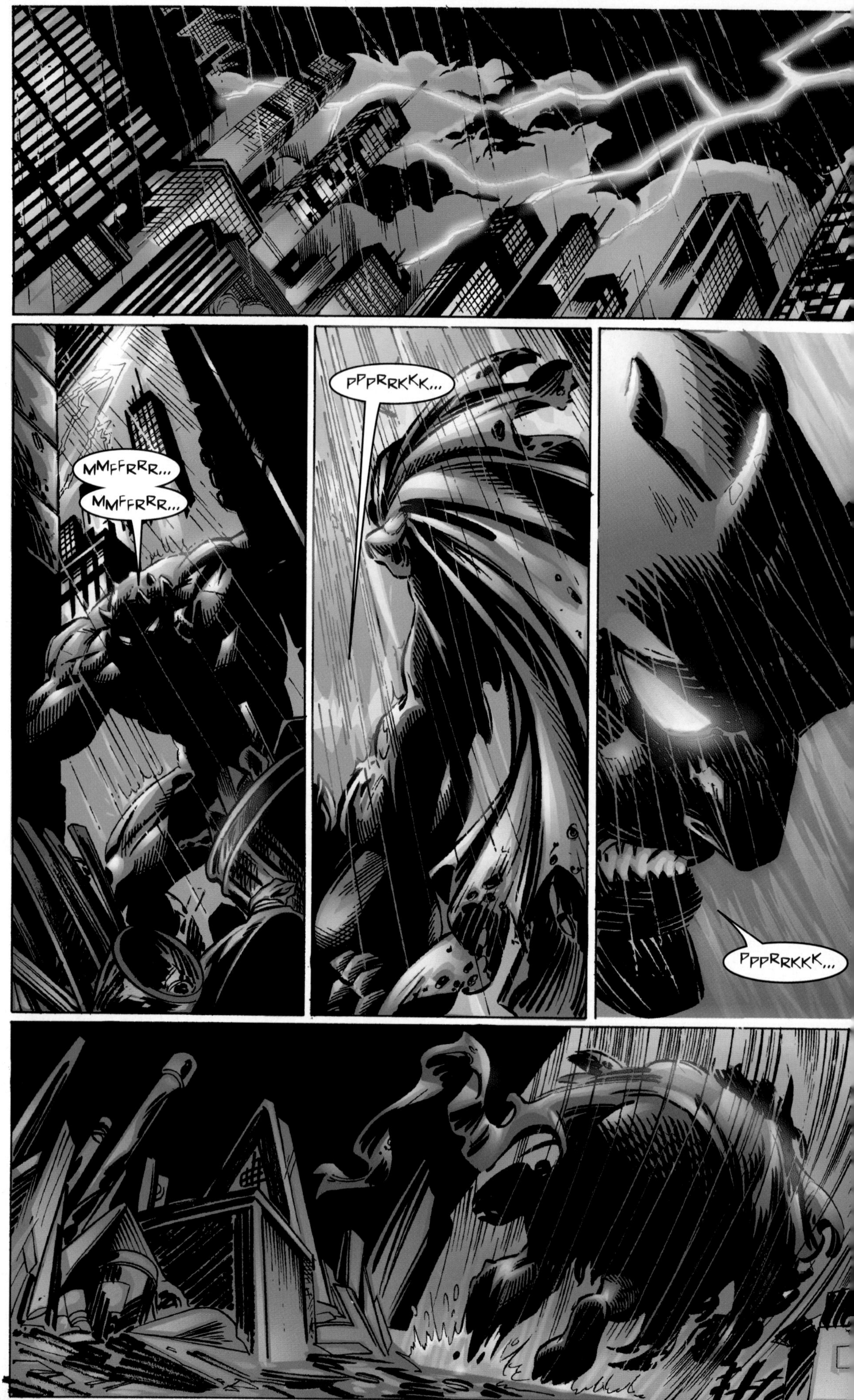
MMFFRRR...
MMFFRRR...
PPPRRKKK...
PPPRRKKK...

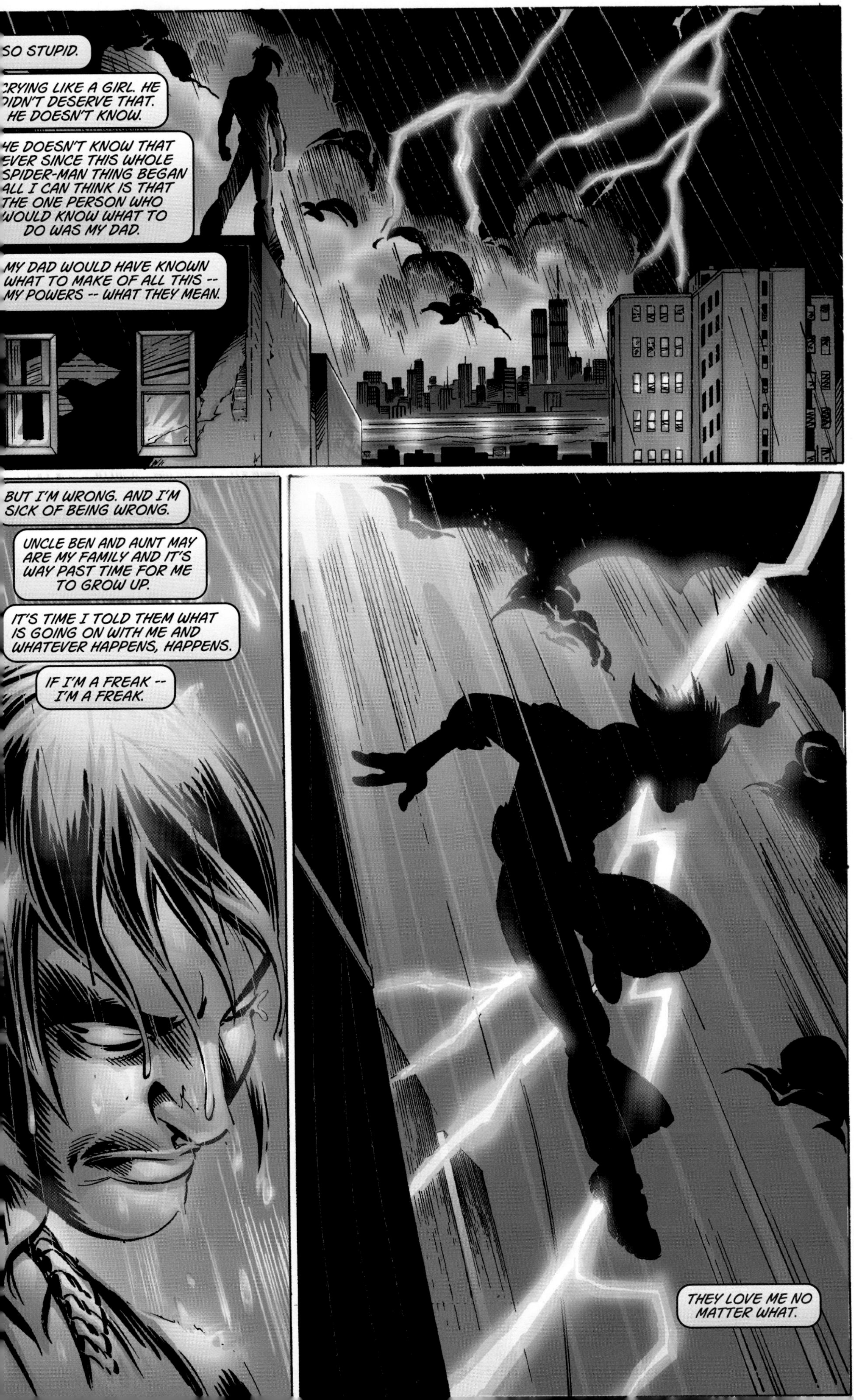
SO STUPID.
CRYING LIKE A GIRL. HE DIDN'T DESERVE THAT. HE DOESN'T KNOW.
HE DOESN'T KNOW THAT EVER SINCE THIS WHOLE SPIDER-MAN THING BEGAN ALL I CAN THINK IS THAT THE ONE PERSON WHO WOULD KNOW WHAT TO DO WAS MY DAD.
MY DAD WOULD HAVE KNOWN WHAT TO MAKE OF ALL THIS -- MY POWERS -- WHAT THEY MEAN.
BUT I'M WRONG. AND I'M SICK OF BEING WRONG.
UNCLE BEN AND AUNT MAY ARE MY FAMILY AND IT'S WAY PAST TIME FOR ME TO GROW UP.
IT'S TIME I TOLD THEM WHAT IS GOING ON WITH ME AND WHATEVER HAPPENS, HAPPENS.
IF I'M A FREAK -- I'M A FREAK.
THEY LOVE ME NO MATTER WHAT.

OH, NO...

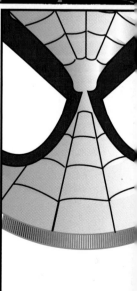

ULTIM

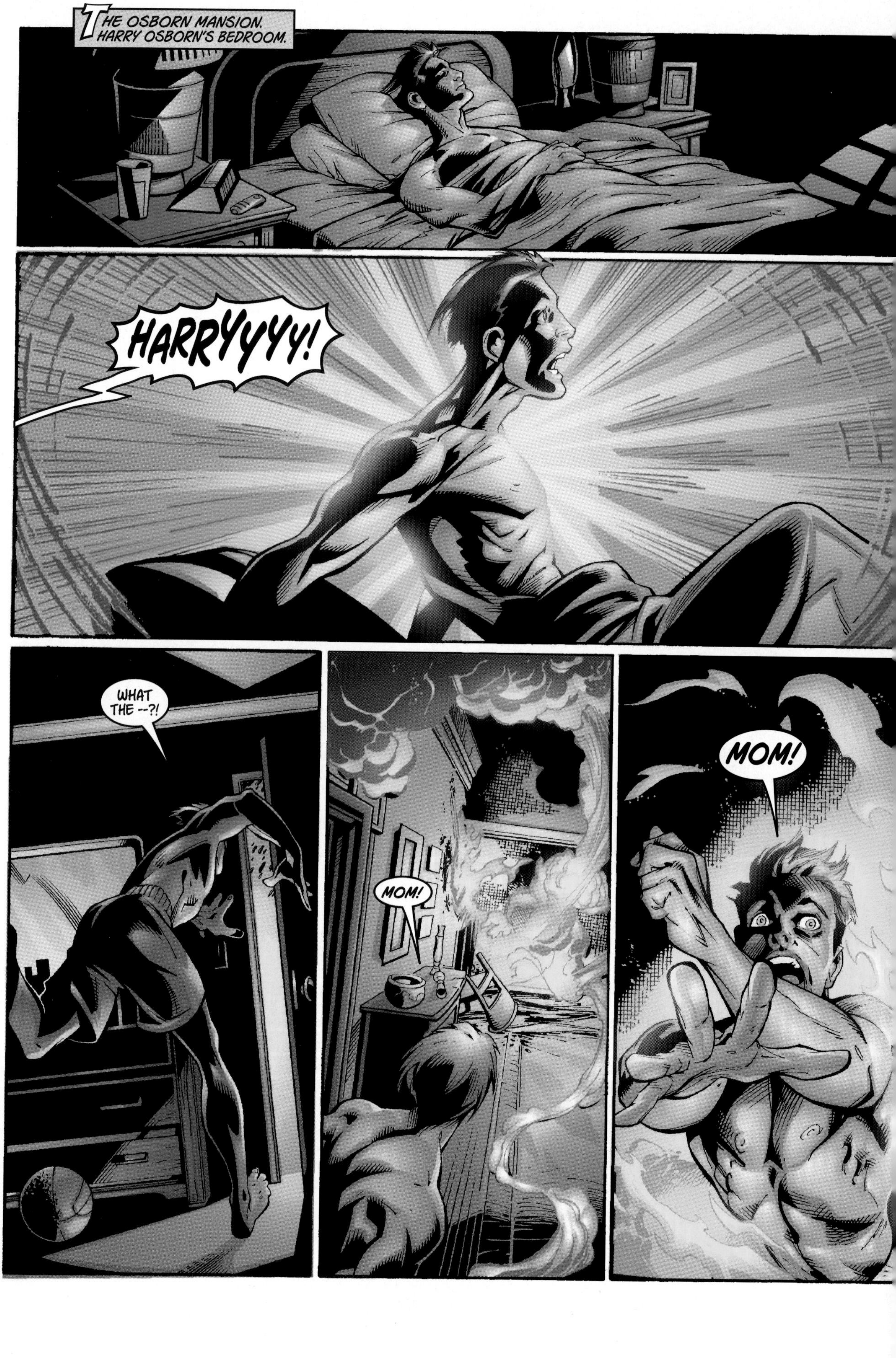
THE OSBORN MANSION.
HARRY OSBORN'S BEDROOM.
HARRYYYY!
WHAT THE --?!
MOM!
MOM!

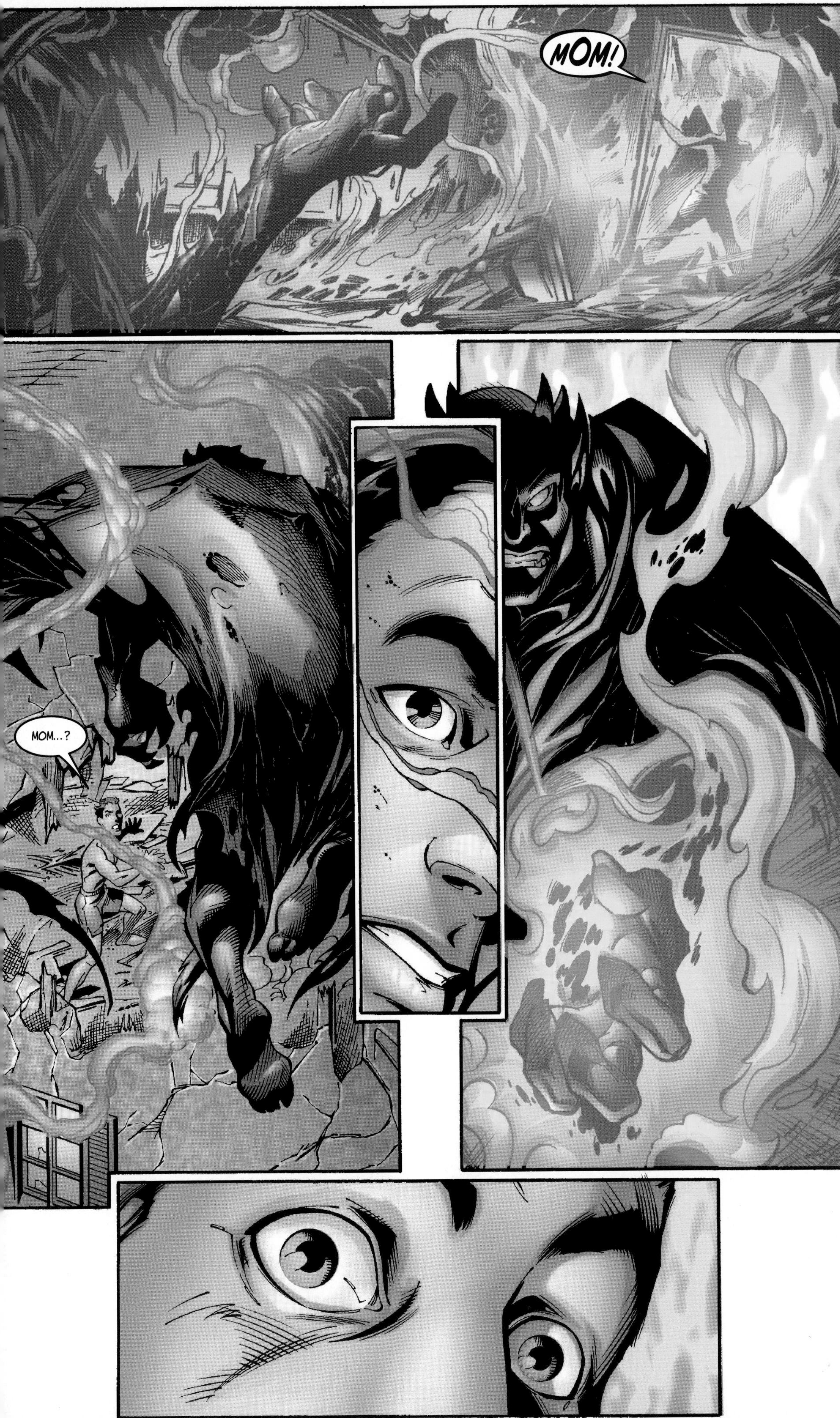
MOM!
MOM...?

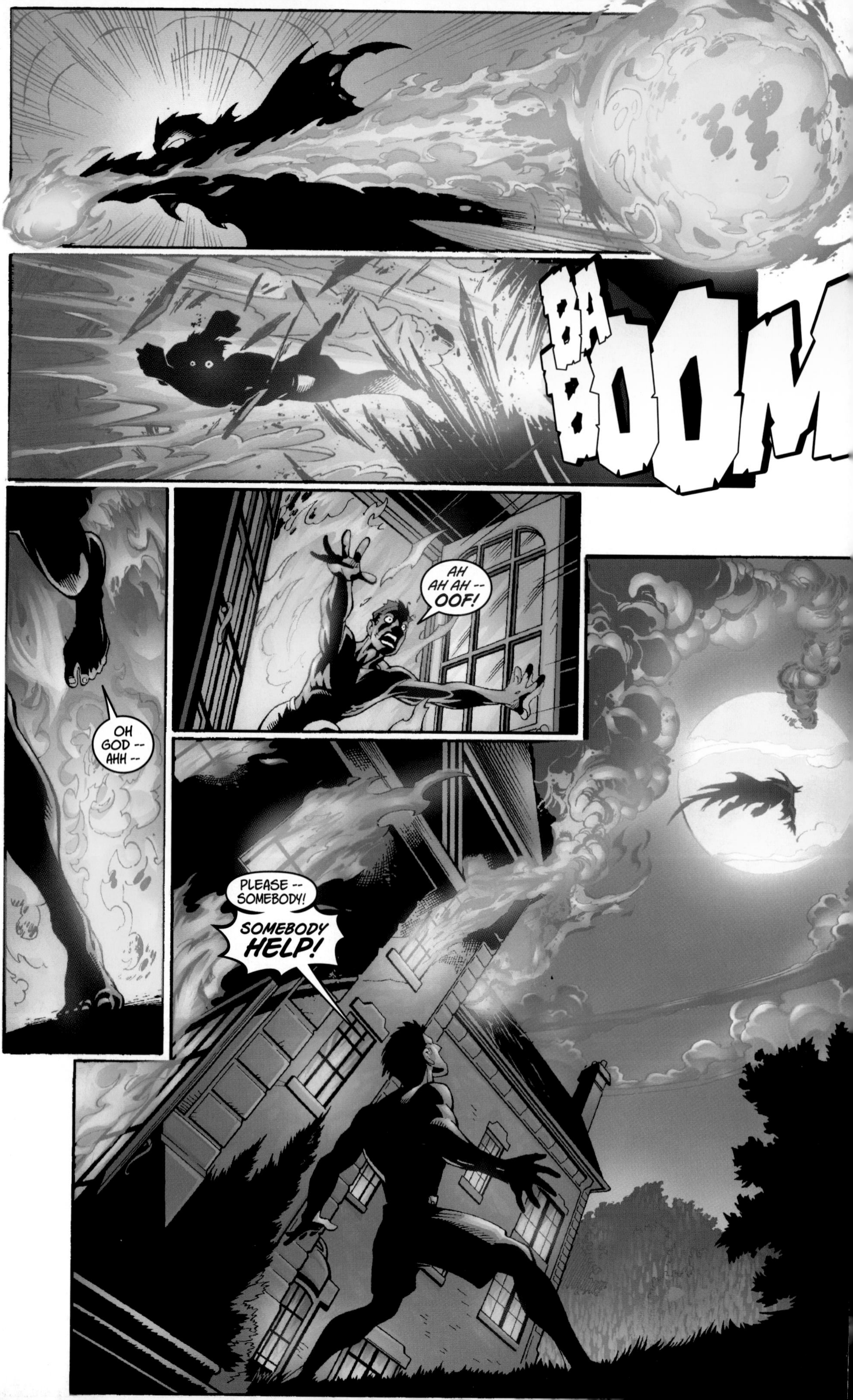
BA
BOOM
AH
AH AH --
OOF!
OH
GOD --
AHH --
PLEASE --
SOMEBODY!
SOMEBODY
HELP!

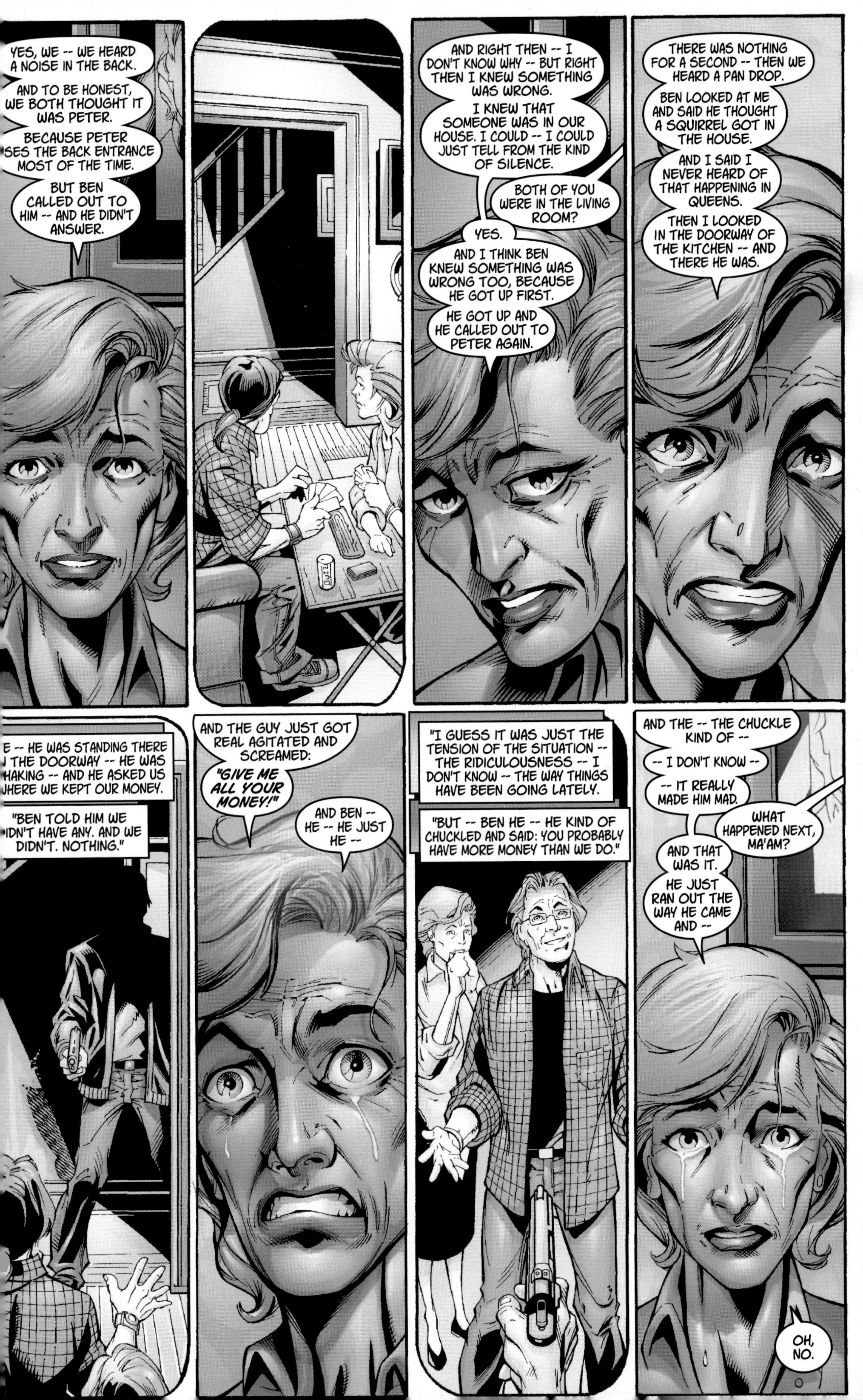
YES, WE -- WE HEARD A NOISE IN THE BACK.
AND TO BE HONEST, WE BOTH THOUGHT IT WAS PETER.
BECAUSE PETER USES THE BACK ENTRANCE MOST OF THE TIME.
BUT BEN CALLED OUT TO HIM -- AND HE DIDN'T ANSWER.
BUZZ
AND RIGHT THEN -- I DON'T KNOW WHY -- BUT RIGHT THEN I KNEW SOMETHING WAS WRONG.
I KNEW THAT SOMEONE WAS IN OUR HOUSE. I COULD -- I COULD JUST TELL FROM THE KIND OF SILENCE.
BOTH OF YOU WERE IN THE LIVING ROOM?
YES.
AND I THINK BEN KNEW SOMETHING WAS WRONG TOO, BECAUSE HE GOT UP FIRST.
HE GOT UP AND HE CALLED OUT TO PETER AGAIN.
THERE WAS NOTHING FOR A SECOND -- THEN WE HEARD A PAN DROP.
BEN LOOKED AT ME AND SAID HE THOUGHT A SQUIRREL GOT IN THE HOUSE.
AND I SAID I NEVER HEARD OF THAT HAPPENING IN QUEENS.
THEN I LOOKED IN THE DOORWAY OF THE KITCHEN -- AND THERE HE WAS.
E -- HE WAS STANDING THERE N THE DOORWAY -- HE WAS HAKING -- AND HE ASKED US WHERE WE KEPT OUR MONEY.
"BEN TOLD HIM WE IDN'T HAVE ANY. AND WE DIDN'T. NOTHING."
AND THE GUY JUST GOT REAL AGITATED AND SCREAMED:
"GIVE ME ALL YOUR MONEY!"
AND BEN -- HE -- HE JUST HE --
"I GUESS IT WAS JUST THE TENSION OF THE SITUATION -- THE RIDICULOUSNESS -- I DON'T KNOW -- THE WAY THINGS HAVE BEEN GOING LATELY.
"BUT -- BEN HE -- HE KIND OF CHUCKLED AND SAID: YOU PROBABLY HAVE MORE MONEY THAN WE DO."
AND THE -- THE CHUCKLE KIND OF --
-- I DON'T KNOW --
-- IT REALLY MADE HIM MAD.
WHAT HAPPENED NEXT, MA'AM?
AND THAT WAS IT.
HE JUST RAN OUT THE WAY HE CAME AND --
OH, NO.

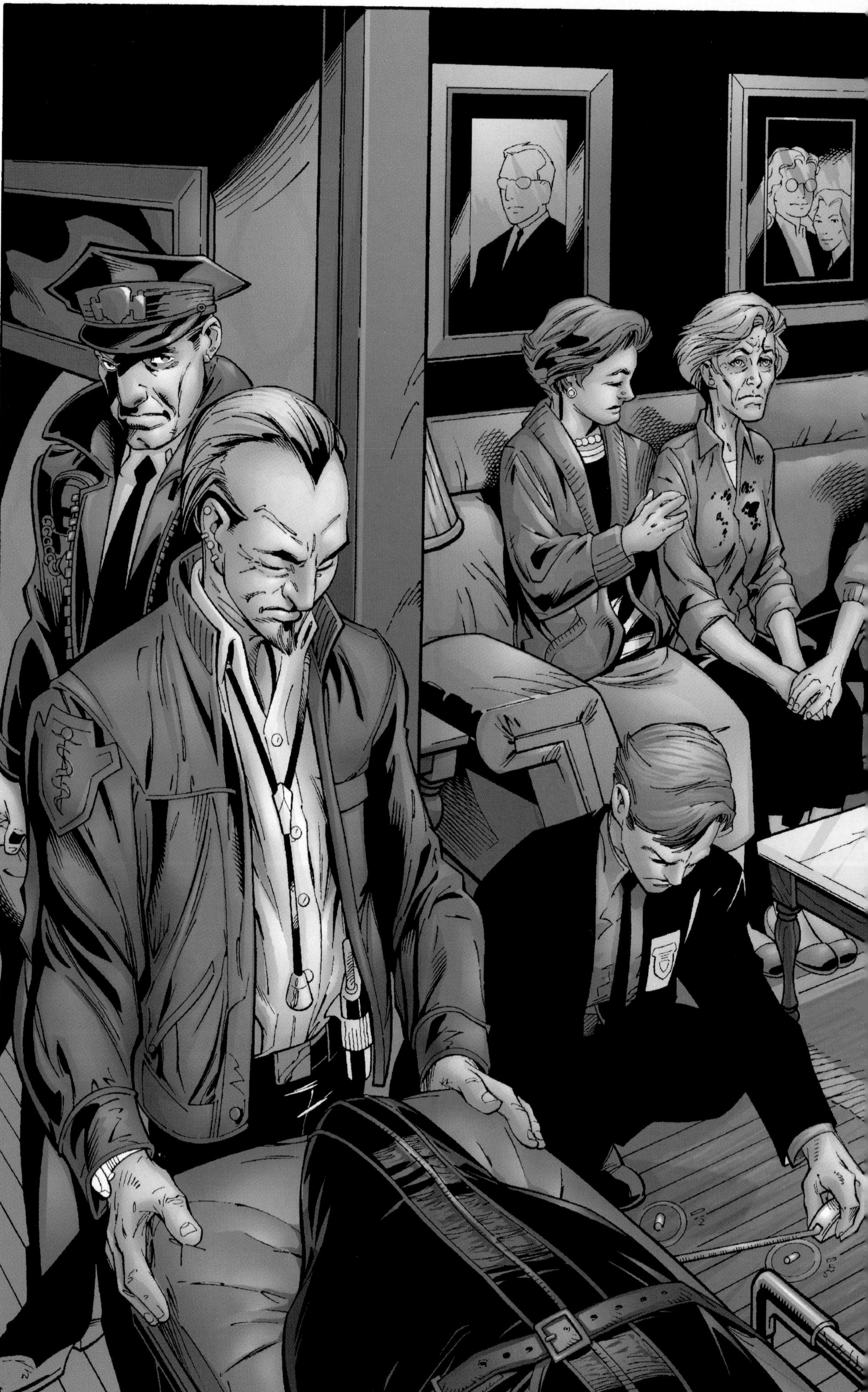

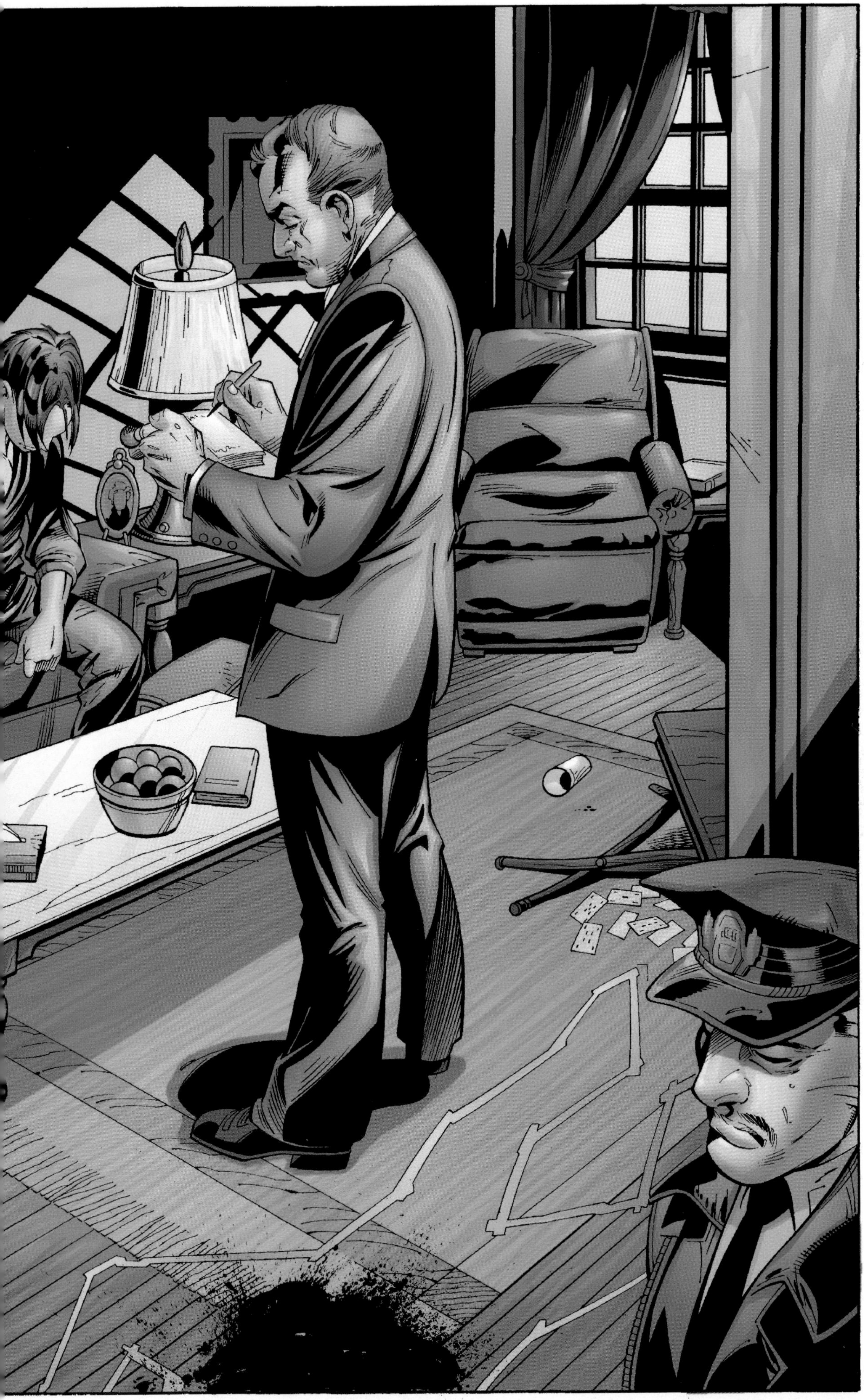

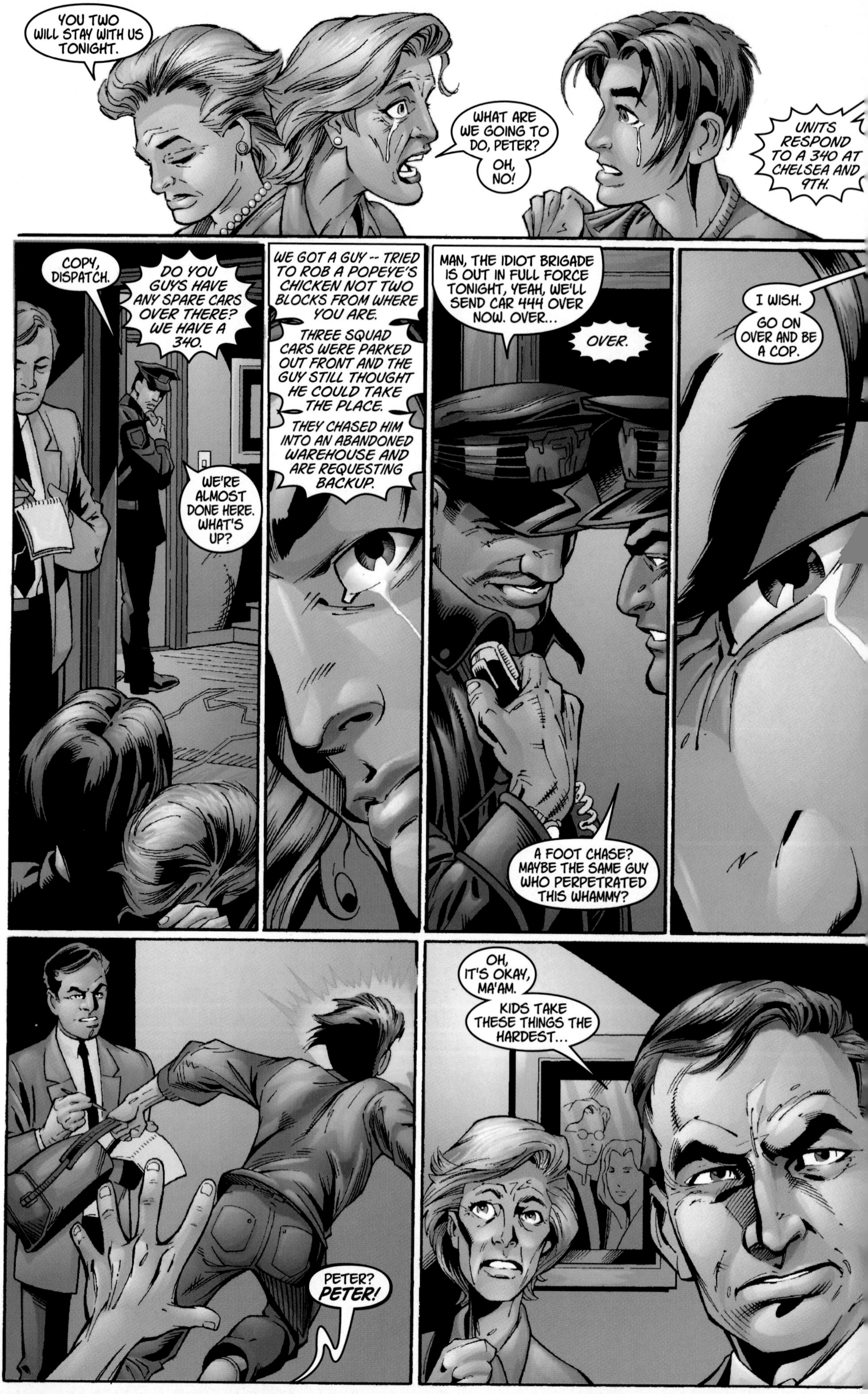
YOU TWO WILL STAY WITH US TONIGHT.
WHAT ARE WE GOING TO DO, PETER?
OH, NO!
UNITS RESPOND TO A 340 AT CHELSEA AND 9TH.
COPY, DISPATCH.
DO YOU GUYS HAVE ANY SPARE CARS OVER THERE? WE HAVE A 340.
WE'RE ALMOST DONE HERE. WHAT'S UP?
WE GOT A GUY -- TRIED TO ROB A POPEYE'S CHICKEN NOT TWO BLOCKS FROM WHERE YOU ARE.
THREE SQUAD CARS WERE PARKED OUT FRONT AND THE GUY STILL THOUGHT HE COULD TAKE THE PLACE.
THEY CHASED HIM INTO AN ABANDONED WAREHOUSE AND ARE REQUESTING BACKUP.
MAN, THE IDIOT BRIGADE IS OUT IN FULL FORCE TONIGHT, YEAH, WE'LL SEND CAR 444 OVER NOW. OVER...
OVER.
A FOOT CHASE? MAYBE THE SAME GUY WHO PERPETRATED THIS WHAMMY?
I WISH.
GO ON OVER AND BE A COP.
PETER? PETER!
OH, IT'S OKAY, MA'AM.
KIDS TAKE THESE THINGS THE HARDEST...

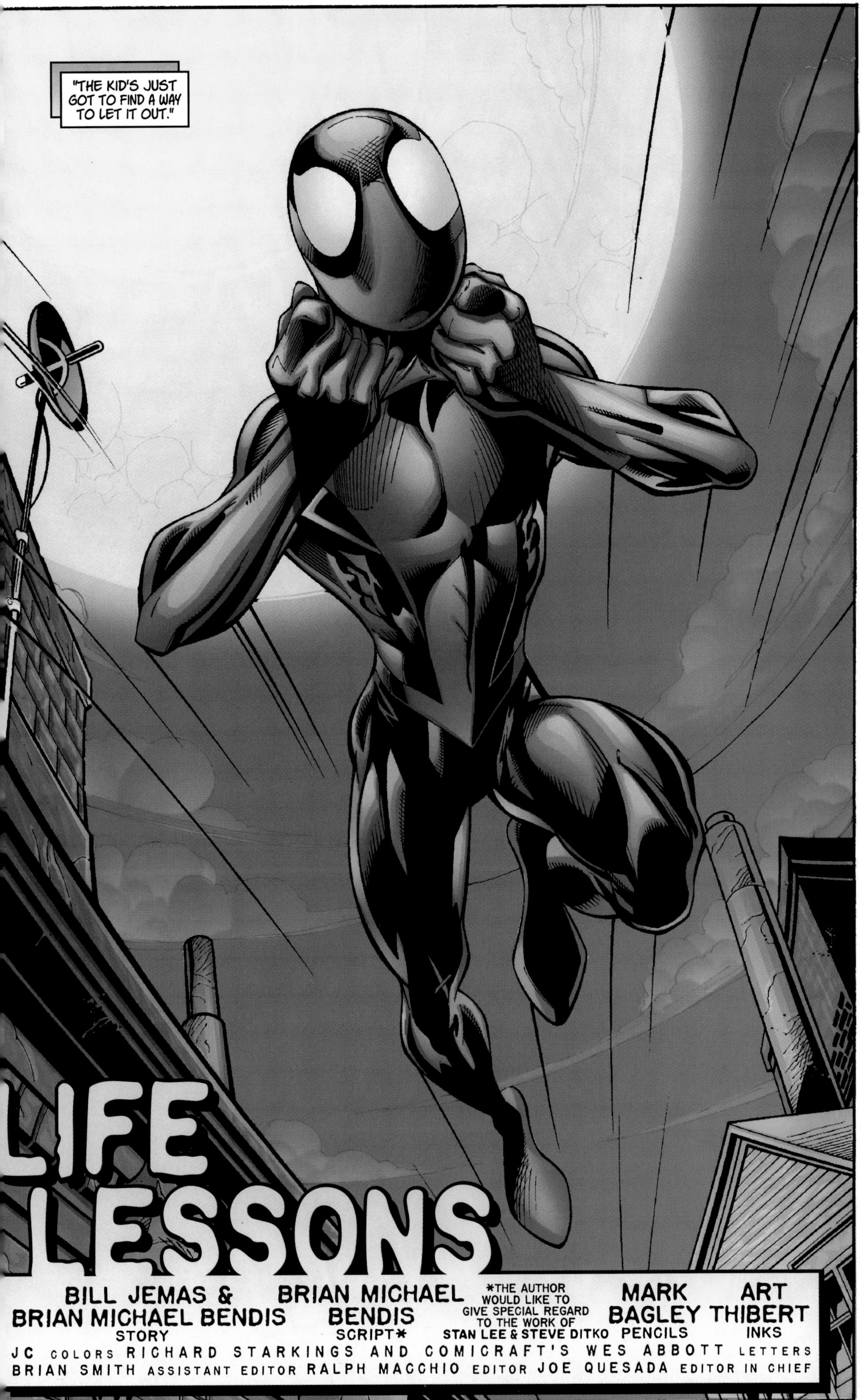
"THE KID'S JUST GOT TO FIND A WAY TO LET IT OUT."
LIFE LESSONS
BILL JEMAS & BRIAN MICHAEL BENDIS STORY
BRIAN MICHAEL BENDIS SCRIPT*
*THE AUTHOR WOULD LIKE TO GIVE SPECIAL REGARD TO THE WORK OF STAN LEE & STEVE DITKO
MARK BAGLEY PENCILS
ART THIBERT INKS
JC COLORS RICHARD STARKINGS AND COMICRAFT'S WES ABBOTT LETTERS
BRIAN SMITH ASSISTANT EDITOR RALPH MACCHIO EDITOR JOE QUESADA EDITOR IN CHIEF

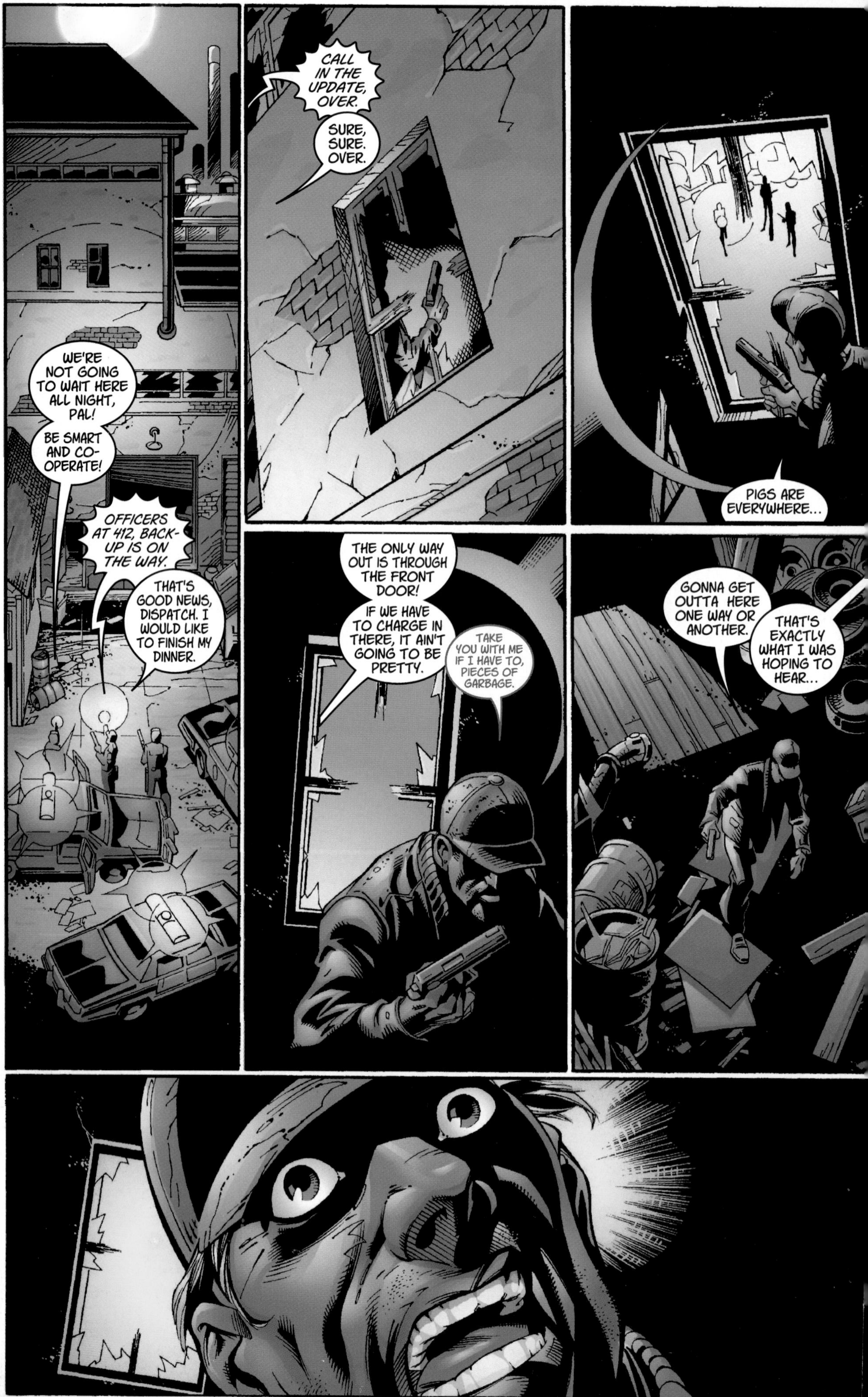

WE'RE NOT GOING TO WAIT HERE ALL NIGHT, PAL!
BE SMART AND CO-OPERATE!
OFFICERS AT 412, BACK-UP IS ON THE WAY.
THAT'S GOOD NEWS, DISPATCH. I WOULD LIKE TO FINISH MY DINNER.
CALL IN THE UPDATE, OVER.
SURE, SURE. OVER.
PIGS ARE EVERYWHERE...
THE ONLY WAY OUT IS THROUGH THE FRONT DOOR!
IF WE HAVE TO CHARGE IN THERE, IT AIN'T GOING TO BE PRETTY.
TAKE YOU WITH ME IF I HAVE TO, PIECES OF GARBAGE.
GONNA GET OUTTA HERE ONE WAY OR ANOTHER.
THAT'S EXACTLY WHAT I WAS HOPING TO HEAR...

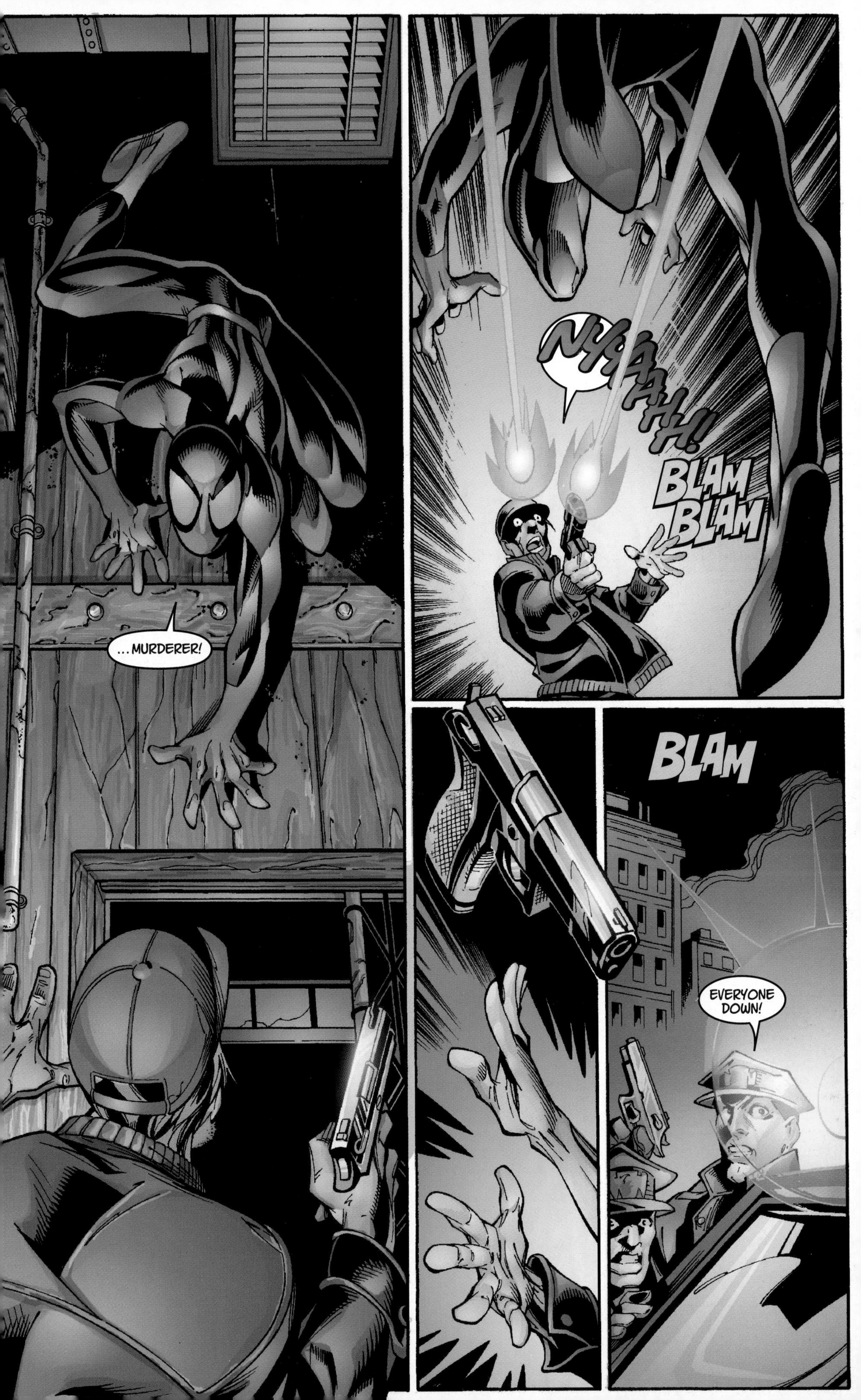
...MURDERER!
NYAAAHH!
BLAM
BLAM
BLAM
EVERYONE DOWN!

I-I MUST BE SEEIN' THINGS. I --

MUST BE OUT OF MY --

THUMP

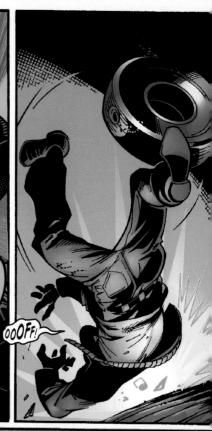

OOOFF!

MAYBE HE POPPED HIMSELF?

YOU WISH.

WHAT IS THIS? WH-WHAT'S GOIN' ON? I GOTTA -- I GOTTA HIDE --

I GOTTA --

MISTER, THERE IS NOWHERE ON EARTH YOU WILL BE ABLE TO HIDE FROM ME!

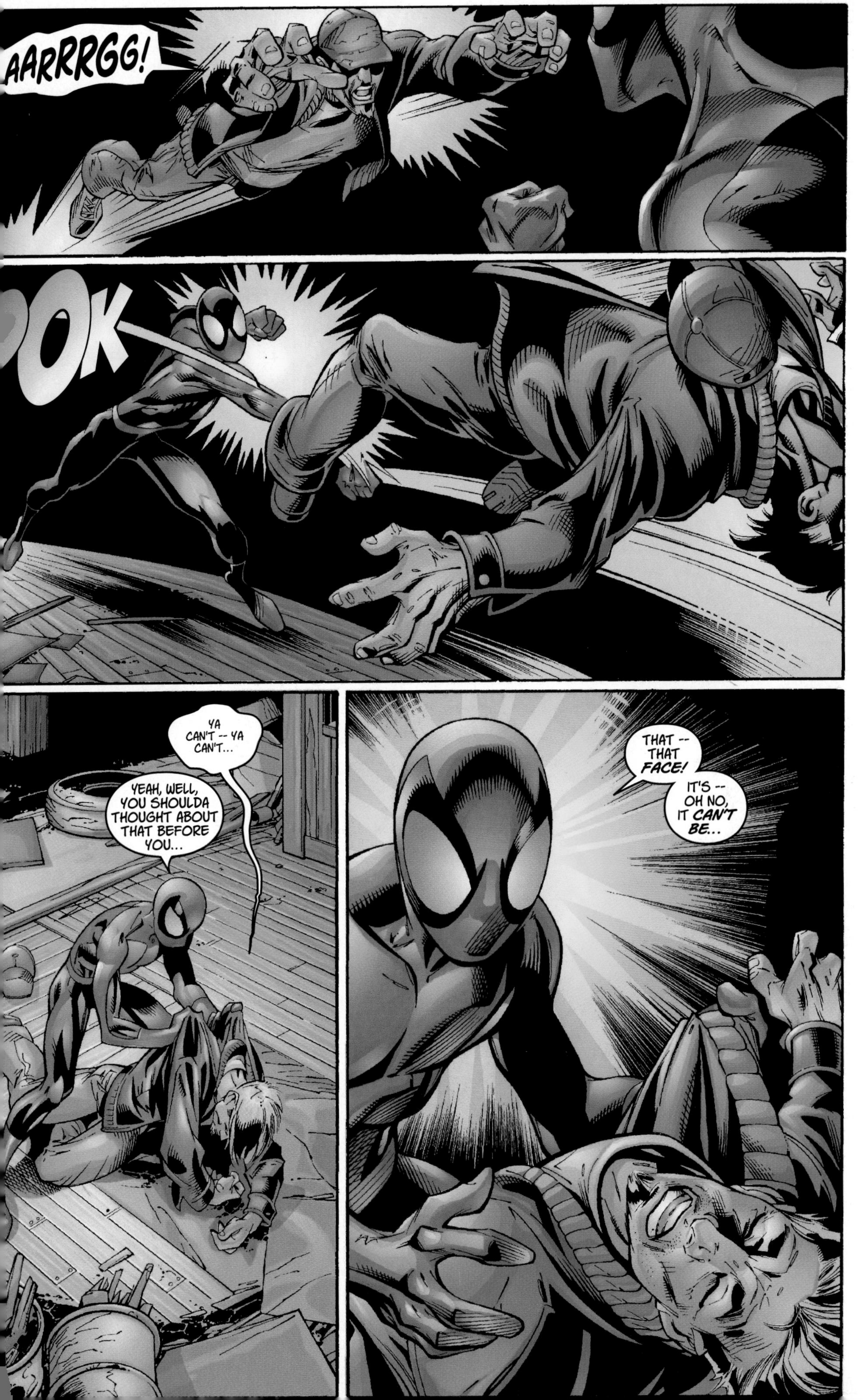
AARRRGG!
OOK
YA CAN'T -- YA CAN'T...
YEAH, WELL, YOU SHOULDA THOUGHT ABOUT THAT BEFORE YOU...
THAT -- THAT FACE!
IT'S -- OH NO, IT CAN'T BE...

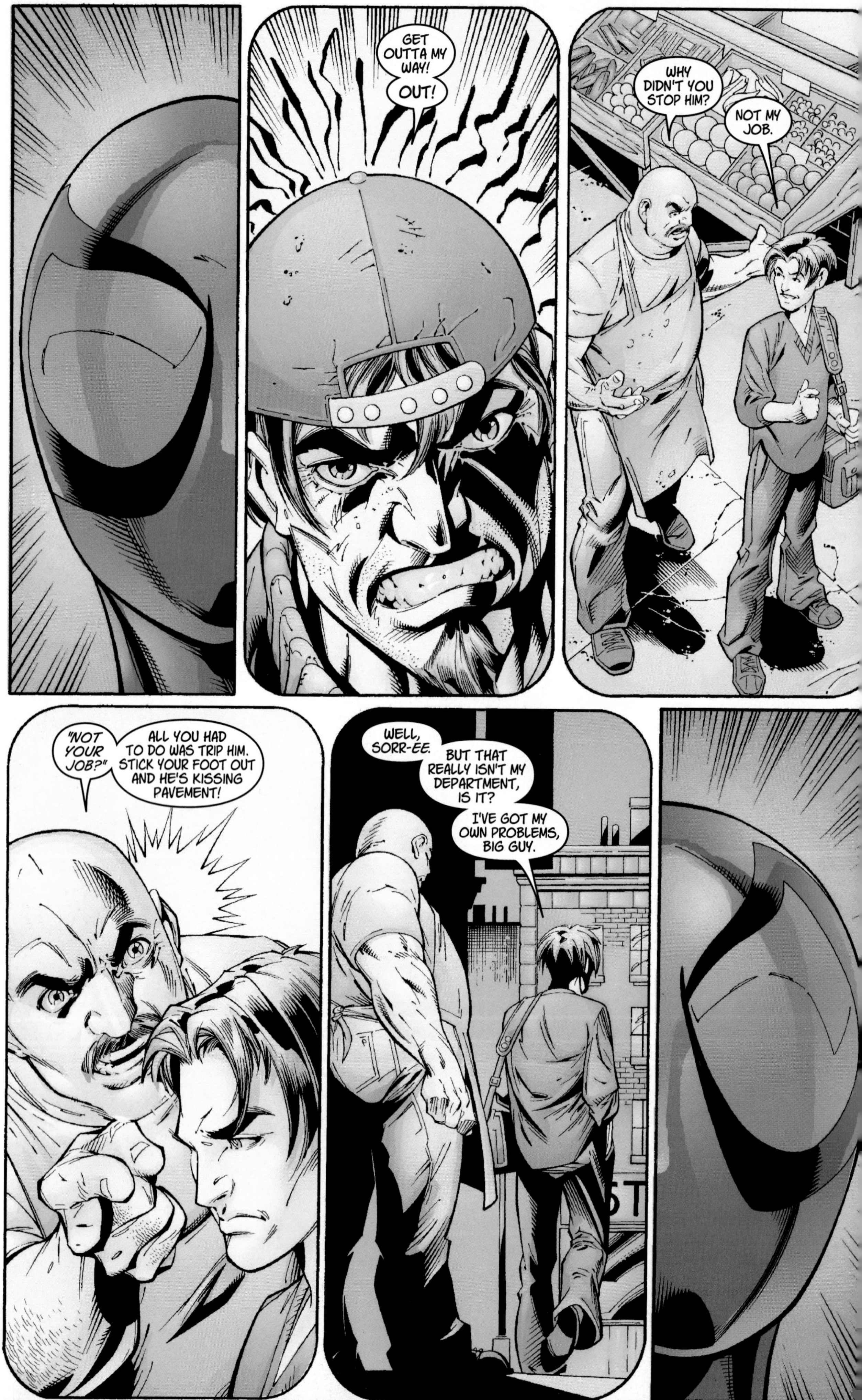
GET OUTTA MY WAY!
OUT!
WHY DIDN'T YOU STOP HIM?
NOT MY JOB.
"NOT YOUR JOB?"
ALL YOU HAD TO DO WAS TRIP HIM. STICK YOUR FOOT OUT AND HE'S KISSING PAVEMENT!
WELL, SORR-EE.
BUT THAT REALLY ISN'T MY DEPARTMENT, IS IT?
I'VE GOT MY OWN PROBLEMS, BIG GUY.

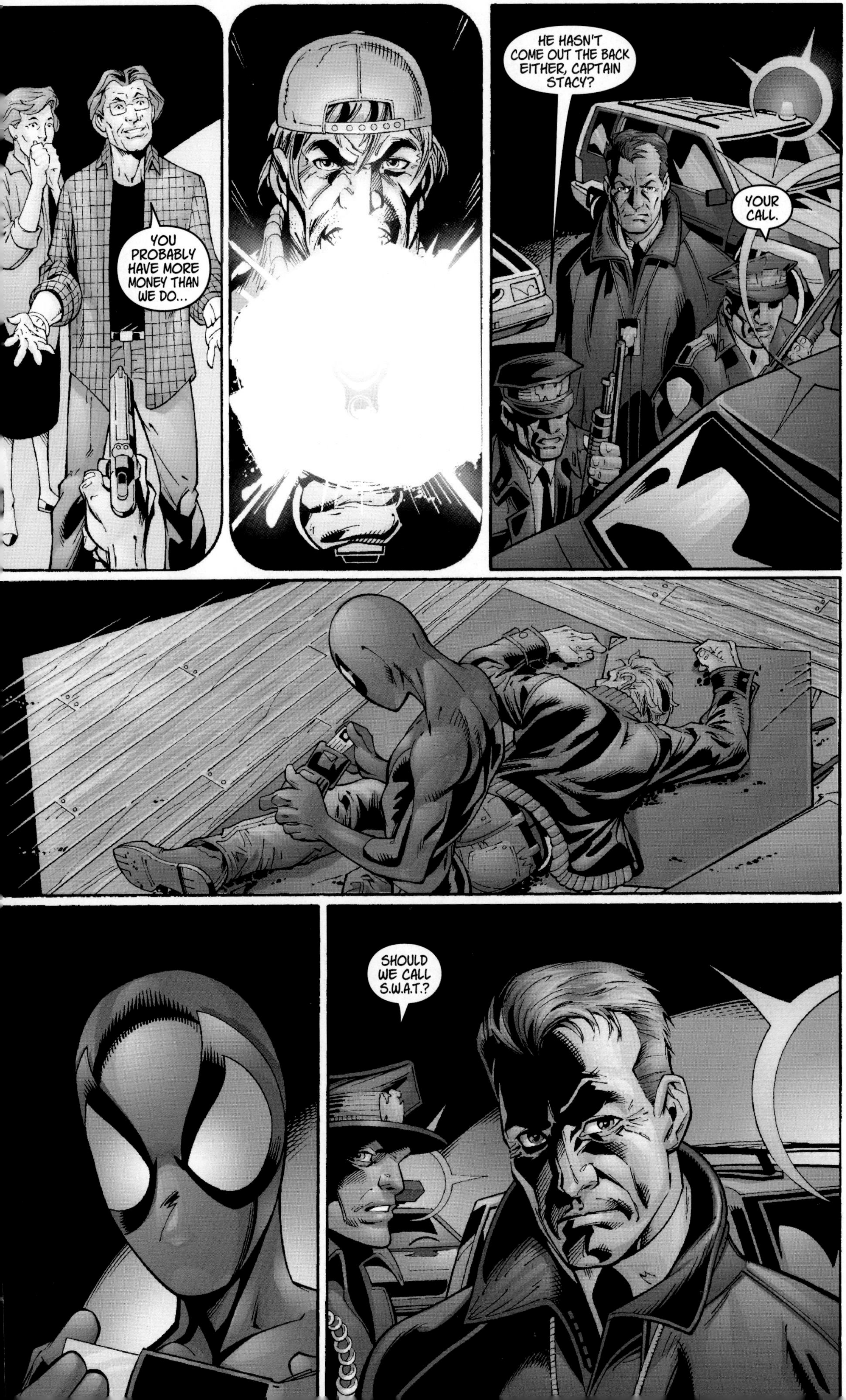
YOU PROBABLY HAVE MORE MONEY THAN WE DO...
HE HASN'T COME OUT THE BACK EITHER, CAPTAIN STACY?
YOUR CALL.
SHOULD WE CALL S.W.A.T.?

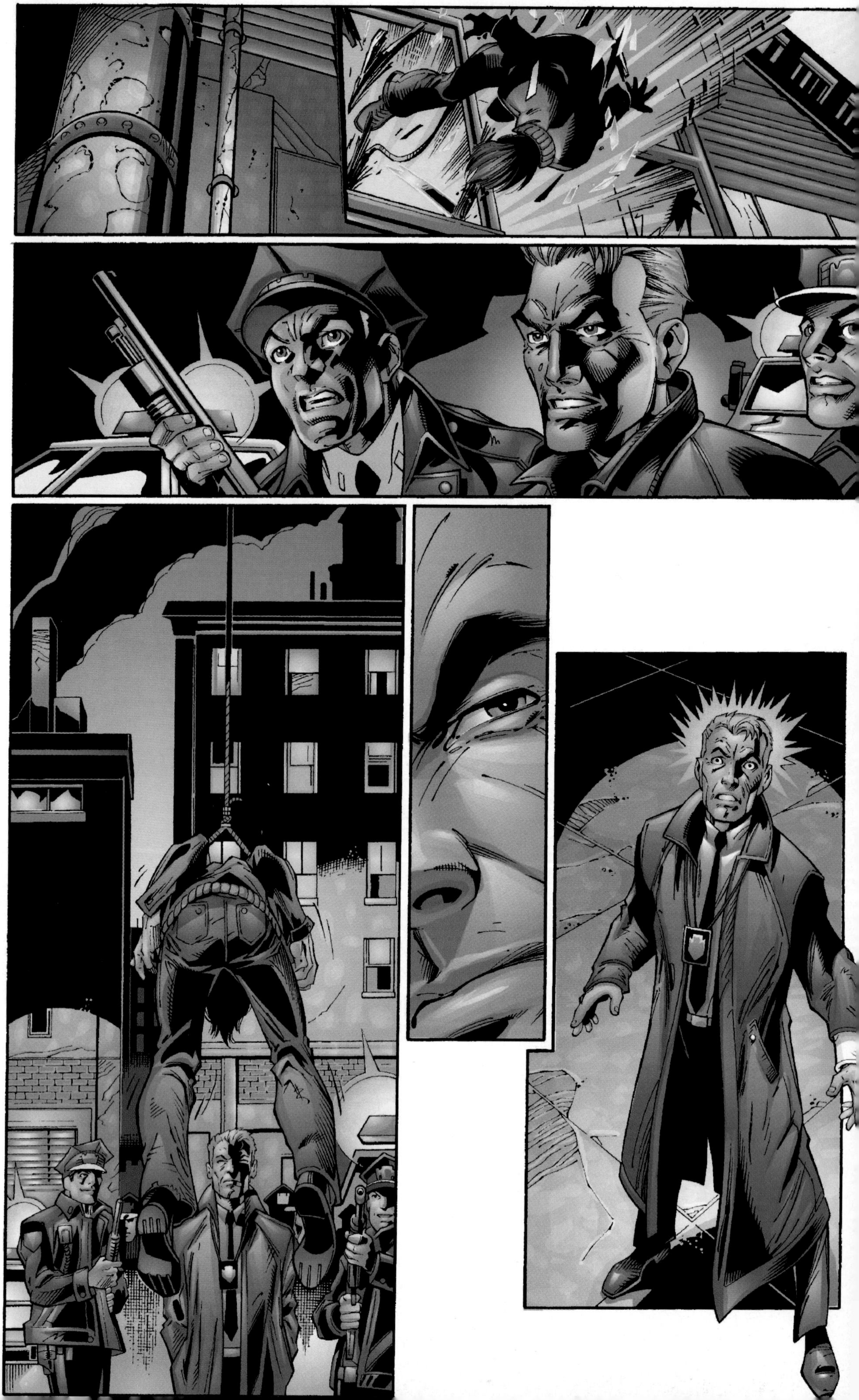

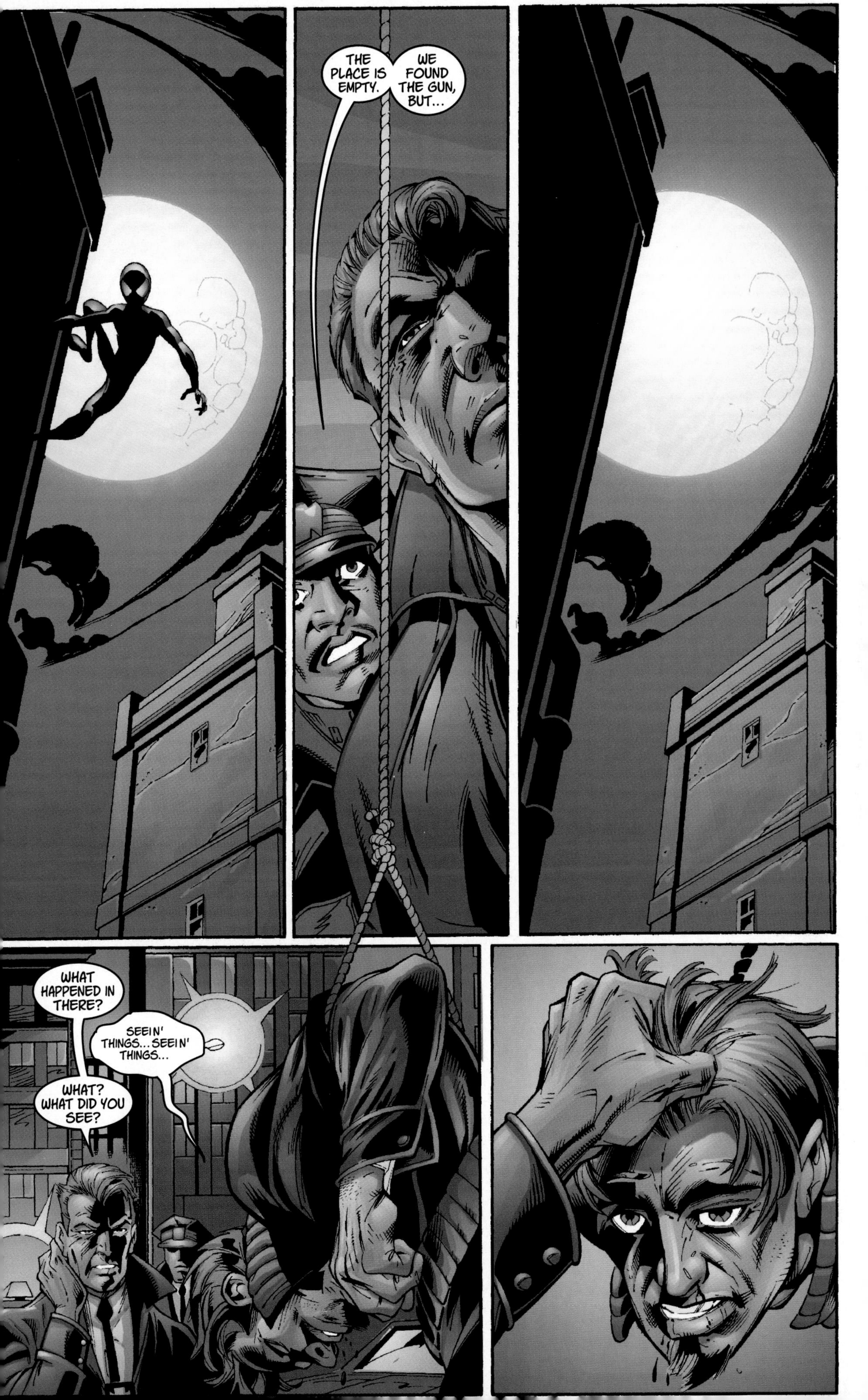
THE PLACE IS EMPTY.
WE FOUND THE GUN, BUT...
WHAT HAPPENED IN THERE?
SEEIN' THINGS... SEEIN' THINGS...
WHAT? WHAT DID YOU SEE?

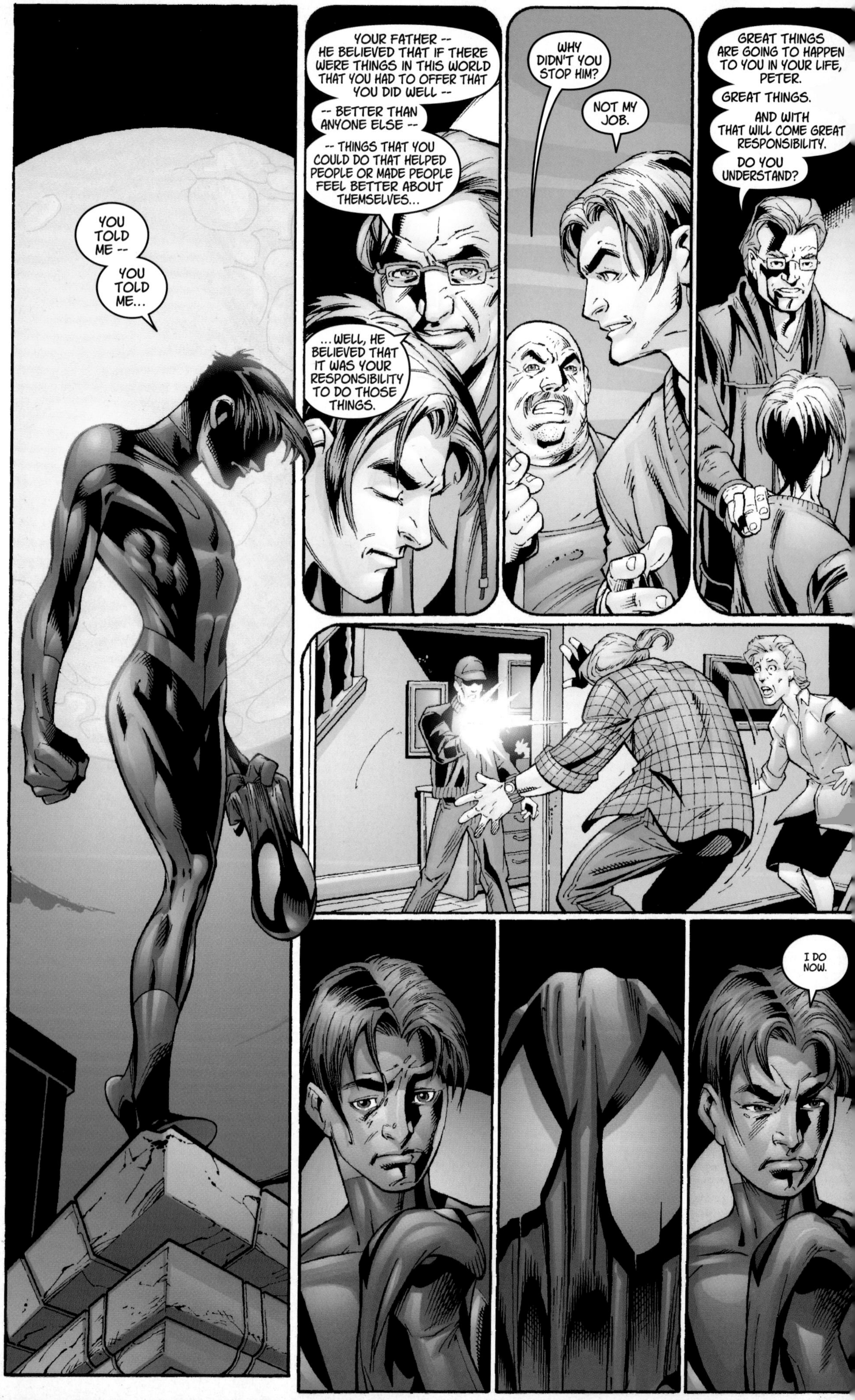
YOU TOLD ME --
YOU TOLD ME...
YOUR FATHER -- HE BELIEVED THAT IF THERE WERE THINGS IN THIS WORLD THAT YOU HAD TO OFFER THAT YOU DID WELL --
-- BETTER THAN ANYONE ELSE --
-- THINGS THAT YOU COULD DO THAT HELPED PEOPLE OR MADE PEOPLE FEEL BETTER ABOUT THEMSELVES...
...WELL, HE BELIEVED THAT IT WAS YOUR RESPONSIBILITY TO DO THOSE THINGS.
WHY DIDN'T YOU STOP HIM?
NOT MY JOB.
GREAT THINGS ARE GOING TO HAPPEN TO YOU IN YOUR LIFE, PETER.
GREAT THINGS.
AND WITH THAT WILL COME GREAT RESPONSIBILITY.
DO YOU UNDERSTAND?
I DO NOW.

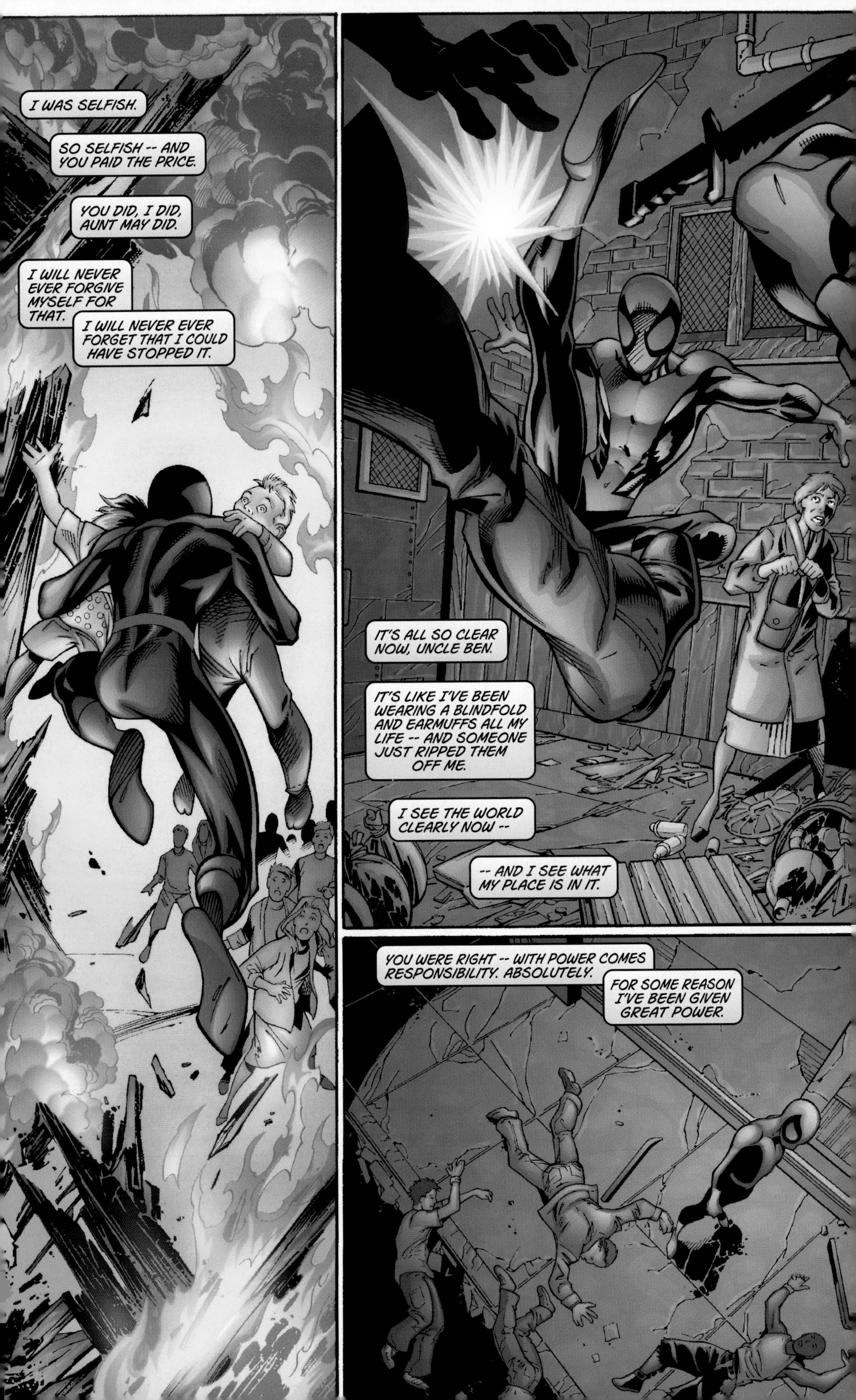
I WAS SELFISH.
SO SELFISH -- AND YOU PAID THE PRICE.
YOU DID, I DID, AUNT MAY DID.
I WILL NEVER EVER FORGIVE MYSELF FOR THAT.
I WILL NEVER EVER FORGET THAT I COULD HAVE STOPPED IT.
IT'S ALL SO CLEAR NOW, UNCLE BEN.
IT'S LIKE I'VE BEEN WEARING A BLINDFOLD AND EARMUFFS ALL MY LIFE -- AND SOMEONE JUST RIPPED THEM OFF ME.
I SEE THE WORLD CLEARLY NOW --
-- AND I SEE WHAT MY PLACE IS IN IT.
YOU WERE RIGHT -- WITH POWER COMES RESPONSIBILITY. ABSOLUTELY.
FOR SOME REASON I'VE BEEN GIVEN GREAT POWER.

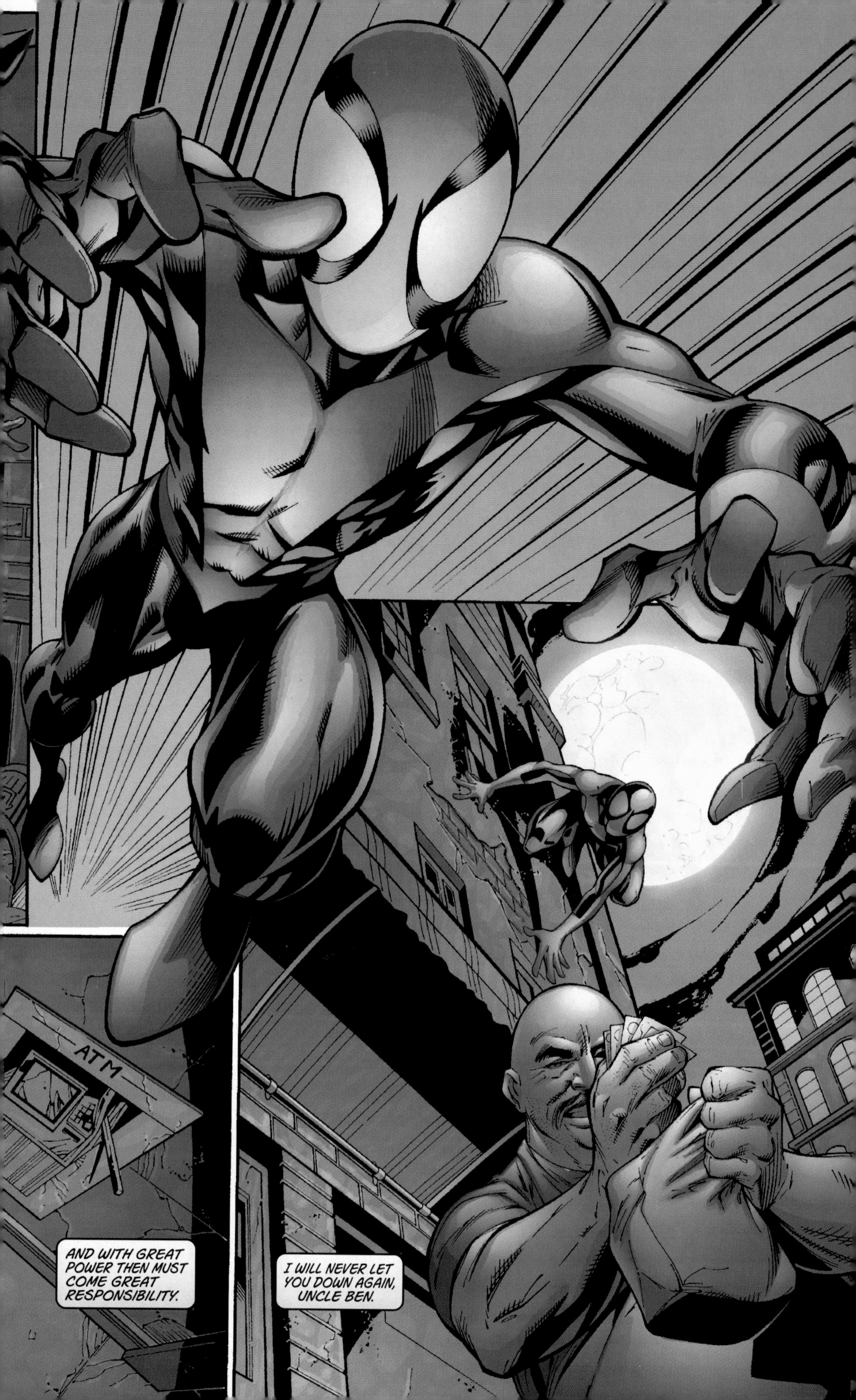
ATM
AND WITH GREAT POWER THEN MUST COME GREAT RESPONSIBILITY.
I WILL NEVER LET YOU DOWN AGAIN, UNCLE BEN.

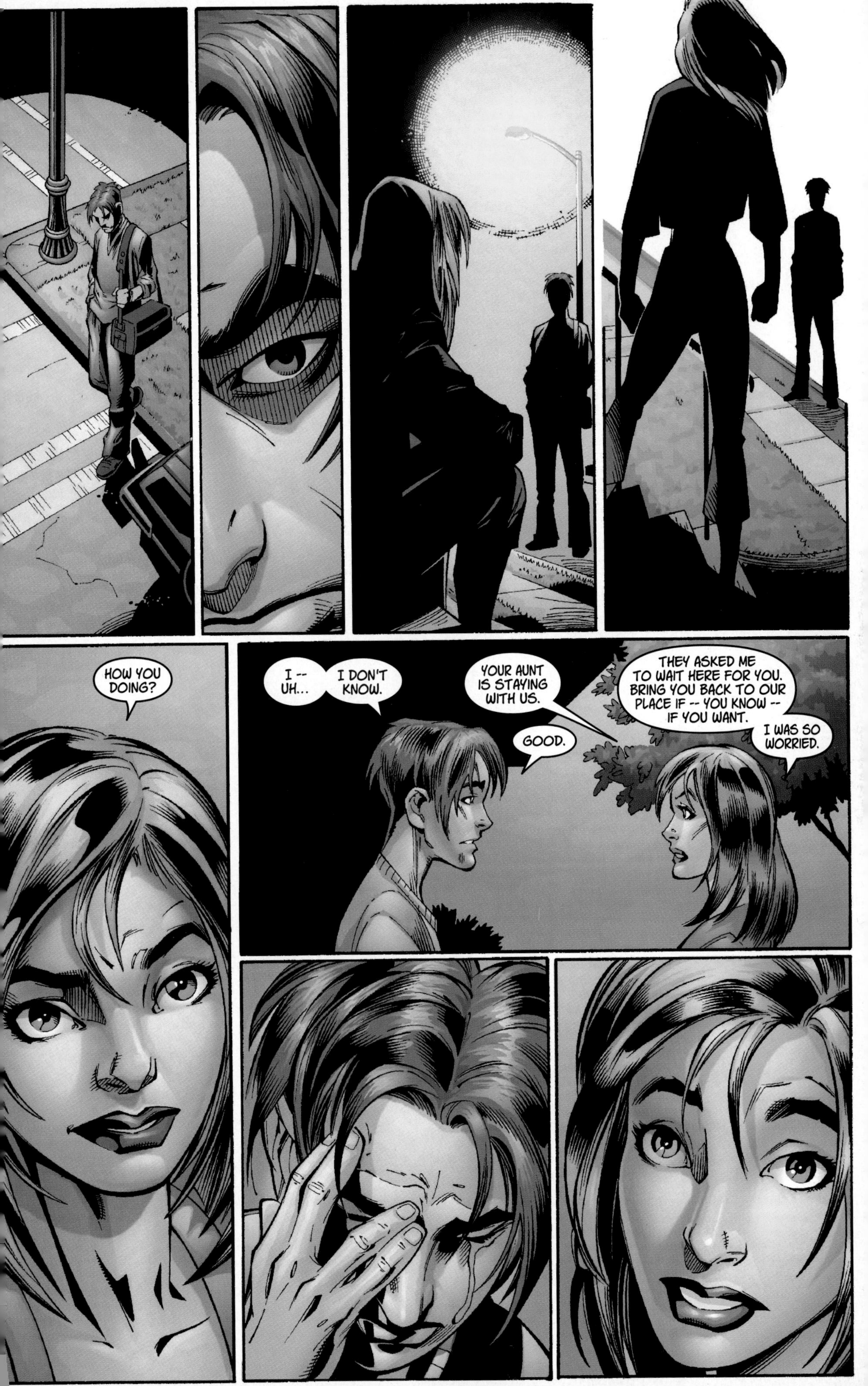
HOW YOU DOING?
I -- UH...
I DON'T KNOW.
YOUR AUNT IS STAYING WITH US.
GOOD.
THEY ASKED ME TO WAIT HERE FOR YOU. BRING YOU BACK TO OUR PLACE IF -- YOU KNOW -- IF YOU WANT.
I WAS SO WORRIED.

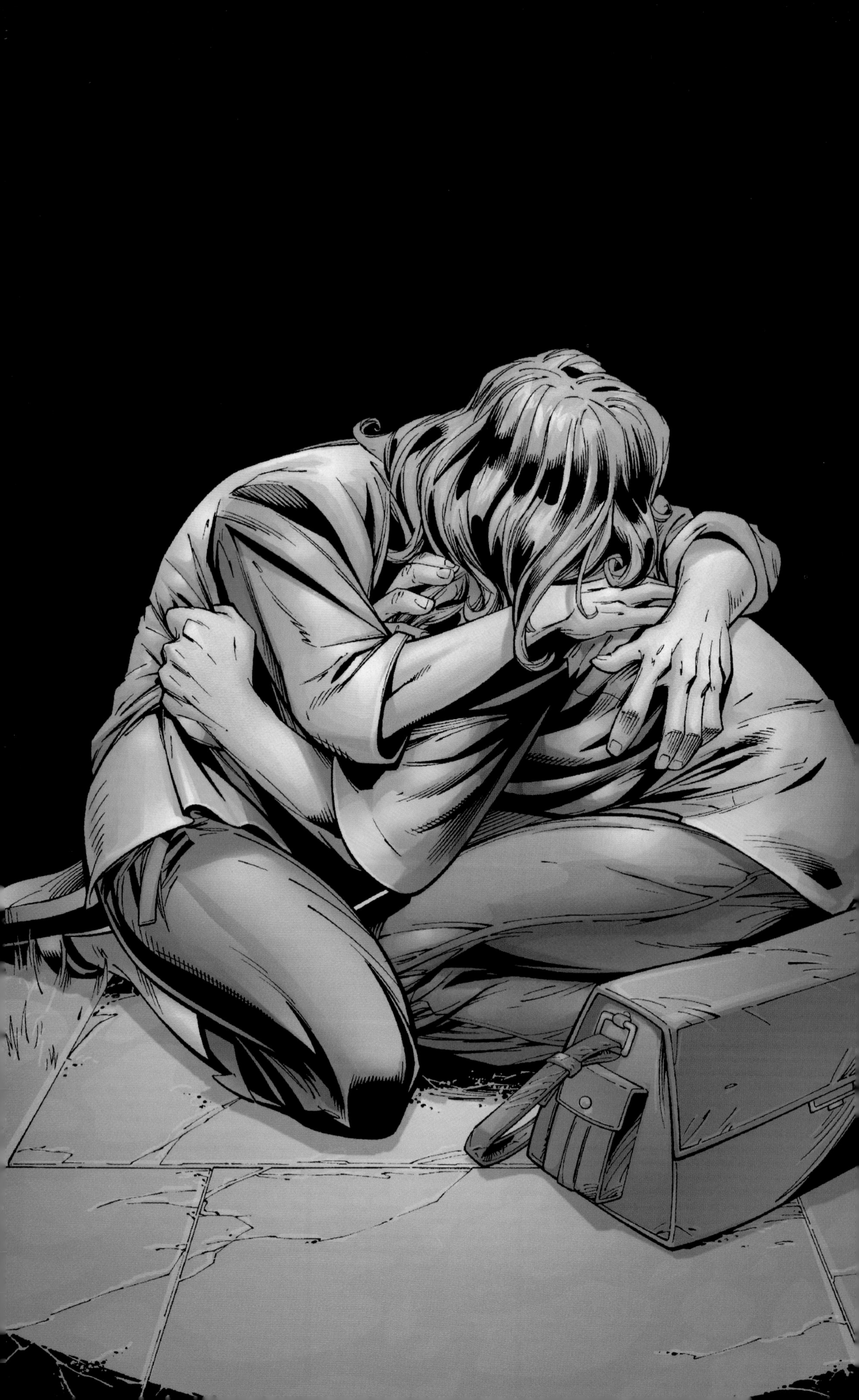

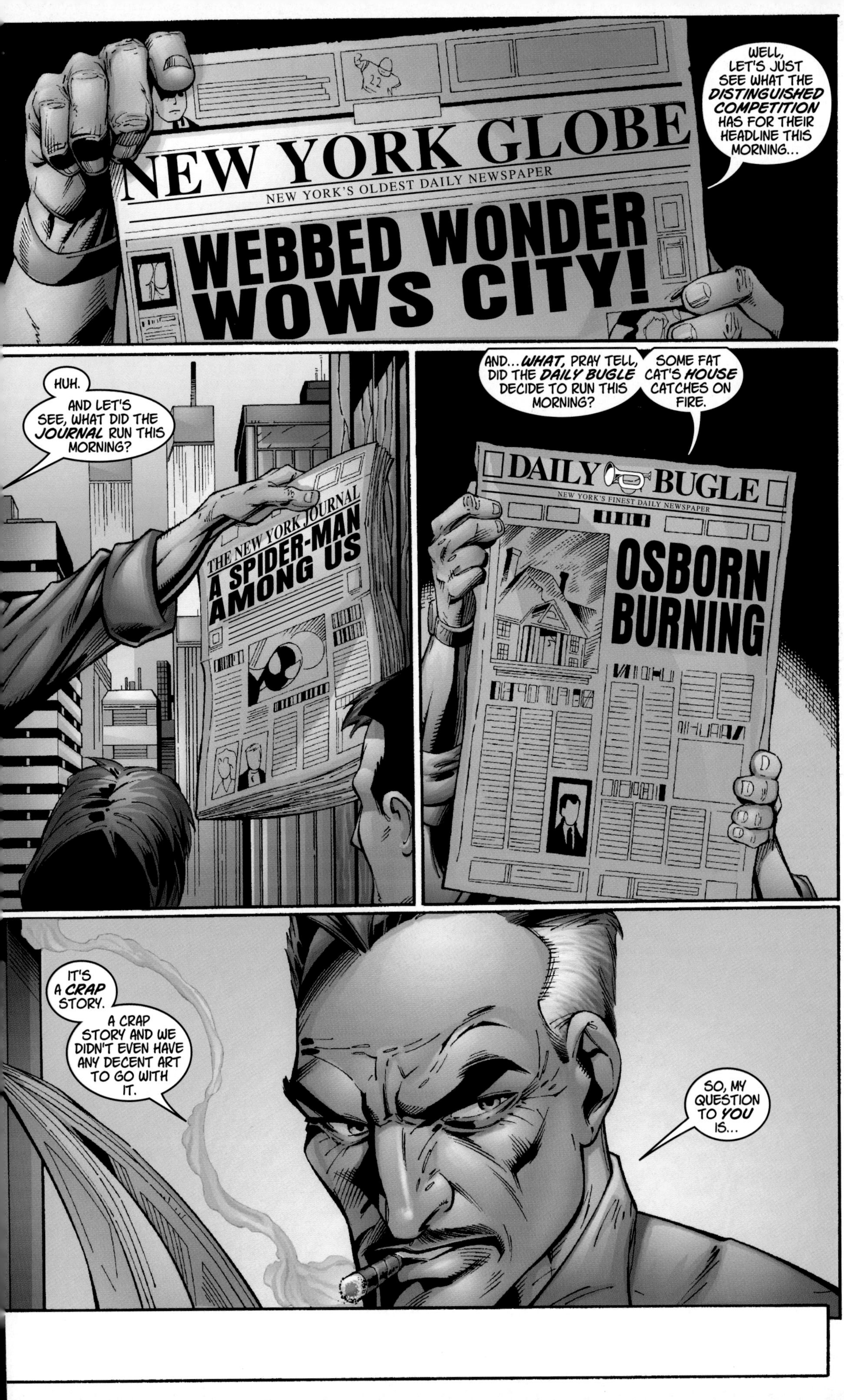
NEW YORK GLOBE
NEW YORK'S OLDEST DAILY NEWSPAPER
WEBBED WONDER WOWS CITY!
WELL, LET'S JUST SEE WHAT THE DISTINGUISHED COMPETITION HAS FOR THEIR HEADLINE THIS MORNING...
HUH.
AND LET'S SEE, WHAT DID THE JOURNAL RUN THIS MORNING?
THE NEW YORK JOURNAL
A SPIDER-MAN AMONG US
AND... WHAT, PRAY TELL, DID THE DAILY BUGLE DECIDE TO RUN THIS MORNING?
SOME FAT CAT'S HOUSE CATCHES ON FIRE.
DAILY BUGLE
NEW YORK'S FINEST DAILY NEWSPAPER
OSBORN BURNING
IT'S A CRAP STORY.
A CRAP STORY AND WE DIDN'T EVEN HAVE ANY DECENT ART TO GO WITH IT.
SO, MY QUESTION TO YOU IS...

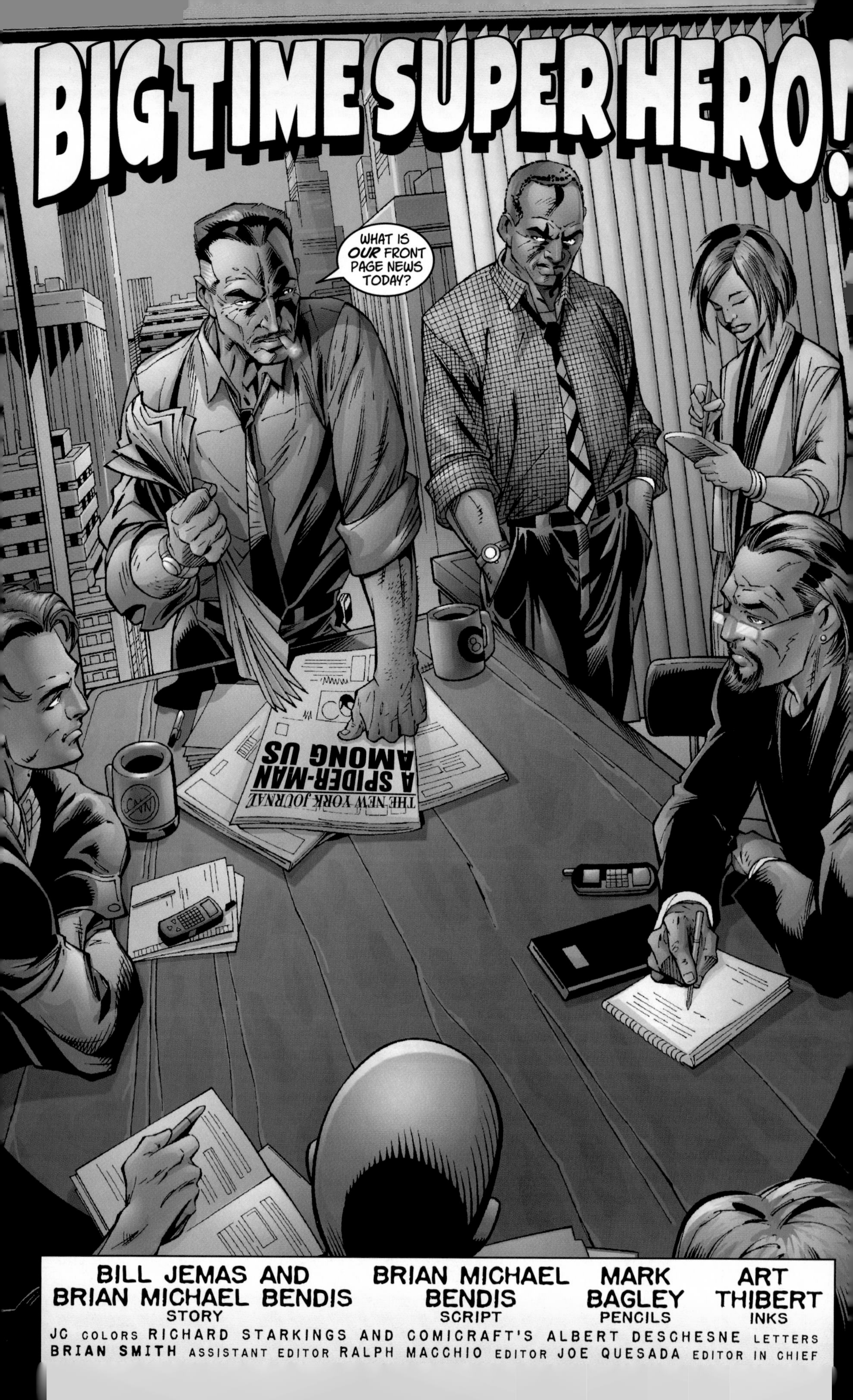
BIG TIME SUPER HERO!
WHAT IS OUR FRONT PAGE NEWS TODAY?
THE NEW YORK JOURNAL
A SPIDER-MAN AMONG US
BILL JEMAS AND BRIAN MICHAEL BENDIS STORY
BRIAN MICHAEL BENDIS SCRIPT
MARK BAGLEY PENCILS
ART THIBERT INKS
JC COLORS RICHARD STARKINGS AND COMICRAFT'S ALBERT DESCHESNE LETTERS
BRIAN SMITH ASSISTANT EDITOR RALPH MACCHIO EDITOR JOE QUESADA EDITOR IN CHIEF

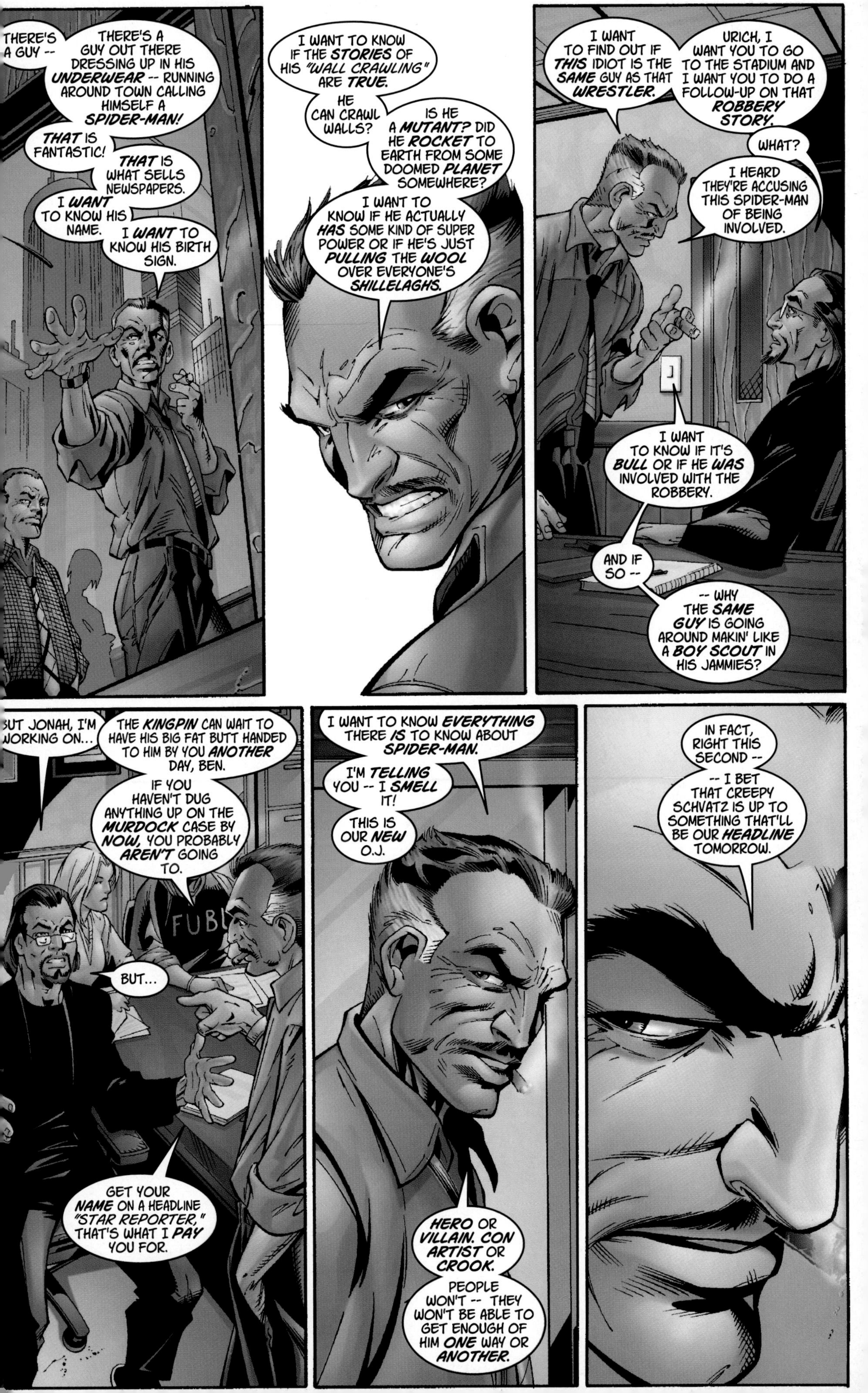
THERE'S A GUY --
THERE'S A GUY OUT THERE DRESSING UP IN HIS UNDERWEAR -- RUNNING AROUND TOWN CALLING HIMSELF A SPIDER-MAN!
THAT IS FANTASTIC!
THAT IS WHAT SELLS NEWSPAPERS.
I WANT TO KNOW HIS NAME.
I WANT TO KNOW HIS BIRTH SIGN.
I WANT TO KNOW IF THE STORIES OF HIS "WALL CRAWLING" ARE TRUE.
HE CAN CRAWL WALLS?
IS HE A MUTANT? DID HE ROCKET TO EARTH FROM SOME DOOMED PLANET SOMEWHERE?
I WANT TO KNOW IF HE ACTUALLY HAS SOME KIND OF SUPER POWER OR IF HE'S JUST PULLING THE WOOL OVER EVERYONE'S SHILLELAGHS.
I WANT TO FIND OUT IF THIS IDIOT IS THE SAME GUY AS THAT WRESTLER.
URICH, I WANT YOU TO GO TO THE STADIUM AND I WANT YOU TO DO A FOLLOW-UP ON THAT ROBBERY STORY.
WHAT?
I HEARD THEY'RE ACCUSING THIS SPIDER-MAN OF BEING INVOLVED.
I WANT TO KNOW IF IT'S BULL OR IF HE WAS INVOLVED WITH THE ROBBERY.
AND IF SO --
-- WHY THE SAME GUY IS GOING AROUND MAKIN' LIKE A BOY SCOUT IN HIS JAMMIES?
BUT JONAH, I'M WORKING ON...
THE KINGPIN CAN WAIT TO HAVE HIS BIG FAT BUTT HANDED TO HIM BY YOU ANOTHER DAY, BEN.
IF YOU HAVEN'T DUG ANYTHING UP ON THE MURDOCK CASE BY NOW, YOU PROBABLY AREN'T GOING TO.
FUBU
BUT...
GET YOUR NAME ON A HEADLINE "STAR REPORTER," THAT'S WHAT I PAY YOU FOR.
I WANT TO KNOW EVERYTHING THERE IS TO KNOW ABOUT SPIDER-MAN.
I'M TELLING YOU -- I SMELL IT!
THIS IS OUR NEW O.J.
HERO OR VILLAIN. CON ARTIST OR CROOK.
PEOPLE WON'T -- THEY WON'T BE ABLE TO GET ENOUGH OF HIM ONE WAY OR ANOTHER.
IN FACT, RIGHT THIS SECOND --
-- I BET THAT CREEPY SCHVATZ IS UP TO SOMETHING THAT'LL BE OUR HEADLINE TOMORROW.

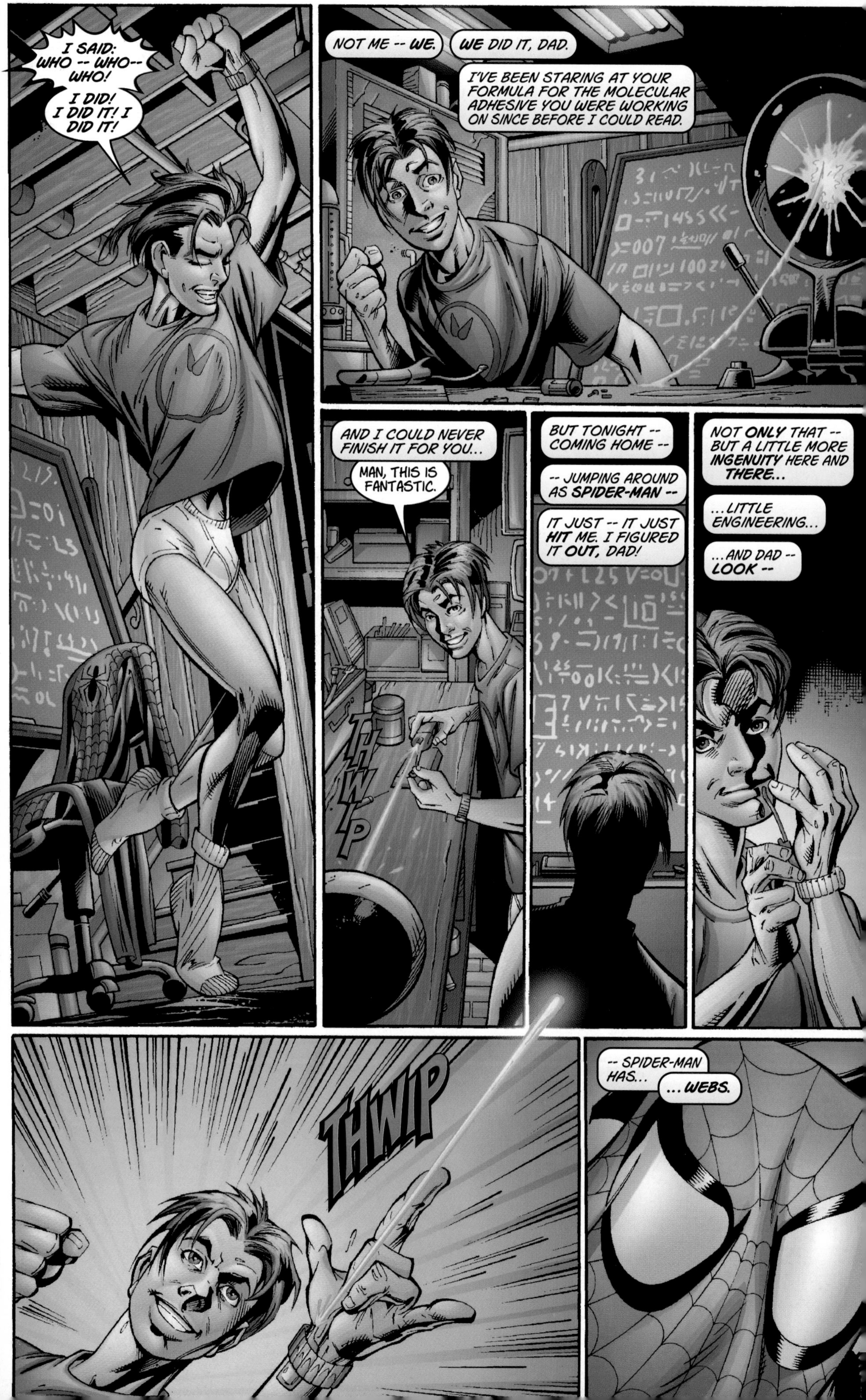
I SAID: WHO -- WHO-- WHO!
I DID! I DID IT! I DID IT!
NOT ME -- WE.
WE DID IT, DAD.
I'VE BEEN STARING AT YOUR FORMULA FOR THE MOLECULAR ADHESIVE YOU WERE WORKING ON SINCE BEFORE I COULD READ.
AND I COULD NEVER FINISH IT FOR YOU...
MAN, THIS IS FANTASTIC.
THWIP
BUT TONIGHT -- COMING HOME --
-- JUMPING AROUND AS SPIDER-MAN --
IT JUST -- IT JUST HIT ME. I FIGURED IT OUT, DAD!
NOT ONLY THAT -- BUT A LITTLE MORE INGENUITY HERE AND THERE...
...LITTLE ENGINEERING...
...AND DAD -- LOOK --
THWIP
-- SPIDER-MAN HAS...
... WEBS.

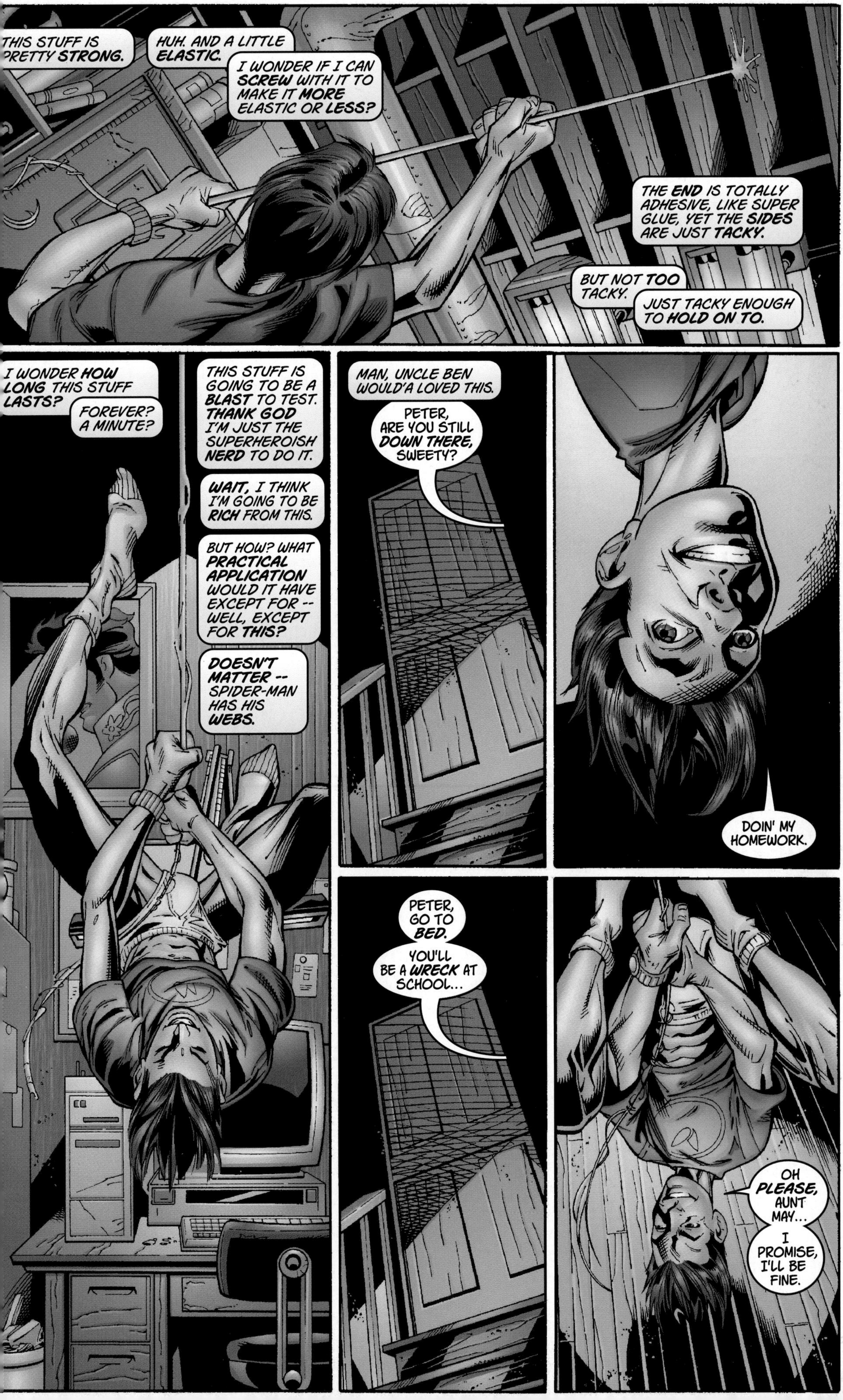
THIS STUFF IS PRETTY STRONG.
HUH. AND A LITTLE ELASTIC.
I WONDER IF I CAN SCREW WITH IT TO MAKE IT MORE ELASTIC OR LESS?
THE END IS TOTALLY ADHESIVE, LIKE SUPER GLUE, YET THE SIDES ARE JUST TACKY.
BUT NOT TOO TACKY.
JUST TACKY ENOUGH TO HOLD ON TO.
I WONDER HOW LONG THIS STUFF LASTS?
FOREVER? A MINUTE?
THIS STUFF IS GOING TO BE A BLAST TO TEST. THANK GOD I'M JUST THE SUPERHEROISH NERD TO DO IT.
WAIT, I THINK I'M GOING TO BE RICH FROM THIS.
BUT HOW? WHAT PRACTICAL APPLICATION WOULD IT HAVE EXCEPT FOR -- WELL, EXCEPT FOR THIS?
DOESN'T MATTER -- SPIDER-MAN HAS HIS WEBS.
MAN, UNCLE BEN WOULD'A LOVED THIS.
PETER, ARE YOU STILL DOWN THERE, SWEETY?
DOIN' MY HOMEWORK.
PETER, GO TO BED.
YOU'LL BE A WRECK AT SCHOOL...
OH PLEASE, AUNT MAY...
I PROMISE, I'LL BE FINE.

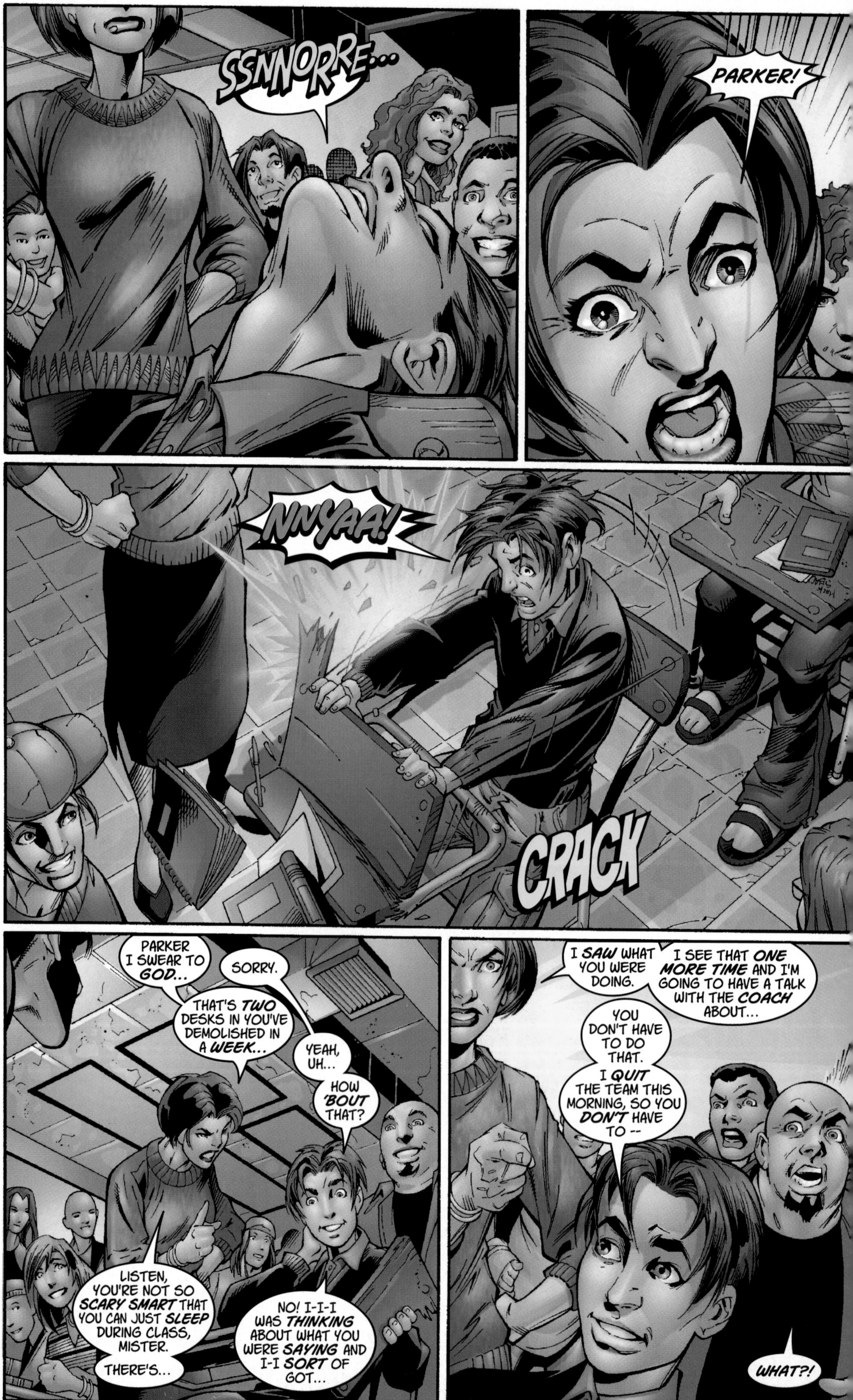
SSNNORRE...
PARKER!
NNYAA!
CRACK
PARKER I SWEAR TO GOD...
SORRY.
THAT'S TWO DESKS IN YOU'VE DEMOLISHED IN A WEEK...
YEAH, UH...
HOW 'BOUT THAT?
LISTEN, YOU'RE NOT SO SCARY SMART THAT YOU CAN JUST SLEEP DURING CLASS, MISTER.
THERE'S...
NO! I-I-I WAS THINKING ABOUT WHAT YOU WERE SAYING AND I-I SORT OF GOT...
I SAW WHAT YOU WERE DOING.
I SEE THAT ONE MORE TIME AND I'M GOING TO HAVE A TALK WITH THE COACH ABOUT...
YOU DON'T HAVE TO DO THAT.
I QUIT THE TEAM THIS MORNING, SO YOU DON'T HAVE TO --
WHAT?!

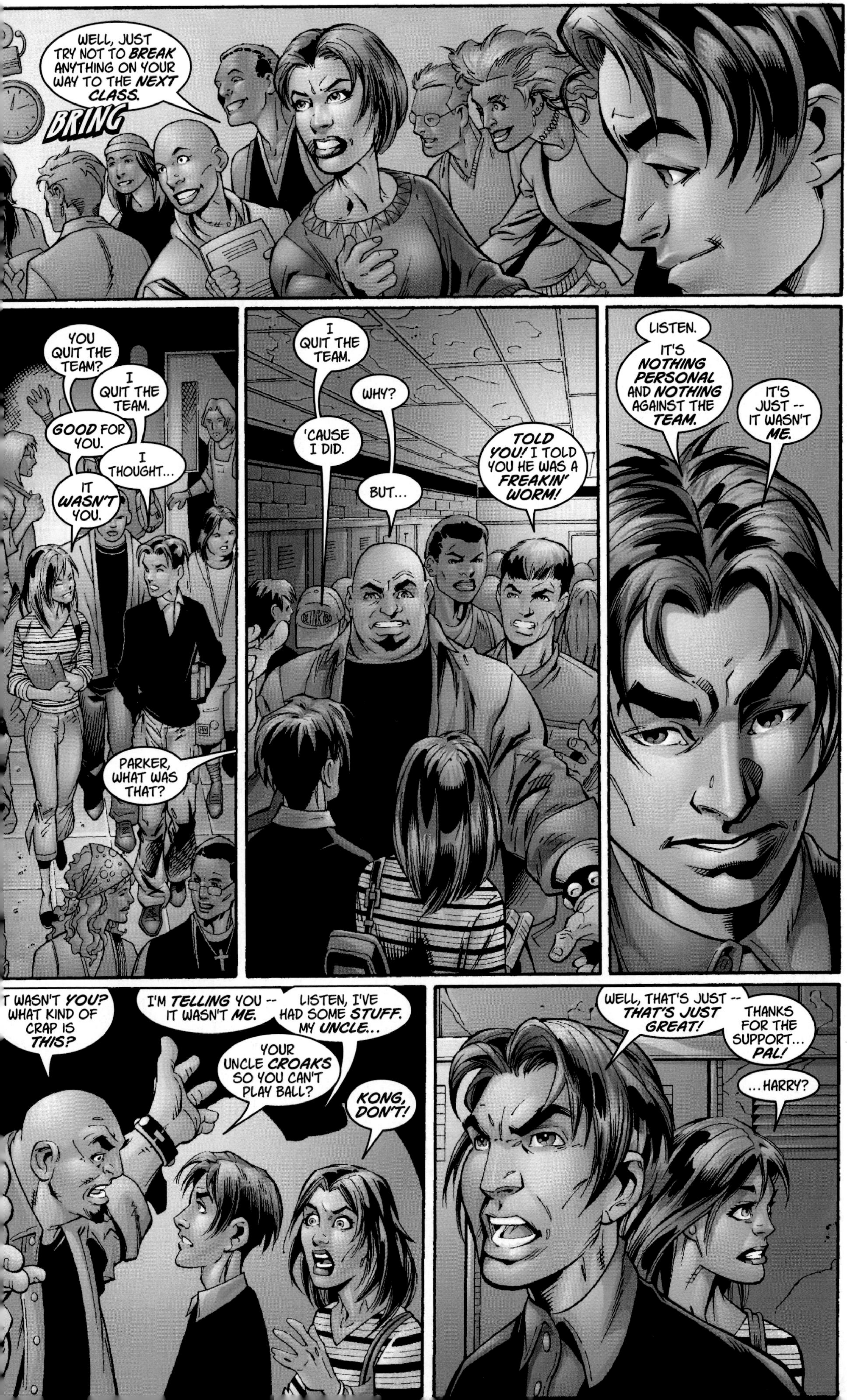
WELL, JUST TRY NOT TO BREAK ANYTHING ON YOUR WAY TO THE NEXT CLASS.
BRING
YOU QUIT THE TEAM?
I QUIT THE TEAM.
GOOD FOR YOU.
I THOUGHT...
IT WASN'T YOU.
PARKER, WHAT WAS THAT?
I QUIT THE TEAM.
WHY?
'CAUSE I DID.
BUT...
TOLD YOU! I TOLD YOU HE WAS A FREAKIN' WORM!
LISTEN.
IT'S NOTHING PERSONAL AND NOTHING AGAINST THE TEAM.
IT'S JUST -- IT WASN'T ME.
T WASN'T YOU? WHAT KIND OF CRAP IS THIS?
I'M TELLING YOU -- IT WASN'T ME.
LISTEN, I'VE HAD SOME STUFF. MY UNCLE...
YOUR UNCLE CROAKS SO YOU CAN'T PLAY BALL?
KONG, DON'T!
WELL, THAT'S JUST -- THAT'S JUST GREAT!
THANKS FOR THE SUPPORT... PAL!
...HARRY?

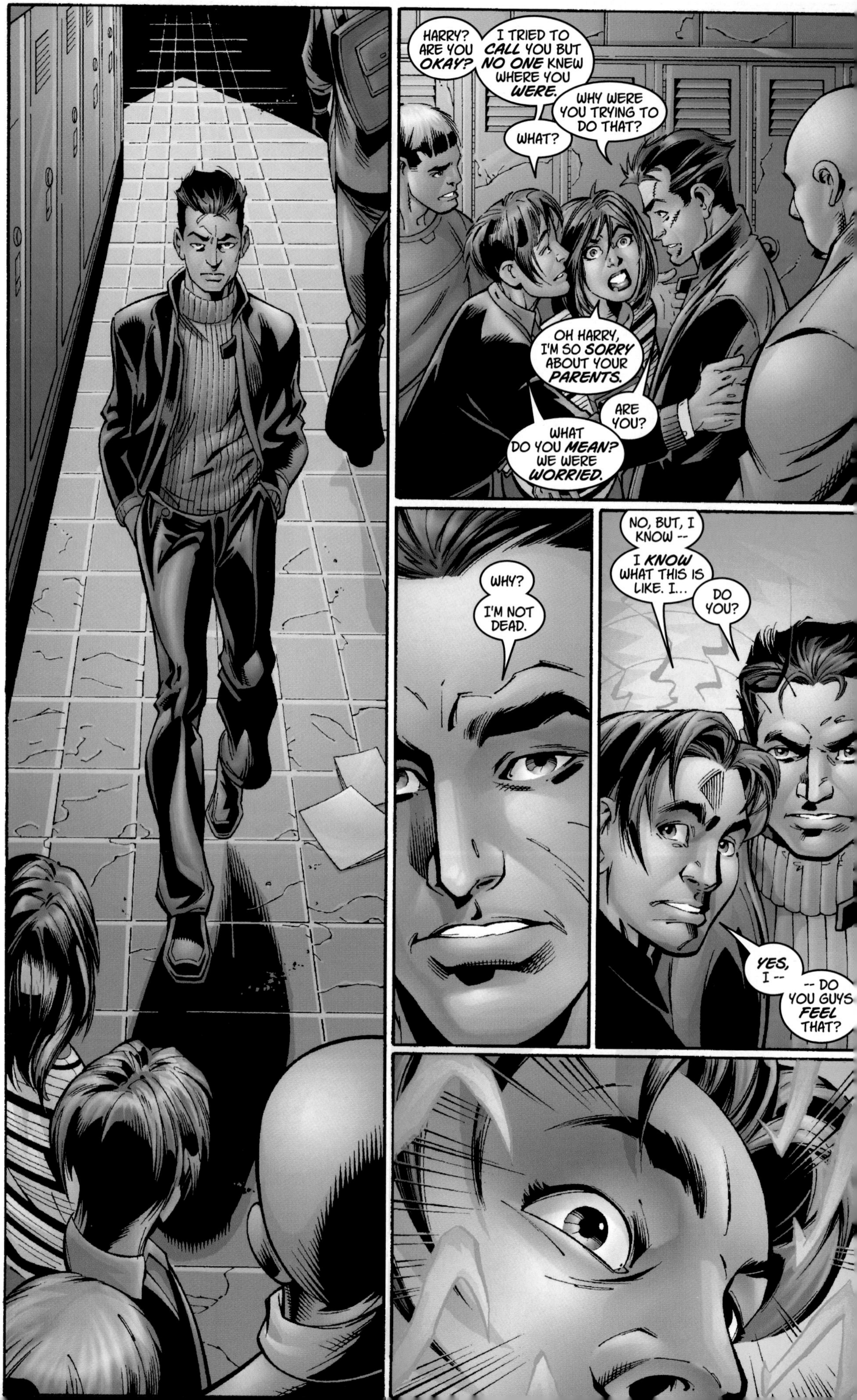
HARRY? ARE YOU OKAY?
I TRIED TO CALL YOU BUT NO ONE KNEW WHERE YOU WERE.
WHAT?
WHY WERE YOU TRYING TO DO THAT?
OH HARRY, I'M SO SORRY ABOUT YOUR PARENTS.
ARE YOU?
WHAT DO YOU MEAN? WE WERE WORRIED.
WHY?
I'M NOT DEAD.
NO, BUT, I KNOW --
I KNOW WHAT THIS IS LIKE. I...
DO YOU?
YES, I --
-- DO YOU GUYS FEEL THAT?

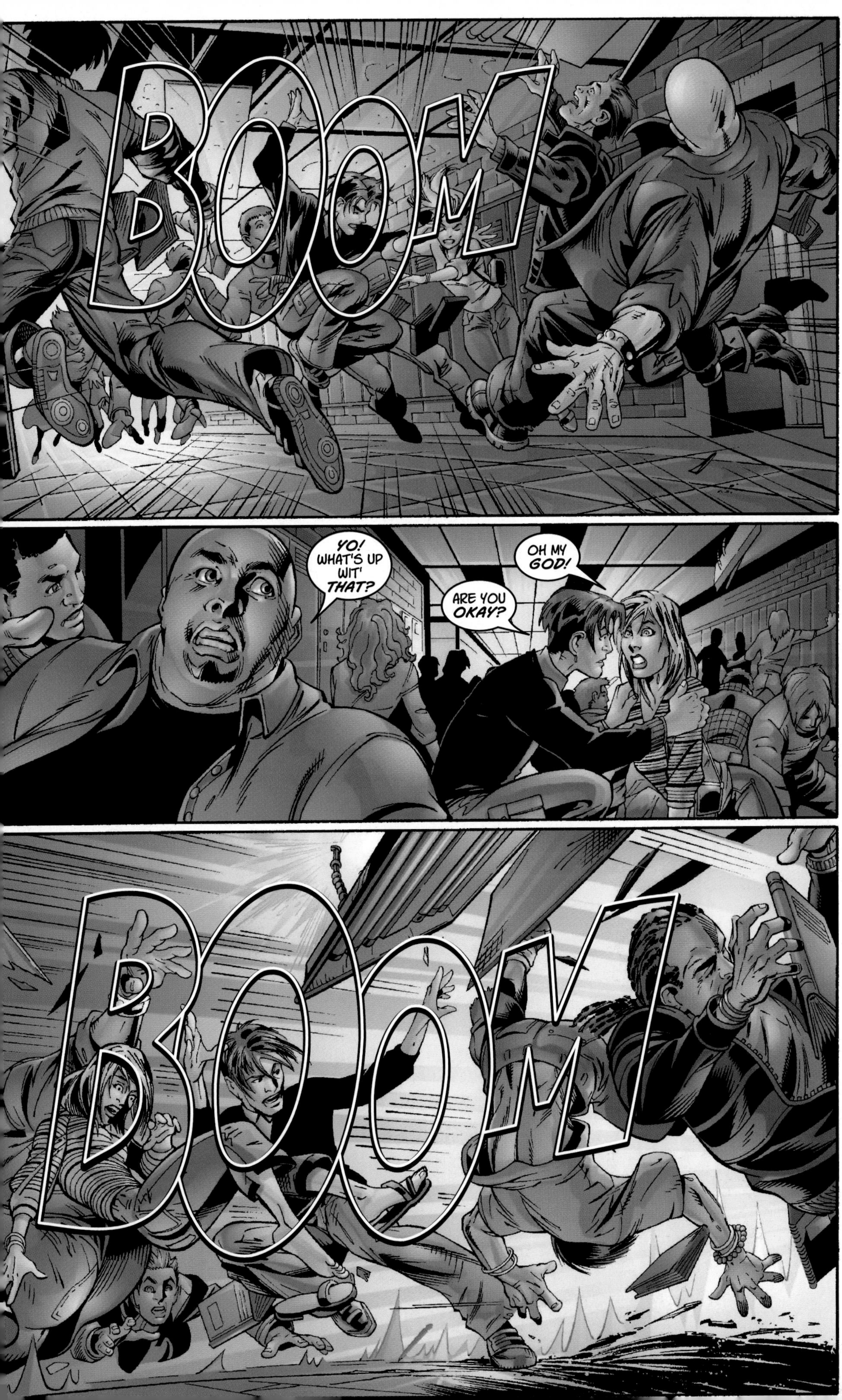
BOOM
YO! WHAT'S UP WIT' THAT?
OH MY GOD!
ARE YOU OKAY?
BOOM

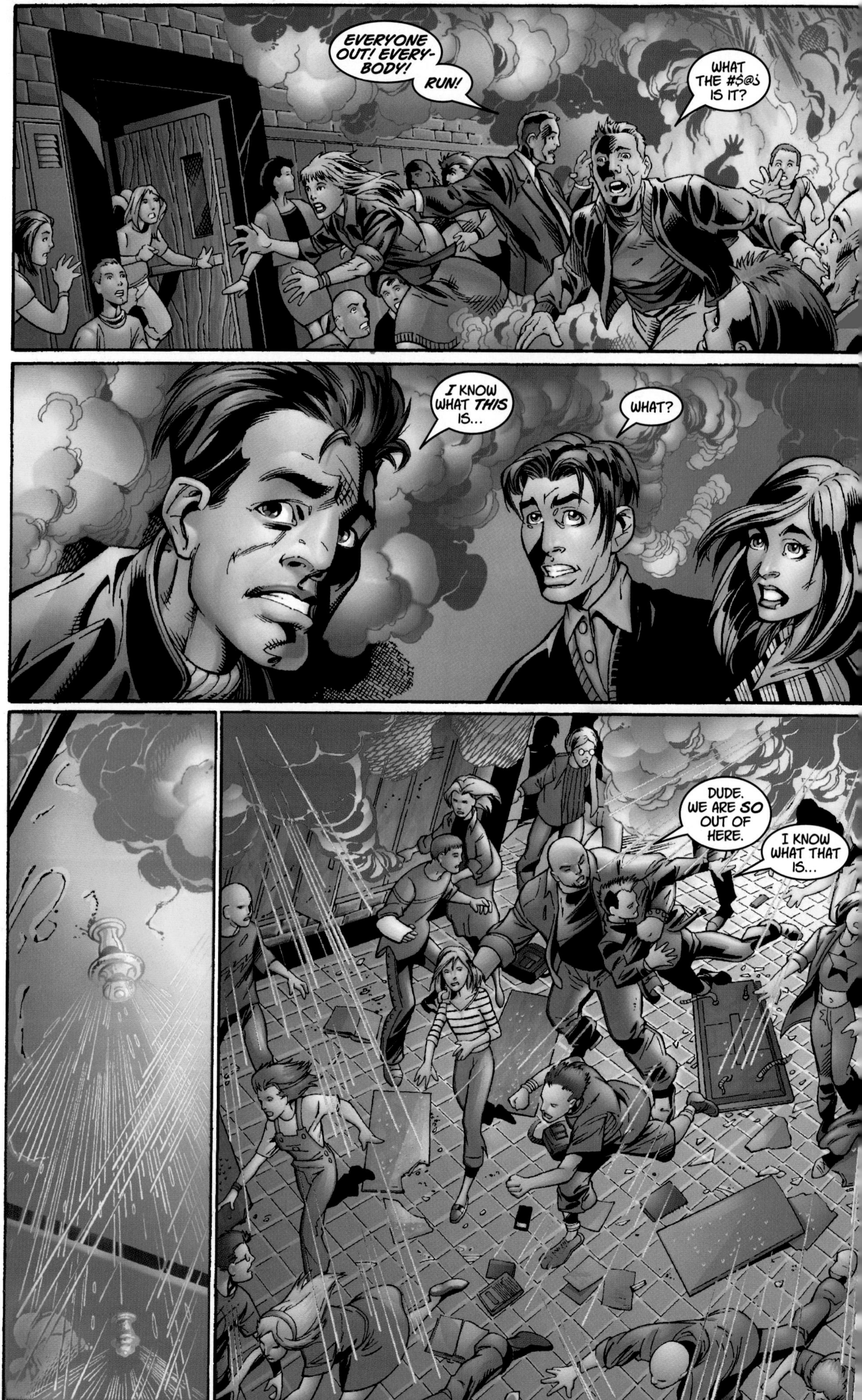
EVERYONE OUT! EVERY-BODY!
RUN!
WHAT THE #$@¿ IS IT?
I KNOW WHAT THIS IS...
WHAT?
DUDE. WE ARE SO OUT OF HERE.
I KNOW WHAT THAT IS...

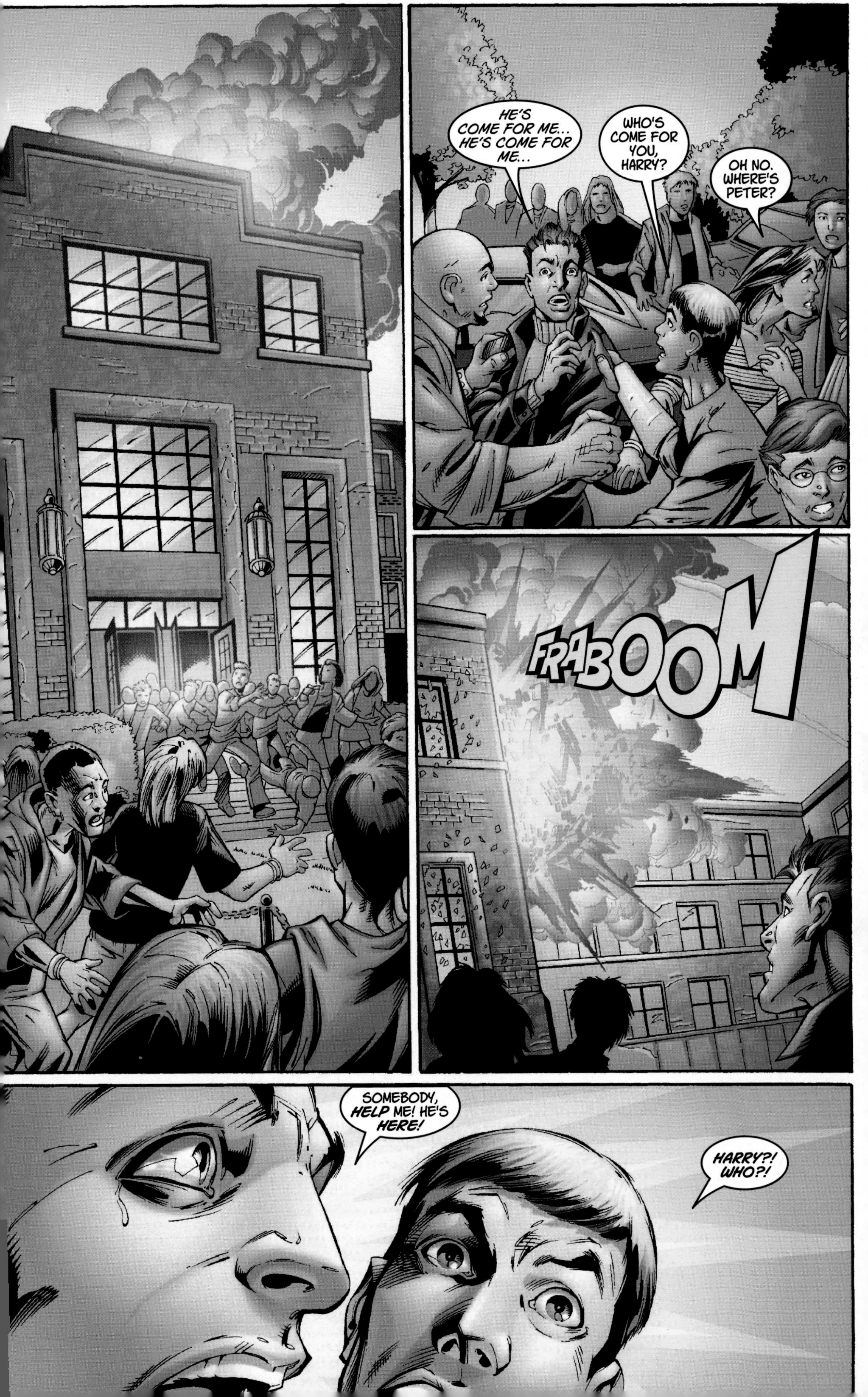
HE'S COME FOR ME... HE'S COME FOR ME...
WHO'S COME FOR YOU, HARRY?
OH NO. WHERE'S PETER?
FRABOOOM
SOMEBODY, HELP ME! HE'S HERE!
HARRY?! WHO?!

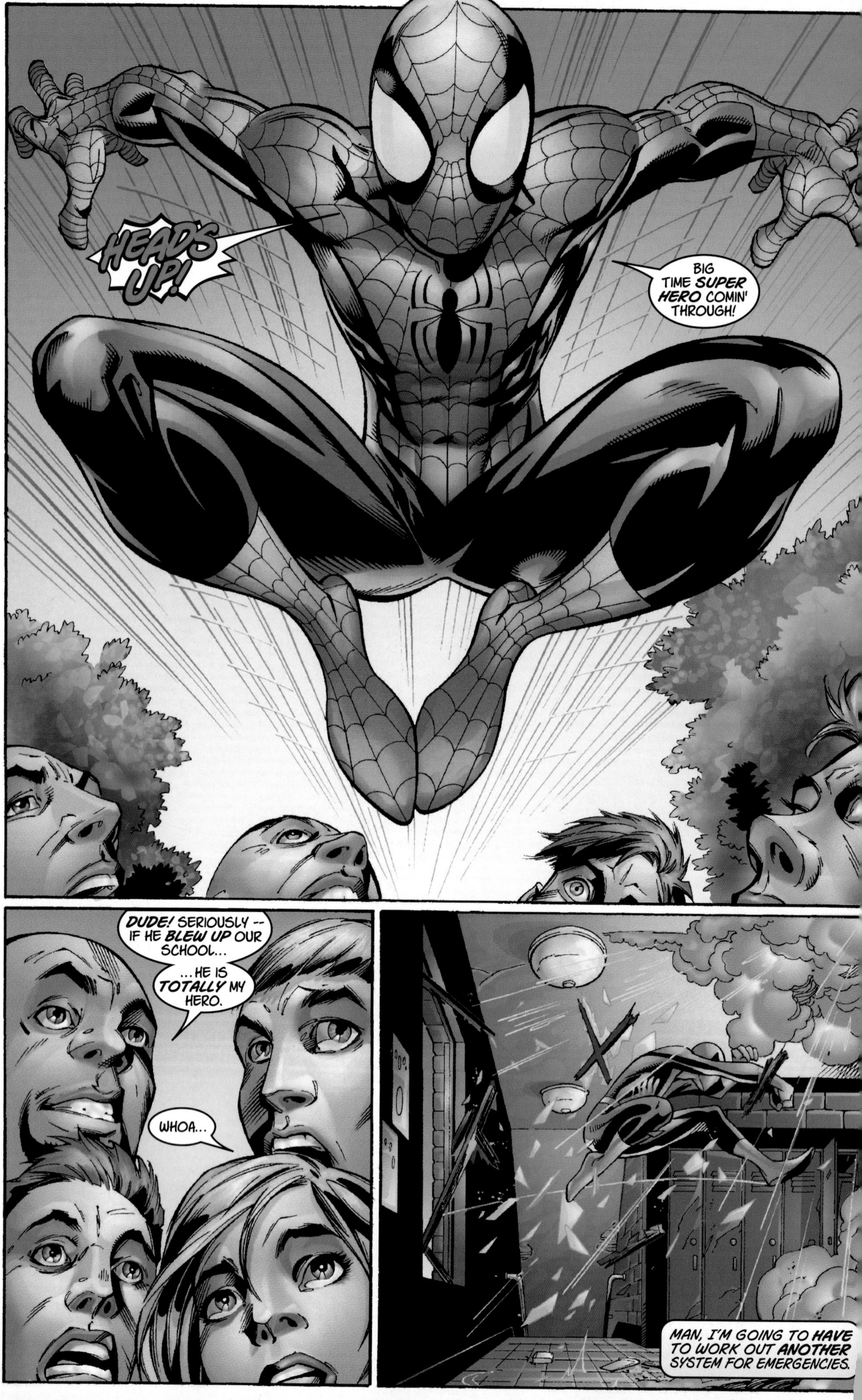
HEAD'S UP!
BIG TIME SUPER HERO COMIN' THROUGH!
DUDE! SERIOUSLY -- IF HE BLEW UP OUR SCHOOL...
...HE IS TOTALLY MY HERO.
WHOA...
MAN, I'M GOING TO HAVE TO WORK OUT ANOTHER SYSTEM FOR EMERGENCIES.

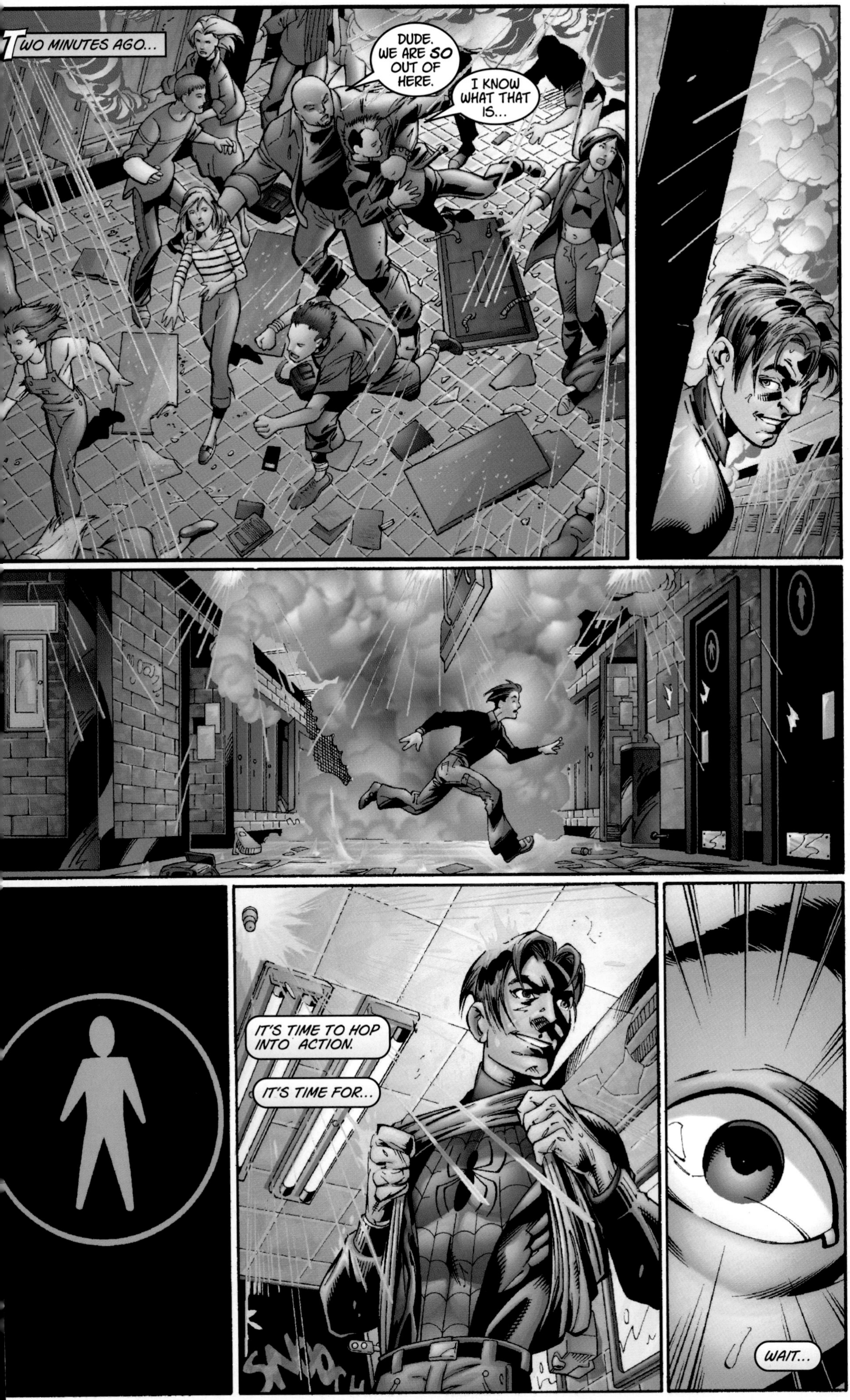

TWO MINUTES AGO...
DUDE. WE ARE SO OUT OF HERE.
I KNOW WHAT THAT IS...
IT'S TIME TO HOP INTO ACTION.
IT'S TIME FOR...
WAIT...

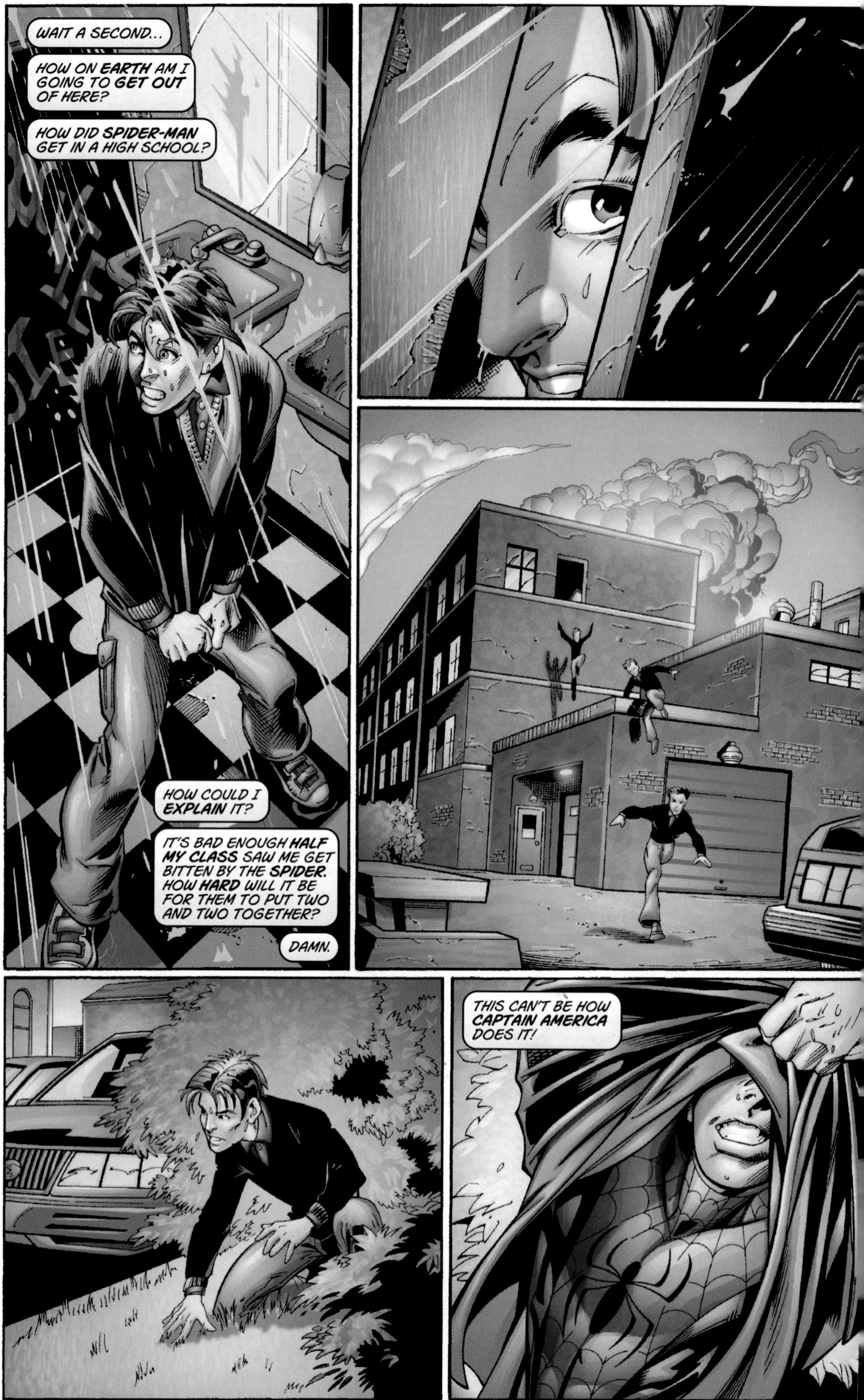
WAIT A SECOND...
HOW ON EARTH AM I GOING TO GET OUT OF HERE?
HOW DID SPIDER-MAN GET IN A HIGH SCHOOL?
HOW COULD I EXPLAIN IT?
IT'S BAD ENOUGH HALF MY CLASS SAW ME GET BITTEN BY THE SPIDER. HOW HARD WILL IT BE FOR THEM TO PUT TWO AND TWO TOGETHER?
DAMN.
THIS CAN'T BE HOW CAPTAIN AMERICA DOES IT!

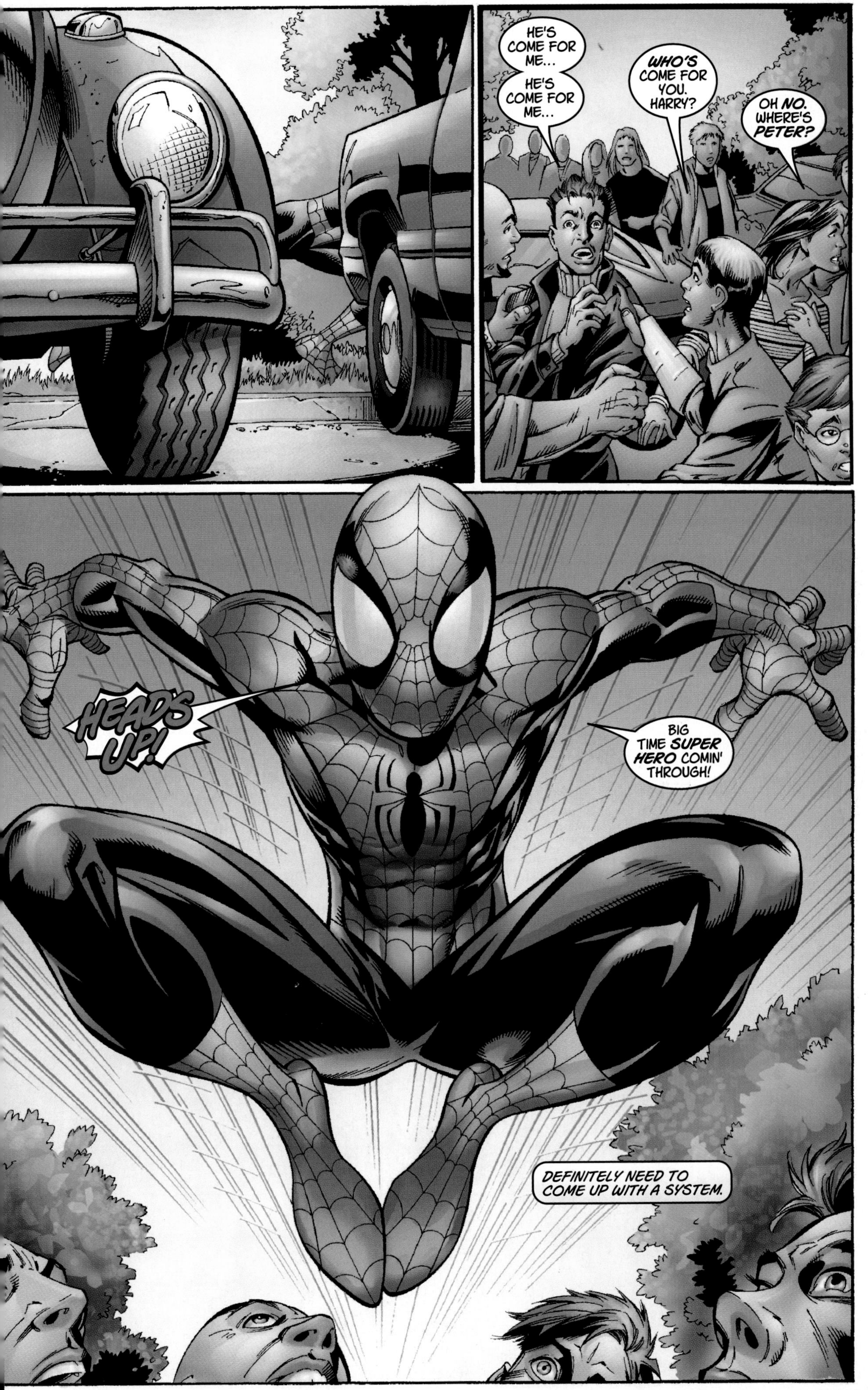
HE'S COME FOR ME...
HE'S COME FOR ME...
WHO'S COME FOR YOU. HARRY?
OH NO. WHERE'S PETER?
HEAD'S UP!
BIG TIME SUPER HERO COMIN' THROUGH!
DEFINITELY NEED TO COME UP WITH A SYSTEM.

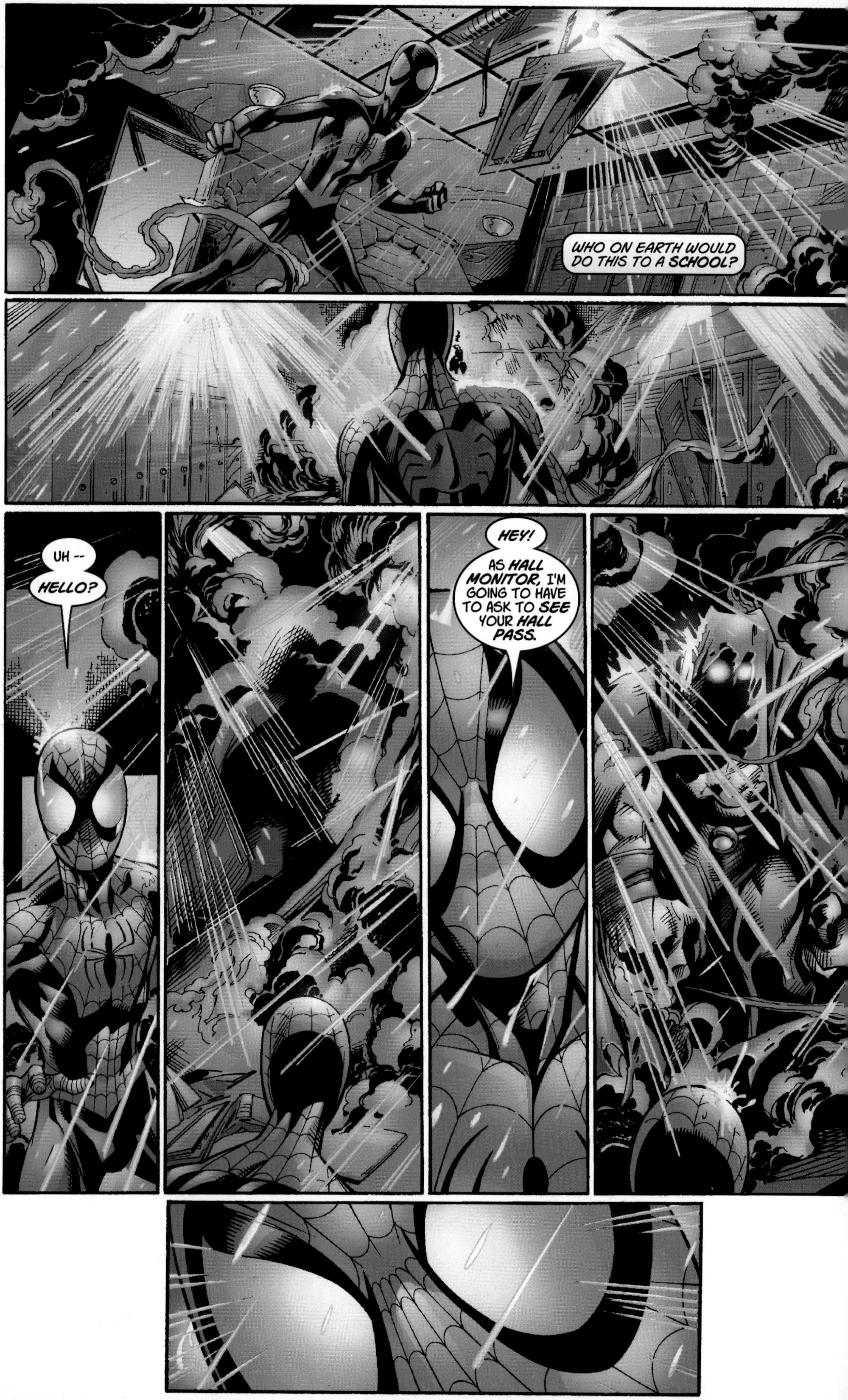

WHO ON EARTH WOULD DO THIS TO A SCHOOL?
UH --
HELLO?
HEY!
AS HALL MONITOR, I'M GOING TO HAVE TO ASK TO SEE YOUR HALL PASS.

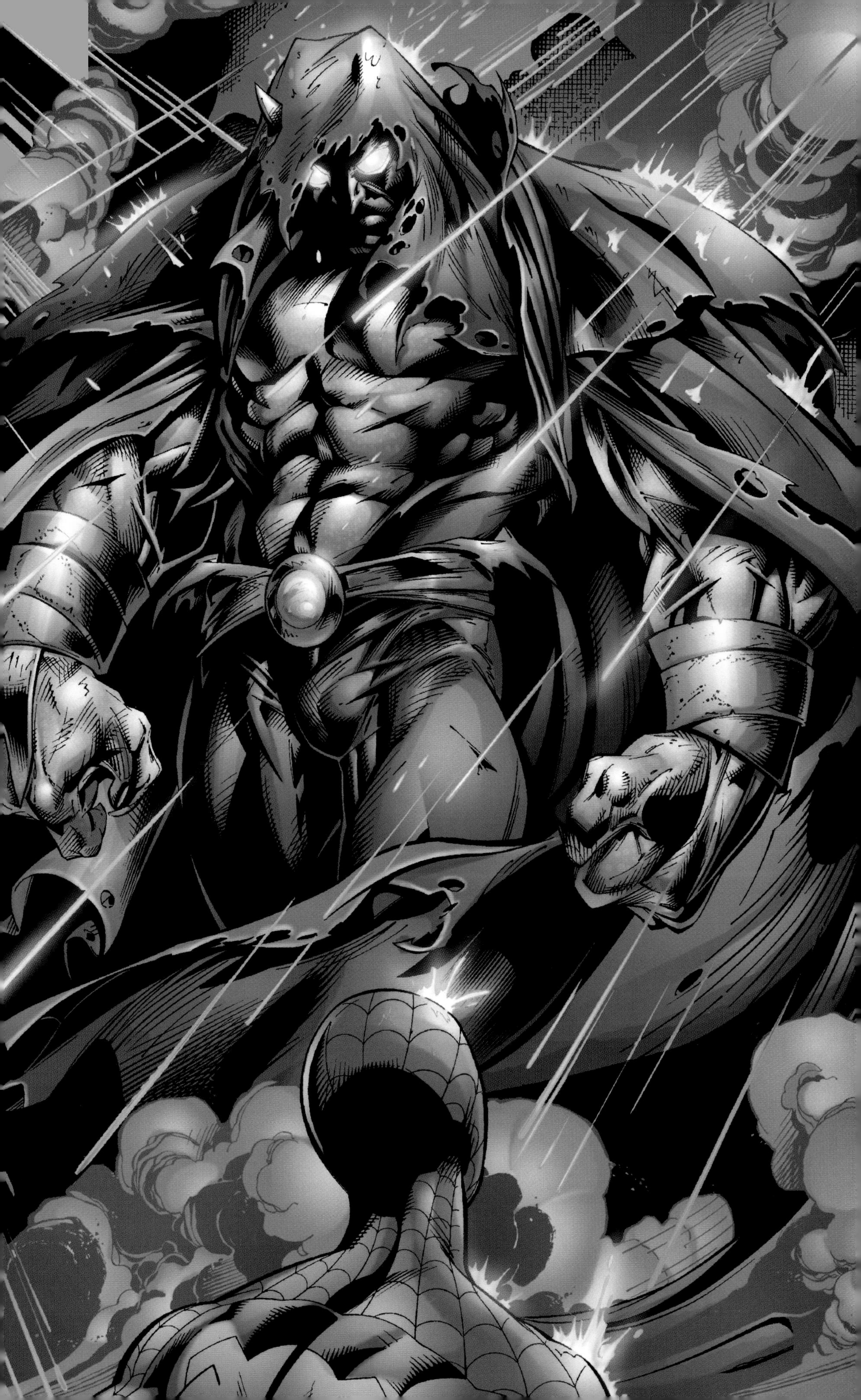

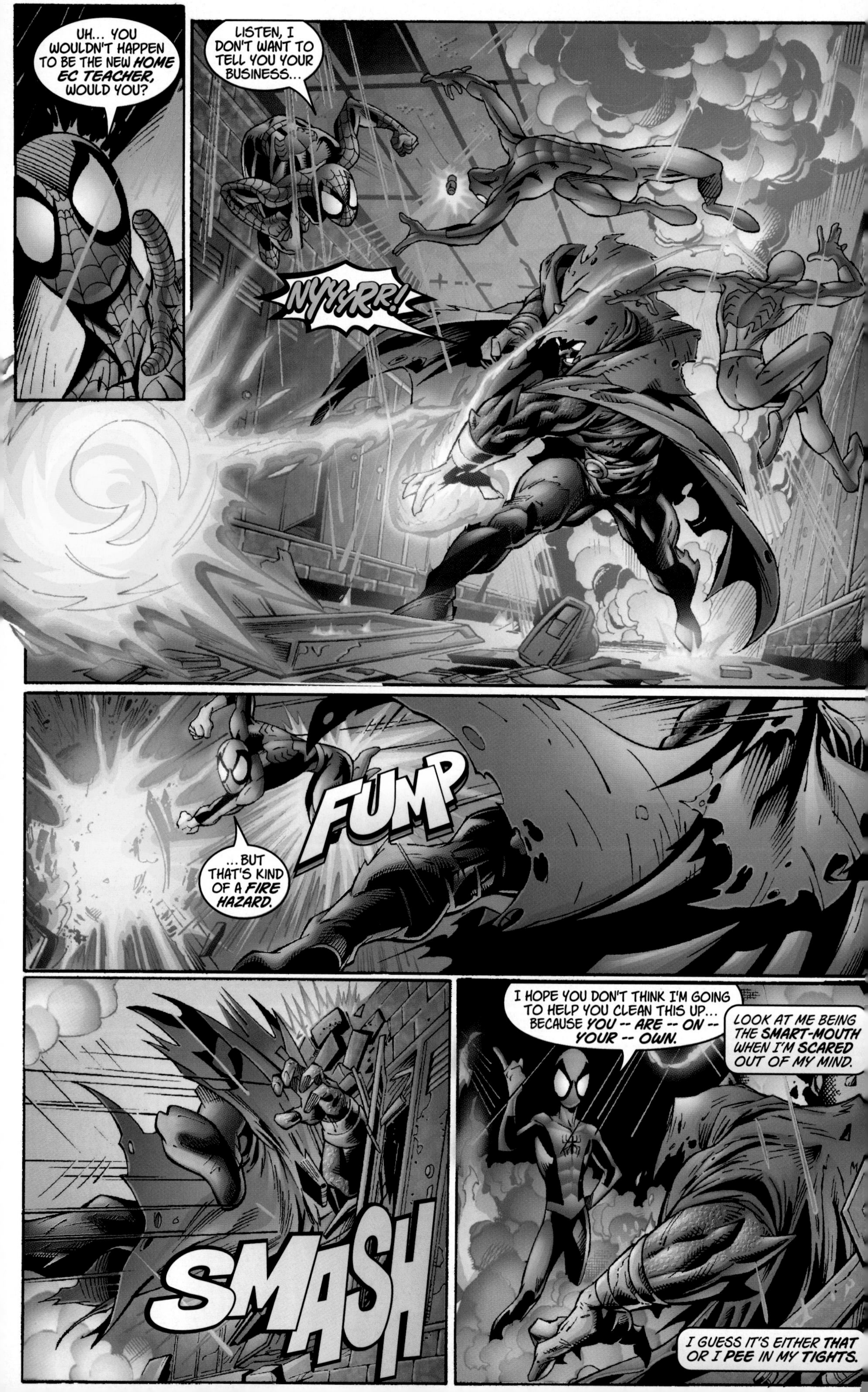
UH... YOU WOULDN'T HAPPEN TO BE THE NEW HOME EC TEACHER, WOULD YOU?
LISTEN, I DON'T WANT TO TELL YOU YOUR BUSINESS...
NYYYRR!
FUMP
...BUT THAT'S KIND OF A FIRE HAZARD.
SMASH
I HOPE YOU DON'T THINK I'M GOING TO HELP YOU CLEAN THIS UP... BECAUSE YOU -- ARE -- ON -- YOUR -- OWN.
LOOK AT ME BEING THE SMART-MOUTH WHEN I'M SCARED OUT OF MY MIND.
I GUESS IT'S EITHER THAT OR I PEE IN MY TIGHTS.

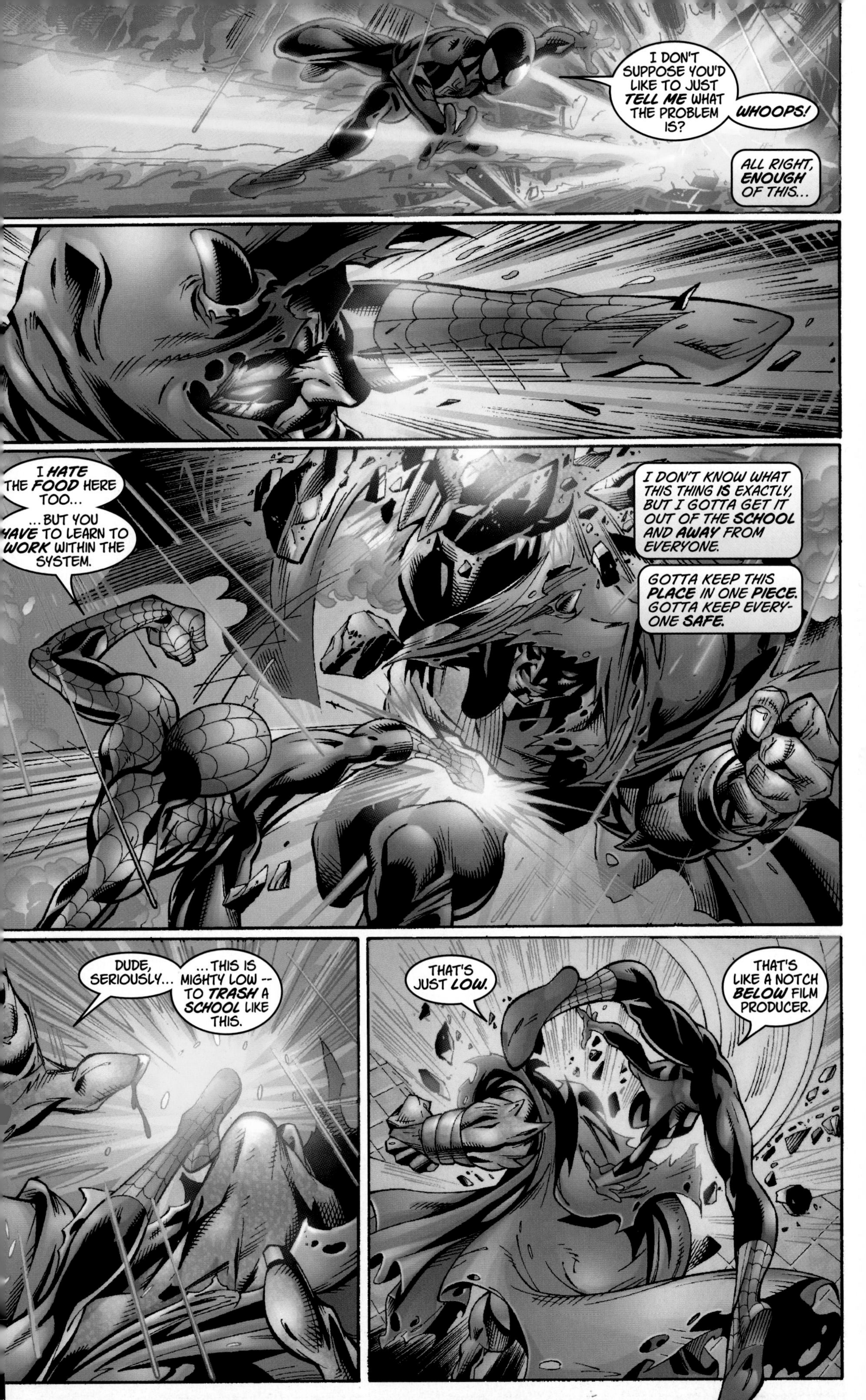

I DON'T SUPPOSE YOU'D LIKE TO JUST TELL ME WHAT THE PROBLEM IS?
WHOOPS!
ALL RIGHT, ENOUGH OF THIS...
I HATE THE FOOD HERE TOO...
...BUT YOU HAVE TO LEARN TO WORK WITHIN THE SYSTEM.
I DON'T KNOW WHAT THIS THING IS EXACTLY, BUT I GOTTA GET IT OUT OF THE SCHOOL AND AWAY FROM EVERYONE.
GOTTA KEEP THIS PLACE IN ONE PIECE. GOTTA KEEP EVERYONE SAFE.
DUDE, SERIOUSLY...
...THIS IS MIGHTY LOW -- TO TRASH A SCHOOL LIKE THIS.
THAT'S JUST LOW.
THAT'S LIKE A NOTCH BELOW FILM PRODUCER.

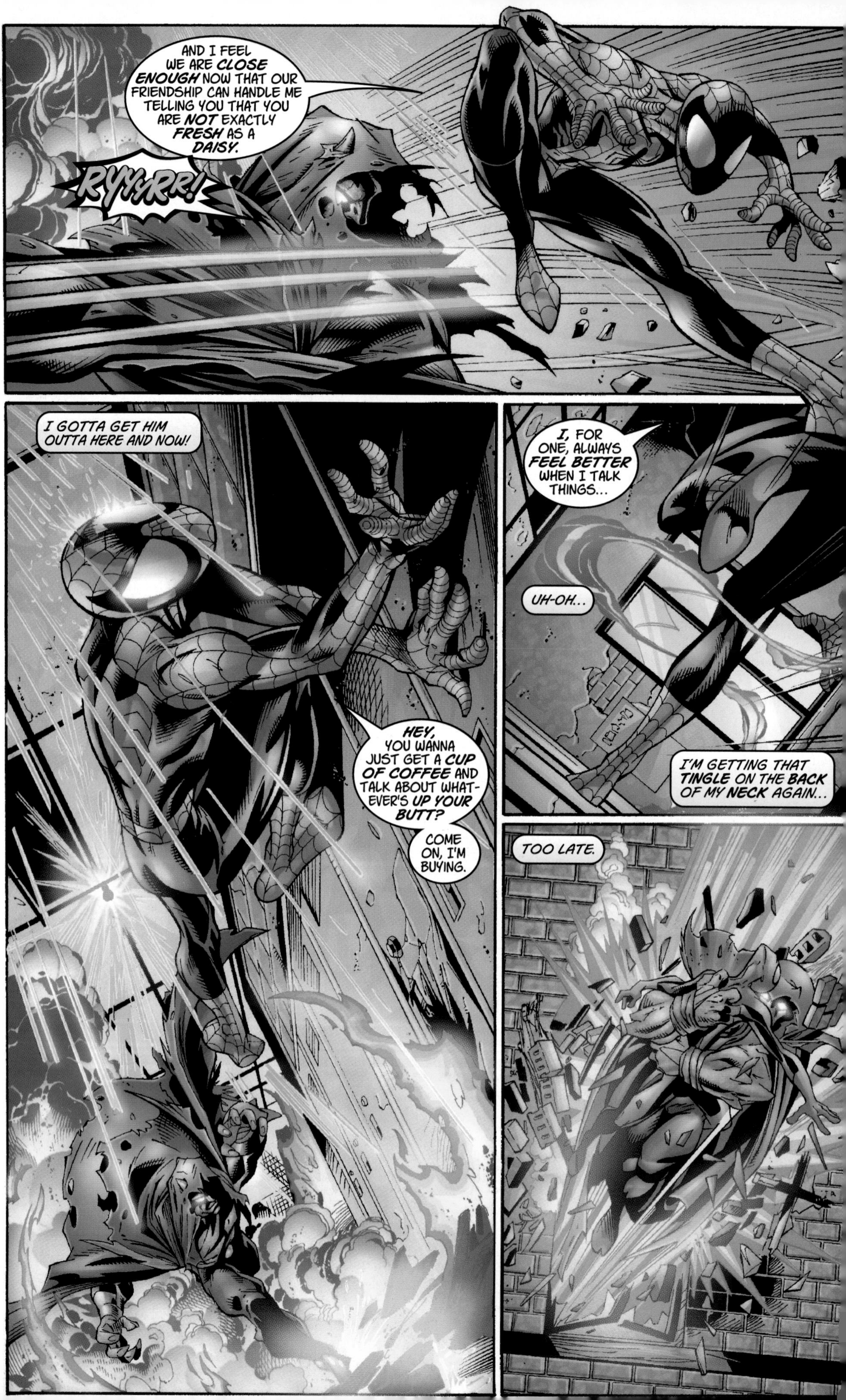
AND I FEEL WE ARE CLOSE ENOUGH NOW THAT OUR FRIENDSHIP CAN HANDLE ME TELLING YOU THAT YOU ARE NOT EXACTLY FRESH AS A DAISY.
RYYYRR!
I GOTTA GET HIM OUTTA HERE AND NOW!
HEY, YOU WANNA JUST GET A CUP OF COFFEE AND TALK ABOUT WHATEVER'S UP YOUR BUTT?
COME ON, I'M BUYING.
I, FOR ONE, ALWAYS FEEL BETTER WHEN I TALK THINGS...
UH-OH...
I'M GETTING THAT TINGLE ON THE BACK OF MY NECK AGAIN...
TOO LATE.

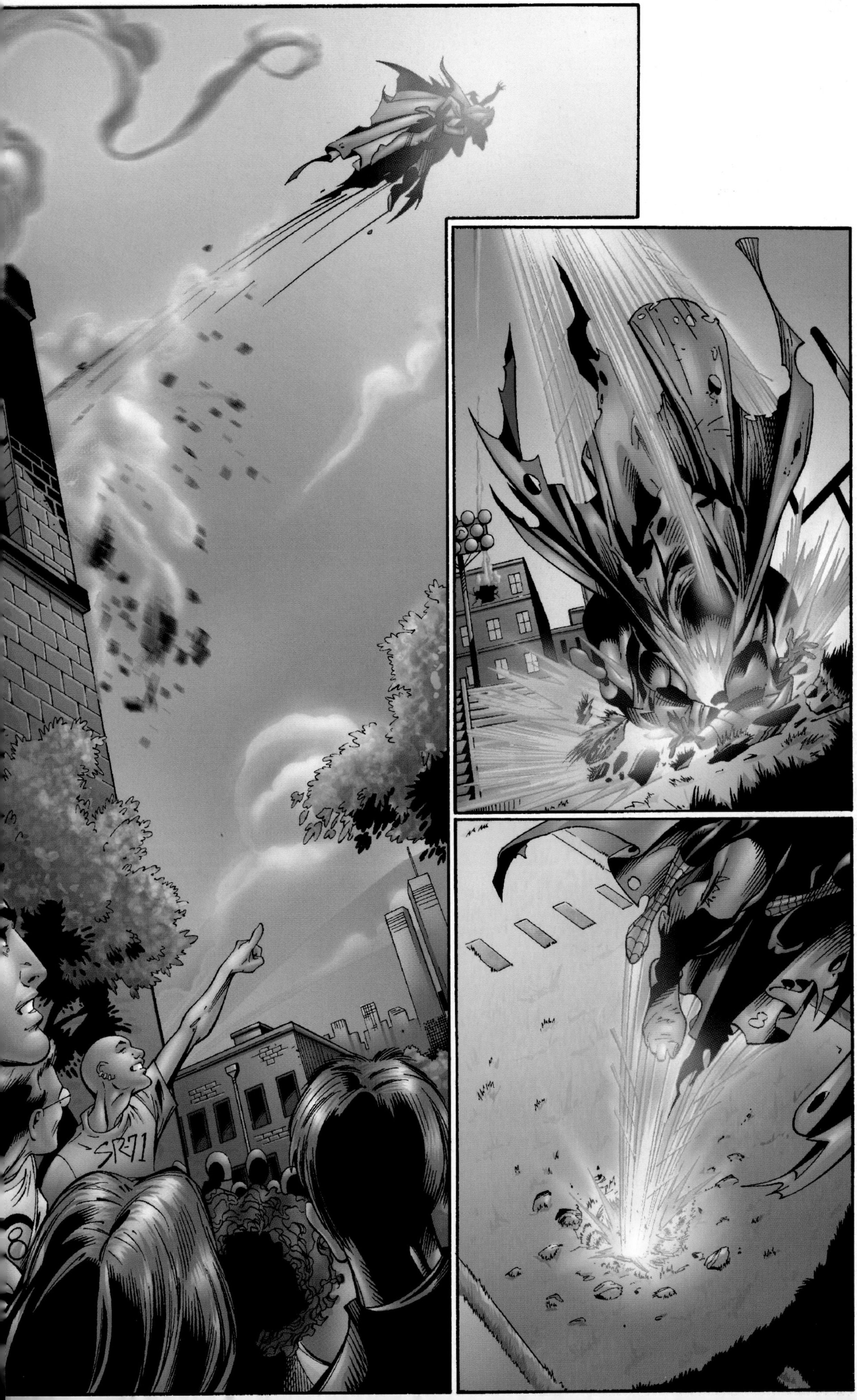
SR-71

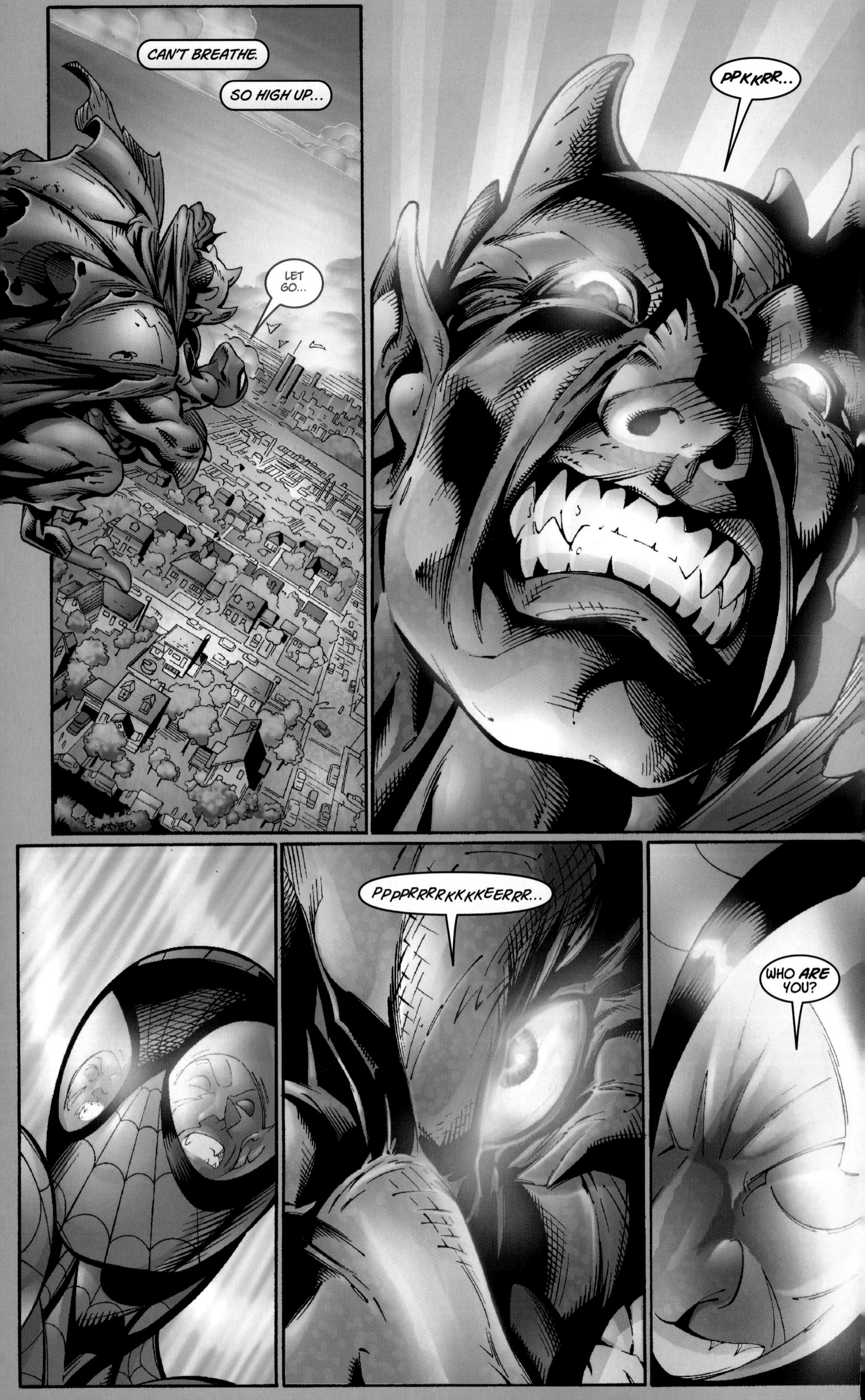
CAN'T BREATHE.
SO HIGH UP...
LET GO...
PPKKRR...
PPPPRRRRKKKKEERRR...
WHO ARE YOU?

TE S

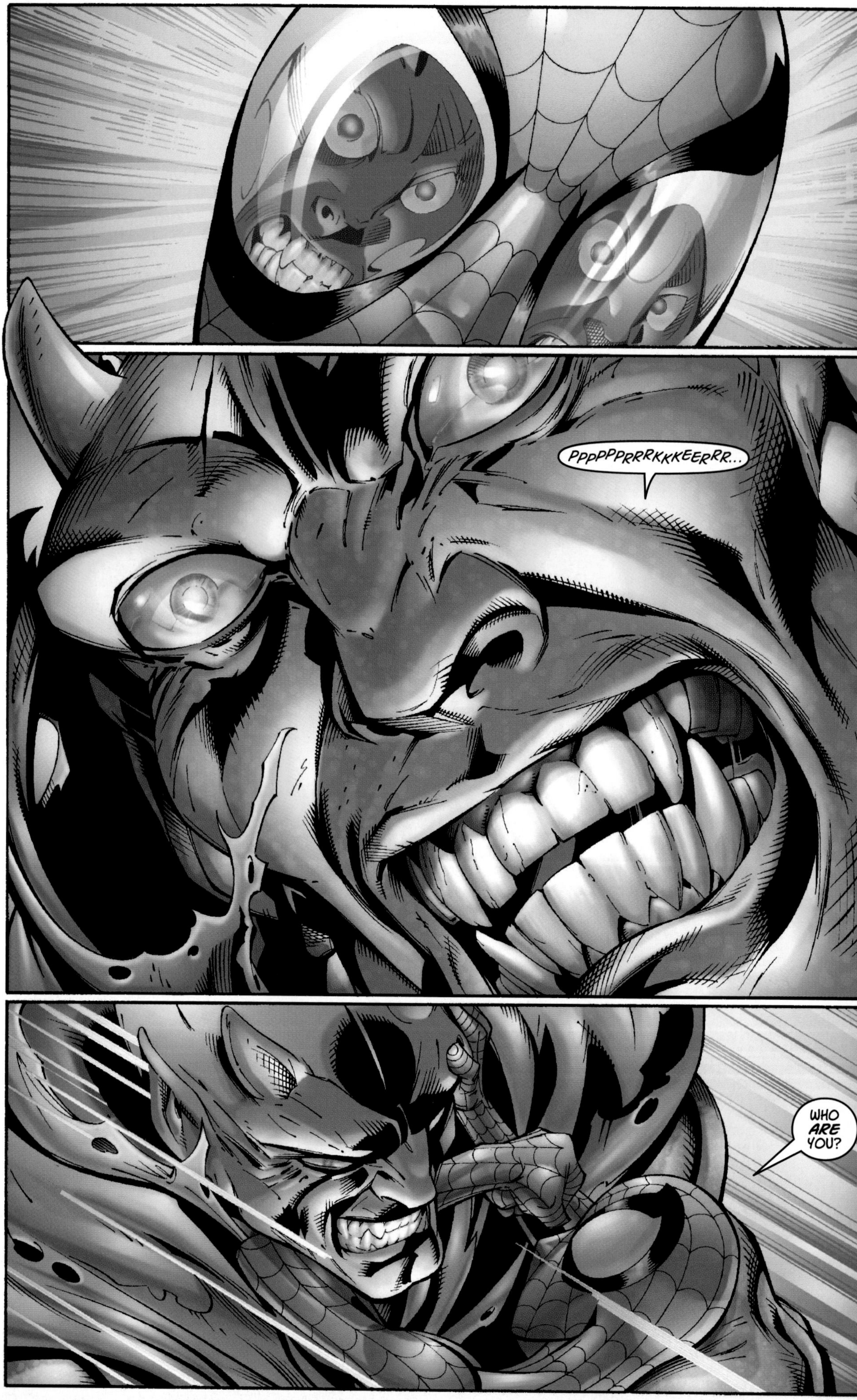
PPPPPPRRRKKKEERRR...
WHO ARE YOU?

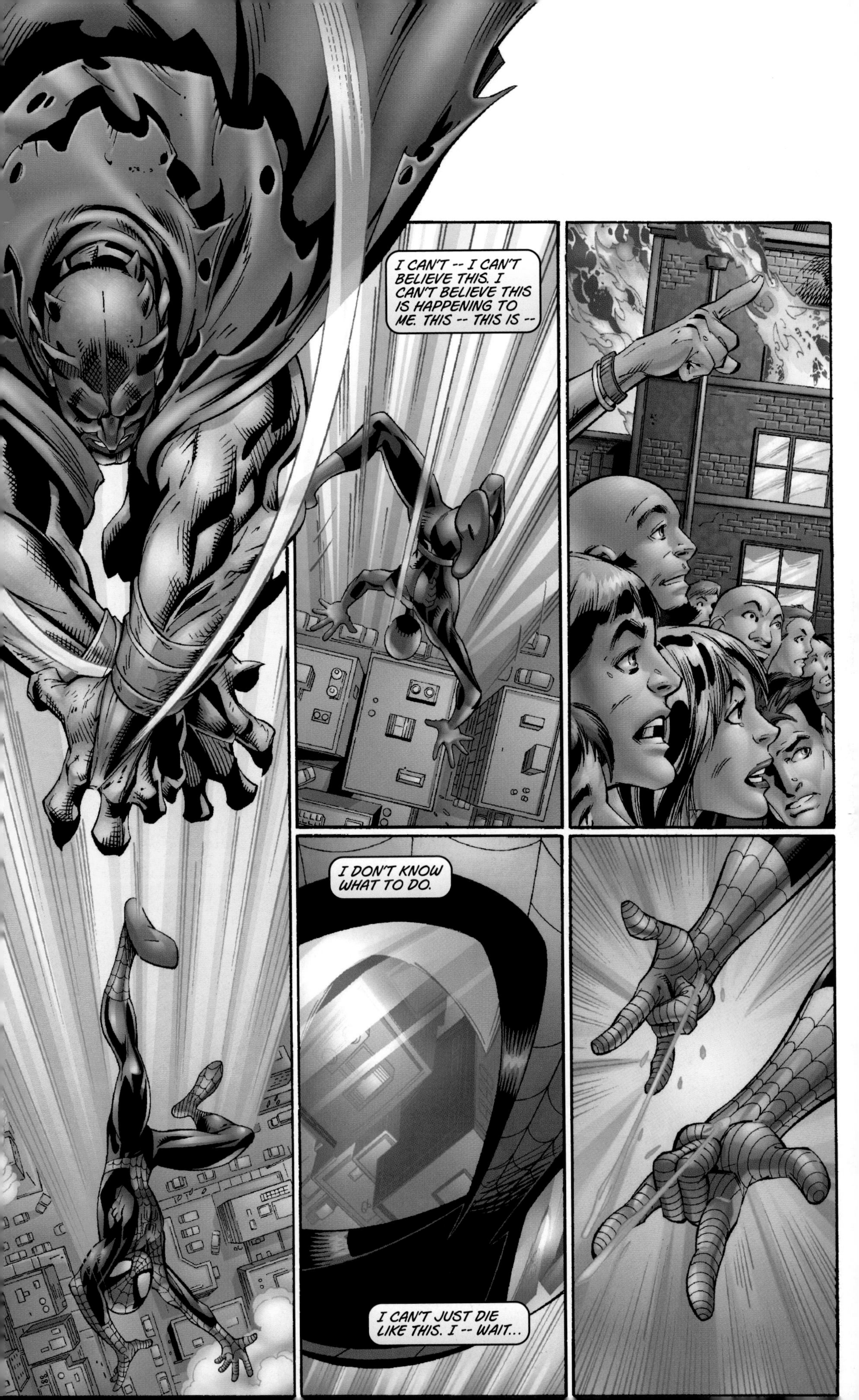
I CAN'T -- I CAN'T BELIEVE THIS. I CAN'T BELIEVE THIS IS HAPPENING TO ME. THIS -- THIS IS --
I DON'T KNOW WHAT TO DO.
I CAN'T JUST DIE LIKE THIS. I -- WAIT...

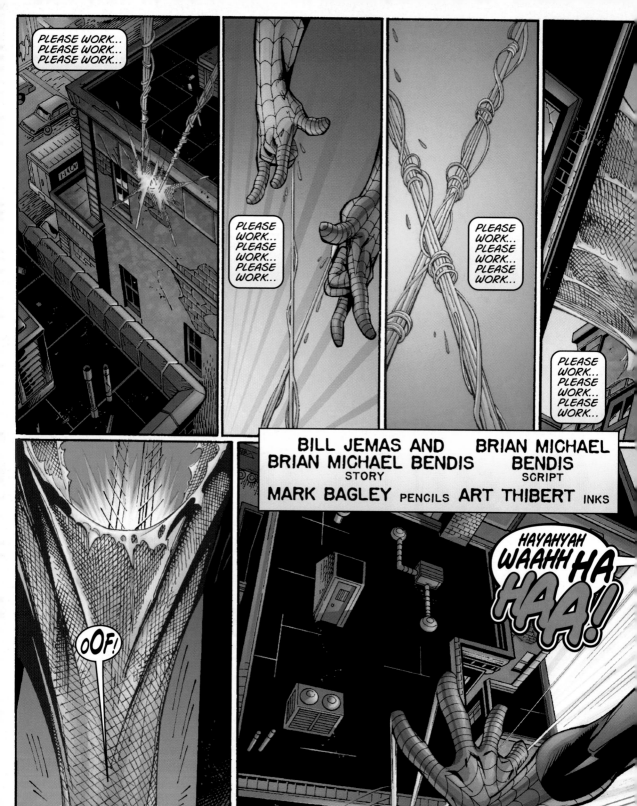

PLEASE WORK...
PLEASE WORK...
PLEASE WORK...

PLEASE WORK...
PLEASE WORK...
PLEASE WORK...

PLEASE WORK...
PLEASE WORK...
PLEASE WORK...

PLEASE WORK...
PLEASE WORK...
PLEASE WORK...

BILL JEMAS AND BRIAN MICHAEL BENDIS STORY
BRIAN MICHAEL BENDIS SCRIPT
MARK BAGLEY PENCILS ART THIBERT INKS

oOF!

HAYAHYAH WAAHH HA HAA!

RS & COMICRAFT'S ALBERT DESCHESNE LETTERS
JC COLORS BRIAN SMITH ASSISTANT EDITOR
RALPH MACCHIO EDITOR JOE QUESADA EDITOR IN CHIEF

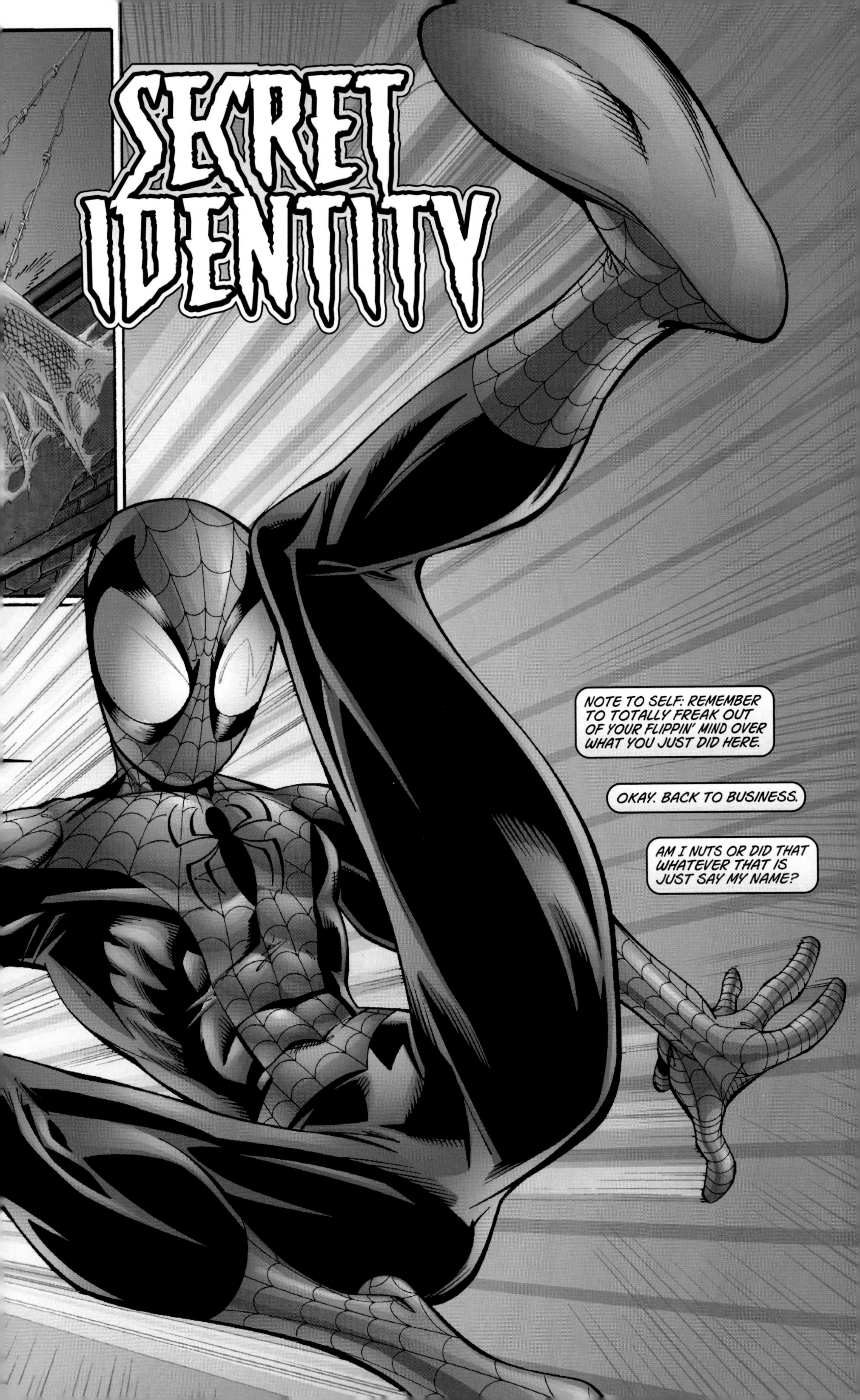
SECRET IDENTITY
NOTE TO SELF: REMEMBER TO TOTALLY FREAK OUT OF YOUR FLIPPIN' MIND OVER WHAT YOU JUST DID HERE.
OKAY. BACK TO BUSINESS.
AM I NUTS OR DID THAT WHATEVER THAT IS JUST SAY MY NAME?

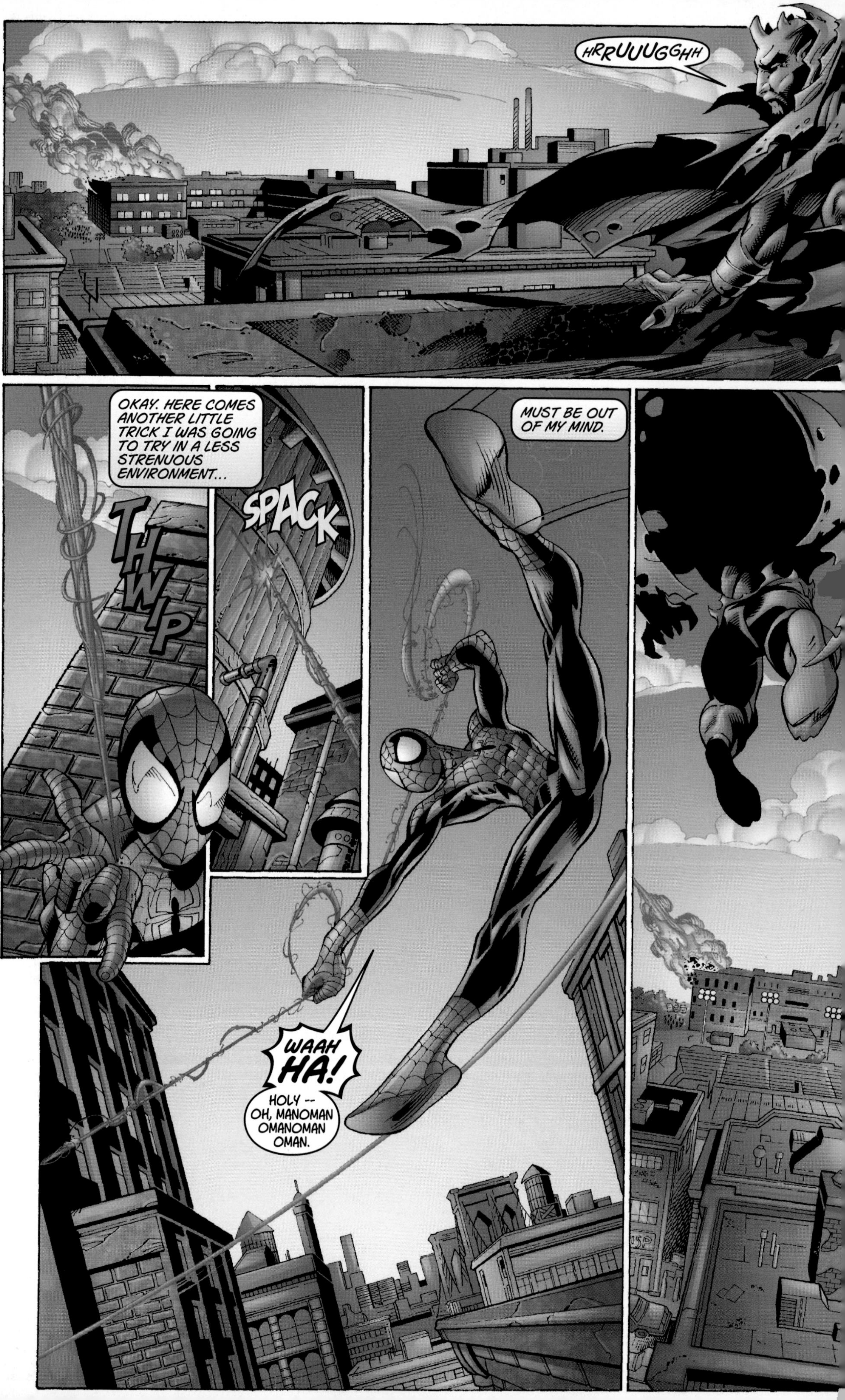
HRRUUUGGHH
OKAY. HERE COMES ANOTHER LITTLE TRICK I WAS GOING TO TRY IN A LESS STRENUOUS ENVIRONMENT...
THWIP
SPACK
MUST BE OUT OF MY MIND.
WAAH HA!
HOLY -- OH, MANOMAN OMANOMAN OMAN.

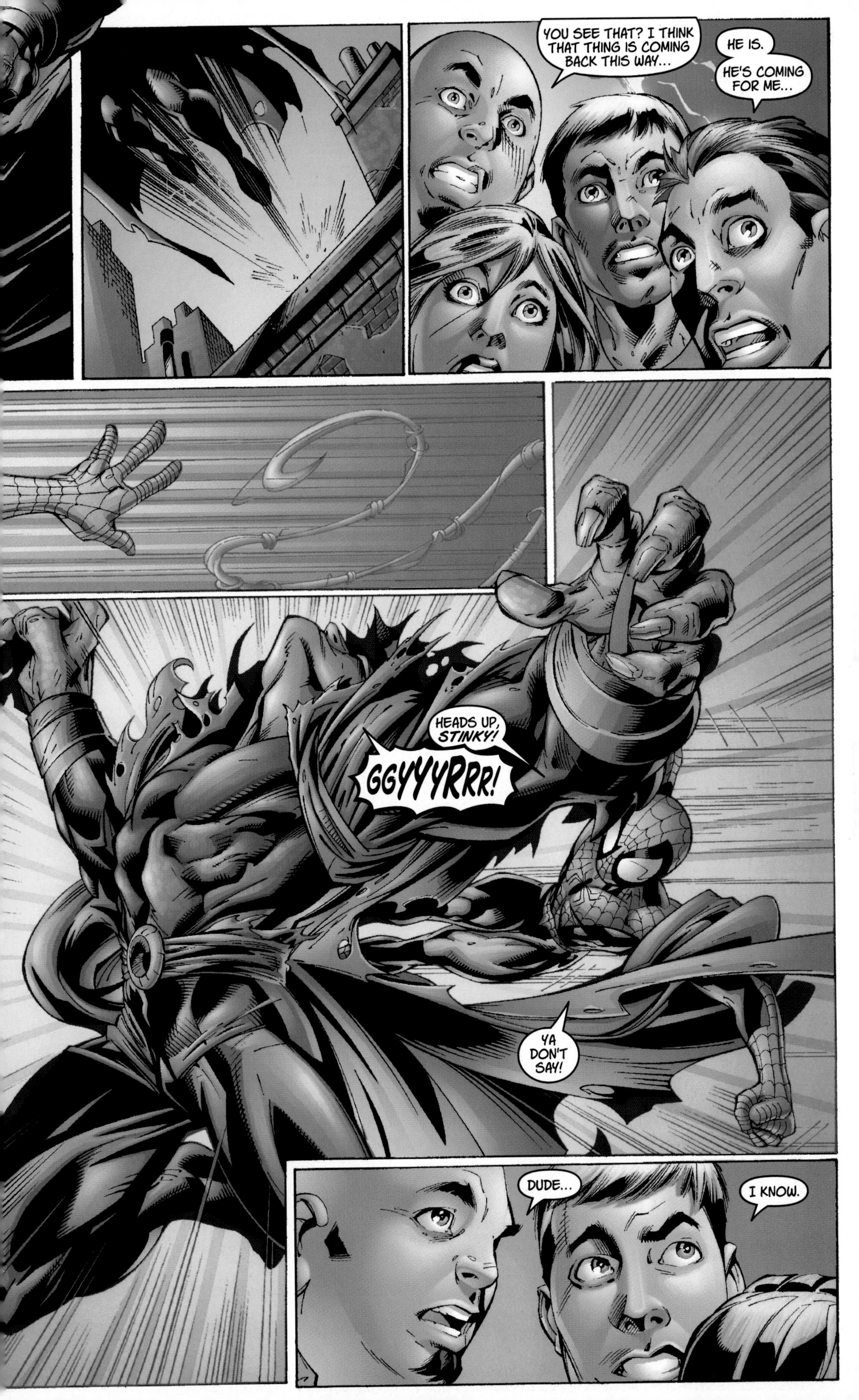
YOU SEE THAT? I THINK THAT THING IS COMING BACK THIS WAY...
HE IS.
HE'S COMING FOR ME...
HEADS UP, STINKY!
GGYYYRRR!
YA DON'T SAY!
DUDE...
I KNOW.

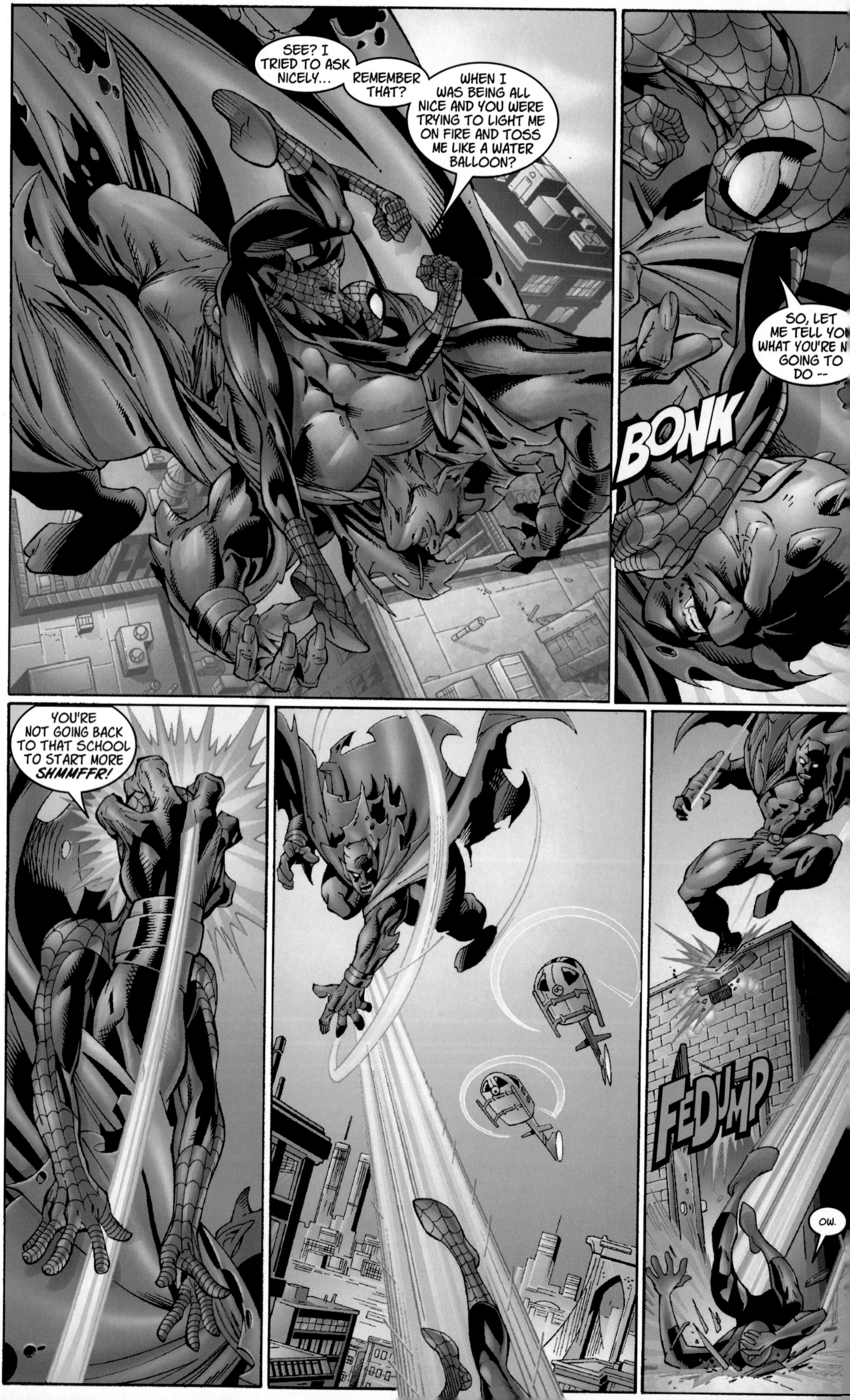

SEE? I TRIED TO ASK NICELY...
REMEMBER THAT?
WHEN I WAS BEING ALL NICE AND YOU WERE TRYING TO LIGHT ME ON FIRE AND TOSS ME LIKE A WATER BALLOON?
SO, LET ME TELL YO WHAT YOU'RE N GOING TO DO --
BONK
YOU'RE NOT GOING BACK TO THAT SCHOOL TO START MORE *SHMMFFR!*
FEDUMP
OW.

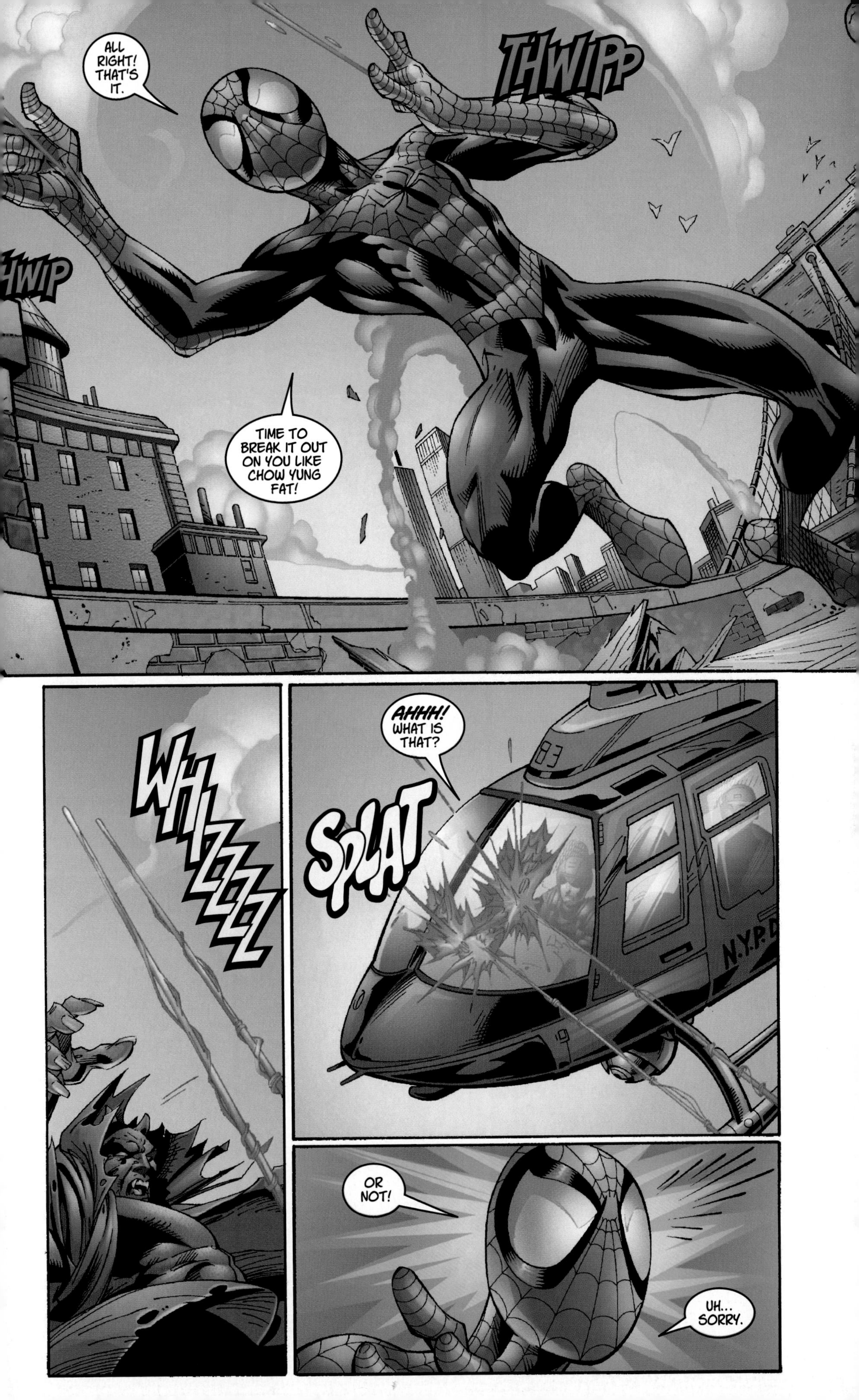
ALL RIGHT! THAT'S IT.
THWIPP
THWIP
TIME TO BREAK IT OUT ON YOU LIKE CHOW YUNG FAT!
WHIZZZZZ
AHHH! WHAT IS THAT?
SPLAT
N.Y.P.D.
OR NOT!
UH... SORRY.

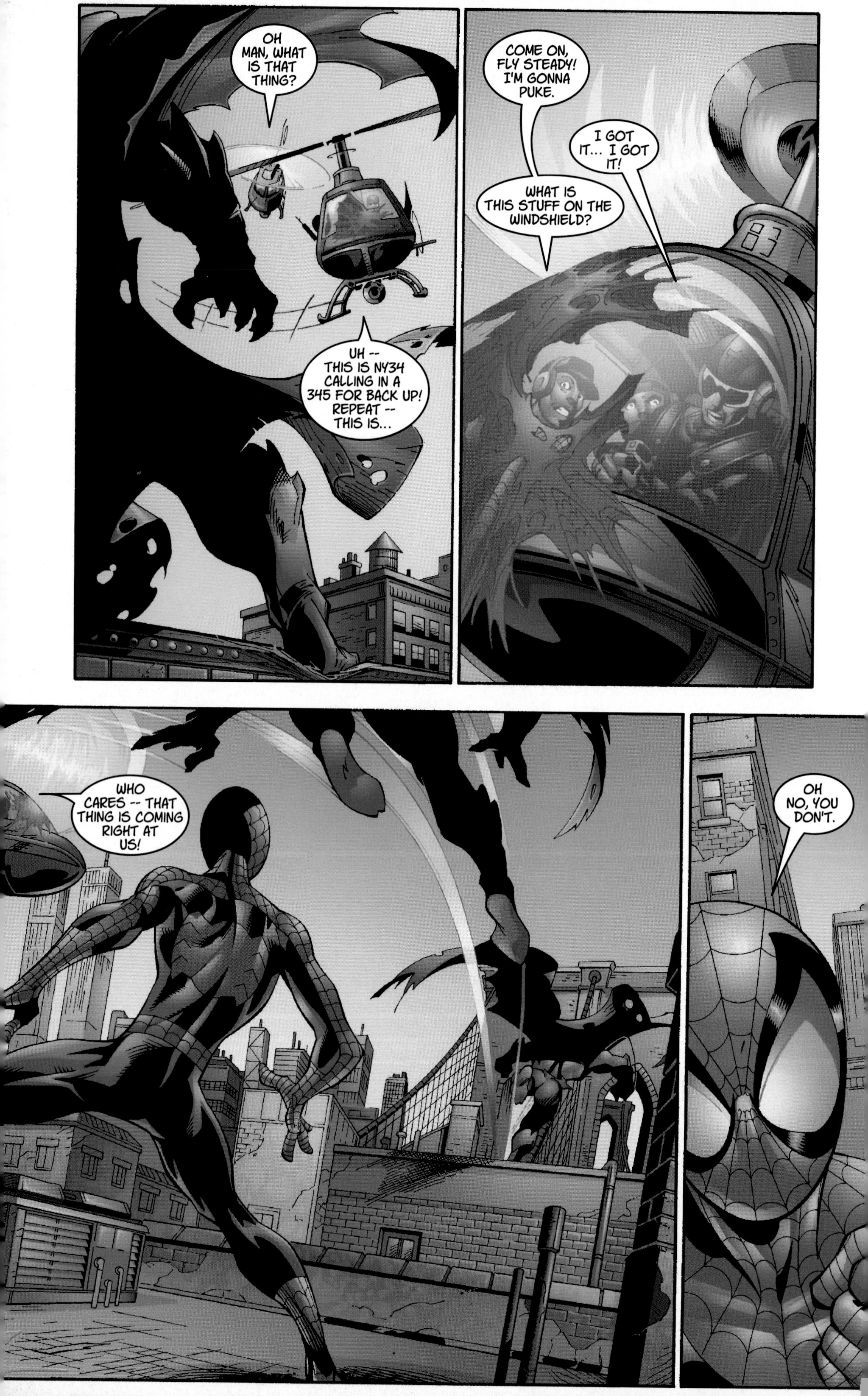
OH MAN, WHAT IS THAT THING?
UH -- THIS IS NY34 CALLING IN A 345 FOR BACK UP! REPEAT -- THIS IS...
COME ON, FLY STEADY! I'M GONNA PUKE.
WHAT IS THIS STUFF ON THE WINDSHIELD?
I GOT IT... I GOT IT!
WHO CARES -- THAT THING IS COMING RIGHT AT US!
OH NO, YOU DON'T.

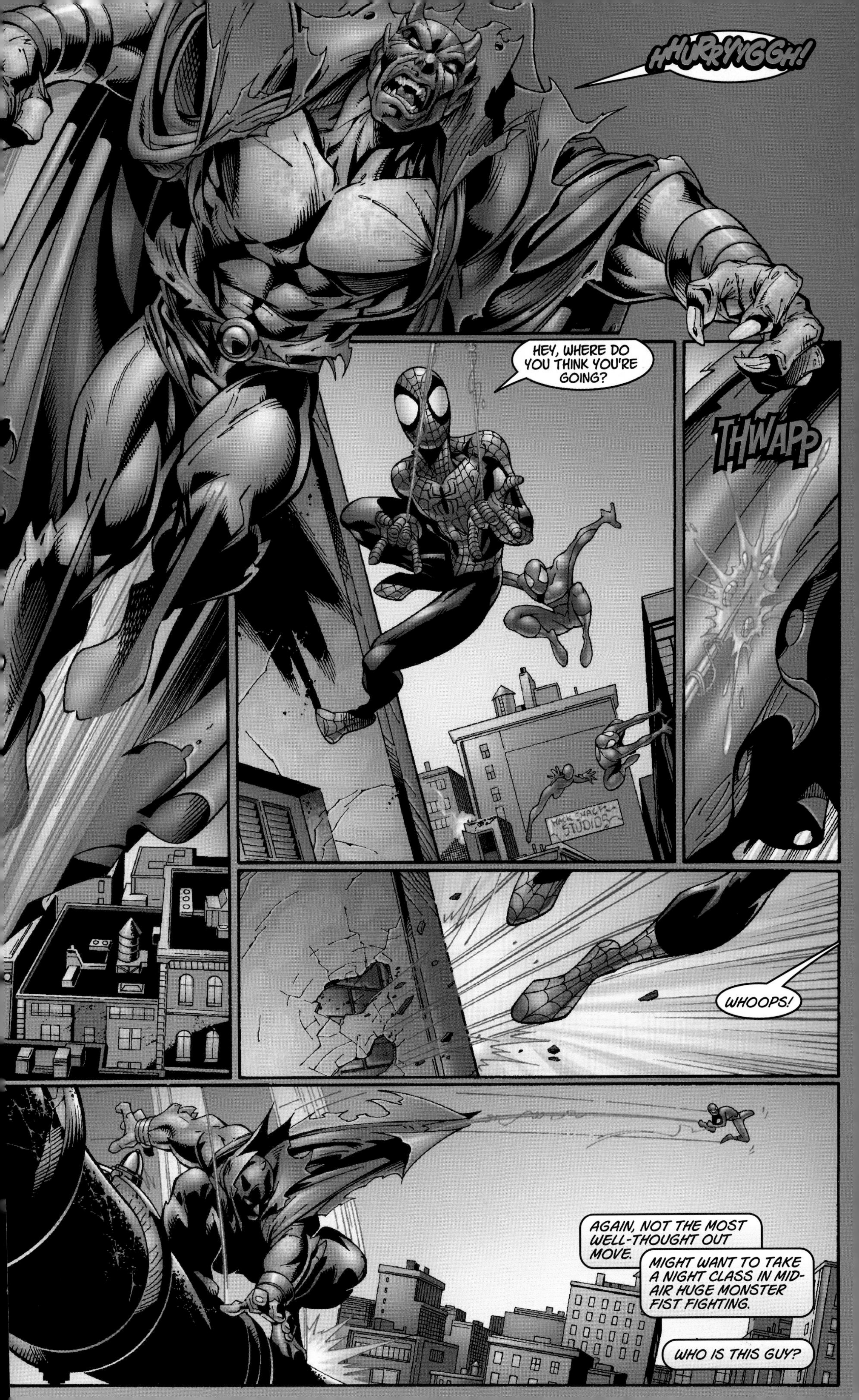
HHURRYYGGH!
HEY, WHERE DO YOU THINK YOU'RE GOING?
THWAPP
HACK SHACK STUDIOS
WHOOPS!
AGAIN, NOT THE MOST WELL-THOUGHT OUT MOVE.
MIGHT WANT TO TAKE A NIGHT CLASS IN MID-AIR HUGE MONSTER FIST FIGHTING.
WHO IS THIS GUY?

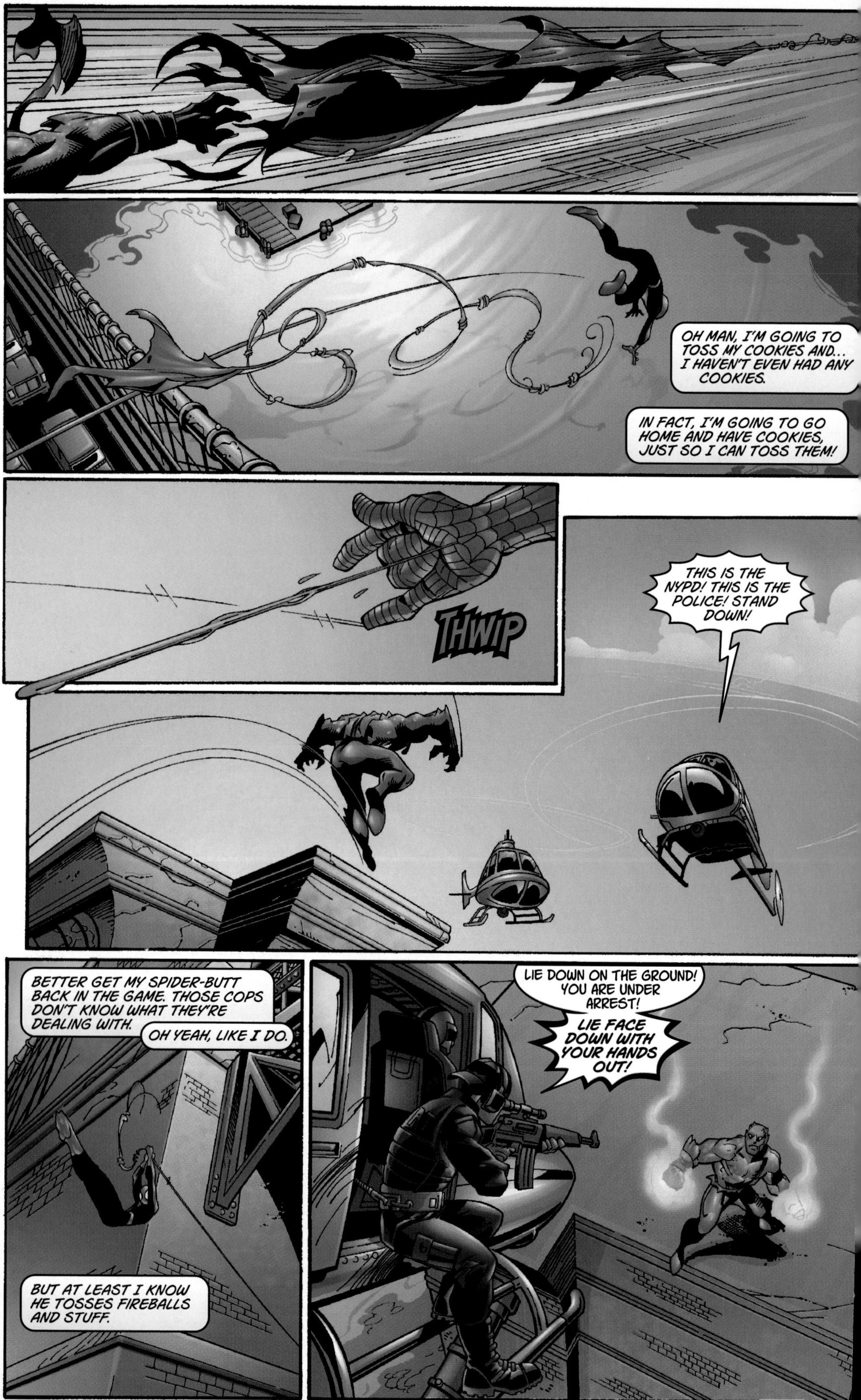

OH MAN, I'M GOING TO TOSS MY COOKIES AND... I HAVEN'T EVEN HAD ANY COOKIES.
IN FACT, I'M GOING TO GO HOME AND HAVE COOKIES, JUST SO I CAN TOSS THEM!
THWIP
THIS IS THE NYPD! THIS IS THE POLICE! STAND DOWN!
BETTER GET MY SPIDER-BUTT BACK IN THE GAME. THOSE COPS DON'T KNOW WHAT THEY'RE DEALING WITH.
OH YEAH, LIKE I DO.
BUT AT LEAST I KNOW HE TOSSES FIREBALLS AND STUFF.
LIE DOWN ON THE GROUND! YOU ARE UNDER ARREST!
LIE FACE DOWN WITH YOUR HANDS OUT!

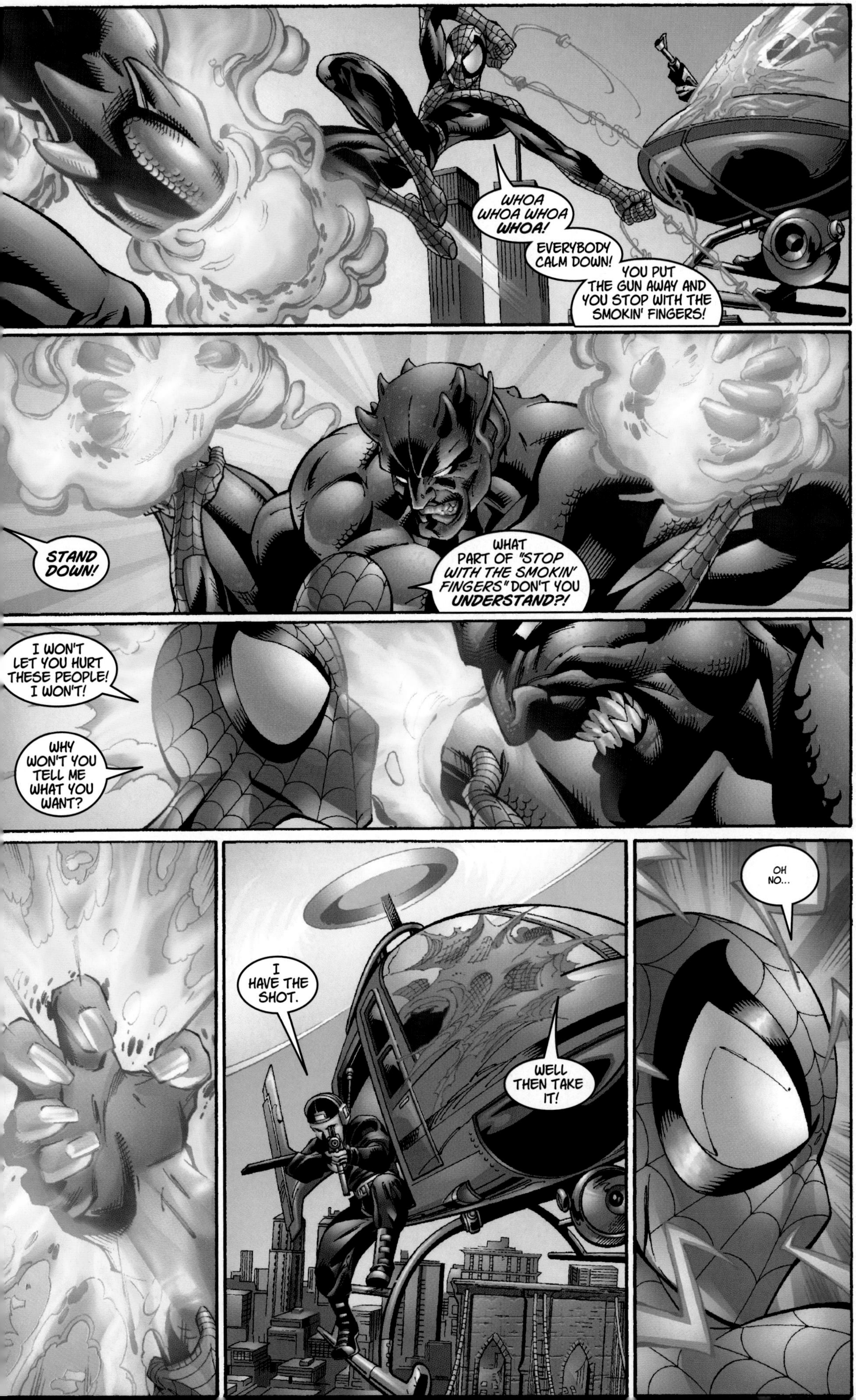
WHOA WHOA WHOA WHOA!
EVERYBODY CALM DOWN!
YOU PUT THE GUN AWAY AND YOU STOP WITH THE SMOKIN' FINGERS!
STAND DOWN!
WHAT PART OF "STOP WITH THE SMOKIN' FINGERS" DON'T YOU UNDERSTAND?!
I WON'T LET YOU HURT THESE PEOPLE! I WON'T!
WHY WON'T YOU TELL ME WHAT YOU WANT?
I HAVE THE SHOT.
WELL THEN TAKE IT!
OH NO...

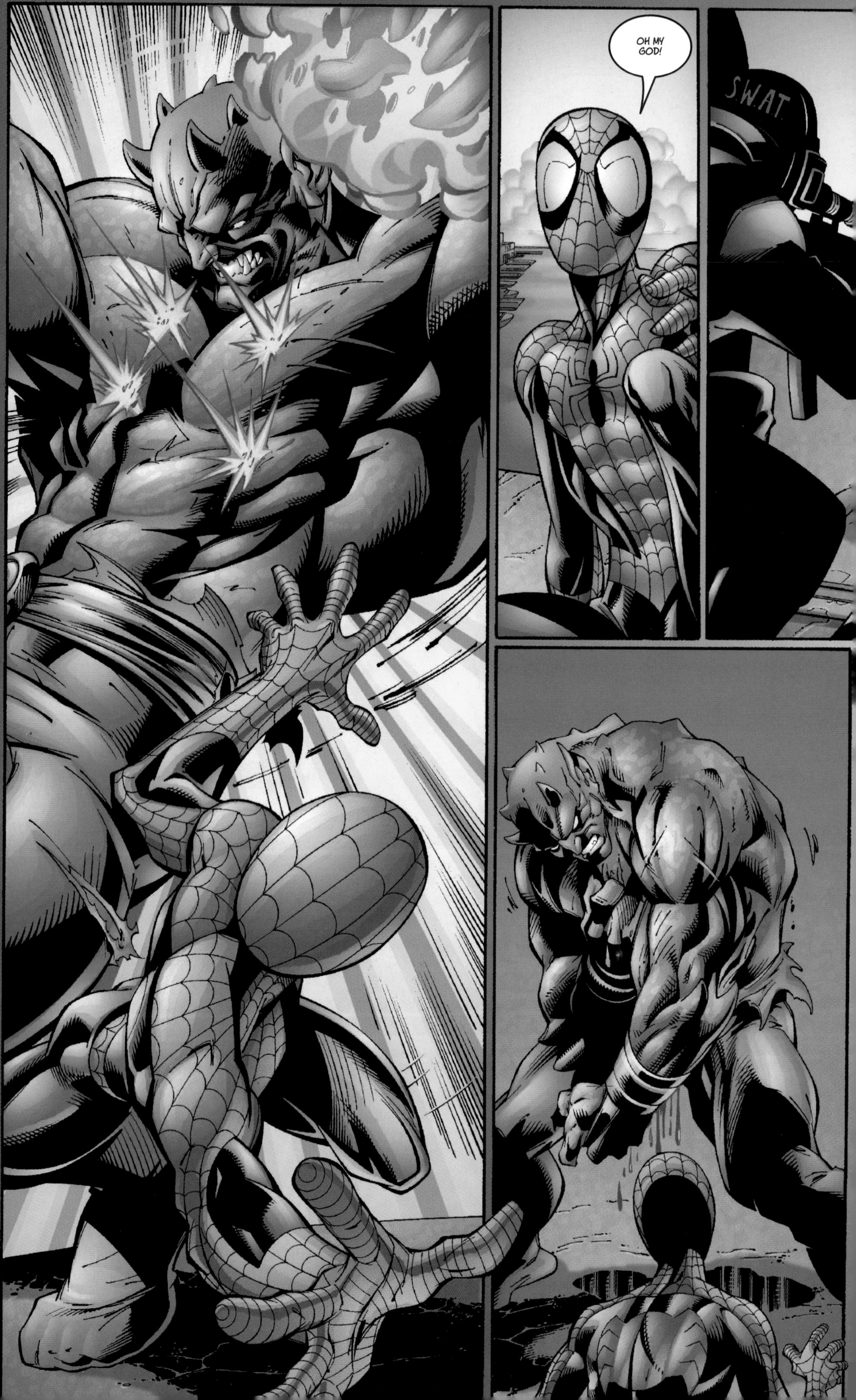
OH MY GOD!
S.W.A.T.

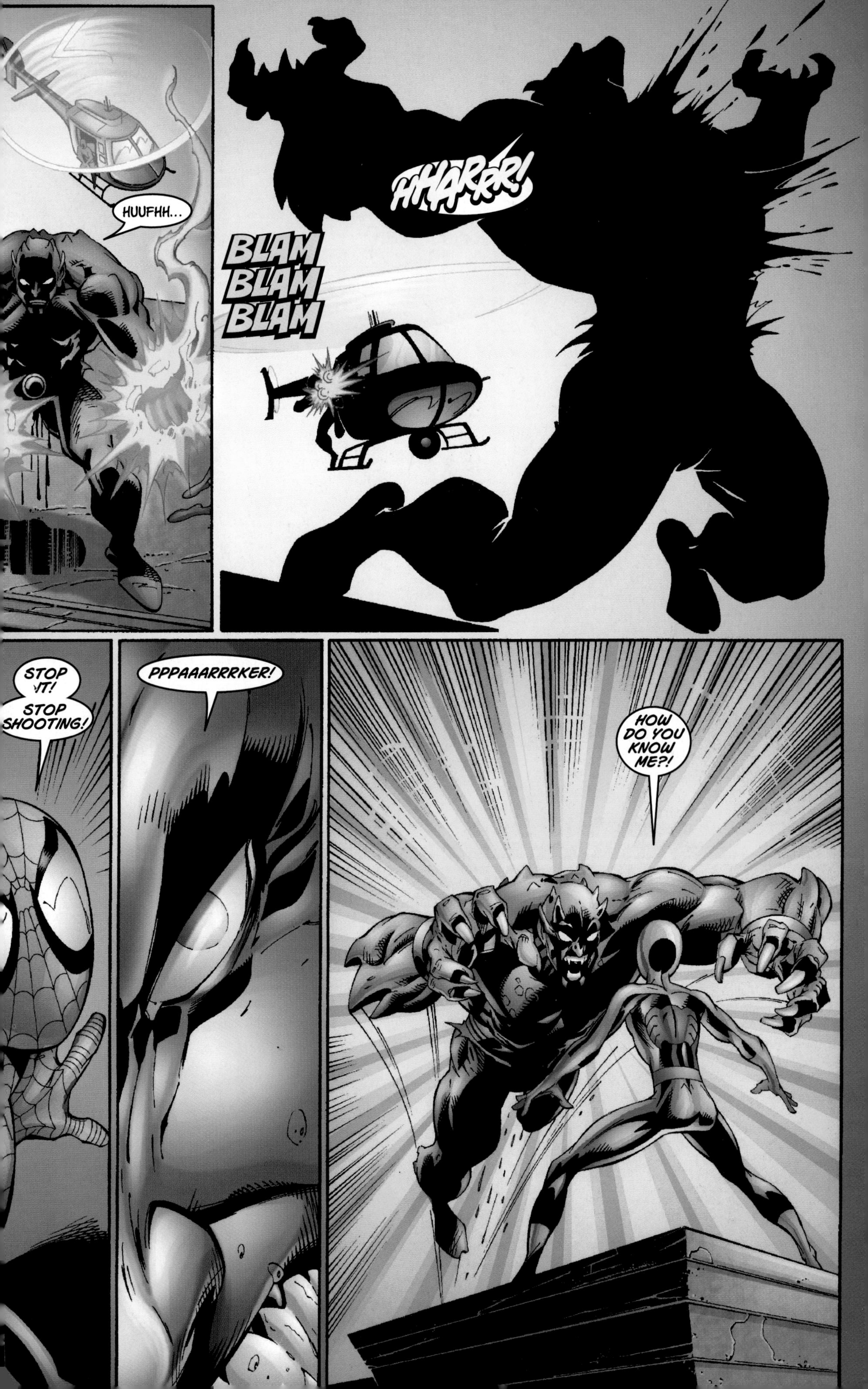
HUUFHH...
HHARRR!
BLAM
BLAM
BLAM
STOP IT! STOP SHOOTING!
PPPAAARRRKER!
HOW DO YOU KNOW ME?!

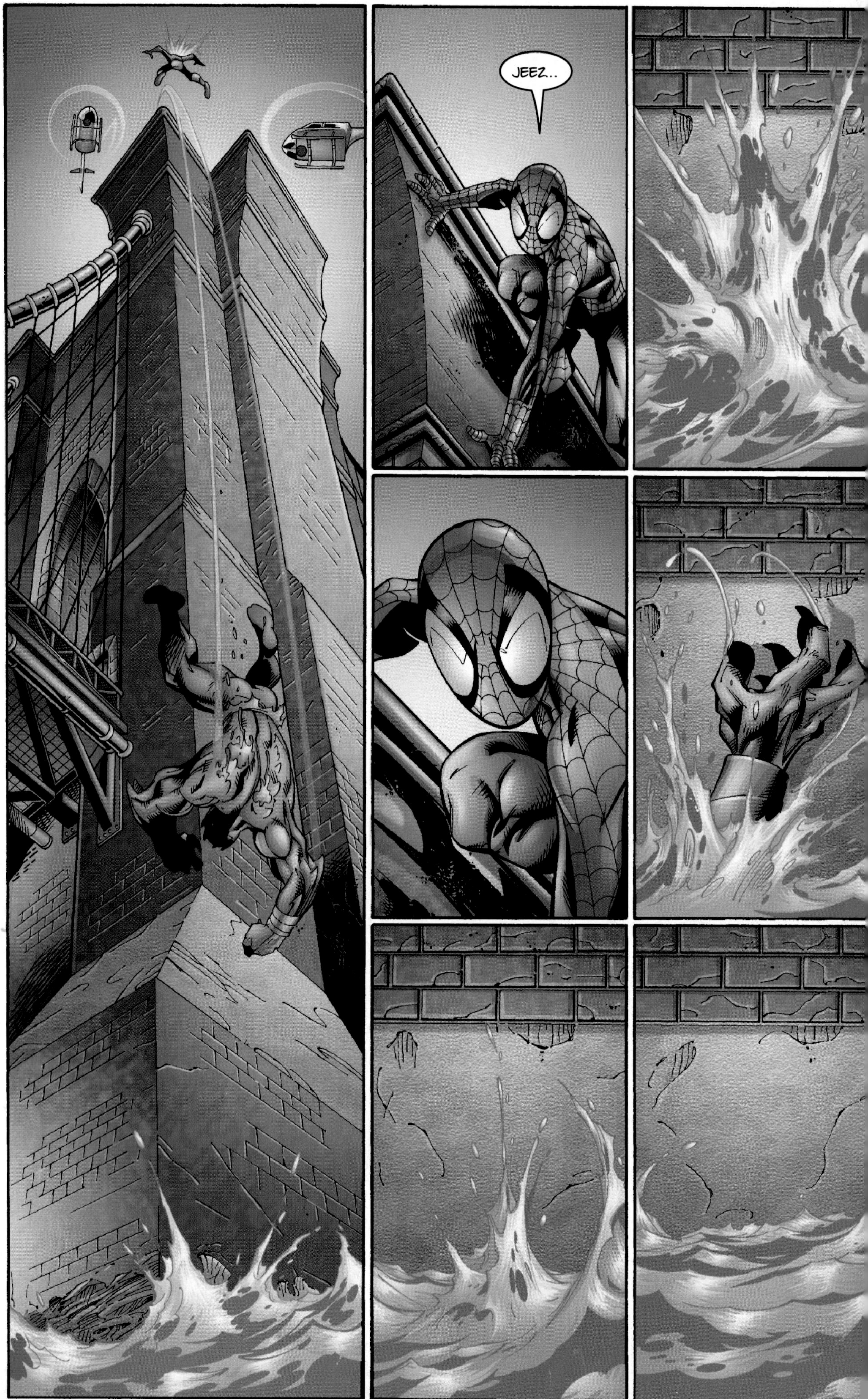
JEEZ...

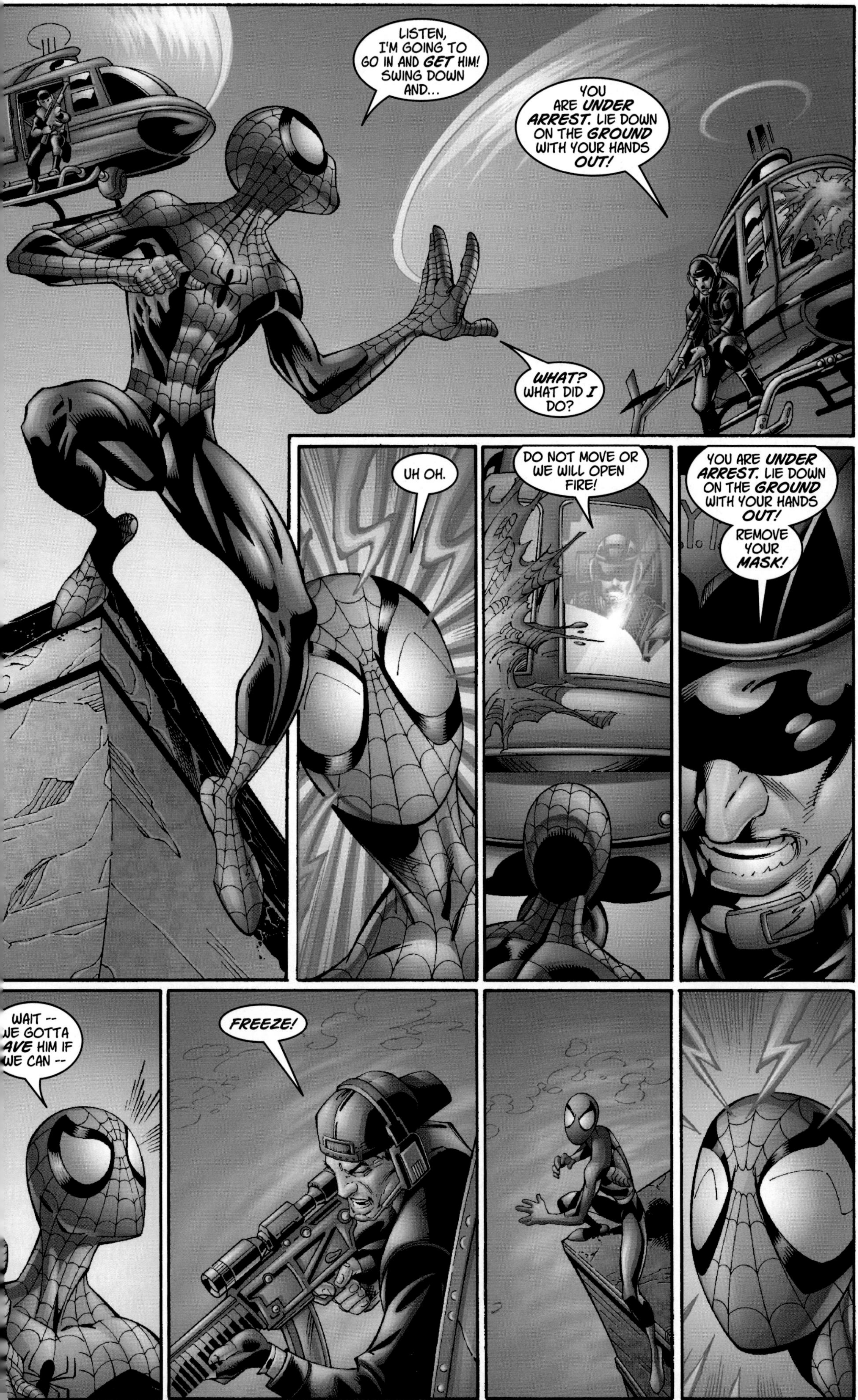
LISTEN, I'M GOING TO GO IN AND GET HIM! SWING DOWN AND...
YOU ARE UNDER ARREST. LIE DOWN ON THE GROUND WITH YOUR HANDS OUT!
WHAT? WHAT DID I DO?
UH OH.
DO NOT MOVE OR WE WILL OPEN FIRE!
YOU ARE UNDER ARREST. LIE DOWN ON THE GROUND WITH YOUR HANDS OUT!
REMOVE YOUR MASK!
WAIT -- WE GOTTA SAVE HIM IF WE CAN --
FREEZE!

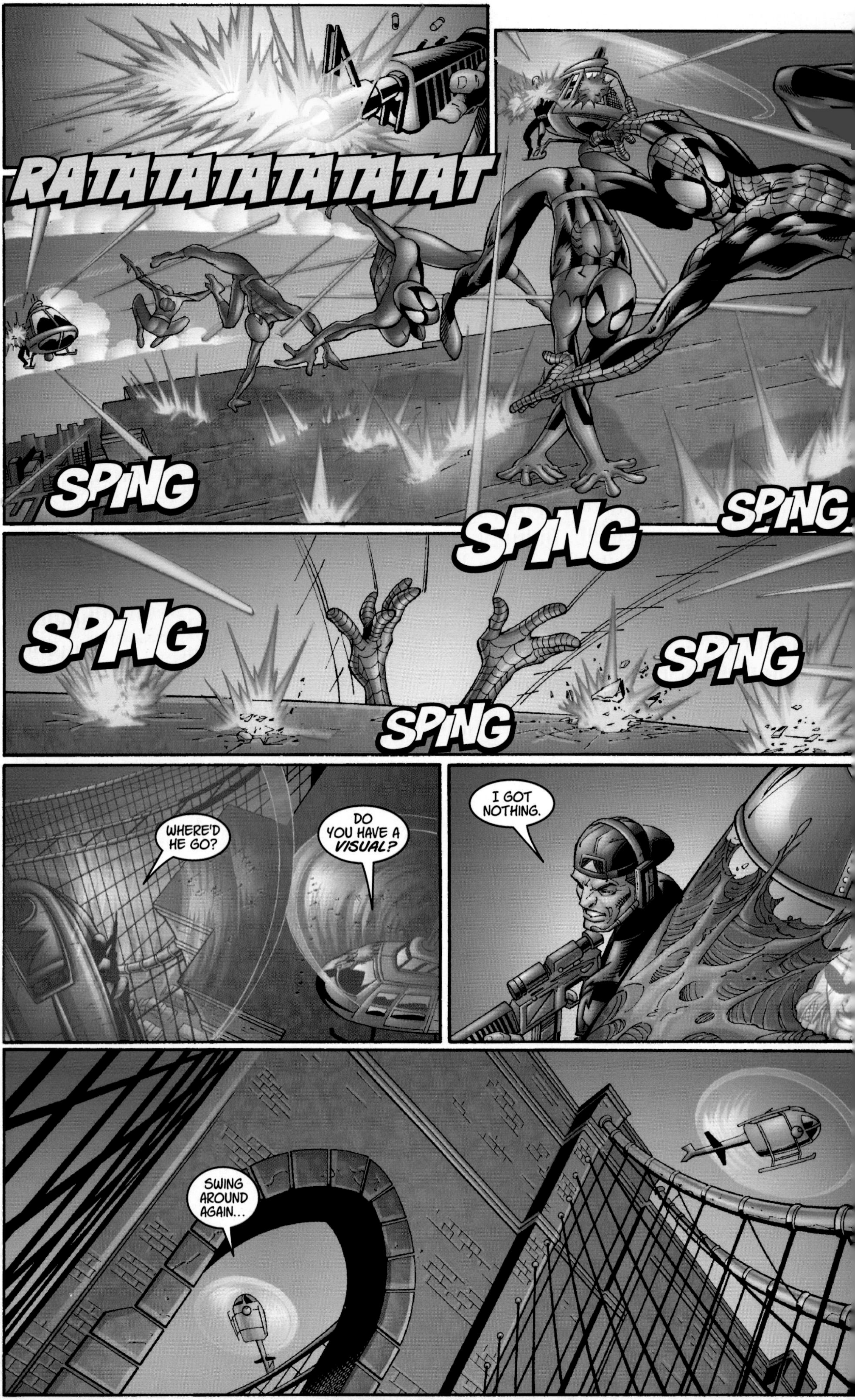
RATATATATATATATAT
SPING
SPING
SPING
SPING
SPING
SPING
WHERE'D HE GO?
DO YOU HAVE A *VISUAL?*
I GOT NOTHING.
SWING AROUND AGAIN...

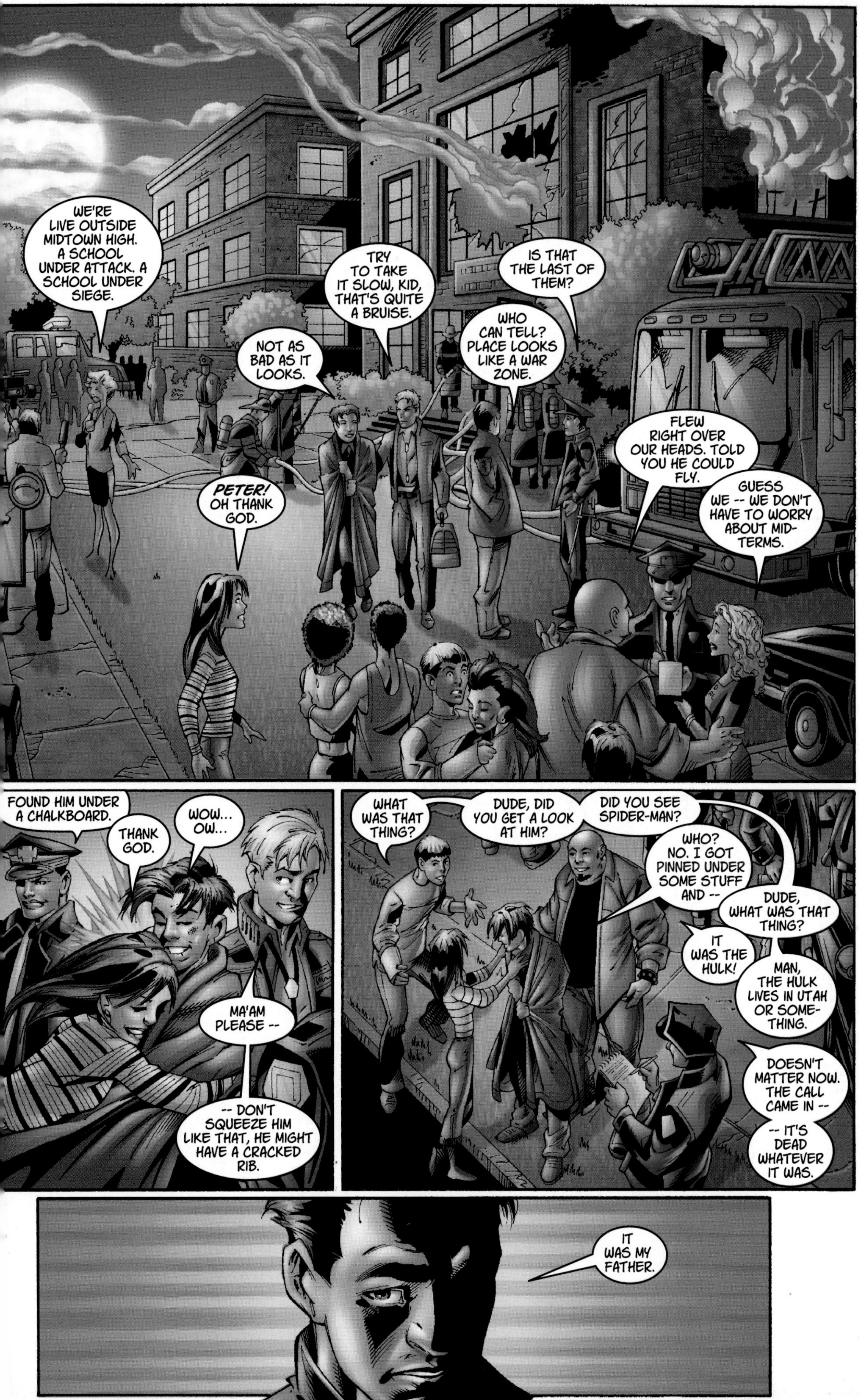
WE'RE LIVE OUTSIDE MIDTOWN HIGH. A SCHOOL UNDER ATTACK. A SCHOOL UNDER SIEGE.
TRY TO TAKE IT SLOW, KID, THAT'S QUITE A BRUISE.
NOT AS BAD AS IT LOOKS.
IS THAT THE LAST OF THEM?
WHO CAN TELL? PLACE LOOKS LIKE A WAR ZONE.
PETER! OH THANK GOD.
FLEW RIGHT OVER OUR HEADS. TOLD YOU HE COULD FLY.
GUESS WE -- WE DON'T HAVE TO WORRY ABOUT MID-TERMS.
FOUND HIM UNDER A CHALKBOARD.
THANK GOD.
WOW... OW...
MA'AM PLEASE --
-- DON'T SQUEEZE HIM LIKE THAT, HE MIGHT HAVE A CRACKED RIB.
WHAT WAS THAT THING?
DUDE, DID YOU GET A LOOK AT HIM?
DID YOU SEE SPIDER-MAN?
WHO? NO. I GOT PINNED UNDER SOME STUFF AND --
DUDE, WHAT WAS THAT THING?
IT WAS THE HULK!
MAN, THE HULK LIVES IN UTAH OR SOME-THING.
DOESN'T MATTER NOW. THE CALL CAME IN --
-- IT'S DEAD WHATEVER IT WAS.
IT WAS MY FATHER.

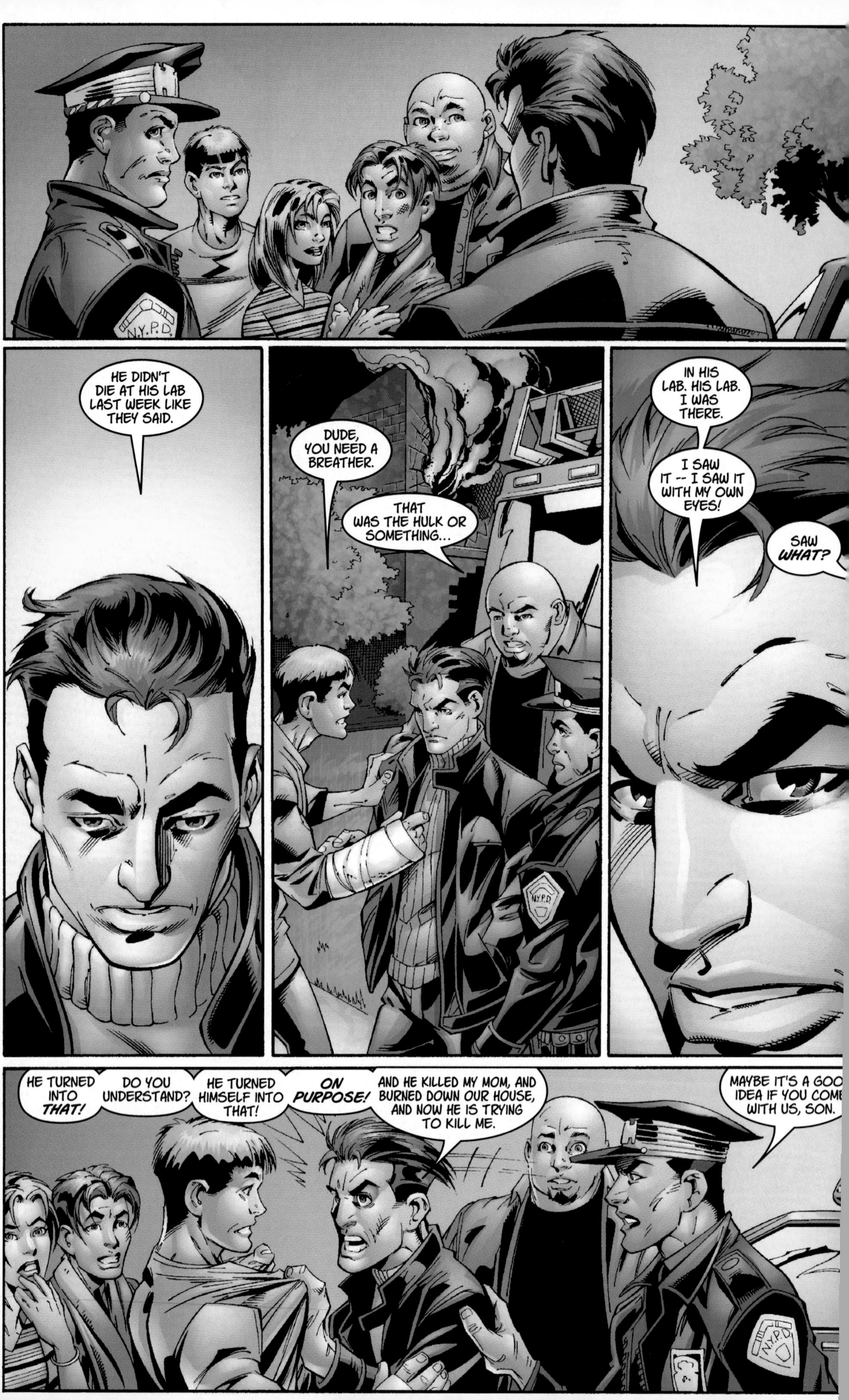
HE DIDN'T DIE AT HIS LAB LAST WEEK LIKE THEY SAID.
DUDE, YOU NEED A BREATHER.
THAT WAS THE HULK OR SOMETHING...
IN HIS LAB. HIS LAB. I WAS THERE.
I SAW IT -- I SAW IT WITH MY OWN EYES!
SAW *WHAT?*
HE TURNED INTO *THAT!*
DO YOU UNDERSTAND?
HE TURNED HIMSELF INTO THAT!
ON PURPOSE!
AND HE KILLED MY MOM, AND BURNED DOWN OUR HOUSE, AND NOW HE IS TRYING TO KILL ME.
MAYBE IT'S A GOO IDEA IF YOU COME WITH US, SON.

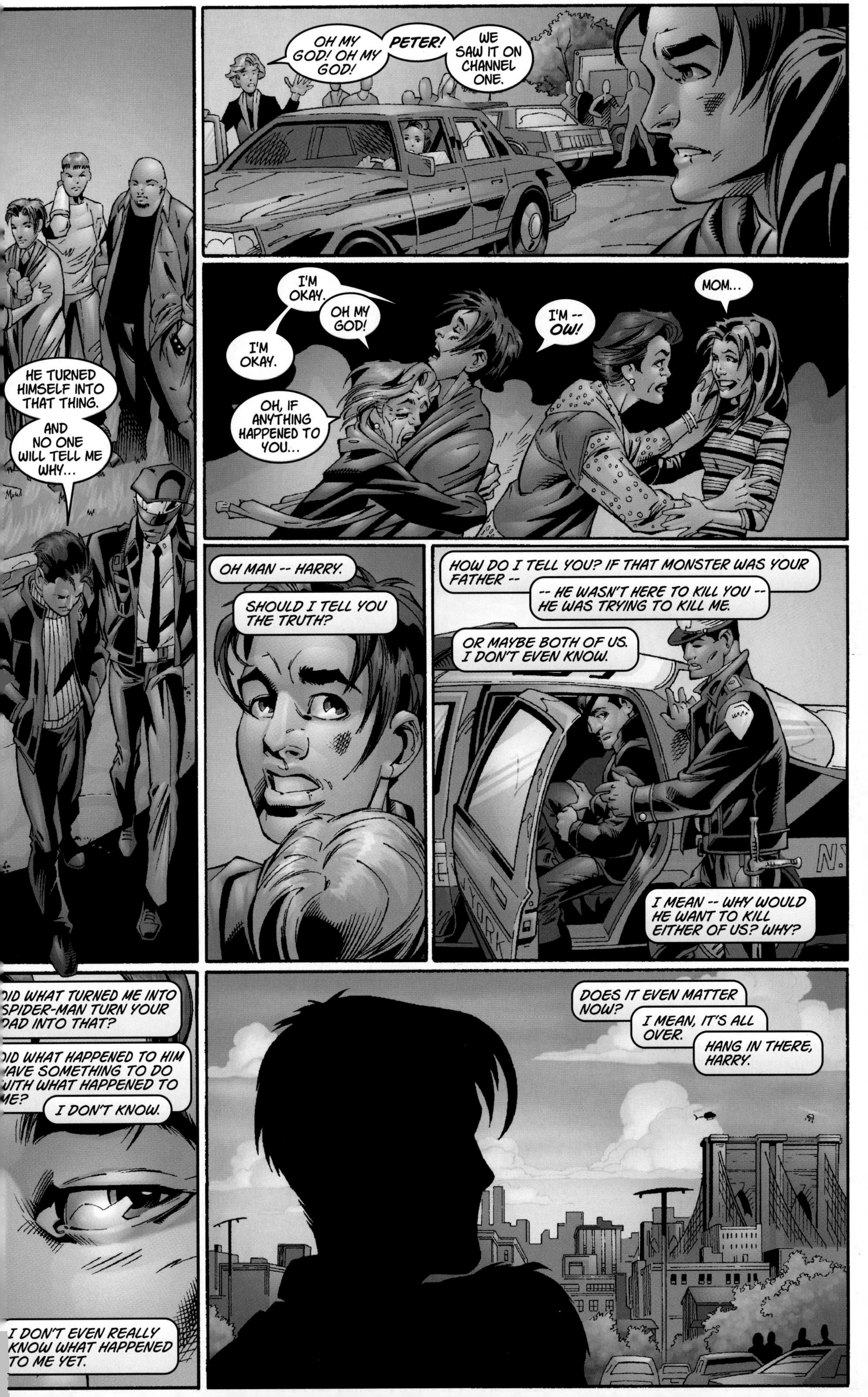
OH MY GOD! OH MY GOD!
PETER!
WE SAW IT ON CHANNEL ONE.
HE TURNED HIMSELF INTO THAT THING.
AND NO ONE WILL TELL ME WHY...
I'M OKAY.
OH MY GOD!
I'M OKAY.
OH, IF ANYTHING HAPPENED TO YOU...
I'M -- OW!
MOM...
OH MAN -- HARRY.
SHOULD I TELL YOU THE TRUTH?
HOW DO I TELL YOU? IF THAT MONSTER WAS YOUR FATHER --
-- HE WASN'T HERE TO KILL YOU -- HE WAS TRYING TO KILL ME.
OR MAYBE BOTH OF US. I DON'T EVEN KNOW.
I MEAN -- WHY WOULD HE WANT TO KILL EITHER OF US? WHY?
DID WHAT TURNED ME INTO SPIDER-MAN TURN YOUR DAD INTO THAT?
DID WHAT HAPPENED TO HIM HAVE SOMETHING TO DO WITH WHAT HAPPENED TO ME?
I DON'T KNOW.
I DON'T EVEN REALLY KNOW WHAT HAPPENED TO ME YET.
DOES IT EVEN MATTER NOW?
I MEAN, IT'S ALL OVER.
HANG IN THERE, HARRY.

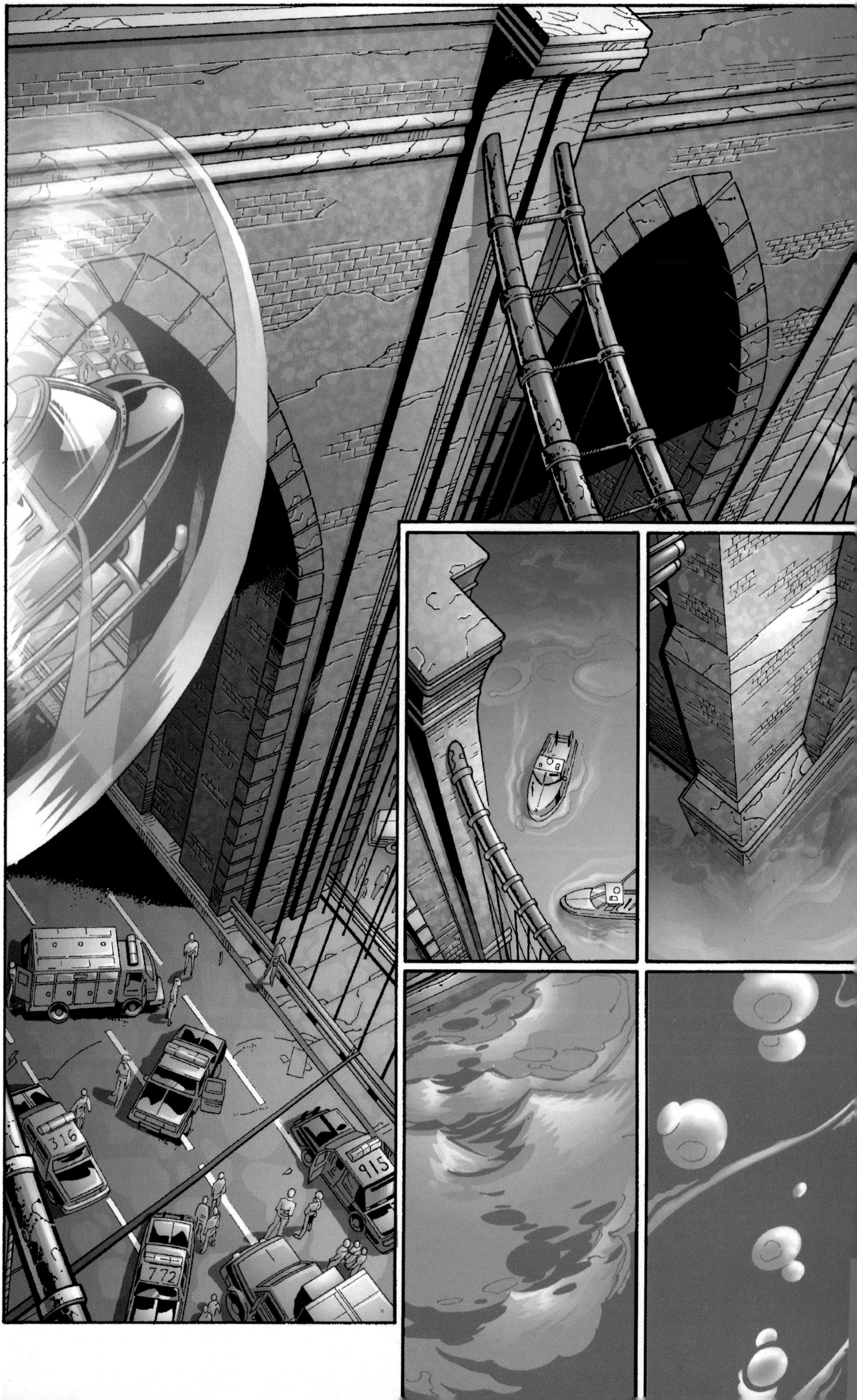
316
915
772

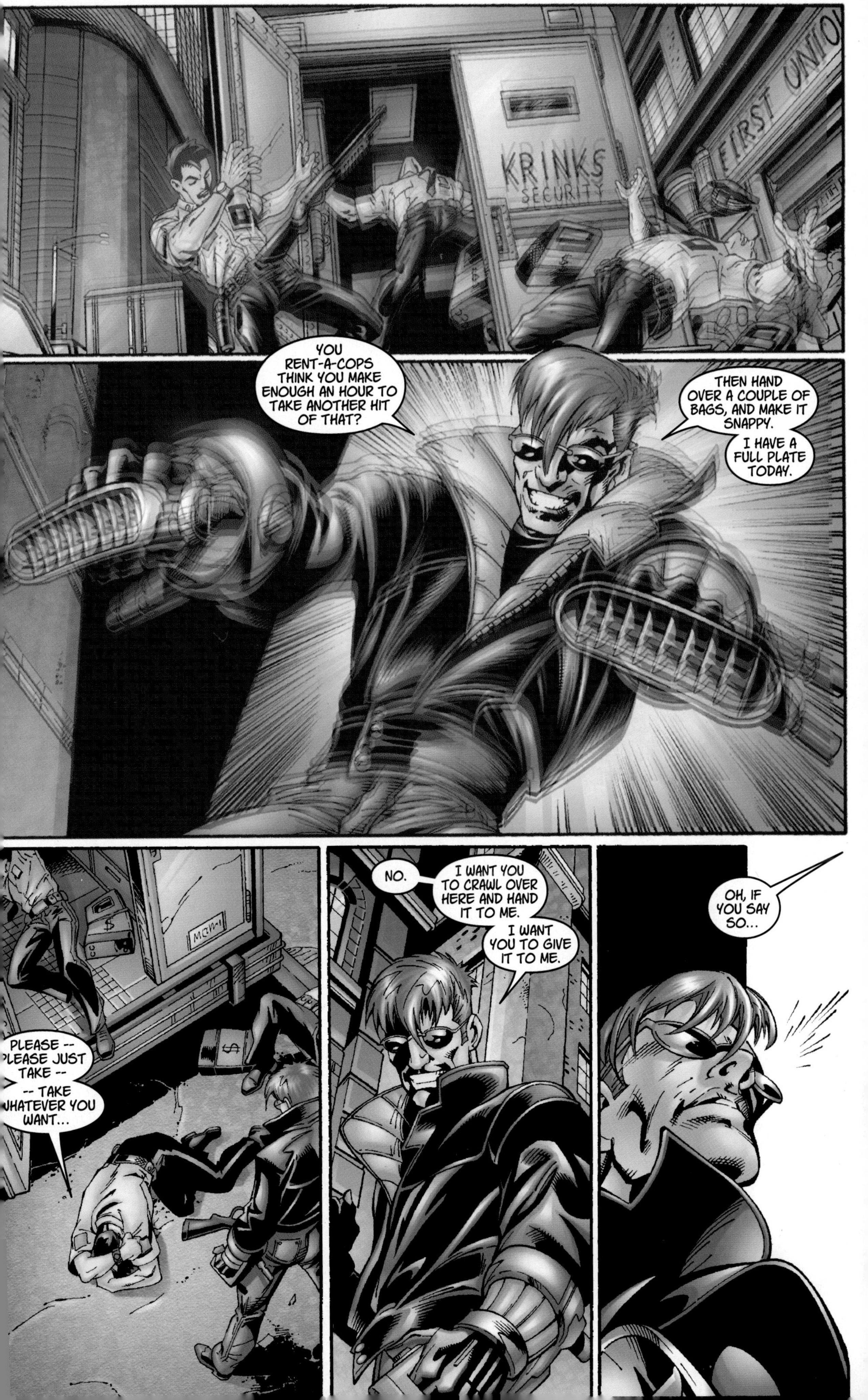
FIRST UNION
KRINKS SECURITY
YOU RENT-A-COPS THINK YOU MAKE ENOUGH AN HOUR TO TAKE ANOTHER HIT OF THAT?
THEN HAND OVER A COUPLE OF BAGS, AND MAKE IT SNAPPY.
I HAVE A FULL PLATE TODAY.
PLEASE -- PLEASE JUST TAKE --
-- TAKE WHATEVER YOU WANT...
NO.
I WANT YOU TO CRAWL OVER HERE AND HAND IT TO ME.
I WANT YOU TO GIVE IT TO ME.
OH, IF YOU SAY SO...

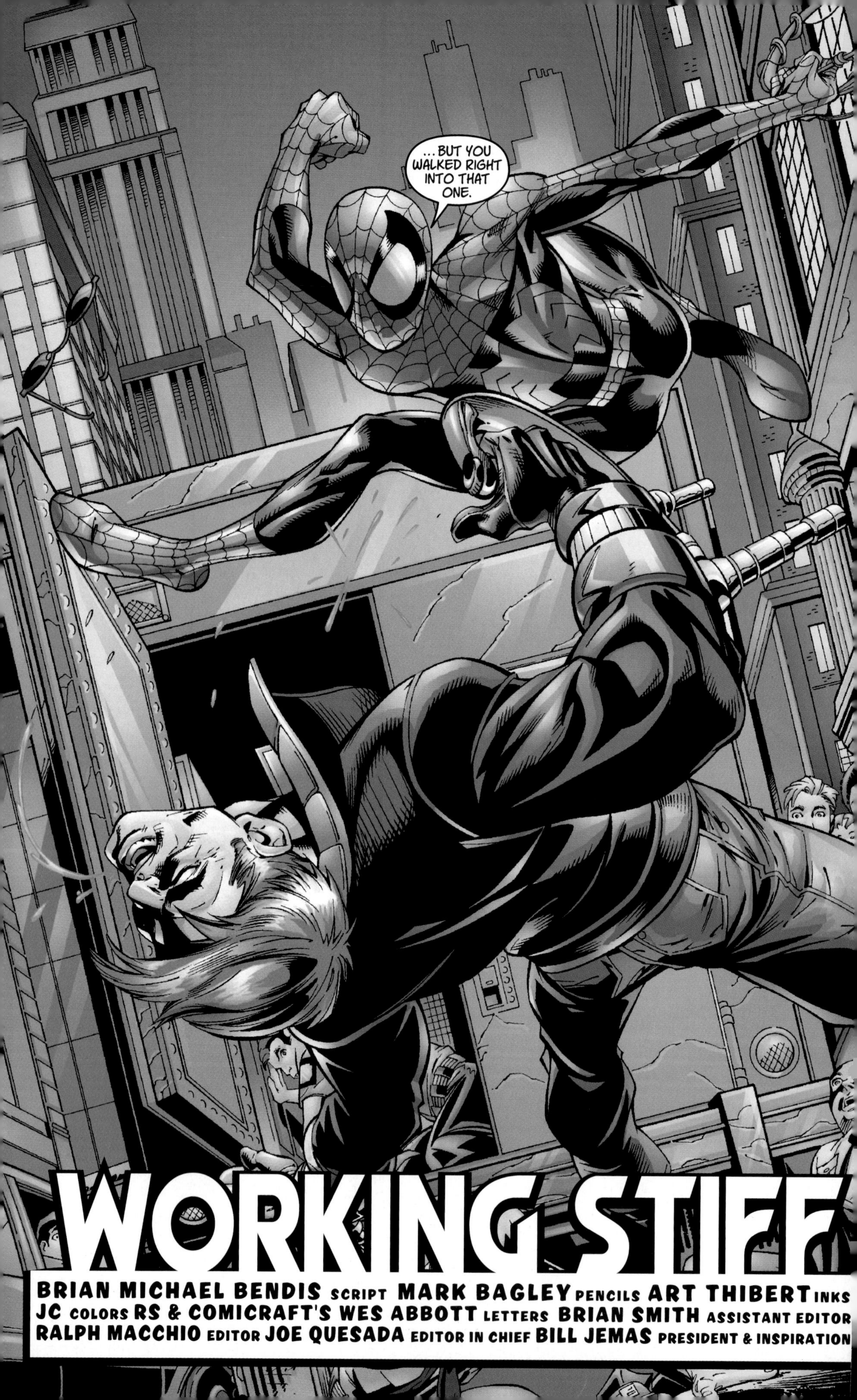

...BUT YOU WALKED RIGHT INTO THAT ONE.
WORKING STIFF
BRIAN MICHAEL BENDIS SCRIPT MARK BAGLEY PENCILS ART THIBERT INKS
JC COLORS RS & COMICRAFT'S WES ABBOTT LETTERS BRIAN SMITH ASSISTANT EDITOR
RALPH MACCHIO EDITOR JOE QUESADA EDITOR IN CHIEF BILL JEMAS PRESIDENT & INSPIRATION

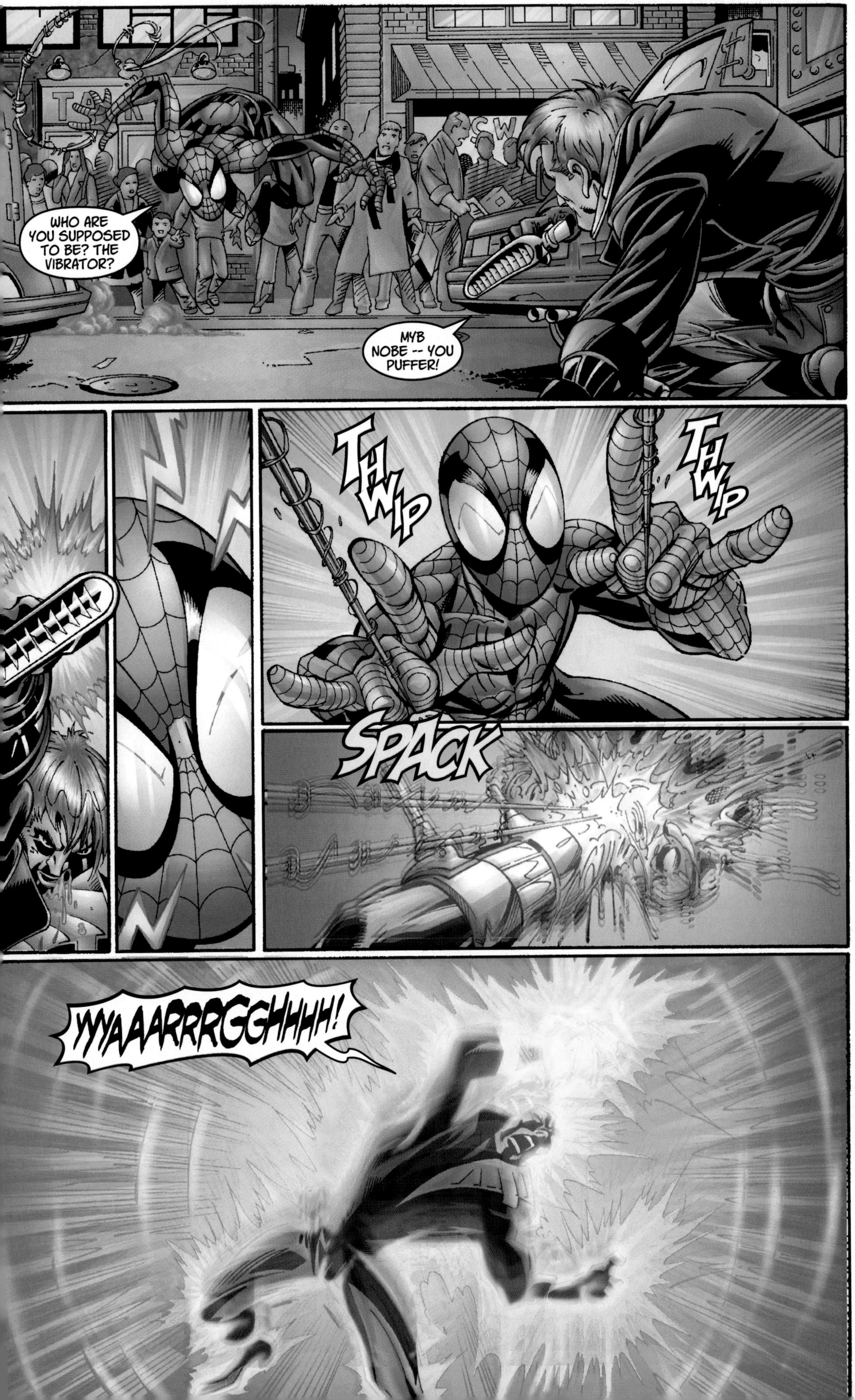
WHO ARE YOU SUPPOSED TO BE? THE VIBRATOR?
MYB NOBE -- YOU PUFFER!
THWIP
THWIP
SPACK
YYYAAARRRGGHHHH!

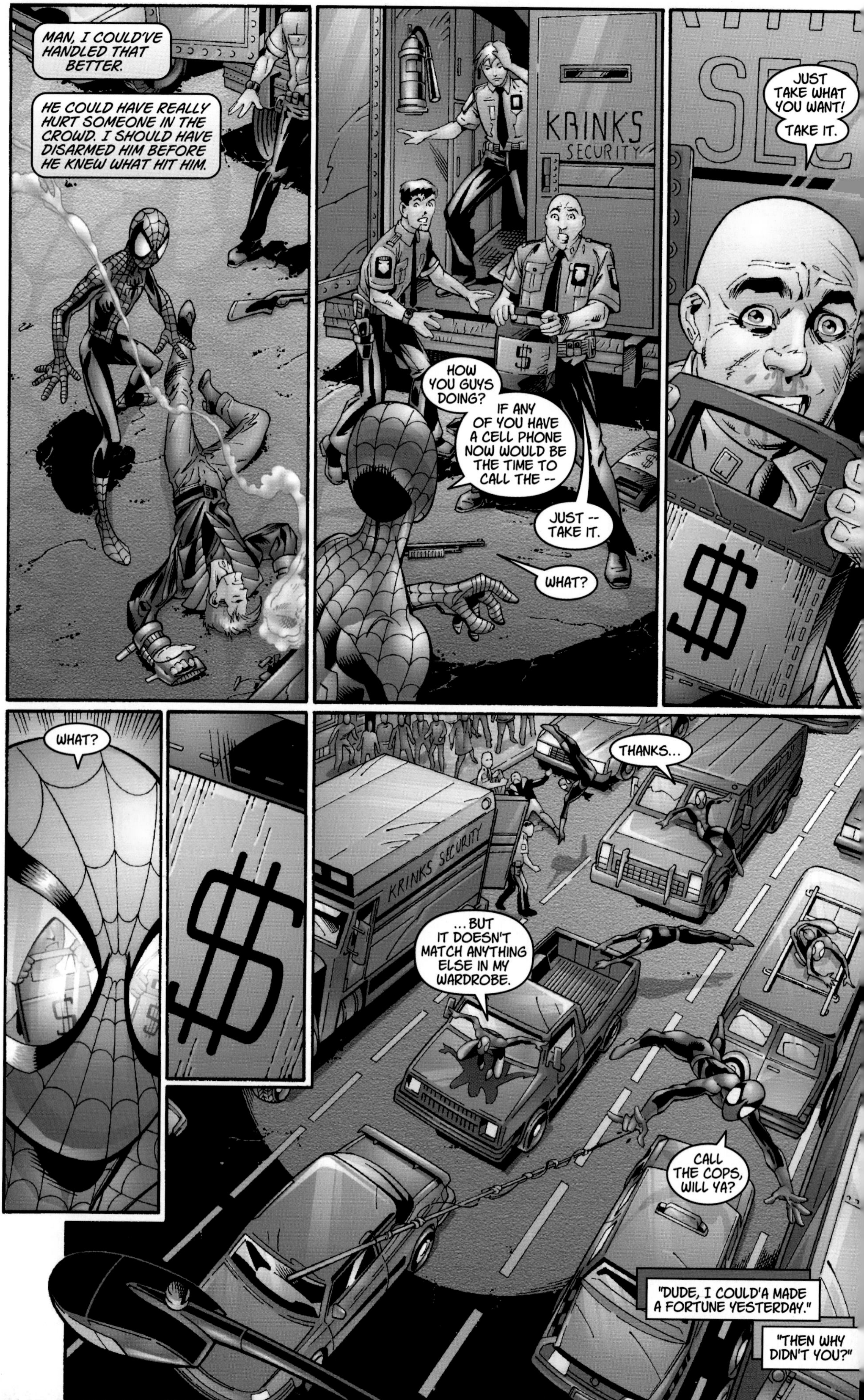
MAN, I COULD'VE HANDLED THAT BETTER.
HE COULD HAVE REALLY HURT SOMEONE IN THE CROWD. I SHOULD HAVE DISARMED HIM BEFORE HE KNEW WHAT HIT HIM.
KRINKS SECURITY
HOW YOU GUYS DOING?
IF ANY OF YOU HAVE A CELL PHONE NOW WOULD BE THE TIME TO CALL THE --
JUST -- TAKE IT.
WHAT?
JUST TAKE WHAT YOU WANT!
TAKE IT.
WHAT?
THANKS...
KRINKS SECURITY
...BUT IT DOESN'T MATCH ANYTHING ELSE IN MY WARDROBE.
CALL THE COPS, WILL YA?
"DUDE, I COULD'A MADE A FORTUNE YESTERDAY."
"THEN WHY DIDN'T YOU?"

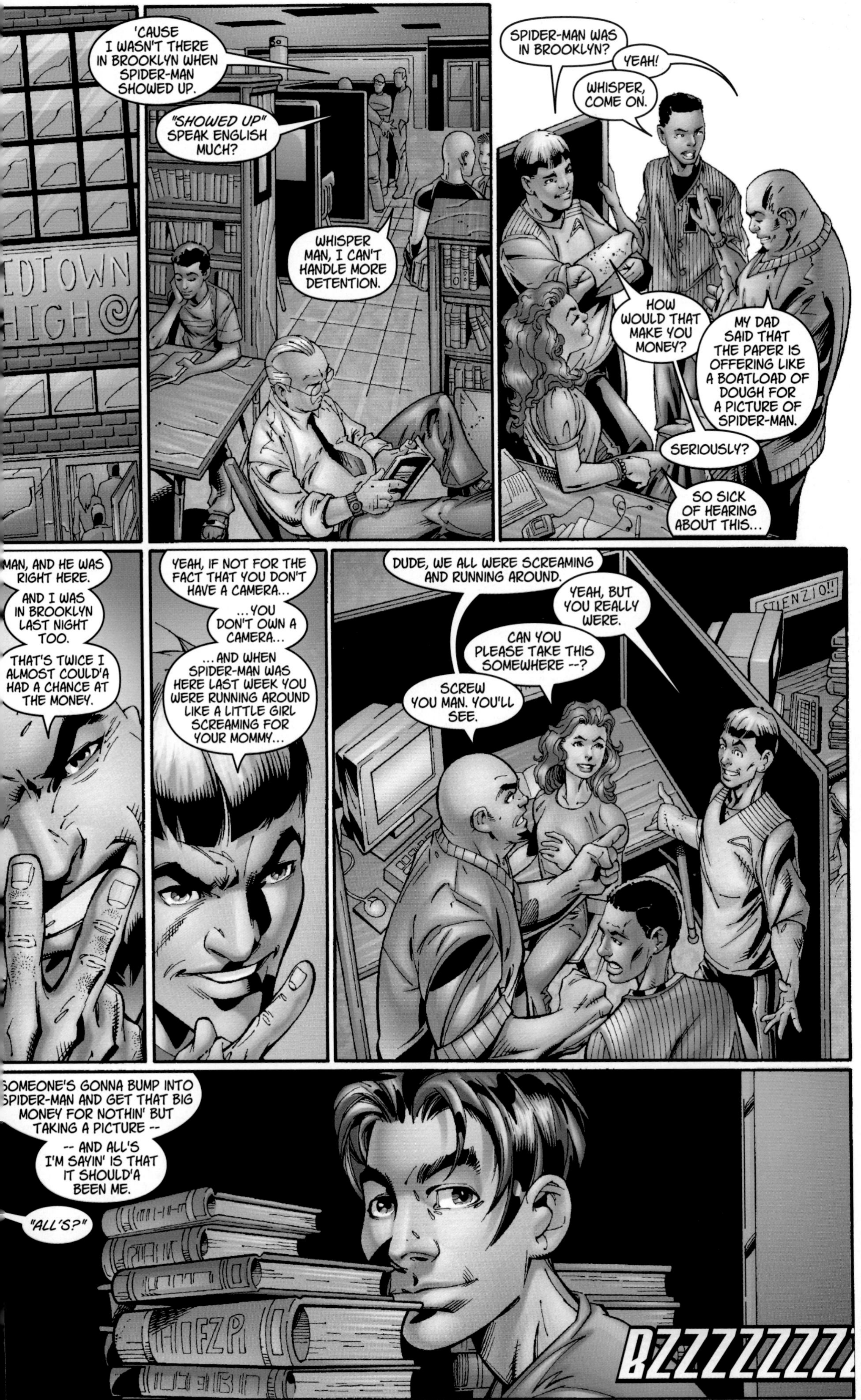
'CAUSE I WASN'T THERE IN BROOKLYN WHEN SPIDER-MAN SHOWED UP.
"SHOWED UP" SPEAK ENGLISH MUCH?
WHISPER MAN, I CAN'T HANDLE MORE DETENTION.
IDTOWN HIGH
SPIDER-MAN WAS IN BROOKLYN?
YEAH!
WHISPER, COME ON.
HOW WOULD THAT MAKE YOU MONEY?
MY DAD SAID THAT THE PAPER IS OFFERING LIKE A BOATLOAD OF DOUGH FOR A PICTURE OF SPIDER-MAN.
SERIOUSLY?
SO SICK OF HEARING ABOUT THIS...
MAN, AND HE WAS RIGHT HERE.
AND I WAS IN BROOKLYN LAST NIGHT TOO.
THAT'S TWICE I ALMOST COULD'A HAD A CHANCE AT THE MONEY.
YEAH, IF NOT FOR THE FACT THAT YOU DON'T HAVE A CAMERA...
...YOU DON'T OWN A CAMERA...
...AND WHEN SPIDER-MAN WAS HERE LAST WEEK YOU WERE RUNNING AROUND LIKE A LITTLE GIRL SCREAMING FOR YOUR MOMMY...
DUDE, WE ALL WERE SCREAMING AND RUNNING AROUND.
YEAH, BUT YOU REALLY WERE.
CAN YOU PLEASE TAKE THIS SOMEWHERE --?
SCREW YOU MAN. YOU'LL SEE.
SILENZIO!!
SOMEONE'S GONNA BUMP INTO SPIDER-MAN AND GET THAT BIG MONEY FOR NOTHIN' BUT TAKING A PICTURE --
-- AND ALL'S I'M SAYIN' IS THAT IT SHOULD'A BEEN ME.
"ALL'S?"
BZZZZZZZZ

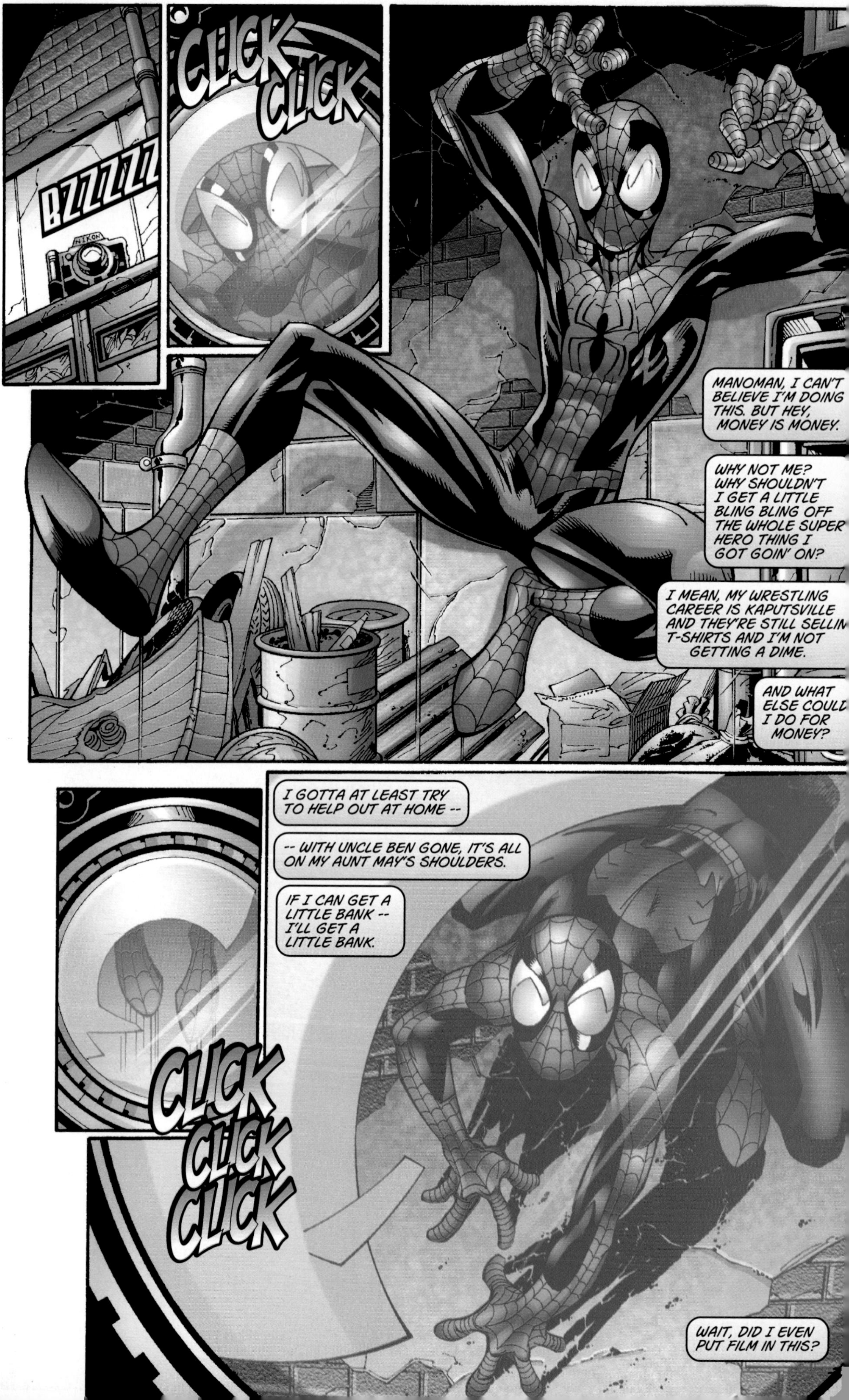
BZZZZZ
NIKON
CLICK CLICK
MANOMAN, I CAN'T BELIEVE I'M DOING THIS. BUT HEY, MONEY IS MONEY.
WHY NOT ME? WHY SHOULDN'T I GET A LITTLE BLING BLING OFF THE WHOLE SUPER HERO THING I GOT GOIN' ON?
I MEAN, MY WRESTLING CAREER IS KAPUTSVILLE AND THEY'RE STILL SELLIN T-SHIRTS AND I'M NOT GETTING A DIME.
AND WHAT ELSE COULD I DO FOR MONEY?
I GOTTA AT LEAST TRY TO HELP OUT AT HOME --
-- WITH UNCLE BEN GONE, IT'S ALL ON MY AUNT MAY'S SHOULDERS.
IF I CAN GET A LITTLE BANK -- I'LL GET A LITTLE BANK.
CLICK CLICK CLICK
WAIT, DID I EVEN PUT FILM IN THIS?

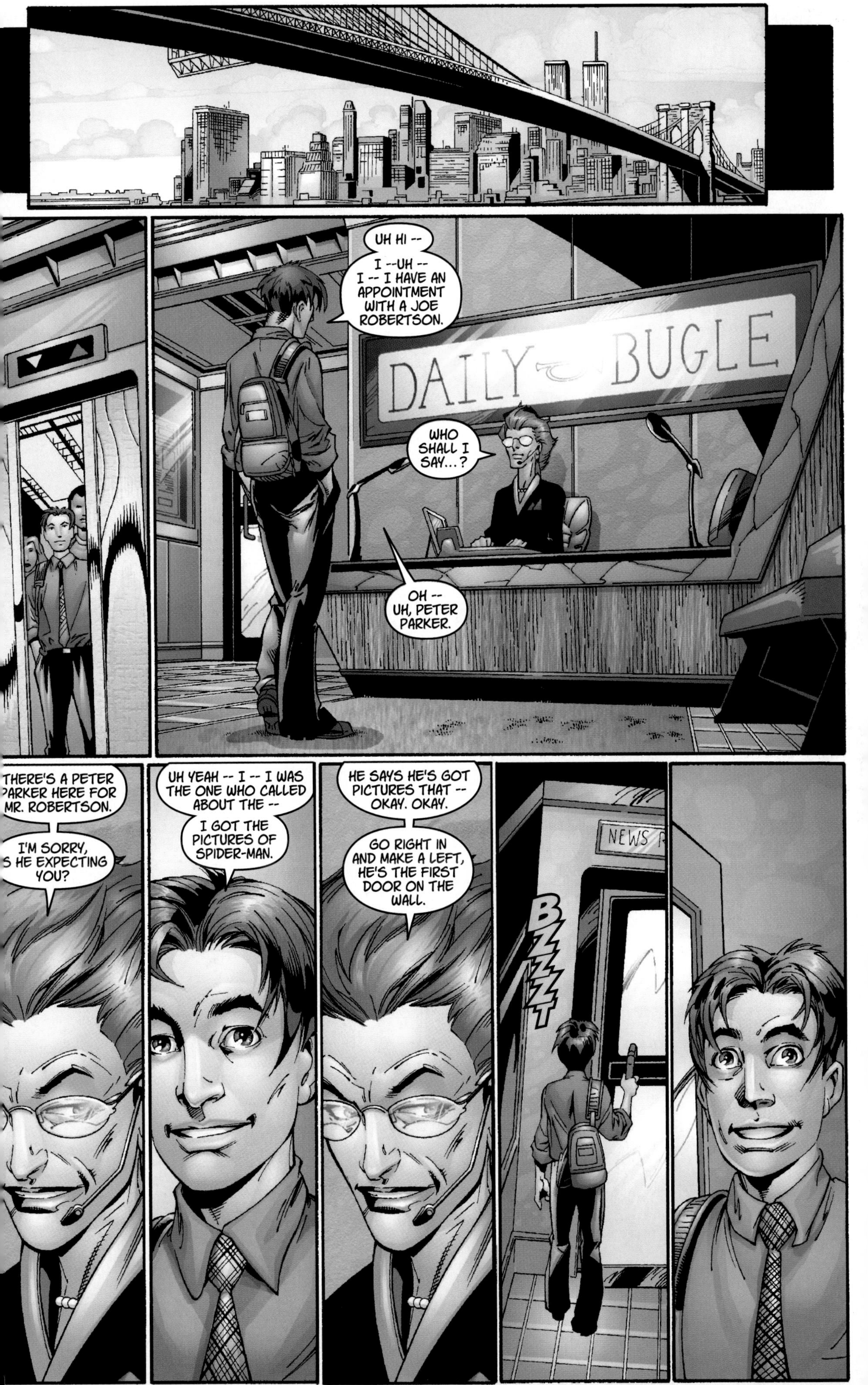

UH HI --
I --UH -- I -- I HAVE AN APPOINTMENT WITH A JOE ROBERTSON.
DAILY BUGLE
WHO SHALL I SAY...?
OH -- UH, PETER PARKER.
THERE'S A PETER PARKER HERE FOR MR. ROBERTSON.
I'M SORRY, S HE EXPECTING YOU?
UH YEAH -- I -- I WAS THE ONE WHO CALLED ABOUT THE --
I GOT THE PICTURES OF SPIDER-MAN.
HE SAYS HE'S GOT PICTURES THAT -- OKAY. OKAY.
GO RIGHT IN AND MAKE A LEFT, HE'S THE FIRST DOOR ON THE WALL.
NEWS R
BZZZT

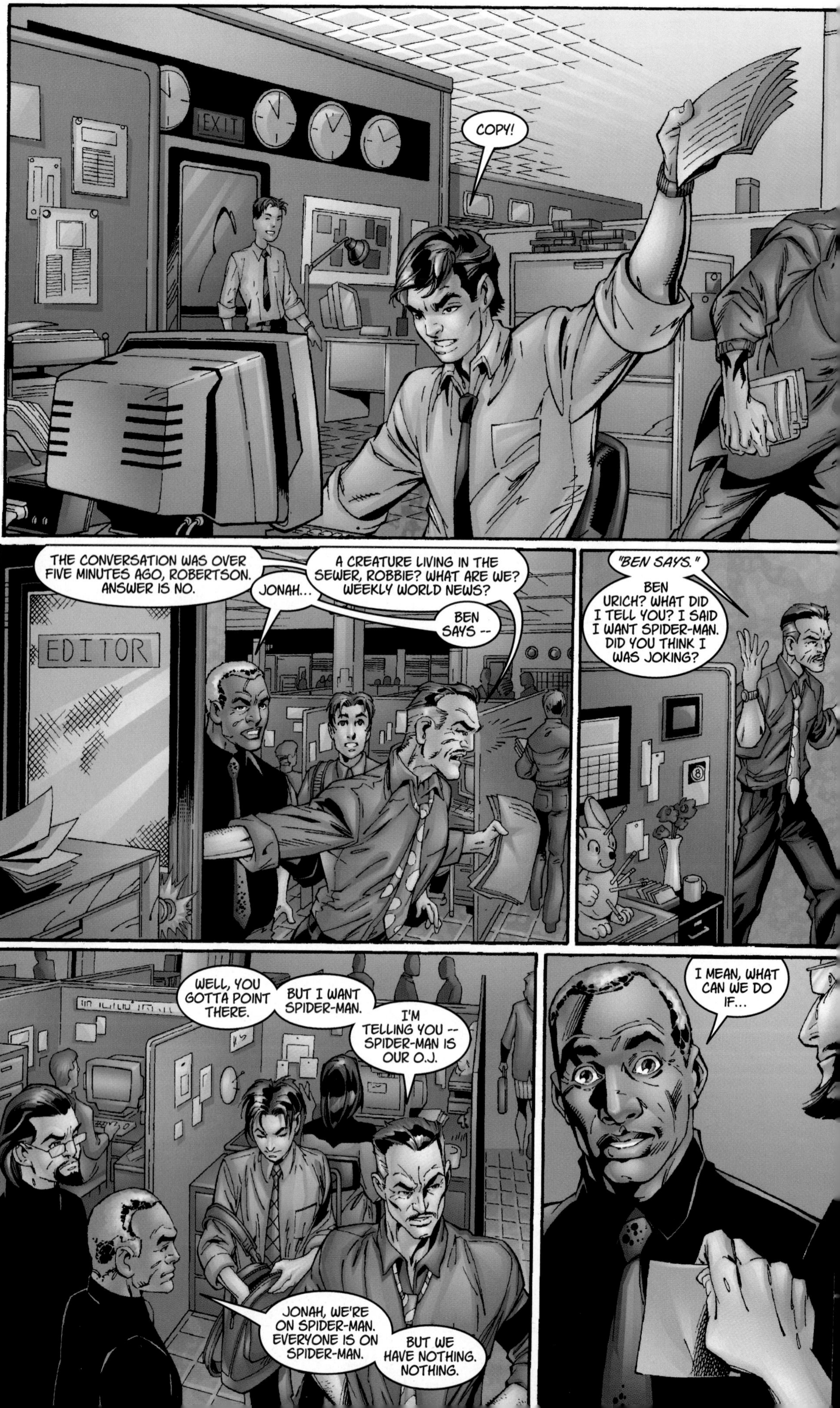
EXIT
COPY!
EDITOR
THE CONVERSATION WAS OVER FIVE MINUTES AGO, ROBERTSON. ANSWER IS NO.
JONAH...
A CREATURE LIVING IN THE SEWER, ROBBIE? WHAT ARE WE? WEEKLY WORLD NEWS?
BEN SAYS --
"BEN SAYS."
BEN URICH? WHAT DID I TELL YOU? I SAID I WANT SPIDER-MAN. DID YOU THINK I WAS JOKING?
WELL, YOU GOTTA POINT THERE.
BUT I WANT SPIDER-MAN.
I'M TELLING YOU -- SPIDER-MAN IS OUR O.J.
JONAH, WE'RE ON SPIDER-MAN. EVERYONE IS ON SPIDER-MAN.
BUT WE HAVE NOTHING. NOTHING.
I MEAN, WHAT CAN WE DO IF...

I'M WORKING ON IT.

"WORKING ON IT."

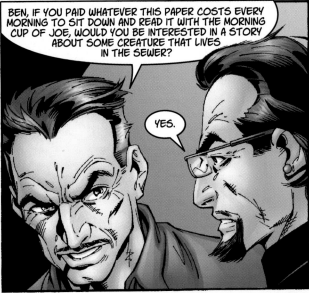
BEN, IF YOU PAID WHATEVER THIS PAPER COSTS EVERY MORNING TO SIT DOWN AND READ IT WITH THE MORNING CUP OF JOE, WOULD YOU BE INTERESTED IN A STORY ABOUT SOME CREATURE THAT LIVES IN THE SEWER?

YES.

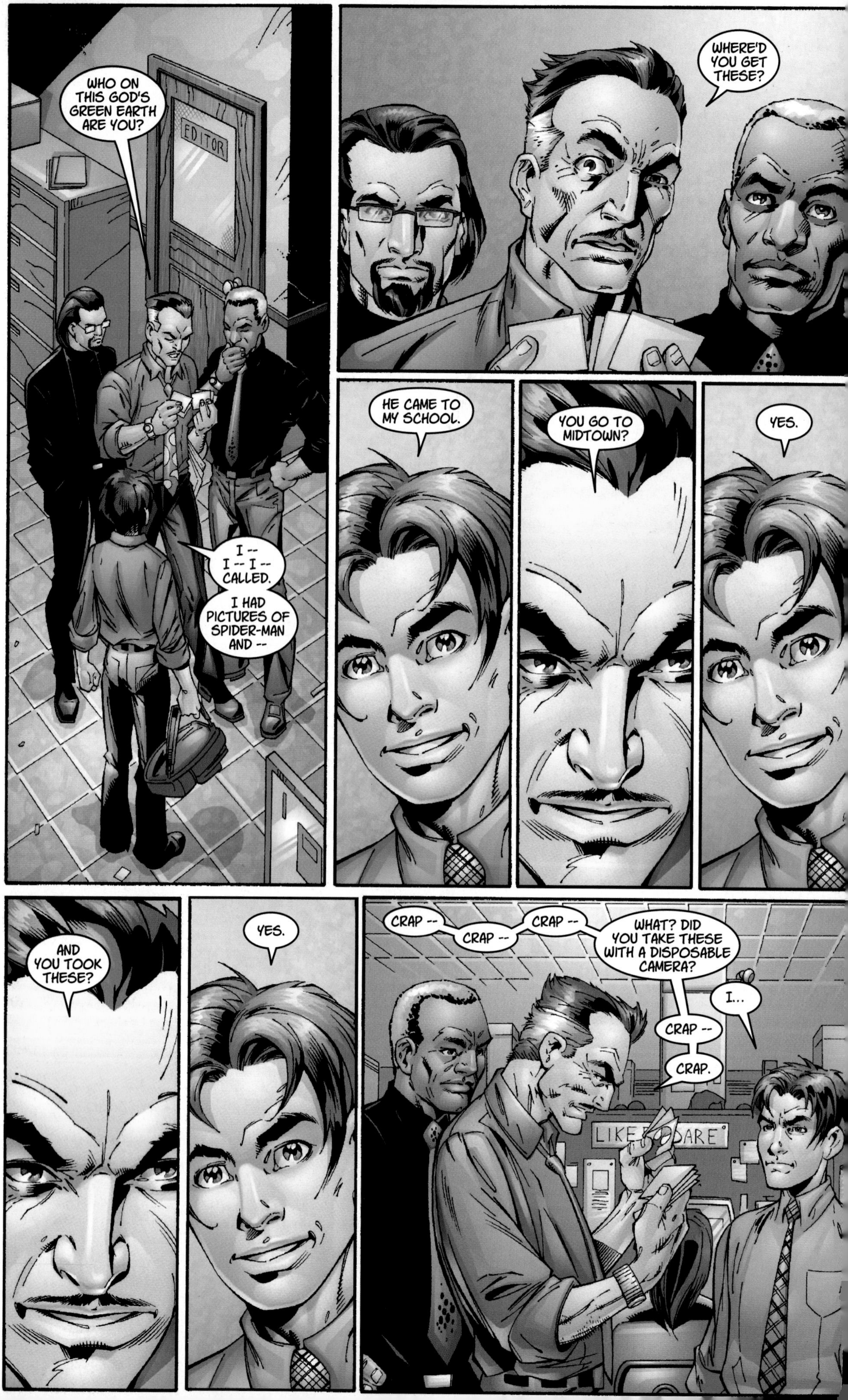
WHO ON THIS GOD'S GREEN EARTH ARE YOU?
EDITOR
I -- I -- I -- CALLED.
I HAD PICTURES OF SPIDER-MAN AND --
WHERE'D YOU GET THESE?
HE CAME TO MY SCHOOL.
YOU GO TO MIDTOWN?
YES.
AND YOU TOOK THESE?
YES.
CRAP --
CRAP --
CRAP --
WHAT? DID YOU TAKE THESE WITH A DISPOSABLE CAMERA?
I...
CRAP --
CRAP.

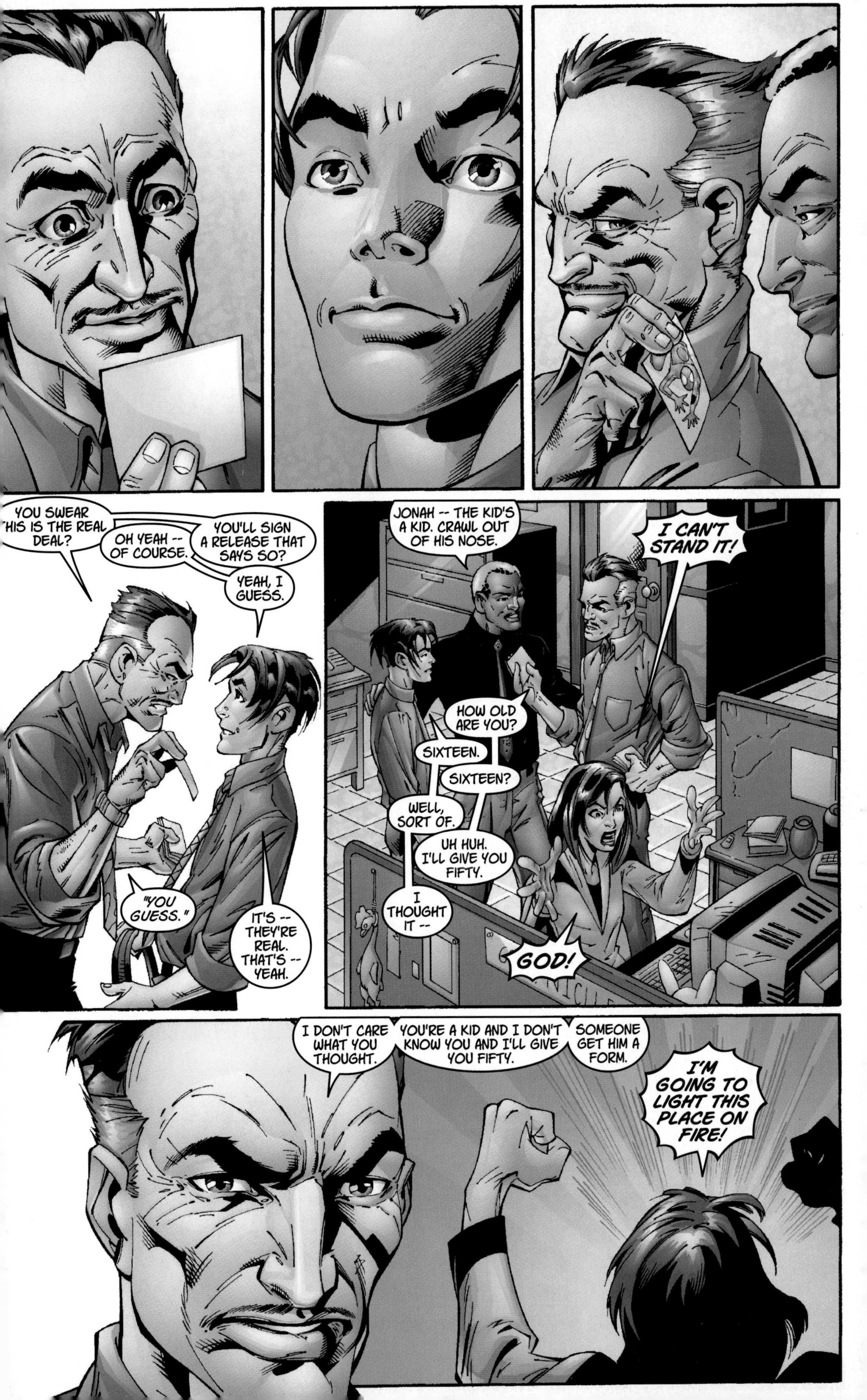
YOU SWEAR THIS IS THE REAL DEAL?
OH YEAH -- OF COURSE.
YOU'LL SIGN A RELEASE THAT SAYS SO?
YEAH, I GUESS.
"YOU GUESS."
IT'S -- THEY'RE REAL. THAT'S -- YEAH.
JONAH -- THE KID'S A KID. CRAWL OUT OF HIS NOSE.
I CAN'T STAND IT!
HOW OLD ARE YOU?
SIXTEEN.
SIXTEEN?
WELL, SORT OF.
UH HUH. I'LL GIVE YOU FIFTY.
I THOUGHT IT --
GOD!
I DON'T CARE WHAT YOU THOUGHT.
YOU'RE A KID AND I DON'T KNOW YOU AND I'LL GIVE YOU FIFTY.
SOMEONE GET HIM A FORM.
I'M GOING TO LIGHT THIS PLACE ON FIRE!

WHAT NOW. MS. BRANT?

I CAN'T -- I'M NOT DOING THIS ANYMORE, JONAH.

YOU'LL DO WHAT I --

NO. NO. I'M THE ASSOCIATE BOOK EDITOR.

I'M NOT A FREAKIN' WEB DESIGNER. I CAN'T GET THIS FREAKIN' THING TO WORK!

IT FREEZES UP ON ME EVERY TIME I TAKE A DEEP BREATH AND I CAN'T I CAN'T -- I CAN'T -- FORGET IT. NOPE.

BUT WE PAID FOR YOU TO TAKE THAT CLASS.

IT WAS A ONE DAY CLASS, JONAH. IF I TOOK A ONE DAY CLASS IN CHINESE -- I WOULDN'T KNOW CHINESE BY THE END OF THE DAY.

I DON'T -- ARRRGH!

HEY, WHAT HAPPENED TO OUR WEB SITE?! IT'S NOT COMING UP ON THE FREAKIN' BROWSER!

I DON'T KNOW! YOU SIT!

YOU CRASHED IT!

YOU SIT!

UH -- IT LOOKS LIKE THE SCRIPT'S IN A RECURSIVE LOOP.

A -- A RECURSIVE LOOP.

THE LINE YOU CHANGED IS CAUSING THE SCRIPT TO CALL ITSELF OVER AND OVER AGAIN WITHOUT A CONDITIONAL STATEMENT TO ALLOW THE SCRIPT TO EXIT OR STOP CALLING ITSELF.

NONE OF THE PAGES ON THE SITE ARE RENDERED BECAUSE THE RESULTS OF THE SCRIPT ARE NEEDED, BUT SINCE THE SCRIPT IS RECURSIVELY CALLING ITSELF, YOU'LL NEVER GET RESULTS AND THE PAGES WILL NEVER RENDER.

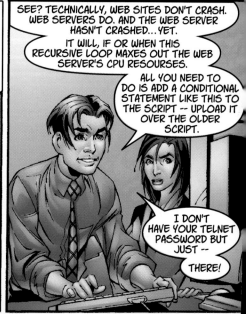

SEE? TECHNICALLY, WEB SITES DON'T CRASH. WEB SERVERS DO. AND THE WEB SERVER HASN'T CRASHED...YET.

IT WILL, IF OR WHEN THIS RECURSIVE LOOP MAXES OUT THE WEB SERVER'S CPU RESOURCES.

ALL YOU NEED TO DO IS ADD A CONDITIONAL STATEMENT LIKE THIS TO THE SCRIPT -- UPLOAD IT OVER THE OLDER SCRIPT.

I DON'T HAVE YOUR TELNET PASSWORD BUT JUST --

THERE!

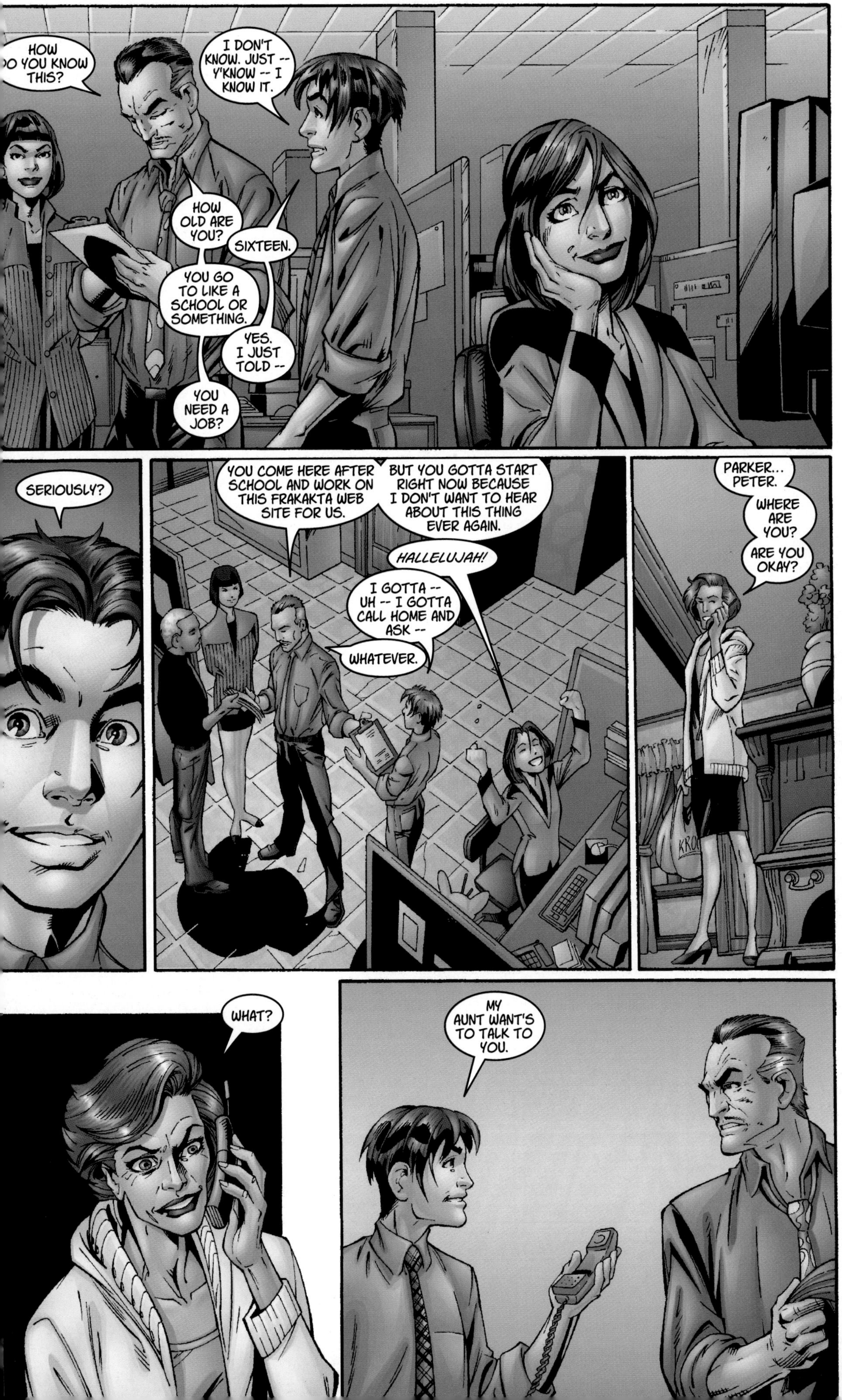
HOW
DO YOU KNOW
THIS?
I DON'T
KNOW. JUST --
Y'KNOW -- I
KNOW IT.
HOW
OLD ARE
YOU?
SIXTEEN.
YOU GO
TO LIKE A
SCHOOL OR
SOMETHING.
YES.
I JUST
TOLD --
YOU
NEED A
JOB?
SERIOUSLY?
YOU COME HERE AFTER
SCHOOL AND WORK ON
THIS FRAKAKTA WEB
SITE FOR US.
BUT YOU GOTTA START
RIGHT NOW BECAUSE
I DON'T WANT TO HEAR
ABOUT THIS THING
EVER AGAIN.
HALLELUJAH!
I GOTTA --
UH -- I GOTTA
CALL HOME AND
ASK --
WHATEVER.
PARKER...
PETER.
WHERE
ARE
YOU?
ARE YOU
OKAY?
WHAT?
MY
AUNT WANT'S
TO TALK TO
YOU.

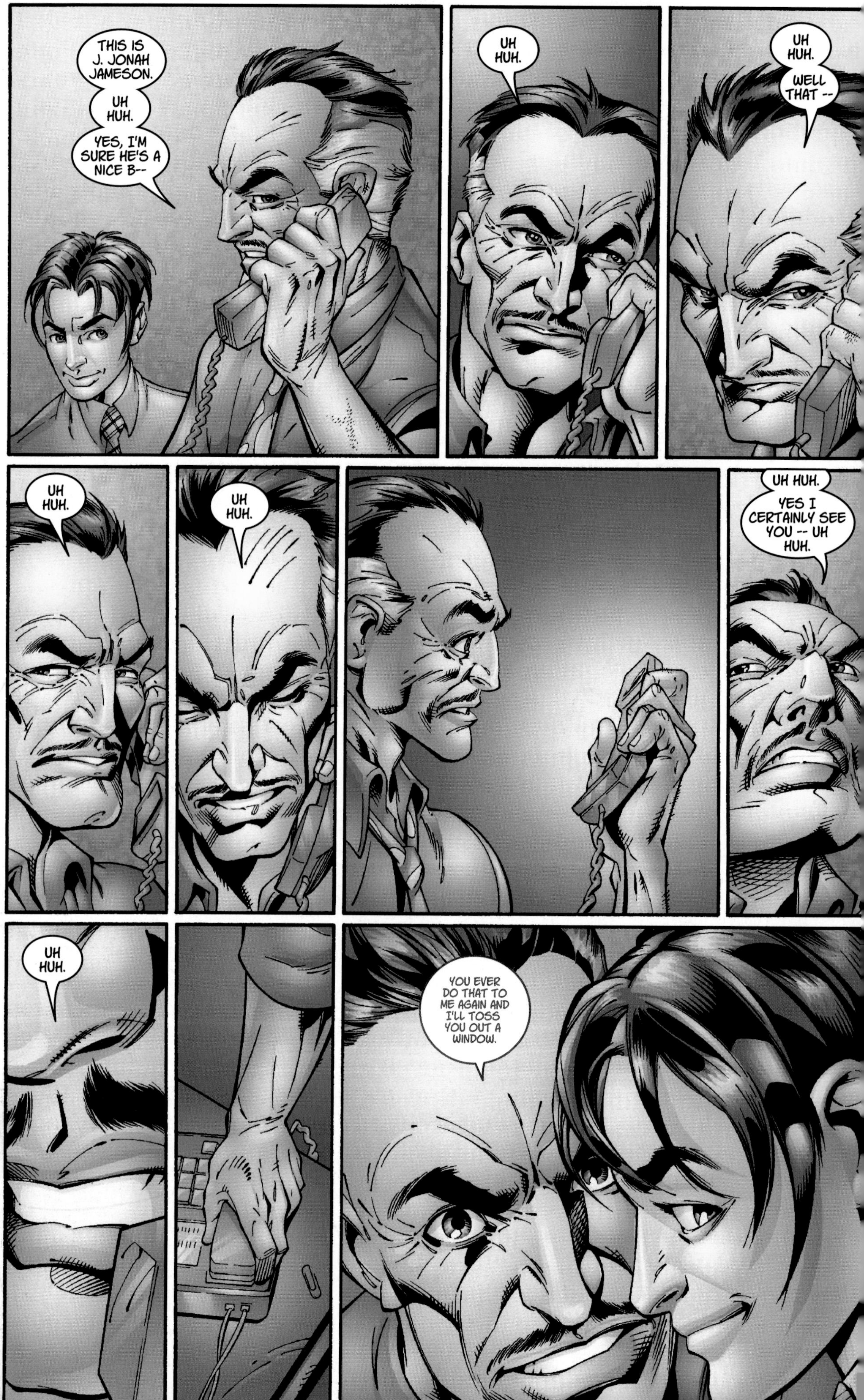
THIS IS J. JONAH JAMESON.
UH HUH.
YES, I'M SURE HE'S A NICE B--
UH HUH.
UH HUH.
WELL THAT --
UH HUH.
UH HUH.
UH HUH.
YES I CERTAINLY SEE YOU -- UH HUH.
UH HUH.
YOU EVER DO THAT TO ME AGAIN AND I'LL TOSS YOU OUT A WINDOW.

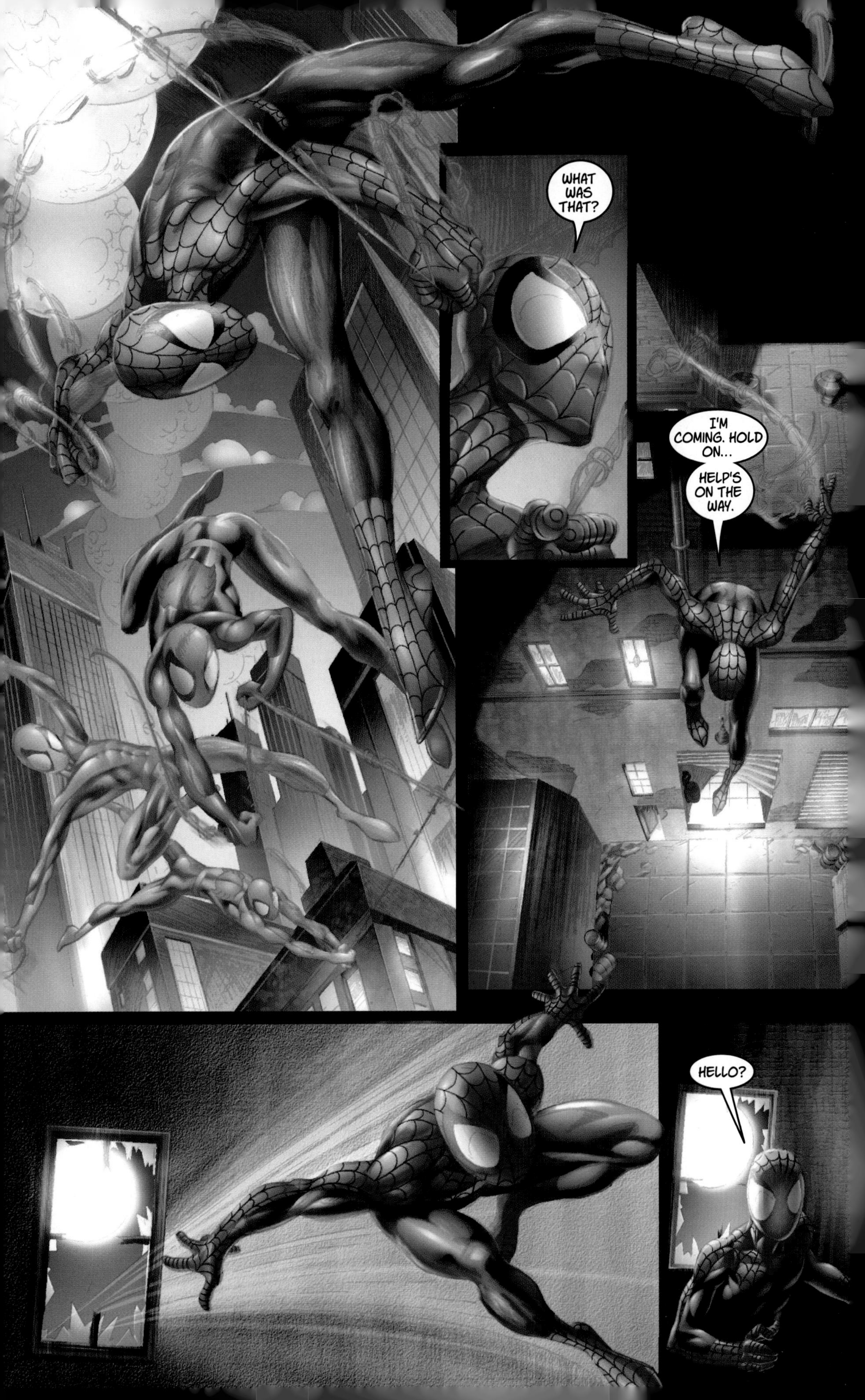
WHAT WAS THAT?
I'M COMING. HOLD ON...
HELP'S ON THE WAY.
HELLO?

THOUGHT YOU SEEN THE LAST OF ME, HUH?

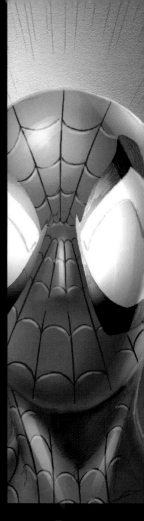

BLAM

PETER...

...I WANTED TO TELL YOU...

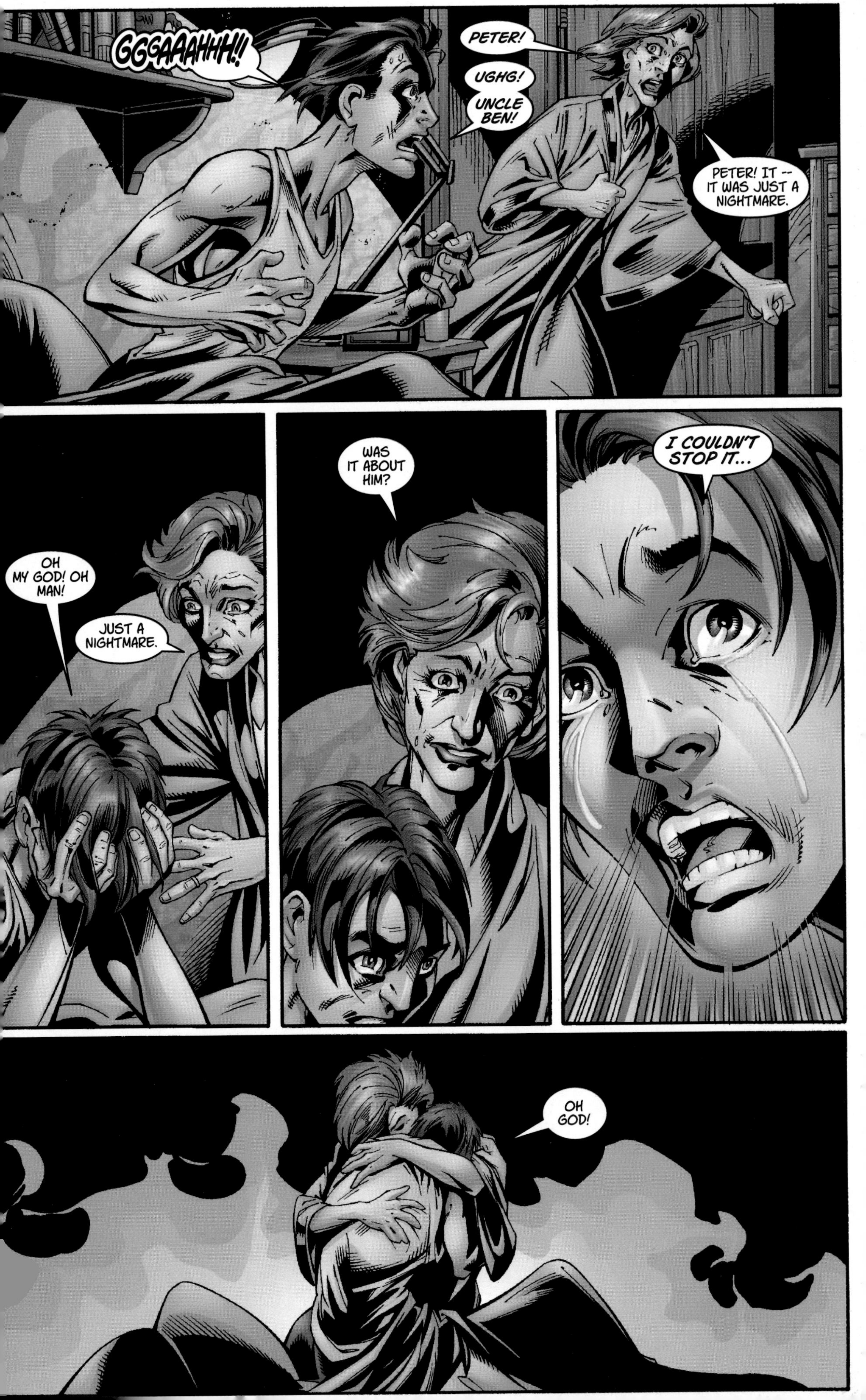
GGGAAAHHH!!
PETER!
UGHG!
UNCLE BEN!
PETER! IT -- IT WAS JUST A NIGHTMARE.
OH MY GOD! OH MAN!
JUST A NIGHTMARE.
WAS IT ABOUT HIM?
I COULDN'T STOP IT...
OH GOD!

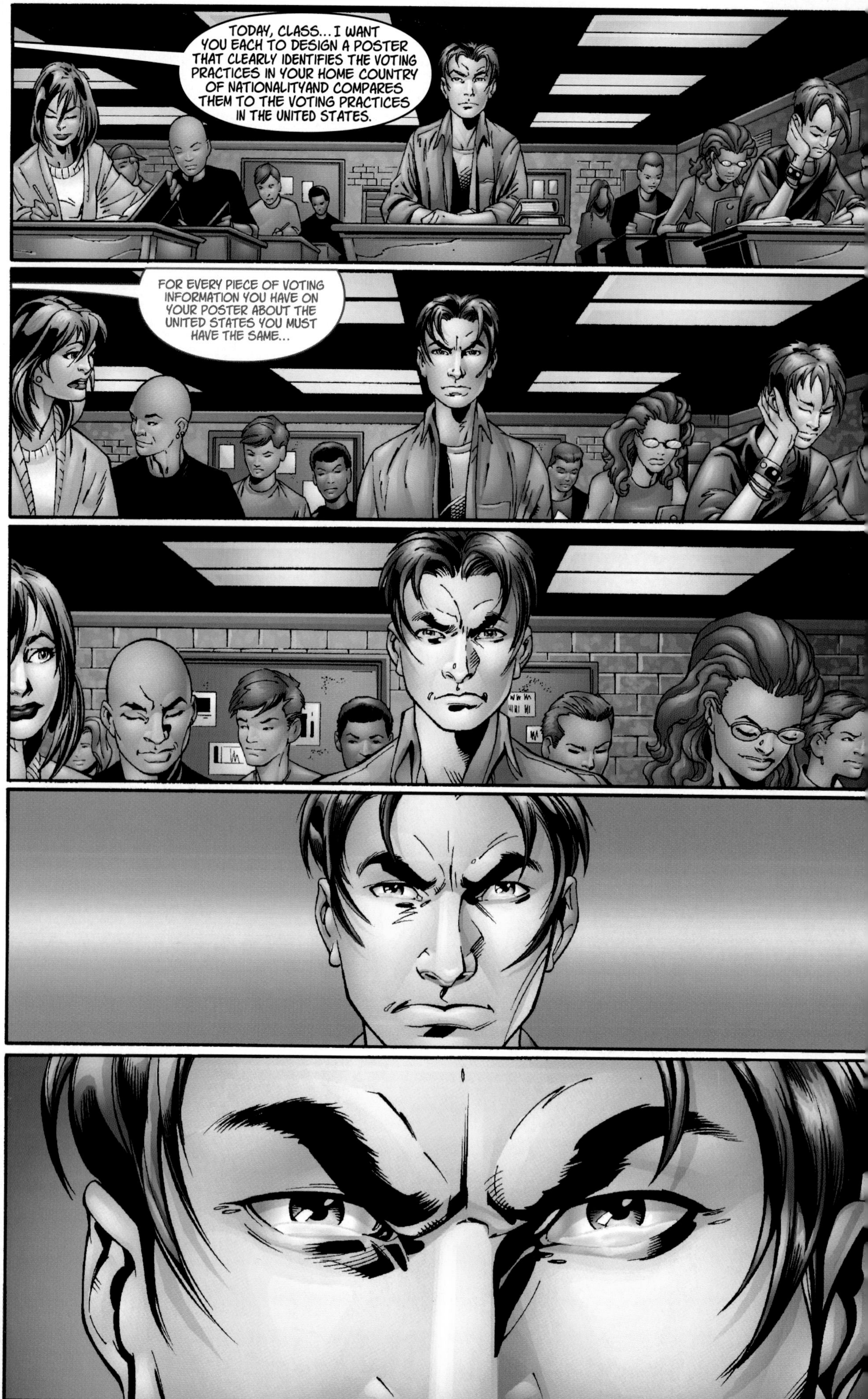
TODAY, CLASS... I WANT YOU EACH TO DESIGN A POSTER THAT CLEARLY IDENTIFIES THE VOTING PRACTICES IN YOUR HOME COUNTRY OF NATIONALITYAND COMPARES THEM TO THE VOTING PRACTICES IN THE UNITED STATES.
FOR EVERY PIECE OF VOTING INFORMATION YOU HAVE ON YOUR POSTER ABOUT THE UNITED STATES YOU MUST HAVE THE SAME...

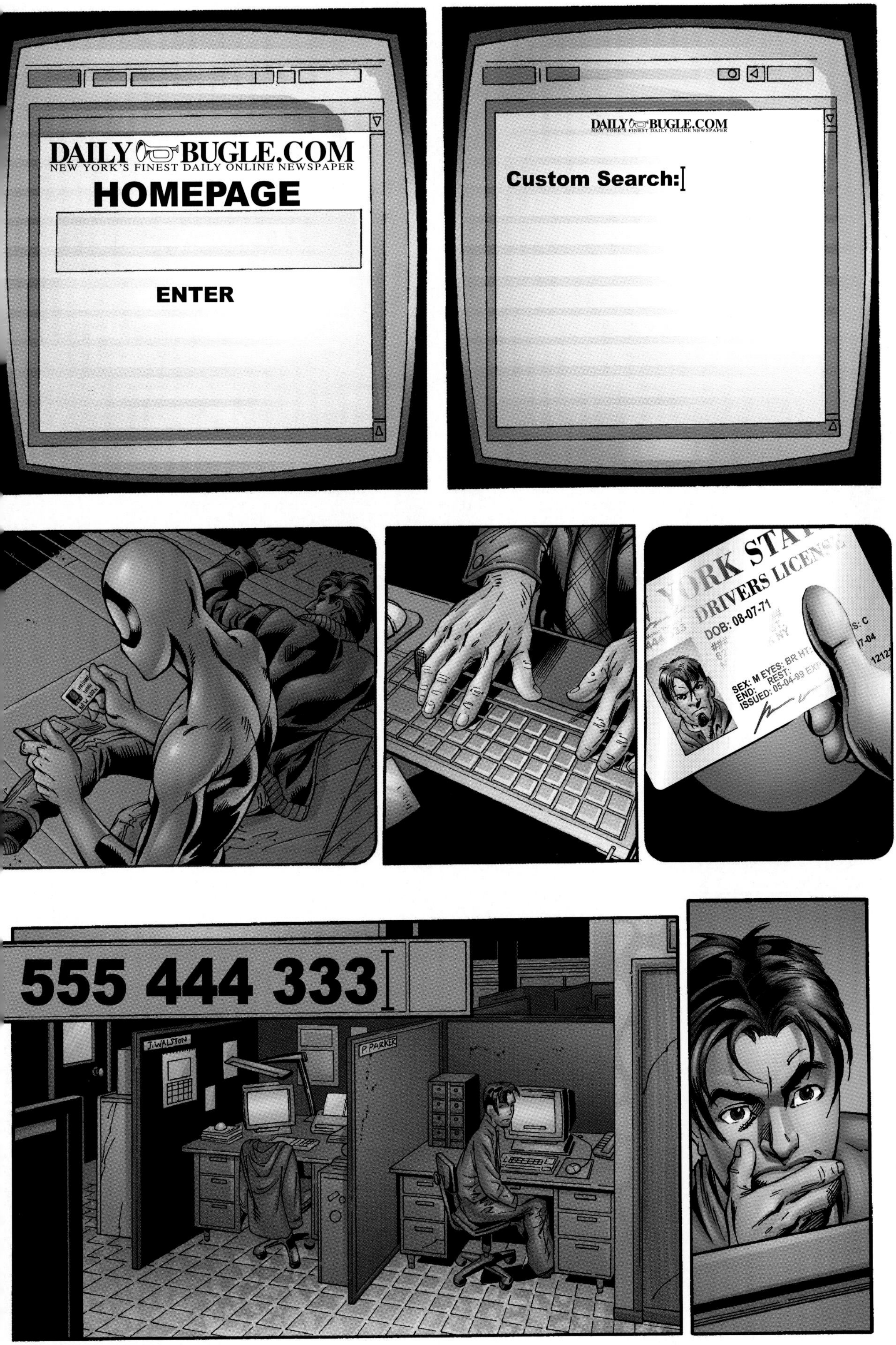

DAILY BUGLE.COM
NEW YORK'S FINEST DAILY ONLINE NEWSPAPER
HOMEPAGE
ENTER
DAILY BUGLE.COM
NEW YORK'S FINEST DAILY ONLINE NEWSPAPER
Custom Search:
DRIVERS LICENSE
DOB: 08-07-71
SEX: M EYES: BR
END:
REST:
ISSUED: 05-04-99
555 444 333
J. WALSTON
P. PARKER

ITEM'S FOUND: 2

Police bust bosses at "The Cage." A hot spot for alleged organized crime.

More?

ITEM: 2

ORGANIZED CRIME IN NEW YORK CITY
an overview by Ben Urich

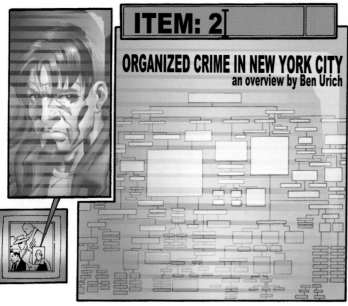

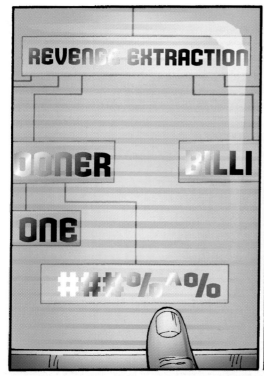

REVENGE EXTRACTION

OONER   BILLI

ONE

#'#'%^%

WILSON FISK
THE KINGPIN

ENFORCER

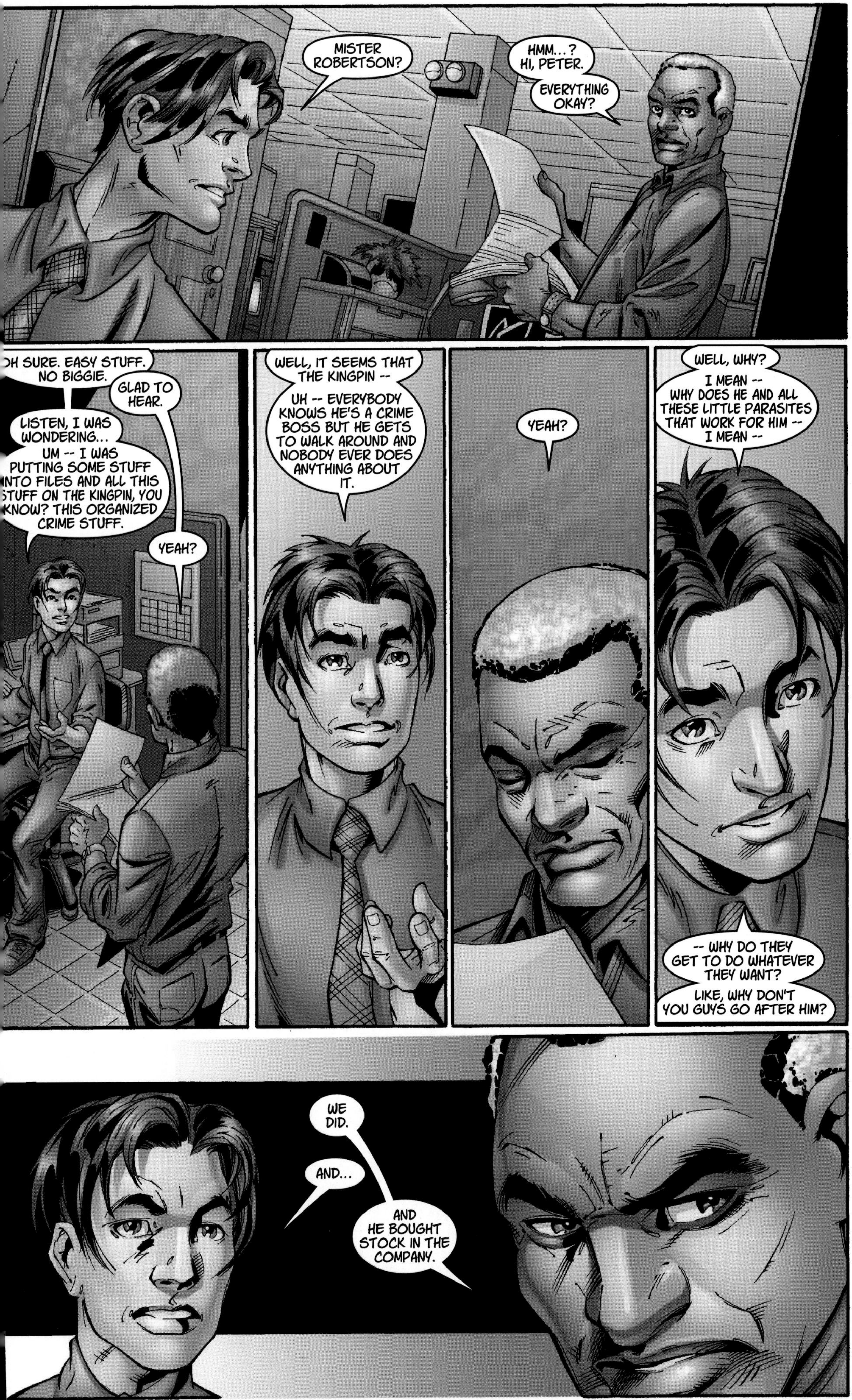
MISTER ROBERTSON?
HMM...? HI, PETER.
EVERYTHING OKAY?
OH SURE. EASY STUFF. NO BIGGIE.
GLAD TO HEAR.
LISTEN, I WAS WONDERING...
UM -- I WAS PUTTING SOME STUFF INTO FILES AND ALL THIS STUFF ON THE KINGPIN, YOU KNOW? THIS ORGANIZED CRIME STUFF.
YEAH?
WELL, IT SEEMS THAT THE KINGPIN --
UH -- EVERYBODY KNOWS HE'S A CRIME BOSS BUT HE GETS TO WALK AROUND AND NOBODY EVER DOES ANYTHING ABOUT IT.
YEAH?
WELL, WHY?
I MEAN -- WHY DOES HE AND ALL THESE LITTLE PARASITES THAT WORK FOR HIM -- I MEAN --
-- WHY DO THEY GET TO DO WHATEVER THEY WANT?
LIKE, WHY DON'T YOU GUYS GO AFTER HIM?
WE DID.
AND...
AND HE BOUGHT STOCK IN THE COMPANY.

LISTEN...

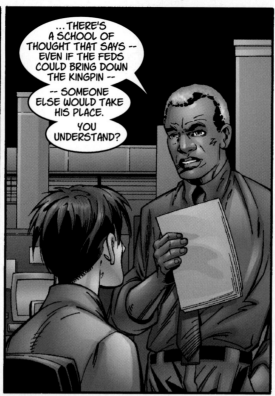

...THERE'S A SCHOOL OF THOUGHT THAT SAYS -- EVEN IF THE FEDS COULD BRING DOWN THE KINGPIN --

-- SOMEONE ELSE WOULD TAKE HIS PLACE.

YOU UNDERSTAND?

JUST THE WAY IT IS.

WILSON FISK
THE KINGPIN

OH YEAH? WELL, WE'LL SEE.

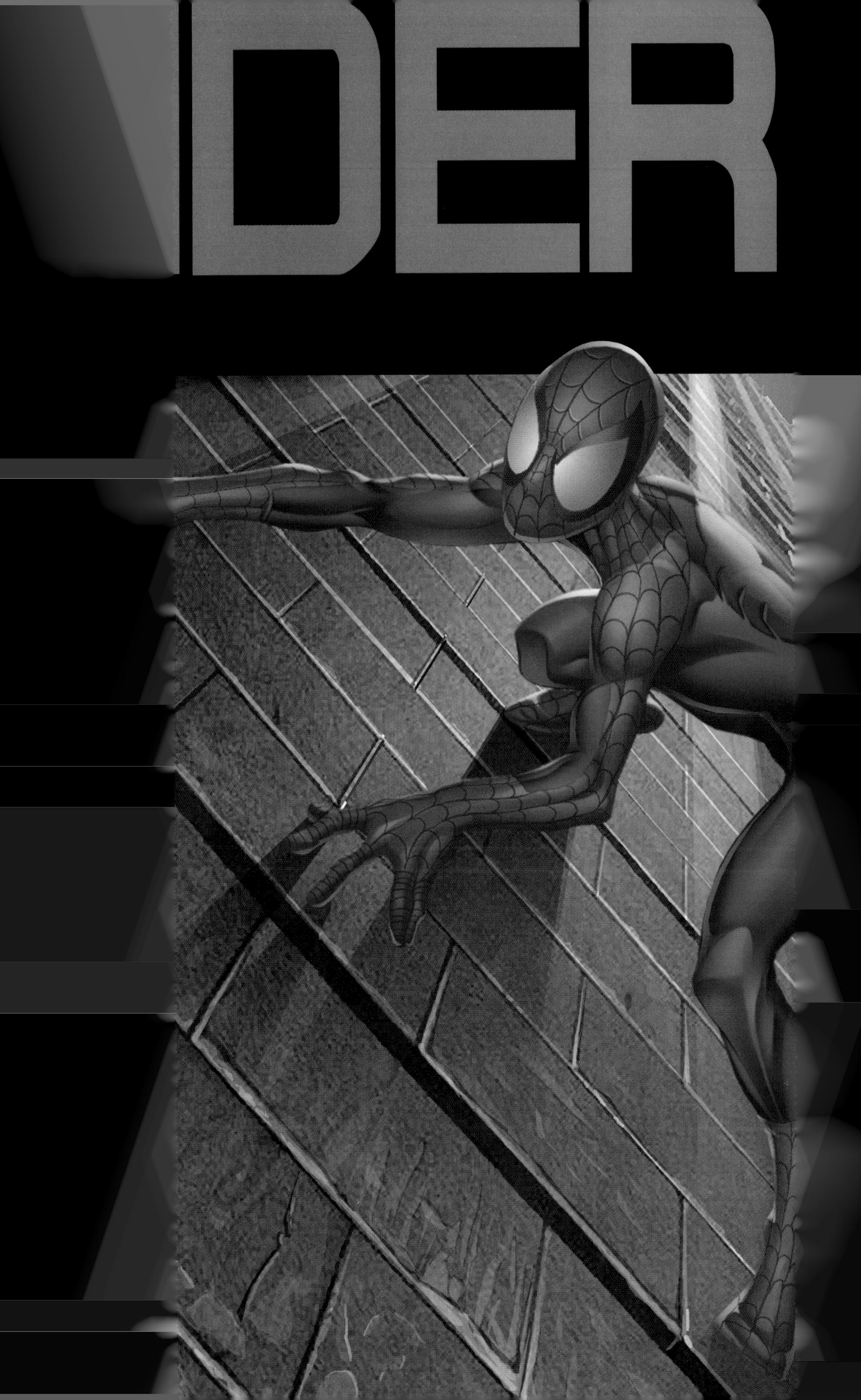
DER

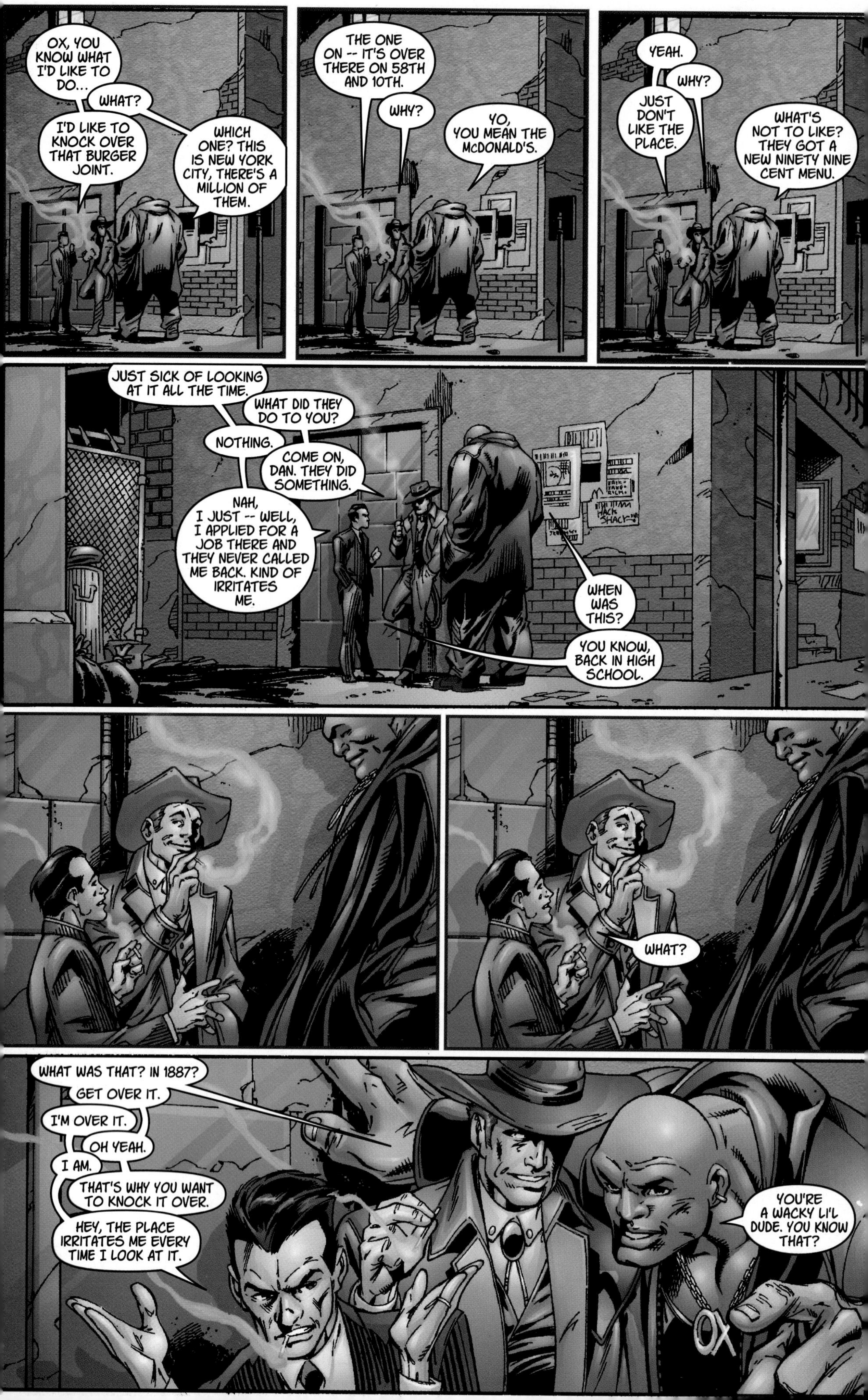
OX, YOU KNOW WHAT I'D LIKE TO DO...
WHAT?
I'D LIKE TO KNOCK OVER THAT BURGER JOINT.
WHICH ONE? THIS IS NEW YORK CITY, THERE'S A MILLION OF THEM.
THE ONE ON -- IT'S OVER THERE ON 58TH AND 10TH.
WHY?
YO, YOU MEAN THE McDONALD'S.
YEAH.
WHY?
JUST DON'T LIKE THE PLACE.
WHAT'S NOT TO LIKE? THEY GOT A NEW NINETY NINE CENT MENU.
JUST SICK OF LOOKING AT IT ALL THE TIME.
WHAT DID THEY DO TO YOU?
NOTHING.
COME ON, DAN. THEY DID SOMETHING.
NAH, I JUST -- WELL, I APPLIED FOR A JOB THERE AND THEY NEVER CALLED ME BACK. KIND OF IRRITATES ME.
WHEN WAS THIS?
YOU KNOW, BACK IN HIGH SCHOOL.
WHAT?
WHAT WAS THAT? IN 1887?
GET OVER IT.
I'M OVER IT.
OH YEAH.
I AM.
THAT'S WHY YOU WANT TO KNOCK IT OVER.
HEY, THE PLACE IRRITATES ME EVERY TIME I LOOK AT IT.
YOU'RE A WACKY LI'L DUDE. YOU KNOW THAT?

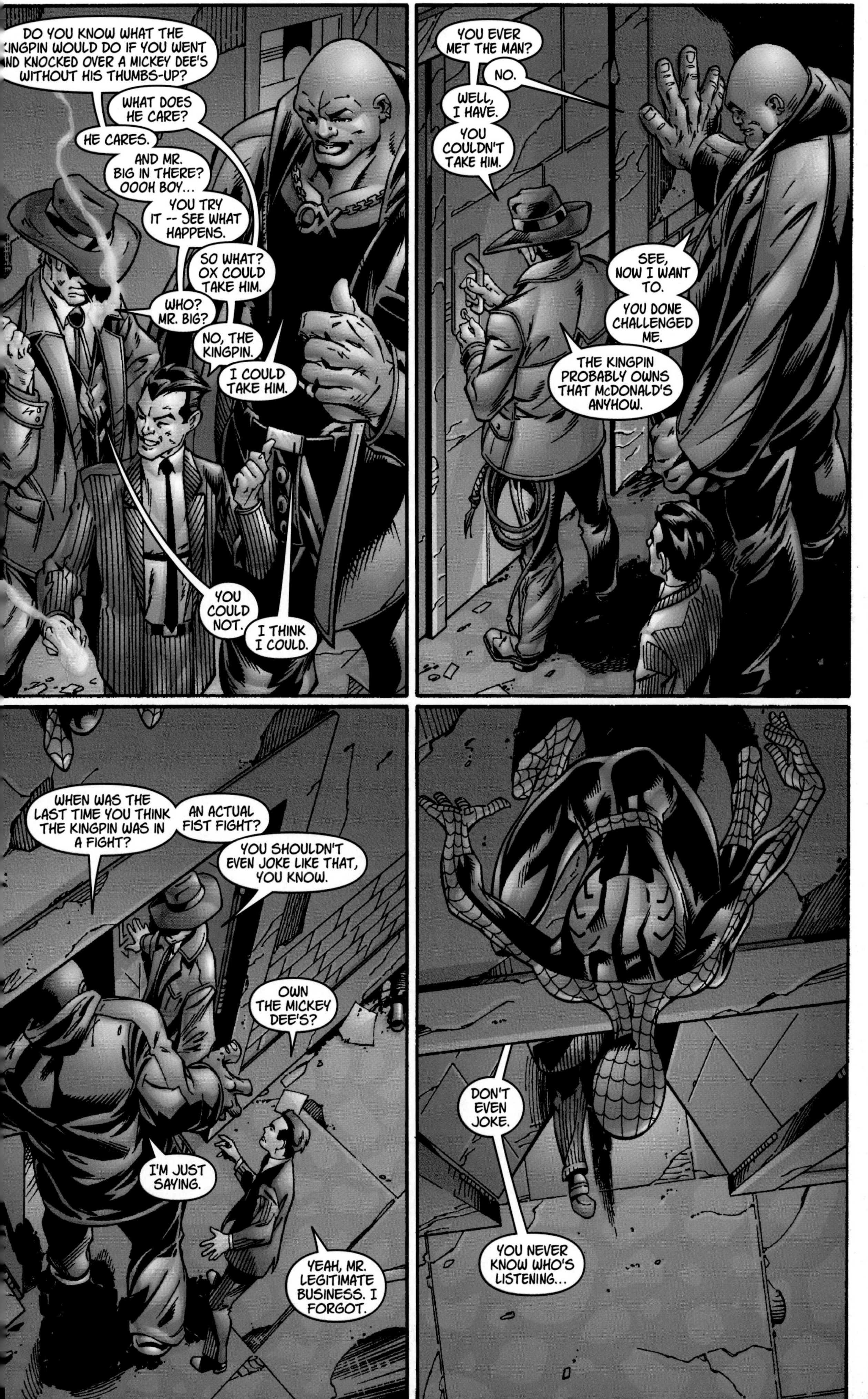

DO YOU KNOW WHAT THE KINGPIN WOULD DO IF YOU WENT AND KNOCKED OVER A MICKEY DEE'S WITHOUT HIS THUMBS-UP?
WHAT DOES HE CARE?
HE CARES.
AND MR. BIG IN THERE? OOOH BOY...
YOU TRY IT -- SEE WHAT HAPPENS.
SO WHAT? OX COULD TAKE HIM.
WHO? MR. BIG?
NO, THE KINGPIN.
I COULD TAKE HIM.
YOU COULD NOT.
I THINK I COULD.
YOU EVER MET THE MAN?
NO.
WELL, I HAVE.
YOU COULDN'T TAKE HIM.
SEE, NOW I WANT TO.
YOU DONE CHALLENGED ME.
THE KINGPIN PROBABLY OWNS THAT McDONALD'S ANYHOW.
WHEN WAS THE LAST TIME YOU THINK THE KINGPIN WAS IN A FIGHT?
AN ACTUAL FIST FIGHT?
YOU SHOULDN'T EVEN JOKE LIKE THAT, YOU KNOW.
OWN THE MICKEY DEE'S?
I'M JUST SAYING.
YEAH, MR. LEGITIMATE BUSINESS. I FORGOT.
DON'T EVEN JOKE.
YOU NEVER KNOW WHO'S LISTENING...

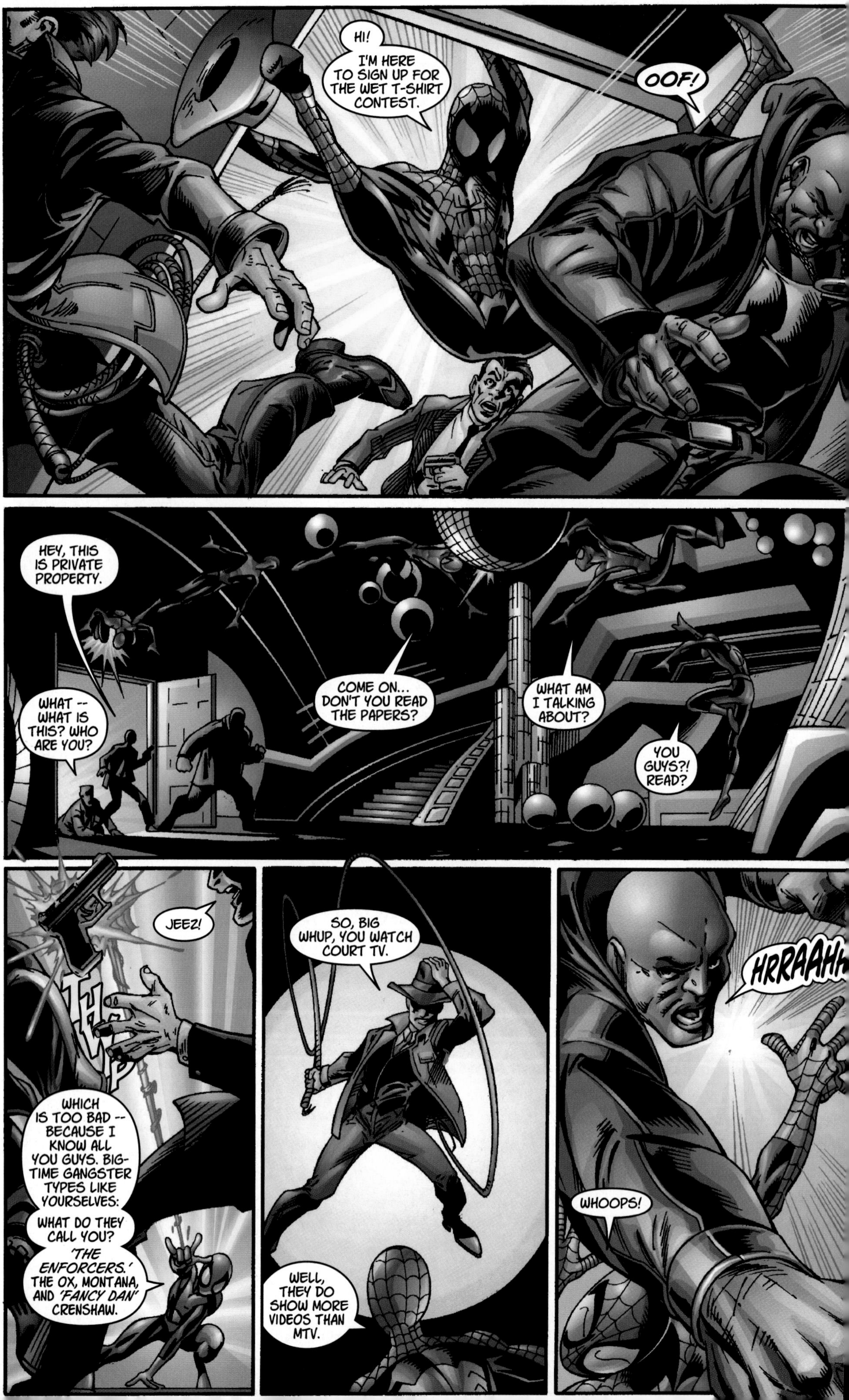
HI! I'M HERE TO SIGN UP FOR THE WET T-SHIRT CONTEST.
OOF!
HEY, THIS IS PRIVATE PROPERTY.
WHAT -- WHAT IS THIS? WHO ARE YOU?
COME ON... DON'T YOU READ THE PAPERS?
WHAT AM I TALKING ABOUT?
YOU GUYS?! READ?
JEEZ!
THWIP
WHICH IS TOO BAD -- BECAUSE I KNOW ALL YOU GUYS. BIG-TIME GANGSTER TYPES LIKE YOURSELVES:
WHAT DO THEY CALL YOU?
'THE ENFORCERS.' THE OX, MONTANA, AND 'FANCY DAN' CRENSHAW.
SO, BIG WHUP, YOU WATCH COURT TV.
WELL, THEY DO SHOW MORE VIDEOS THAN MTV.
HRRAAHH
WHOOPS!

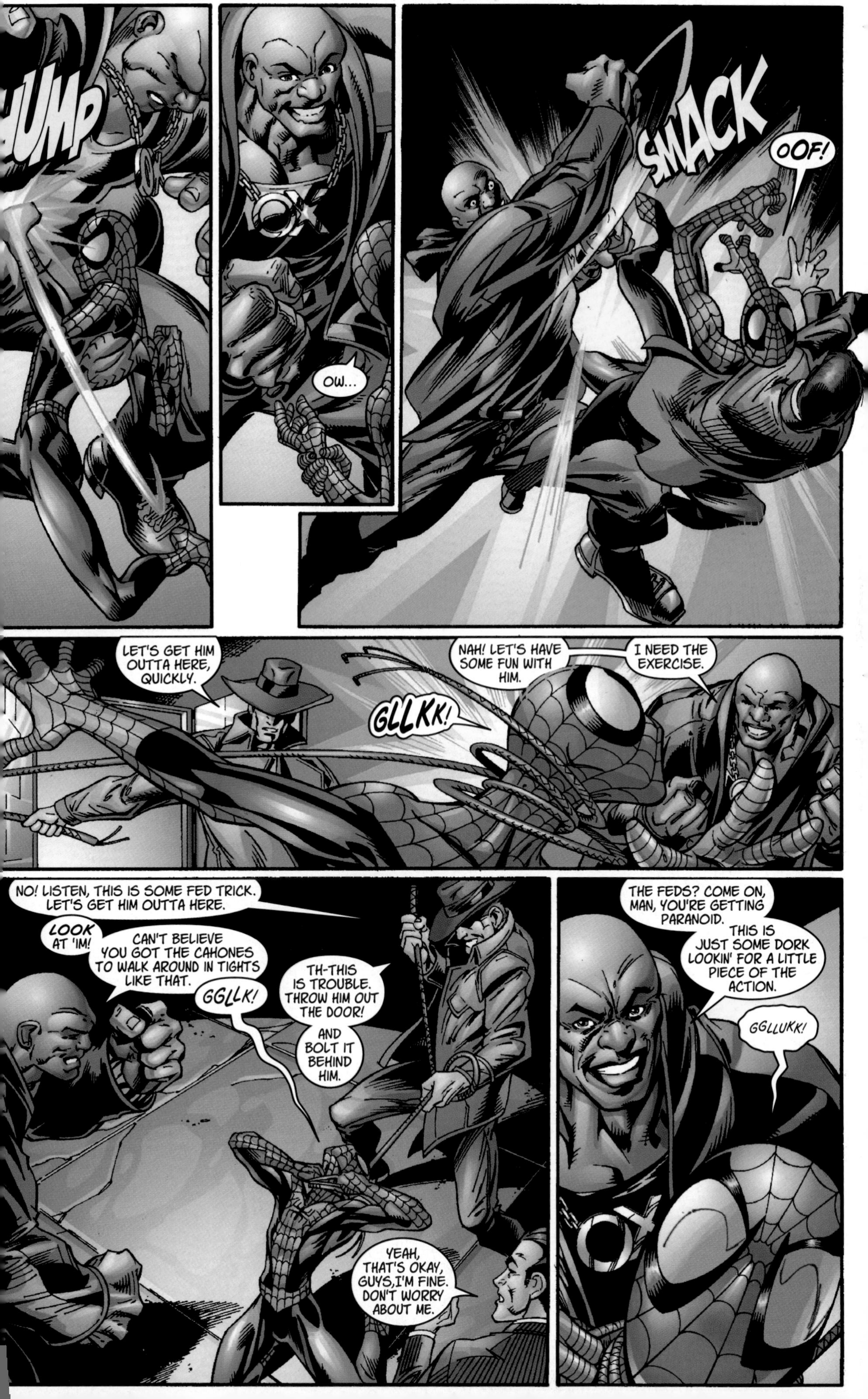

THUMP
OW...
SMACK
OOF!
LET'S GET HIM OUTTA HERE, QUICKLY.
GLLKK!
NAH! LET'S HAVE SOME FUN WITH HIM.
I NEED THE EXERCISE.
NO! LISTEN, THIS IS SOME FED TRICK. LET'S GET HIM OUTTA HERE.
LOOK AT 'IM!
CAN'T BELIEVE YOU GOT THE CAHONES TO WALK AROUND IN TIGHTS LIKE THAT.
GGLLK!
TH-THIS IS TROUBLE. THROW HIM OUT THE DOOR!
AND BOLT IT BEHIND HIM.
YEAH, THAT'S OKAY, GUYS, I'M FINE. DON'T WORRY ABOUT ME.
THE FEDS? COME ON, MAN, YOU'RE GETTING PARANOID.
THIS IS JUST SOME DORK LOOKIN' FOR A LITTLE PIECE OF THE ACTION.
GGLLUKK!

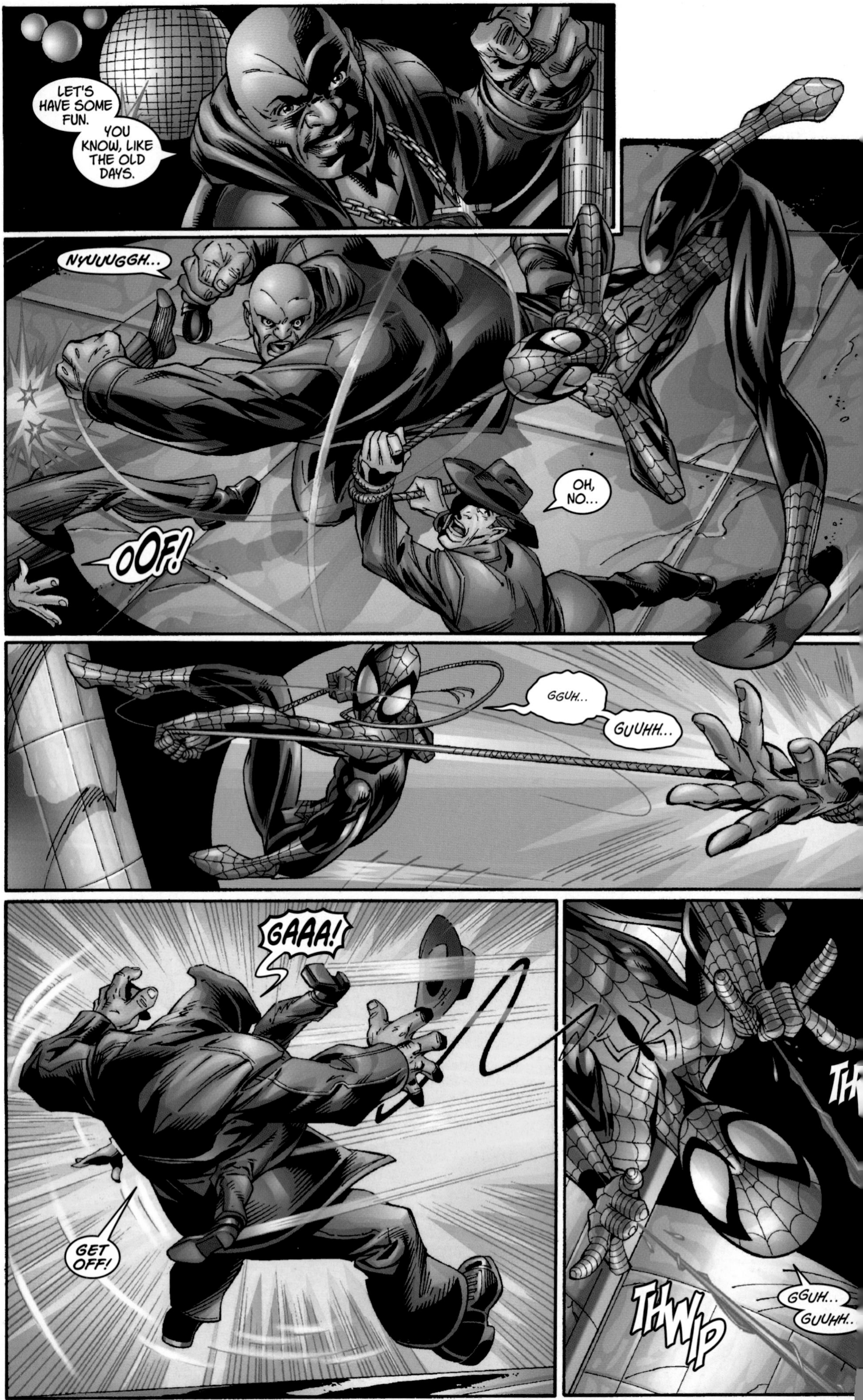
LET'S HAVE SOME FUN.
YOU KNOW, LIKE THE OLD DAYS.
NYUUUGGH...
OH, NO...
OOF!
GGUH...
GUUHH...
GAAA!
GET OFF!
THWIP
GGUH...
GUUHH...

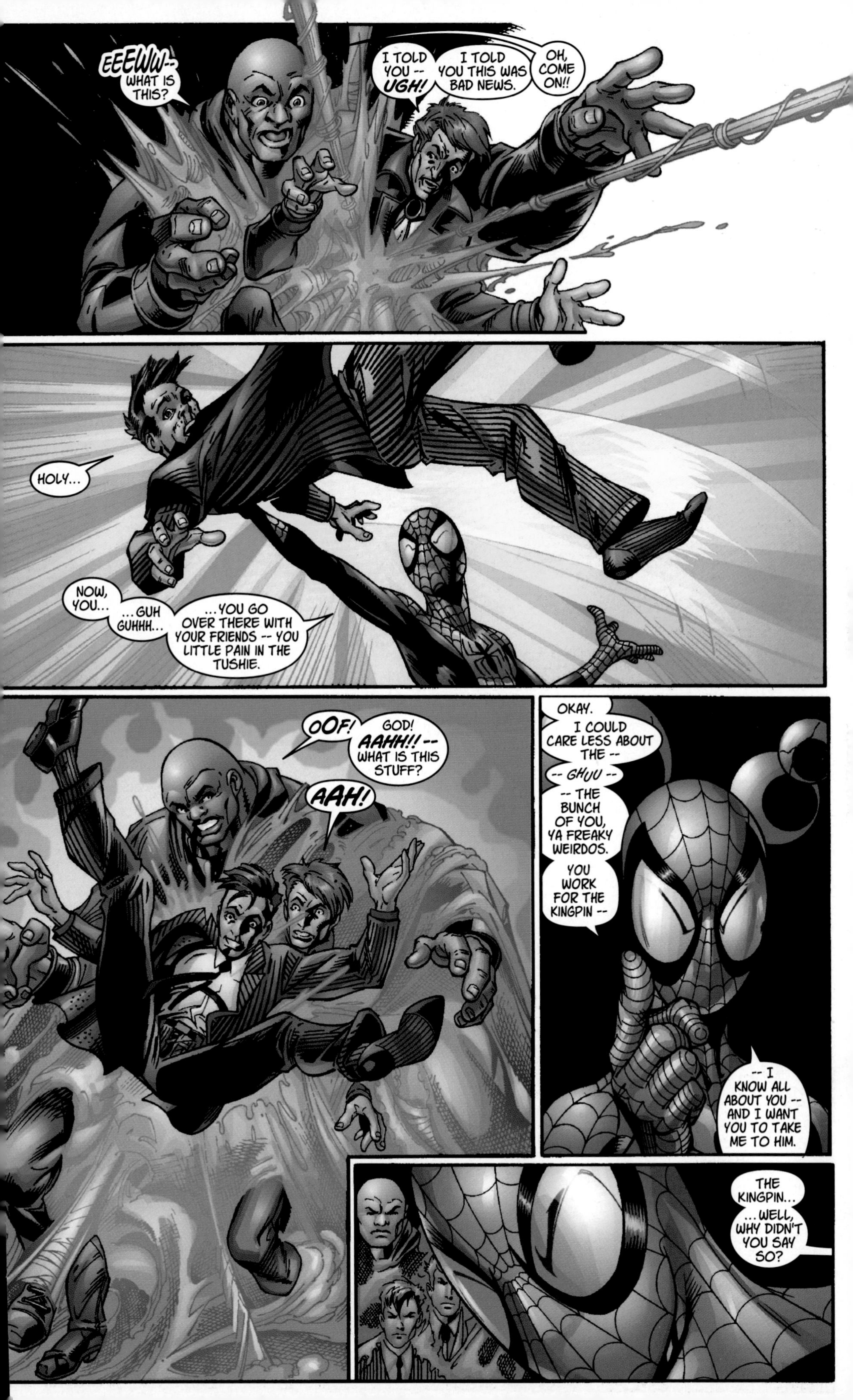
EEEWW-- WHAT IS THIS?
I TOLD YOU -- UGH!
I TOLD YOU THIS WAS BAD NEWS.
OH, COME ON!!
HOLY...
NOW, YOU...
...GUH GUHHH...
...YOU GO OVER THERE WITH YOUR FRIENDS -- YOU LITTLE PAIN IN THE TUSHIE.
OOF!
GOD! AAHH!! -- WHAT IS THIS STUFF?
AAH!
OKAY.
I COULD CARE LESS ABOUT THE --
-- GHUU --
-- THE BUNCH OF YOU, YA FREAKY WEIRDOS.
YOU WORK FOR THE KINGPIN --
-- I KNOW ALL ABOUT YOU -- AND I WANT YOU TO TAKE ME TO HIM.
THE KINGPIN...
...WELL, WHY DIDN'T YOU SAY SO?

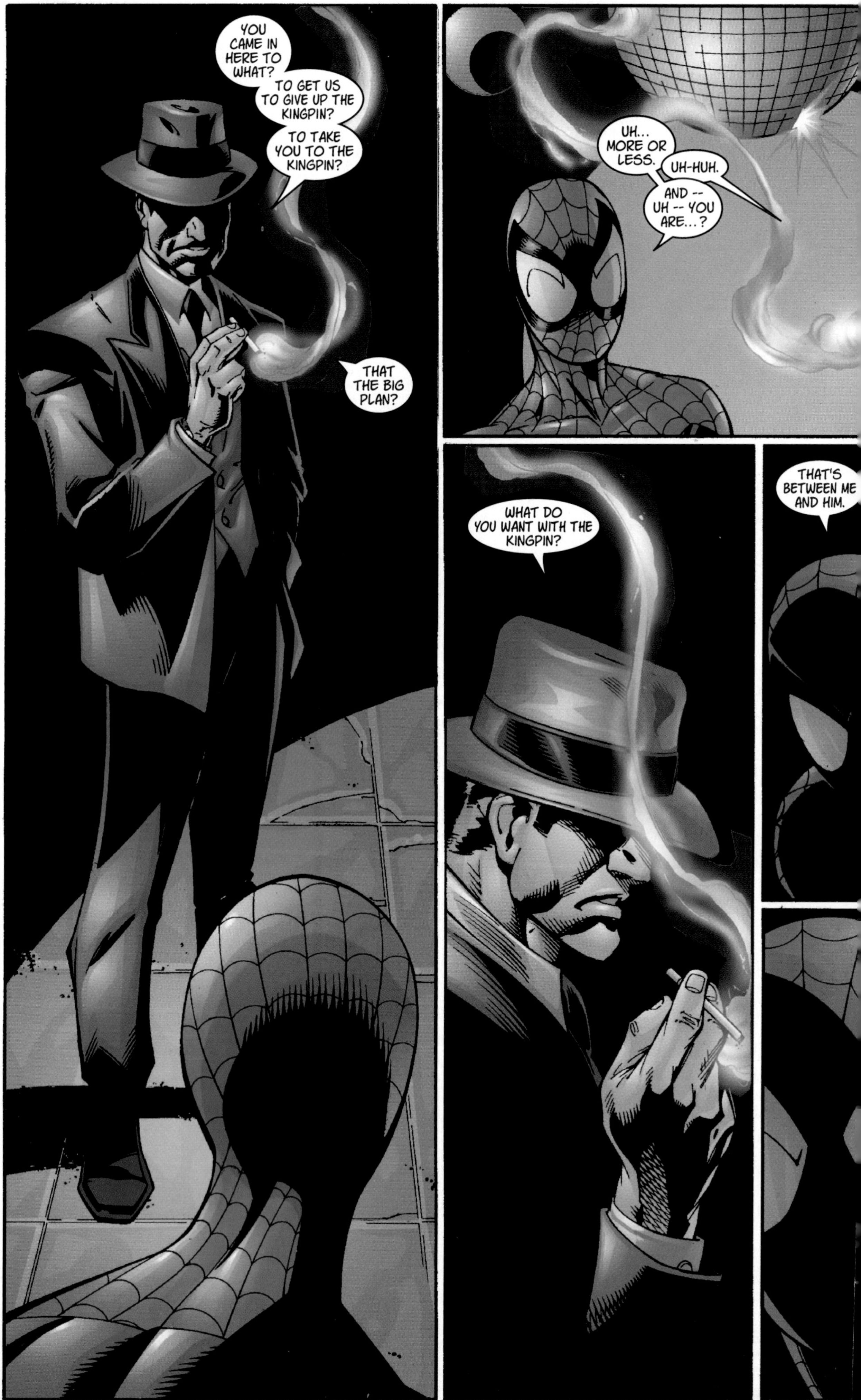
YOU CAME IN HERE TO WHAT?
TO GET US TO GIVE UP THE KINGPIN?
TO TAKE YOU TO THE KINGPIN?
THAT THE BIG PLAN?
UH... MORE OR LESS.
UH-HUH.
AND -- UH -- YOU ARE...?
WHAT DO YOU WANT WITH THE KINGPIN?
THAT'S BETWEEN ME AND HIM.

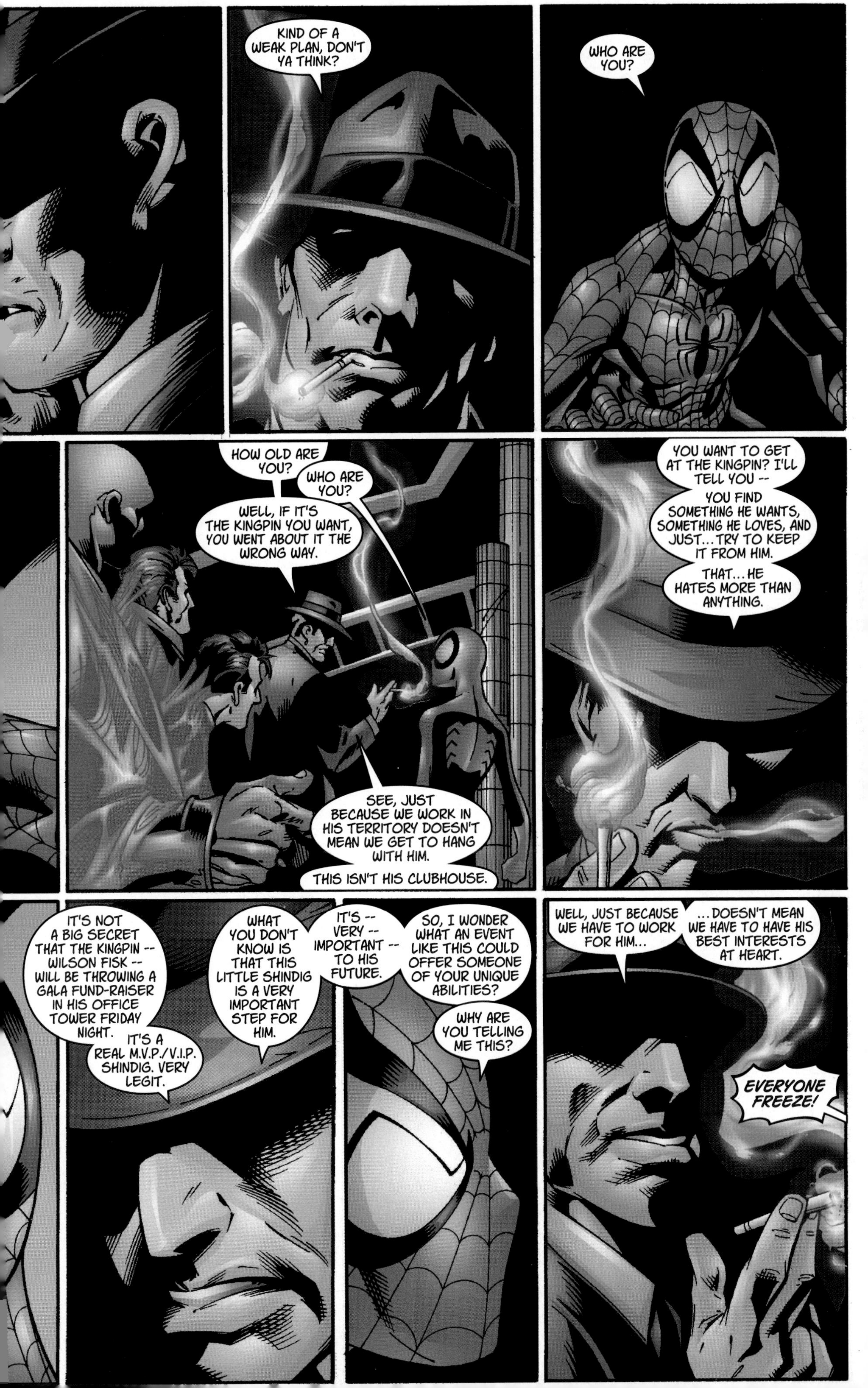
KIND OF A WEAK PLAN, DON'T YA THINK?
WHO ARE YOU?
HOW OLD ARE YOU?
WHO ARE YOU?
WELL, IF IT'S THE KINGPIN YOU WANT, YOU WENT ABOUT IT THE WRONG WAY.
SEE, JUST BECAUSE WE WORK IN HIS TERRITORY DOESN'T MEAN WE GET TO HANG WITH HIM.
THIS ISN'T HIS CLUBHOUSE.
YOU WANT TO GET AT THE KINGPIN? I'LL TELL YOU --
YOU FIND SOMETHING HE WANTS, SOMETHING HE LOVES, AND JUST...TRY TO KEEP IT FROM HIM.
THAT... HE HATES MORE THAN ANYTHING.
IT'S NOT A BIG SECRET THAT THE KINGPIN -- WILSON FISK -- WILL BE THROWING A GALA FUND-RAISER IN HIS OFFICE TOWER FRIDAY NIGHT.
IT'S A REAL M.V.P./V.I.P. SHINDIG. VERY LEGIT.
WHAT YOU DON'T KNOW IS THAT THIS LITTLE SHINDIG IS A VERY IMPORTANT STEP FOR HIM.
IT'S -- VERY -- IMPORTANT -- TO HIS FUTURE.
SO, I WONDER WHAT AN EVENT LIKE THIS COULD OFFER SOMEONE OF YOUR UNIQUE ABILITIES?
WHY ARE YOU TELLING ME THIS?
WELL, JUST BECAUSE WE HAVE TO WORK FOR HIM...
...DOESN'T MEAN WE HAVE TO HAVE HIS BEST INTERESTS AT HEART.
EVERYONE FREEZE!

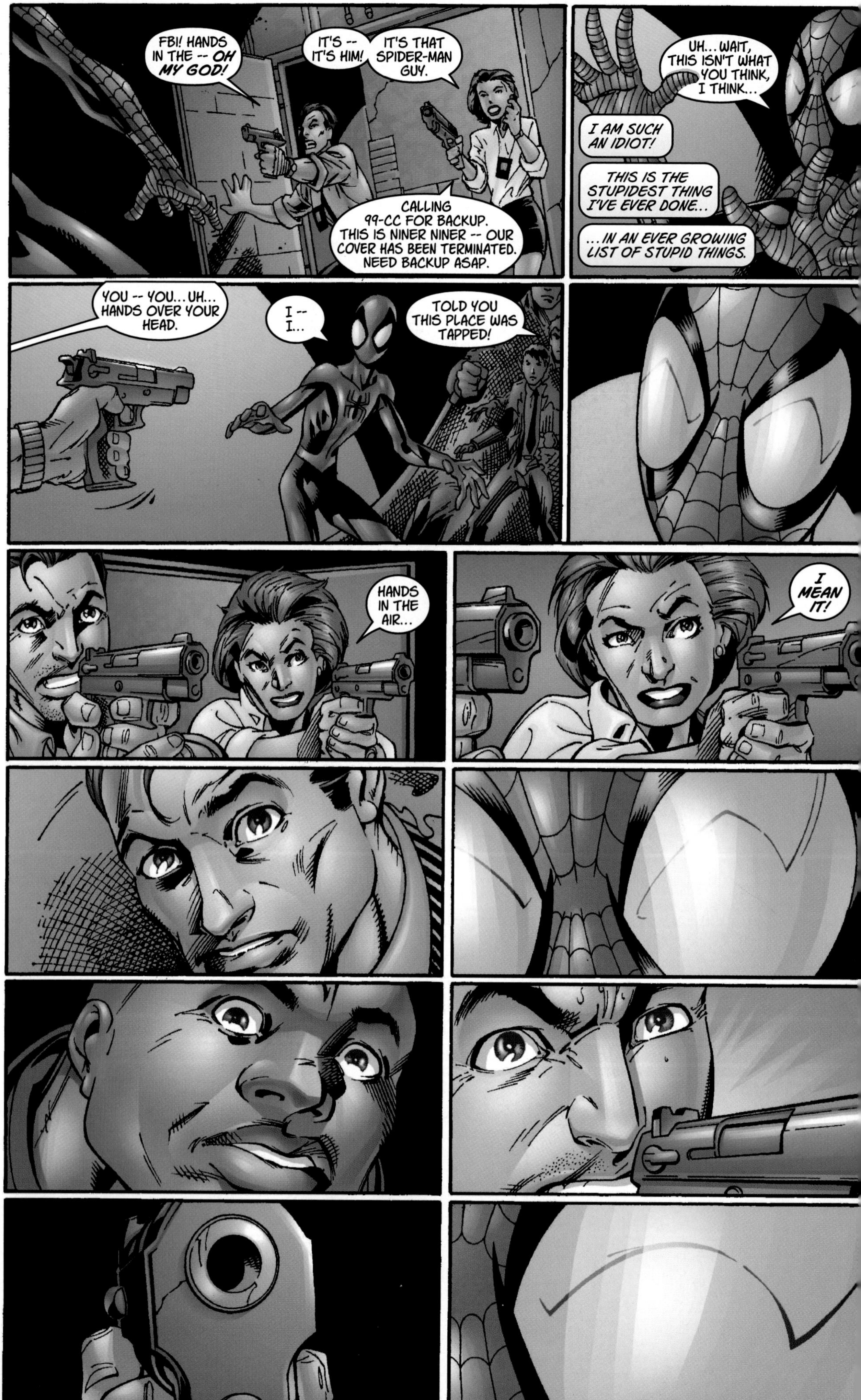
FBI! HANDS IN THE -- OH MY GOD!
IT'S -- IT'S HIM!
IT'S THAT SPIDER-MAN GUY.
CALLING 99-CC FOR BACKUP. THIS IS NINER NINER -- OUR COVER HAS BEEN TERMINATED. NEED BACKUP ASAP.
UH... WAIT, THIS ISN'T WHAT YOU THINK, I THINK...
I AM SUCH AN IDIOT!
THIS IS THE STUPIDEST THING I'VE EVER DONE...
...IN AN EVER GROWING LIST OF STUPID THINGS.
YOU -- YOU... UH... HANDS OVER YOUR HEAD.
I -- I...
TOLD YOU THIS PLACE WAS TAPPED!
HANDS IN THE AIR...
I MEAN IT!

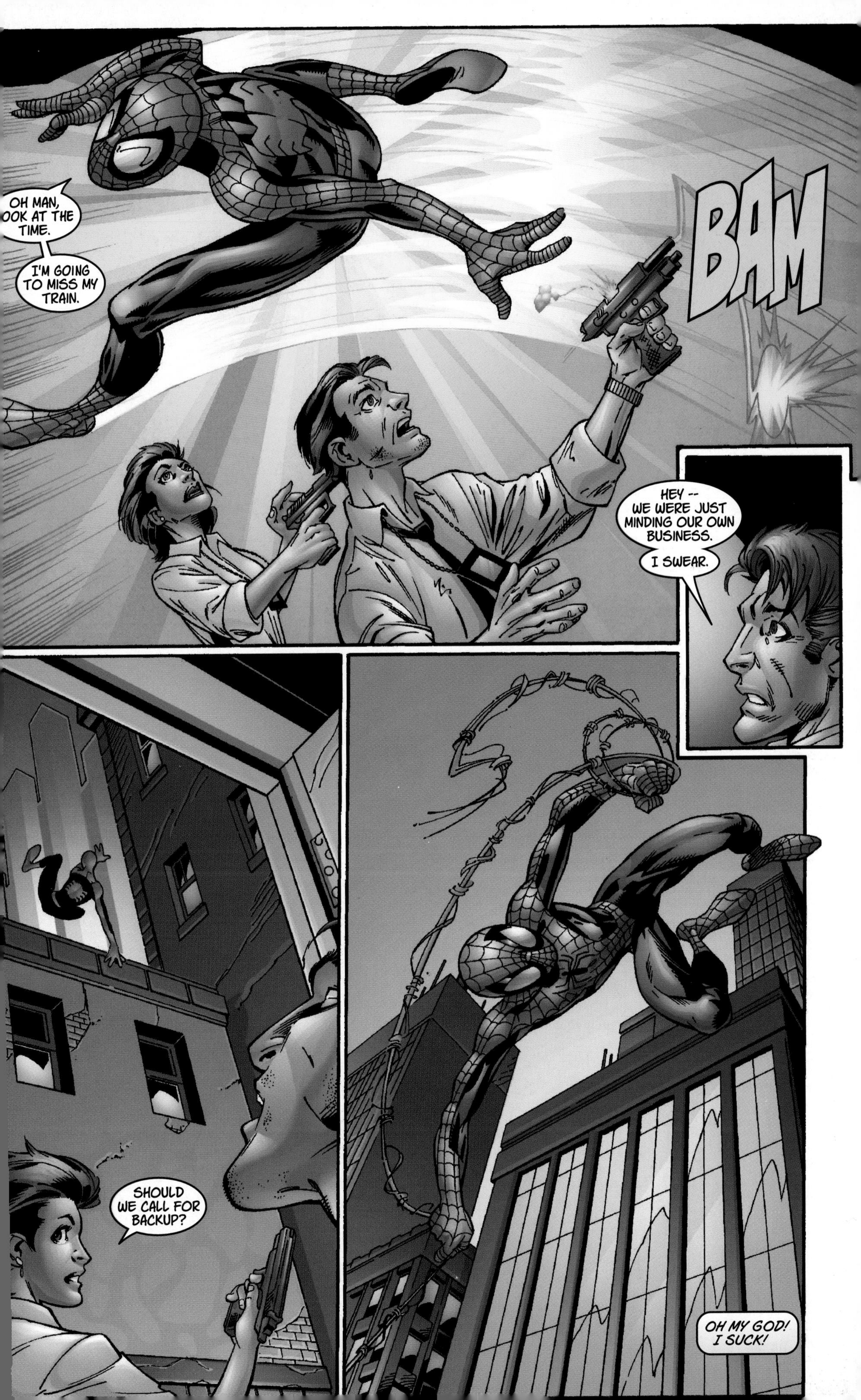
OH MAN, LOOK AT THE TIME.
I'M GOING TO MISS MY TRAIN.
BAM
HEY -- WE WERE JUST MINDING OUR OWN BUSINESS.
I SWEAR.
SHOULD WE CALL FOR BACKUP?
OH MY GOD! I SUCK!

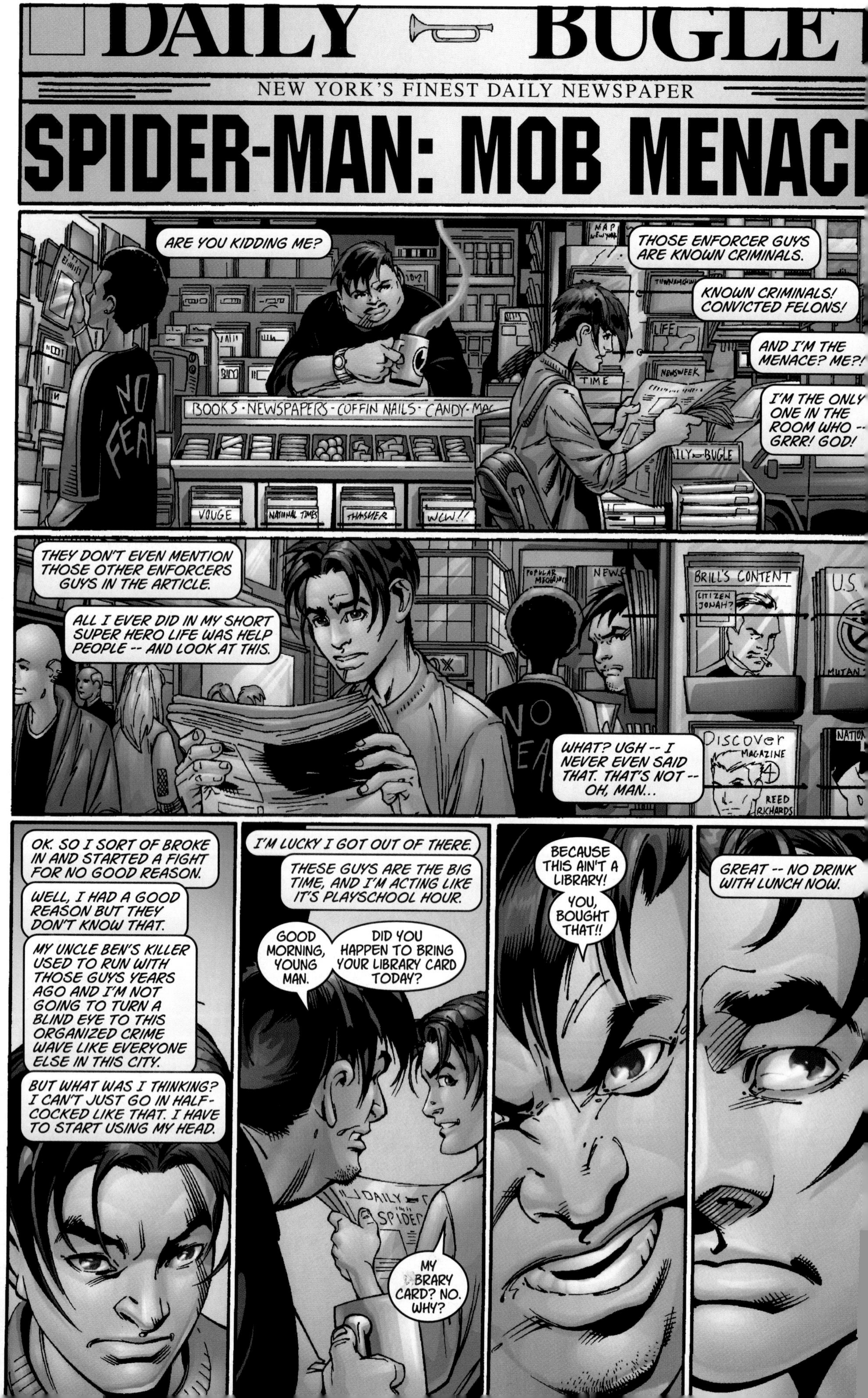
DAILY BUGLE
NEW YORK'S FINEST DAILY NEWSPAPER
SPIDER-MAN: MOB MENAC
ARE YOU KIDDING ME?
THOSE ENFORCER GUYS ARE KNOWN CRIMINALS.
KNOWN CRIMINALS! CONVICTED FELONS!
AND I'M THE MENACE? ME?!
I'M THE ONLY ONE IN THE ROOM WHO -- GRRR! GOD!
BOOKS · NEWSPAPERS · COFFIN NAILS · CANDY · MAG
THEY DON'T EVEN MENTION THOSE OTHER ENFORCERS GUYS IN THE ARTICLE.
ALL I EVER DID IN MY SHORT SUPER HERO LIFE WAS HELP PEOPLE -- AND LOOK AT THIS.
BRILL'S CONTENT
CITIZEN JONAH?
WHAT? UGH -- I NEVER EVEN SAID THAT. THAT'S NOT -- OH, MAN...
Discover MAGAZINE
REED RICHARDS
OK. SO I SORT OF BROKE IN AND STARTED A FIGHT FOR NO GOOD REASON.
WELL, I HAD A GOOD REASON BUT THEY DON'T KNOW THAT.
MY UNCLE BEN'S KILLER USED TO RUN WITH THOSE GUYS YEARS AGO AND I'M NOT GOING TO TURN A BLIND EYE TO THIS ORGANIZED CRIME WAVE LIKE EVERYONE ELSE IN THIS CITY.
BUT WHAT WAS I THINKING? I CAN'T JUST GO IN HALF-COCKED LIKE THAT. I HAVE TO START USING MY HEAD.
I'M LUCKY I GOT OUT OF THERE.
THESE GUYS ARE THE BIG TIME, AND I'M ACTING LIKE IT'S PLAYSCHOOL HOUR.
GOOD MORNING, YOUNG MAN.
DID YOU HAPPEN TO BRING YOUR LIBRARY CARD TODAY?
MY BRARY CARD? NO. WHY?
BECAUSE THIS AIN'T A LIBRARY!
YOU, BOUGHT THAT!!
GREAT -- NO DRINK WITH LUNCH NOW.

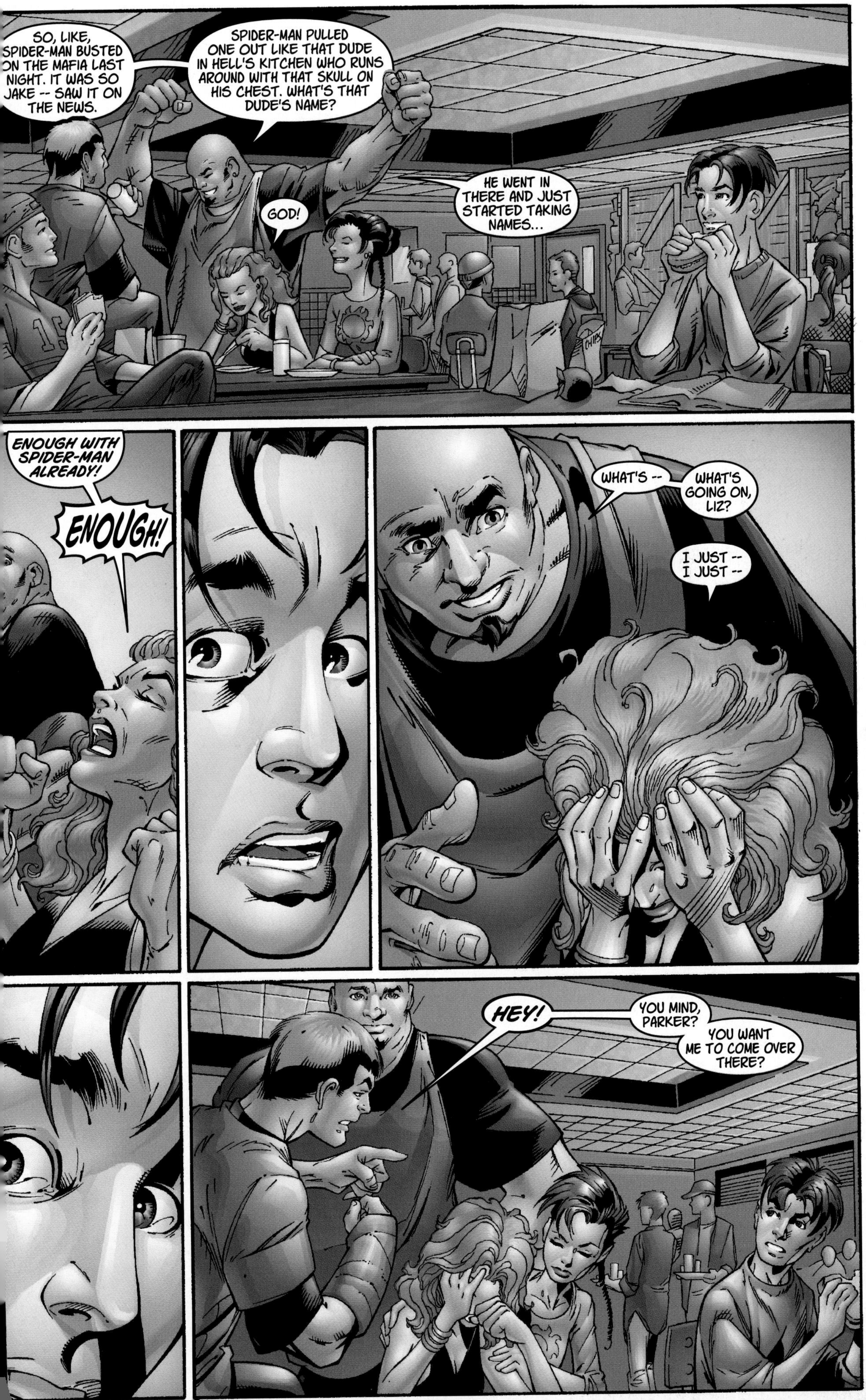

SO, LIKE, SPIDER-MAN BUSTED ON THE MAFIA LAST NIGHT. IT WAS SO JAKE -- SAW IT ON THE NEWS.
SPIDER-MAN PULLED ONE OUT LIKE THAT DUDE IN HELL'S KITCHEN WHO RUNS AROUND WITH THAT SKULL ON HIS CHEST. WHAT'S THAT DUDE'S NAME?
GOD!
HE WENT IN THERE AND JUST STARTED TAKING NAMES...
ENOUGH WITH SPIDER-MAN ALREADY!
ENOUGH!
WHAT'S --
WHAT'S GOING ON, LIZ?
I JUST -- I JUST --
HEY!
YOU MIND, PARKER?
YOU WANT ME TO COME OVER THERE?

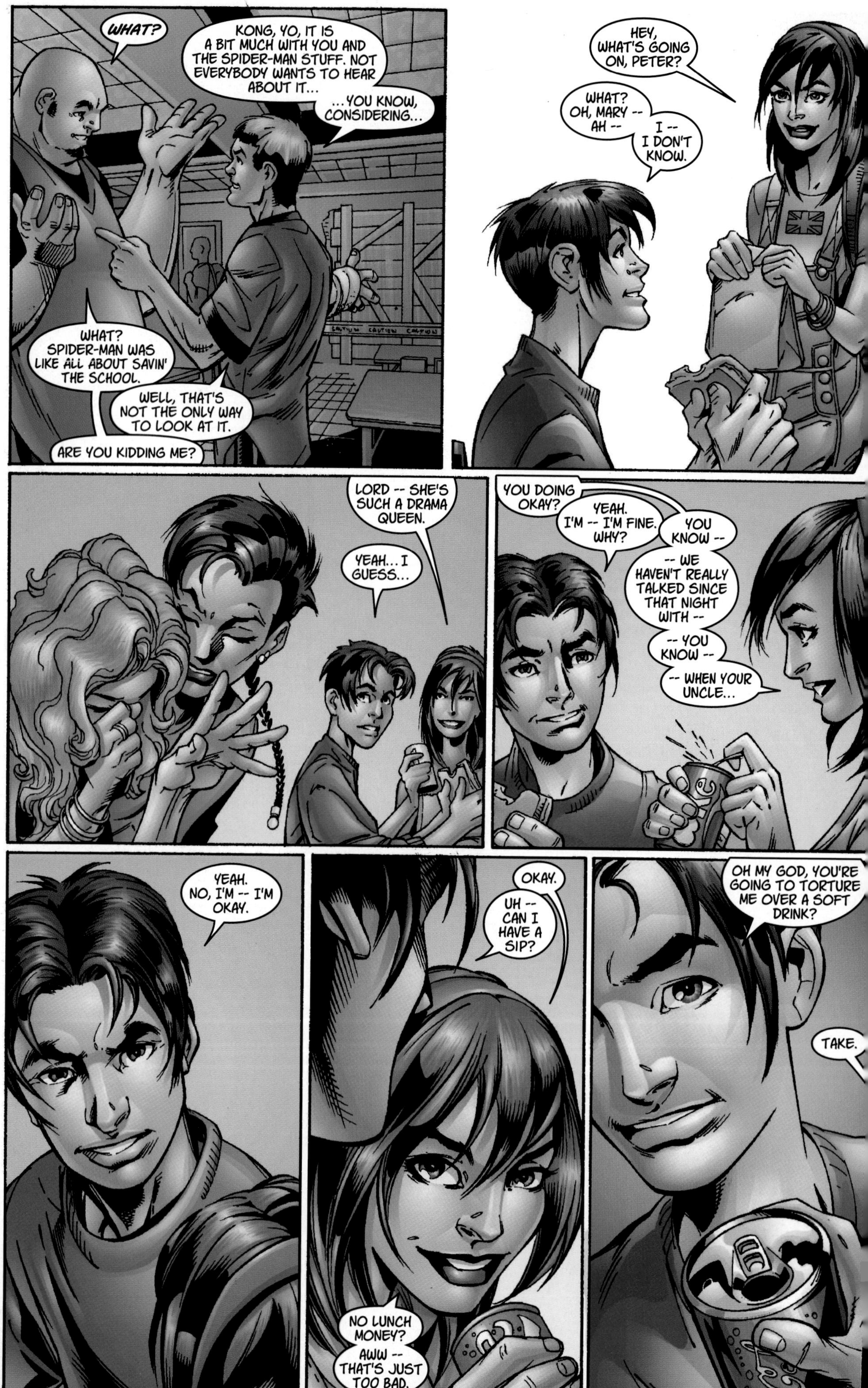
WHAT?
KONG, YO, IT IS A BIT MUCH WITH YOU AND THE SPIDER-MAN STUFF. NOT EVERYBODY WANTS TO HEAR ABOUT IT...
...YOU KNOW, CONSIDERING...
WHAT? SPIDER-MAN WAS LIKE ALL ABOUT SAVIN' THE SCHOOL.
WELL, THAT'S NOT THE ONLY WAY TO LOOK AT IT.
ARE YOU KIDDING ME?
HEY, WHAT'S GOING ON, PETER?
WHAT? OH, MARY -- AH --
I -- I DON'T KNOW.
LORD -- SHE'S SUCH A DRAMA QUEEN.
YEAH... I GUESS...
YOU DOING OKAY?
YEAH. I'M -- I'M FINE. WHY?
YOU KNOW --
-- WE HAVEN'T REALLY TALKED SINCE THAT NIGHT WITH --
-- YOU KNOW --
-- WHEN YOUR UNCLE...
YEAH. NO, I'M -- I'M OKAY.
OKAY.
UH -- CAN I HAVE A SIP?
NO LUNCH MONEY? AWW -- THAT'S JUST TOO BAD.
OH MY GOD, YOU'RE GOING TO TORTURE ME OVER A SOFT DRINK?
TAKE.

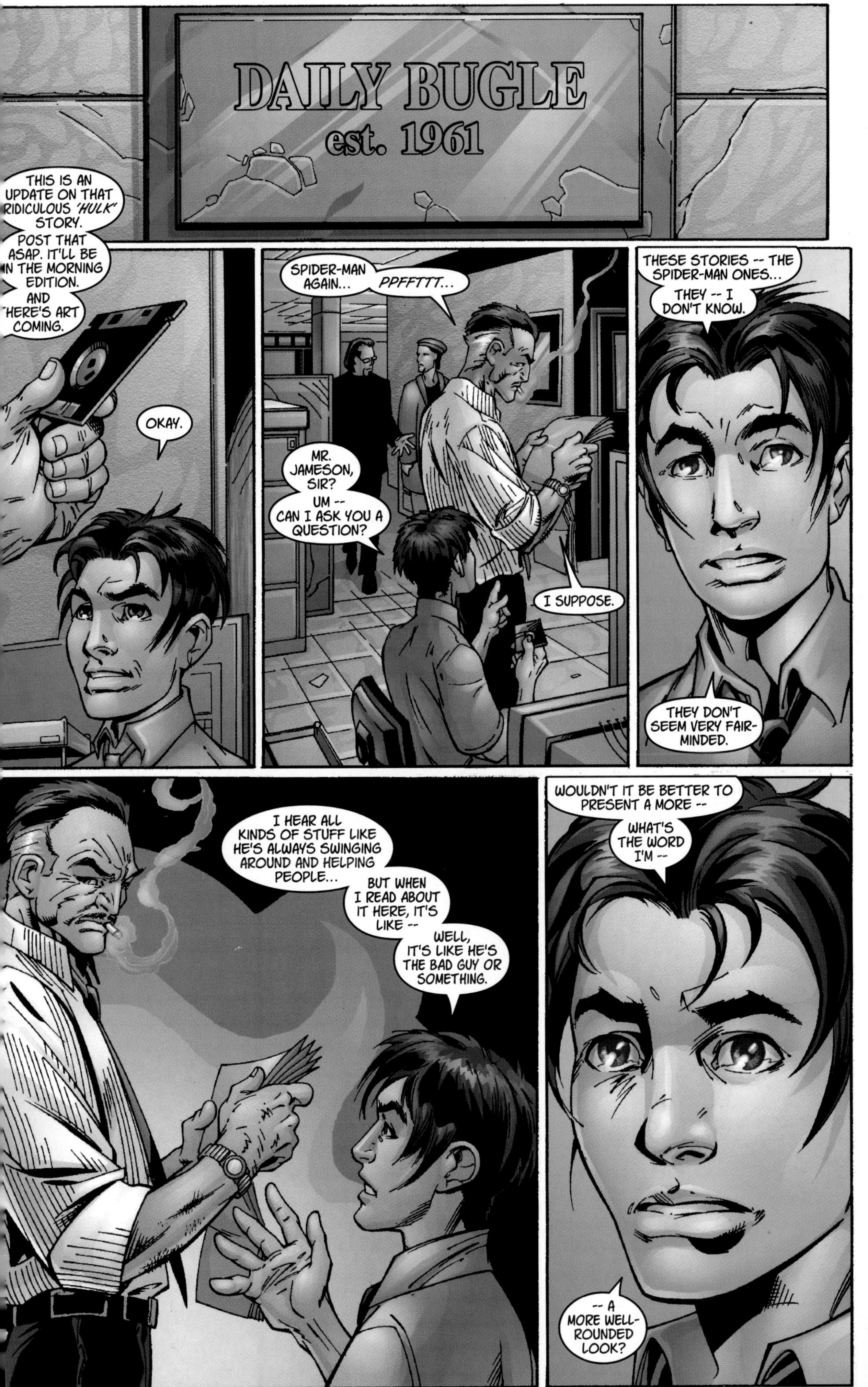

DAILY BUGLE
est. 1961
THIS IS AN UPDATE ON THAT RIDICULOUS 'HULK' STORY.
POST THAT ASAP. IT'LL BE IN THE MORNING EDITION.
AND THERE'S ART COMING.
OKAY.
SPIDER-MAN AGAIN...
PPFFTTT...
MR. JAMESON, SIR?
UM -- CAN I ASK YOU A QUESTION?
I SUPPOSE.
THESE STORIES -- THE SPIDER-MAN ONES...
THEY -- I DON'T KNOW.
THEY DON'T SEEM VERY FAIR-MINDED.
I HEAR ALL KINDS OF STUFF LIKE HE'S ALWAYS SWINGING AROUND AND HELPING PEOPLE...
BUT WHEN I READ ABOUT IT HERE, IT'S LIKE --
WELL, IT'S LIKE HE'S THE BAD GUY OR SOMETHING.
WOULDN'T IT BE BETTER TO PRESENT A MORE --
WHAT'S THE WORD I'M --
-- A MORE WELL-ROUNDED LOOK?

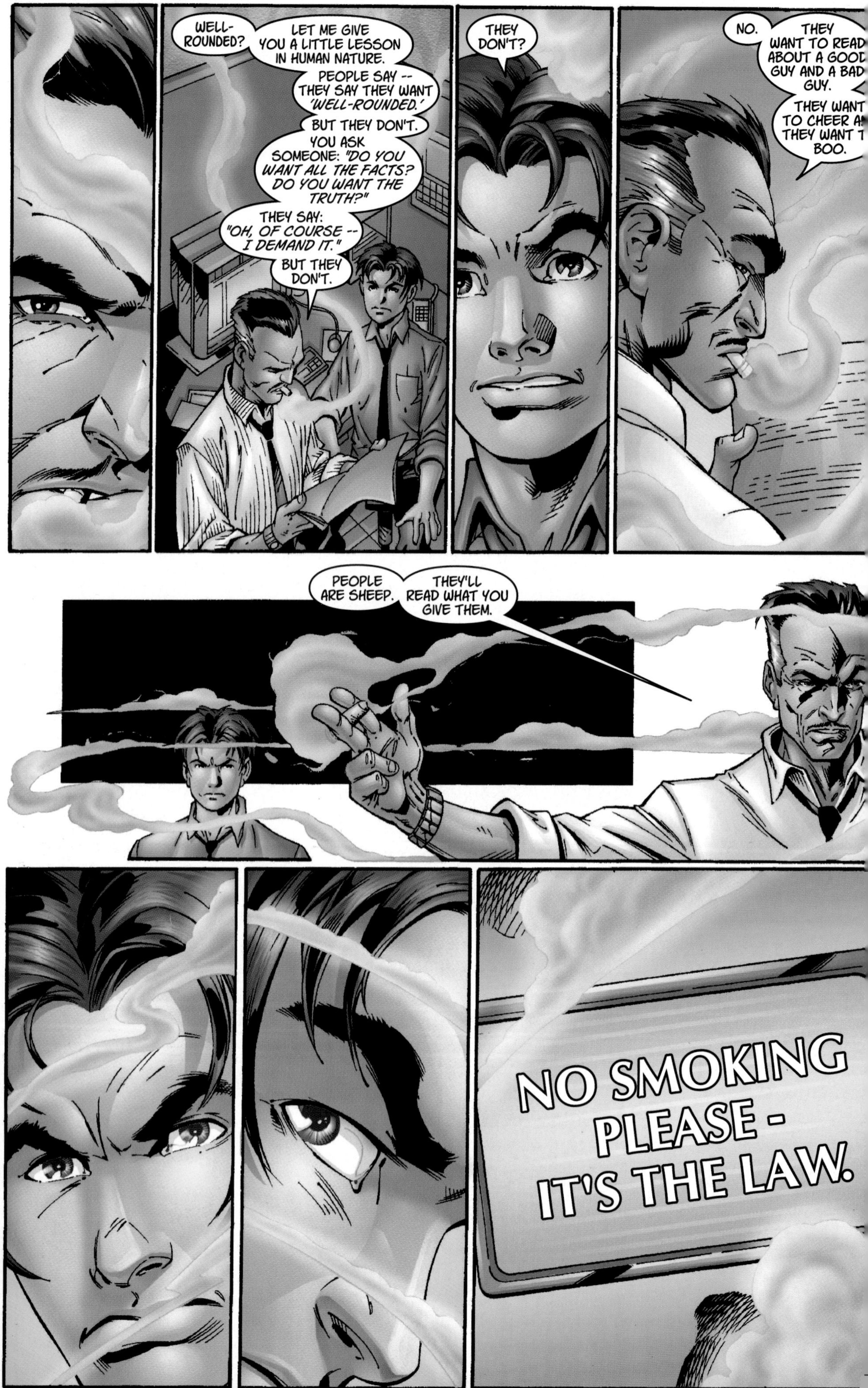
WELL-ROUNDED?
LET ME GIVE YOU A LITTLE LESSON IN HUMAN NATURE.
PEOPLE SAY -- THEY SAY THEY WANT 'WELL-ROUNDED.'
BUT THEY DON'T.
YOU ASK SOMEONE: "DO YOU WANT ALL THE FACTS? DO YOU WANT THE TRUTH?"
THEY SAY: "OH, OF COURSE -- I DEMAND IT."
BUT THEY DON'T.
THEY DON'T?
NO.
THEY WANT TO READ ABOUT A GOOD GUY AND A BAD GUY.
THEY WANT TO CHEER AND THEY WANT TO BOO.
PEOPLE ARE SHEEP.
THEY'LL READ WHAT YOU GIVE THEM.
NO SMOKING PLEASE - IT'S THE LAW.

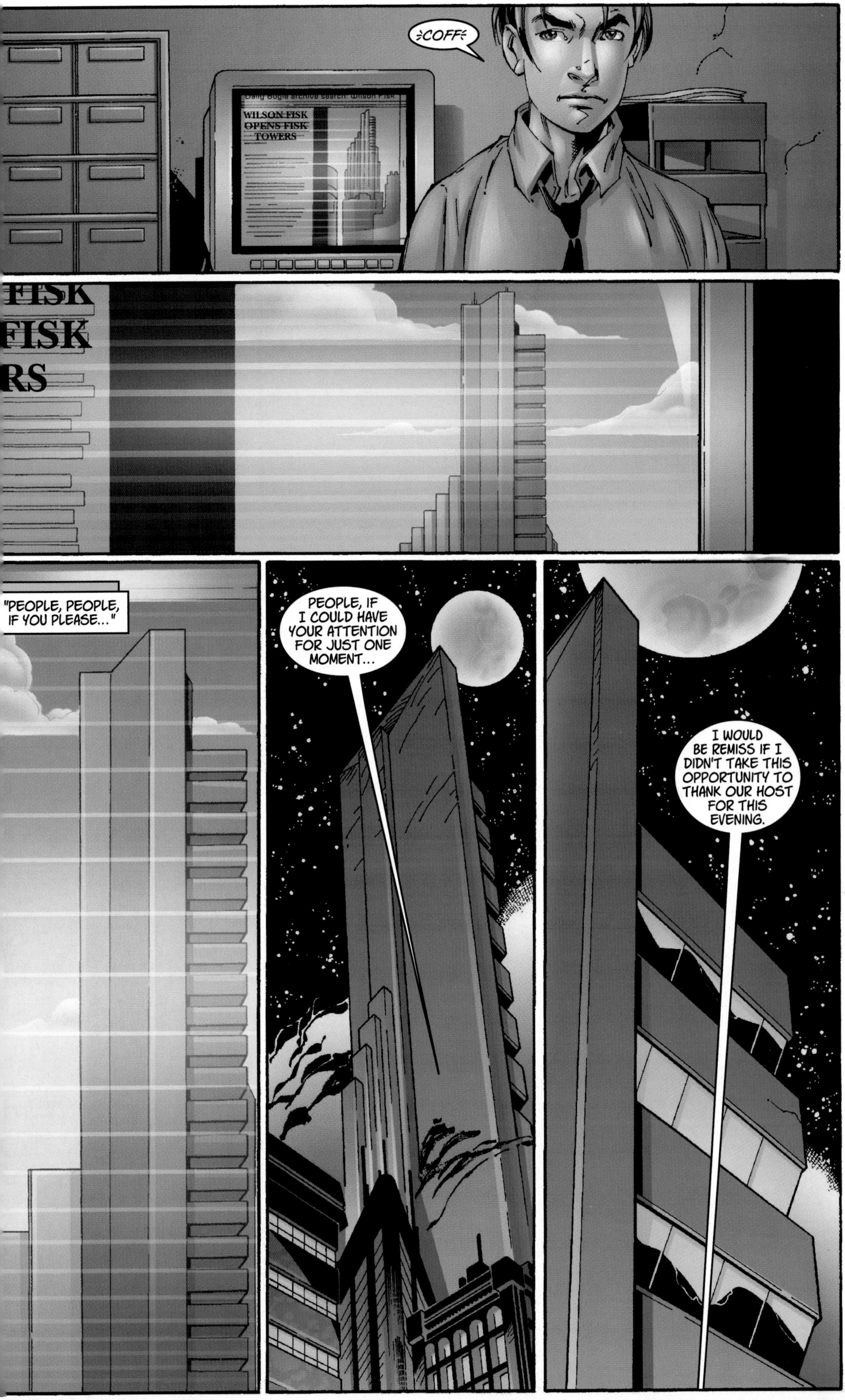

COFF
Daily Bugle archive search: Wilson Fisk
WILSON FISK OPENS FISK TOWERS
"PEOPLE, PEOPLE, IF YOU PLEASE..."
PEOPLE, IF I COULD HAVE YOUR ATTENTION FOR JUST ONE MOMENT...
I WOULD BE REMISS IF I DIDN'T TAKE THIS OPPORTUNITY TO THANK OUR HOST FOR THIS EVENING.

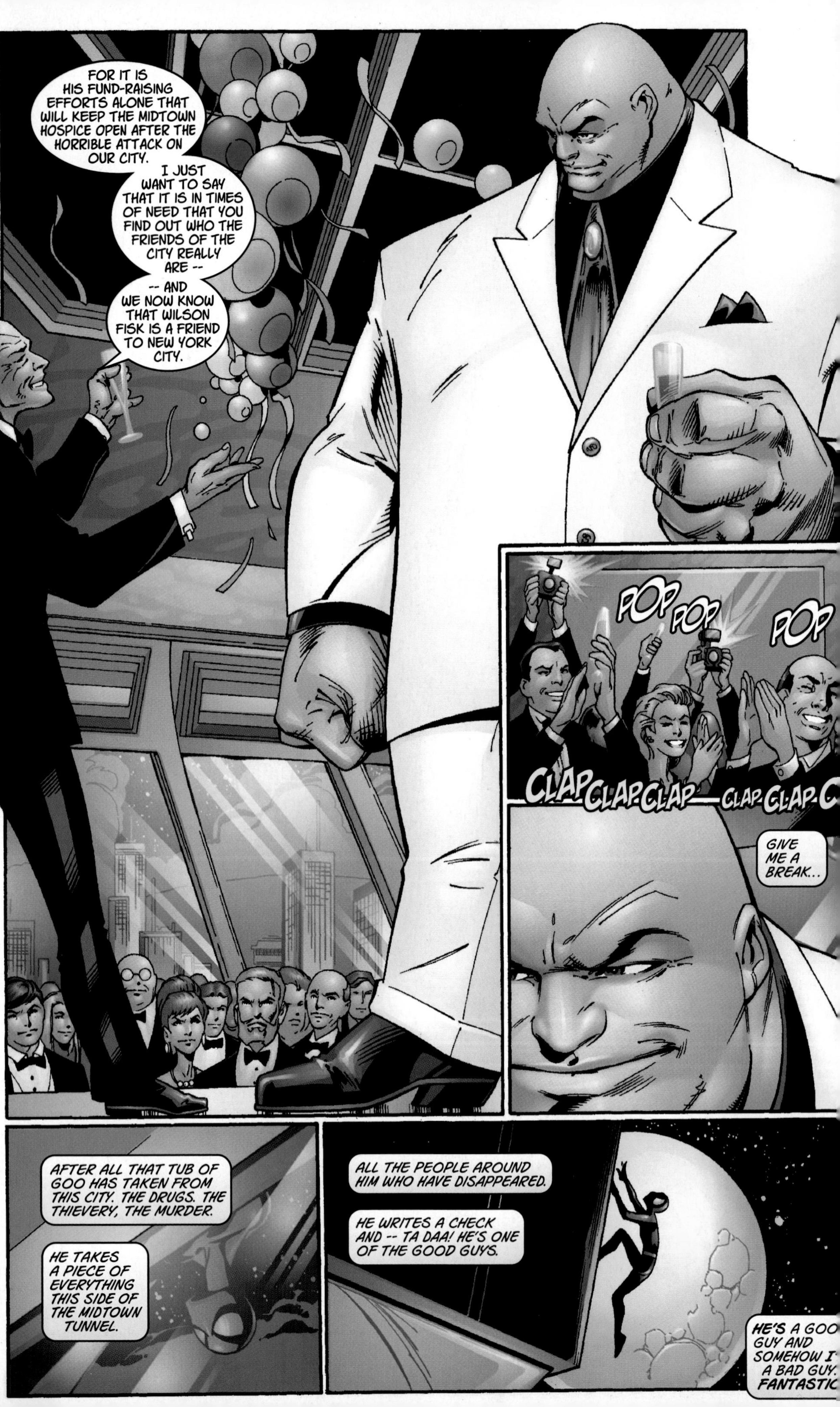
FOR IT IS HIS FUND-RAISING EFFORTS ALONE THAT WILL KEEP THE MIDTOWN HOSPICE OPEN AFTER THE HORRIBLE ATTACK ON OUR CITY.
I JUST WANT TO SAY THAT IT IS IN TIMES OF NEED THAT YOU FIND OUT WHO THE FRIENDS OF THE CITY REALLY ARE --
-- AND WE NOW KNOW THAT WILSON FISK IS A FRIEND TO NEW YORK CITY.
POP POP
POP
CLAP CLAP CLAP CLAP CLAP
GIVE ME A BREAK...
AFTER ALL THAT TUB OF GOO HAS TAKEN FROM THIS CITY. THE DRUGS. THE THIEVERY, THE MURDER.
HE TAKES A PIECE OF EVERYTHING THIS SIDE OF THE MIDTOWN TUNNEL.
ALL THE PEOPLE AROUND HIM WHO HAVE DISAPPEARED.
HE WRITES A CHECK AND -- TA DAA! HE'S ONE OF THE GOOD GUYS.

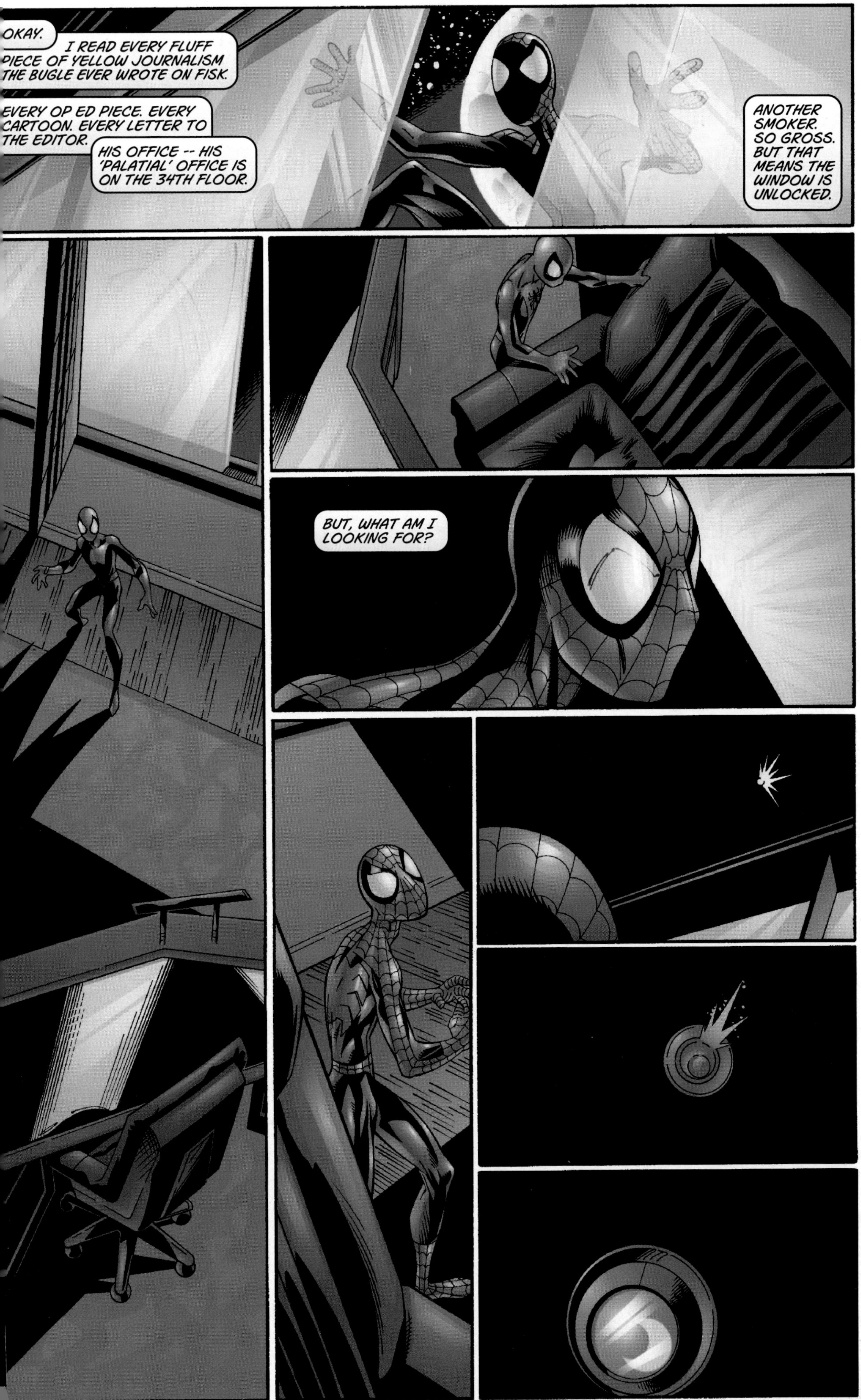
OKAY.
I READ EVERY FLUFF PIECE OF YELLOW JOURNALISM THE BUGLE EVER WROTE ON FISK.
EVERY OP ED PIECE. EVERY CARTOON. EVERY LETTER TO THE EDITOR.
HIS OFFICE -- HIS 'PALATIAL' OFFICE IS ON THE 34TH FLOOR.
ANOTHER SMOKER. SO GROSS. BUT THAT MEANS THE WINDOW IS UNLOCKED.
BUT, WHAT AM I LOOKING FOR?

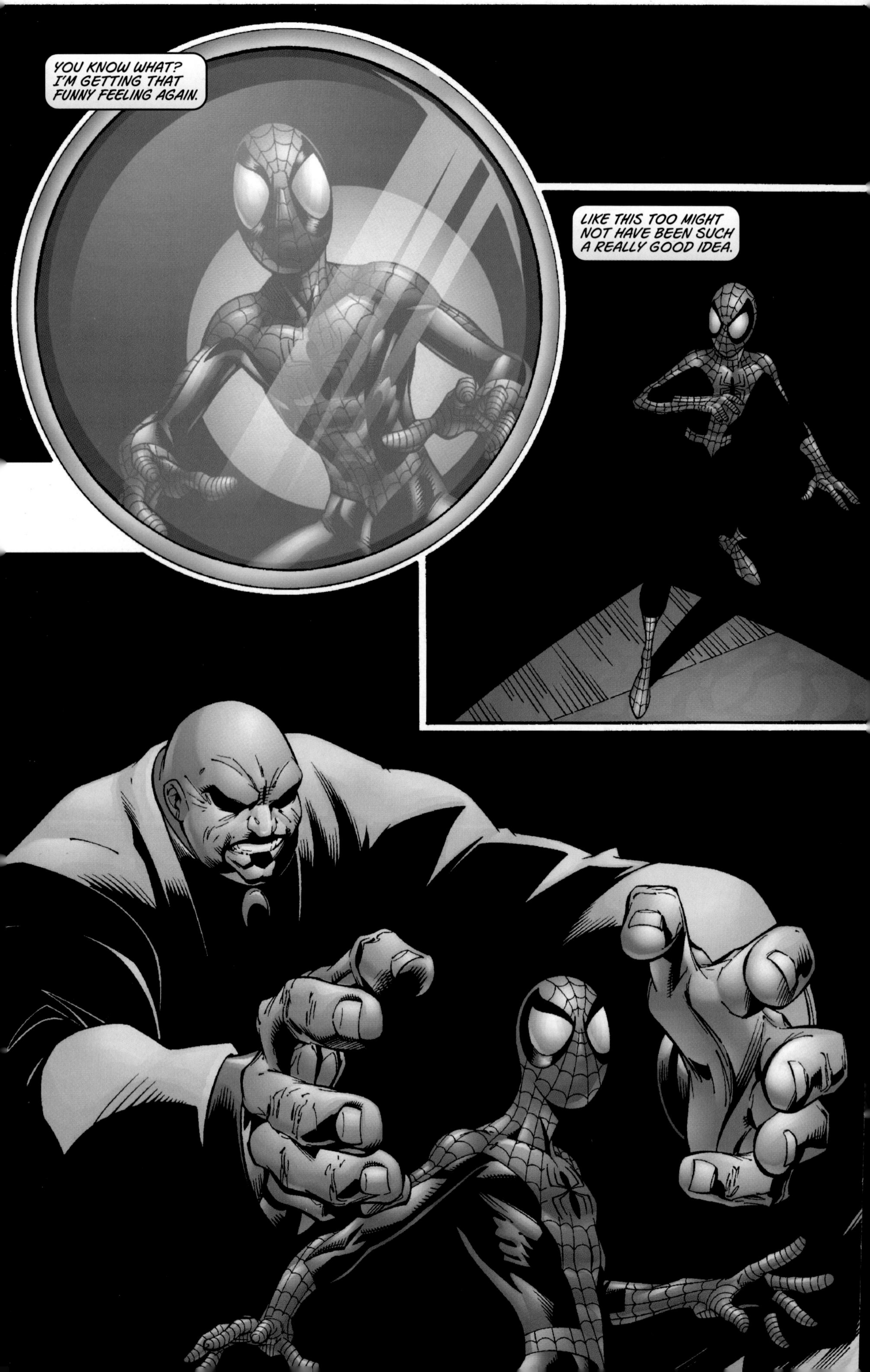
YOU KNOW WHAT? I'M GETTING THAT FUNNY FEELING AGAIN.
LIKE THIS TOO MIGHT NOT HAVE BEEN SUCH A REALLY GOOD IDEA.

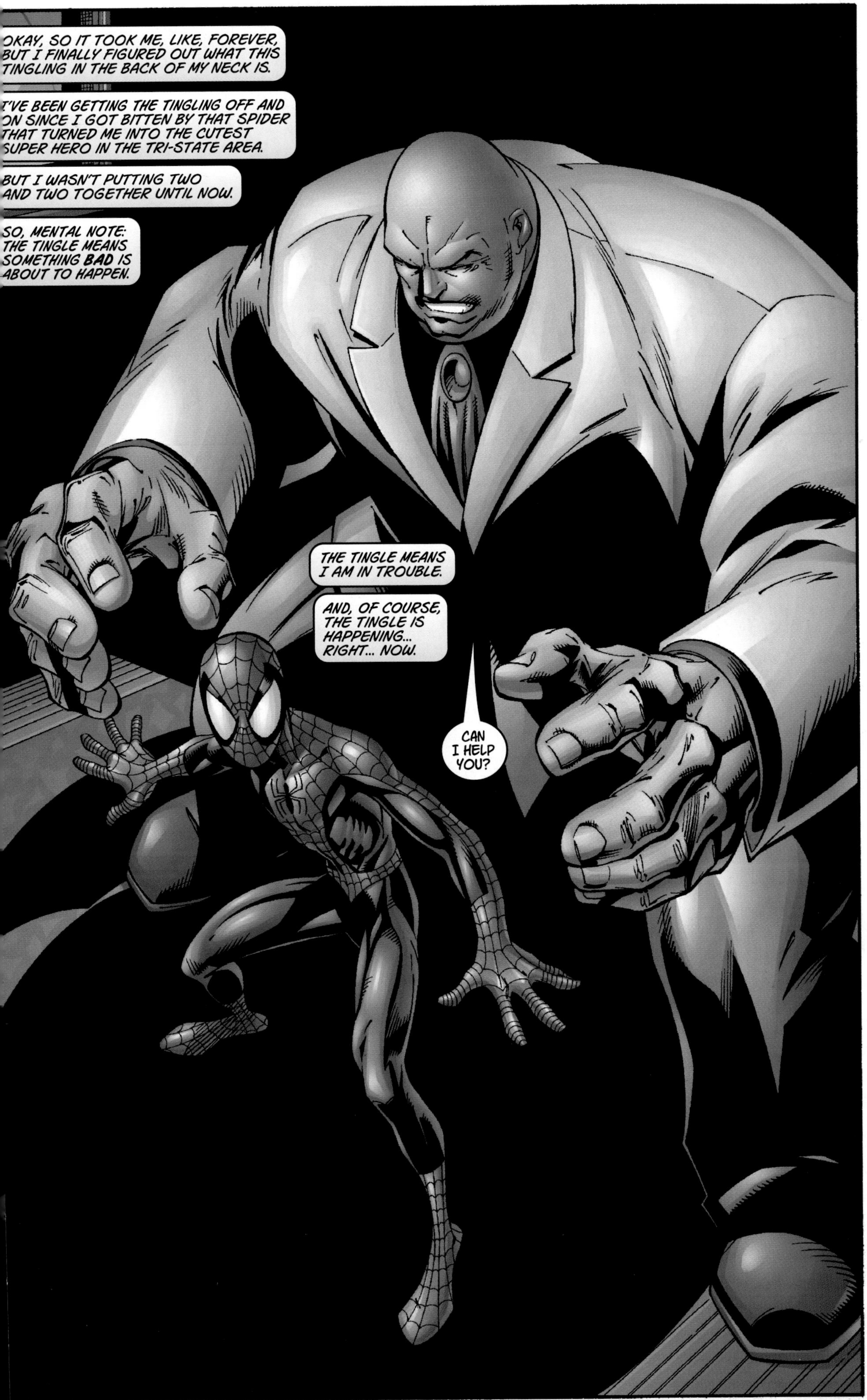
OKAY, SO IT TOOK ME, LIKE, FOREVER, BUT I FINALLY FIGURED OUT WHAT THIS TINGLING IN THE BACK OF MY NECK IS.
I'VE BEEN GETTING THE TINGLING OFF AND ON SINCE I GOT BITTEN BY THAT SPIDER THAT TURNED ME INTO THE CUTEST SUPER HERO IN THE TRI-STATE AREA.
BUT I WASN'T PUTTING TWO AND TWO TOGETHER UNTIL NOW.
SO, MENTAL NOTE: THE TINGLE MEANS SOMETHING **BAD** IS ABOUT TO HAPPEN.
THE TINGLE MEANS I AM IN TROUBLE.
AND, OF COURSE, THE TINGLE IS HAPPENING... RIGHT... NOW.
CAN I HELP YOU?

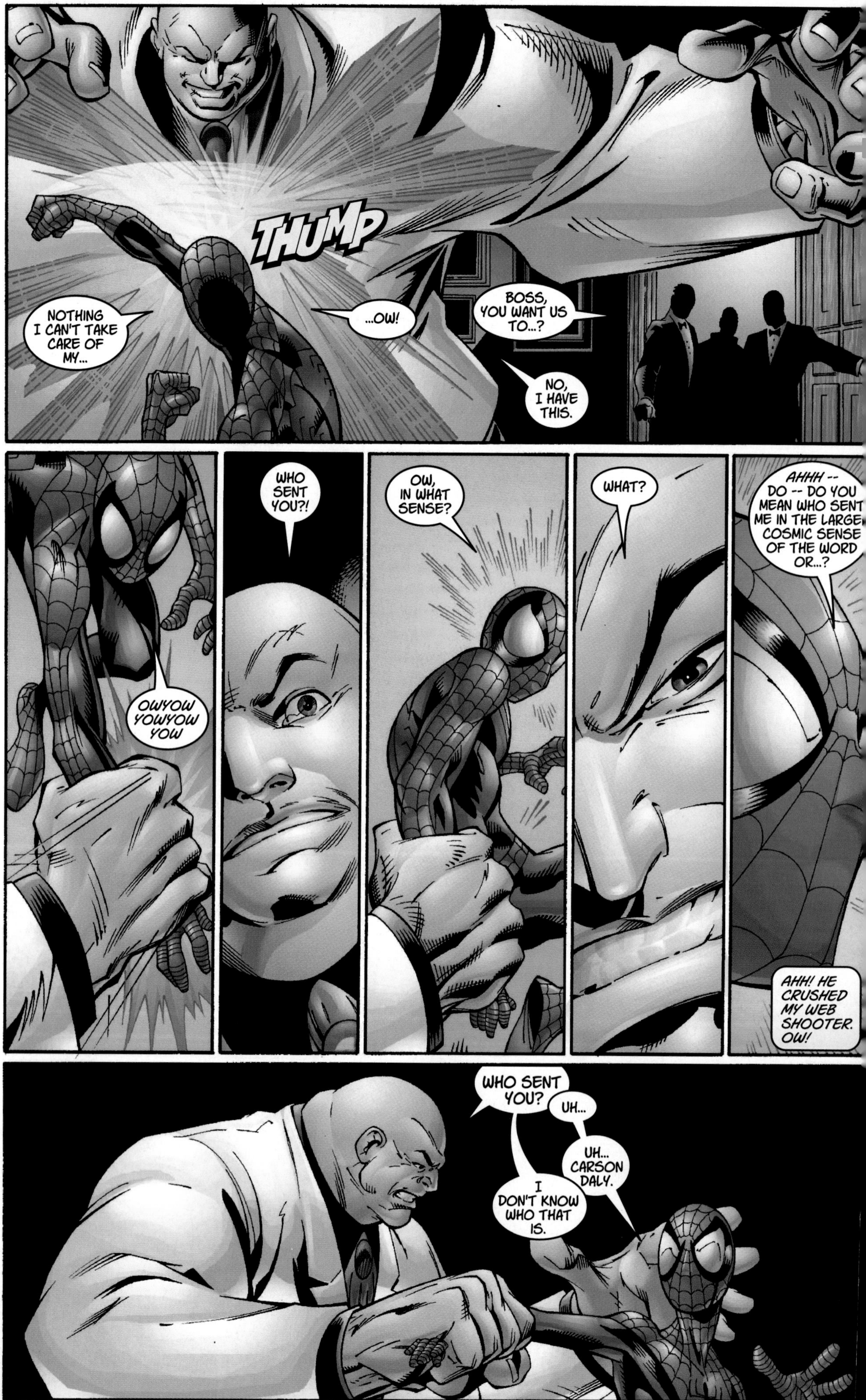
THUMP
NOTHING I CAN'T TAKE CARE OF MY...
...OW!
BOSS, YOU WANT US TO...?
NO, I HAVE THIS.
OWYOW YOWYOW YOW
WHO SENT YOU?!
OW, IN WHAT SENSE?
WHAT?
AHHH -- DO -- DO YOU MEAN WHO SENT ME IN THE LARGE COSMIC SENSE OF THE WORD OR...?
AHH! HE CRUSHED MY WEB SHOOTER. OW!
WHO SENT YOU?
UH...
UH... CARSON DALY.
I DON'T KNOW WHO THAT IS.

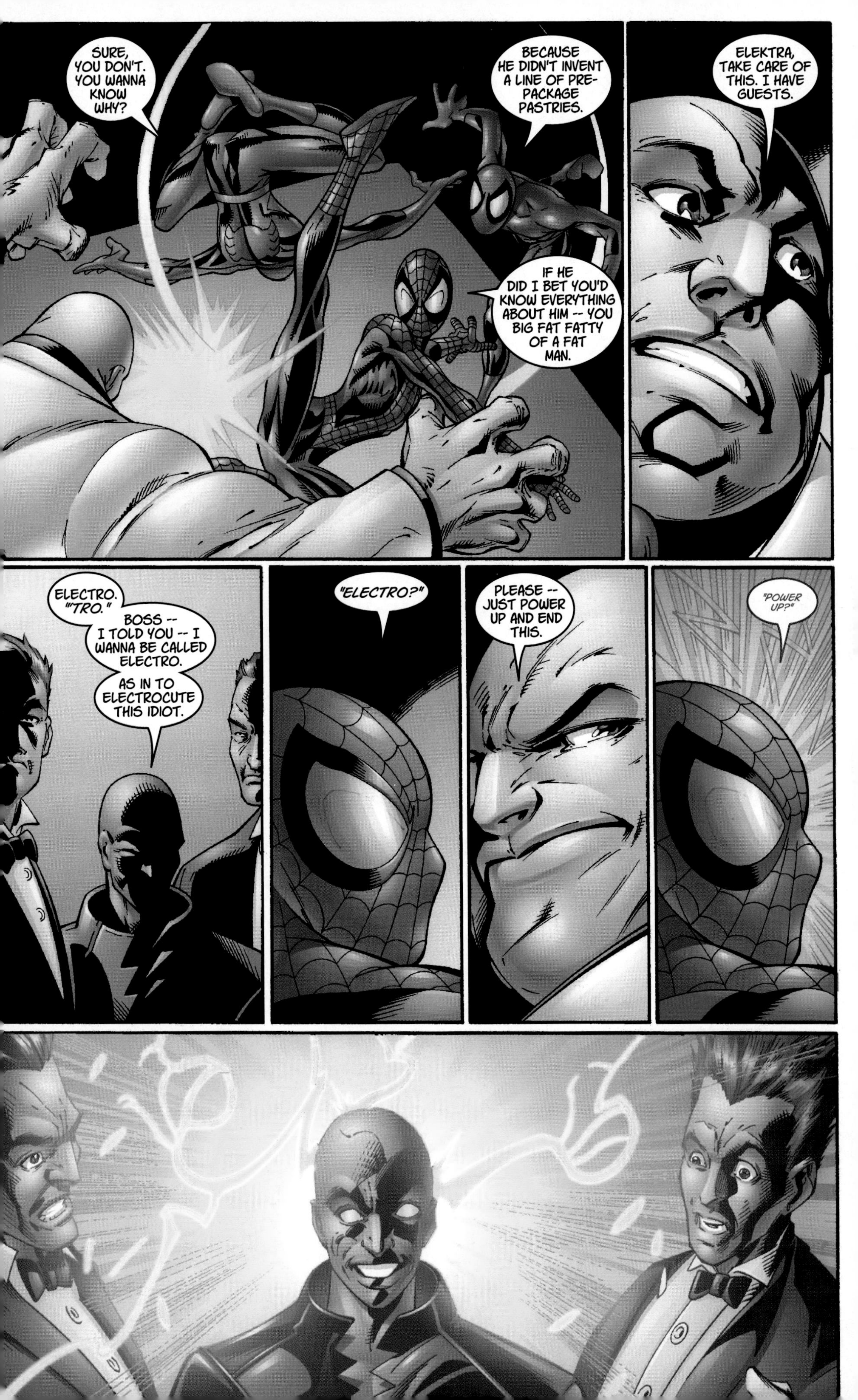
SURE, YOU DON'T. YOU WANNA KNOW WHY?
BECAUSE HE DIDN'T INVENT A LINE OF PRE-PACKAGE PASTRIES.
IF HE DID I BET YOU'D KNOW EVERYTHING ABOUT HIM -- YOU BIG FAT FATTY OF A FAT MAN.
ELEKTRA, TAKE CARE OF THIS. I HAVE GUESTS.
ELECTRO. "TRO."
BOSS -- I TOLD YOU -- I WANNA BE CALLED ELECTRO.
AS IN TO ELECTROCUTE THIS IDIOT.
"ELECTRO?"
PLEASE -- JUST POWER UP AND END THIS.
"POWER UP?"

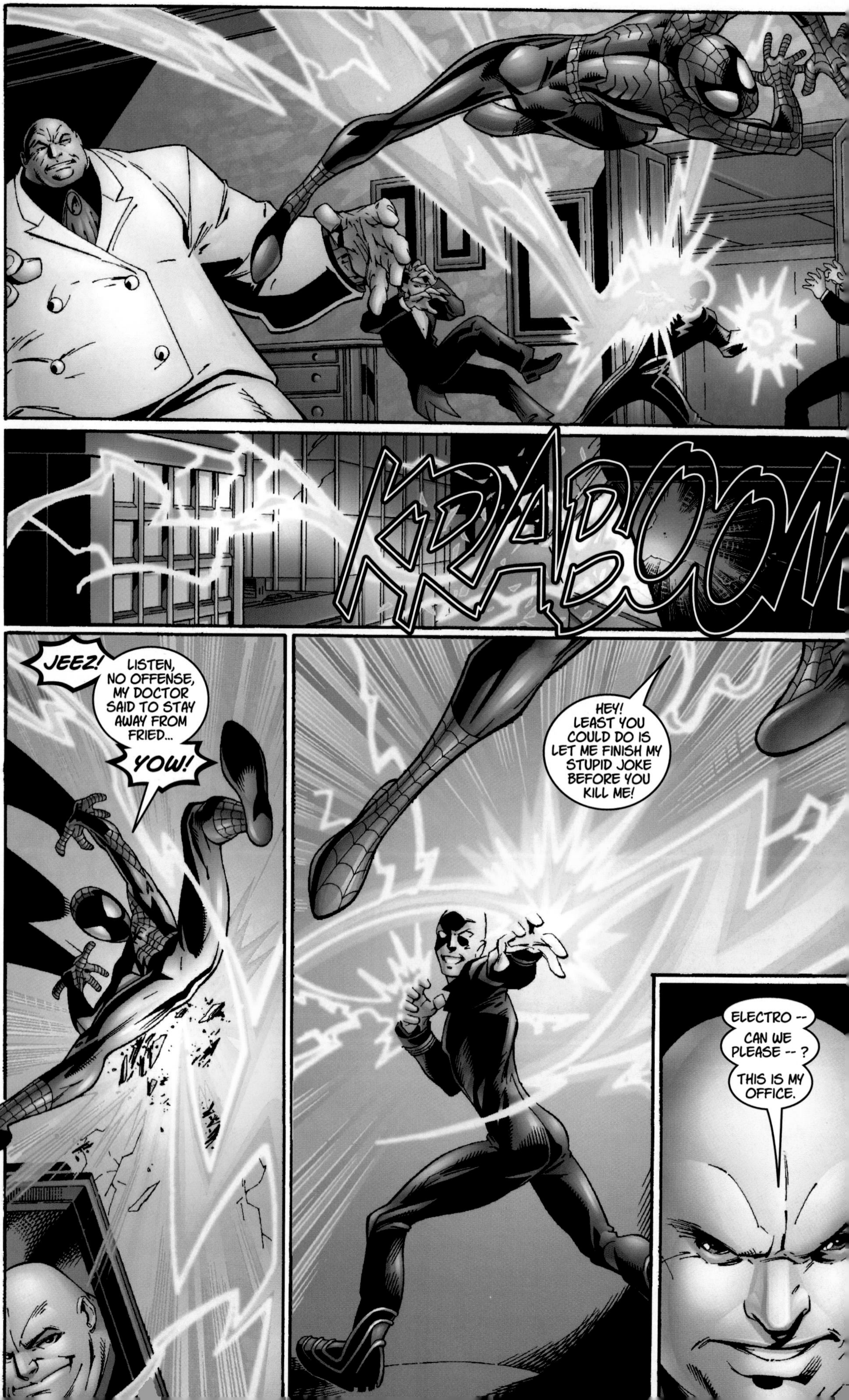
KRABOOM
JEEZ!
LISTEN, NO OFFENSE, MY DOCTOR SAID TO STAY AWAY FROM FRIED...
YOW!
HEY! LEAST YOU COULD DO IS LET ME FINISH MY STUPID JOKE BEFORE YOU KILL ME!
ELECTRO --
CAN WE PLEASE -- ?
THIS IS MY OFFICE.

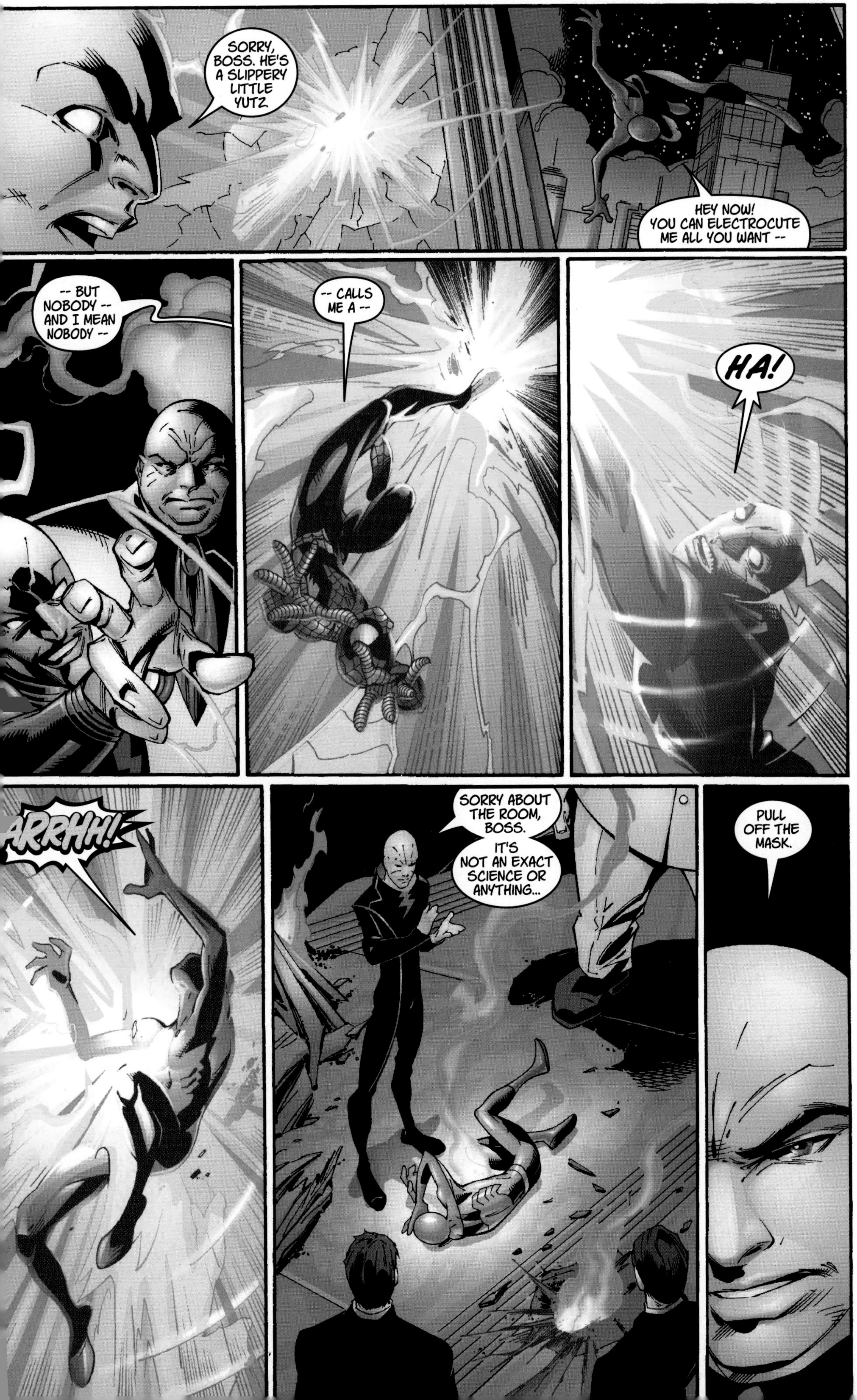
SORRY, BOSS. HE'S A SLIPPERY LITTLE YUTZ.
HEY NOW! YOU CAN ELECTROCUTE ME ALL YOU WANT --
-- BUT NOBODY -- AND I MEAN NOBODY --
-- CALLS ME A --
HA!
ARRHH!
SORRY ABOUT THE ROOM, BOSS.
IT'S NOT AN EXACT SCIENCE OR ANYTHING...
PULL OFF THE MASK.

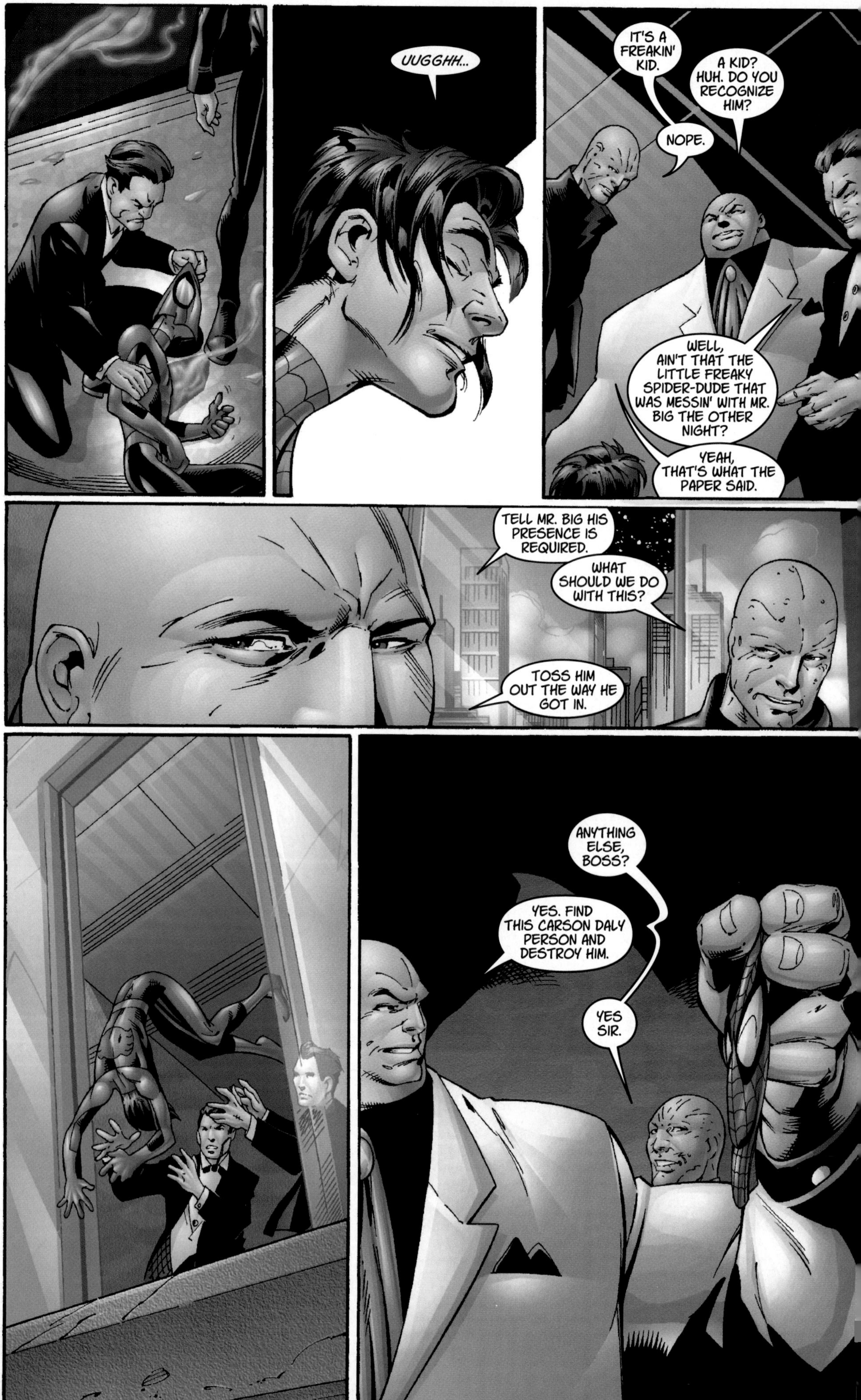
UUGGHH...
IT'S A FREAKIN' KID.
A KID? HUH. DO YOU RECOGNIZE HIM?
NOPE.
WELL, AIN'T THAT THE LITTLE FREAKY SPIDER-DUDE THAT WAS MESSIN' WITH MR. BIG THE OTHER NIGHT?
YEAH, THAT'S WHAT THE PAPER SAID.
TELL MR. BIG HIS PRESENCE IS REQUIRED.
WHAT SHOULD WE DO WITH THIS?
TOSS HIM OUT THE WAY HE GOT IN.
ANYTHING ELSE, BOSS?
YES. FIND THIS CARSON DALY PERSON AND DESTROY HIM.
YES SIR.

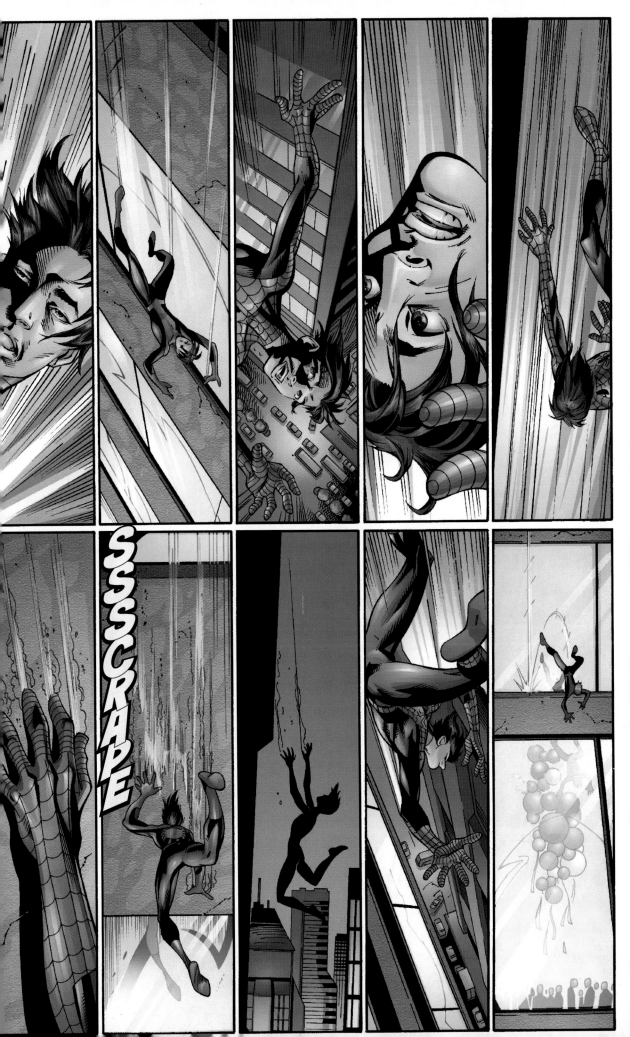

SSSCRAPE

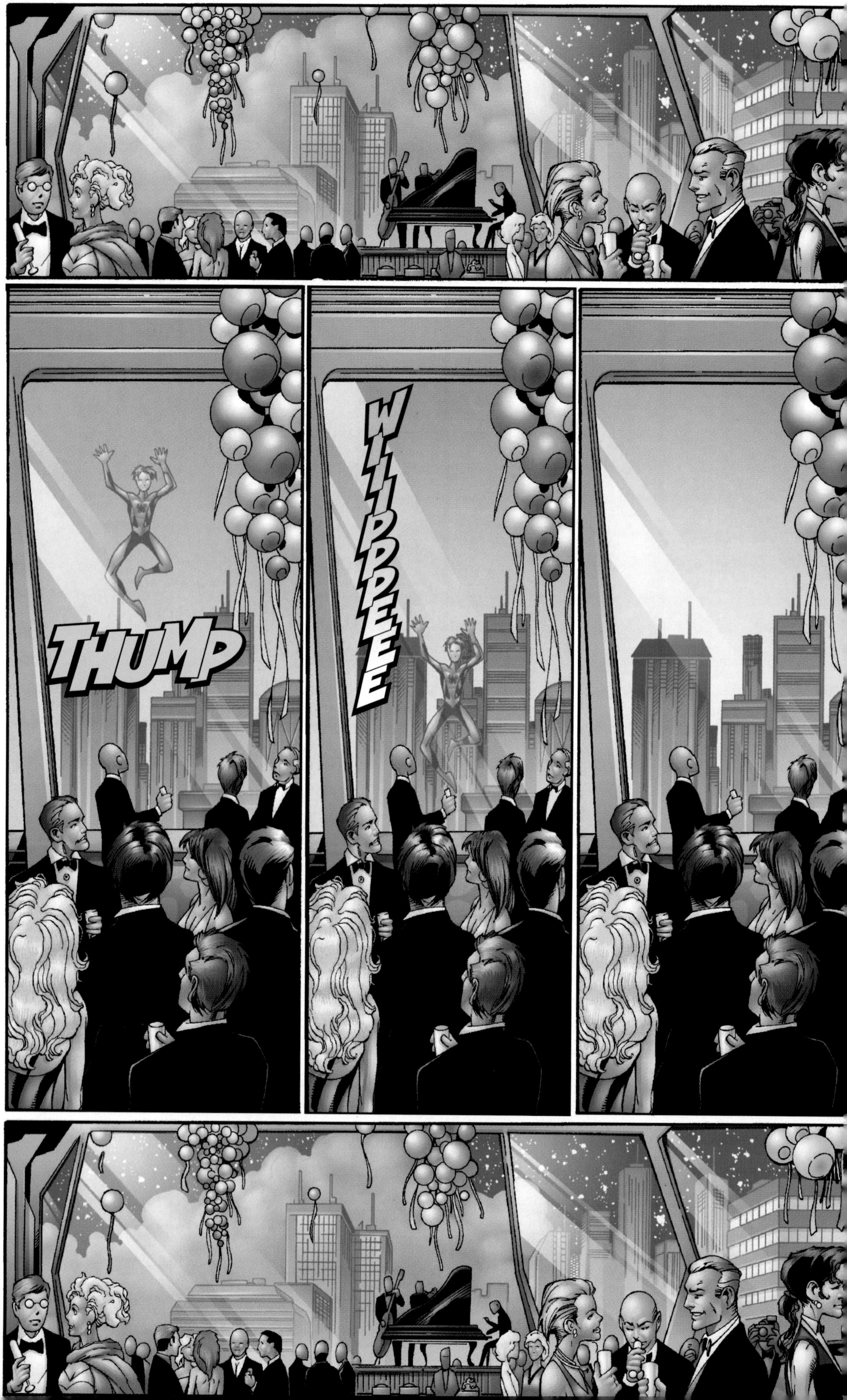
THUMP
WHIPPEEE

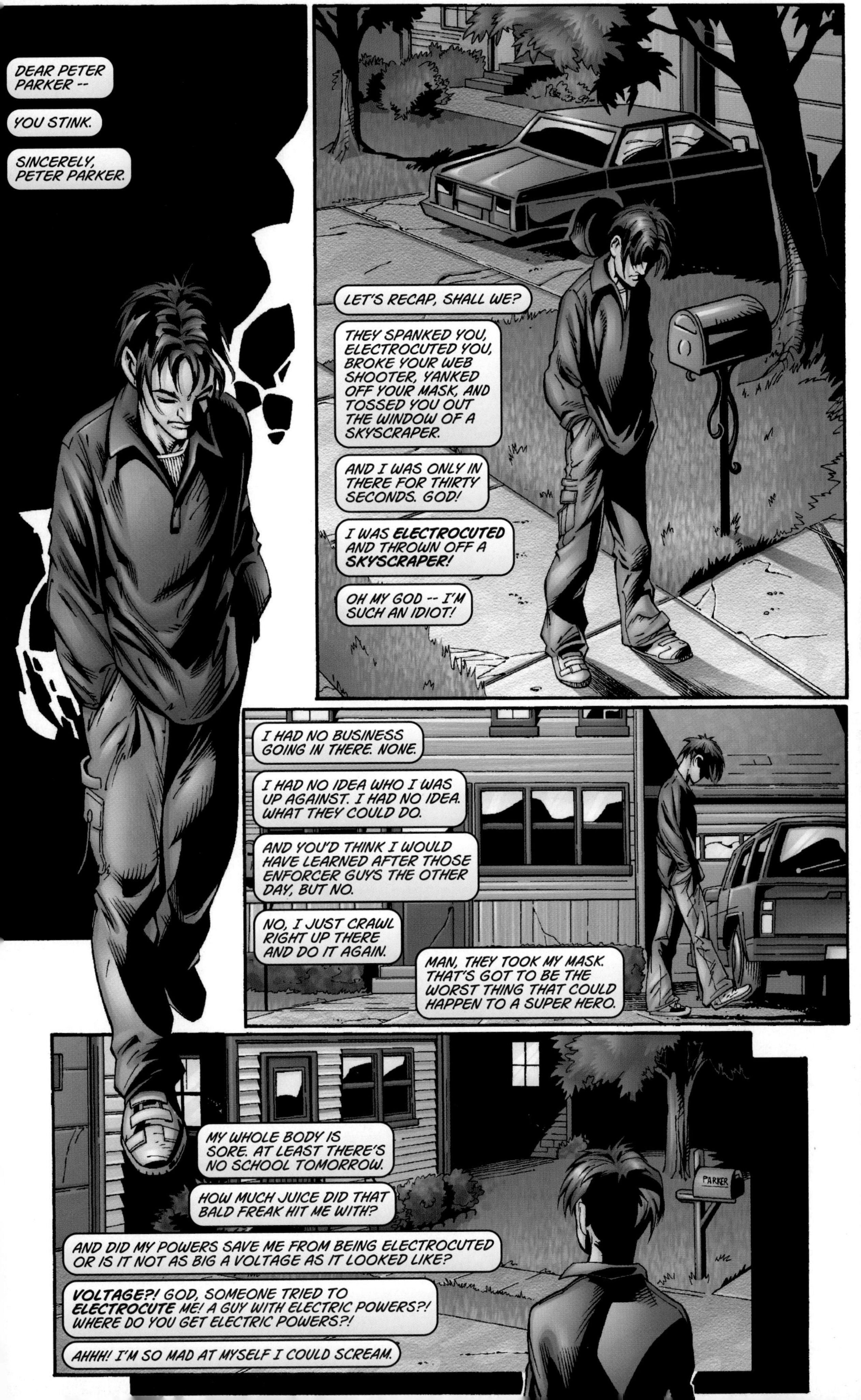
DEAR PETER PARKER --
YOU STINK.
SINCERELY, PETER PARKER.
LET'S RECAP, SHALL WE?
THEY SPANKED YOU, ELECTROCUTED YOU, BROKE YOUR WEB SHOOTER, YANKED OFF YOUR MASK, AND TOSSED YOU OUT THE WINDOW OF A SKYSCRAPER.
AND I WAS ONLY IN THERE FOR THIRTY SECONDS. GOD!
I WAS ELECTROCUTED AND THROWN OFF A SKYSCRAPER!
OH MY GOD -- I'M SUCH AN IDIOT!
I HAD NO BUSINESS GOING IN THERE. NONE.
I HAD NO IDEA WHO I WAS UP AGAINST. I HAD NO IDEA. WHAT THEY COULD DO.
AND YOU'D THINK I WOULD HAVE LEARNED AFTER THOSE ENFORCER GUYS THE OTHER DAY, BUT NO.
NO, I JUST CRAWL RIGHT UP THERE AND DO IT AGAIN.
MAN, THEY TOOK MY MASK. THAT'S GOT TO BE THE WORST THING THAT COULD HAPPEN TO A SUPER HERO.
MY WHOLE BODY IS SORE. AT LEAST THERE'S NO SCHOOL TOMORROW.
HOW MUCH JUICE DID THAT BALD FREAK HIT ME WITH?
AND DID MY POWERS SAVE ME FROM BEING ELECTROCUTED OR IS IT NOT AS BIG A VOLTAGE AS IT LOOKED LIKE?
VOLTAGE?! GOD, SOMEONE TRIED TO ELECTROCUTE ME! A GUY WITH ELECTRIC POWERS?! WHERE DO YOU GET ELECTRIC POWERS?!
AHHH! I'M SO MAD AT MYSELF I COULD SCREAM.
PARKER

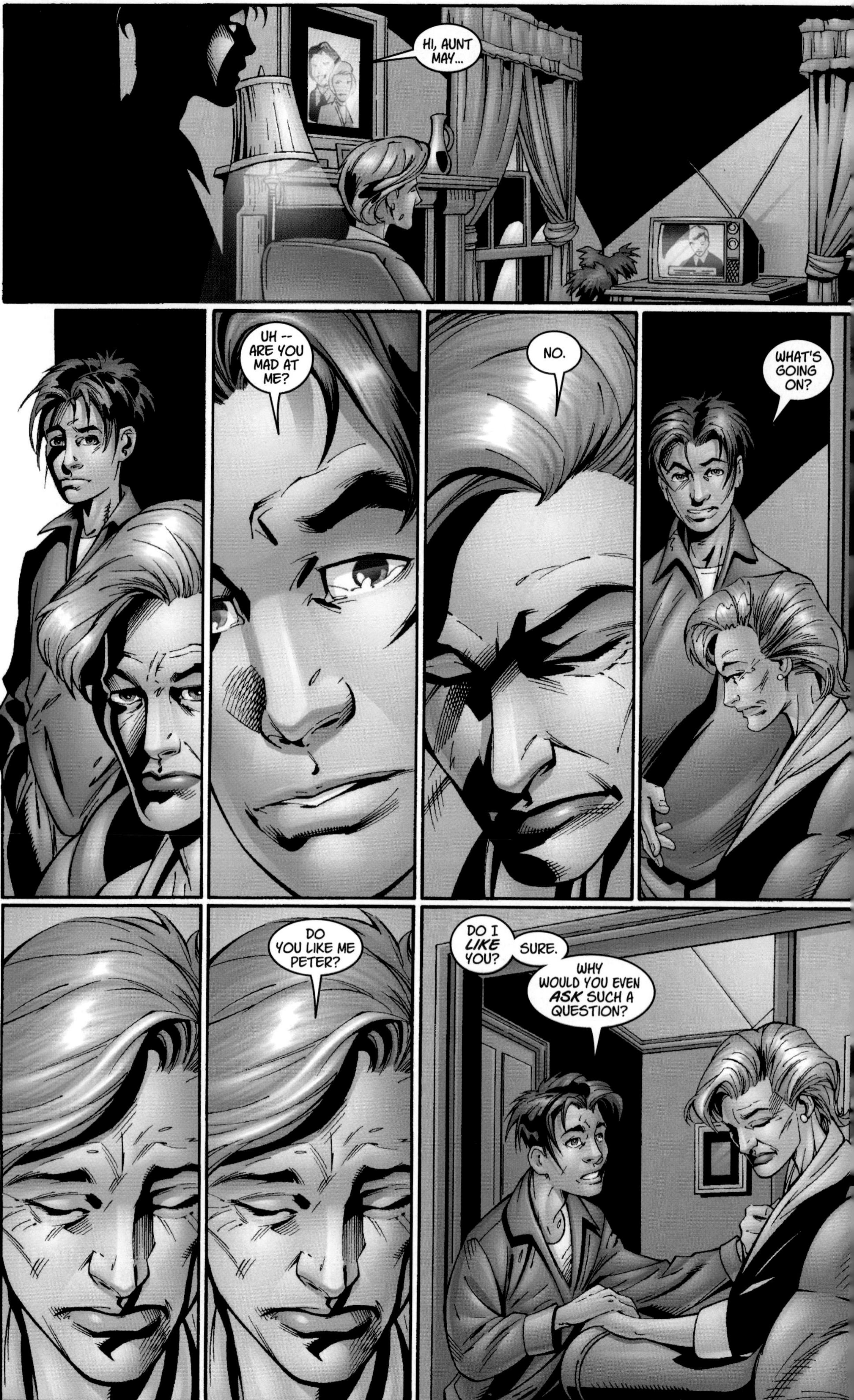
HI, AUNT MAY...
UH -- ARE YOU MAD AT ME?
NO.
WHAT'S GOING ON?
DO YOU LIKE ME PETER?
DO I *LIKE* YOU?
SURE.
WHY WOULD YOU EVEN *ASK* SUCH A QUESTION?

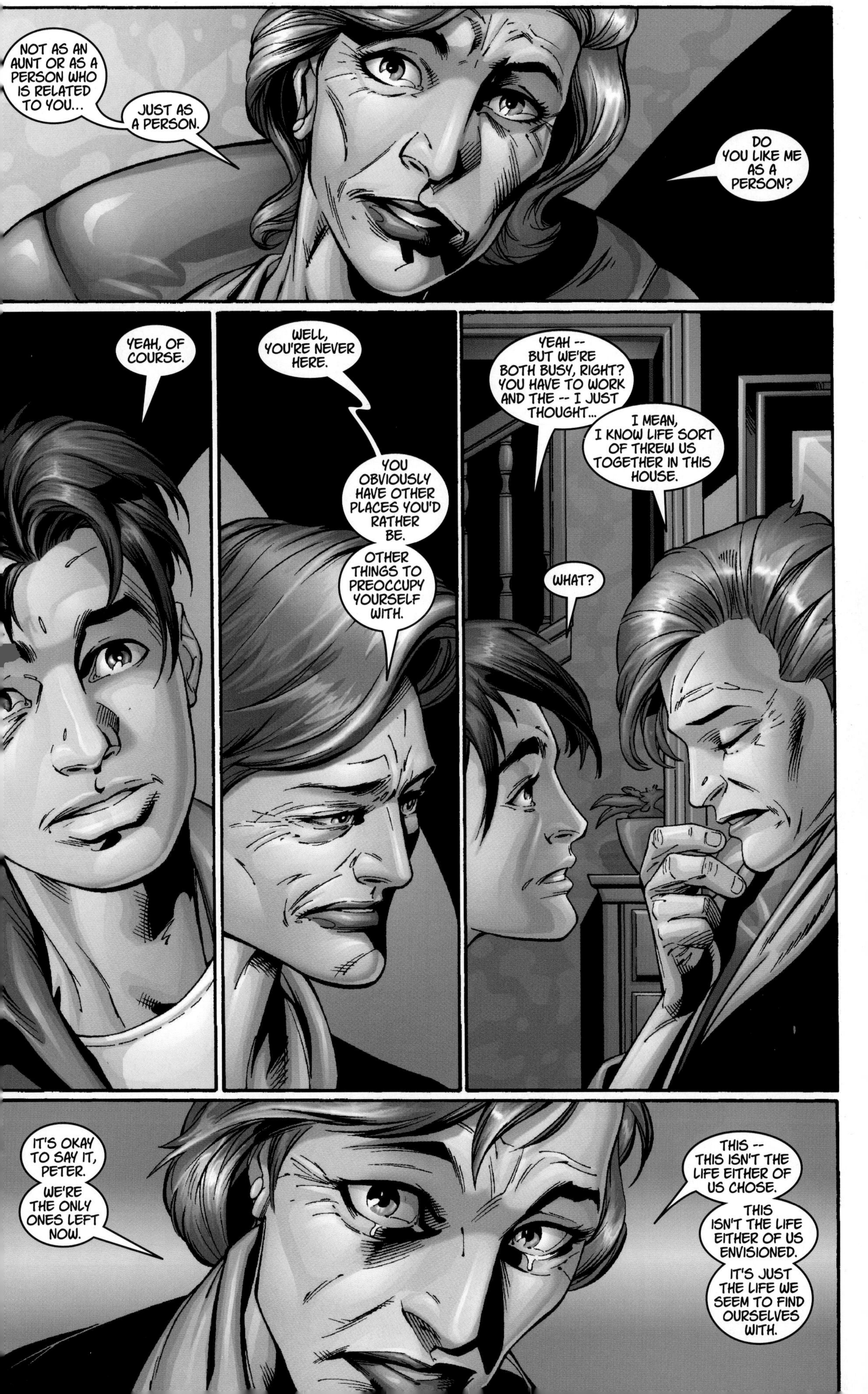
NOT AS AN AUNT OR AS A PERSON WHO IS RELATED TO YOU...
JUST AS A PERSON.
DO YOU LIKE ME AS A PERSON?
YEAH, OF COURSE.
WELL, YOU'RE NEVER HERE.
YOU OBVIOUSLY HAVE OTHER PLACES YOU'D RATHER BE.
OTHER THINGS TO PREOCCUPY YOURSELF WITH.
YEAH -- BUT WE'RE BOTH BUSY, RIGHT? YOU HAVE TO WORK AND THE -- I JUST THOUGHT...
I MEAN, I KNOW LIFE SORT OF THREW US TOGETHER IN THIS HOUSE.
WHAT?
IT'S OKAY TO SAY IT, PETER.
WE'RE THE ONLY ONES LEFT NOW.
THIS -- THIS ISN'T THE LIFE EITHER OF US CHOSE.
THIS ISN'T THE LIFE EITHER OF US ENVISIONED.
IT'S JUST THE LIFE WE SEEM TO FIND OURSELVES WITH.

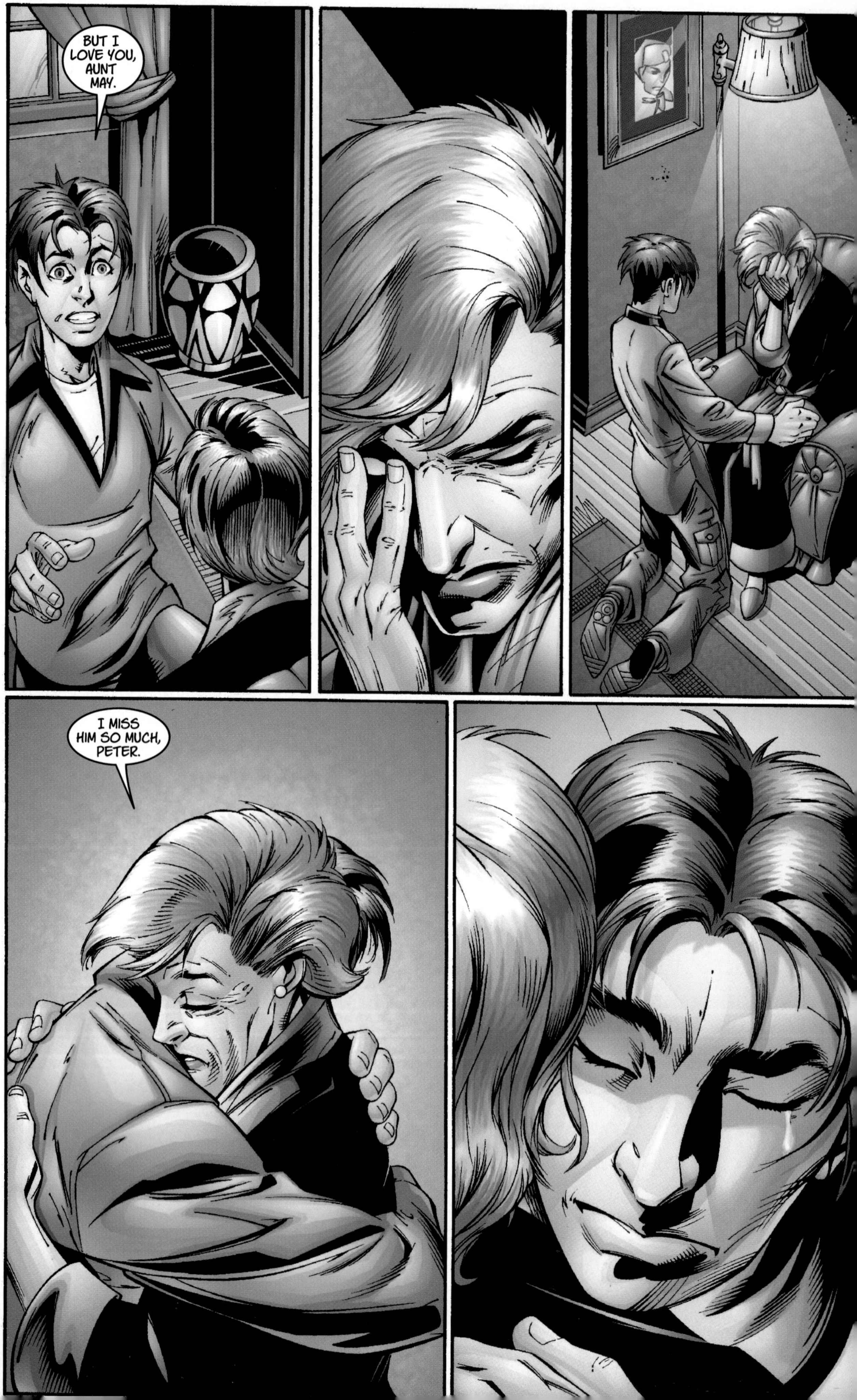
BUT I LOVE YOU, AUNT MAY.
I MISS HIM SO MUCH, PETER.

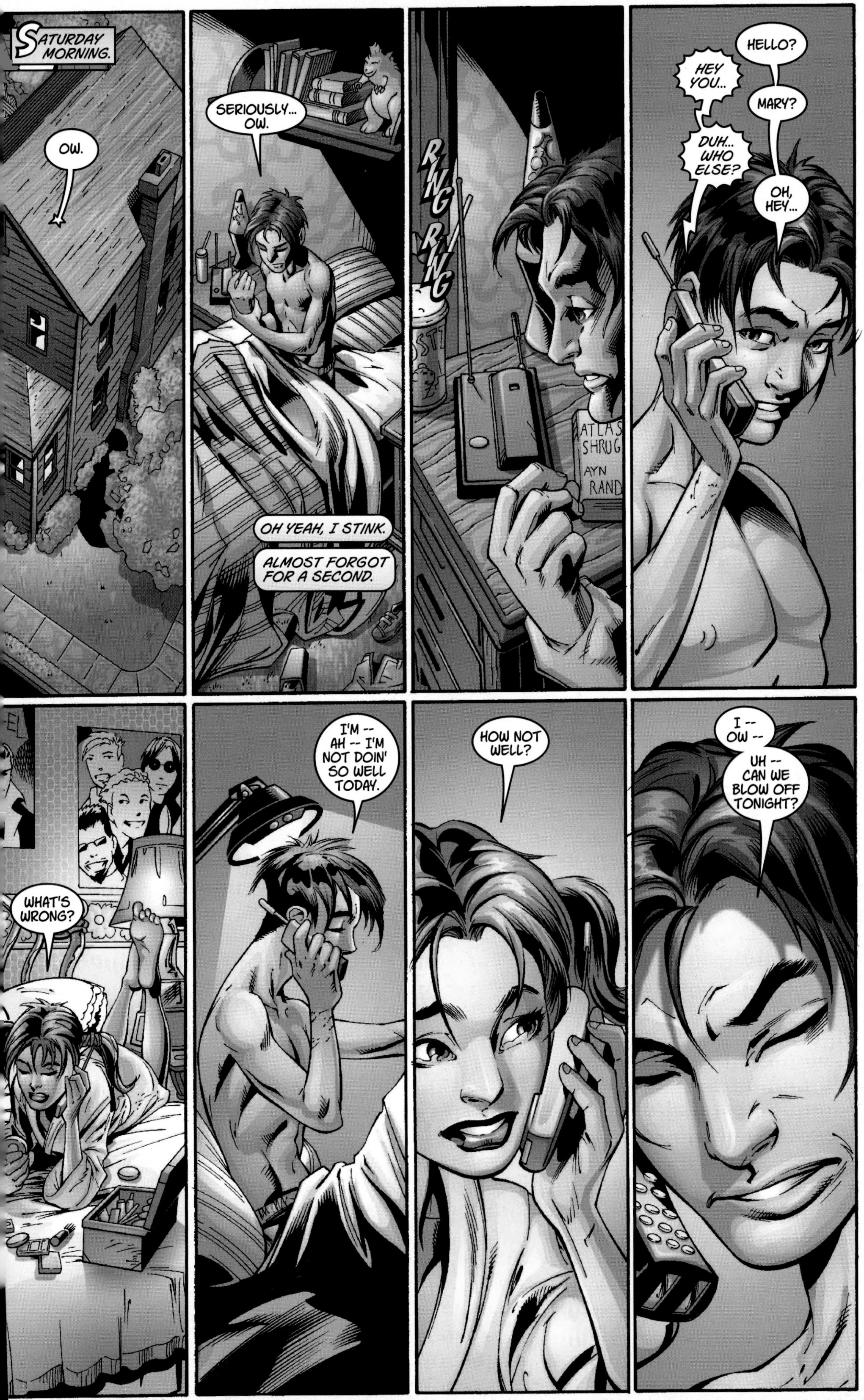
SATURDAY MORNING.
OW.
SERIOUSLY... OW.
OH YEAH, I STINK.
ALMOST FORGOT FOR A SECOND.
RING RING
ATLAS SHRUG AYN RAND
HELLO?
HEY YOU...
MARY?
DUH... WHO ELSE?
OH, HEY...
WHAT'S WRONG?
I'M -- AH -- I'M NOT DOIN' SO WELL TODAY.
HOW NOT WELL?
I -- OW --
UH -- CAN WE BLOW OFF TONIGHT?

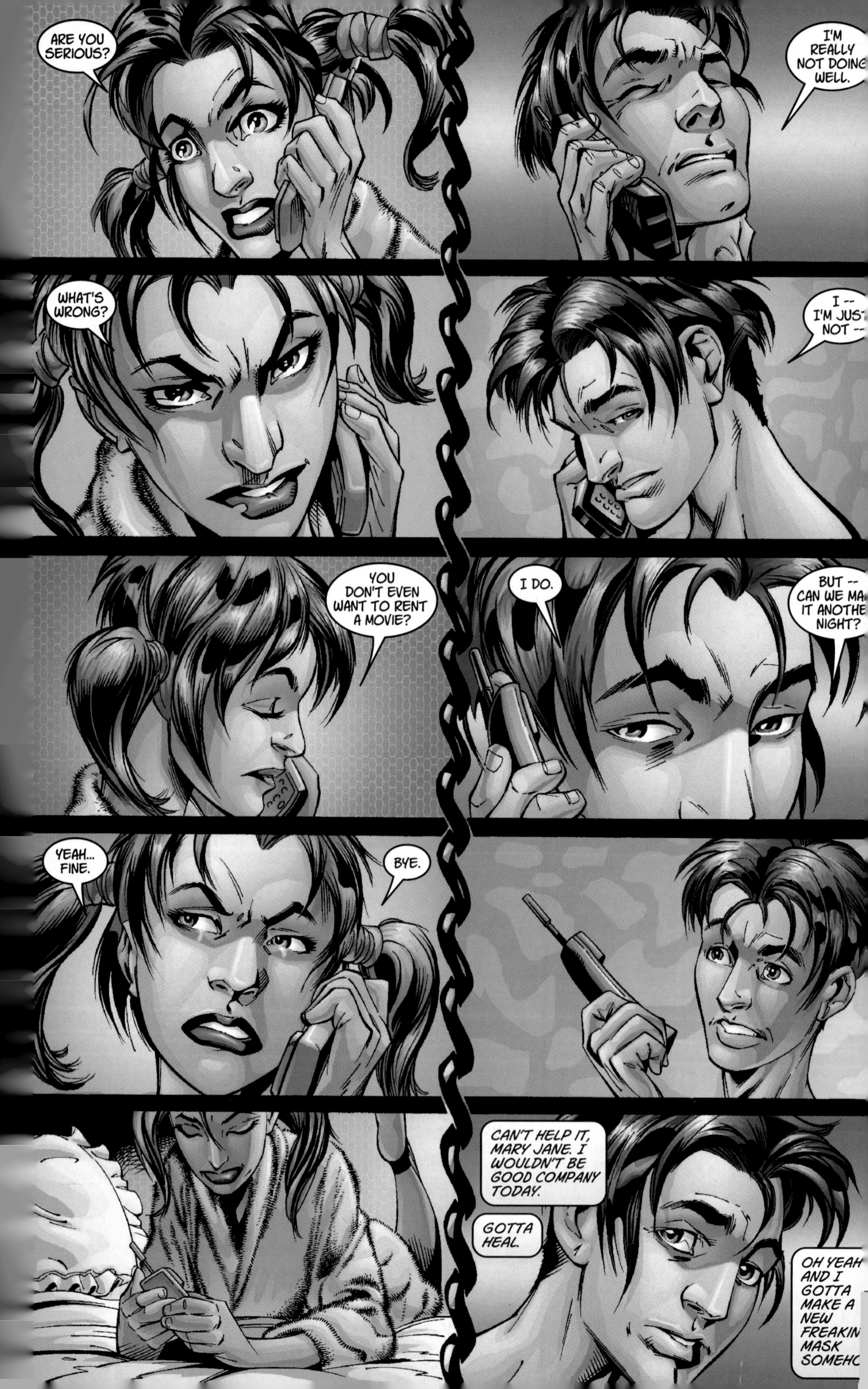
ARE YOU SERIOUS?
I'M REALLY NOT DOING WELL.
WHAT'S WRONG?
I -- I'M JUST NOT --
YOU DON'T EVEN WANT TO RENT A MOVIE?
I DO.
BUT -- CAN WE MA IT ANOTHE NIGHT?
YEAH... FINE.
BYE.
CAN'T HELP IT, MARY JANE. I WOULDN'T BE GOOD COMPANY TODAY.
GOTTA HEAL.
OH YEAH AND I GOTTA MAKE A NEW FREAKIN MASK SOMEHO

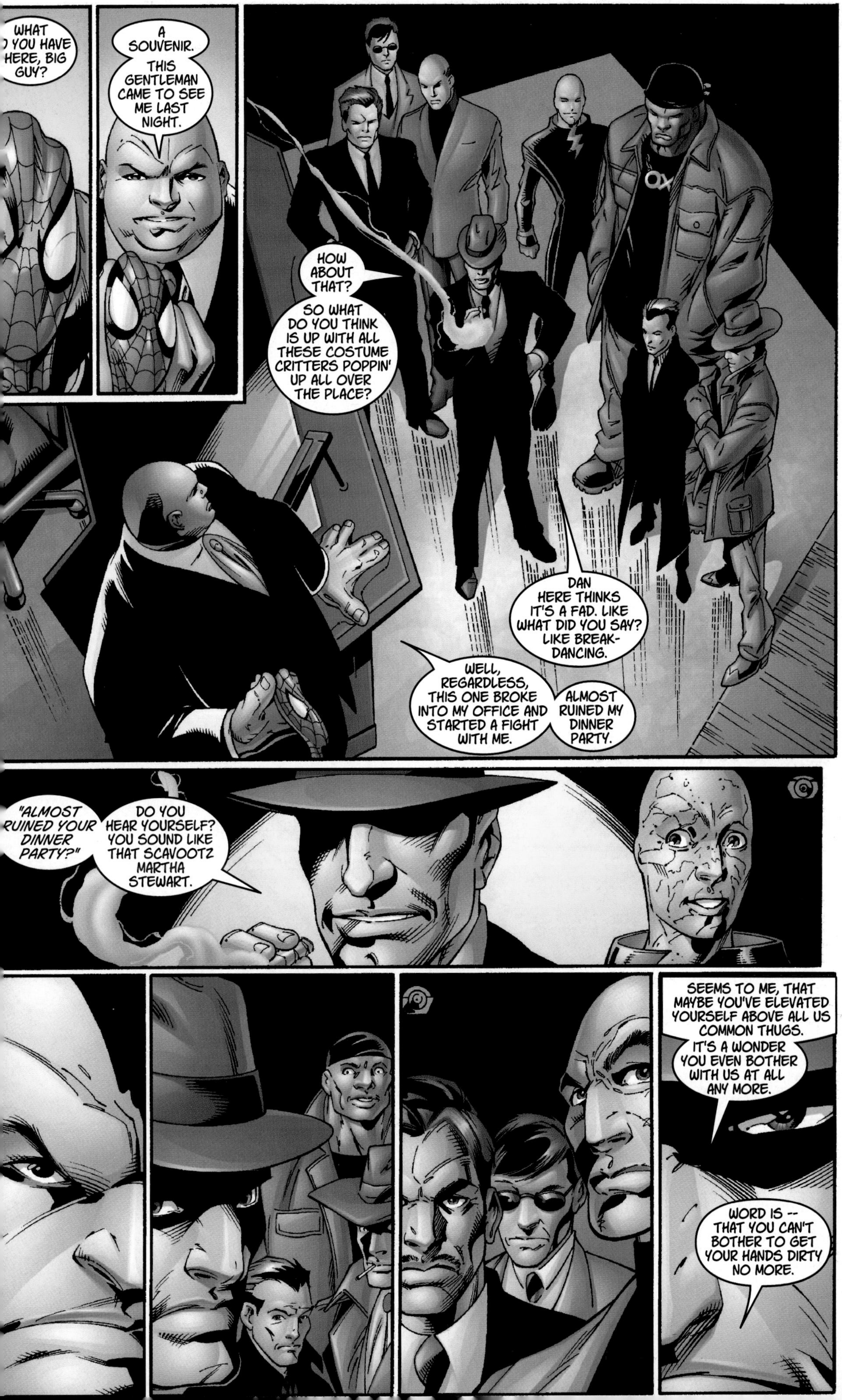
WHAT DO YOU HAVE HERE, BIG GUY?
A SOUVENIR.
THIS GENTLEMAN CAME TO SEE ME LAST NIGHT.
HOW ABOUT THAT?
SO WHAT DO YOU THINK IS UP WITH ALL THESE COSTUME CRITTERS POPPIN' UP ALL OVER THE PLACE?
DAN HERE THINKS IT'S A FAD. LIKE WHAT DID YOU SAY? LIKE BREAK-DANCING.
WELL, REGARDLESS, THIS ONE BROKE INTO MY OFFICE AND STARTED A FIGHT WITH ME.
ALMOST RUINED MY DINNER PARTY.
"ALMOST RUINED YOUR DINNER PARTY?"
DO YOU HEAR YOURSELF? YOU SOUND LIKE THAT SCAVOOTZ MARTHA STEWART.
SEEMS TO ME, THAT MAYBE YOU'VE ELEVATED YOURSELF ABOVE ALL US COMMON THUGS.
IT'S A WONDER YOU EVEN BOTHER WITH US AT ALL ANY MORE.
WORD IS -- THAT YOU CAN'T BOTHER TO GET YOUR HANDS DIRTY NO MORE.

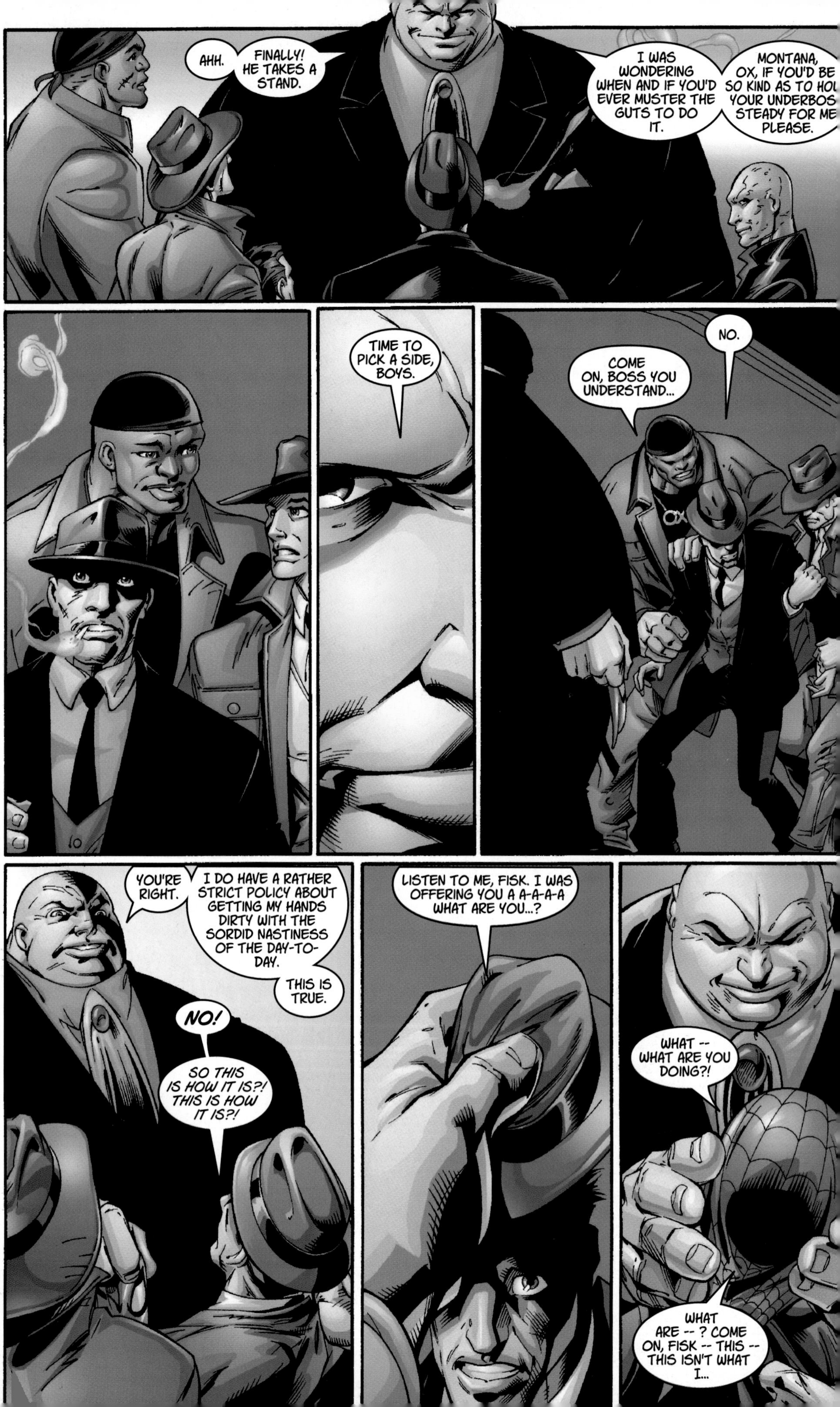
AHH.
FINALLY! HE TAKES A STAND.
I WAS WONDERING WHEN AND IF YOU'D EVER MUSTER THE GUTS TO DO IT.
MONTANA, OX, IF YOU'D BE SO KIND AS TO HOL YOUR UNDERBOS STEADY FOR ME PLEASE.
TIME TO PICK A SIDE, BOYS.
COME ON, BOSS YOU UNDERSTAND...
NO.
YOU'RE RIGHT.
I DO HAVE A RATHER STRICT POLICY ABOUT GETTING MY HANDS DIRTY WITH THE SORDID NASTINESS OF THE DAY-TO-DAY.
THIS IS TRUE.
NO!
SO THIS IS HOW IT IS?! THIS IS HOW IT IS?!
LISTEN TO ME, FISK. I WAS OFFERING YOU A A-A-A-A WHAT ARE YOU...?
WHAT -- WHAT ARE YOU DOING?!
WHAT ARE -- ? COME ON, FISK -- THIS -- THIS ISN'T WHAT I...

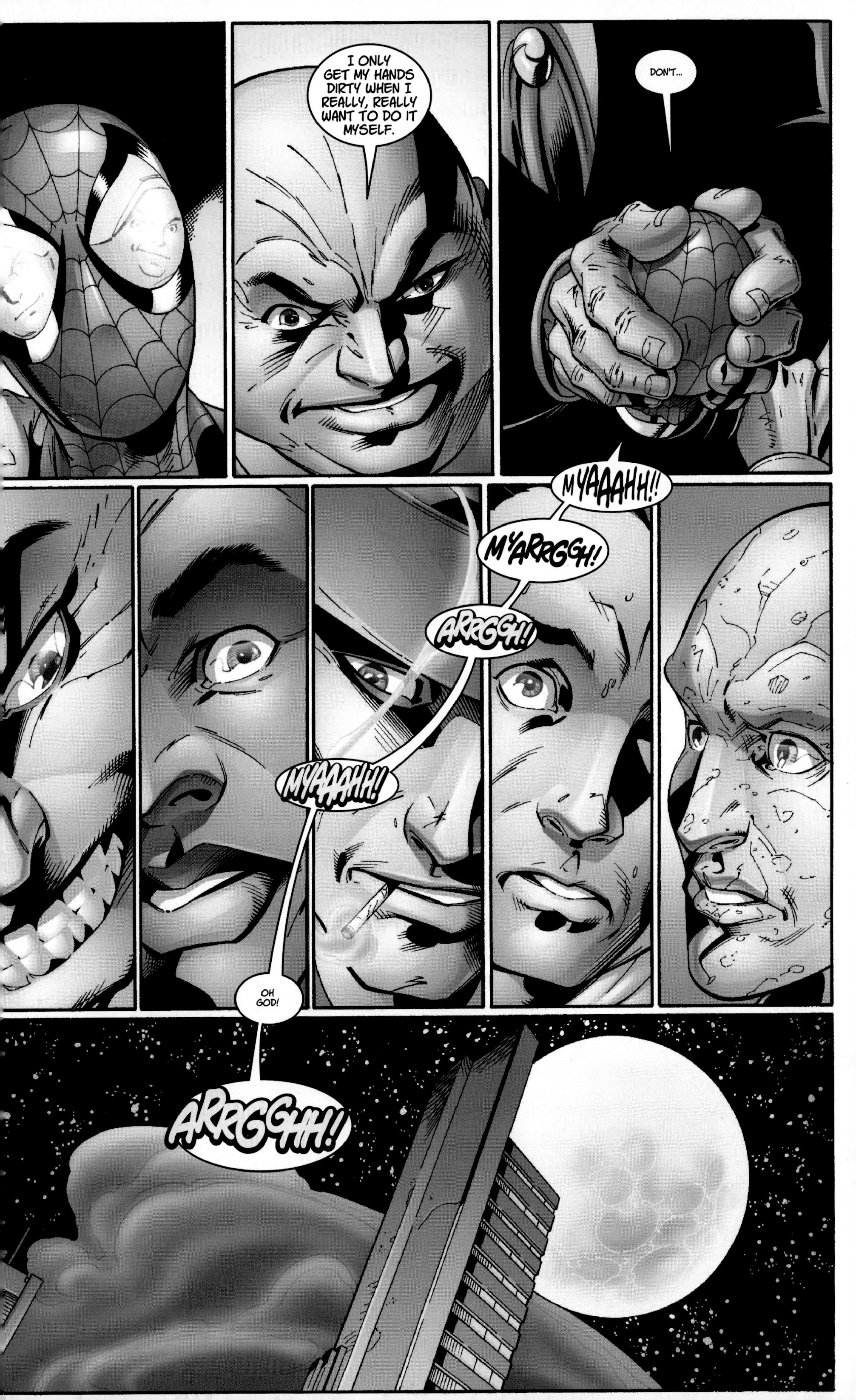
I ONLY GET MY HANDS DIRTY WHEN I REALLY, REALLY WANT TO DO IT MYSELF.
DON'T...
MYAAAHH!!
MYARRGGH!
ARRGGH!
MYAAAHH!
OH GOD!
ARRGGHH!

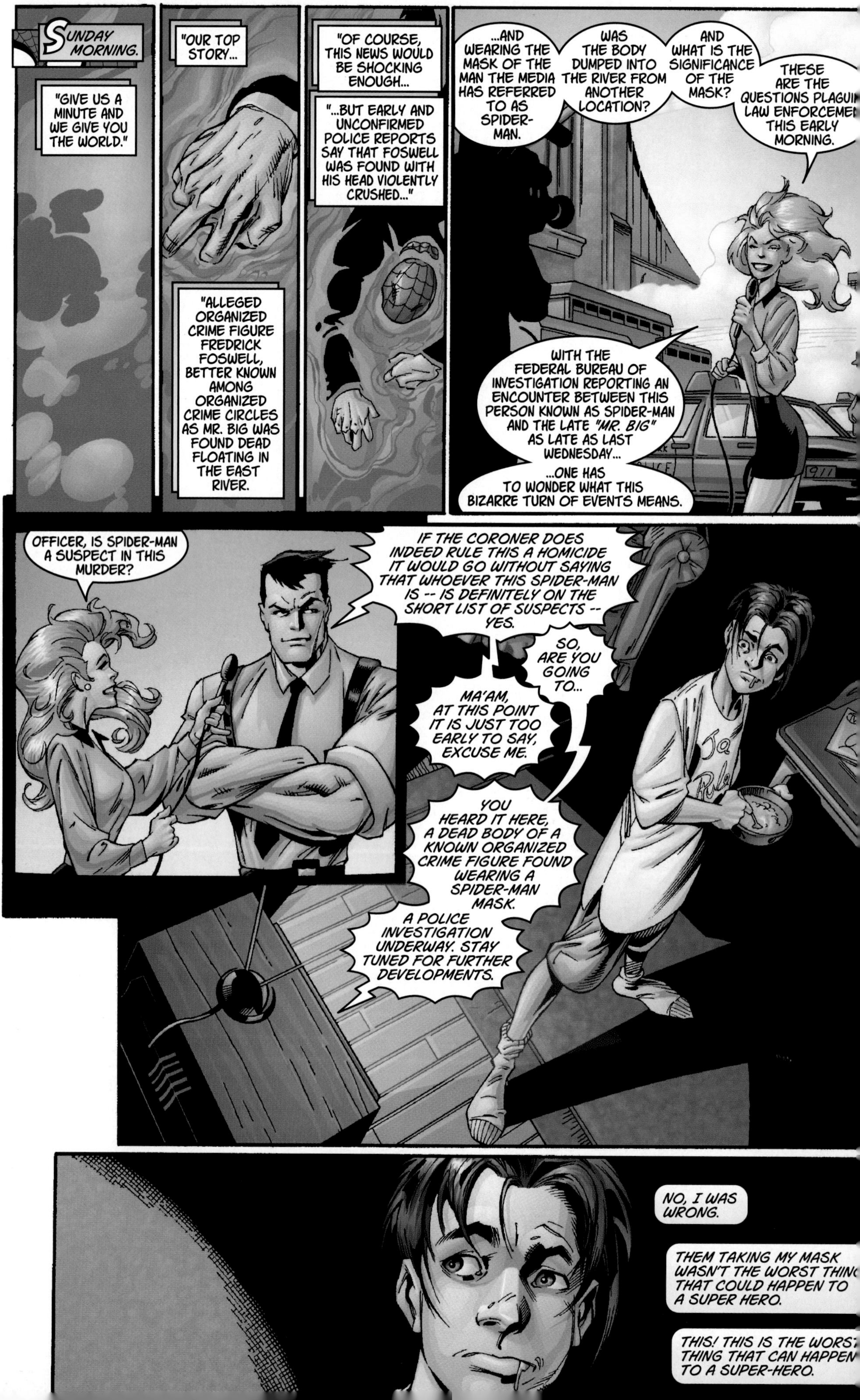
SUNDAY MORNING.
"GIVE US A MINUTE AND WE GIVE YOU THE WORLD."
"OUR TOP STORY...
"ALLEGED ORGANIZED CRIME FIGURE FREDRICK FOSWELL, BETTER KNOWN AMONG ORGANIZED CRIME CIRCLES AS MR. BIG WAS FOUND DEAD FLOATING IN THE EAST RIVER.
"OF COURSE, THIS NEWS WOULD BE SHOCKING ENOUGH...
"...BUT EARLY AND UNCONFIRMED POLICE REPORTS SAY THAT FOSWELL WAS FOUND WITH HIS HEAD VIOLENTLY CRUSHED..."
...AND WEARING THE MASK OF THE MAN THE MEDIA HAS REFERRED TO AS SPIDER-MAN.
WAS THE BODY DUMPED INTO THE RIVER FROM ANOTHER LOCATION?
AND WHAT IS THE SIGNIFICANCE OF THE MASK?
THESE ARE THE QUESTIONS PLAGUI LAW ENFORCEME THIS EARLY MORNING.
WITH THE FEDERAL BUREAU OF INVESTIGATION REPORTING AN ENCOUNTER BETWEEN THIS PERSON KNOWN AS SPIDER-MAN AND THE LATE "MR. BIG" AS LATE AS LAST WEDNESDAY...
...ONE HAS TO WONDER WHAT THIS BIZARRE TURN OF EVENTS MEANS.
OFFICER, IS SPIDER-MAN A SUSPECT IN THIS MURDER?
IF THE CORONER DOES INDEED RULE THIS A HOMICIDE IT WOULD GO WITHOUT SAYING THAT WHOEVER THIS SPIDER-MAN IS -- IS DEFINITELY ON THE SHORT LIST OF SUSPECTS -- YES.
SO, ARE YOU GOING TO...
MA'AM, AT THIS POINT IT IS JUST TOO EARLY TO SAY, EXCUSE ME.
YOU HEARD IT HERE, A DEAD BODY OF A KNOWN ORGANIZED CRIME FIGURE FOUND WEARING A SPIDER-MAN MASK.
A POLICE INVESTIGATION UNDERWAY. STAY TUNED FOR FURTHER DEVELOPMENTS.
NO, I WAS WRONG.
THEM TAKING MY MASK WASN'T THE WORST THIN THAT COULD HAPPEN TO A SUPER HERO.
THIS! THIS IS THE WORS THING THAT CAN HAPPEN TO A SUPER-HERO.

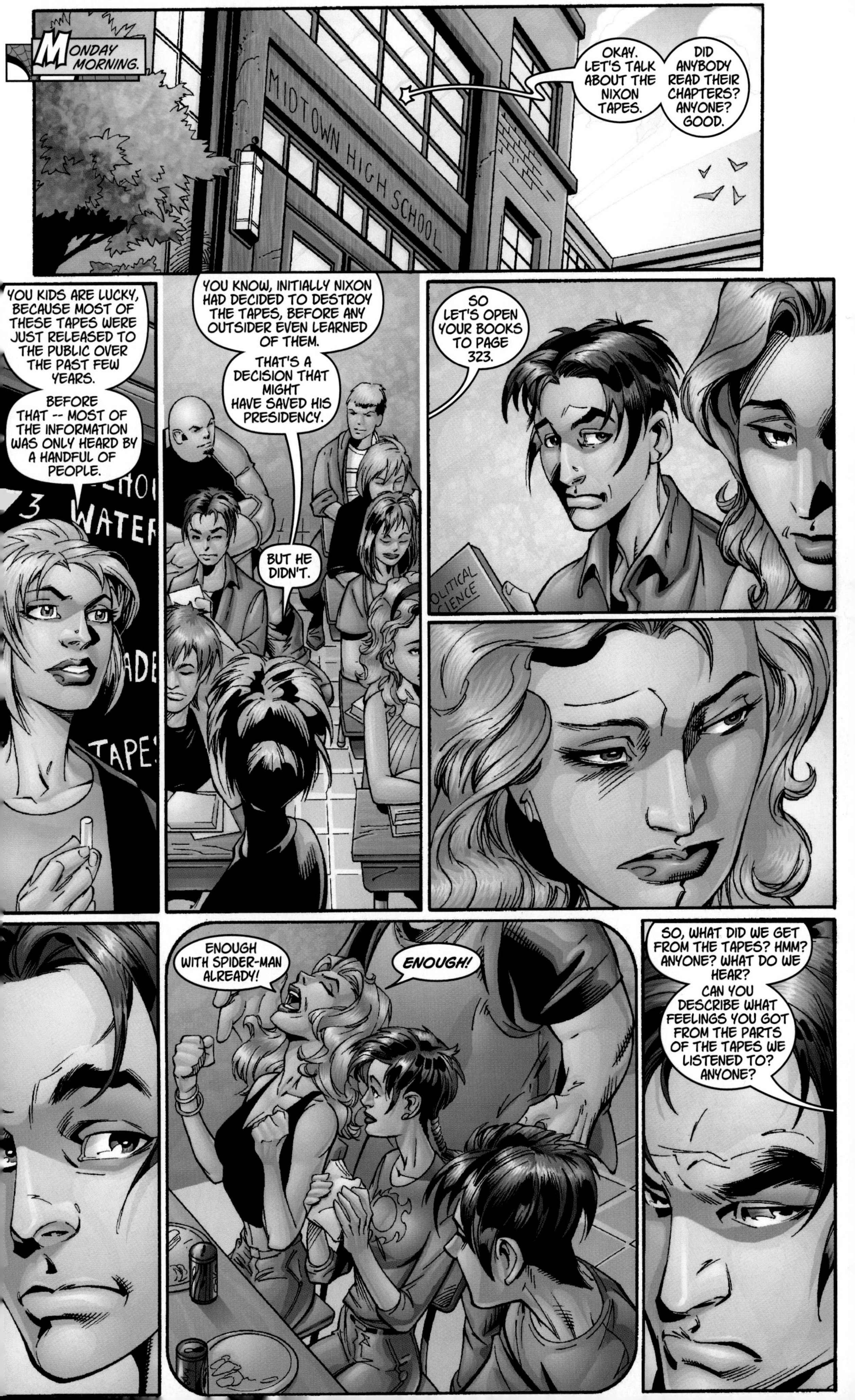
MONDAY MORNING.
MIDTOWN HIGH SCHOOL
OKAY. LET'S TALK ABOUT THE NIXON TAPES.
DID ANYBODY READ THEIR CHAPTERS? ANYONE? GOOD.
YOU KIDS ARE LUCKY, BECAUSE MOST OF THESE TAPES WERE JUST RELEASED TO THE PUBLIC OVER THE PAST FEW YEARS.
BEFORE THAT -- MOST OF THE INFORMATION WAS ONLY HEARD BY A HANDFUL OF PEOPLE.
YOU KNOW, INITIALLY NIXON HAD DECIDED TO DESTROY THE TAPES, BEFORE ANY OUTSIDER EVEN LEARNED OF THEM.
THAT'S A DECISION THAT MIGHT HAVE SAVED HIS PRESIDENCY.
BUT HE DIDN'T.
SO LET'S OPEN YOUR BOOKS TO PAGE 323.
ENOUGH WITH SPIDER-MAN ALREADY!
ENOUGH!
SO, WHAT DID WE GET FROM THE TAPES? HMM? ANYONE? WHAT DO WE HEAR?
CAN YOU DESCRIBE WHAT FEELINGS YOU GOT FROM THE PARTS OF THE TAPES WE LISTENED TO? ANYONE?

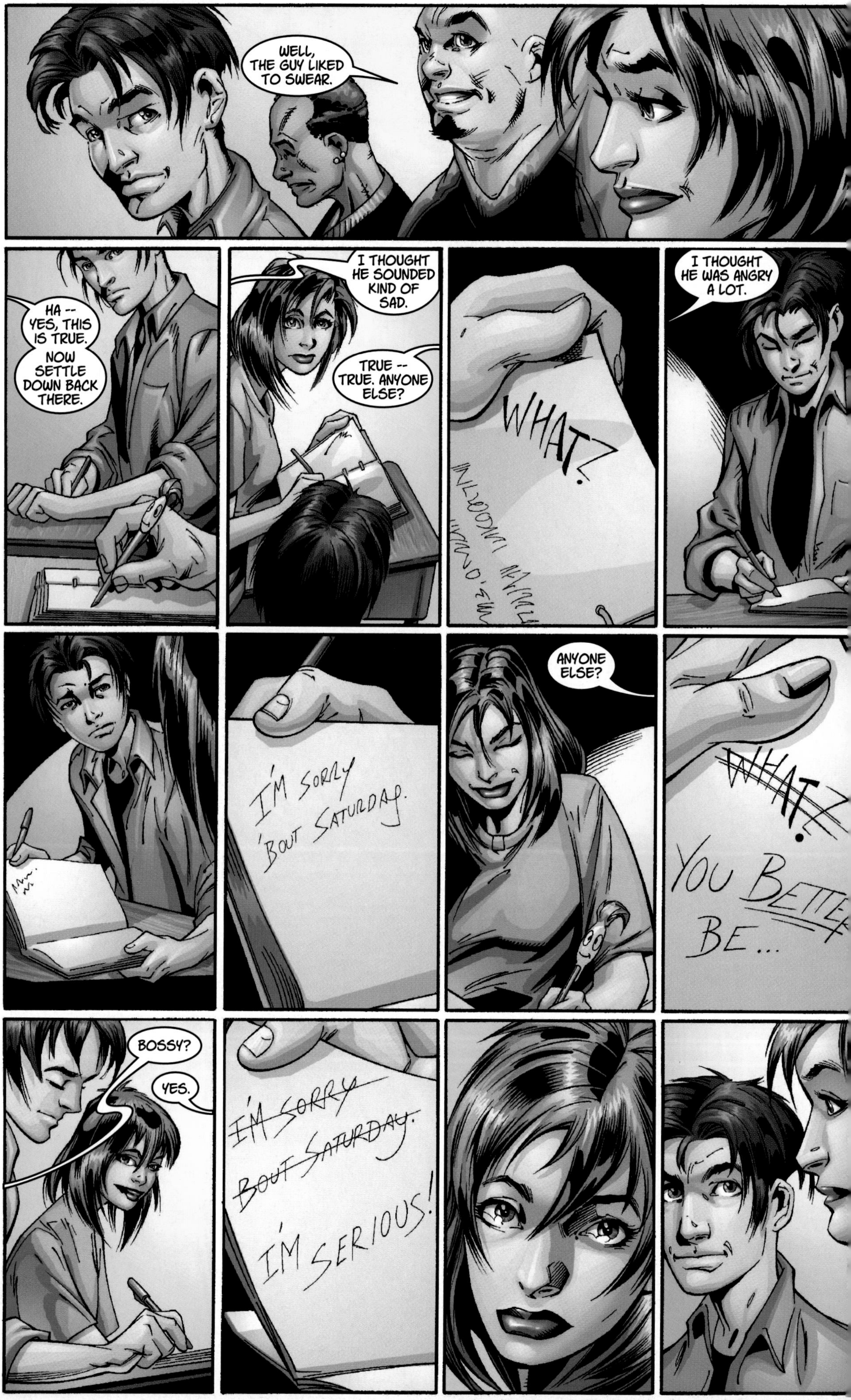
WELL, THE GUY LIKED TO SWEAR.
HA -- YES, THIS IS TRUE.
NOW SETTLE DOWN BACK THERE.
I THOUGHT HE SOUNDED KIND OF SAD.
TRUE -- TRUE. ANYONE ELSE?
WHAT?
I THOUGHT HE WAS ANGRY A LOT.
I'M SORRY 'BOUT SATURDAY.
ANYONE ELSE?
WHAT?
YOU BETTER BE...
BOSSY?
YES.
I'M SORRY 'BOUT SATURDAY.
I'M SERIOUS!

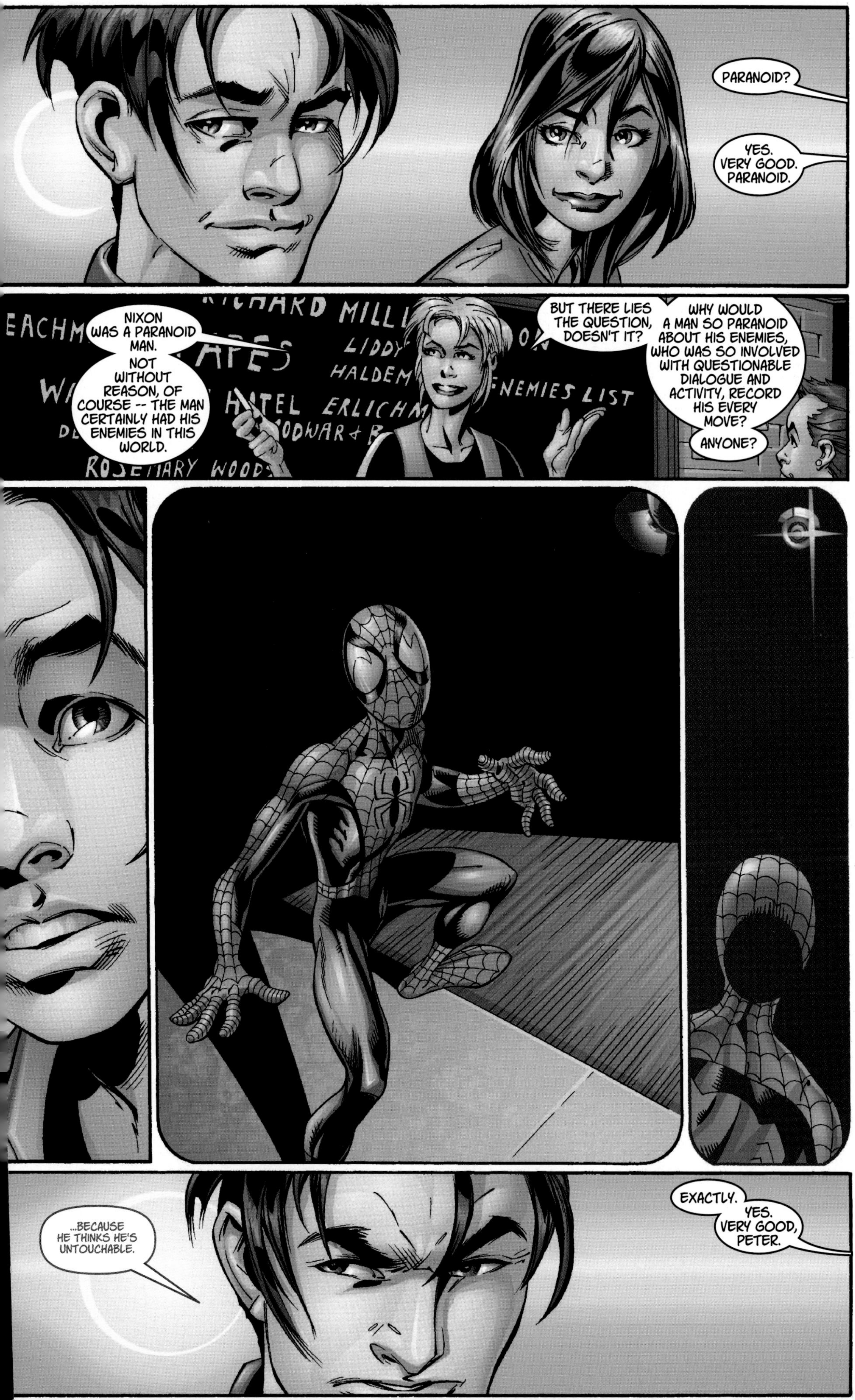
PARANOID?
YES. VERY GOOD. PARANOID.
NIXON WAS A PARANOID MAN.
NOT WITHOUT REASON, OF COURSE -- THE MAN CERTAINLY HAD HIS ENEMIES IN THIS WORLD.
BUT THERE LIES THE QUESTION, DOESN'T IT?
WHY WOULD A MAN SO PARANOID ABOUT HIS ENEMIES, WHO WAS SO INVOLVED WITH QUESTIONABLE DIALOGUE AND ACTIVITY, RECORD HIS EVERY MOVE?
ANYONE?
...BECAUSE HE THINKS HE'S UNTOUCHABLE.
EXACTLY.
YES. VERY GOOD, PETER.

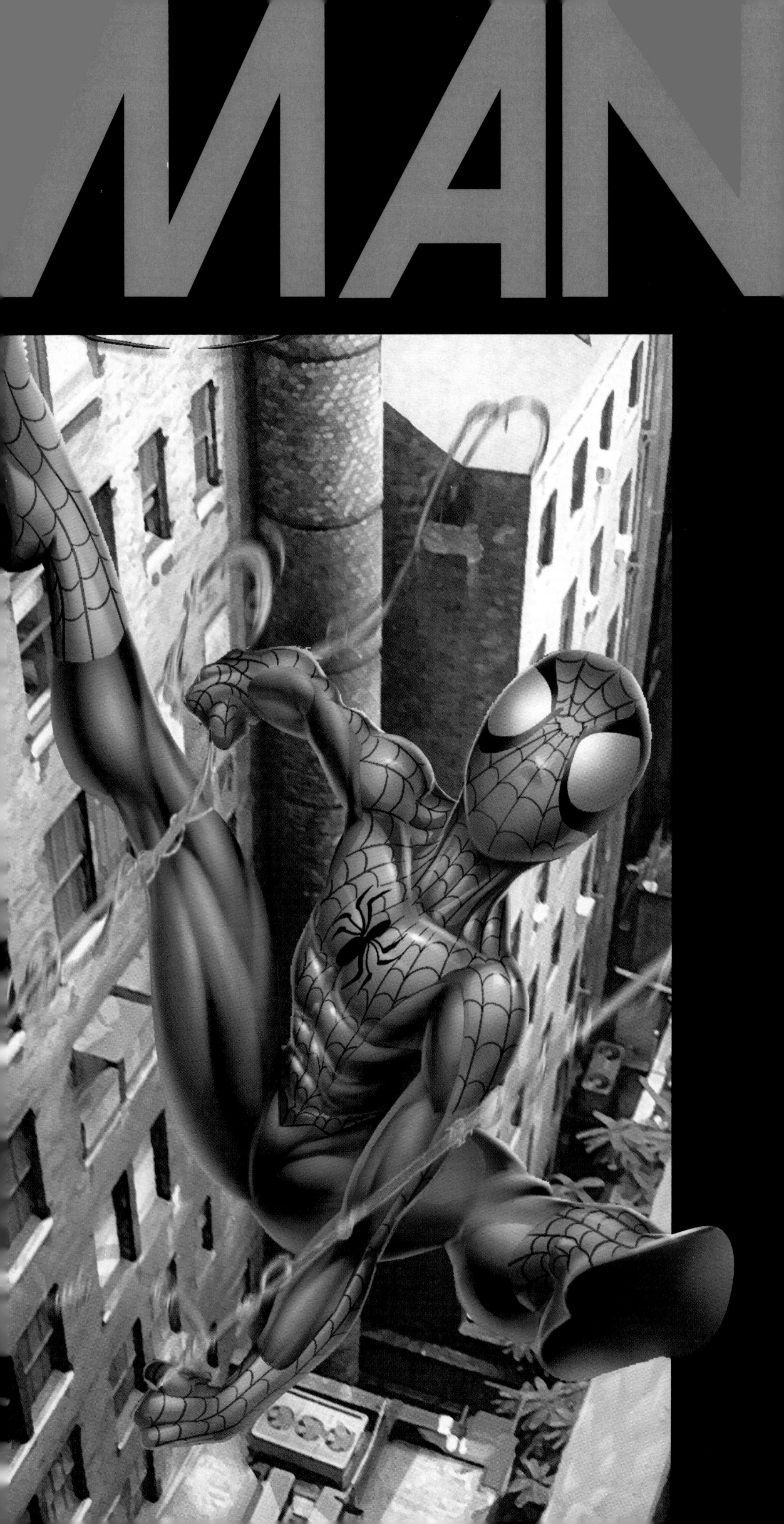
MAN

I HAVE BEEN SUCH A PINHEAD.

JUST BECAUSE I HAVE THESE SPIDER-POWERS DOESN'T MEAN I SHOULD STOP USING MY BRAIN.

I HAVE TOTALLY BEEN HITTING THE PAUSE BUTTON ON MY CRANIUM EVERY TIME I PUT ON THE SPIDEY COSTUME...

...AND THAT AIN'T GONNA FLY NO MORE.

I'M LUCKY TO BE ALIVE.

OW MANY TIMES AM I GOING TO SCAPE SOMETHING LIKE WHAT APPENED AT THE KINGPIN'S TOWER EFORE I GET MYSELF INTO GEAR?

ND SPEAKING OF WHICH, WHERE OES SOMEONE LIKE THE KINGPIN ET SOMETHING LIKE ELECTRIC ODYGUARDS?

ND MAN, THAT LECTRO GUY REEPED ME UT TO NO END.

S HE ONE F THOSE UTANTS R WHAT?

HE REALLY TRIED TO FRY ME. I'M STILL ACHY.

OOOF -- IF I'M EVER GOING TO TRY TO GO BACK IN THERE -- I NEED TO KNOW FOR SURE WHY AND HOW!

THE COMPANY THAT MAKES THE SURVEILLANCE EQUIPMENT THE KINGPIN USES IS A HUGE COMPANY AND I FIND THE CAMERA ONLINE JUST LIKE THAT.

GOD BLESS SEARCH ENGINES.

AND THERE IS A CUSTOMER SERVICE E-MAIL ADDRESS.

AND SETTING UP A FAKE E-MAIL ACCOUNT AND E-MAILING THE COMPANY FOR INFORMATION --

-- WELL, THAT IS USING THE OLD AWARD-WINNING PARKER NOGGIN.

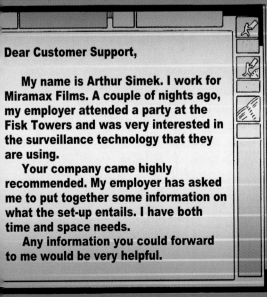

Dear Customer Support,

My name is Arthur Simek. I work for Miramax Films. A couple of nights ago, my employer attended a party at the Fisk Towers and was very interested in the surveillance technology that they are using.

Your company came highly recommended. My employer has asked me to put together some information on what the set-up entails. I have both time and space needs.

Any information you could forward to me would be very helpful.

CROSS YOUR FINGERS...

SEND

OH MAN, ENGLISH LIT STARTED FIVE MINUTES AGO.

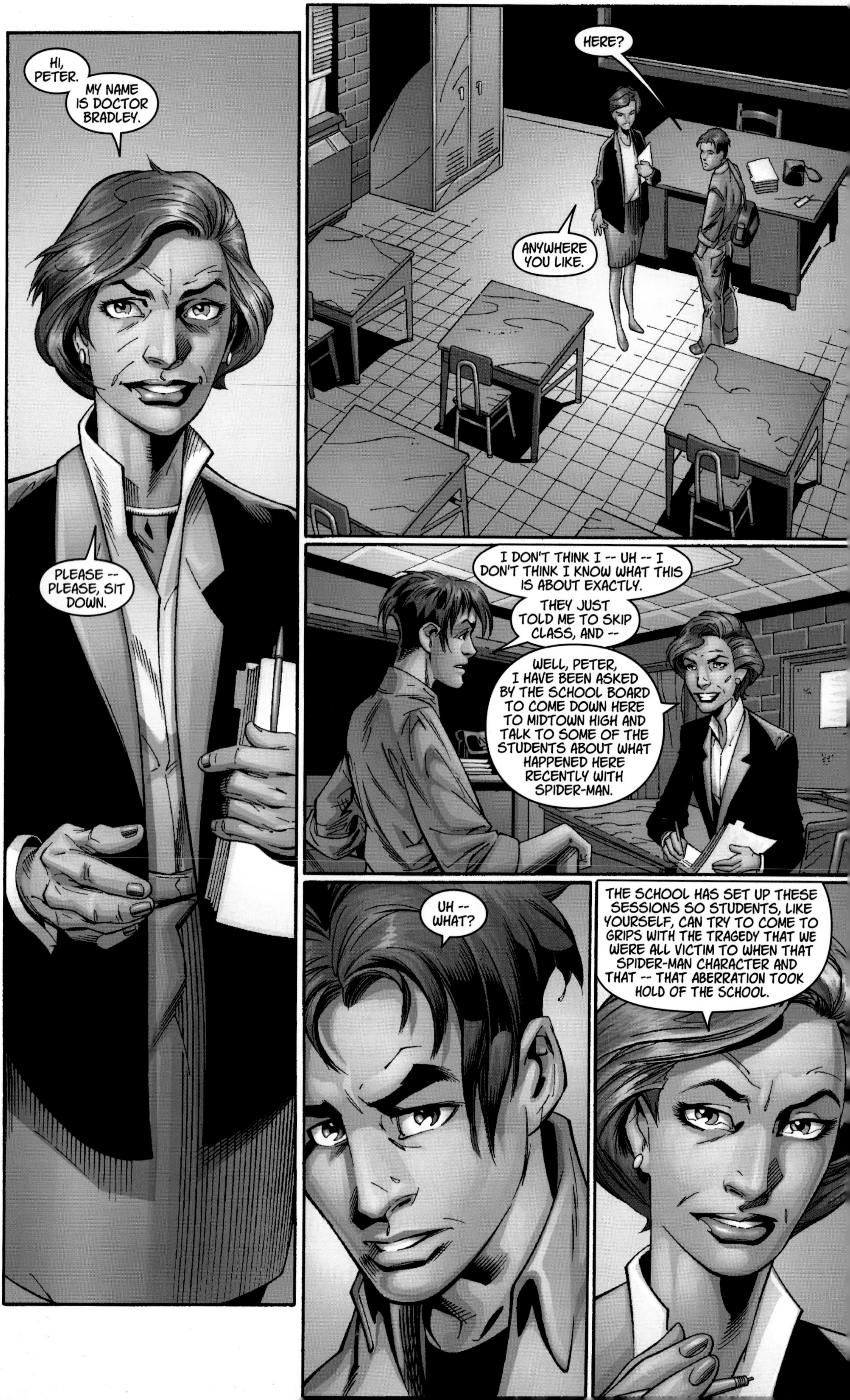
HI, PETER.
MY NAME IS DOCTOR BRADLEY.
PLEASE -- PLEASE, SIT DOWN.
HERE?
ANYWHERE YOU LIKE.
I DON'T THINK I -- UH -- I DON'T THINK I KNOW WHAT THIS IS ABOUT EXACTLY.
THEY JUST TOLD ME TO SKIP CLASS, AND --
WELL, PETER, I HAVE BEEN ASKED BY THE SCHOOL BOARD TO COME DOWN HERE TO MIDTOWN HIGH AND TALK TO SOME OF THE STUDENTS ABOUT WHAT HAPPENED HERE RECENTLY WITH SPIDER-MAN.
UH -- WHAT?
THE SCHOOL HAS SET UP THESE SESSIONS SO STUDENTS, LIKE YOURSELF, CAN TRY TO COME TO GRIPS WITH THE TRAGEDY THAT WE WERE ALL VICTIM TO WHEN THAT SPIDER-MAN CHARACTER AND THAT -- THAT ABERRATION TOOK HOLD OF THE SCHOOL.

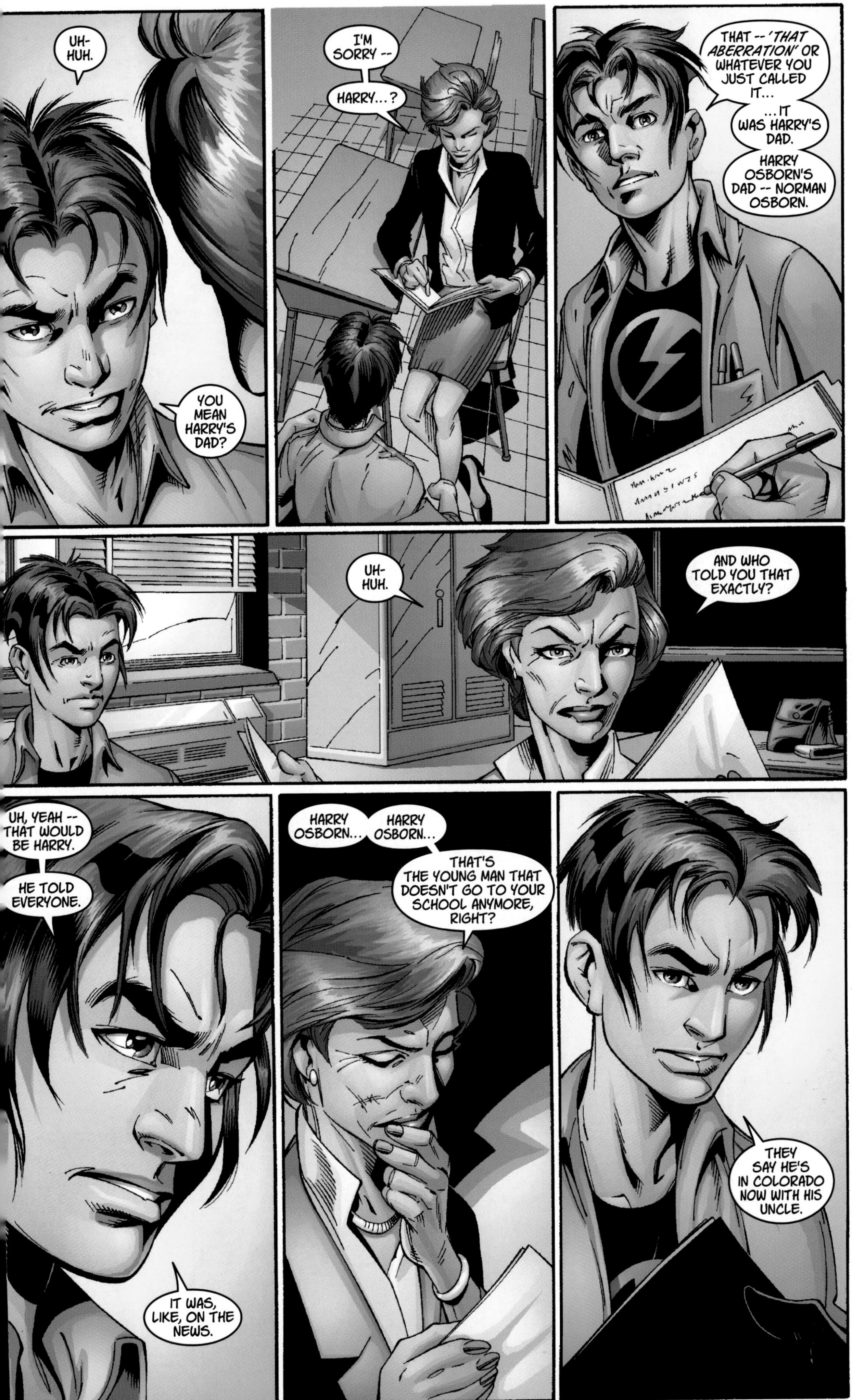
UH-HUH.
YOU MEAN HARRY'S DAD?
I'M SORRY --
HARRY...?
THAT -- 'THAT ABERRATION' OR WHATEVER YOU JUST CALLED IT...
...IT WAS HARRY'S DAD.
HARRY OSBORN'S DAD -- NORMAN OSBORN.
UH-HUH.
AND WHO TOLD YOU THAT EXACTLY?
UH, YEAH -- THAT WOULD BE HARRY.
HE TOLD EVERYONE.
IT WAS, LIKE, ON THE NEWS.
HARRY OSBORN...
HARRY OSBORN...
THAT'S THE YOUNG MAN THAT DOESN'T GO TO YOUR SCHOOL ANYMORE, RIGHT?
THEY SAY HE'S IN COLORADO NOW WITH HIS UNCLE.

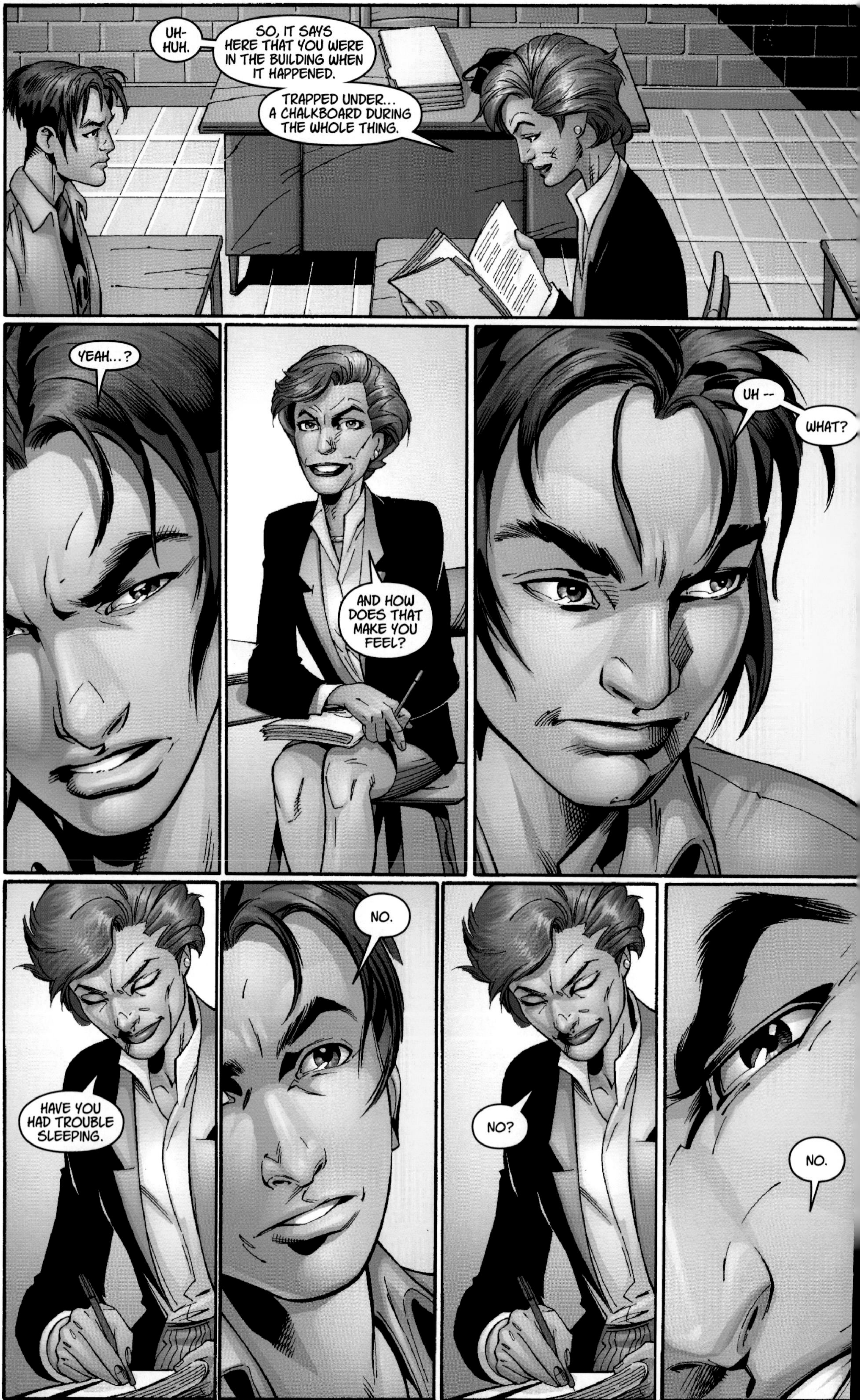
UH-HUH.
SO, IT SAYS HERE THAT YOU WERE IN THE BUILDING WHEN IT HAPPENED.
TRAPPED UNDER... A CHALKBOARD DURING THE WHOLE THING.
YEAH...?
AND HOW DOES THAT MAKE YOU FEEL?
UH --
WHAT?
HAVE YOU HAD TROUBLE SLEEPING.
NO.
NO?
NO.

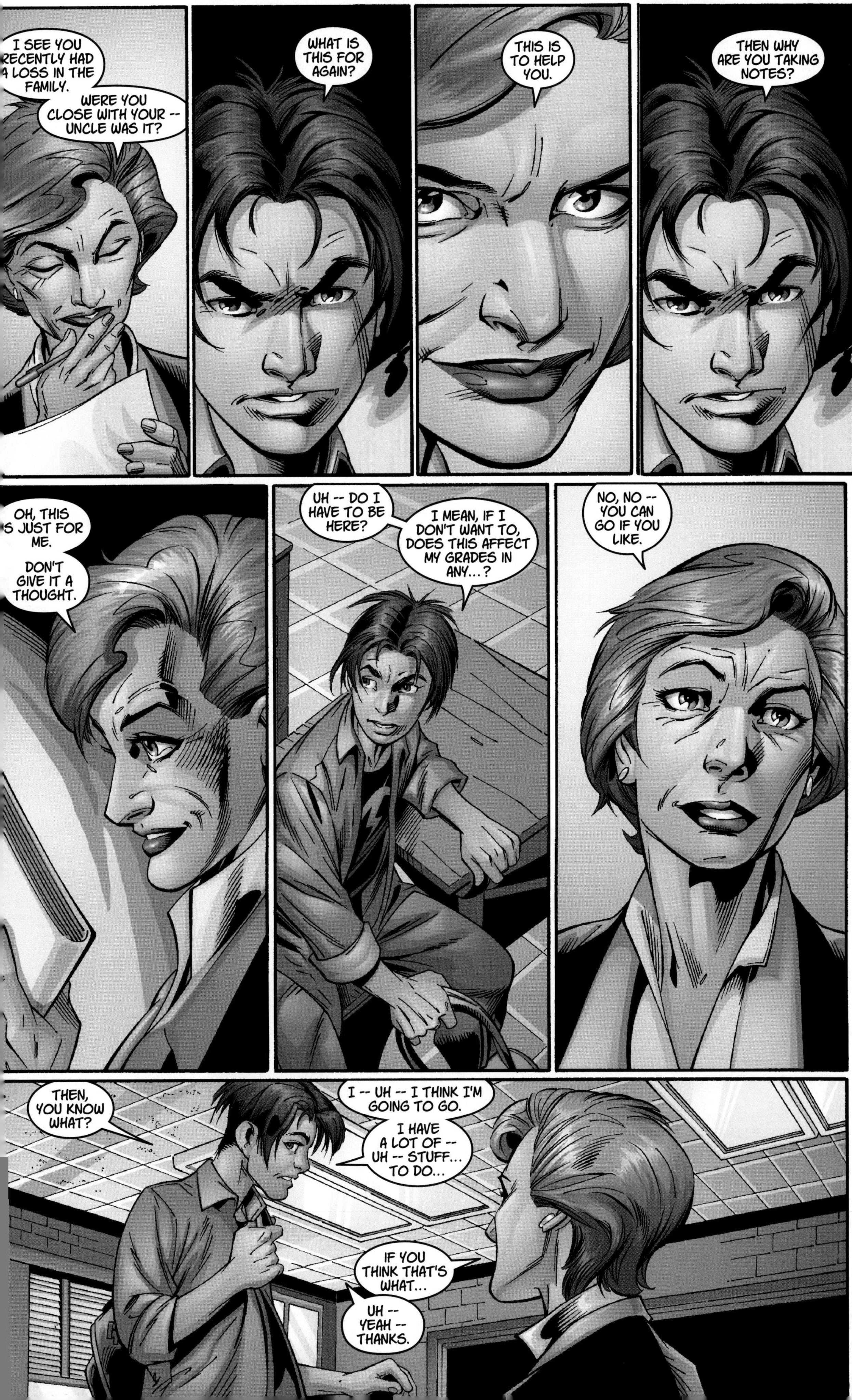
I SEE YOU RECENTLY HAD A LOSS IN THE FAMILY.
WERE YOU CLOSE WITH YOUR -- UNCLE WAS IT?
WHAT IS THIS FOR AGAIN?
THIS IS TO HELP YOU.
THEN WHY ARE YOU TAKING NOTES?
OH, THIS IS JUST FOR ME.
DON'T GIVE IT A THOUGHT.
UH -- DO I HAVE TO BE HERE?
I MEAN, IF I DON'T WANT TO, DOES THIS AFFECT MY GRADES IN ANY...?
NO, NO -- YOU CAN GO IF YOU LIKE.
THEN, YOU KNOW WHAT?
I -- UH -- I THINK I'M GOING TO GO.
I HAVE A LOT OF -- UH -- STUFF... TO DO...
IF YOU THINK THAT'S WHAT...
UH -- YEAH -- THANKS.

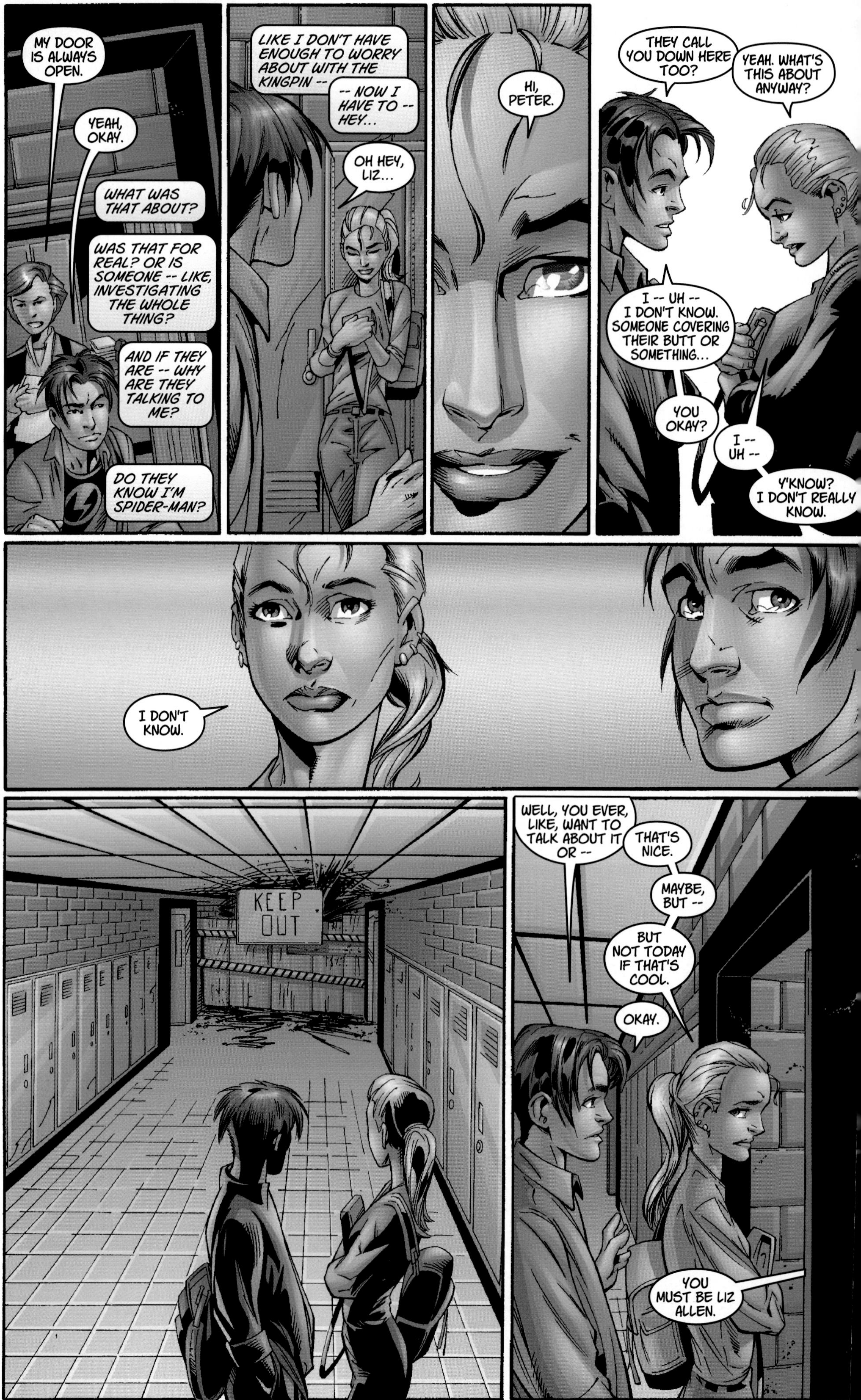
MY DOOR IS ALWAYS OPEN.
YEAH, OKAY.
WHAT WAS THAT ABOUT?
WAS THAT FOR REAL? OR IS SOMEONE -- LIKE, INVESTIGATING THE WHOLE THING?
AND IF THEY ARE -- WHY ARE THEY TALKING TO ME?
DO THEY KNOW I'M SPIDER-MAN?
LIKE I DON'T HAVE ENOUGH TO WORRY ABOUT WITH THE KINGPIN --
-- NOW I HAVE TO -- HEY...
OH HEY, LIZ...
HI, PETER.
THEY CALL YOU DOWN HERE TOO?
YEAH. WHAT'S THIS ABOUT ANYWAY?
I -- UH -- I DON'T KNOW. SOMEONE COVERING THEIR BUTT OR SOMETHING...
YOU OKAY?
I -- UH --
Y'KNOW? I DON'T REALLY KNOW.
I DON'T KNOW.
KEEP OUT
WELL, YOU EVER, LIKE, WANT TO TALK ABOUT IT OR --
THAT'S NICE.
MAYBE, BUT --
BUT NOT TODAY IF THAT'S COOL.
OKAY.
YOU MUST BE LIZ ALLEN.

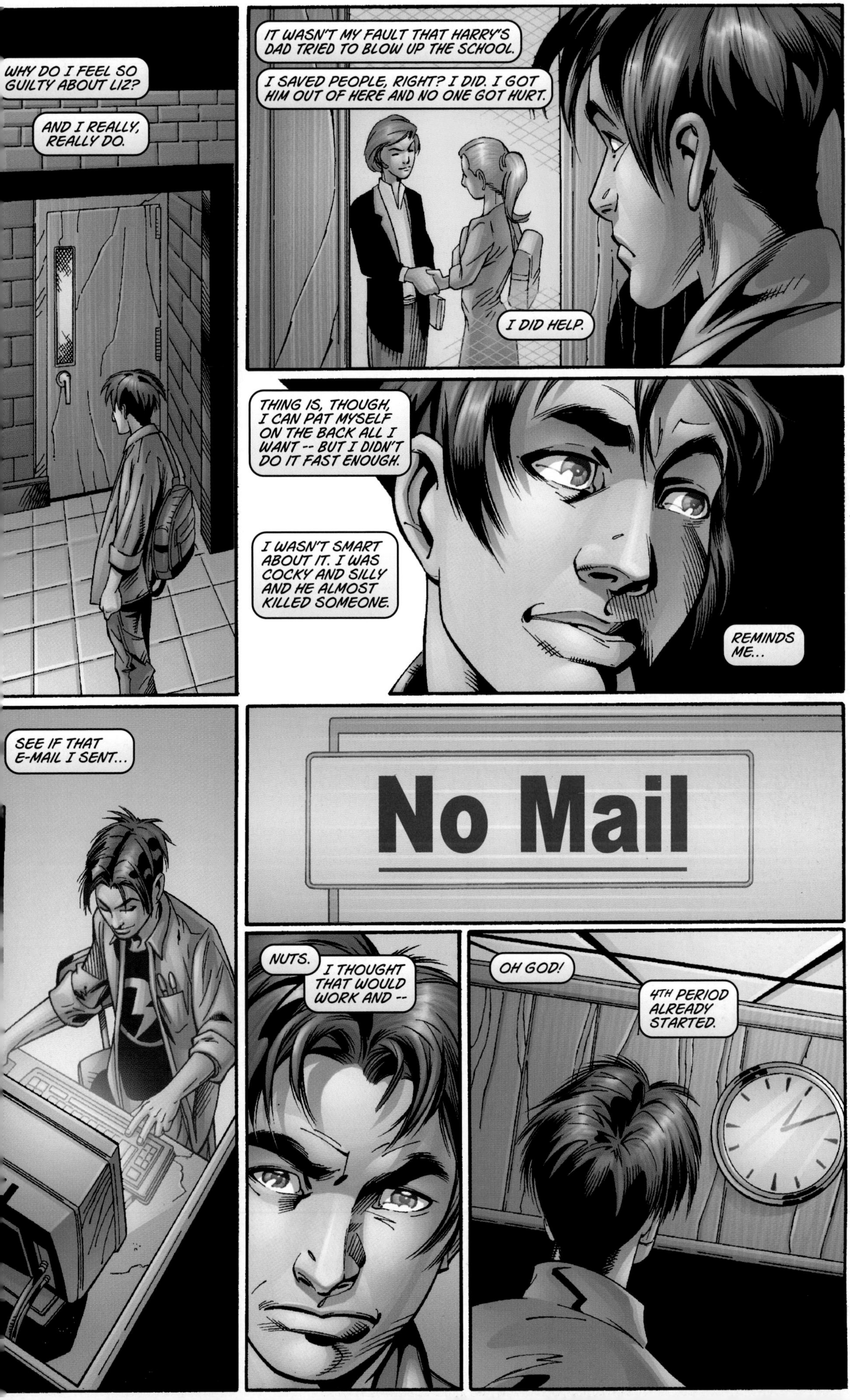
WHY DO I FEEL SO GUILTY ABOUT LIZ?
AND I REALLY, REALLY DO.
IT WASN'T MY FAULT THAT HARRY'S DAD TRIED TO BLOW UP THE SCHOOL.
I SAVED PEOPLE, RIGHT? I DID. I GOT HIM OUT OF HERE AND NO ONE GOT HURT.
I DID HELP.
THING IS, THOUGH, I CAN PAT MYSELF ON THE BACK ALL I WANT -- BUT I DIDN'T DO IT FAST ENOUGH.
I WASN'T SMART ABOUT IT. I WAS COCKY AND SILLY AND HE ALMOST KILLED SOMEONE.
REMINDS ME...
SEE IF THAT E-MAIL I SENT...
No Mail
NUTS.
I THOUGHT THAT WOULD WORK AND --
OH GOD!
4TH PERIOD ALREADY STARTED.

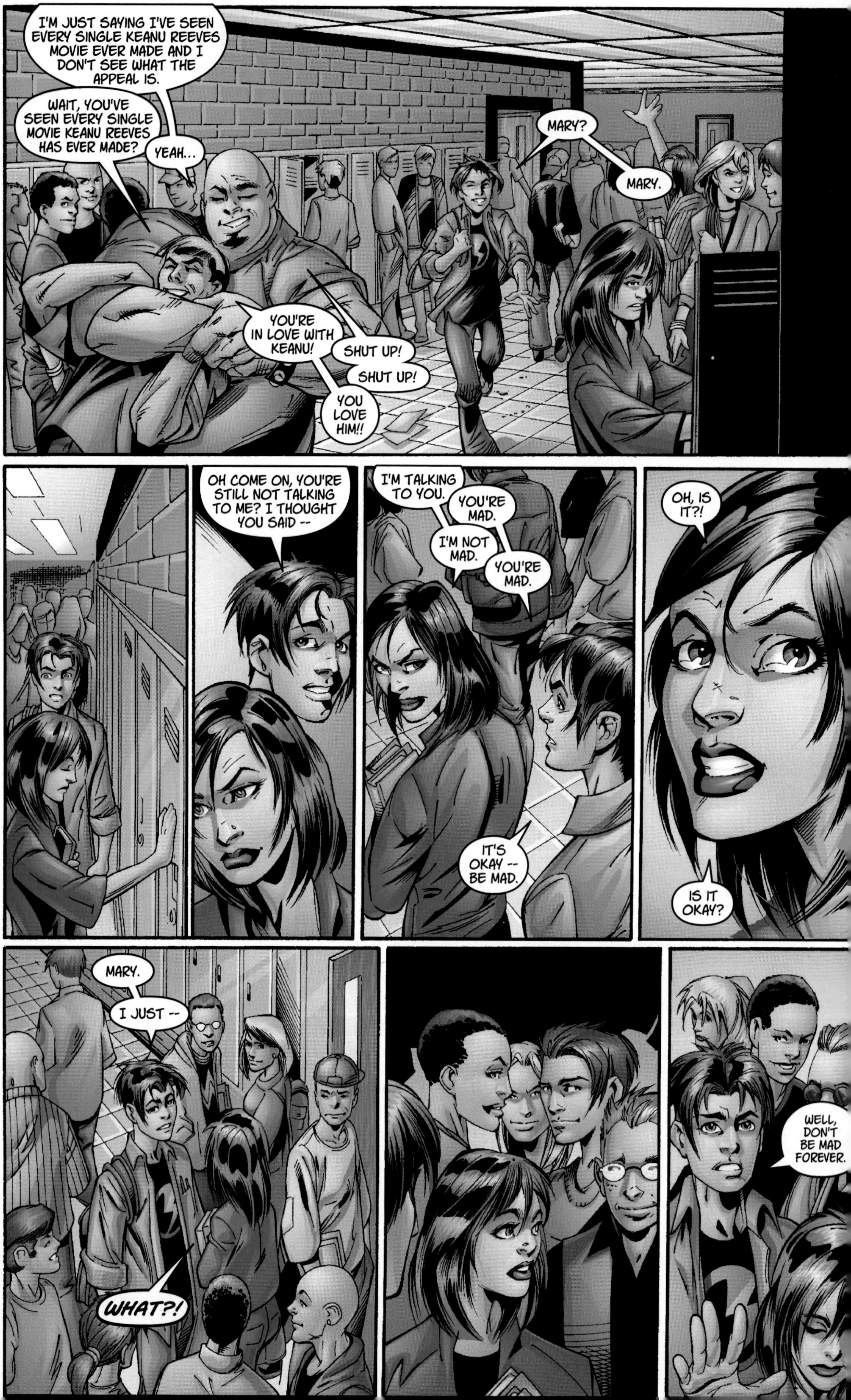
I'M JUST SAYING I'VE SEEN EVERY SINGLE KEANU REEVES MOVIE EVER MADE AND I DON'T SEE WHAT THE APPEAL IS.
WAIT, YOU'VE SEEN EVERY SINGLE MOVIE KEANU REEVES HAS EVER MADE?
YEAH...
MARY?
MARY.
YOU'RE IN LOVE WITH KEANU!
SHUT UP!
SHUT UP!
YOU LOVE HIM!!
OH COME ON, YOU'RE STILL NOT TALKING TO ME? I THOUGHT YOU SAID --
I'M TALKING TO YOU.
YOU'RE MAD.
I'M NOT MAD.
YOU'RE MAD.
IT'S OKAY -- BE MAD.
OH, IS IT?!
IS IT OKAY?
MARY.
I JUST --
WHAT?!
WELL, DON'T BE MAD FOREVER.

...AN, SINCE WHEN DID ...ARY JANE GET SO ...RITATED BY ME?

...MEAN, WE'VE NEVER ...VEN HAD A FIGHT IN ...UR ENTIRE LIVES AND I ...EED TO STAND HER UP ...OR ONE LOUSY MOVIE, ...ND ALL OF A SUDDEN ...M CHARLIE SHEEN.

...ND -- HEY -- I DID ...AVE A GOOD REASON.

...NEEDED TO HEAL FROM ...Y SPECTACULAR BUTT-...CKING AT THE KINGPIN'S ...HE NIGHT BEFORE.

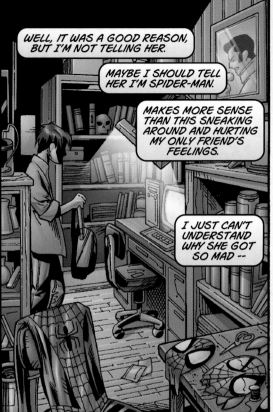

WELL, IT WAS A GOOD REASON, BUT I'M NOT TELLING HER.

MAYBE I SHOULD TELL HER I'M SPIDER-MAN.

MAKES MORE SENSE THAN THIS SNEAKING AROUND AND HURTING MY ONLY FRIEND'S FEELINGS.

I JUST CAN'T UNDERSTAND WHY SHE GOT SO MAD --

You've got mail.

OH MY GOD...

HEY --

-- IT WORKED.

Dear Mr. Simek,

Thank you for your interest in the 4566 Telech System. It is a popular system among many of the Fortune 500 companies and I hope the following information is useful. I have also included links to some of our more technical web pages in hopes that this will help paint a clearer picture of what we can offer you.

If you want to discuss this further or have one of our people come out to you for an evaluation, please feel free to call me directly at 718 555-5567 ext. 23 and I will personally take care of this for you.

Best regards,

Sam Rosen

The 4566 Telech System is the most modern and efficient corporate security system available on the market today.

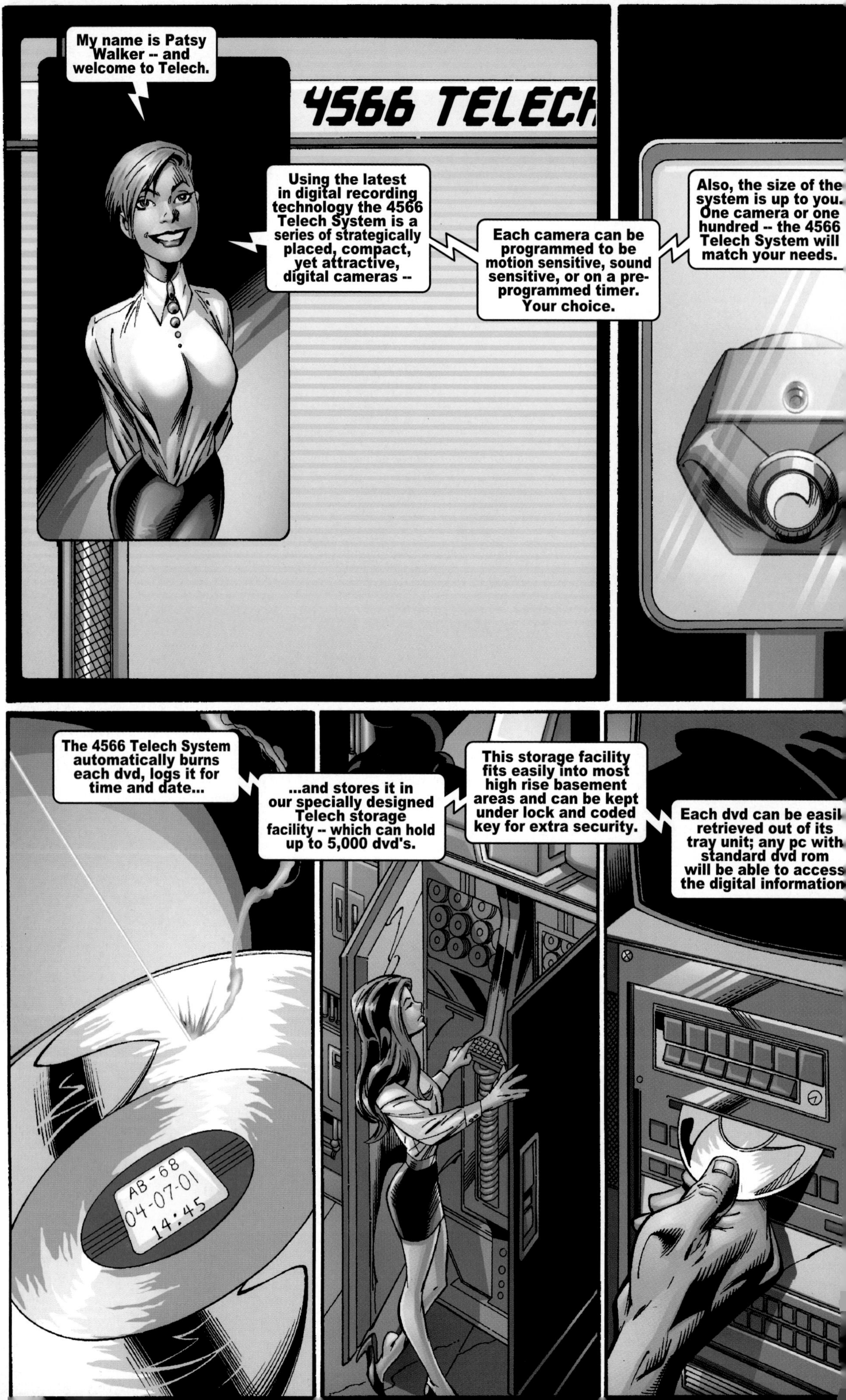
My name is Patsy Walker -- and welcome to Telech.
4566 TELECH
Using the latest in digital recording technology the 4566 Telech System is a series of strategically placed, compact, yet attractive, digital cameras --
Each camera can be programmed to be motion sensitive, sound sensitive, or on a pre-programmed timer. Your choice.
Also, the size of the system is up to you. One camera or one hundred -- the 4566 Telech System will match your needs.
The 4566 Telech System automatically burns each dvd, logs it for time and date...
...and stores it in our specially designed Telech storage facility -- which can hold up to 5,000 dvd's.
AB-68 04-07-01 14:45
This storage facility fits easily into most high rise basement areas and can be kept under lock and coded key for extra security.
Each dvd can be easil retrieved out of its tray unit; any pc with standard dvd rom will be able to access the digital information

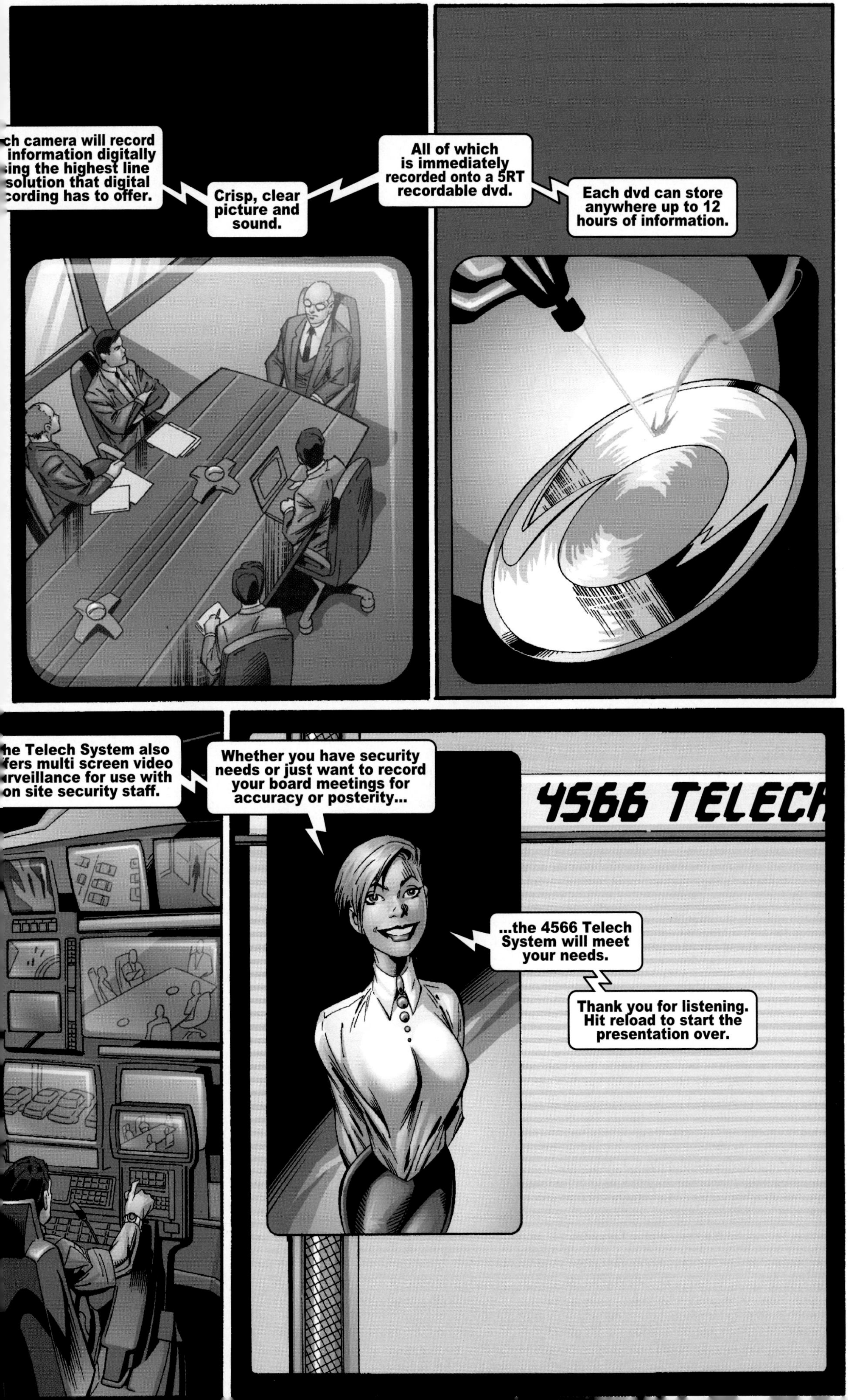
ch camera will record information digitally ɪing the highest line solution that digital cording has to offer.
Crisp, clear picture and sound.
All of which is immediately recorded onto a 5RT recordable dvd.
Each dvd can store anywhere up to 12 hours of information.
he Telech System also fers multi screen video ırveillance for use with on site security staff.
Whether you have security needs or just want to record your board meetings for accuracy or posterity...
4566 TELEC
...the 4566 Telech System will meet your needs.
Thank you for listening. Hit reload to start the presentation over.

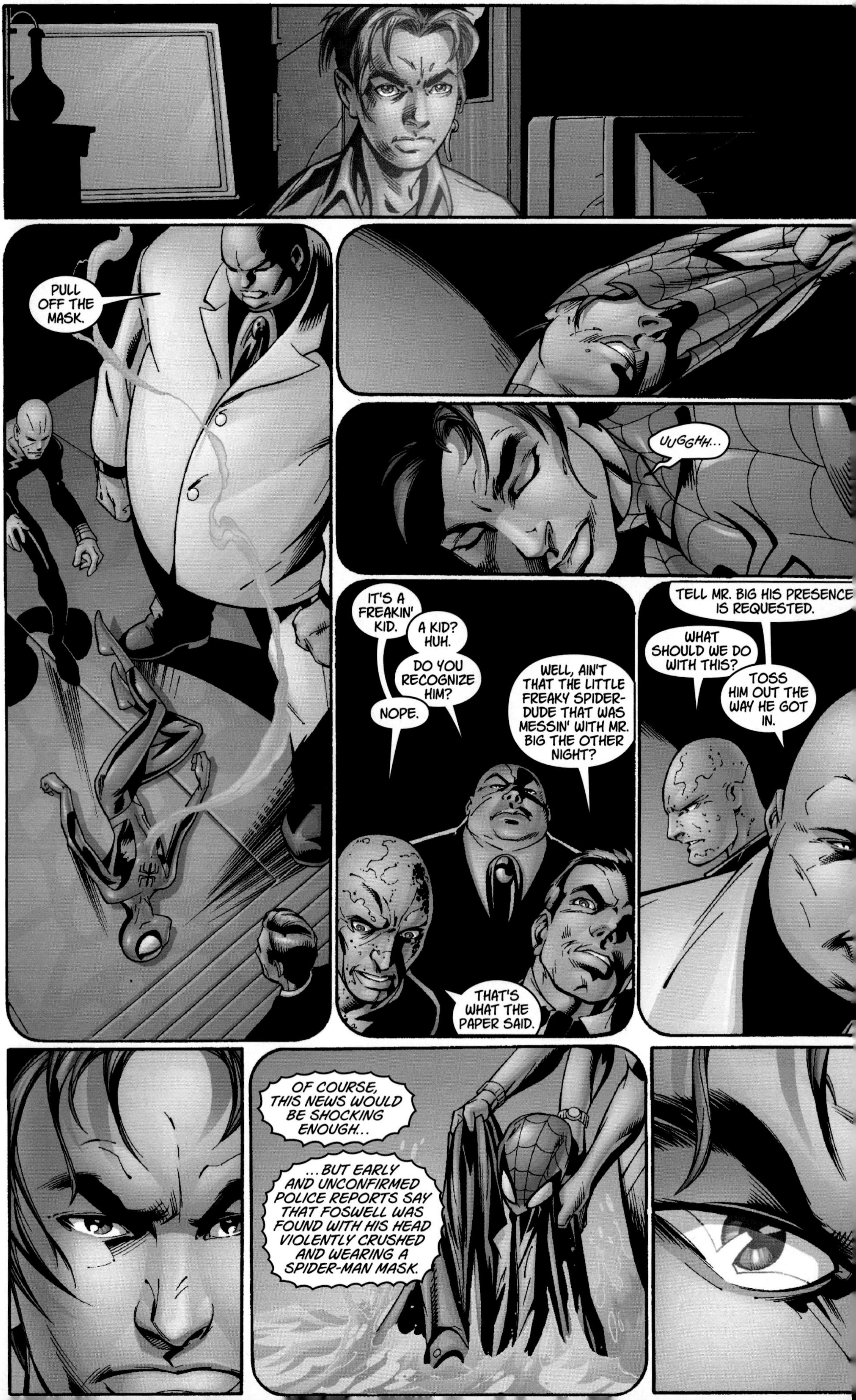
PULL OFF THE MASK.
UUGGHH...
IT'S A FREAKIN' KID.
A KID? HUH.
DO YOU RECOGNIZE HIM?
NOPE.
WELL, AIN'T THAT THE LITTLE FREAKY SPIDER-DUDE THAT WAS MESSIN' WITH MR. BIG THE OTHER NIGHT?
THAT'S WHAT THE PAPER SAID.
TELL MR. BIG HIS PRESENCE IS REQUESTED.
WHAT SHOULD WE DO WITH THIS?
TOSS HIM OUT THE WAY HE GOT IN.
OF COURSE, THIS NEWS WOULD BE SHOCKING ENOUGH...
...BUT EARLY AND UNCONFIRMED POLICE REPORTS SAY THAT FOSWELL WAS FOUND WITH HIS HEAD VIOLENTLY CRUSHED AND WEARING A SPIDER-MAN MASK.

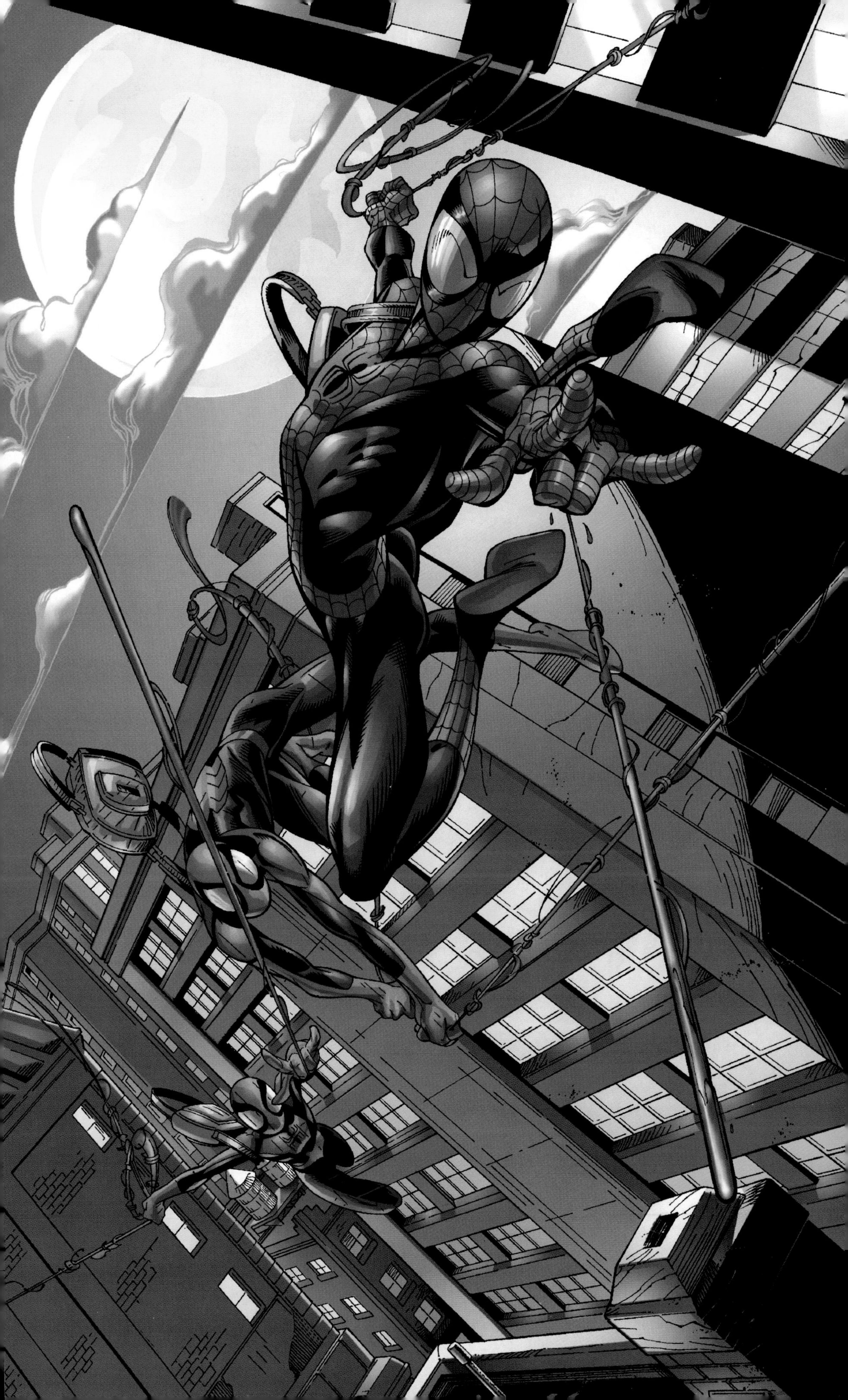

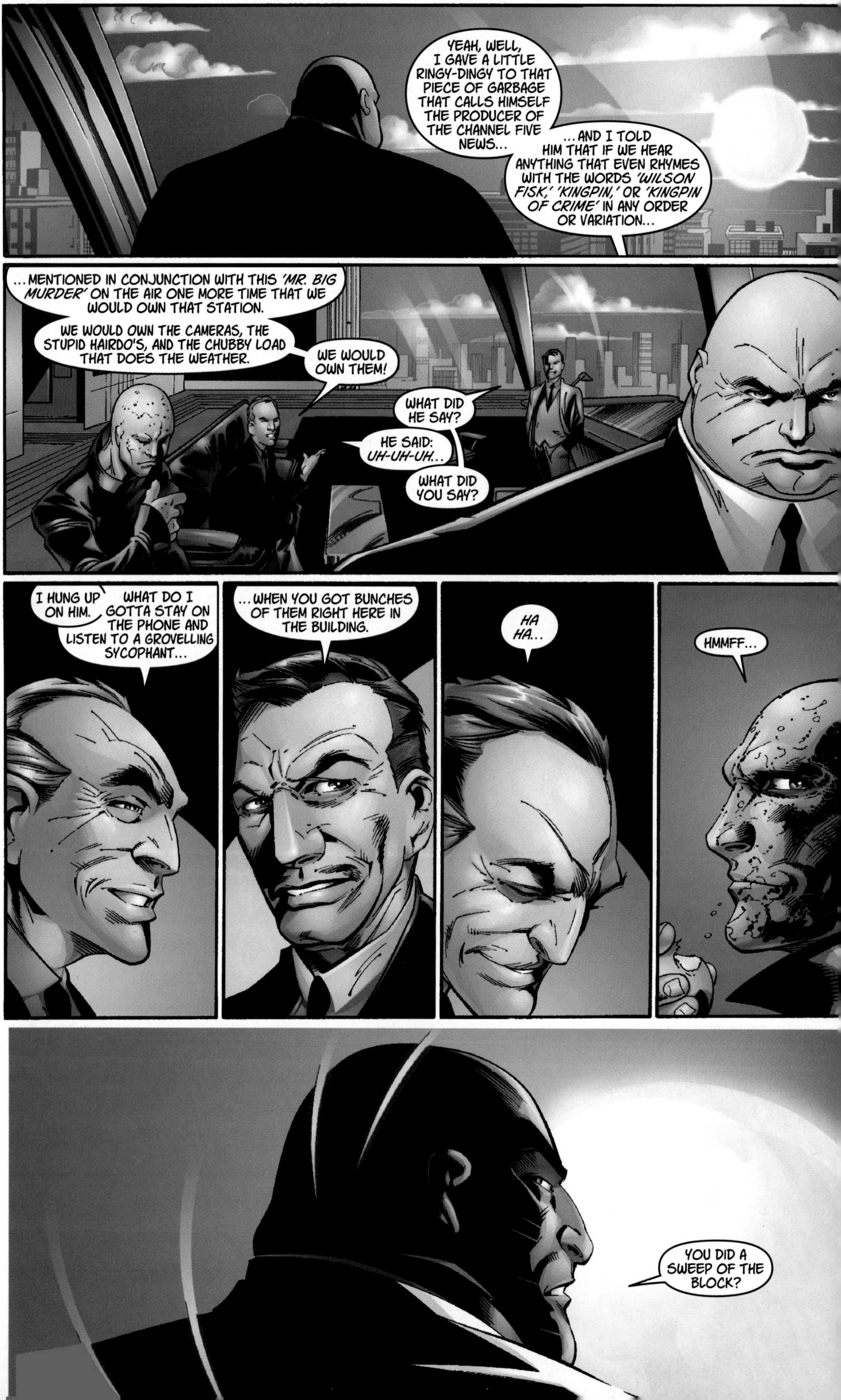
YEAH, WELL, I GAVE A LITTLE RINGY-DINGY TO THAT PIECE OF GARBAGE THAT CALLS HIMSELF THE PRODUCER OF THE CHANNEL FIVE NEWS...
...AND I TOLD HIM THAT IF WE HEAR ANYTHING THAT EVEN RHYMES WITH THE WORDS 'WILSON FISK,' 'KINGPIN,' OR 'KINGPIN OF CRIME' IN ANY ORDER OR VARIATION...
...MENTIONED IN CONJUNCTION WITH THIS 'MR. BIG MURDER' ON THE AIR ONE MORE TIME THAT WE WOULD OWN THAT STATION.
WE WOULD OWN THE CAMERAS, THE STUPID HAIRDO'S, AND THE CHUBBY LOAD THAT DOES THE WEATHER.
WE WOULD OWN THEM!
WHAT DID HE SAY?
HE SAID: UH-UH-UH...
WHAT DID YOU SAY?
I HUNG UP ON HIM.
WHAT DO I GOTTA STAY ON THE PHONE AND LISTEN TO A GROVELLING SYCOPHANT...
...WHEN YOU GOT BUNCHES OF THEM RIGHT HERE IN THE BUILDING.
HA HA...
HMMFF...
YOU DID A SWEEP OF THE BLOCK?

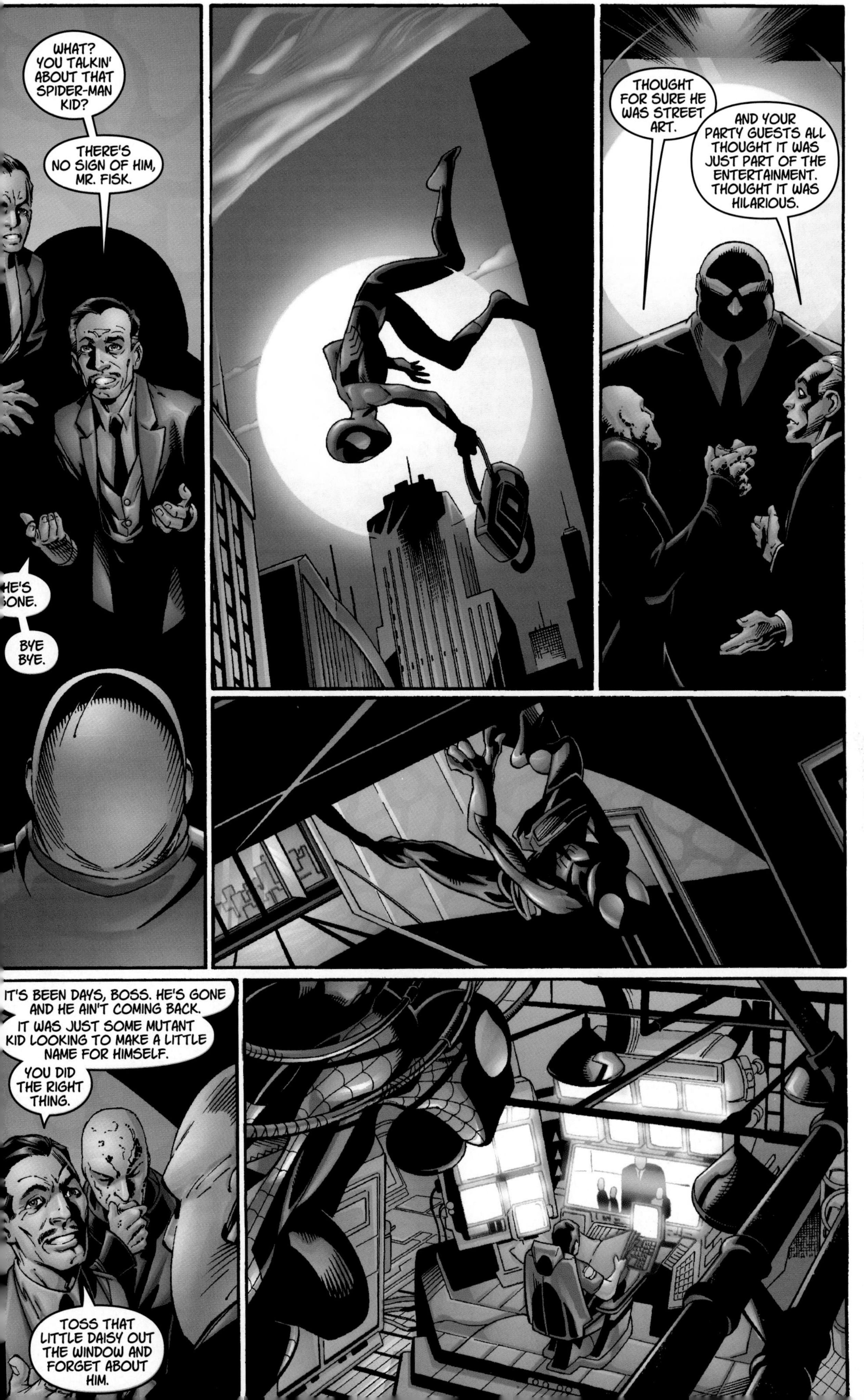
WHAT? YOU TALKIN' ABOUT THAT SPIDER-MAN KID?
THERE'S NO SIGN OF HIM, MR. FISK.
HE'S GONE.
BYE BYE.
THOUGHT FOR SURE HE WAS STREET ART.
AND YOUR PARTY GUESTS ALL THOUGHT IT WAS JUST PART OF THE ENTERTAINMENT. THOUGHT IT WAS HILARIOUS.
IT'S BEEN DAYS, BOSS. HE'S GONE AND HE AIN'T COMING BACK.
IT WAS JUST SOME MUTANT KID LOOKING TO MAKE A LITTLE NAME FOR HIMSELF.
YOU DID THE RIGHT THING.
TOSS THAT LITTLE DAISY OUT THE WINDOW AND FORGET ABOUT HIM.

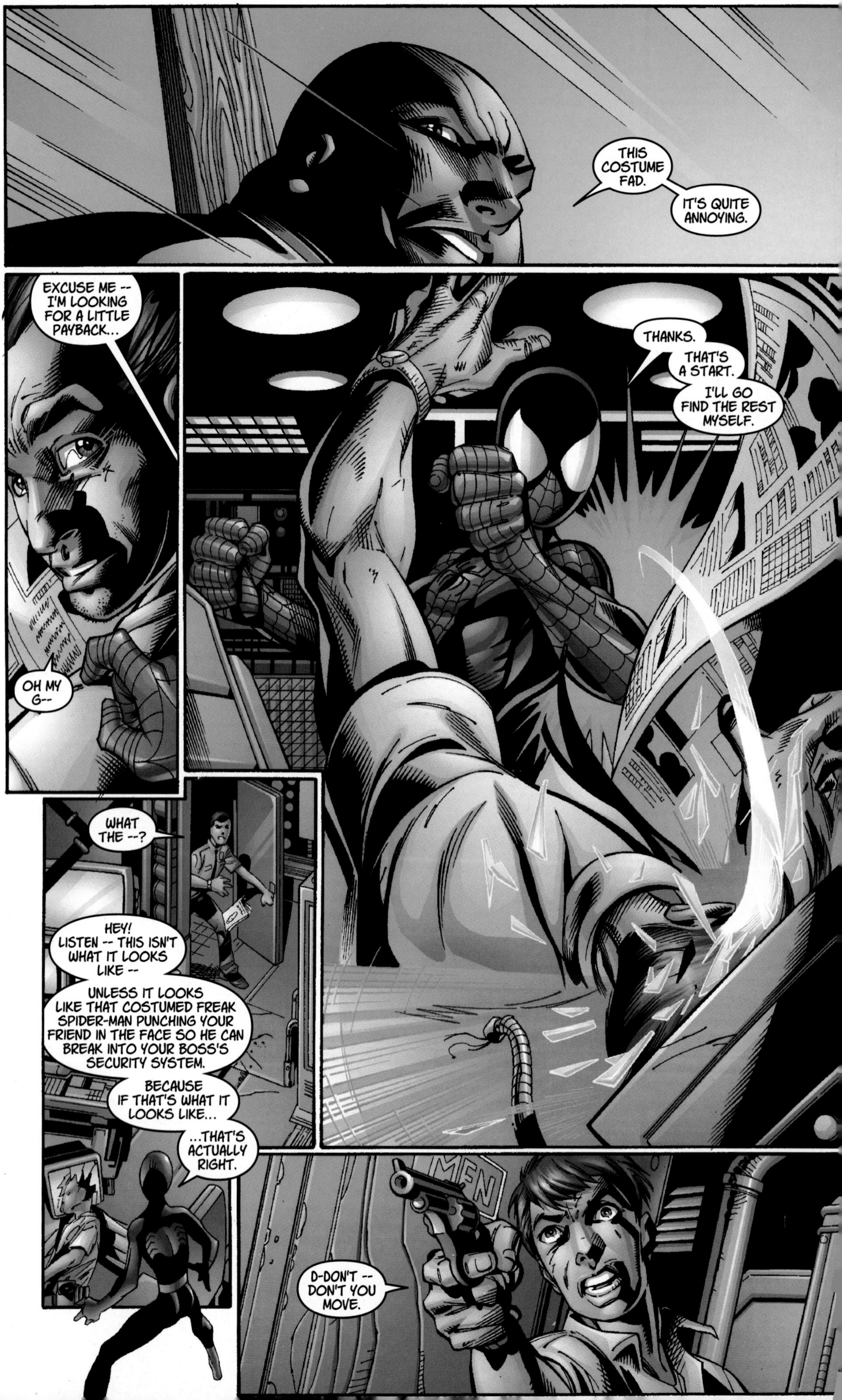

THIS COSTUME FAD.
IT'S QUITE ANNOYING.
EXCUSE ME -- I'M LOOKING FOR A LITTLE PAYBACK...
OH MY G--
THANKS.
THAT'S A START.
I'LL GO FIND THE REST MYSELF.
WHAT THE --?
HEY! LISTEN -- THIS ISN'T WHAT IT LOOKS LIKE --
UNLESS IT LOOKS LIKE THAT COSTUMED FREAK SPIDER-MAN PUNCHING YOUR FRIEND IN THE FACE SO HE CAN BREAK INTO YOUR BOSS'S SECURITY SYSTEM.
BECAUSE IF THAT'S WHAT IT LOOKS LIKE...
...THAT'S ACTUALLY RIGHT.
MEN
D-DON'T -- DON'T YOU MOVE.

MR. FISK, WE WON'T BE HEARING FROM ANY SPIDER-MAN AGAIN.

BAM

BSSSSSSS

SPDZZZ

AND IF WE DID -- I'D SMOKE HIM LIKE A SALMON.

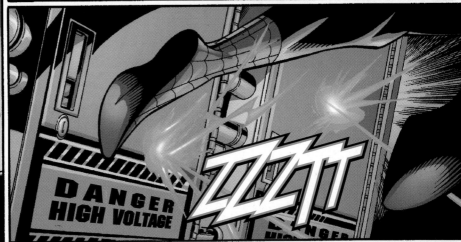

DANGER HIGH VOLTAGE

ZZZTT

SNAP

ZZZTT

UH --

I DIDN'T DO THAT.

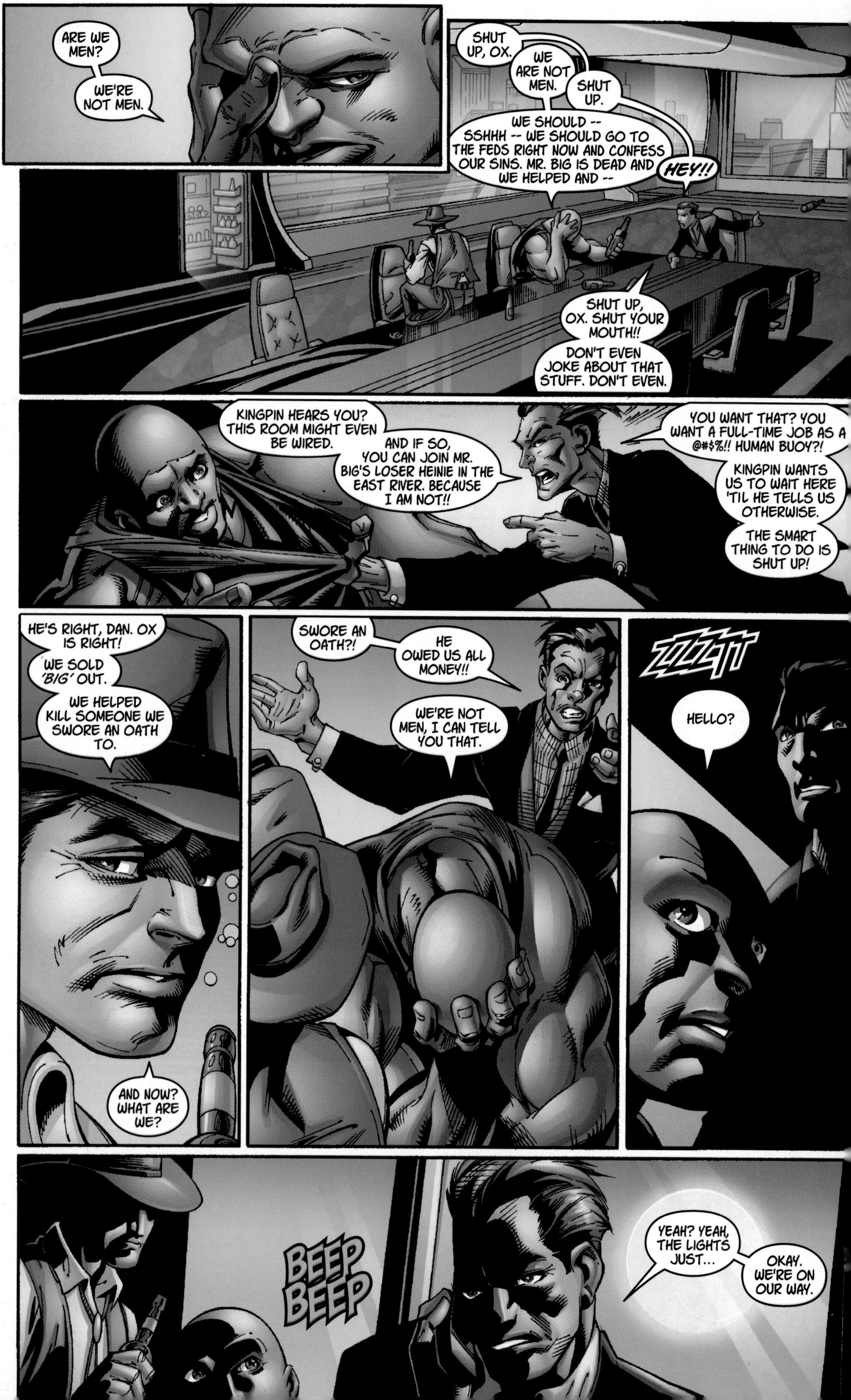
ARE WE MEN?
WE'RE NOT MEN.
SHUT UP, OX.
WE ARE NOT MEN.
SHUT UP.
WE SHOULD -- SSHHH -- WE SHOULD GO TO THE FEDS RIGHT NOW AND CONFESS OUR SINS. MR. BIG IS DEAD AND WE HELPED AND --
HEY!!
SHUT UP, OX. SHUT YOUR MOUTH!!
DON'T EVEN JOKE ABOUT THAT STUFF. DON'T EVEN.
KINGPIN HEARS YOU? THIS ROOM MIGHT EVEN BE WIRED.
AND IF SO, YOU CAN JOIN MR. BIG'S LOSER HEINIE IN THE EAST RIVER. BECAUSE I AM NOT!!
YOU WANT THAT? YOU WANT A FULL-TIME JOB AS A @#$%!! HUMAN BUOY?!
KINGPIN WANTS US TO WAIT HERE 'TIL HE TELLS US OTHERWISE.
THE SMART THING TO DO IS SHUT UP!
HE'S RIGHT, DAN. OX IS RIGHT!
WE SOLD 'BIG' OUT.
WE HELPED KILL SOMEONE WE SWORE AN OATH TO.
AND NOW? WHAT ARE WE?
SWORE AN OATH?!
HE OWED US ALL MONEY!!
WE'RE NOT MEN, I CAN TELL YOU THAT.
ZZZZTT
HELLO?
BEEP BEEP
YEAH? YEAH, THE LIGHTS JUST...
OKAY. WE'RE ON OUR WAY.

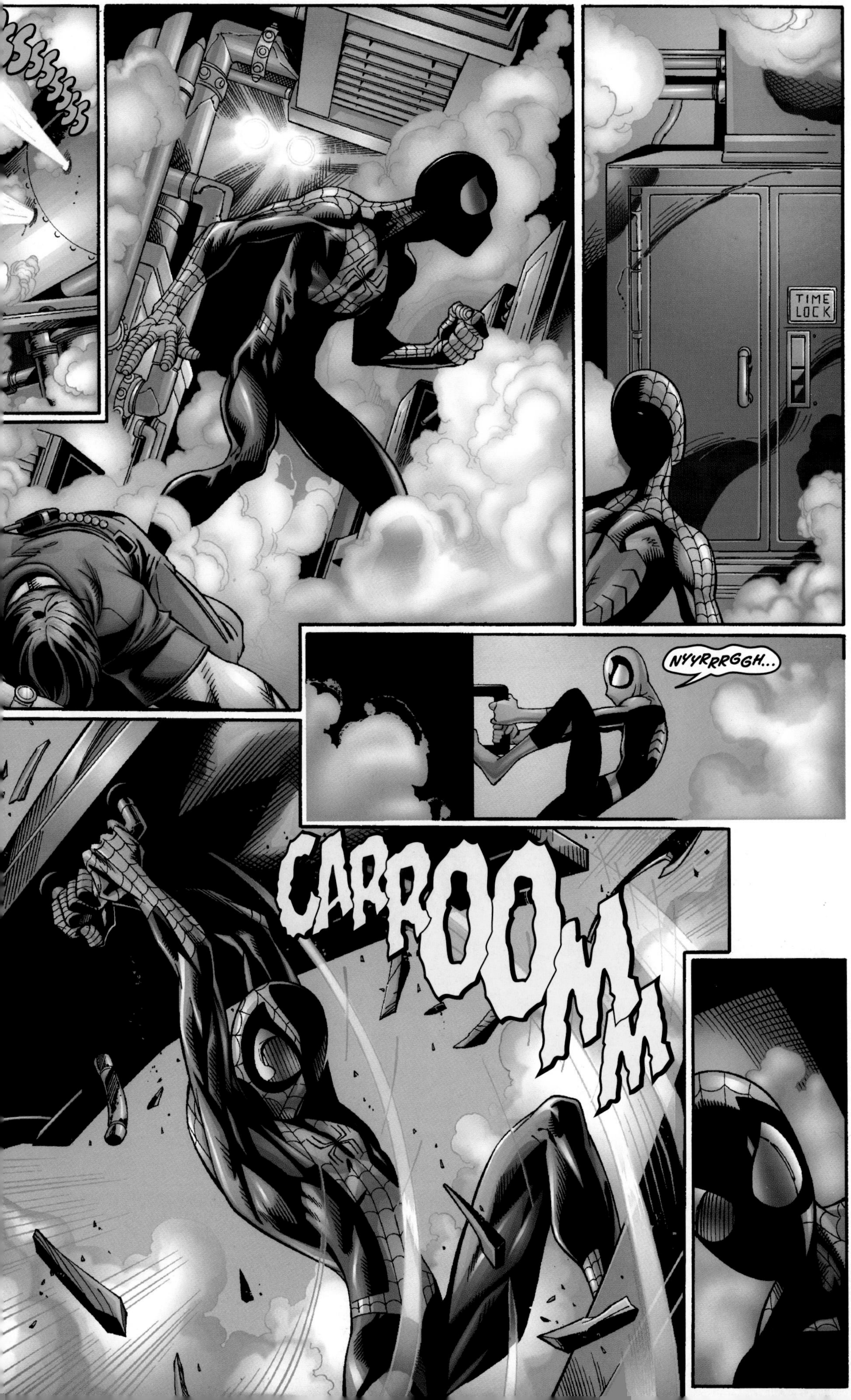
SSSSSSSS
TIME LOCK
NYYRRRGGH...
CARROOM

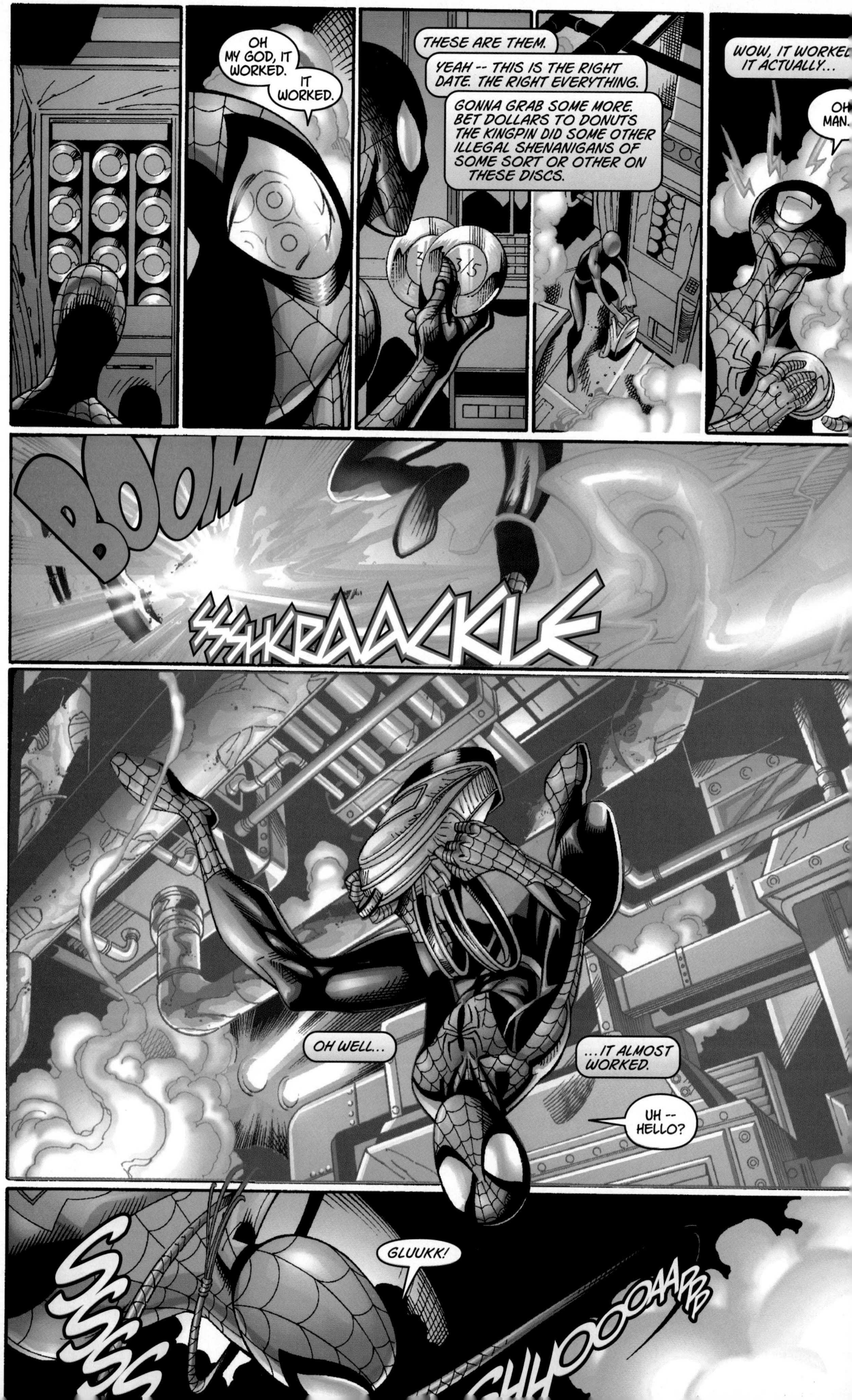
OH MY GOD, IT WORKED.
IT WORKED.
THESE ARE THEM.
YEAH -- THIS IS THE RIGHT DATE. THE RIGHT EVERYTHING.
GONNA GRAB SOME MORE. BET DOLLARS TO DONUTS THE KINGPIN DID SOME OTHER ILLEGAL SHENANIGANS OF SOME SORT OR OTHER ON THESE DISCS.
WOW, IT WORKED IT ACTUALLY...
OH MAN.
BOOM
SSSHKRAACKLE
OH WELL...
...IT ALMOST WORKED.
UH -- HELLO?
GLUUKK!
CHHOOOOAARRP

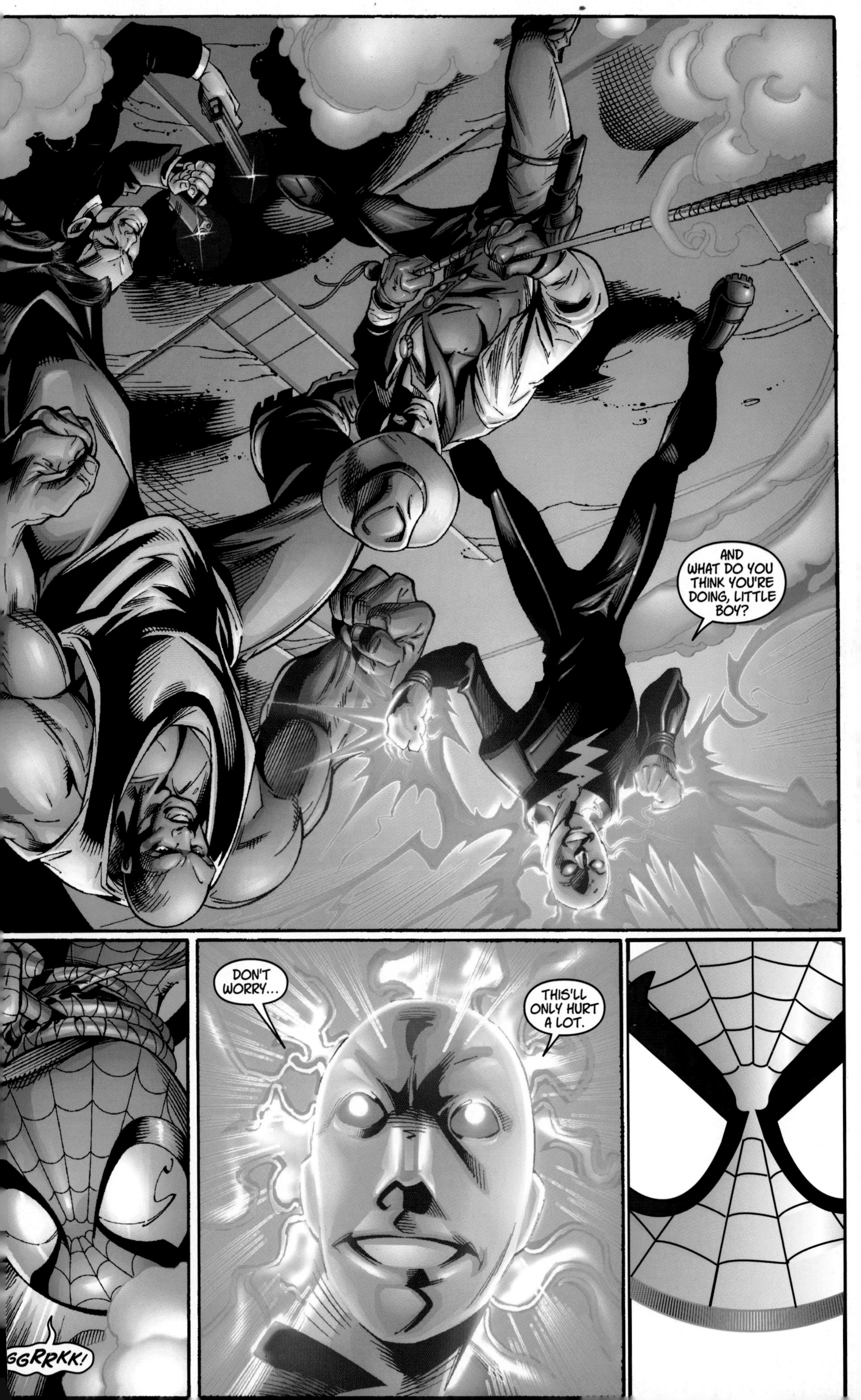
AND WHAT DO YOU THINK YOU'RE DOING, LITTLE BOY?
SGRRKK!
DON'T WORRY...
THIS'LL ONLY HURT A LOT.

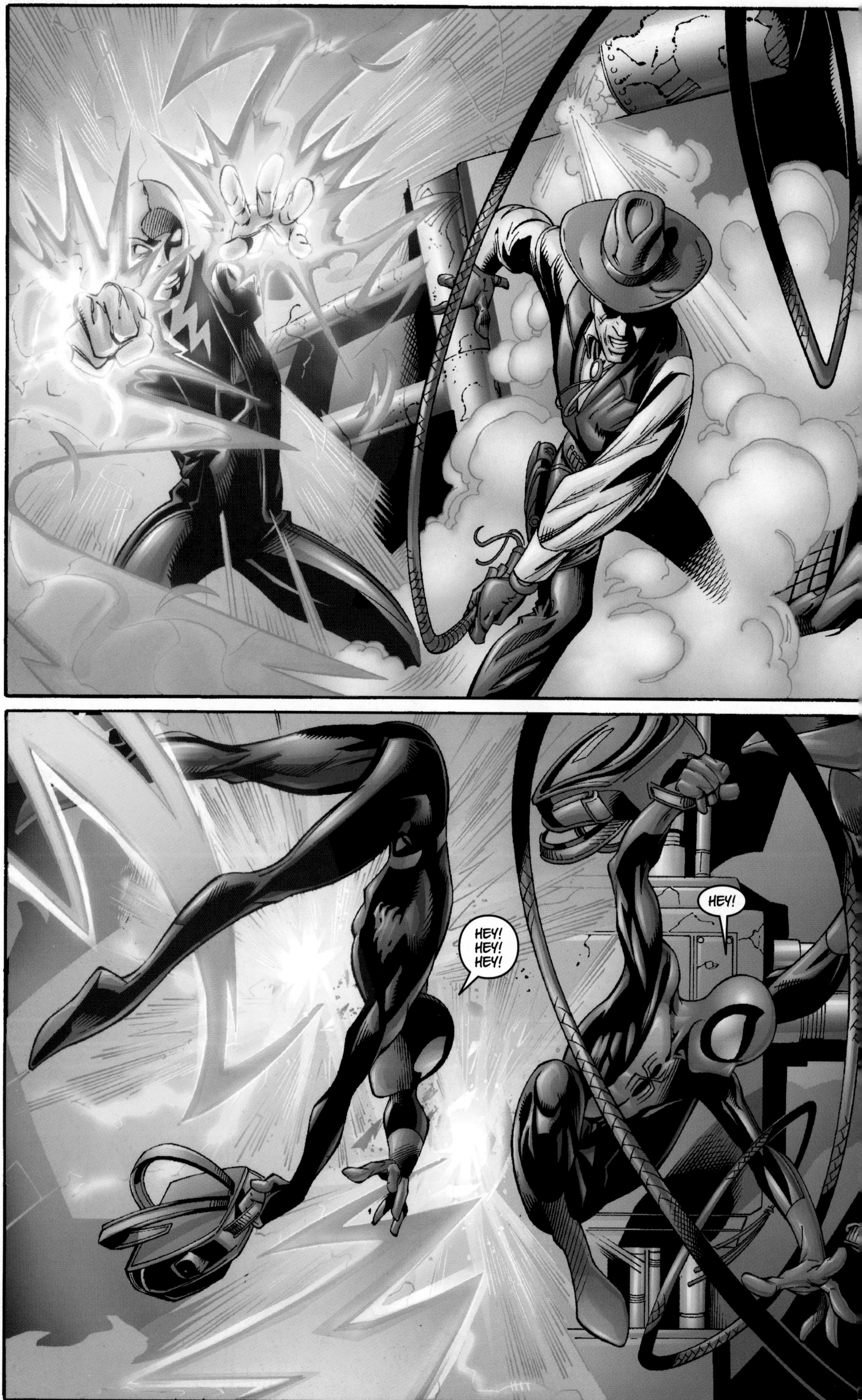
HEY!
HEY!
HEY!
HEY!

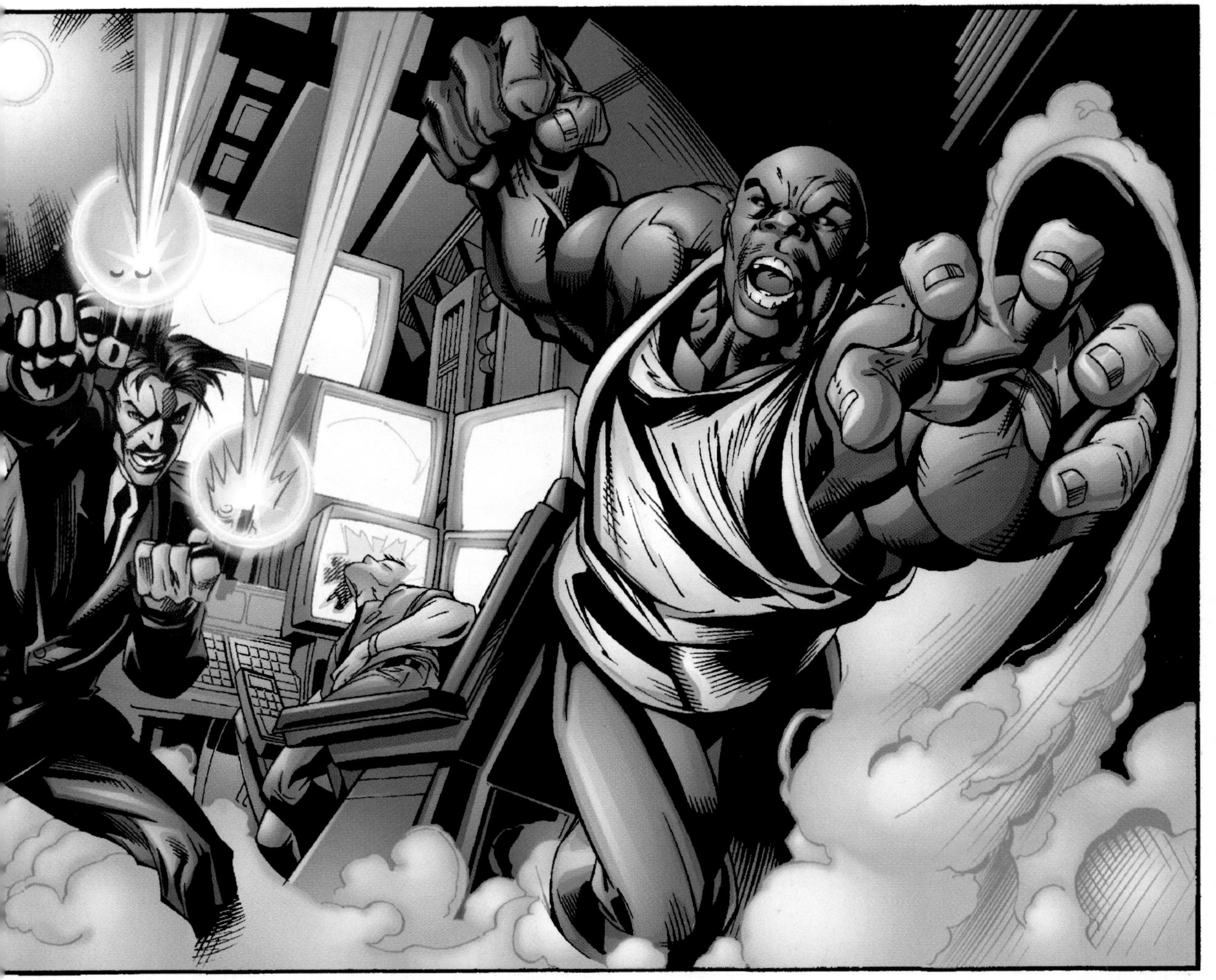

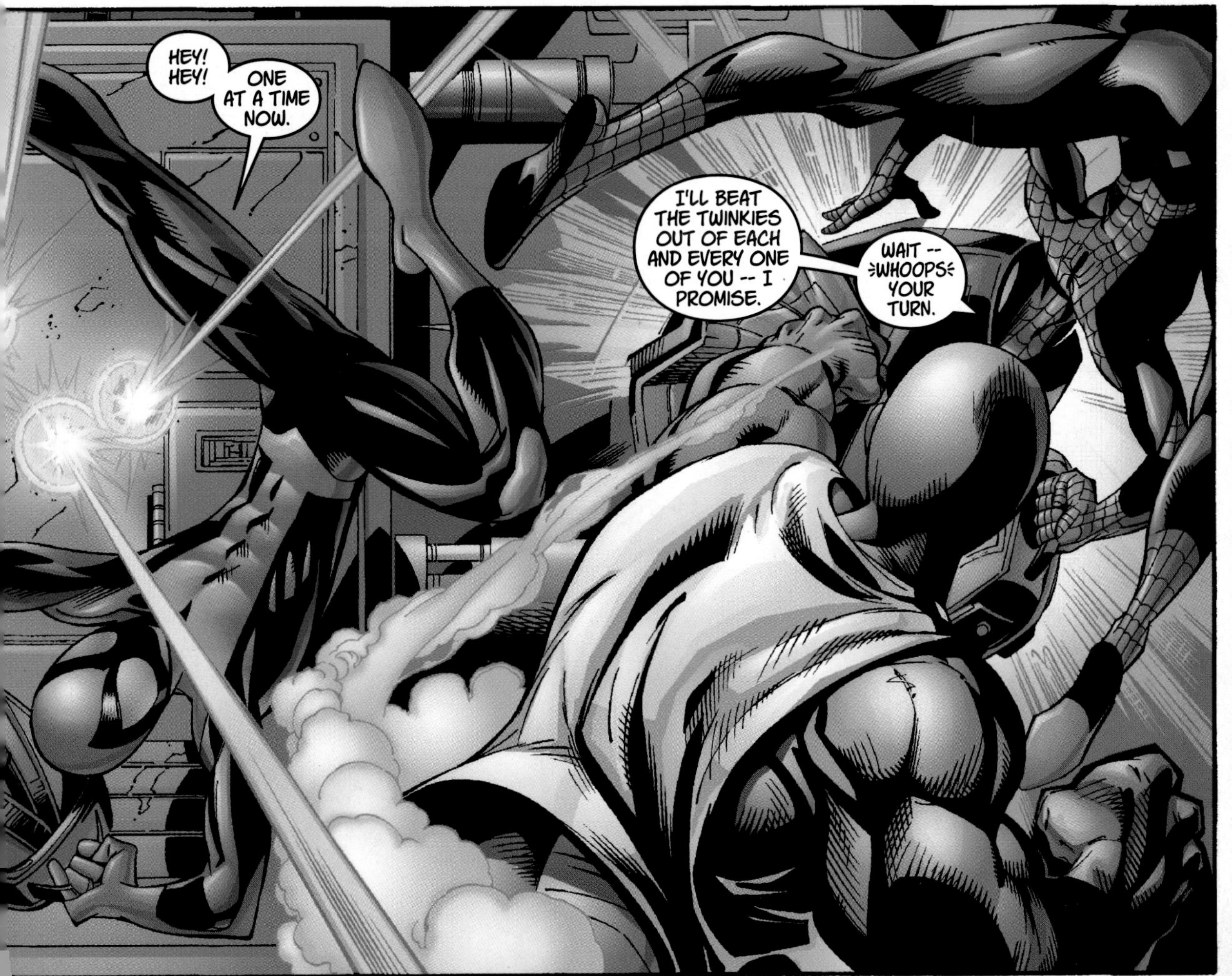
HEY! HEY!
ONE AT A TIME NOW.
I'LL BEAT THE TWINKIES OUT OF EACH AND EVERY ONE OF YOU -- I PROMISE.
WAIT -- WHOOPS YOUR TURN.

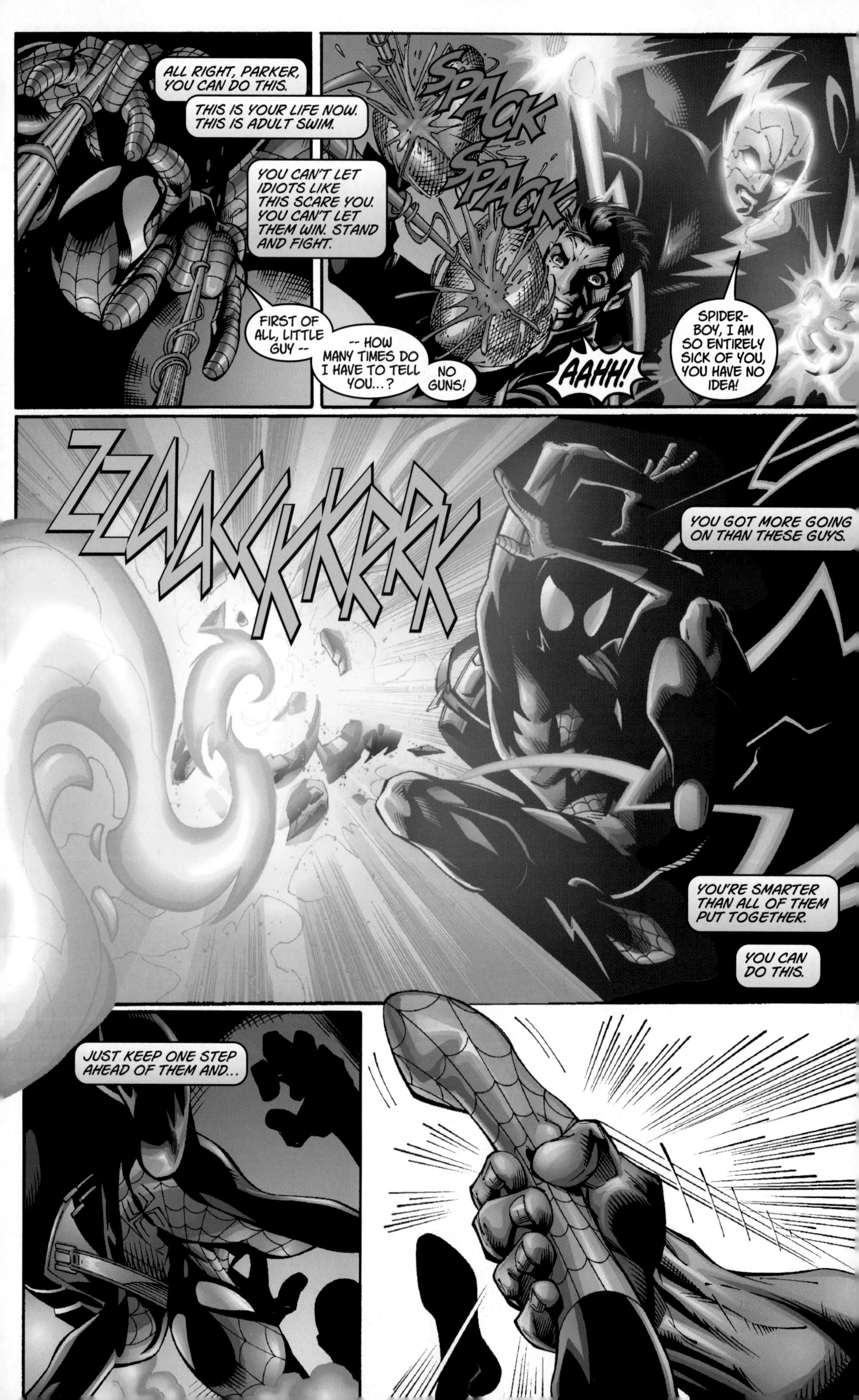
ALL RIGHT, PARKER, YOU CAN DO THIS.
THIS IS YOUR LIFE NOW. THIS IS ADULT SWIM.
YOU CAN'T LET IDIOTS LIKE THIS SCARE YOU. YOU CAN'T LET THEM WIN. STAND AND FIGHT.
SPACK
SPACK
FIRST OF ALL, LITTLE GUY --
-- HOW MANY TIMES DO I HAVE TO TELL YOU...?
NO GUNS!
AAHH!
SPIDER-BOY, I AM SO ENTIRELY SICK OF YOU, YOU HAVE NO IDEA!
ZZAACKKRRK
YOU GOT MORE GOING ON THAN THESE GUYS.
YOU'RE SMARTER THAN ALL OF THEM PUT TOGETHER.
YOU CAN DO THIS.
JUST KEEP ONE STEP AHEAD OF THEM AND...

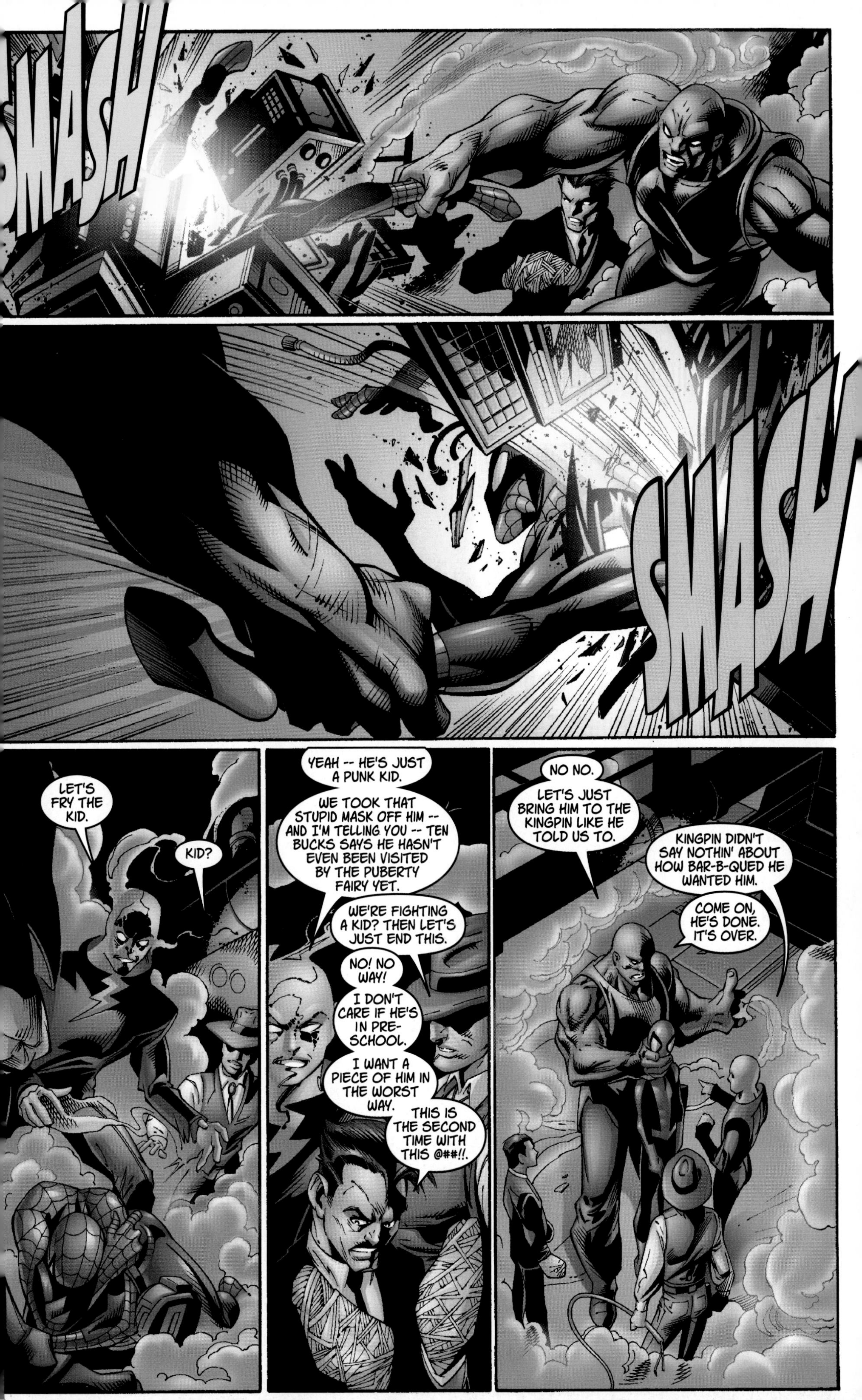
SMASH
SMASH
LET'S FRY THE KID.
KID?
YEAH -- HE'S JUST A PUNK KID.
WE TOOK THAT STUPID MASK OFF HIM -- AND I'M TELLING YOU -- TEN BUCKS SAYS HE HASN'T EVEN BEEN VISITED BY THE PUBERTY FAIRY YET.
WE'RE FIGHTING A KID? THEN LET'S JUST END THIS.
NO! NO WAY!
I DON'T CARE IF HE'S IN PRE-SCHOOL.
I WANT A PIECE OF HIM IN THE WORST WAY.
THIS IS THE SECOND TIME WITH THIS @##!!.
NO NO.
LET'S JUST BRING HIM TO THE KINGPIN LIKE HE TOLD US TO.
KINGPIN DIDN'T SAY NOTHIN' ABOUT HOW BAR-B-QUED HE WANTED HIM.
COME ON, HE'S DONE. IT'S OVER.

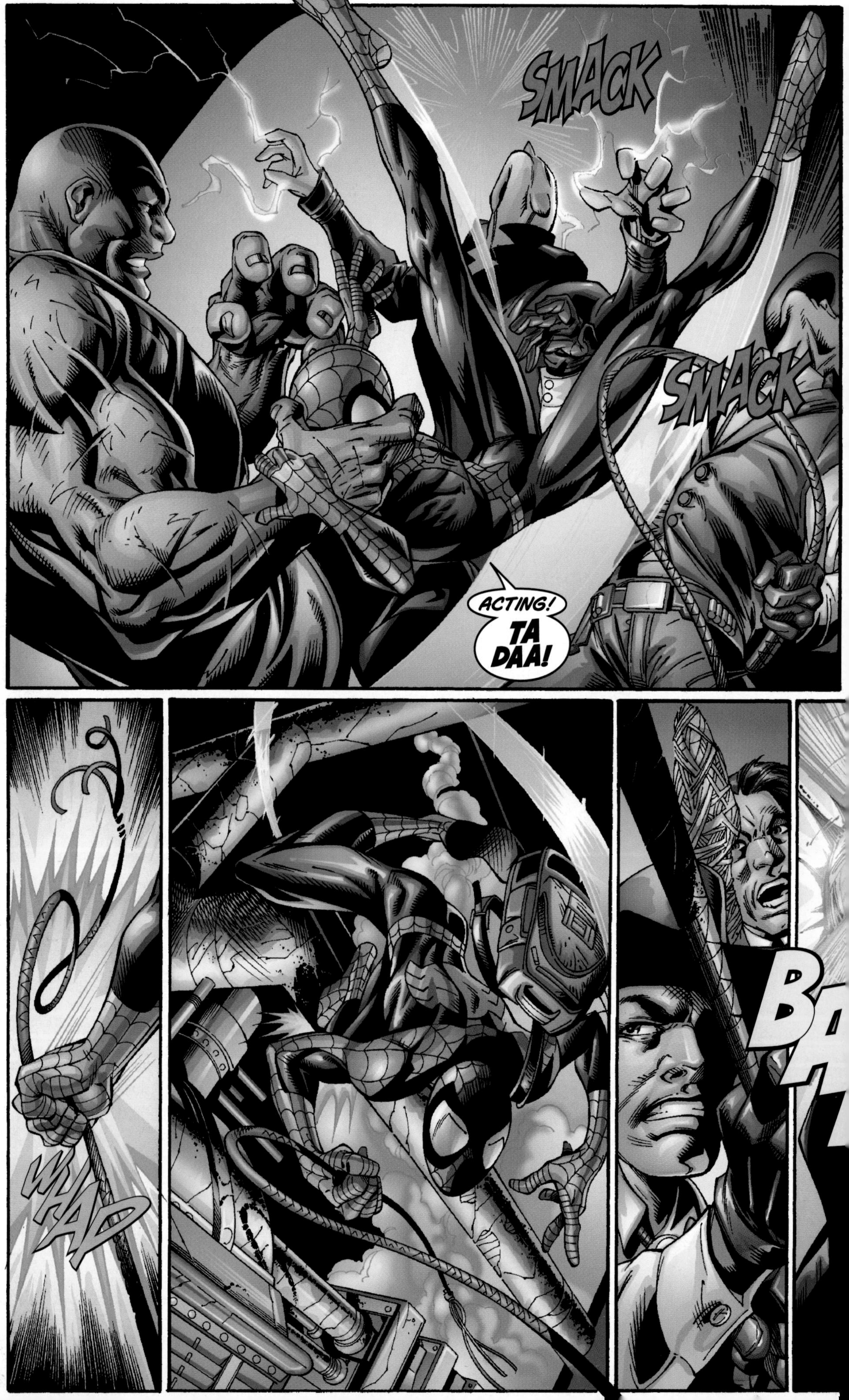
SMACK
SMACK
ACTING! TA DAA!
WHAP

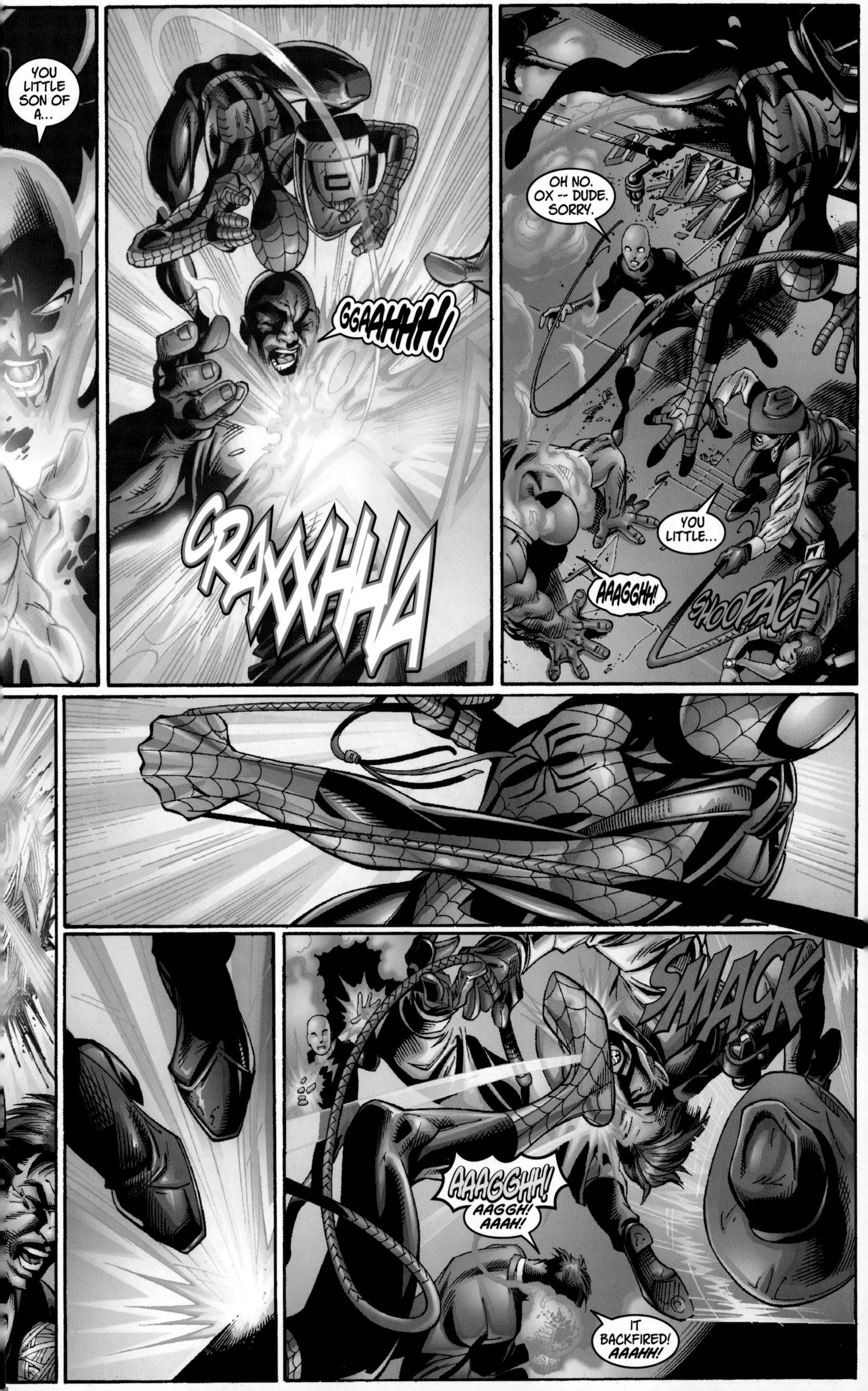
YOU LITTLE SON OF A...
GGAAHHH!
CRAXXHHA
OH NO. OX -- DUDE. SORRY.
YOU LITTLE...
AAAGGHH!
SHOOPACK
SMACK
AAAGGHH! AAGGH! AAAH!
IT BACKFIRED! AAAHH!

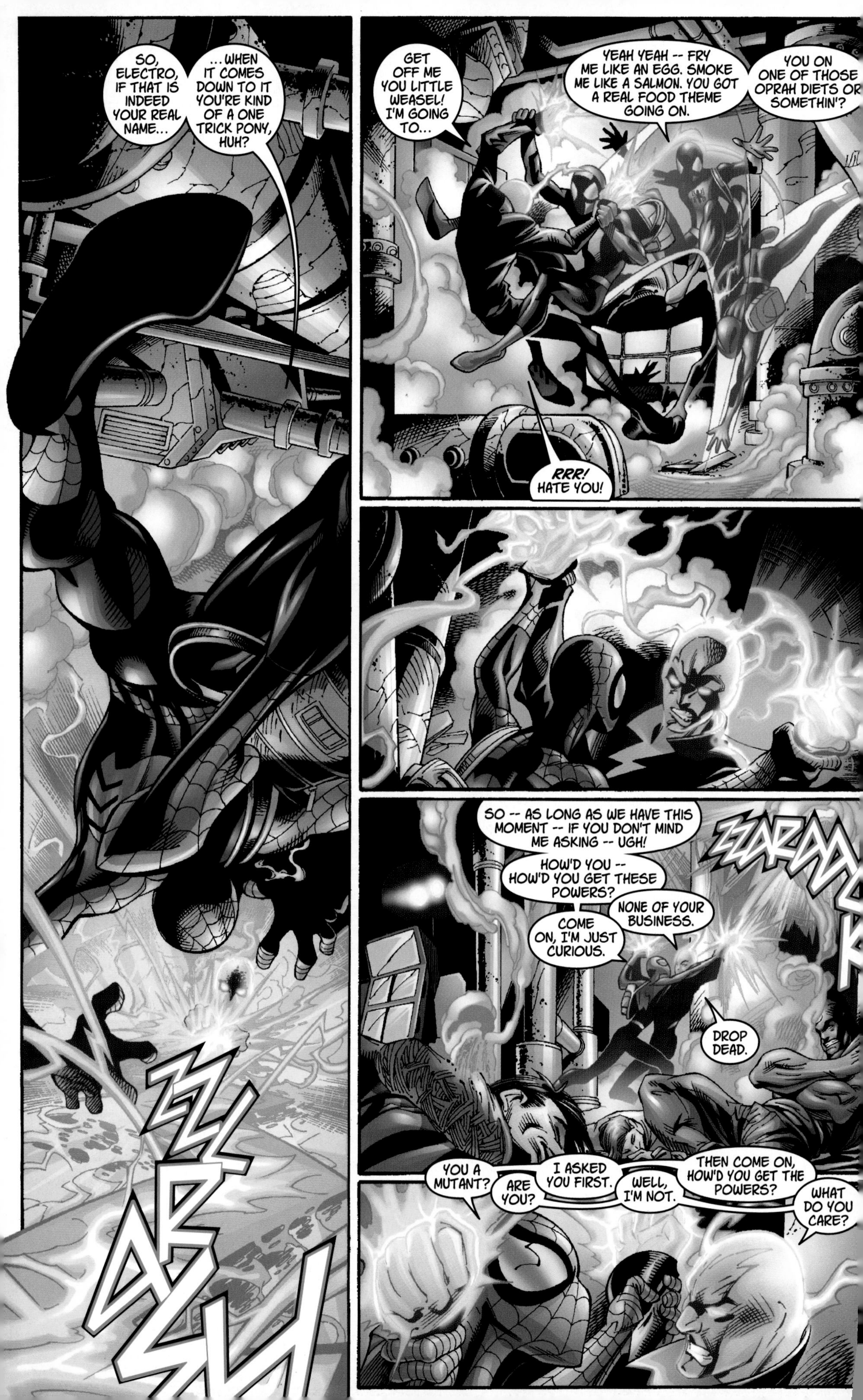
SO, ELECTRO, IF THAT IS INDEED YOUR REAL NAME...
...WHEN IT COMES DOWN TO IT YOU'RE KIND OF A ONE TRICK PONY, HUH?
ZZZARRRAK
GET OFF ME YOU LITTLE WEASEL! I'M GOING TO...
YEAH YEAH -- FRY ME LIKE AN EGG. SMOKE ME LIKE A SALMON. YOU GOT A REAL FOOD THEME GOING ON.
YOU ON ONE OF THOSE OPRAH DIETS OR SOMETHIN'?
RRR! HATE YOU!
SO -- AS LONG AS WE HAVE THIS MOMENT -- IF YOU DON'T MIND ME ASKING -- UGH!
HOW'D YOU -- HOW'D YOU GET THESE POWERS?
NONE OF YOUR BUSINESS.
COME ON, I'M JUST CURIOUS.
DROP DEAD.
YOU A MUTANT?
ARE YOU?
I ASKED YOU FIRST.
WELL, I'M NOT.
THEN COME ON, HOW'D YOU GET THE POWERS?
WHAT DO YOU CARE?

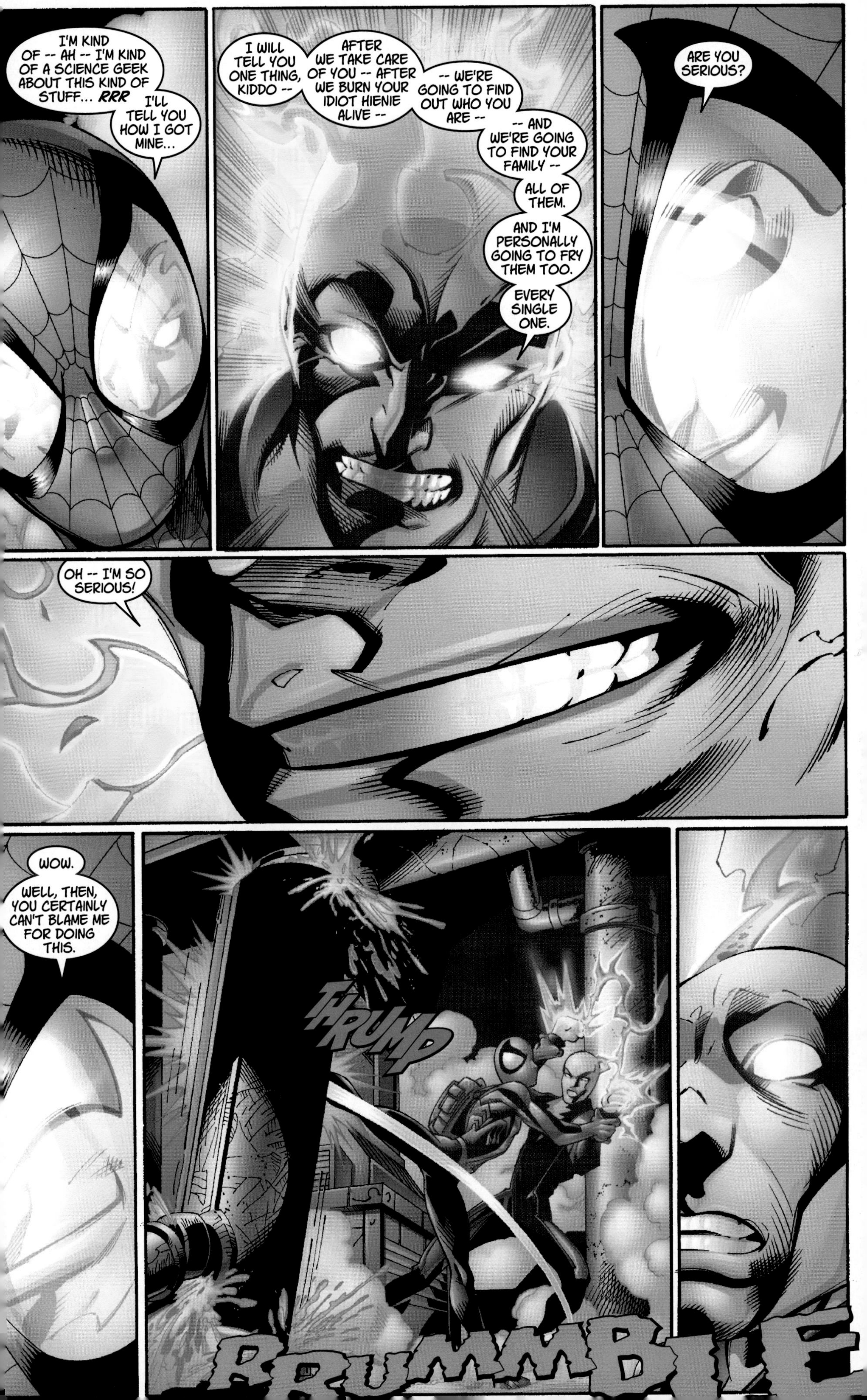
I'M KIND OF -- AH -- I'M KIND OF A SCIENCE GEEK ABOUT THIS KIND OF STUFF... RRR
I'LL TELL YOU HOW I GOT MINE...
I WILL TELL YOU ONE THING, KIDDO --
AFTER WE TAKE CARE OF YOU -- AFTER WE BURN YOUR IDIOT HIENIE ALIVE --
-- WE'RE GOING TO FIND OUT WHO YOU ARE --
-- AND WE'RE GOING TO FIND YOUR FAMILY --
ALL OF THEM.
AND I'M PERSONALLY GOING TO FRY THEM TOO.
EVERY SINGLE ONE.
ARE YOU SERIOUS?
OH -- I'M SO SERIOUS!
WOW.
WELL, THEN, YOU CERTAINLY CAN'T BLAME ME FOR DOING THIS.
THRUMP
BRUMMBLE

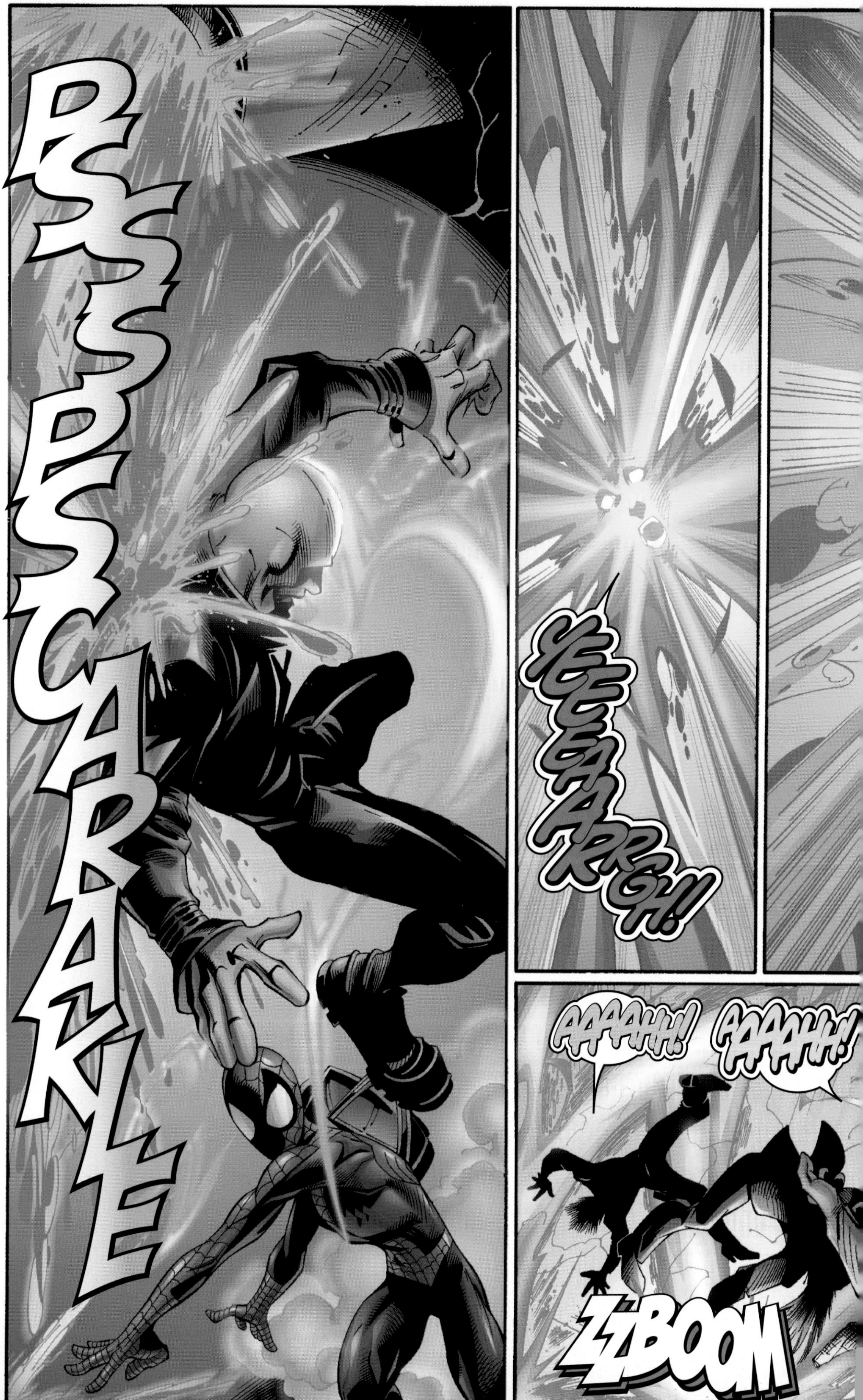
PSSSPSCARAKLE
YEEEAARRGH!!
AAAAHH!
AAAAHH!
ZZBOOM

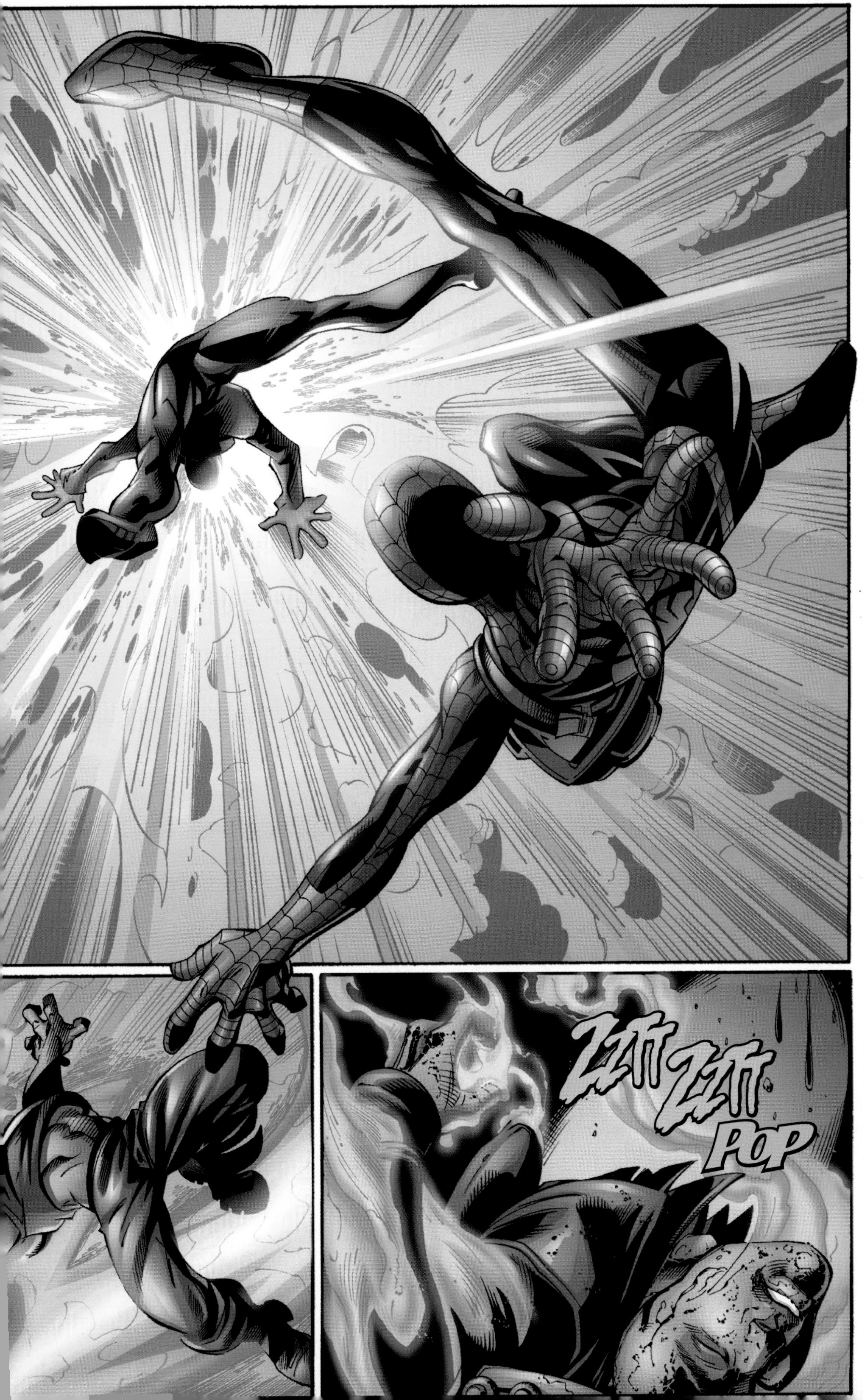
ZZFT ZZFT
POP

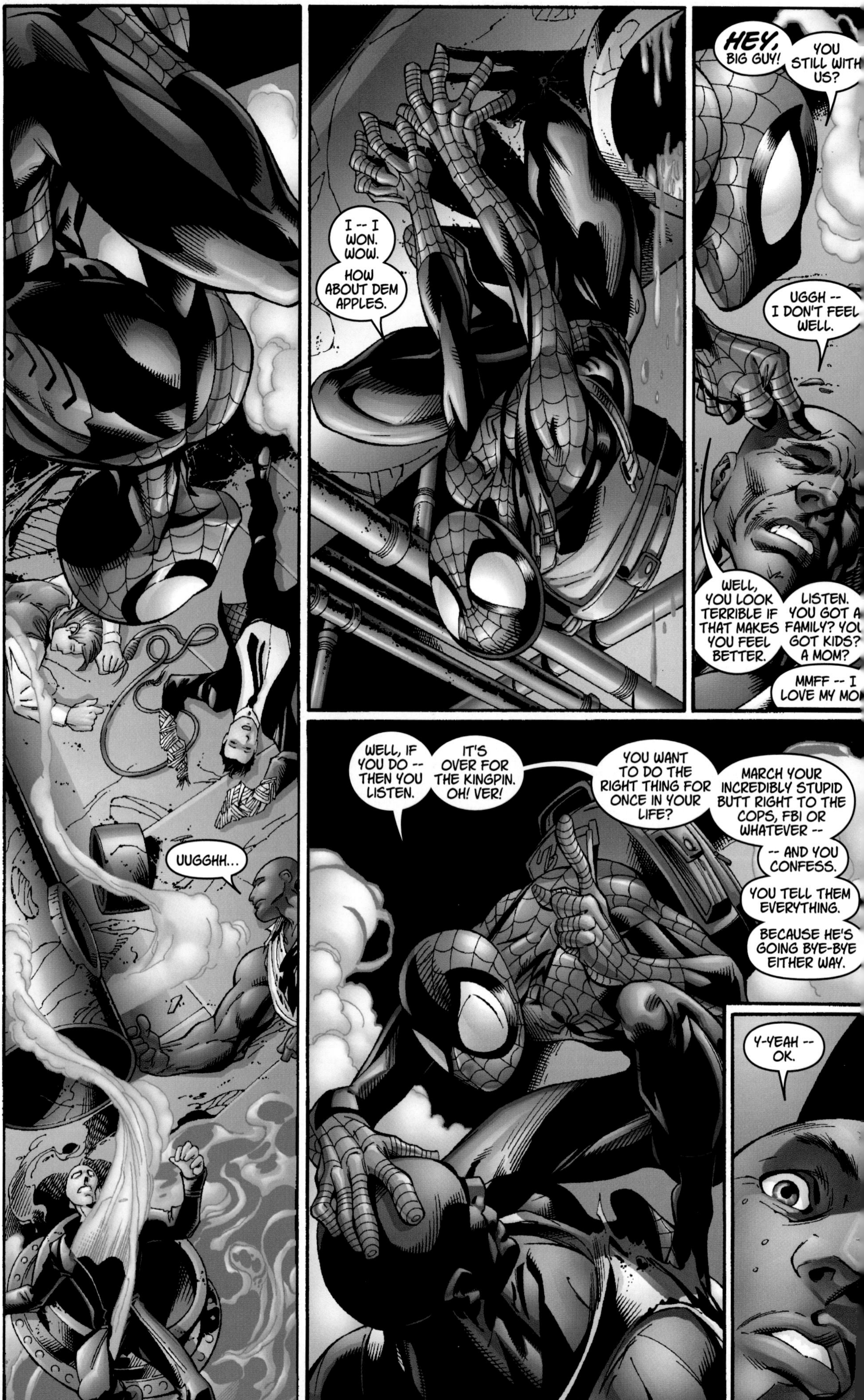
UUGGHH...
I -- I WON. WOW.
HOW ABOUT DEM APPLES.
HEY, BIG GUY!
YOU STILL WITH US?
UGGH -- I DON'T FEEL WELL.
WELL, YOU LOOK TERRIBLE IF THAT MAKES YOU FEEL BETTER.
LISTEN. YOU GOT A FAMILY? YOU GOT KIDS? A MOM?
MMFF -- I LOVE MY MOM
WELL, IF YOU DO -- THEN YOU LISTEN.
IT'S OVER FOR THE KINGPIN. OH! VER!
YOU WANT TO DO THE RIGHT THING FOR ONCE IN YOUR LIFE?
MARCH YOUR INCREDIBLY STUPID BUTT RIGHT TO THE COPS, FBI OR WHATEVER --
-- AND YOU CONFESS.
YOU TELL THEM EVERYTHING.
BECAUSE HE'S GOING BYE-BYE EITHER WAY.
Y-YEAH -- OK.

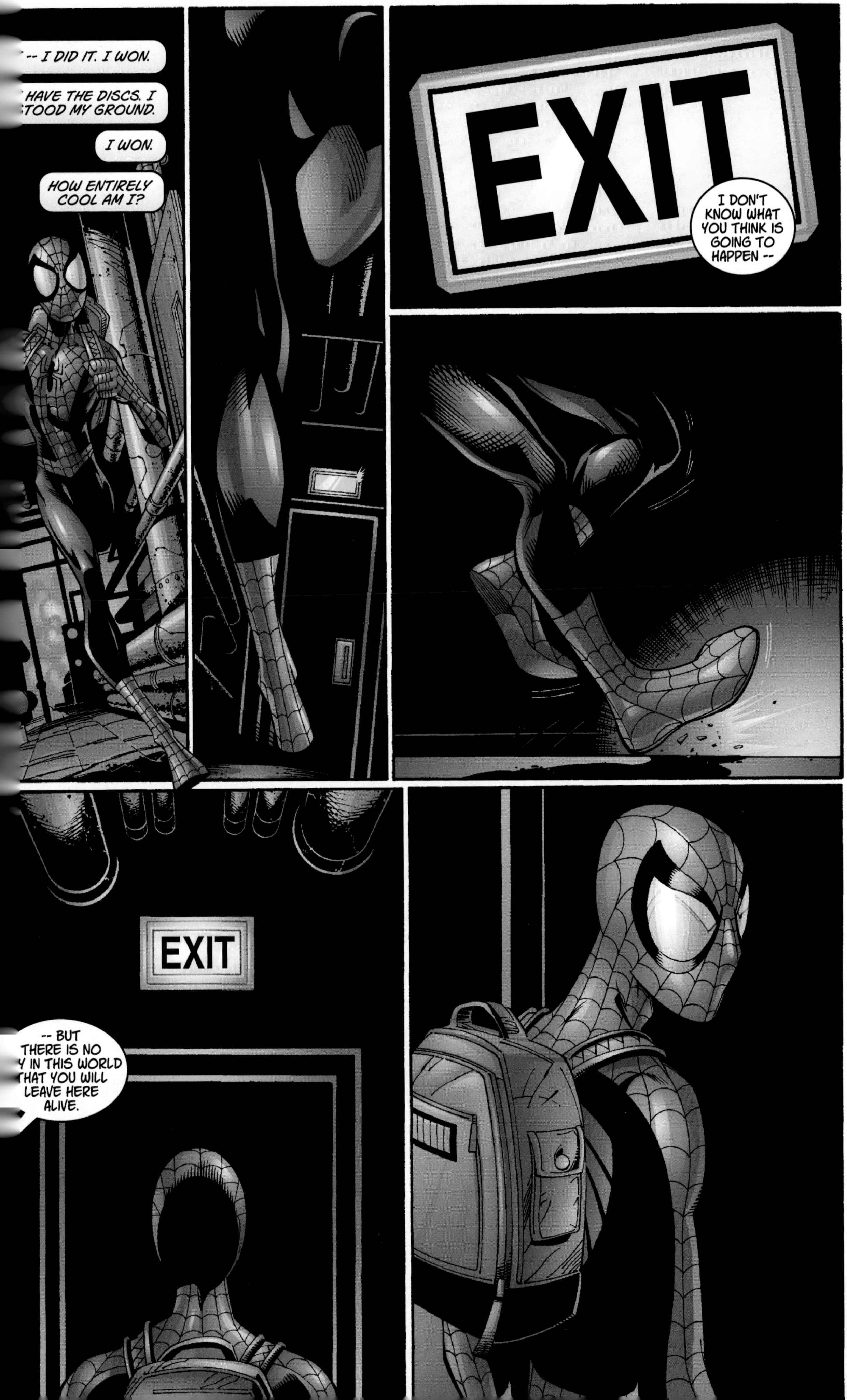
-- I DID IT. I WON.
HAVE THE DISCS. I TOOD MY GROUND.
I WON.
HOW ENTIRELY COOL AM I?
EXIT
I DON'T KNOW WHAT YOU THINK IS GOING TO HAPPEN --
EXIT
-- BUT THERE IS NO Y IN THIS WORLD HAT YOU WILL LEAVE HERE ALIVE.

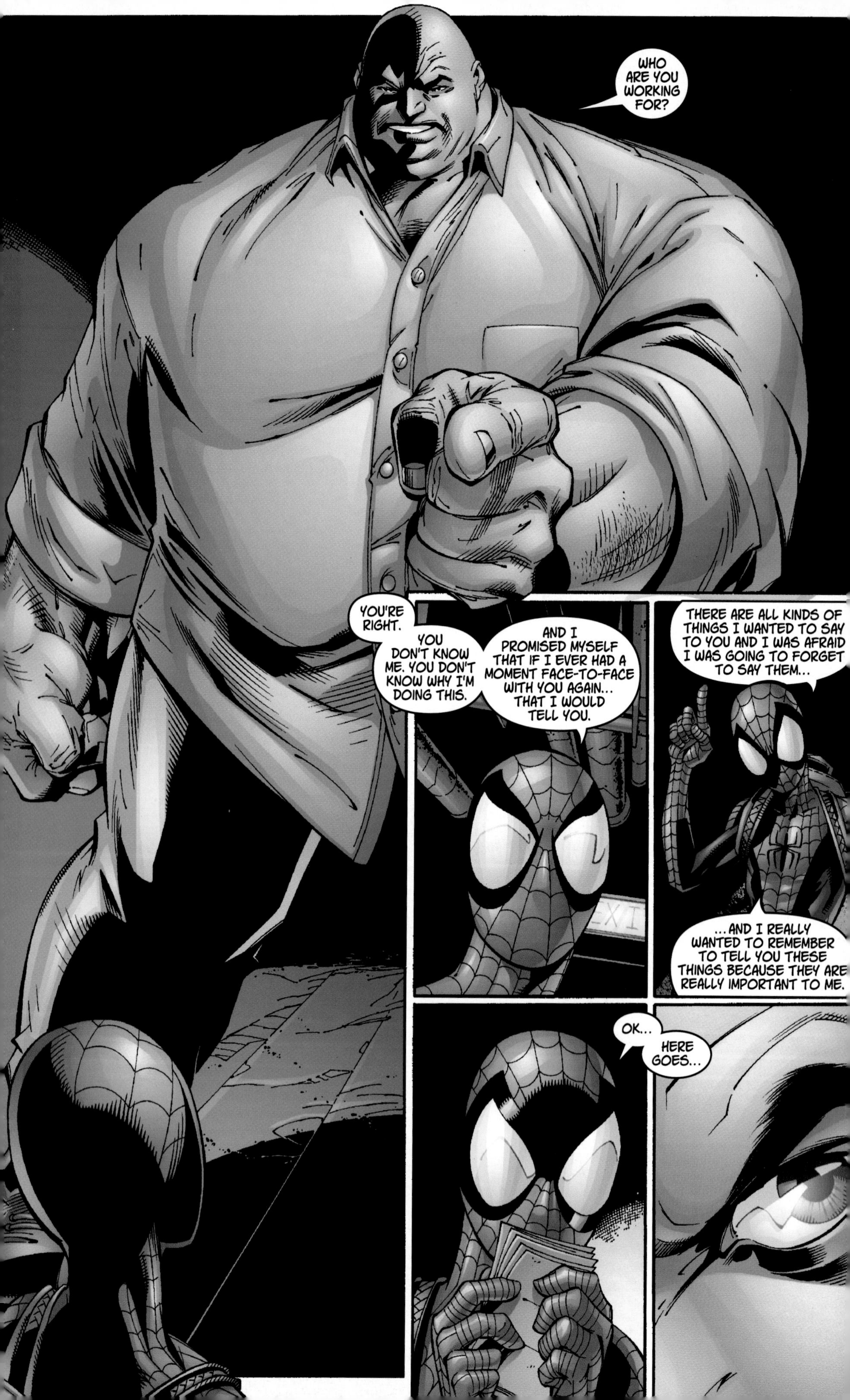
WHO ARE YOU WORKING FOR?
YOU'RE RIGHT.
YOU DON'T KNOW ME. YOU DON'T KNOW WHY I'M DOING THIS.
AND I PROMISED MYSELF THAT IF I EVER HAD A MOMENT FACE-TO-FACE WITH YOU AGAIN... THAT I WOULD TELL YOU.
THERE ARE ALL KINDS OF THINGS I WANTED TO SAY TO YOU AND I WAS AFRAID I WAS GOING TO FORGET TO SAY THEM...
...AND I REALLY WANTED TO REMEMBER TO TELL YOU THESE THINGS BECAUSE THEY ARE REALLY IMPORTANT TO ME.
OK...
HERE GOES...

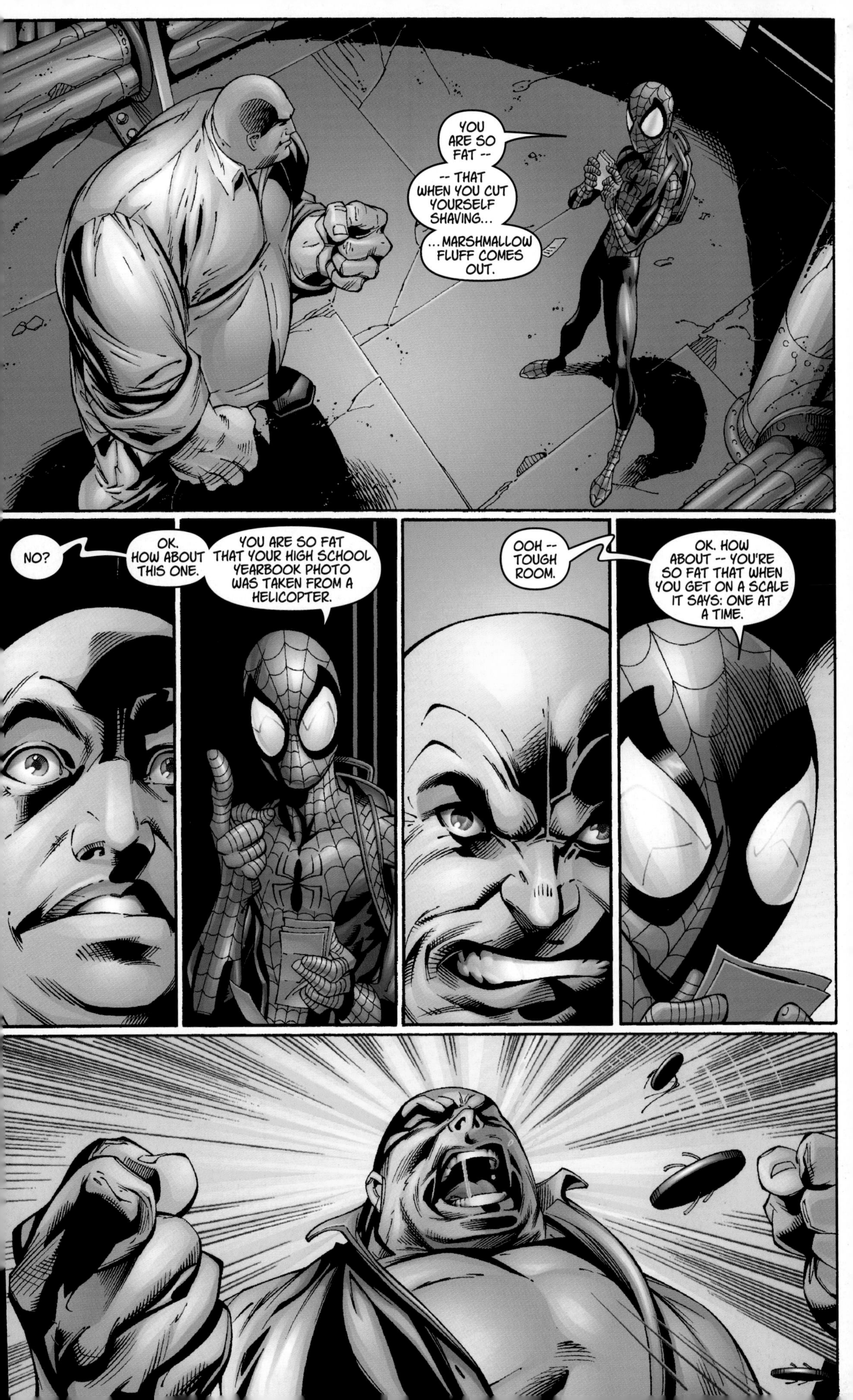

YOU ARE SO FAT --
-- THAT WHEN YOU CUT YOURSELF SHAVING...
...MARSHMALLOW FLUFF COMES OUT.
NO?
OK. HOW ABOUT THIS ONE.
YOU ARE SO FAT THAT YOUR HIGH SCHOOL YEARBOOK PHOTO WAS TAKEN FROM A HELICOPTER.
OOH -- TOUGH ROOM.
OK. HOW ABOUT -- YOU'RE SO FAT THAT WHEN YOU GET ON A SCALE IT SAYS: ONE AT A TIME.

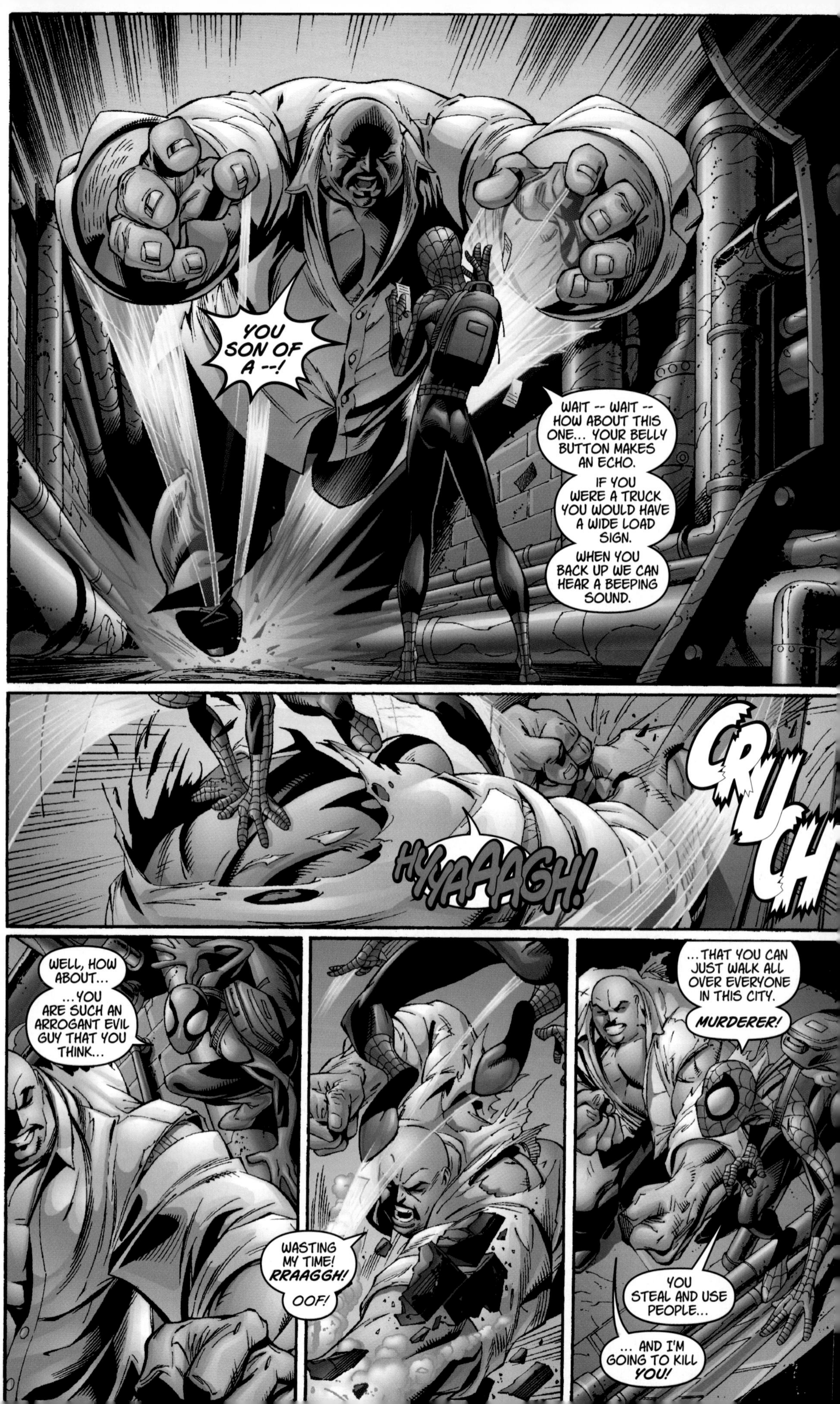
YOU SON OF A --!
WAIT -- WAIT -- HOW ABOUT THIS ONE... YOUR BELLY BUTTON MAKES AN ECHO.
IF YOU WERE A TRUCK YOU WOULD HAVE A WIDE LOAD SIGN.
WHEN YOU BACK UP WE CAN HEAR A BEEPING SOUND.
HYYAAAAGH!
CRUCH
WELL, HOW ABOUT...
...YOU ARE SUCH AN ARROGANT EVIL GUY THAT YOU THINK...
WASTING MY TIME! RRAAGGH!
OOF!
...THAT YOU CAN JUST WALK ALL OVER EVERYONE IN THIS CITY.
MURDERER!
YOU STEAL AND USE PEOPLE...
... AND I'M GOING TO KILL YOU!

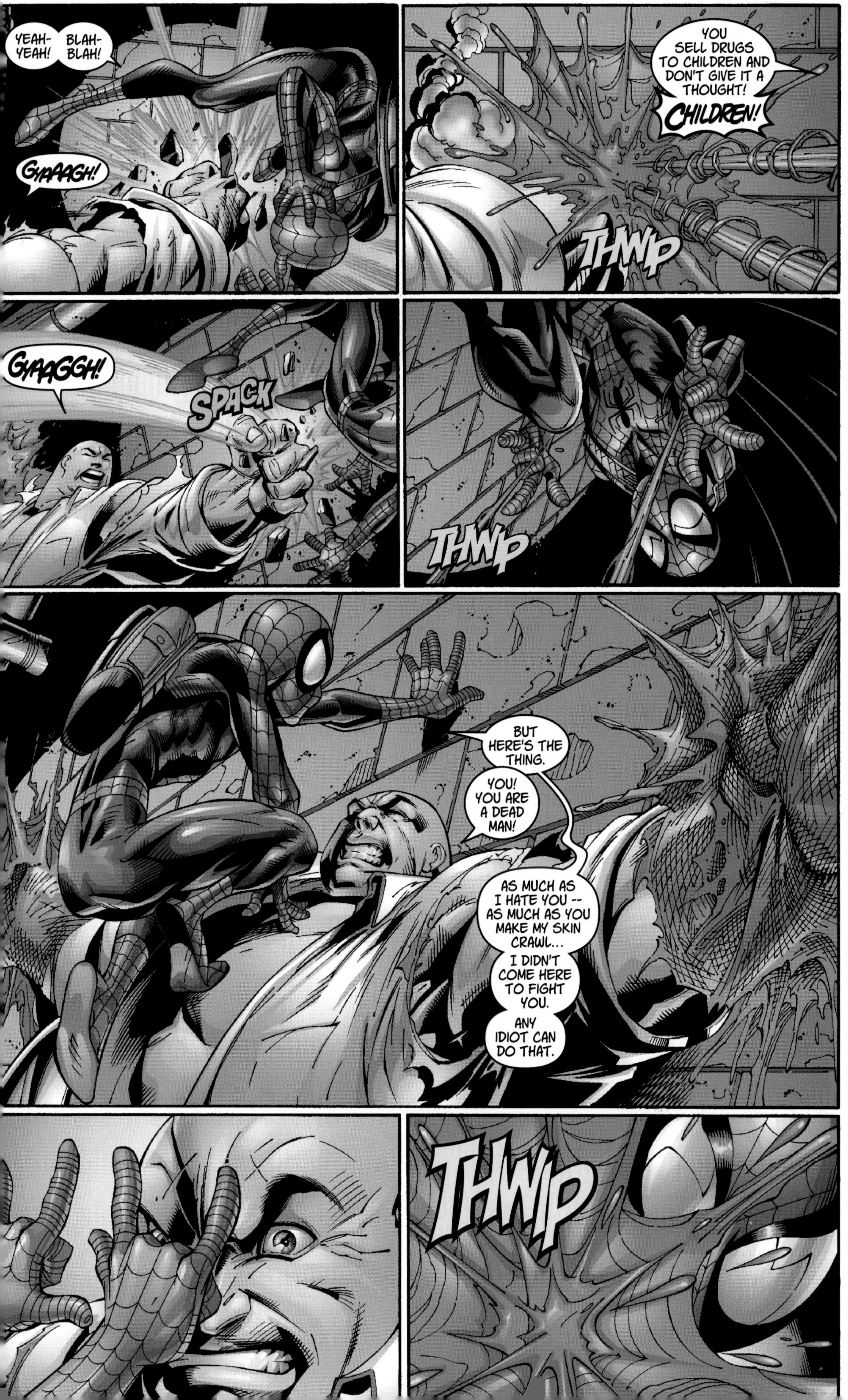
YEAH-YEAH!
BLAH-BLAH!
GYAAAGH!
YOU SELL DRUGS TO CHILDREN AND DON'T GIVE IT A THOUGHT!
CHILDREN!
THWIP
GYAAGGH!
SPACK
THWIP
BUT HERE'S THE THING.
YOU! YOU ARE A DEAD MAN!
AS MUCH AS I HATE YOU -- AS MUCH AS YOU MAKE MY SKIN CRAWL...
I DIDN'T COME HERE TO FIGHT YOU.
ANY IDIOT CAN DO THAT.
THWIP

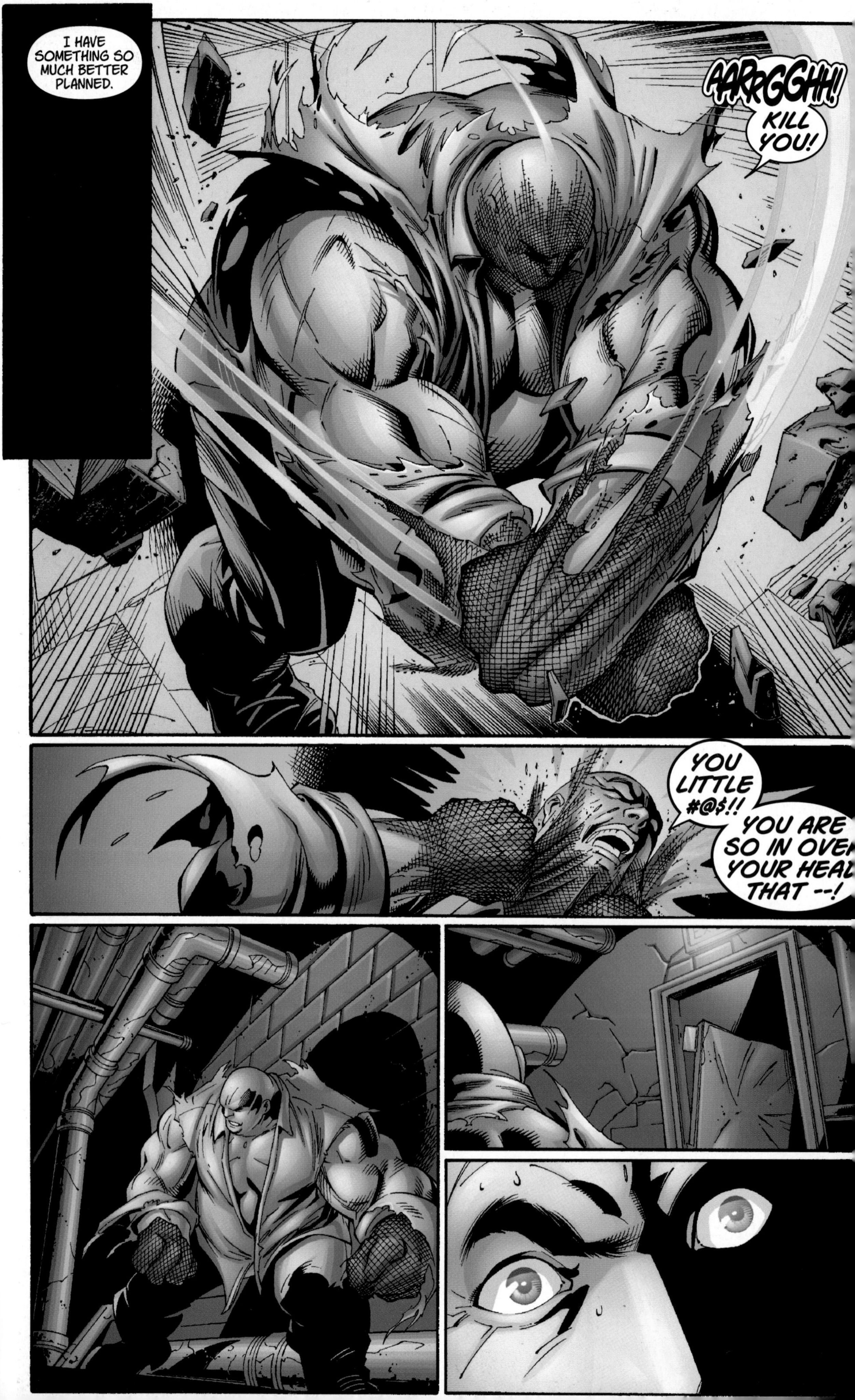

I HAVE SOMETHING SO MUCH BETTER PLANNED.
AARRGGHH!
KILL YOU!
YOU LITTLE #@$!!
YOU ARE SO IN OVER YOUR HEAD THAT --!

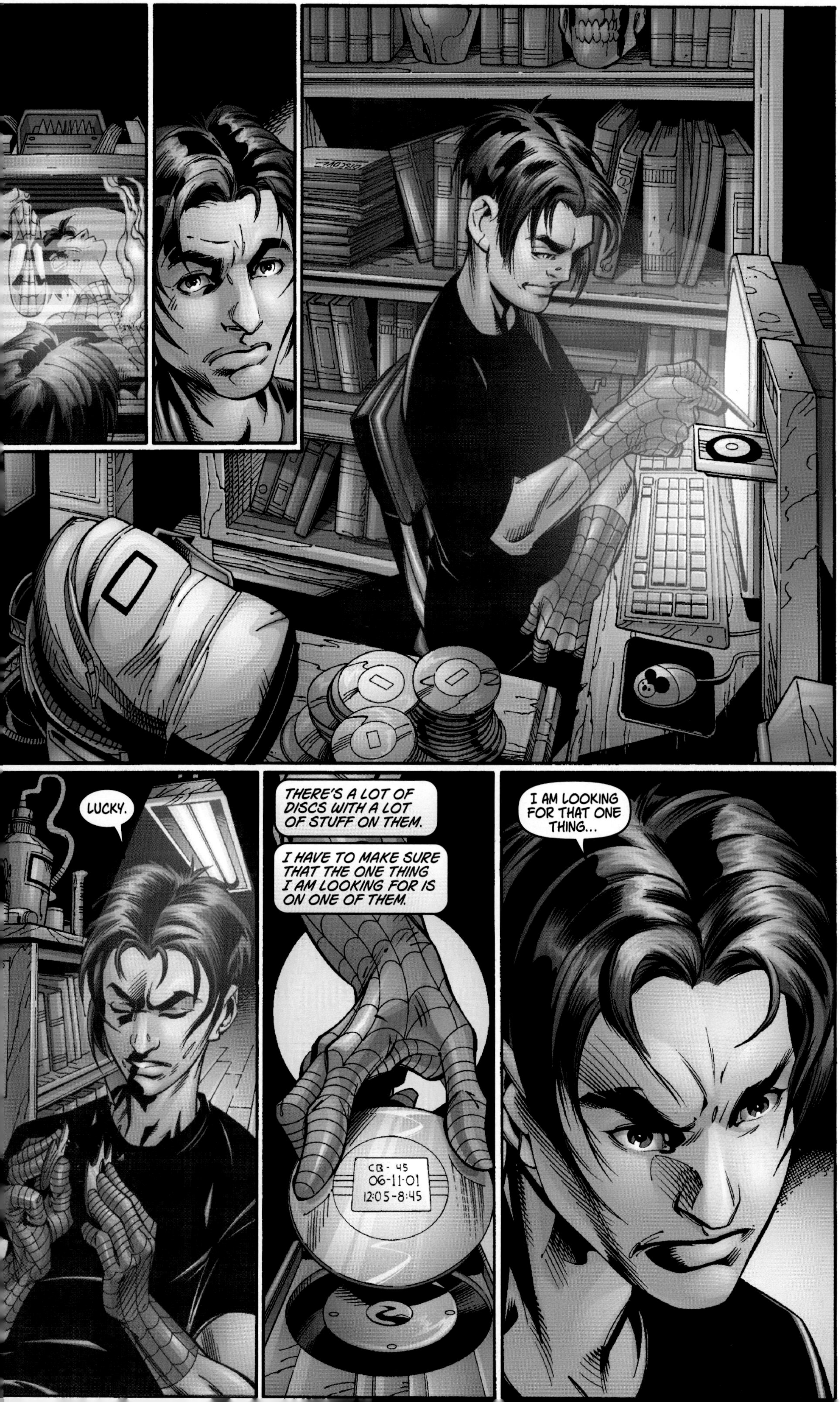
LUCKY.
THERE'S A LOT OF DISCS WITH A LOT OF STUFF ON THEM.
I HAVE TO MAKE SURE THAT THE ONE THING I AM LOOKING FOR IS ON ONE OF THEM.
CB - 45
06-11-01
12:05-8:45
I AM LOOKING FOR THAT ONE THING...

ENCLOSED YOU WILL FIND ALL KINDS OF GOODIES AGAINST THE KINGPIN. I HAVE MARKED A COUPLE OF DISCS THAT SHOULD BE REALLY INTERESTING. PLEASE DO THE R... THING. SIGNED, ... A FRIEND.

P.S. ...OT FOR THE ...QUEAMISH.

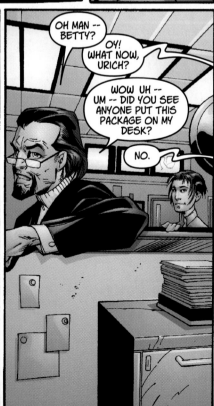

OH MAN -- BETTY?

OY! WHAT NOW, URICH?

WOW UH -- UM -- DID YOU SEE ANYONE PUT THIS PACKAGE ON MY DESK?

NO.

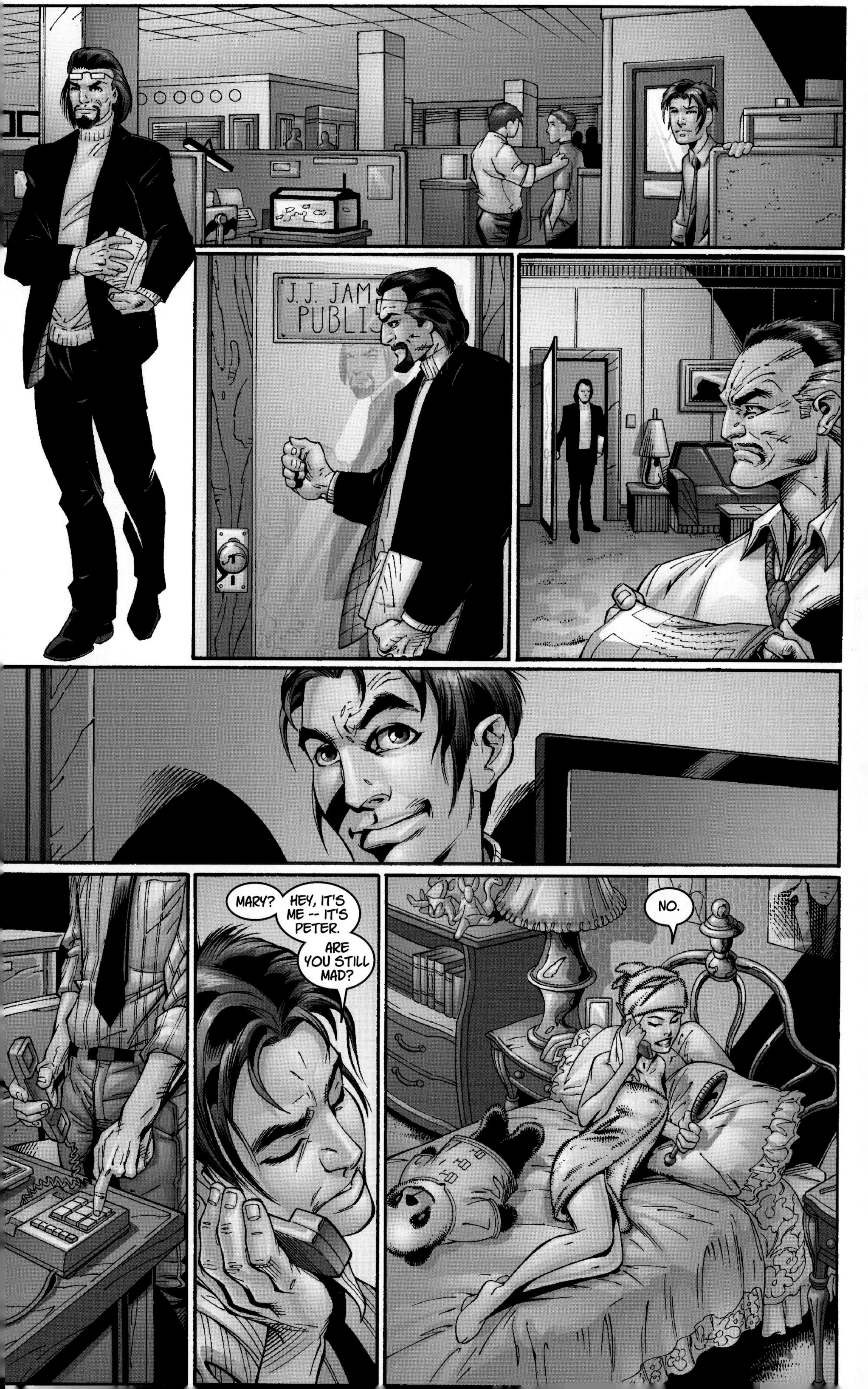
J.J. JAM
PUBLIS
MARY?
HEY, IT'S ME -- IT'S PETER.
ARE YOU STILL MAD?
NO.

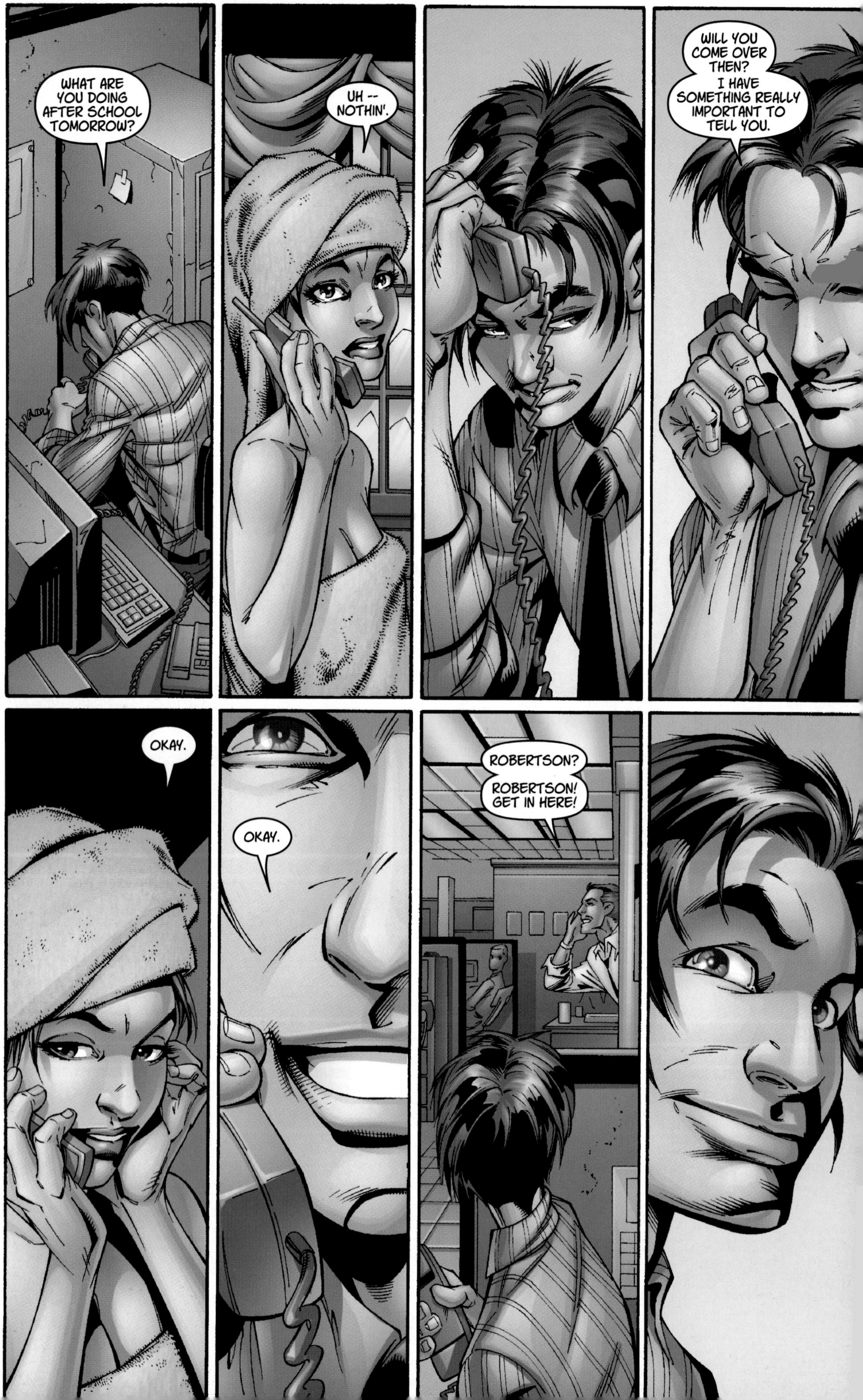
WHAT ARE YOU DOING AFTER SCHOOL TOMORROW?
UH -- NOTHIN'.
WILL YOU COME OVER THEN?
I HAVE SOMETHING REALLY IMPORTANT TO TELL YOU.
OKAY.
OKAY.
ROBERTSON?
ROBERTSON! GET IN HERE!

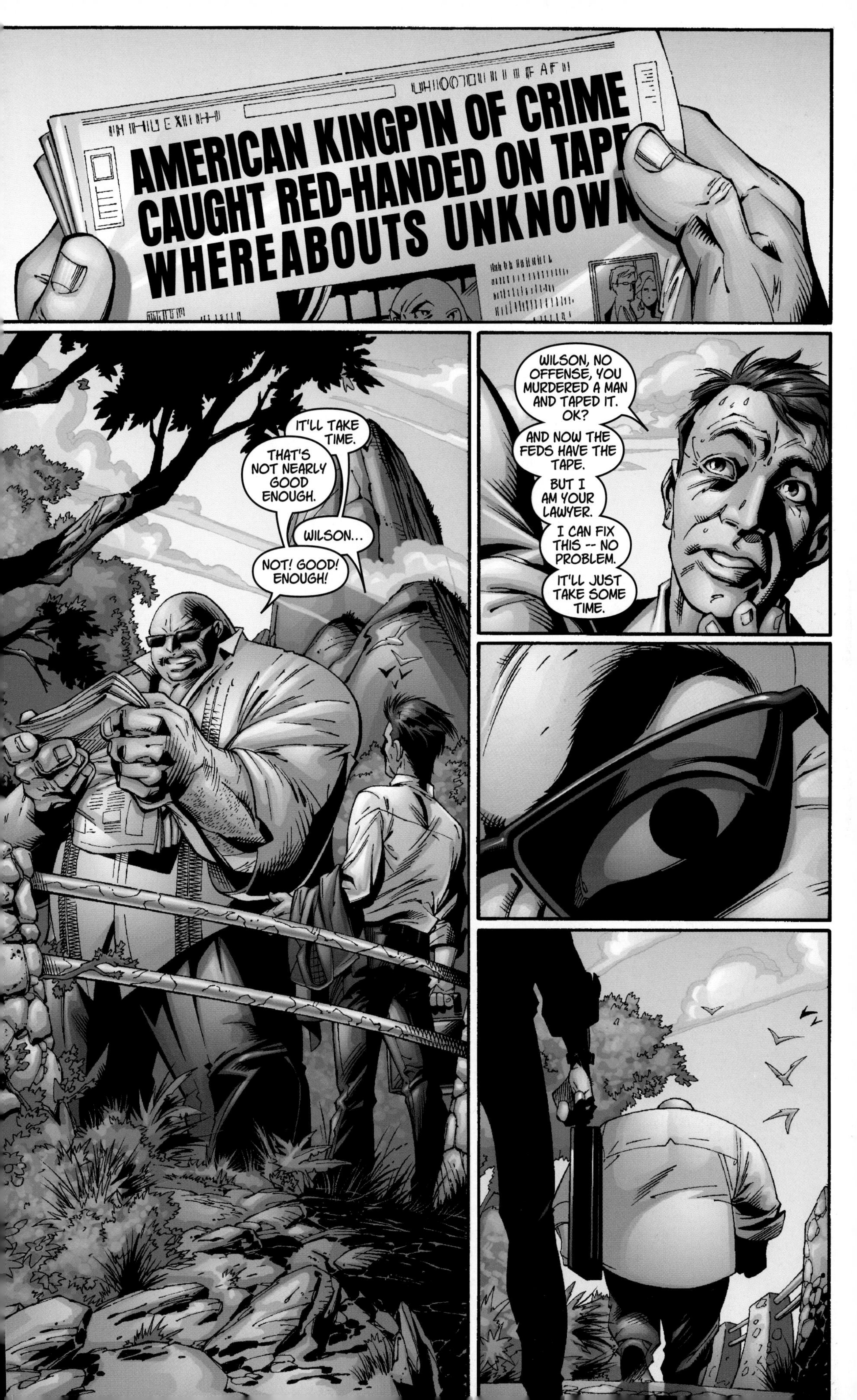
AMERICAN KINGPIN OF CRIME CAUGHT RED-HANDED ON TAPE WHEREABOUTS UNKNOWN
IT'LL TAKE TIME.
THAT'S NOT NEARLY GOOD ENOUGH.
WILSON...
NOT! GOOD! ENOUGH!
WILSON, NO OFFENSE, YOU MURDERED A MAN AND TAPED IT. OK?
AND NOW THE FEDS HAVE THE TAPE.
BUT I AM YOUR LAWYER.
I CAN FIX THIS -- NO PROBLEM.
IT'LL JUST TAKE SOME TIME.

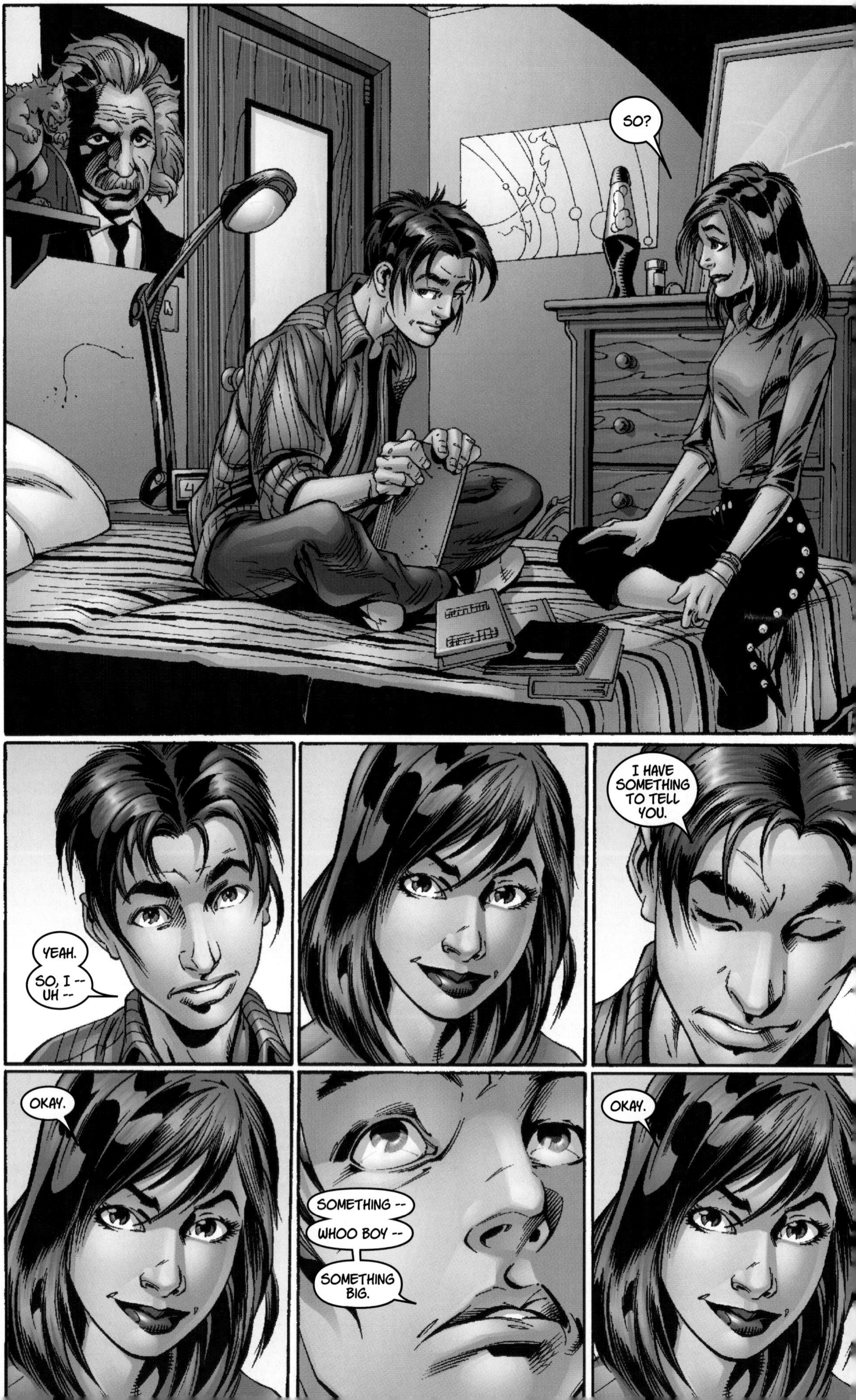
SO?
YEAH.
SO, I -- UH --
I HAVE SOMETHING TO TELL YOU.
OKAY.
SOMETHING --
WHOO BOY --
SOMETHING BIG.
OKAY.

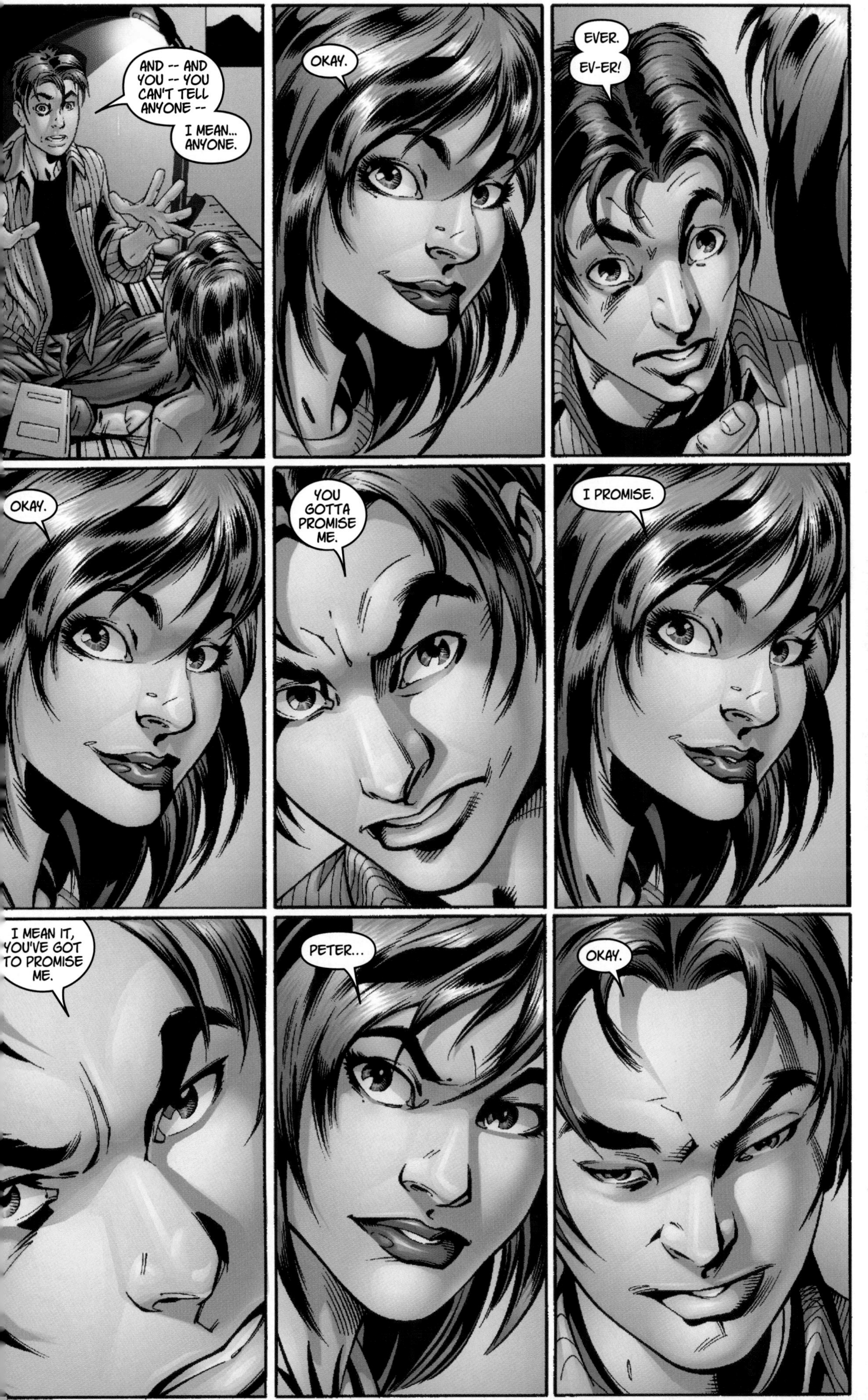
AND -- AND YOU -- YOU CAN'T TELL ANYONE --
I MEAN... ANYONE.
OKAY.
EVER.
EV-ER!
OKAY.
YOU GOTTA PROMISE ME.
I PROMISE.
I MEAN IT, YOU'VE GOT TO PROMISE ME.
PETER...
OKAY.

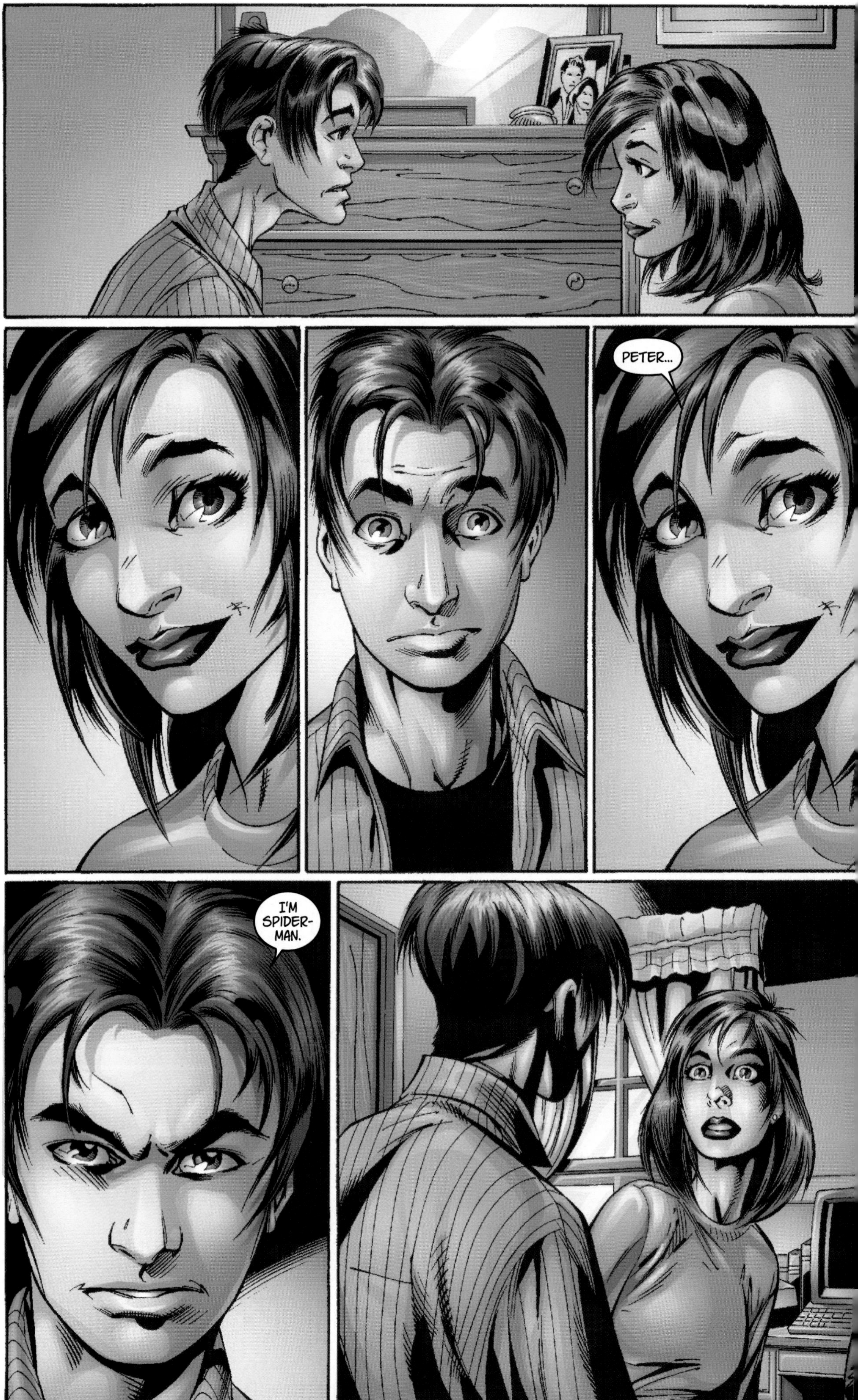
PETER...
I'M SPIDER-MAN.

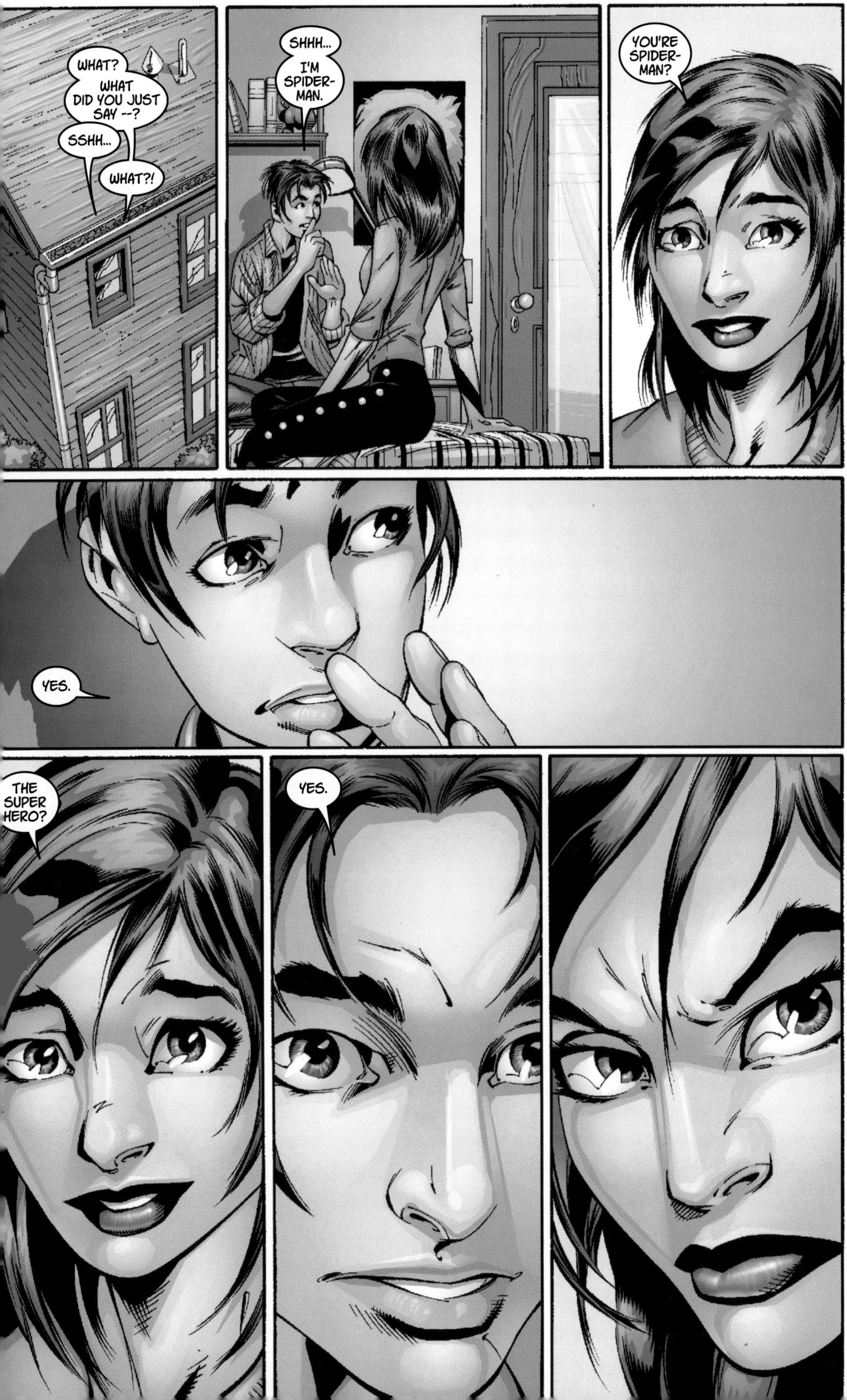
WHAT?
WHAT DID YOU JUST SAY --?
SSHH...
WHAT?!
SHHH... I'M SPIDER-MAN.
YOU'RE SPIDER-MAN?
YES.
THE SUPER HERO?
YES.

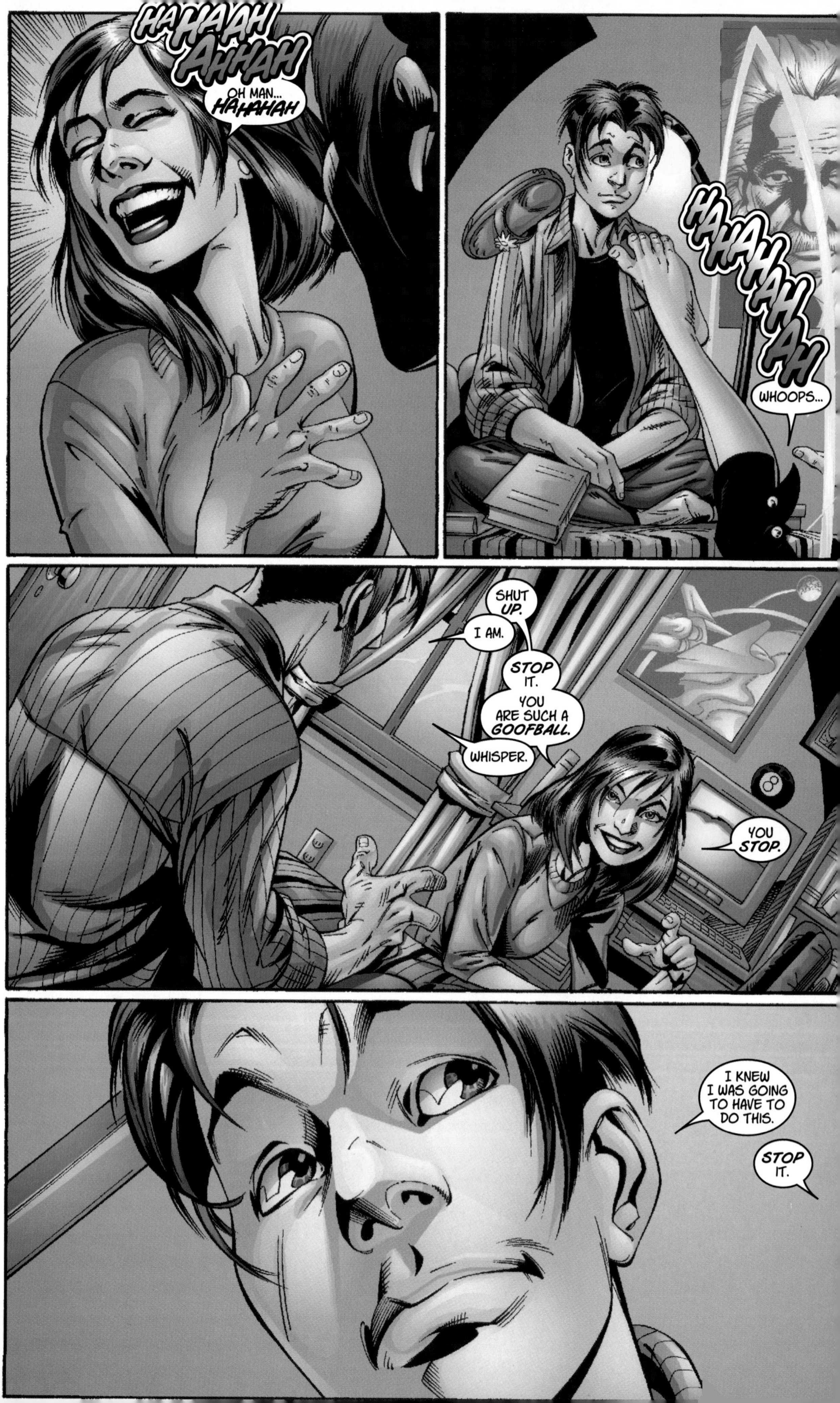

HAHAAAH AHHAH
OH MAN... HAHAHAH
HAHAHAHAHAH
WHOOPS...
SHUT UP.
I AM.
STOP IT.
YOU ARE SUCH A GOOFBALL.
WHISPER.
YOU STOP.
I KNEW I WAS GOING TO HAVE TO DO THIS.
STOP IT.

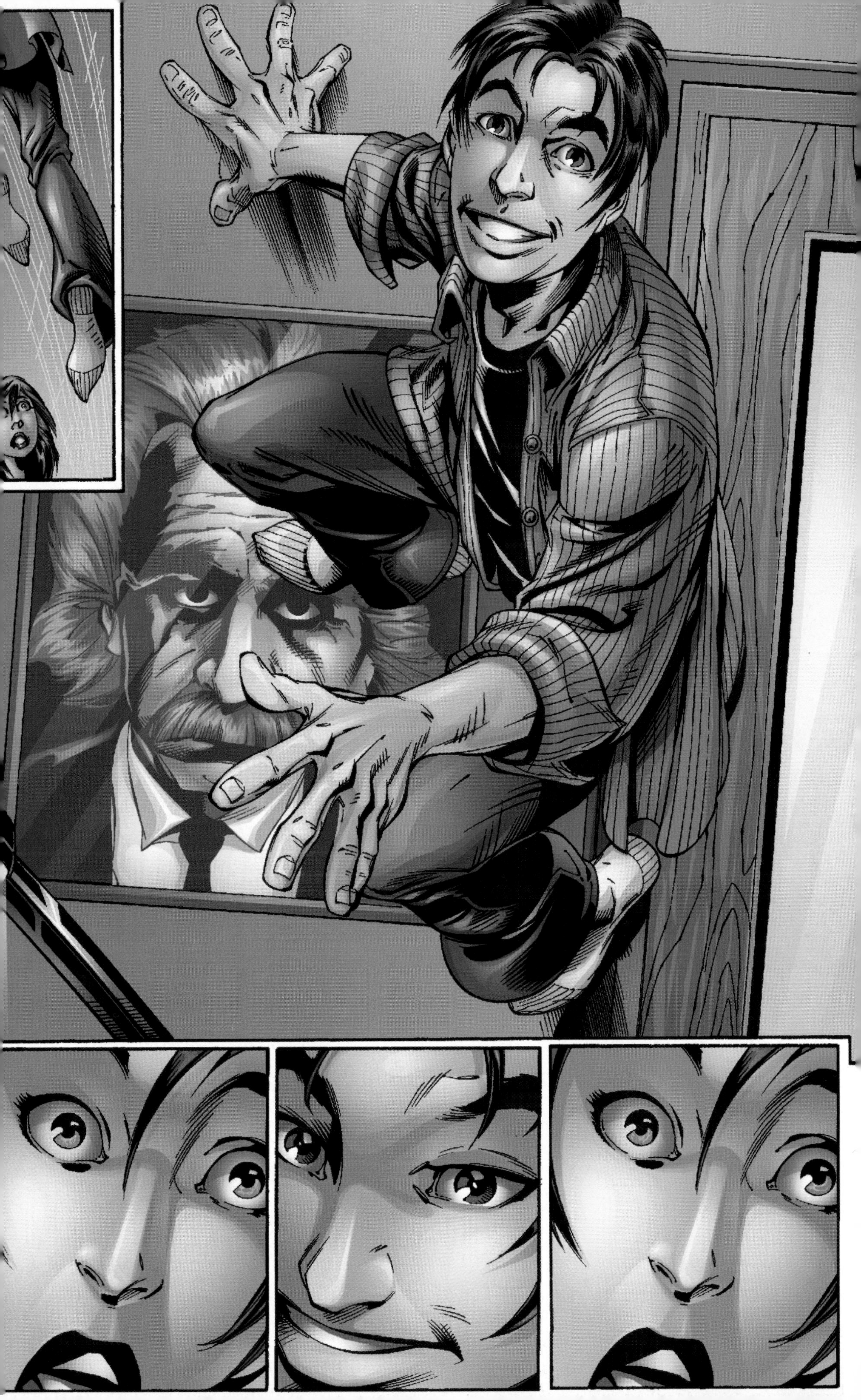

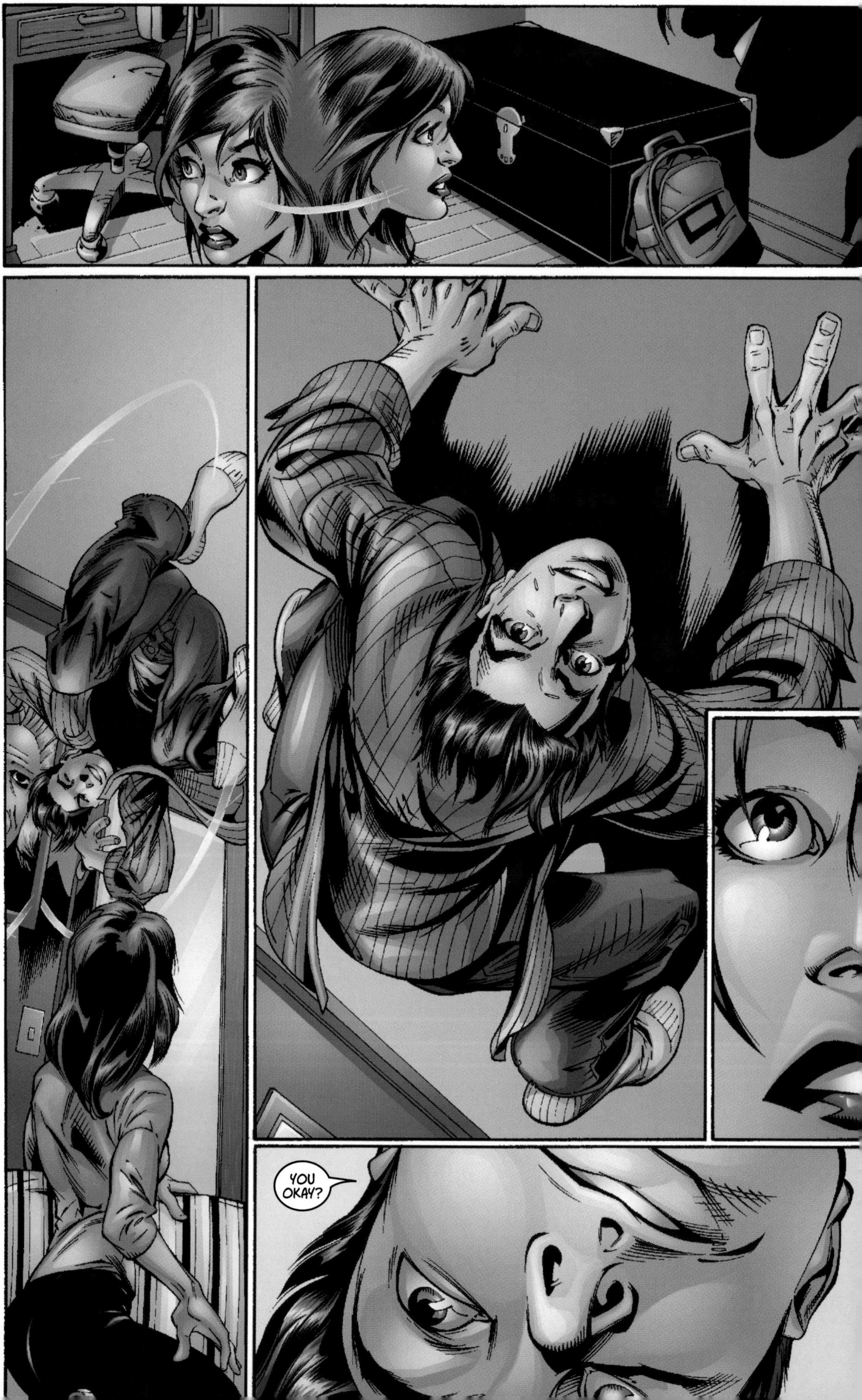
YOU OKAY?

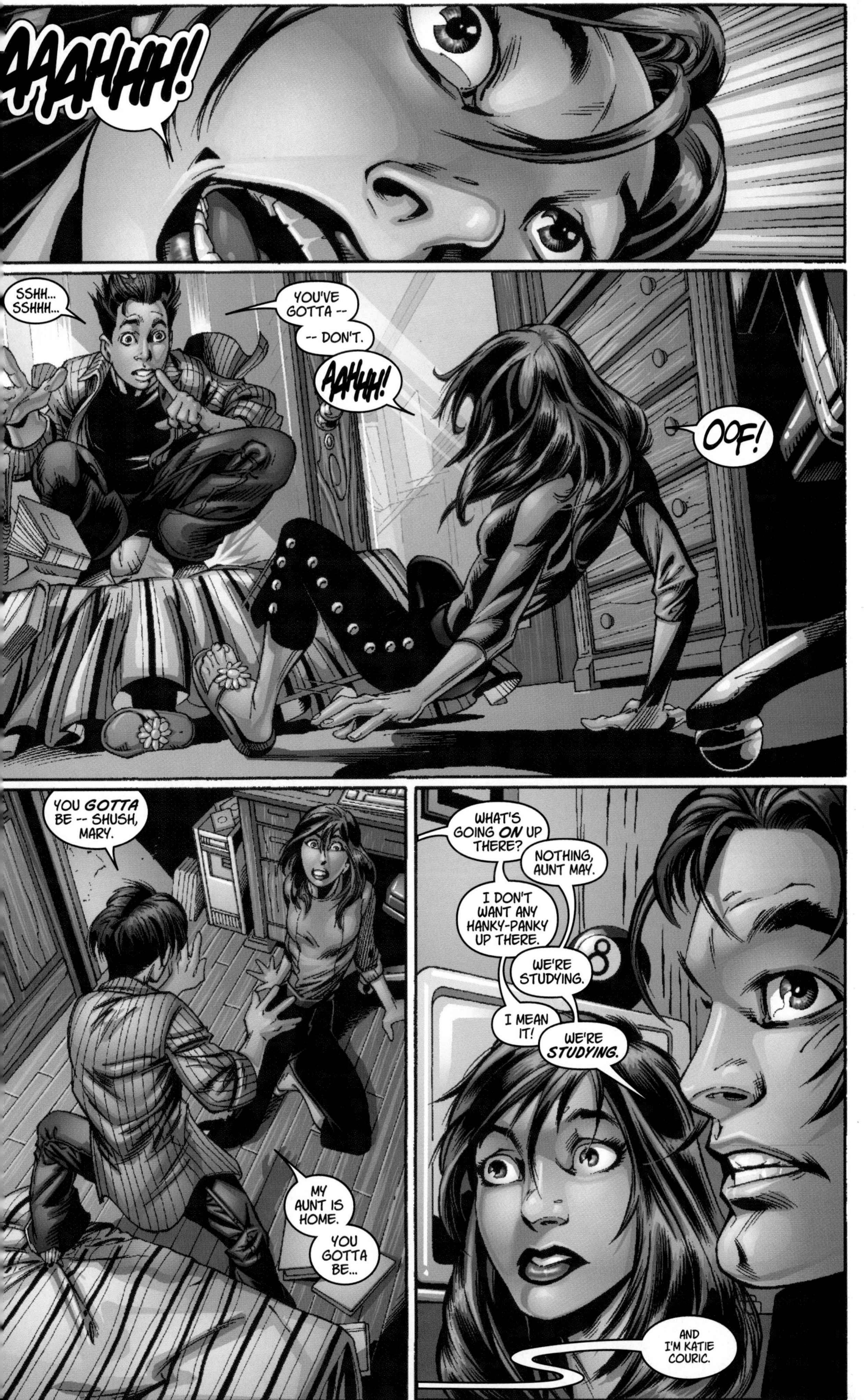
AAAHHH!
SSHH... SSHHH...
YOU'VE GOTTA --
-- DON'T.
AAHHH!
OOF!
YOU GOTTA BE -- SHUSH, MARY.
MY AUNT IS HOME.
YOU GOTTA BE...
WHAT'S GOING ON UP THERE?
NOTHING, AUNT MAY.
I DON'T WANT ANY HANKY-PANKY UP THERE.
WE'RE STUDYING.
I MEAN IT!
WE'RE STUDYING.
AND I'M KATIE COURIC.

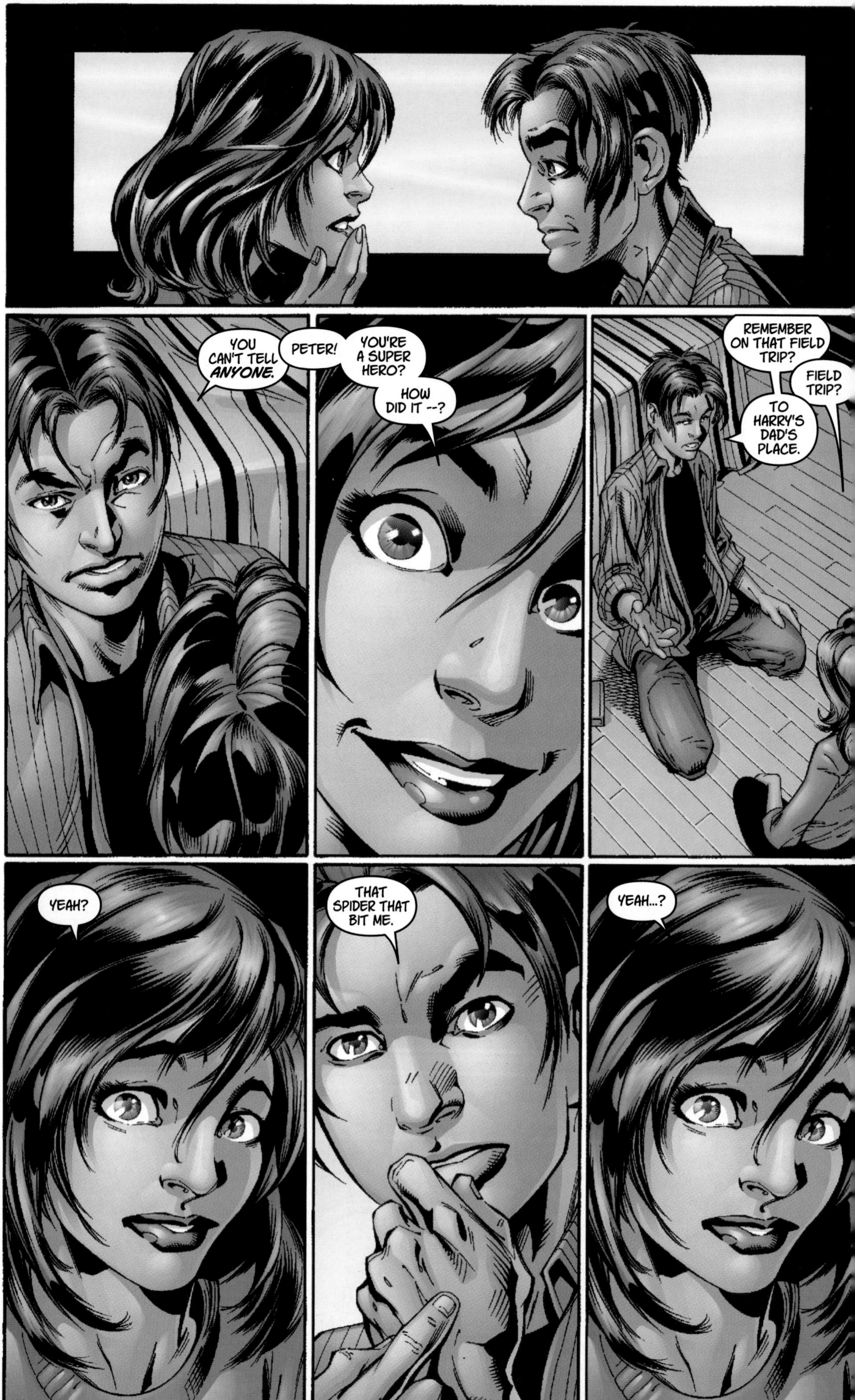

YOU CAN'T TELL *ANYONE*.
PETER!
YOU'RE A SUPER HERO?
HOW DID IT --?
REMEMBER ON THAT FIELD TRIP?
FIELD TRIP?
TO HARRY'S DAD'S PLACE.
YEAH?
THAT SPIDER THAT BIT ME.
YEAH...?

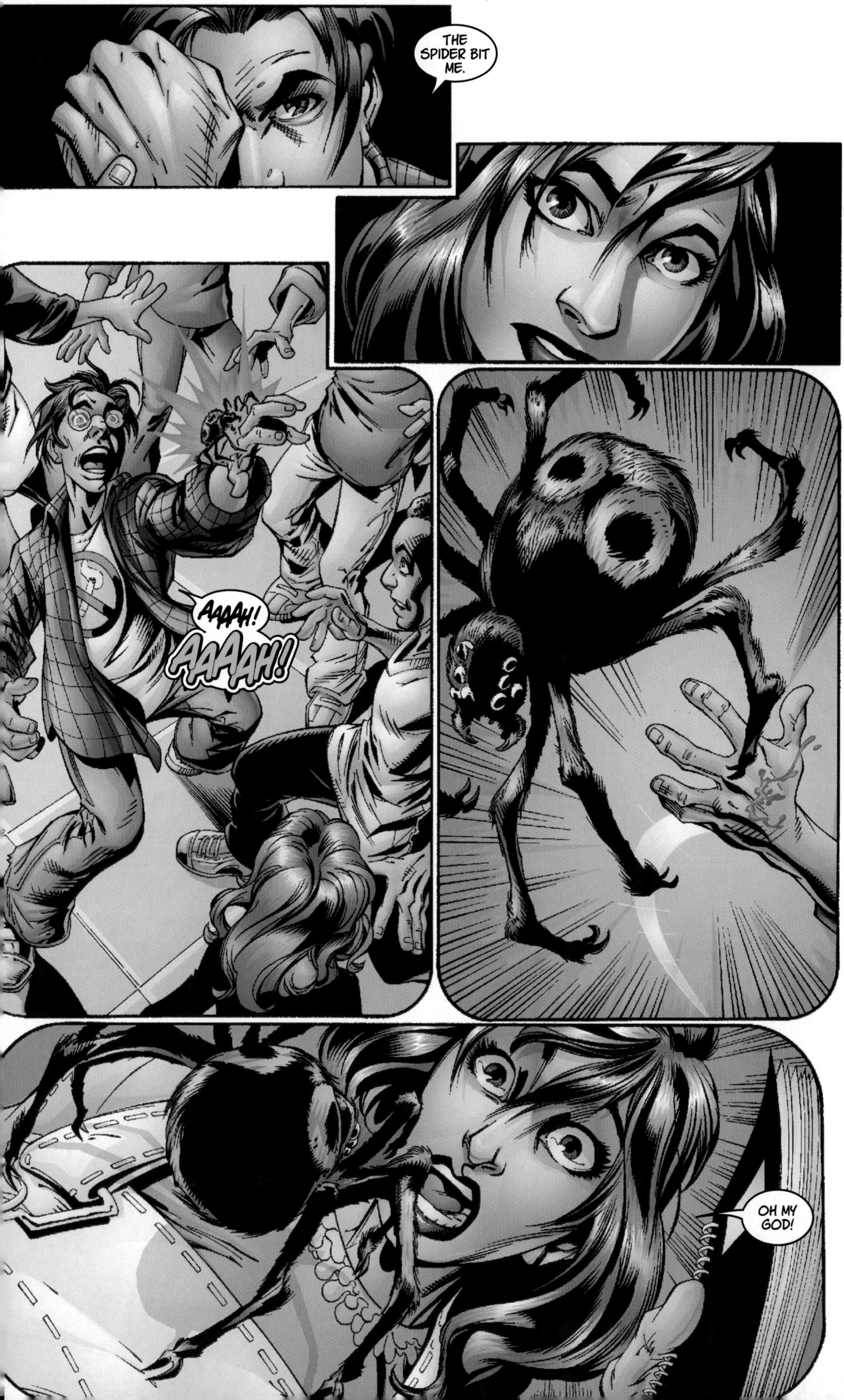
THE SPIDER BIT ME.
AAAAH!
AAAAH!
OH MY GOD!

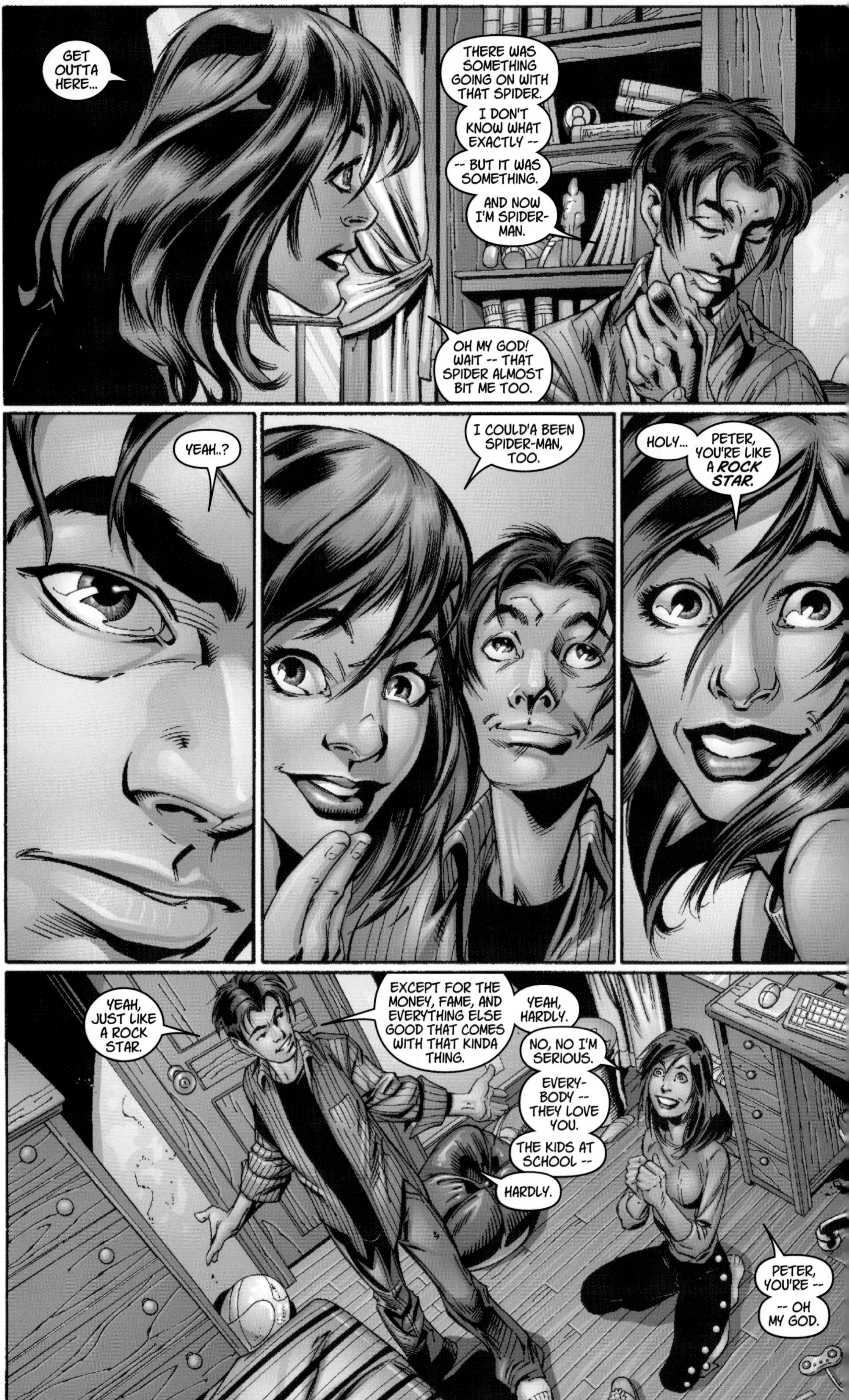
GET OUTTA HERE...
THERE WAS SOMETHING GOING ON WITH THAT SPIDER.
I DON'T KNOW WHAT EXACTLY --
-- BUT IT WAS SOMETHING.
AND NOW I'M SPIDER-MAN.
OH MY GOD! WAIT -- THAT SPIDER ALMOST BIT ME TOO.
YEAH..?
I COULD'A BEEN SPIDER-MAN, TOO.
HOLY...
PETER, YOU'RE LIKE A ROCK STAR.
YEAH, JUST LIKE A ROCK STAR.
EXCEPT FOR THE MONEY, FAME, AND EVERYTHING ELSE GOOD THAT COMES WITH THAT KINDA THING.
YEAH, HARDLY.
NO, NO I'M SERIOUS.
EVERY-BODY -- THEY LOVE YOU.
THE KIDS AT SCHOOL --
HARDLY.
PETER, YOU'RE --
-- OH MY GOD.

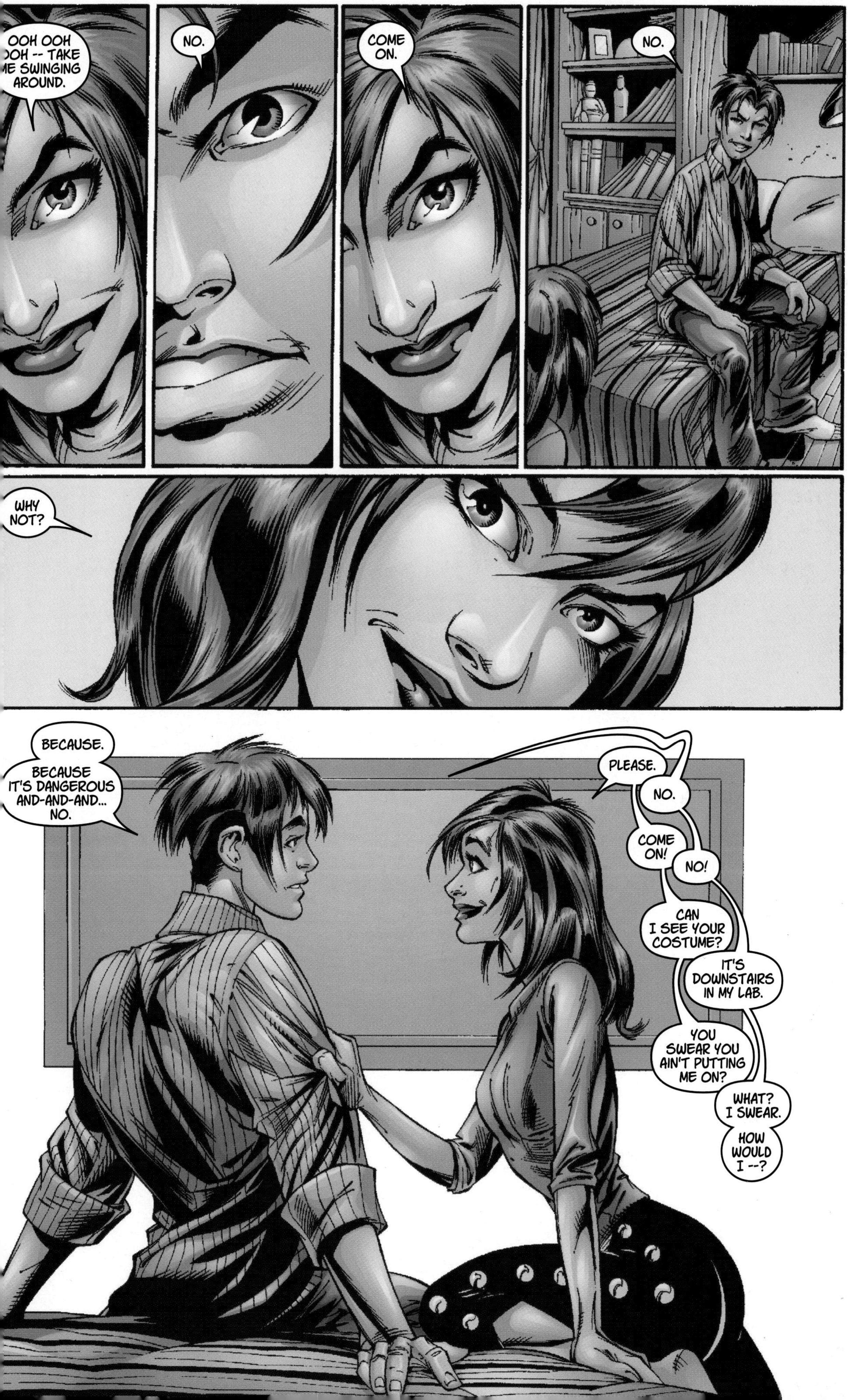
OOH OOH OOH -- TAKE ME SWINGING AROUND.
NO.
COME ON.
NO.
WHY NOT?
BECAUSE.
BECAUSE IT'S DANGEROUS AND-AND-AND... NO.
PLEASE.
NO.
COME ON!
NO!
CAN I SEE YOUR COSTUME?
IT'S DOWNSTAIRS IN MY LAB.
YOU SWEAR YOU AIN'T PUTTING ME ON?
WHAT? I SWEAR.
HOW WOULD I --?

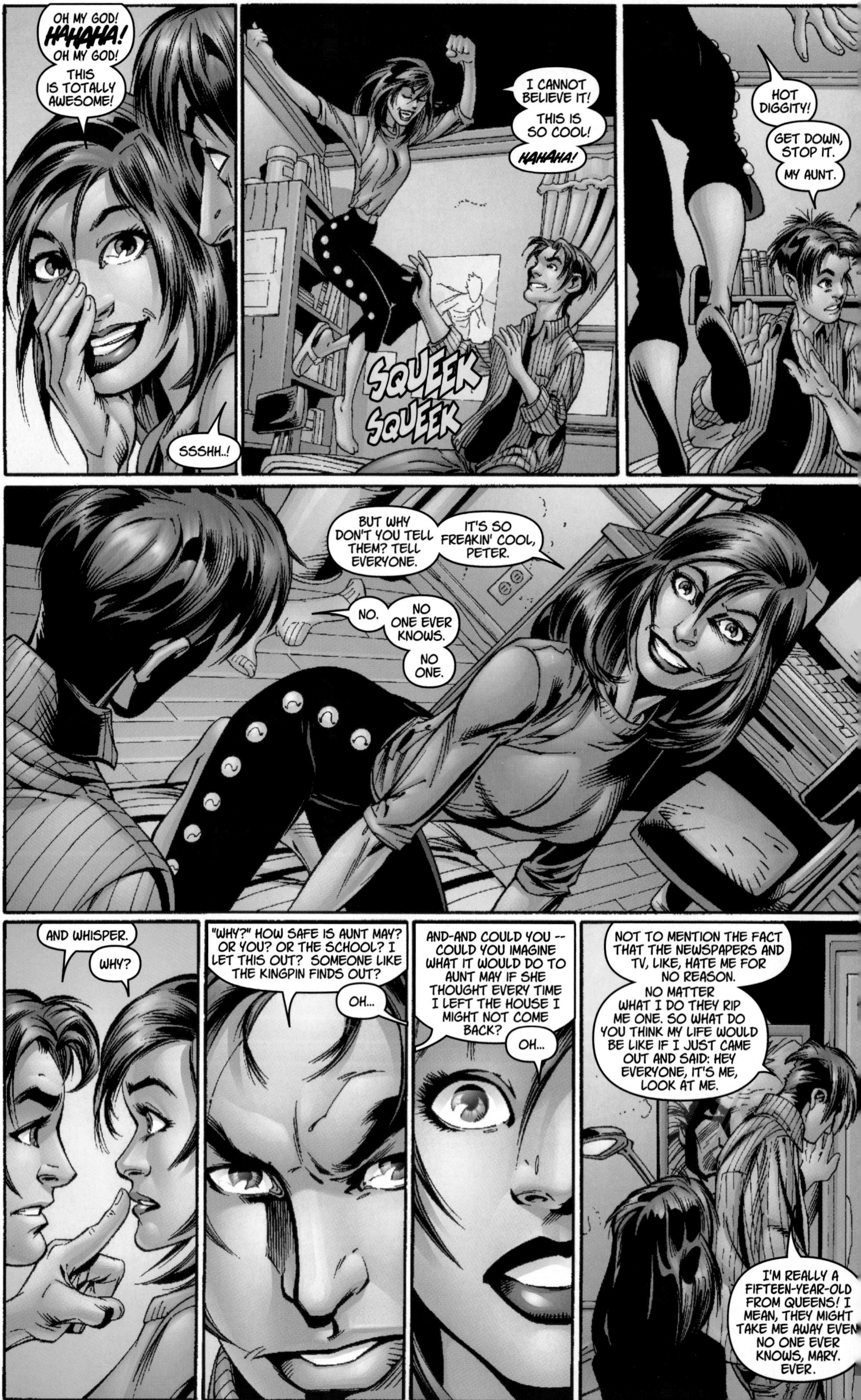

OH MY GOD!
HAHAHA!
OH MY GOD!
THIS IS TOTALLY AWESOME!
SSSHH..!
I CANNOT BELIEVE IT!
THIS IS SO COOL!
HAHAHA!
SQUEEK SQUEEK
HOT DIGGITY!
GET DOWN, STOP IT.
MY AUNT.
BUT WHY DON'T YOU TELL THEM? TELL EVERYONE.
IT'S SO FREAKIN' COOL, PETER.
NO.
NO ONE EVER KNOWS.
NO ONE.
AND WHISPER.
WHY?
"WHY?" HOW SAFE IS AUNT MAY? OR YOU? OR THE SCHOOL? I LET THIS OUT? SOMEONE LIKE THE KINGPIN FINDS OUT?
OH...
AND-AND COULD YOU -- COULD YOU IMAGINE WHAT IT WOULD DO TO AUNT MAY IF SHE THOUGHT EVERY TIME I LEFT THE HOUSE I MIGHT NOT COME BACK?
OH...
NOT TO MENTION THE FACT THAT THE NEWSPAPERS AND TV, LIKE, HATE ME FOR NO REASON.
NO MATTER WHAT I DO THEY RIP ME ONE. SO WHAT DO YOU THINK MY LIFE WOULD BE LIKE IF I JUST CAME OUT AND SAID: HEY EVERYONE, IT'S ME, LOOK AT ME.
I'M REALLY A FIFTEEN-YEAR-OLD FROM QUEENS! I MEAN, THEY MIGHT TAKE ME AWAY EVEN
NO ONE EVER KNOWS, MARY. EVER.

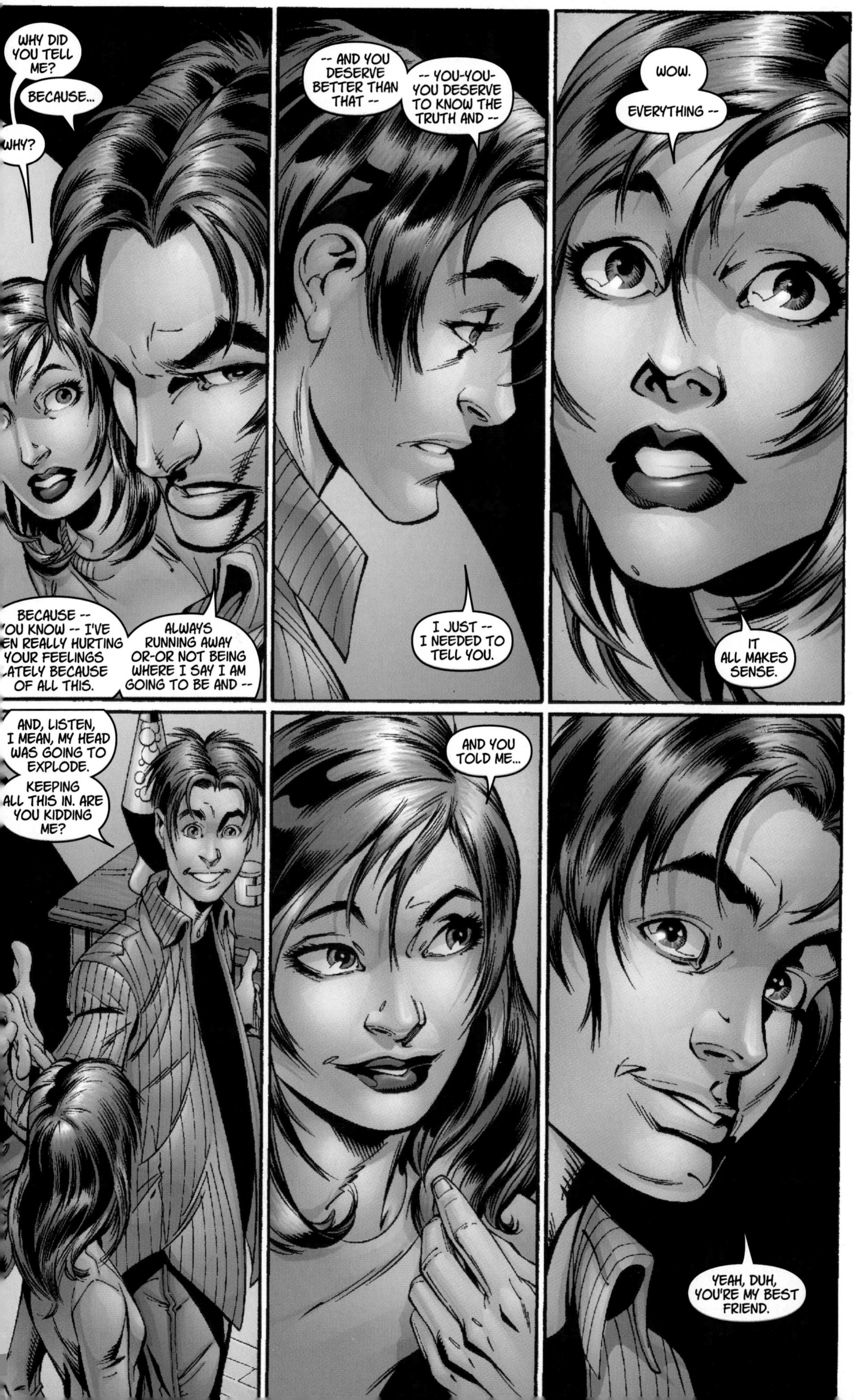
WHY DID YOU TELL ME?
BECAUSE...
WHY?
BECAUSE -- YOU KNOW -- I'VE BEEN REALLY HURTING YOUR FEELINGS LATELY BECAUSE OF ALL THIS.
ALWAYS RUNNING AWAY OR-OR NOT BEING WHERE I SAY I AM GOING TO BE AND --
-- AND YOU DESERVE BETTER THAN THAT --
-- YOU-YOU-YOU DESERVE TO KNOW THE TRUTH AND --
I JUST -- I NEEDED TO TELL YOU.
WOW.
EVERYTHING --
IT ALL MAKES SENSE.
AND, LISTEN, I MEAN, MY HEAD WAS GOING TO EXPLODE.
KEEPING ALL THIS IN. ARE YOU KIDDING ME?
AND YOU TOLD ME...
YEAH, DUH, YOU'RE MY BEST FRIEND.

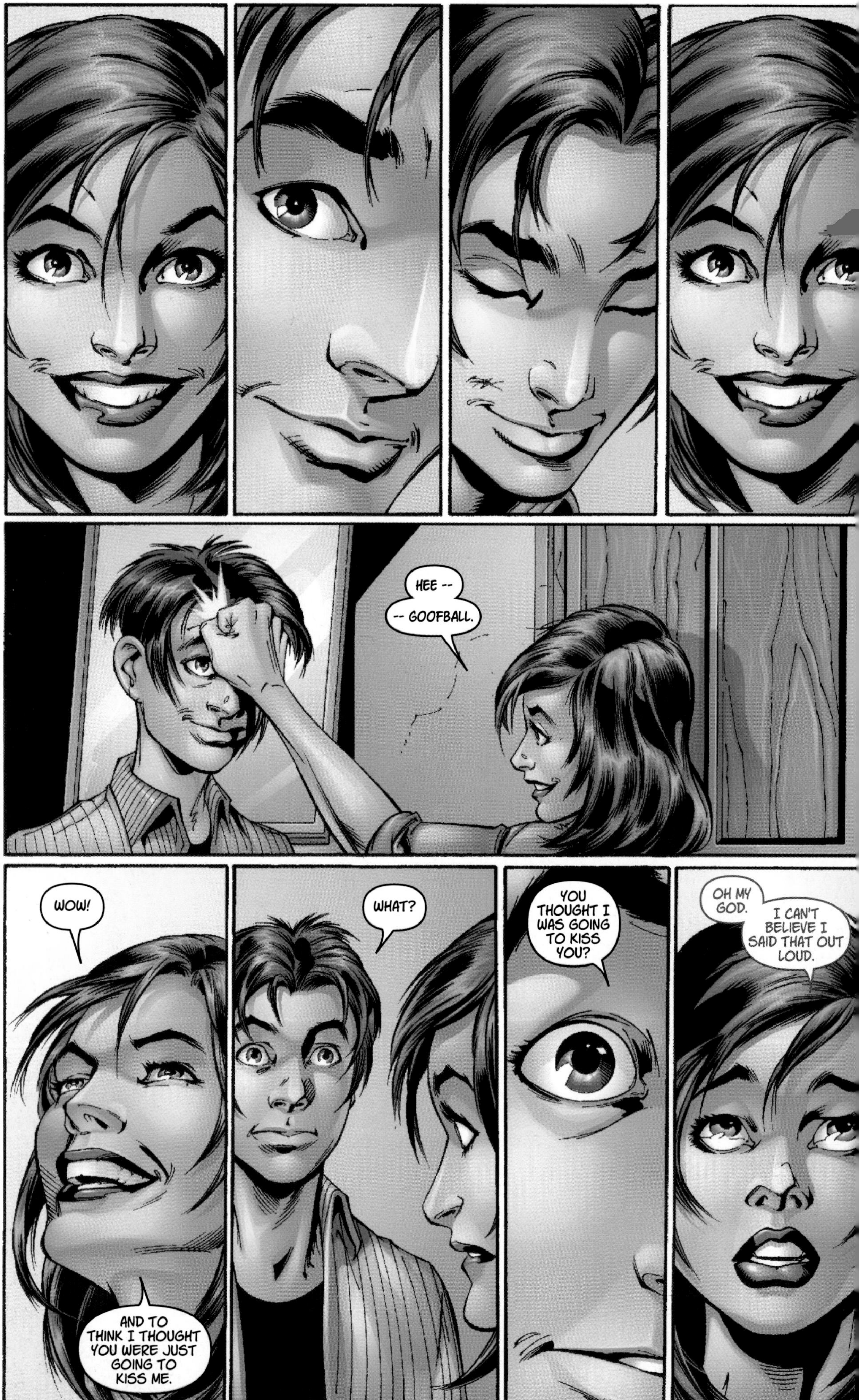
HEE --
-- GOOFBALL.
WOW!
AND TO THINK I THOUGHT YOU WERE JUST GOING TO KISS ME.
WHAT?
YOU THOUGHT I WAS GOING TO KISS YOU?
OH MY GOD.
I CAN'T BELIEVE I SAID THAT OUT LOUD.

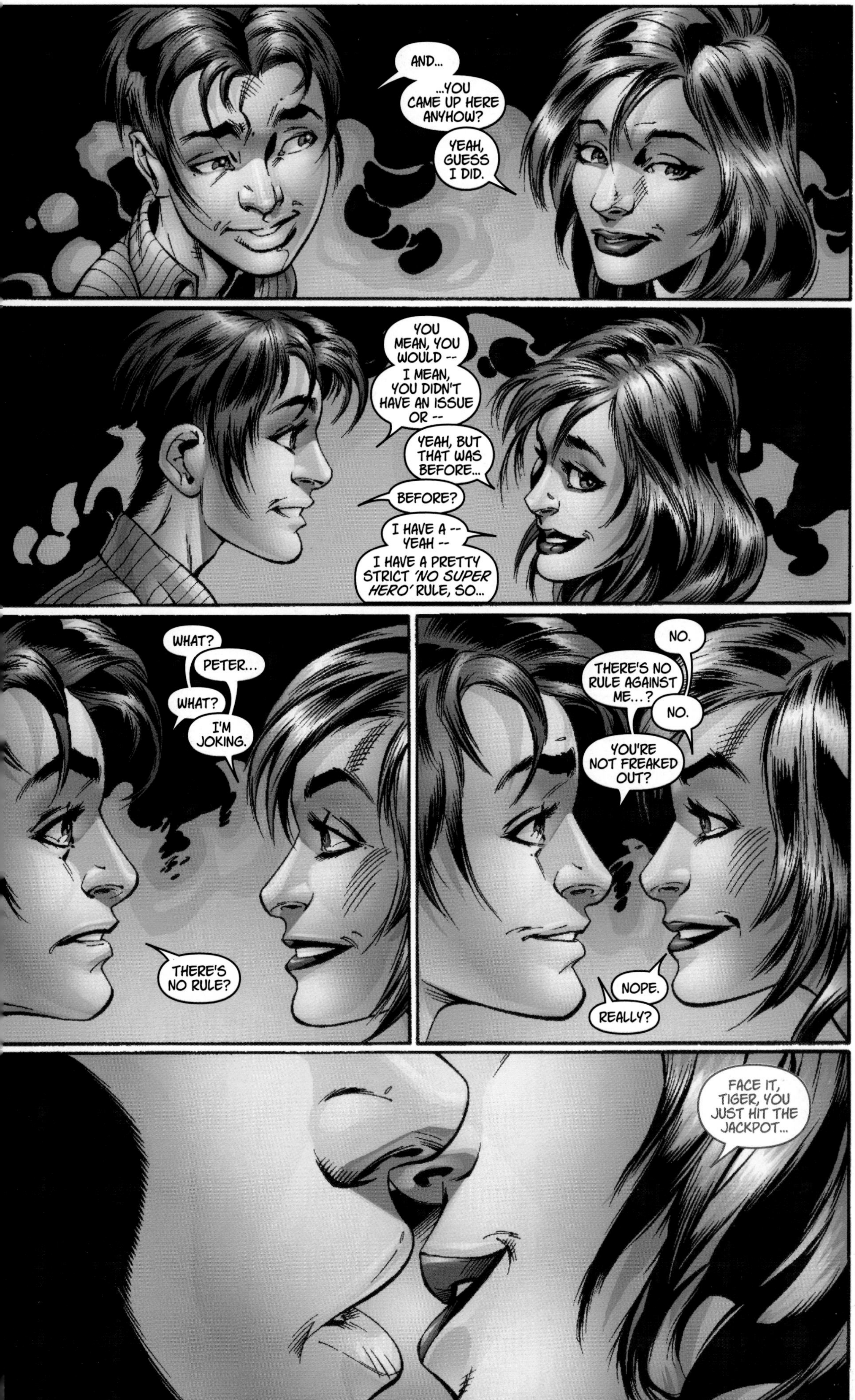
AND...
...YOU CAME UP HERE ANYHOW?
YEAH, GUESS I DID.
YOU MEAN, YOU WOULD -- I MEAN, YOU DIDN'T HAVE AN ISSUE OR --
YEAH, BUT THAT WAS BEFORE...
BEFORE?
I HAVE A -- YEAH -- I HAVE A PRETTY STRICT 'NO SUPER HERO' RULE, SO...
WHAT?
PETER...
WHAT?
I'M JOKING.
THERE'S NO RULE?
NO.
THERE'S NO RULE AGAINST ME...?
NO.
YOU'RE NOT FREAKED OUT?
NOPE.
REALLY?
FACE IT, TIGER, YOU JUST HIT THE JACKPOT...

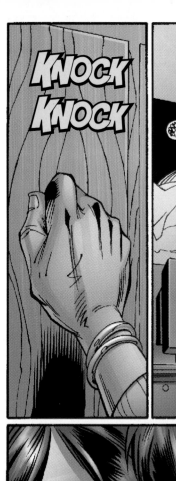

KNOCK KNOCK

PHONE!

WHAT?

THE PHONE. IT'S MARY'S MOM.

I DIDN'T HEAR THE PHONE RING.

IT DIDN'T. I CALLED HER.

HELLO? MOM?

WE -- WE WEREN'T.

WE WERE NOT.

NO -- NO!

WE WERE STUDYING.

GOD! WHAT?! WHY?

IT'S 4:30 IN THE AFTERNOON.

WHAT? OH, COME ON. WE'RE IN THE MIDDLE OF SOMETHING *IMPORTANT*!

UGGH!

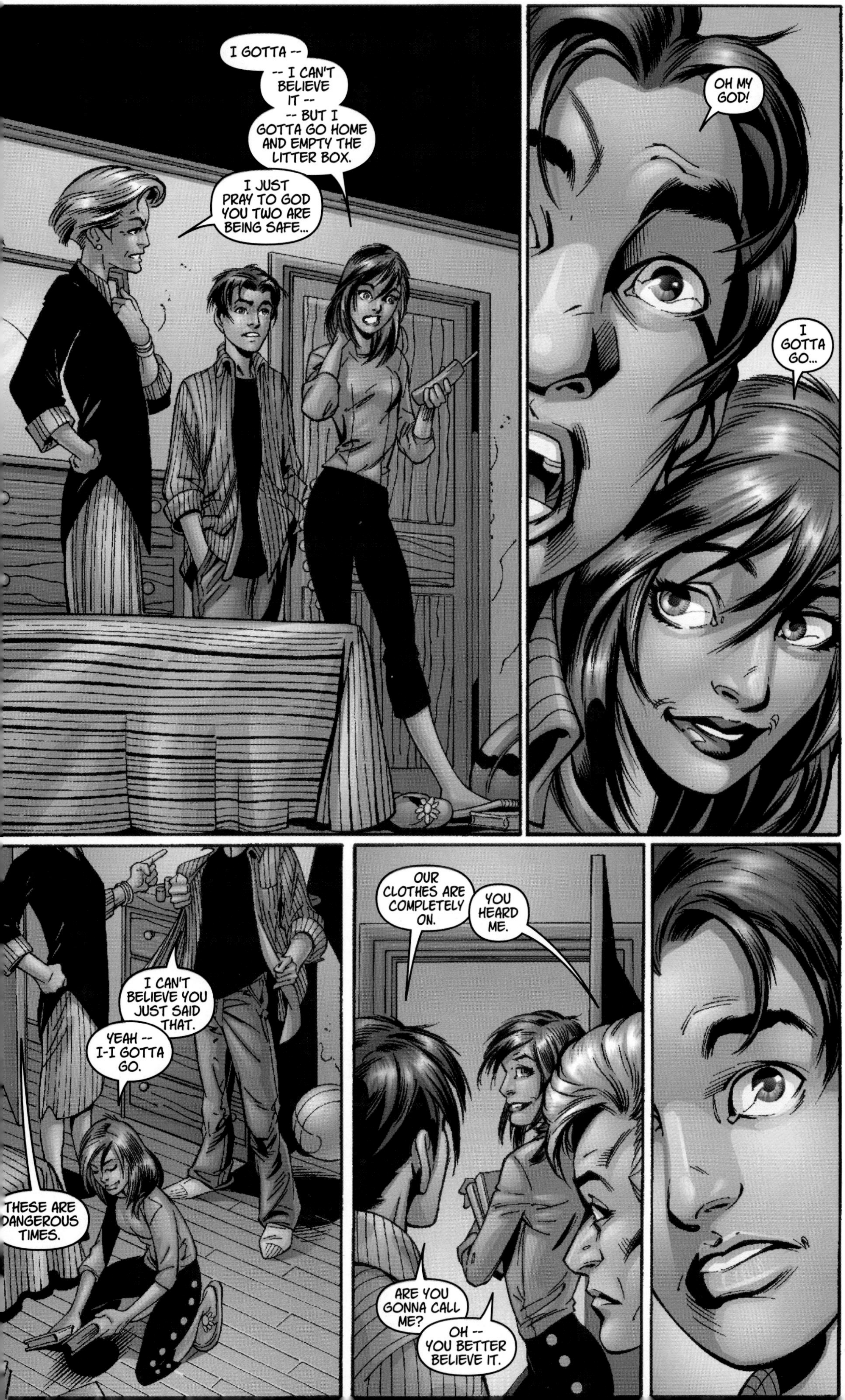
I GOTTA --
-- I CAN'T BELIEVE IT --
-- BUT I GOTTA GO HOME AND EMPTY THE LITTER BOX.
I JUST PRAY TO GOD YOU TWO ARE BEING SAFE...
OH MY GOD!
I GOTTA GO...
I CAN'T BELIEVE YOU JUST SAID THAT.
YEAH -- I-I GOTTA GO.
THESE ARE DANGEROUS TIMES.
OUR CLOTHES ARE COMPLETELY ON.
YOU HEARD ME.
ARE YOU GONNA CALL ME?
OH -- YOU BETTER BELIEVE IT.

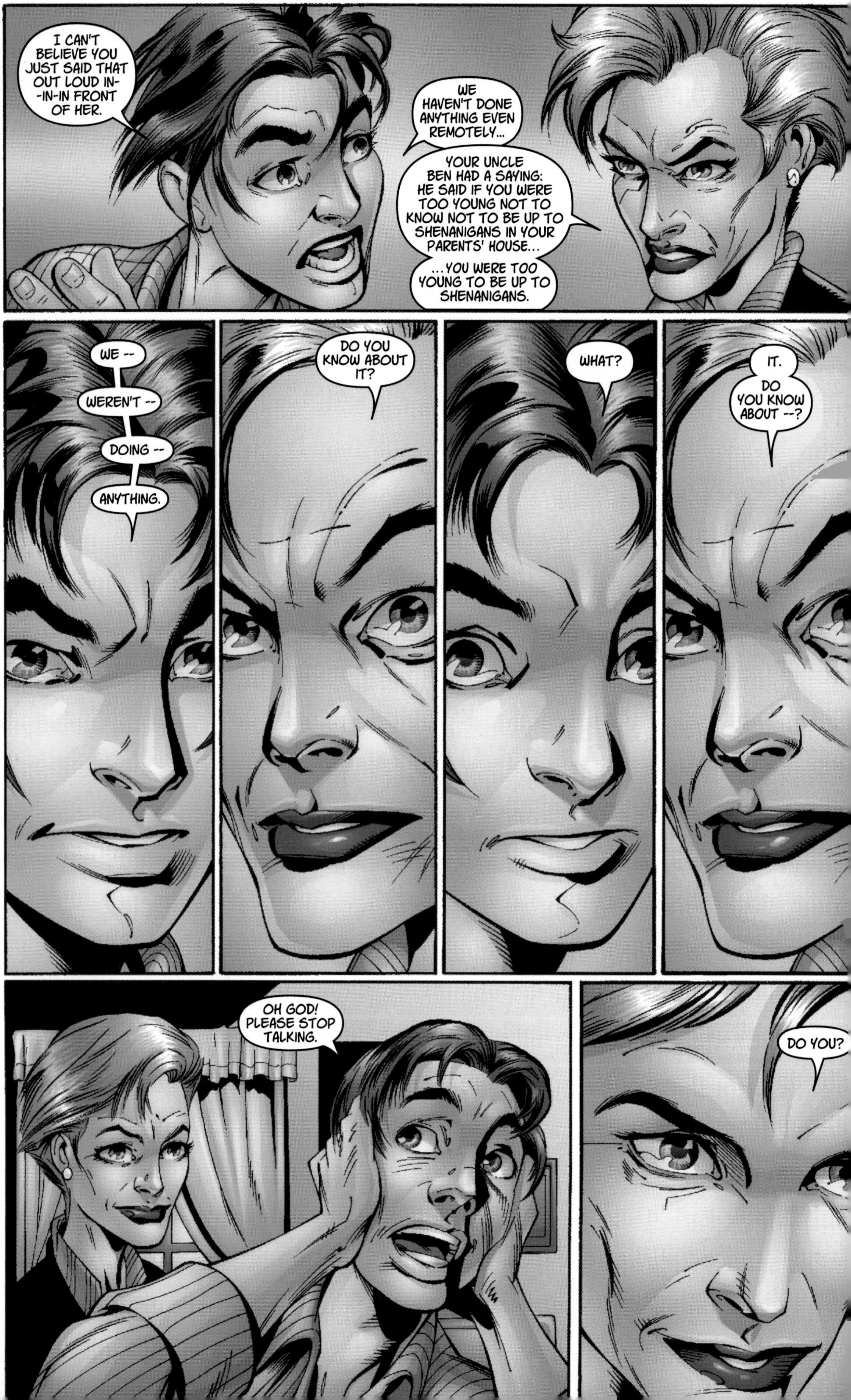
I CAN'T BELIEVE YOU JUST SAID THAT OUT LOUD IN- -IN-IN FRONT OF HER.
WE HAVEN'T DONE ANYTHING EVEN REMOTELY...
YOUR UNCLE BEN HAD A SAYING: HE SAID IF YOU WERE TOO YOUNG NOT TO KNOW NOT TO BE UP TO SHENANIGANS IN YOUR PARENTS' HOUSE...
...YOU WERE TOO YOUNG TO BE UP TO SHENANIGANS.
WE --
WEREN'T --
DOING --
ANYTHING.
DO YOU KNOW ABOUT IT?
WHAT?
IT.
DO YOU KNOW ABOUT --?
OH GOD! PLEASE STOP TALKING.
DO YOU?

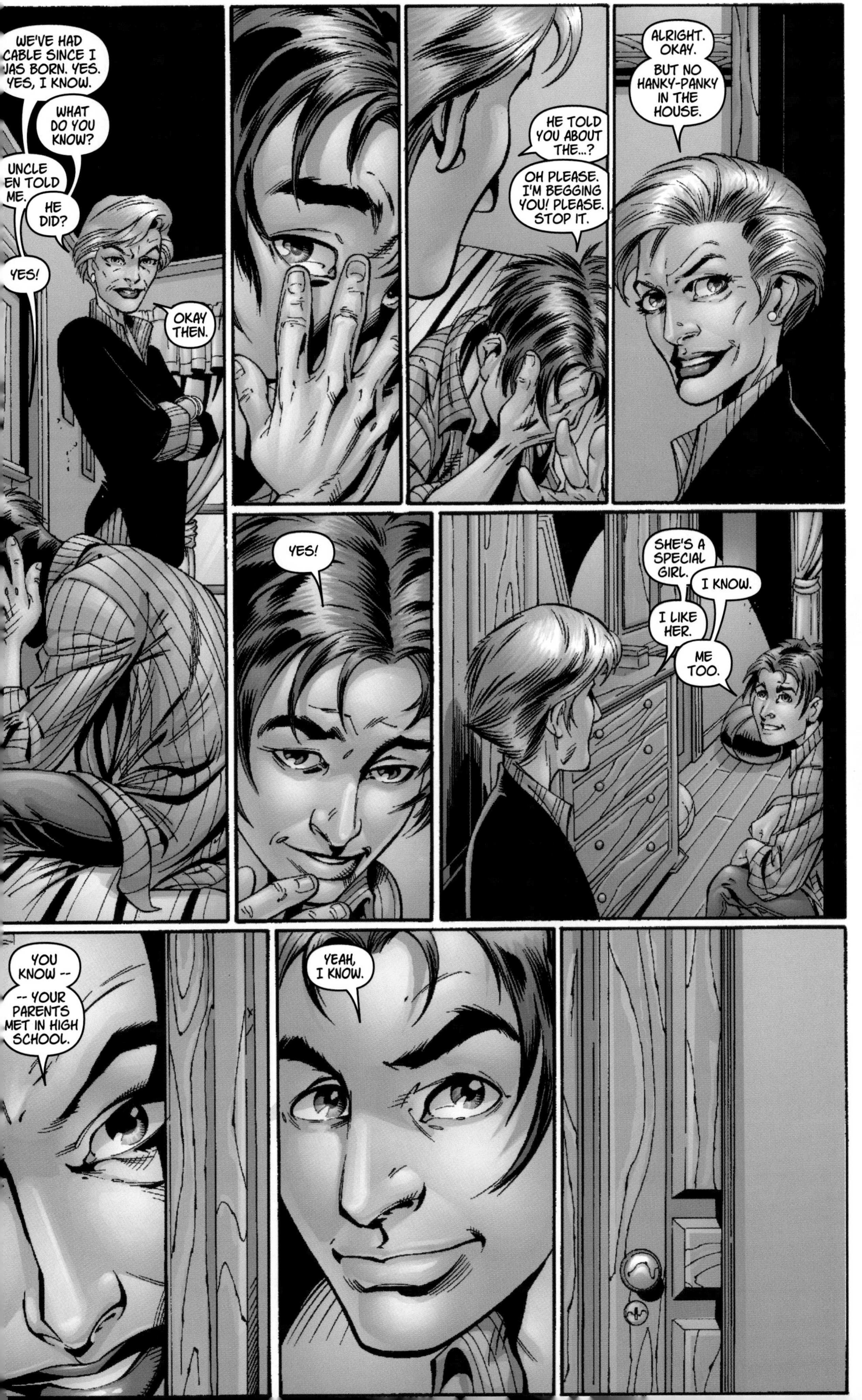
WE'VE HAD CABLE SINCE I WAS BORN. YES. YES, I KNOW.
WHAT DO YOU KNOW?
UNCLE BEN TOLD ME.
HE DID?
YES!
OKAY THEN.
HE TOLD YOU ABOUT THE...?
OH PLEASE. I'M BEGGING YOU! PLEASE. STOP IT.
ALRIGHT. OKAY.
BUT NO HANKY-PANKY IN THE HOUSE.
YES!
SHE'S A SPECIAL GIRL.
I KNOW.
I LIKE HER.
ME TOO.
YOU KNOW --
-- YOUR PARENTS MET IN HIGH SCHOOL.
YEAH, I KNOW.

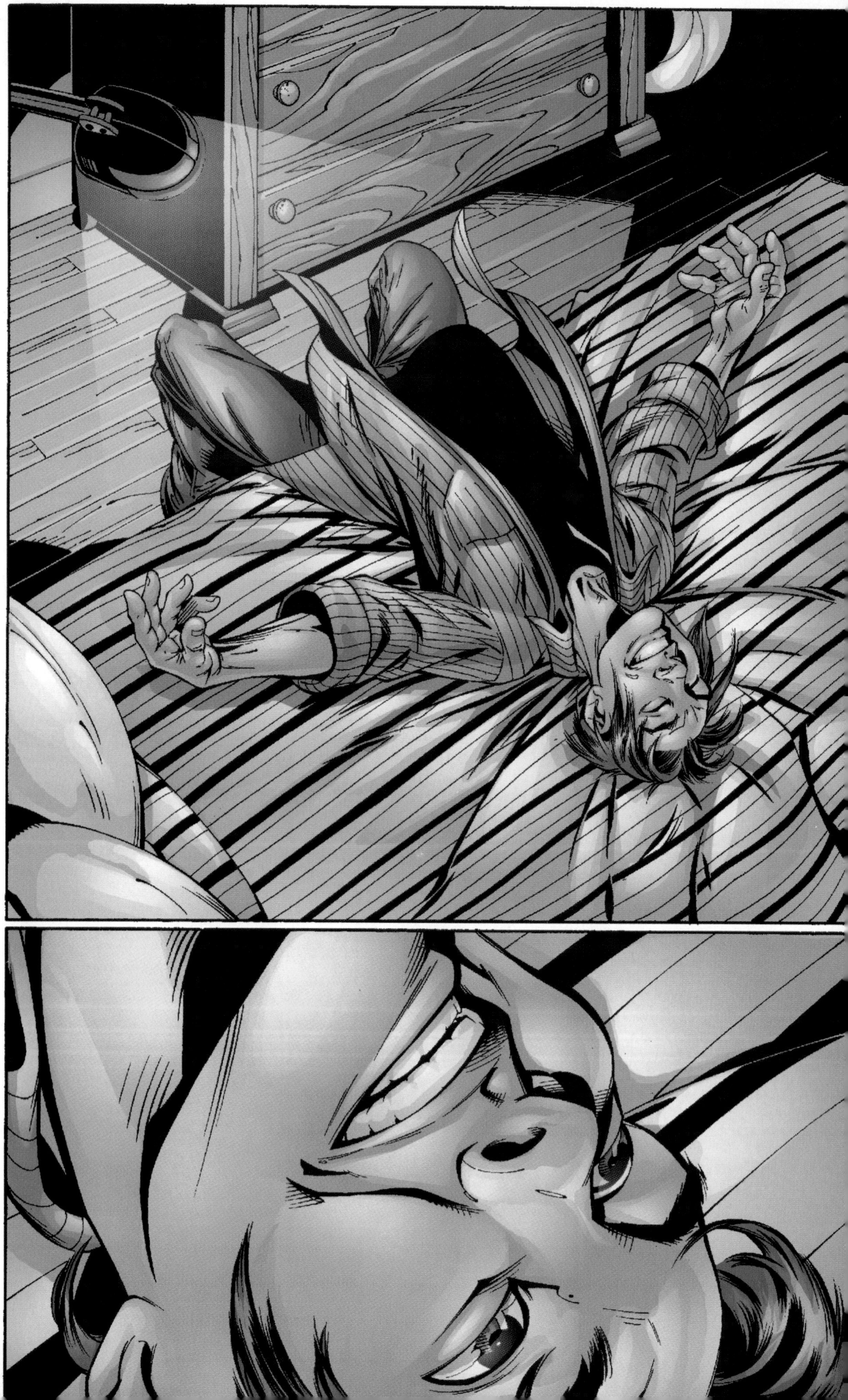

The Ultimate Marvel Universe

Nobody knows this except Gareb Shamus (the CEO of Wizard, The Guide to Comics) and me, but the basic principle for the Ultimate Universe came from our conversation in January 2000 – days after I accepted the job as Marvel's President. In a nutshell, Marvel's greatest teen characters – Spidey and the X-Men started as teenagers in the 1960's and won the hearts of a generation of teens. 40 years later, the characters had aged along with most of Marvel's editors, writers, artists and readers. The way to win new, younger readers – said Gareb and me – would be to recast them as year 2000 teenagers. Gareb tells me it was my idea, so I'll like him more and Marvel will buy more ad pages in Wizard, and I tell him it was his, so he'll like me more and give Marvel more coverage in Wizard.

Anyway that conversation got me thinking about the difference that the past 40 years had made in the lifestyle of an American kid. Stan Lee's Peter Parker showed up in 1961, and the 60s were a different world for kids. The "play date" had not been invented. It was a safer, more innocent era. Back then, close parental supervision ended as soon as you could figure out how to work the front door knob. You ran out of the house after breakfast and lived amongst the pack of neighborhood kids – checking back in for meals and boo boos. This is not to say that parents were less loving than they are now – just that they were less protective and less involved. After about a week of focusing on Ultimate Peter Parker showing up in 2000, living in the new millennium and facing modern kids issues, the basic plot for Ultimate Spider-Man hit me like a ton of bricks. And it revolved around the relationship between Peter and his foster parents.

All through that February, I worked on the plot with input from Lou Aronica, Bob Harras, Mark Powers and Joe Quesada. (At that time, Joe and his wife Nancy were running the Marvel Knights as independent contractors.) You can read the final outline – it's printed in its entirety a few pages down.

We all agreed that the outline was good and that the Ultimates concept was great.

We believed that a new Ultimate Marvel imprint could help rebuild our teen audience. And, then my mouth got me in trouble. Without enough ducks in a row, I made Marvel make some very expensive moves – we would launch the Ultimate Spider-Man and Ultimate X-Men in conjunction with the X-Men movie in July 2000. And we made this very bold announcement in February.

....

Marvel's Teen Initiative

The Ultimate Marvel comic book line will be our most comprehensive, focused and well-financed imprint. During the next 18 months, the X-Men Movie from 20th Century Fox and the Spider-Man Movie from Columbia Tri-Star will raise Marvel exposure and excitement to an all-time high. Marvel plans to leverage the growing demand for our characters into new readership for our comics.

Everybody in the industry knows that this is not an easy task. For the past ten years, comic publishers have been talking about bringing in new fans. But the cold truth is that the collective efforts of publishers and distributors have failed. Readership continues to drop and stores continue to suffer financially. Marvel is not giving up on comic books. In fact, Ultimate Marvel is on the ultimate industry mission – new customers.

The Ultimates will be great Marvel comic stories.

Loyal comic fans have earned an inside knowledge and insight through five, ten or twenty years of reading. The Marvel Universe is the longest-running continuous story in history, and it's very difficult, in that context, to do anything new that's not tied in to that continuity. Lose the continuity and you lose your most important customers.

This is the dilemma. Loyal fans embrace the complexities of the forty-year history, but new fans are baffled by it. This is an industry-wide issue. It is all but impossible for a new reader to comprehend (let alone enjoy) any main line comic from any main line publisher.

Marvel believes that the Ultimate Spider-

Man and X-Men lines are the answer. Core comic fans will love these books. The characters are pure and true to themselves. The stories are strong, complete, compelling, and produced by our best artists and writers. But, any new reader can pick up any one of these books and start reading. Essentially, the Ultimates swap out the traditional backstory and replace it with a rich, self-contained, Year-2000 context.

The Ultimates will be marketed to new readers.

Let's face facts. New readers are not going to find us. We can't to sit back and wait for a 12 year old kid to wander into a comic shop, drift over to the right rack and find the Ultimate X-Men. Marvel will reach out through aggressive marketing and sampling programs. Our goal is to distribute 12 million sample comics over a 12-month launch period. We believe that the books will hook new readers into the Ultimates line and that they will expand their horizons to traditional titles. We are willing to invest heavily in this program.

Marvel.com will play a major role in the rebuilding of our comic book business. Marvel has developed our graphic and storytelling skills and earned our reputation as America's storytellers. Now we are putting those skills to work in the on-line environment to reach out to a new generation of readers. Again, the goal is to build comic book readership by introducing them to the beauty of comic book storytelling and promoting the purchase of hard copy books at retail.

....

On one level, it all started to come true. Licensees were signing up to make Ultimates products — t-shirts, sneakers, underoos, pajamas...you name it. We got the graphic look down — all based on Joe Quesada's (there's that name again) covers – for Ultimate Spider-Man #1 and Ultimate X-Men. #1. The press coverage was spectacular — with full coverage by industry press and widespread stories in mainstream media — even the New York Times and Wall Street Journal ran Ultimates articles. By the way, the Journal reporter showed up to cover Marvel's business prospects (somewhat shaky at the time) and had

rolled her eyes when she heard about Ultimate Spider-Man reaching modern kids. Just to get her goat, I said Stan Lee put Peter to work for a newspaper, because that was a cool job — like 40 years ago. New Peter would be a webmaster, because that's hot now. Whether she knew I made that up on the spot or not, she laughed and got into the spirit. And, by the way, Brian was a little surprised when he read the article, but he liked the webmaster thing enough to get it into the second arc.

Everything was on a roll — except, of course, the most important thing.

We could not find the right writer. We tried like crazy, but many of Marvel's top guns passed on the project. In retrospect (given the current success of the Ultimates line) that may seem strange. But the modern history of Marvel is marked (scarred?) by many failed teen initiatives. To industry insiders, Ultimates promised sure to be one more. Several very good writers did take a shot at a script, but none of them hit the mark. The clock kept ticking, days and weeks kept passing. We were going to miss the X-Men movie premier by a mile, and nothing good was happening. Then, thank goodness, Joe (you remember Joe) showed up in my office with this nasty comic about a serial killer written by this adult-oriented Indy comic unknown (except to Indy fans) guy named Brian Bendis. I saw what Joe saw — this man had the lights on.

We showed Brian the outline and he saw the light. In his own words —

A CONFESSION

BY BRIAN MICHAEL BENDIS

So the question is, what qualifies an admitted alternative comics artist and crime fiction writer to get a gig helping to revamp a classic the likes of Spider-Man.

Okay. All right, I am going to confess something to you here, and by doing so I am going to ruin my reputation. For eight long years I have spent every waking moment creating this public persona of a tough talking, smart mouthed writer/artist and I am kissing it goodbye.

It was whatever year it was that I was 10 or 11 years old. And man, I was all about the Marvel Comics. You name it! I was immersed. I never read a bad comic. They were all equally perfect.

But my favorite thing to buy was the comic book with the record attached. It was like a read-along. You read the comic and actors and such acted it out along on the record. I loved them! I remember having a Star Trek comic book and record set and thinking in awe: "Wow, how did they ever get William Shatner himself to reprise the role for this record?!?"

My favorite one was an issue of the Fantastic Four that John Buscema drew where the FF basically relived their origin. I had a couple of others too, but I wanted all my comics to have a record.

So, I took my crappy little Radio Shack tape recorder and my crappy little cetron 60 minute audio tapes and I convinced my brother to join me in our own vocal interpretation of my collection of Marvel Comics.

We would take all the toys that we had that actually produced a noise (toy guns, trucks) and create a real theater of the mind. We would sit there for hours and work on each character's vocal stylings and decide which toy went with which sound effect.

One comic in particular that I remember spending a lot of time on, I mean a lot of time, was the issue of Amazing Spider-Man where Peter Parker goes to France for something only Gerry Conway would think of and sees the clone of Gwen Stacy. I don't remember what issue it was, but that's what editor Ralph Macchio gets paid for. He'll insert the exact issue number right... about... here. [Amazing Spider-Man #141]

It would take forever, but we eventually perfected our one take recording of the entire issue. I was the voice of Peter, Gwen, and Robbie Robertson. My brother would be the Cyclone and various henchmen. And all the French people sounded like... well, like 10 year olds doing French accents. It became a real art form.

I don't know exactly when we stopped making them, but I'm pretty sure it was around the same time my mom came across one of the tapes. She didn't know what it was, popped it in only to hear my brother and I reenacting an intimate scene between Reed Richards and Sue Storm. Basically it was me doing both voices and then kissing my hand for sound effect, but regardless, it creeped my mom out.

Here is the following interaction between my mom and myself. She is standing in the doorway to my room holding the tape.

"Is this you?"

"Yes?"

"What is this?"

"It's mine!"

"How are you making the kissing noises?"

"With my hand?"

"You're not kissing your brother like that, are you?"

"Oh God, no. Eeww!"

"You know, that's not appropriate."

"Can I have my tape please?"

"Uh- maybe you should go outside and play or something."

So, I think you can clearly see why I was the perfect choice to write the pages you just read.

Okay, not really, but it made me feel better in an odd way.

Brian Michael Bendis
Cleveland, Ohio

p.s. I was relating this story to one of my best friends, John, who isn't in the comics biz, and he told me that when he was that age he and his best friend had a super secret West Coast Avengers Club.

Now that's just weird.

BRIAN CAME BACK WITH AN INCREDIBLE FIRST ISSUE. WE SENT THAT FIRST ISSUE TO MARK BAGLEY WHO RANKED AMONG THE BEST — AND BUSIEST — ARTISTS. HE NEEDED SOME PERSUADING TO TAKE THE JOB. IT CAME FROM A WONDERFUL SOURCE.. MARK SHOWED THE SCRIPT TO HIS HIGH-SCHOOL DAUGHTER WHO REALLY LIKED IT AND CONVINCED HIM TO DO IT. MARK DID WHAT MANY FEEL IS THE BEST WORK OF HIS CAREER AND SOME OF THE BEST PENCILS IN THE BUSINESS. ART THIBERT, AS INKER, AND JUNG CHOI, AS COLORIST, FILLED OUT THE CREATIVE TEAM. RALPH MACCHIO AND BRIAN SMITH TOOK ON THE EDITORIAL ASSIGNMENT.

BENDIS TOOK THE HELM.

RAMBLINGS *BY BRIAN MICHAEL BENDIS*

Hey kids… so, yes I am totally thrilled out of my mind to be doing Spider-Man.

Why? I am Peter Parker.

And not just Spider-Man, but to be given the keys to a new car like this… but more on that in a minute.

And now onto the Spider-Man issue.

First off, the ground zero/ Ultimate idea is a fantastic idea. You don't know the whole picture yet. Most of it is big business stuff and it's all pretty exciting. And it ain't gonna look too shabby on the resumé.

Everyone is screaming: "It's the death knell of comics and why isn't Marvel or DC doing something about it!!" and now someone is. Will it work? Don't know. Doesn't matter. What matters is someone is trying. And not just talking about it, doing it. And I am thrilled to be part of that.

And if it does? FANTASTIC! All I want is for people to read comics and enjoy them and talk about them.

Here's the deal: a lot of people don't like to admit this but there are just simply not enough people reading mainstream comics in North America to justify their existence financially. And it is a business, let's not kid. DC obviously has some cushion from Time Warner and Marvel's losses are public record. SOMETHING MUST BE DONE! NOW!!

X-Men, Spider-Man; they are very popular characters and icons. And not just in the world of comics. People know them. So, we need to make people want to read about them in the artform in which they were invented.

It's such an amazing way to tell a story. Comics. I love them so much. And look how many of you feel the same way. It will turn around. This many of us can't be wrong.

Marvel had, to my understanding, been working on this idea in-house for quite some time before I had anything to do with it. What was missing basically was character and style. I was approached to do it based on Bill Jemas reading some of Joe Quesada's copies of my creator-owned comics. Yes, Joe Quesada is the thread that holds everything in mainstream comics together. And thank God!

They came to me with a clear and really good idea of what the book should be and what it is about. And I know it is a good idea because I hear about 19 bad ideas a week and I know this wasn't one of those.

And I am not saying this to brag, but I didn't need the gig. Right? I have a gig. I am doing okay. I have a roof over my head. So, when this was offered, I was able to decide if I really wanted to do it based on the pure joy of it, and I really did.

Also, I have a horrible DVD addiction that needs constant feeding. I need help. Someone, please help.

It is what they say. It is a relaunching of Spider-Man as Stan Lee envisioned him, but written as dramatically and entertainingly as possible, as if the events that shaped the young Peter Parker started today.

There is nothing we are doing to Spider-Man that isn't in the spirit of the theme and characters that were originally invented. The only thing we are doing is freeing the characters from forty loooong years of sometimes four Spidey titles a month continuity.

If you want to get new readers and a new generation of readers, then continuity is an anchor and an obstacle. I am in no way saying that the material is bad or unappealing in any way. What I am saying is that from a commercial standpoint, from outside of comics, there is no way to get someone to spend their money on something that you NEED 1000 issues of back story to fully appreciate.

Think of it from a non fanboy or completist point of view. Forty years! Has a television show or book series or movie series lasted that long? Can't think of one. Nope. Closest thing I can think of is James Bond or Star Trek and we are on our forth or fifth versions. Most TV shows buckle under the weight of their own premise. Even the best and long lasting ones.

So, it is only natural that comics would need to do it as well. And it is not unprecedented. DC did it in the sixties with their long-in-the-tooth Golden Age Flash and Green Lantern characters. Sales were in the dumper, so they took it back to step one with a modern twist.

And for those of you upset by this idea, don't worry about it. Your comics are continuing business as usual, I hear. So I don't understand why someone would get irritated by the idea of this new book.

But none of this is really a concern to me. All I care about is making the comic.

I don't want to dip too much into what our take is or what the story is because I am looking forward to you guys reading it fresh with no expectations. But a couple of you on the board have read the script as a test audience and I think you can rest assured that I gave it my all.

This Daily Bugle website thing is just one part of a much, much bigger picture and not in the first issues. I think when you see the overall arc you will see how it fits in.

Peter working at the Daily Bugle website is just a logical and faithful way to keep him in that setting. Major newspapers do not hire fifteen and sixteen year old boys to be staff photographers. Just doesn't happen. But they do hire whiz kids and such to work this kind of stuff. My brother was working for major companies as a freelance web guy while still very young.

Also, the first issue is a big 48 pager. We get a lot of story and development in on the first issue. I am pretty excited about that.

I have in my hands a chunk of the art for the first issue and it's a handsome mainstream book. A lot of my writing relies an the artist's ability to have the characters emote without voice-over or caption, and Bagley is very, very good at that.

No, I am not doing layouts, when you see Bagley go at it you will see it is unnecessary. I am also, as of yet, not doing the obnoxious letter column on this like I do on *Sam and Twitch*. I think three letter columns a month is enough, don't you?

What Bill said about me hanging with kids was him relating the fact that I am treating this book the way I treat the work I do on *Sam and Twitch* and *Jinx* etc. I am a writer and I research. You get into the heads of the subjects a little. I am not a teenager as I am not a bounty hunter or cop. It brings so much vitality to the work to get out there and discover stuff on your own.

I hate these writers that just steal stuff off TV and other comics and decide that now it is their work. Only in comics is that considered okay. I don't do it. I do my homework. The good news is I was a teenager and can easily tap into that box of unresolved neurosis any time I want. As I said, I am Peter Parker. Except for the cool powers and hip job.

But I know Bill's comment made me look like one scary, bald, stalker guy. Not what he meant… I think.

So, my manifest of comments is at an end. This was a very fun week.

It is going to be a lot of fun to open the catalogue in a couple of months and see the solicitation for this along with my other buds who are now finding themselves working for the Big Two all of a sudden.

And I am looking forward to talking to all of you about the book when it hits the stands starting in September.

And I promise that this is it for the big announcements… :)

Oh, and the reason I haven't said much about X-Men is that it really is still in development and there isn't much to say yet. Spider-Man is IN production. That could change as early as this week.

I will answer any questions… shoot.

Brian Bendis

COMMUNICATIONS

Bill Jemas continues...

As to working with Brian, it's been a blast. This project has been an ego-free team effort. Here's a sneak peek at a typical interchange. It started with a meeting at the San Diego Comicon between Brian and Ralph Macchio. It's pretty-much self-explanatory, up until the debate about the burglar who wound up killing Uncle Ben. Brian liked the way Stan had handled the infamous burglar in Amazing Fantasy #15, i.e., the burglar had just robbed the wrestling manager and Peter (then dressed as Spider-Man) could have captured him on the spot. I liked everything about Amazing #15 except that scene.

——-Original Message——-
From: Bendis
Sent: Monday, July 17, 2000 4:34 AM

Hi Bill...

Had a nice meeting with Ralph today and I wanted to explain a couple of things that are on my mind and politely debate a couple of other things for Ultimate Spidey. These are all really small in the span of things but I know how you feel about the book and wanted to share.

Firstly, the harsh language and violence is a non issue. I really wasn't sure where the line was drawn here and in the beginning you seemed to be leaning towards a slightly more PG version. I think reading the 'damns' in script form was one thing, but seeing the cartoon and balloons with 'damns' in it was another. I won't be putting those in anymore if I can help it.

The slang terms are another issue. It's hard to know what will fly and what won't. My job is to keep it colorful so I don't want to censor myself, I will let you and Ralph do it for me.

Secondly, the multiple word balloons in one panel was not my first choice but was necessary after getting Mark's pages in. Sometimes, not always, but sometimes, he went for a two or group shot when I asked for a bunch of small, cutting-back-and-forth, one-shot panels. Not a big deal and I will discuss itwith him.

Thirdly, the beginning of issue four has the devastation of the OSBORN LAB scene but the dialogue of a news report. Let me explain what the idea is here. What I am doing here is juxtaposing the public's perception of the events vs. what we the reader know to be horrible fact.

This aspect will play out on a larger scale as the Green Goblin and his legacy become more public. It even shows up a little in this issue with Kong having the TV on and the kids gossiping about it. I could easily have little TV screens going down the side of the first page, but that is a technique done to death, but if it will make you more comfortable, I can put it in.

Fourthly, the one note neither I or Ralph could read was the note you wrote on the page where Peter is confronted by Ben and May. We just can't read what you wrote. I thought it was a prescription from my doctor but I am told it is a story note from you... :)

If you want to e-mail me or call me to explain what the issue is here, feel free to.

And finally, the biggest problem is the coincidence of the robbery at the wrestling arena. I know you hate this and I know it is a storytelling leap, but it is a huge part of what makes up Spider-Man, and I wanted to show you what I have planned for it in the future before you give up on it.

First off, the Spider-Man letting the crook go will be the catalyst for Spidey not being understood in the media. The wrestling guys will accuse him publicly for the theft and it will follow him around and grow in the media. He will be an underdog. When we introduce the Bugle in the next storyline it will give Jonah the angle to harp on the negative Spidey stuff.

Also, and this is something I was really hoping to do, the unbelievable coincidence of the death of Ben will really pull at Peter. He will feel that the murder is a lesson all the more so because his callous act affected him so personally. And he will NEVER let it happen again.

After Peter starts working at the Bugle, he will start looking up stuff about this guy who killed Ben and will find out that he was part of the Kingpin's territory in the underground mob scene of New York - and that no one touches the Kingpin. Not the paper, not the cops. He is untouchable so Peter decides to fixate his new life as a superhero on screwing with Kingpin. We will then slide into one of the best Kingpin storylines which is the tablet story. Spidey will find what Kingpin wants and get in the way.

So my point is that the coincidence is so big that it haunts Peter's actions for many issues and easily motivates Peter into the next storyline. By the end of which Peter has grown by leaps and bounds into his new role as superhero. And he will be misunderstood in the press for it, as well. All of the Spidey things flowing logically into one another from the big well-planned origin story.

Is it very obvious that I have been giving this much thought? :)

I certainly hope that you see these rambling notes as friendly and thoughtful debate and not in any way me being a pain in the ass. It is my belief that you are hiring me to think, and this is what I think.

So let me know your decisions on the last bit and what the story note about Ben was and I will tidy up issue four. I think five is going to be a really popular one. I have some nice human moments planned.

Will you be at San Diego ?

....

[7/17/00 response from Bill J to Brian B and Ralph M]

Brian,

Hope you are enjoying the San Diego show. If you are going to Chicago, I would appreciate it if we could spend a couple of hours together.

Thanks for your understanding and cooperation about the hundred and one shifts that I keep throwing at you.

Here's what I think.

LANGUAGE: You are right, seeing it in balloons was a different feeling than seeing a script, and I agree that the back & forth among you and Ralph and me will be better for the process than you trying to censor yourself.

MULTIPLE BALLOONS: Please don't over-react to my comment on this, in the whole 48 page first book, there were only one or two points where the balloons got confusing, and they looked fixable with better spacing.

#4 OPENING SCENE: The concept is cool — public perception vs. reality. I'm just worried that we may not be able to execute it. You are right, the TV screens are done to death. If you are comfortable that it will work, as written, then I trust you.

MAY AND BEN:

Sorry for the illegible note. Here's the issue, and it applies to the scenes in books 2 and 4 where

Ben, May and Peter fight about grades and Flash.

I must have said the following lines about Uncle Ben and Aunt May a hundred times, but I don't really know if I ever said them to you. Uncle Ben gives Peter absolutely unconditional love. Ben and May don't want to live through Peter, the way a lot of parents want to live through their kids. Parents want their kids to be Little League superstars, be class president, become a doctor, write for Marvel Comics. Uncle Ben wants Peter to be happy. He doesn't really care about grades. Peter is the one who is driven about grades because he's on a mission to fill his missing father's missing shoes. Peter's dad was the studier, his brother Ben was off to Woodstock. I don't like the idea of Ben and May picking a fight with Peter over grades and sending him to his room all the time. He gets bad grades, OK. He got himself out of the basement, that's fine with Ben. He defended himself against Flash, that's OK with Ben. It's really Peter that blows off Ben for no good reason, not that Ben drives Peter away by over-hassling him.

Brian, I know I'm ranting, and that you have Ben and May nailed 90% of the time. They are very likeable people. This is just about the tone of the two confrontation scenes. Peter should be blowing them off, and Ben should be trying to pull him back.

THE BURGLAR:

Your point is well-taken about the importance of the tragedy, but I do think that the more credible the story, the more significant the tragedy. If Peter fails to stop another old man in his own neighborhood from getting mugged, we would go from entirely unbelievable to completely believable.

By the way, the scene where the wrestlers going after Spidey is priceless. Suppose they fight about something else, Spider-Man hurts Crusher in the ring or one of the ring girls makes a move on the kid, and her boyfriend gets mad.

So let's talk.

....

AND NOW, FOR YOUR READING PLEASURE — HERE ARE THE ORIGINAL CHARACTER PROFILES AND THE FIRST PLOT. YOU HAVE JUST READ THE GREAT JOB THAT BRIAN DID ON THE SCRIPT. I HOPE YOU ALL AGREE THAT HE ALSO HAD THE PERFECT SENSE OF WHAT TO LEAVE IN AND WHAT TO LEAVE OUT.

BEST,
BILL J

MARK BAGLEY
SKETCHBOOK

SPIDER-MAN

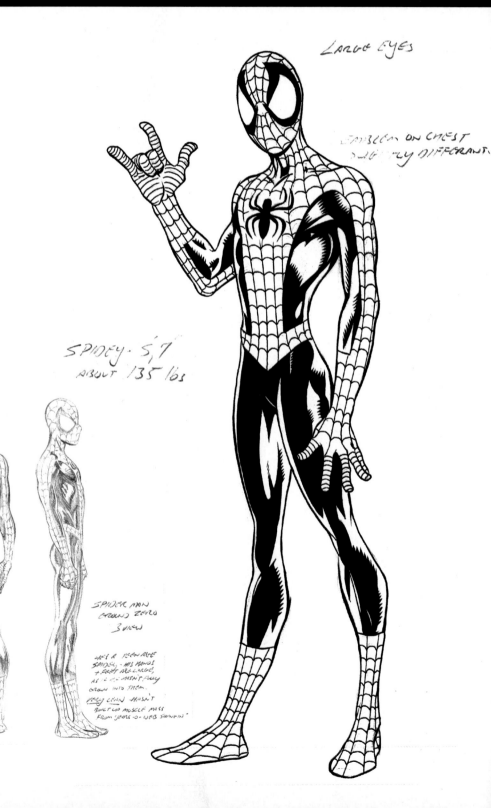

LARGE EYES

EMBLEM ON CHEST SLIGHTLY DIFFERENT

SPIDEY · 5'7
ABOUT 135 lbs

SPIDER MAN
GROUND ZERO
3 VIEW

HE'S A TEENAGE
SANDEE - HIS HANDS
+ FEET ARE LARGE,
AS HE HASN'T FULLY
GROWN INTO THEM.

HE'S LEAN - HASN'T
BUILT UP MUSCLE MASS
FROM YEARS-O-WEB SWINGIN'

HERE'S A REAL PEEK BEHIND THE CURTAIN AS WE PRESENT BILL JEMAS' INITIAL CHARACTER DESCRIPTIONS FOR ALL THE MAJOR FIGURES POPULATING *ULTIMATE SPIDER-MAN*. PLUS, JEMAS' FIRST PASS AT THE ACTUAL PLOTS THAT FORMED THE STORY FRAMEWORK FOR OUR FIRST SEVEN ISSUES. IT'S A FASCINATING FORAY INTO WHAT MIGHT HAVE BEEN, WITH ACCOMPANYING ILLUSTRATIONS BY PENCILLER MARK BAGLEY.

PETER PARKER -
5FT-9IN.
140 lbs
CUTE
ACCORDING TO MY
DAUGHTER

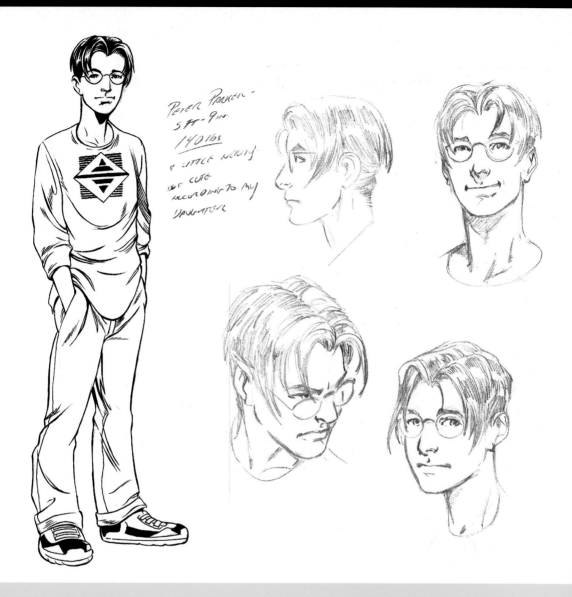

Peter Parker

An outcast: Peter is a bookish, nerdy high school freshman, and the kind of earnest, solemn kid who makes a conspicuous victim for high school bullies. Peter doesn't crave "popularity," but he would like to have a few friends. Unfortunately, this is high school and Peter is no good at sports, has no spending money and is painfully shy around girls.

Peter lost his parents in a plane crash and struggles to reconcile himself with the loss. His father had been a scientist and Peter has kept much of his scientific equipment. He spends hours in the lab every day trying to give life to his father's work. While this studiousness makes him one of the top students in the entire school, it only serves to isolate him more.

Violence: Like every wimp, Peter fantasizes about being stronger to defend himself and pay back those who've picked on him. And, as his spider powers develop, Peter does enjoy being a tough guy and even elicits a positive response from some of the people who have been tormenting him over the years. Still, even when Peter is most full of himself, there is always that good, sad kid underneath the bold new exterior. Even when he is the most "out of control" he will never become truly violent. Moreover, as his powers grow, Spider-Man finds that there will always be a more powerful foe, and he learns that sheer physical force is seldom the right approach to any problem.

Mary Jane Watson —
she's a hottie!
still red haired —
sort a in aguilera do

Mary Jane

Mary Jane and Peter: They were close friends through grammar school, but started running in separate circles in junior high. Then, Peter withdrew from everyone when his parents died, and months later, slowly, painfully re-emerged. Now, they connect on almost every level. They always start toward each other with the best of intentions; but often stumble along the way.

Independence: She is drop-dead gorgeous but she does a good job of hiding it under nondescript clothing, pulled back hair, and no makeup Even with her best efforts to hide her beauty, she could have her pick of young men if she didn't give off a very clear signal to stay away. There's a lot of darkness in her past, including an abusive [alcoholic, workaholic, violent?] father, and she has no interest in boys other than as casual acquaintances. She is friendly and well liked, but she doesn't belong to any one group. Rather, she walks a line between the popular kids and the nerds, the brains and the jocks. Mary Jane may not be dying to get close to people, but she is graceful in just about any social situation. She's great at small talk before class and in the lunchroom and attends a lot of school functions. But her afternoons are spent doing homework, working on social projects (she has a strong desire to make the world a better place, which is common with kids in her situation) and she rarely goes out on the weekends. Mary Jane will begin to come out of her shell and project herself into the world more. She will come to realize how much she cares for Peter before he realizes how much he cares for her.

Harry Osborn

Harry and Peter: The only other person Peter can call a "friend" is Harry Osborn. Osborn's father is one of the richest men in New York and he is constantly on top of his son to excel. Harry doesn't handle the pressure very well and uses Peter because Peter can help him with his schoolwork and keep his grades up. Harry is a smooth talker and he's wealthy. Many want to be friends with him for all of those shallow reasons why teenagers want certain kinds of friends. Peter knows that he's being used by Harry, but figures any kind of friend is better than no friend at all.

Poor little rich kid: Underneath, Harry is a decent kid, but he stands absolutely no chance. His father can't stop telling him how much of a disappointment he is, so Harry therefore can't stop trying to do everything he can to please his father. He's gotten everything he's wanted (except love) from his parents from the day he was born, so he has no sense of values. And he's just plain not very smart.

Aunt May—
cross B-tween
Gena Rowland +
Corkie Roberts

Uncle Ben?
looks a lil' like
Tom Palmer
Maybe too handsome!

Uncle Ben & Aunt May

Open arms: They are actually Peter's great-uncle and great-aunt. Peter's parents' siblings and grandparents are all either dead or unavailable to Peter for some other reason. But Uncle Ben and Aunt May would have welcomed Peter with open arms under any circumstances. They never had children of their own and spent a lot of time with Peter well before his parents died. After the plane crash, they took Peter in immediately and helped him through the grieving process. They know that Peter lost a piece of his soul the day that plane went down, but they have never once withheld love from him. They have always felt that the boy needed a safe harbor, a place where he knew he would be loved unconditionally and they never expected the same love in return.

They were at Woodstock: In a lot of ways, Uncle Ben and Aunt May are cooler than Peter– even though outward appearances make them seem like Fred Mertz from I Love Lucy and Granny from the Beverly Hillbillies. Though they are in their sixties, they have felt it was essential to raise Peter with as much knowledge of the popular culture, contemporary thought and current mores as possible. They have limited financial means, but they are extremely well read and there's a certain young-at-heart attitude to them that makes them very appealing to the few of Peter's contemporaries who have gotten to know them. This is especially true of Uncle Ben who sees it as his role to be Peter's rock. He goes to great lengths to support Peter's interests and celebrate his scholastic successes. He doesn't put any pressure on him to become more popular even though he knows the kid needs to socialize more.

Ironically, Uncle Ben and Aunt May are part of Peter's social problem. They look so old and out of it and appearances mean everything to kids. So not only is Peter a loser, but he's a loser who lives with these elderly people. It just adds to Peter's overall image of total sad sack.

FLASH THOMPSON

Flash Thompson

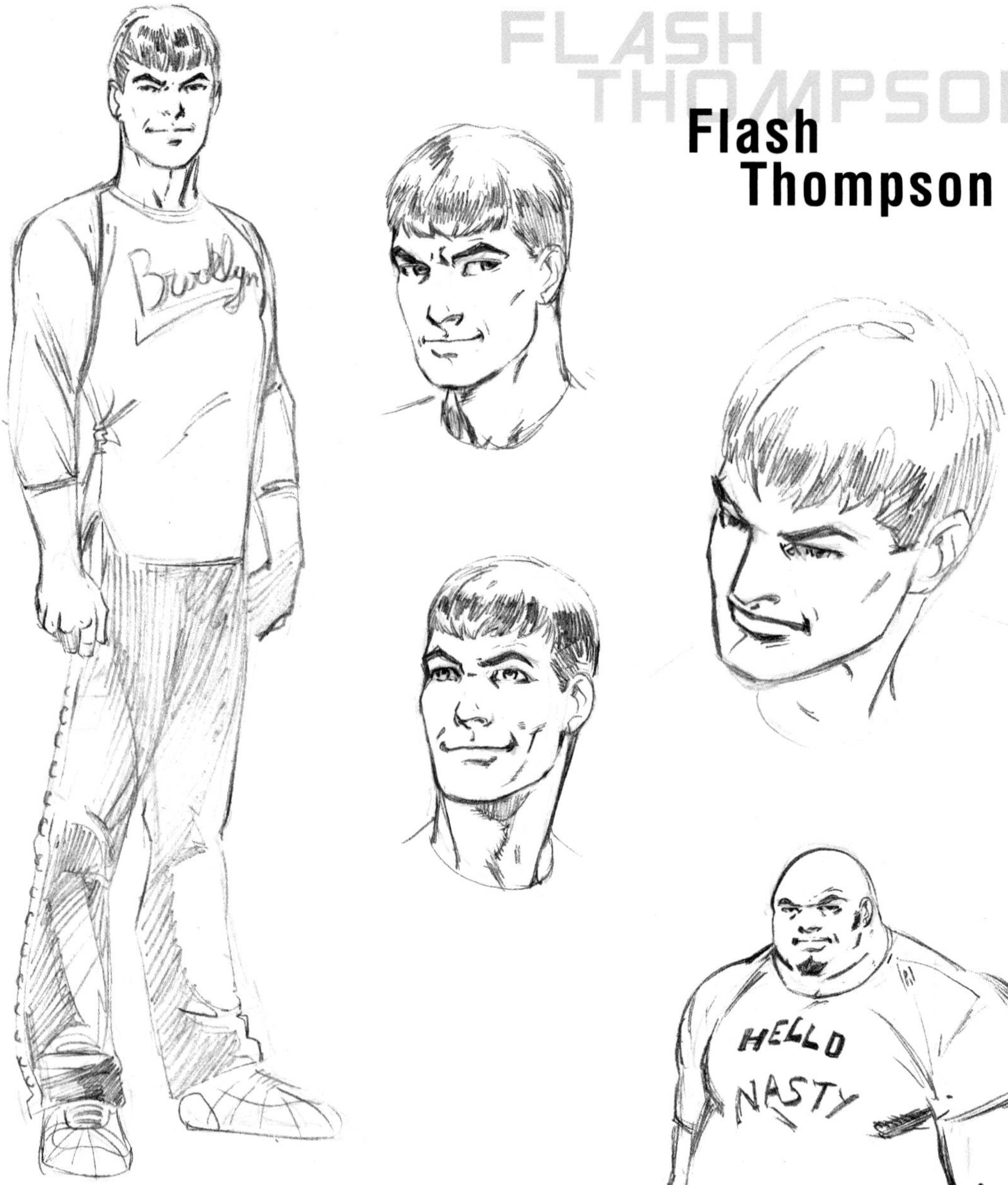

KING KONG

King Kong

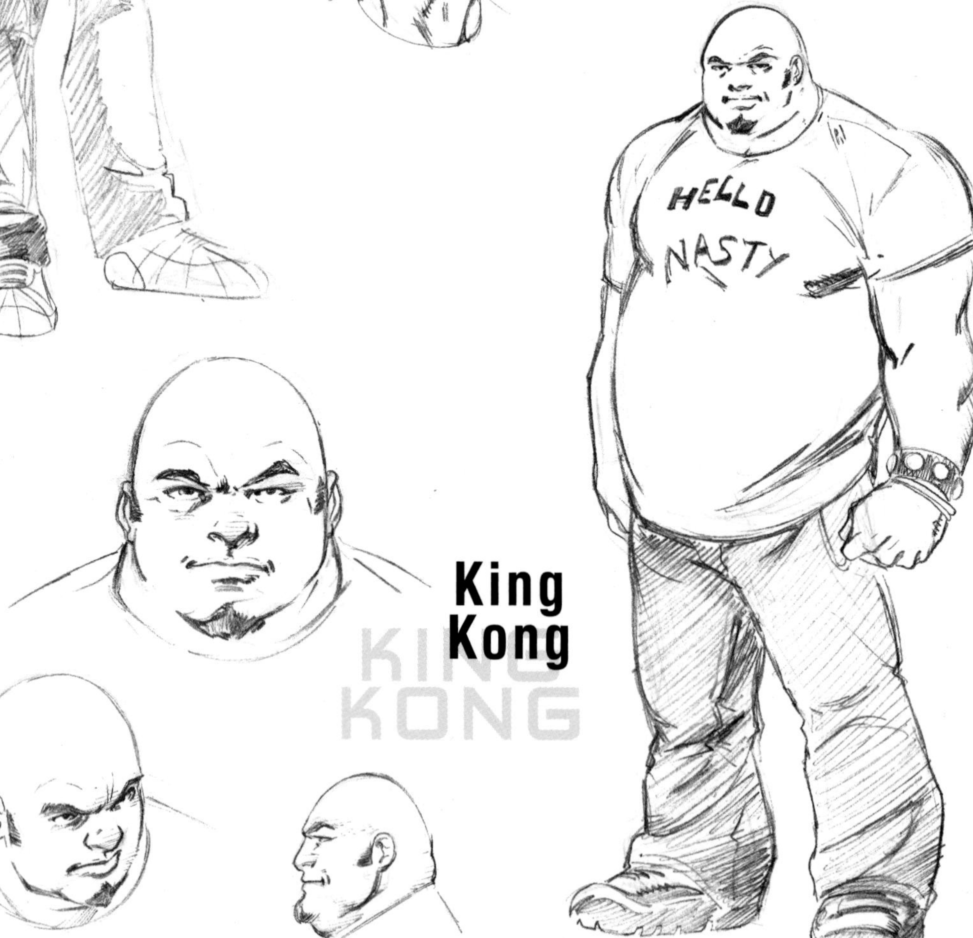
HELLO
NASTY

NORMAN OSBORN

Norman Osborn

GREEN GOBLIN

Green Goblin

THE ORIGINAL ULTIMATE SPIDER-MAN PLOT OUTLINE BY BILL JEMAS...

FIRST ISSUE — POWERLESS

Norman Osborn's Spider

Norman Osborn concentrates on a massive computer monitor in the midst of his fantastic laboratory. He runs through a series of computer images showing him the changes that a new chemical "00" has wrought on a number of different animals and insects. Nothing much to learn from the fly, but a ladybug showed some interesting changes, so he takes a spider from a tank, marks a minute "00" on its back and doses it with the drug. He continues to review scans of a rat and the rabbit and the (gasp!) dog, then turns and realizes that Spider 00 is gone.

Peter, MJ & Uncle Ben

"Look at Parker having lunch with all his friends," says a nearby teen loud enough for Peter to hear. Peter Parker is, of course, eating alone. Uncle Ben had dropped Peter off at Taco Bell where he was supposed to meet Harry Osborn. After lunch, Harry and Peter would catch a movie; then Harry would drive Peter home so they could do their homework together. Harry never showed up.

Mary Jane is at a nearby table crowded in with the "in-crowd" kids.

He wants to join her, but is way too shy. Peter is also hurt, that his friend Mary Jane hasn't invited him. She was his childhood friend and still lives next door, but now she thinks she's too cool for him.

She wants him to join her, and has been trying to save a little room at the table, but Mary thinks that he thinks he's too smart and important to sit around with her and her friends.

Uncle Ben had been shopping next door, and as he's returning to his car to drive home, he sees Peter through the window. The old man decides to join his nephew for lunch. Peter is at once relieved to have the company and embarrassed that he is sitting in the middle of teen land with his sixty-year old relative. Ben understands; he invites Mary Jane to join them at the table. With the ice broken, the kids have a great conversation.

High School Hell

In the morning, Harry Osborn (wearing a soccer jersey) comes to Peter's locker with a lame excuse. He invites himself to Peter's house tonight for homework help. Peter agrees, but asks Harry to tell his soccer teammates to leave him alone. Harry tells Peter to lighten up, and splits.

As Peter walks down the hall in a crowd, he gets a kick in the butt, but couldn't see who did it. The school soccer team is pretty mediocre but the best athletic group in the school. The captain has a great idea, a contest to see who can kick Parker the most times without his being spotted—if you get caught your point total goes back to zero.

The school principal looms over Peter as he picks up his books. Peter tells him that the soccer team is harassing him. The principal tells Peter not to make trouble.

At lunch, Peter is alone again, Harry eats with the soccer team and MJ is at an all-girls table. A huge, tough kid called Kingpin looms over Peter's seat, Peter quietly reaches into his pocket and hands over $5.00.

Gym is loads of fun for top science students—not. Peter is doing his best to hide on the basketball court, but when the ball comes this way, the opposing team yanks it from him. The gym teacher (also the school basketball coach) hurls insults. "Parker you crapper, your muscles are like wet dishrags." In the locker room, Peter returns from the shower, wearing only a towel, to find his locker busted open and empty. His clothes are piled next to a nearby door. As he scoops them up, a bunch of guys pushes him through the door and into the girls' locker room.

Aunt May & Uncle Ben

In the kitchen after dinner, Aunt May reads aloud from a ladies' magazine about "Social Anxiety Disorder." She is sure that Peter has it. Uncle Ben says that Peter is just a nice smart kid and all nice smart kids have a tough time in high school. Aunt May goes on-line (from her laptop) for more "SAD" information.

Harry arrives with Italian pastries (Aunt May's favorite), and his science homework. As the kids do homework, May chirps in with interesting (and embarrassing) tidbits from the SAD Parent's chat room.

When the work's finished, Peter invites Harry to his basement lab, and starts in on a boring explanation of his work. Harry prefers to hang out and eat with May and Ben. He stays and Peter goes.

Peter's Computer Lab

Work in this old-fashioned lab is a nightly ritual for Peter. When his parents were killed in a plane crash, his father was on the verge of a breakthrough in the cure for cancer. He has the notes that his father kept at home, many of which are still too complex for a boy of 15 (albeit a brilliant one) to understand.

Regardless, Peter has been banging away at the project for the last five years, ever since he found the notebooks while nostalgically unpacking his father's lab equipment in Aunt May and Uncle Ben's house. They let him cordon off half of the basement to use as a lab because they thought it would be good therapy for the boy. They didn't expect it to become an obsession.

Peter doesn't have money to buy new lab equipment, but he does have his father's old computer, which he constantly upgrades. He doesn't mix chemicals, what he does is 3-D molecular modeling on his computer, and he uses the Internet to reach out around the world to adult scientists.

Norman's Lab and Family

Harry returns to his home, where we meet Norman Osborn. He is an unbelievably wealthy high-tech industrialist. Norman is also in his lab—a massive nuclear research facility attached to his massive mansion. He buys and sells companies and people every day, but at night, he secretly dabbles with questionable experiments. As Peter labors in his tiny lab seeking something to aid humanity, Norman spends his resources on purely commercial ventures.

As Norman tries to concentrate on his work, his wife yaps away about things he should be doing around the house (mansion). Norman's assistant takes notes and promises to get everything done. Both parents do their best to ignore Harry. Harry reminds Norman that his science class is visiting this lab tomorrow and begs Norman to make an appearance. Norman will not play tour guide at the lab for a bunch of brats, but his assistant will take care of this as well.

Field trip to Osborn Industries

The radiation equipment is awesome. Harry sticks close to Peter throughout the tour, quietly asking him questions, and loudly repeating the answers to the class.

We get a secret peek at Spider 00 in the nuclear lab. It had built its nest next to the plutonium beam, it now hops on the tour guide's lab coat and takes a ride back to the insect (and arachnid) lab. These bugs have been treated with new wonder drugs. The scientist running the demon-

stration asks for a volunteer. Peter sticks his hand up immediately. Spider 00 is now outside the spider tank trying to get in. It chomps Peter's hand; he faints, and the spider gets crushed in the shuffle. No one ever finds out that the creature had been exposed to a massive dose of radiation, not just the wonder drugs.

Peter comes-to right away. The soccer guys think this is hilarious, and Harry can't bring himself to come to Peter's aid. But, Mary Jane is there and doesn't care what anyone thinks. Peter is her friend, and he needs help. She pushes through the crowd, puts her arm around him, and spends the rest of the afternoon by his side. Peter Parker is a little queasy, but he's in heaven.

They sit together on the bus ride back to school. She slips off her shoes and cuddles up next to him. But, he starts feeling very dizzy, then really nauseous and as he's trying to stand up, he throws up right into her Nikes.

Osborn's Private Detective

Flash over to Norman being debriefed about the accident, with Harry nearby. Norman's first reaction is to wonder about the legal implications. Will this Parker kid sue? Geez, everything his son touches turns into a disaster. Norman tells Harry to get lost, asks his lawyer to build up a case protecting him, and has his private investigator keep a close watch on Peter Parker to see if he's showing any signs of impairment. Norman does not want any negative publicity; he is experimenting with a new mood-altering drug that could change his—and our—world forever.

Bad Morning at School

The next day, Peter is even more of a laughingstock than usual with kids pretending to vomit as they pass him in the halls. Mary Jane is taking a fair share of abuse herself. The other kids on the bus thought it was pitiful that she went to the geek's aid and hilarious when he paid her back by blowing chunks into her sneakers. She quickly gets the nickname "spew shoes."

Rushed to the Emergency Room

Peter passes out during gym class, the basketball coach tells him to walk it off, but it is MJ who gets the girls' gym teacher to take Peter to the nurse. Peter is taken to the hospital, tailed by Norman's PI, who nabs his blood sample.

Aunt May's Diagnosis

Peter has environmental allergies explains Aunt May reading from a massive homeopathic health manual. She will bake banana bread—bananas are full of potassium and that counteracts allergies. Ben thinks Peter needs some rest and relaxation and plans a trip to the mountains.

Norman's Prognosis

Norman reads Peter's blood analysis from his computer monitor—it's a train wreck. This kid's so sick he's going to die, and his blood is loaded with the basic active ingredient in Oz. The sickness could surely be traced back to Osborn industries. Norman orders the PI see to it that Peter has "an accident." To Norman, it's not murder because the kid is going to die anyway.

Spider sense is tingling

The PI, parked in a stolen van, waits for Peter on his daily walk home from school. Norman watches from his Lexus; he will anonymously call the right ambulance company to collect the body.

Peter senses danger and turns to see a van jumping the curb tear right at him. Peter springs 6 feet up and 8 feet back and clings to the side of the brick building.

On walkie-talkie, the PI asks Norman if he should go back and kill Peter now. Norman says no and thinks, "This kid was bitten by my spider, now he can stick like a spider. He may have to die, but I want to dissect him first."

ISSUE TWO — PETER PUSHED ASIDE

Sticky & Twitchy

Ben, May and Peter are finishing their dinner. May had noticed that Peter has developed twitches and ticks. (She doesn't know that this is from rapid muscle growth due to the spider venom). She thinks it may be Tourette's Syndrome, except that Peter's speech hasn't been affected.

Peter is leaning against the wall listening to his aunt, when the doorbell rings. As he moves to answer it, he finds a chunk of wallpaper and plaster clinging to his hand.

It's Harry. Over hot chocolate, Harry suggests that Peter go to his Osborn Industries internist, and says that his father will be happy to pick up the bill. He quietly hands Peter his homework assignment and tells him to just do it and give it back before class tomorrow.

Harry & Norman

Back home, Harry reports that Peter will indeed see Doctor Octavius. Norman is pleased, but Harry's mom butts in about how they are wasting their family money on charity cases.

Mary Jane — friend in need

Mary Jane opens her locker and finds an old sneaker filled with pea soup. She turns around to see the soccer captain laughing. He had asked her out, she had refused, and he's been leaving the shoes all around school. Fortunately, she doesn't blame Peter for any of this. In fact, she spots him at lunch, twitching and sticking all alone at his table, and joins him. He spills his milk, drops his food and bites his own fingers. She tells him about a party on Saturday, but Peter, May and Ben will be going up to the mountains for the weekend.

Peter at the Doctor

Doctor Octavius drains two pints of Peter's blood and runs him through a long, sometimes painful, set of tests.

Peter rambles his theory: the spider bite is giving him the proportional strength and speed of a spider, along with extrasensory powers and sticky hands and feet.

While Peter pays a claustrophobic visit to the inside of the CAT scan machine, Doc Ock tells May that Peter's ramblings are probably caused by arachnophobia. Animal phobias are commonplace after an animal attacks…

Norman Osborn, Doc Ock, & Oz the Wonder Drug

We learn that Norman and Doctor Octavius (Doc Ock) have been working on a new, powerful, feel-good drug called Oz. It's a pain killer, but it doesn't make you numb, it makes you feel great. They had been experimenting with insects when Peter got his bite and have moved up to mammals.

Norman has a brilliant scheme; he will not wait out years of safety testing to get FDA approval. He will simply mix Oz into the sugar coating on all of Osborn Industries' versions of aspirin, Tylenol, and Motrin. People would become addicted without even knowing it. That doesn't make him a bad person, this is no worse than what the soft-drink companies do by adding caffeine to soda pop. "Hey, am I genius or what?" asks Norman. "Forget aspirin, it's small time; I'll drop the drug into every Osborn Industries' product from baby food to bran flakes. I will rule the marketplace, and perhaps, one day, the world."

Norman and Doc Ock review Peter's tests, and they are baffled and amazed by the results. The kid's blood has definitely been poisoned, and he should be dying (like some of the unfortunate volunteers), but he is growing incredibly. From Norman's desk, Doc Ock calls Aunt May.

Aunt May & ADD, Uncle Ben & Mountain Air

In a mountain cabin, Aunt May receives a call from Doctor Octavius who tells him that Peter is perfectly fine physically. No allergies, no Tourette's, perfectly normal in every respect. It would be a waste of her money to see any more doctors.

Aunt May reports that there is nothing wrong with Peter's body. She can't believe she had not thought of it sooner—he must have ADD. He keeps dropping things because he can't pay attention. She gets right on the phone to track down the school psychologist to schedule an appointment for next week.

Through all of the bizarre stuff, Uncle Ben stands steadfastly by his nephew's side. As far as he's concerned, this boy needs open mountain air, not a head shrink. Peter and Ben hit the trails, with Ben on a mountain bike and Peter bounding over the countryside.

The Psychologist and the Principal

The next week, May and Peter have their meeting with the school psychologist. The principal shows up at the session; he already "knows all about Parker." With the vomiting and the twitching and the tripping all over himself, (not to mention fighting with the soccer team) Peter is a major disruption. He tells May and the shrink that the boy needs serious help and pulls the school's brightest student out of his AP classes and plops him into the Special Ed room.

The Honor Student Gets Suspended

Peter had always accepted his suffering, but lately he's been getting less afraid and more angry. In a crowded hallway, he senses that he's about to be kicked and reaches back to grab the foot of the soccer captain. In seconds, a ring forms around the two boys. They yell, "Fight! Fight! Fight!" Peter doesn't know how to fight, but he's strong as a bull—err, spider—and pushes the athlete away hard enough to send him flying into the lockers.

The good news is that Peter's daily tormenting at the hands of the "bad" guys comes to an abrupt end. The bad news is that the soccer team's captain has a concussion and separated shoulder.

The Principal is outraged at the damage to the team. He knew all along that Parker was a problem and suspends him on the spot— a 30-day ban from school. He won't even let Peter collect his father's notebooks out of his locker.

In the Suburbs, Soccer Team Payback

For an honor student, getting kicked out of school should be horrible, but for the new Parker, getting booted from school turns out to be cool. It gives him both an excuse to skip his responsibilities and some time to explore his new body and start a new life. He hasn't been chastened by the experience with the authorities but rather emboldened by it. It feels good to fight back.

He can't help himself; Peter knows that the soccer team hangs at the Burger King next to the school. Peter heads over for a Whopper and some payback. Peter lets four soccer players make the first move before he stuffs them in a dumpster behind the building.

Uncle Ben & the Lawyers

When Peter returns home, without a scratch on him, he finds Uncle Ben signing an agreement and handing over a check to a lawyer. Uncle Ben had to pay a hefty settlement to keep Peter out of court. Peter knows where he can get a few hundred dollars for his uncle.

In the City, Kingpin Pays Back with Interest

Peter heads downtown to find the Kingpin. He estimates that the guy has taken $5 a week off of him in the past two years, and he wants it back— with interest.

Peter smacks down a couple of Kingpin's friends. A third pulls a knife, which Peter slaps out of his hand. To Peter's surprise, the Kingpin gets very friendly and hands over a wad of cash. He heard a rumor about Peter taking on the soccer team and now knows it's all true.

Kingpin asks Peter to hang around with him and his friends. Peter declines, but the Kingpin says the door is always open.

Oz & Teenagers

Thanks to Peter's blood work, Norman made an exciting discovery; the drug seems to have a killer side effect. On test subjects in puberty, Oz doesn't just make them feel good, it makes them stronger. To test Oz, Norman mixes it with the Osborn Industries' version of Gatorade and gives the crap to Harry and the other kids on the soccer team to make them play better.

ISSUE THREE — WITH GREAT POWER COMES GOOD TIMES

Oz Works on the Soccer Team

Under the influence of their Oz-laced Gatorade,

the soccer team finishes the season with a string of victories.

Norman Osborn

Norman sees opportunities well beyond big sales of the Oz product; he could build his own private army of super-soldiers with powers like Peter Parker. Pure Oz had good results on the soccer team, but now Norman has found that the drug works best when mixed with venom from spiders, snakes, and lizards—as opposed to being directly ingested. He begins to test teen volunteers on every possible kind of venom/drug mix. (But he is never able to duplicate the exact "Radioactive Spider" effect because he never learns that Spider 00 had been exposed directly to radiation and had mutated before it bit Peter.)

Professional Wrestling

Peter wants cash to help Uncle Ben out of financial trouble. He also likes his new lifestyle, and some spending money would come in handy. Peter hits upon professional wrestling as a way to make some easy cash. He makes the Spidey costume so that the promoters will not know who he is (and that he's only 15). The secret identity will also allow him to keep all the cash he doesn't give to his family.

Peter shows up at the WCW building in costume and is stopped by a security guard before he gets to the elevator. No problem; Peter climbs up 12 stories and in through the president's window.

This skinny little mystery kid in the cool red outfit hops into the ring and wails on those huge pro-wrestlers. Not surprisingly, Spider-Man becomes a WCW overnight sensation. Uncle Ben finds an envelope full of cash in his mailbox one day, and Peter walks around school with his pockets full.

A Great Basketball Player

But making Spidey a star is not enough for Peter. He realizes he can crank his new cool image up to 11 if he does for Peter Parker what he's already done for Spidey. Peter joins his high school basketball team. With the strength, speed and senses of a spider, (and an unbelievable ability to palm the ball), this kid can play like a pro. And, no surprise, Peter develops an NBA ballplayer attitude. He trash talks, abuses fans and skips practice. The coach wants to ride up the college ranks right on Peter's shoulders, so he takes whatever this teenage Alan Iverson hands out.

Mary Jane & the Big Man on Campus

Peter and Mary Jane are growing apart. He is the big man on campus, but she's never been impressed by that kind of thing. MJ wants to treat him the same way she always has, and to talk with him about the same important issues that that they always shared. For Peter that was great when the rest of the world thought he was a dweeb, but that's all just too dull for the new Peter Parker. He doesn't completely blow her off, but the fact is, he just doesn't have the same amount of time to spend with her as he once did.

Harry Osborn gets dumped

Peter comes home one night to find Harry at the kitchen table with Aunt May, Uncle Ben, another box of pastries and a pile of homework. Peter mashes a canolli into Harry's face and sends him packing. Peter wanted this spoiled leech out of his life once and for all. Aunt May is upset that Peter would do such a thing to such a sweet boy. Peter storms out of the kitchen and up to his room.

Uncle Ben understands about Harry, but wants to calm things down in the house. He also has some words of advice for Peter about walking away from fights and keeping sports in perspective. But Peter pushes back with adolescent resistance and resentment. He doesn't want friendly advice and heart-to-heart talks. He wants to be slapped on the back as hard at home as he is in the school halls. Peter's relationship with Uncle Ben deteriorates to the point where they have a huge fight. Hurling insults and abuse at his once beloved uncle, Peter stomps by Aunt May and out of the house.

Living Large

Quick flashes:

Spider-Man as a huge WCW attraction; he wrestles regularly, traveling in style around New York and New Jersey.

Peter surrounded by the "in-crowd" at lunch.

Peter coming late for basketball practice—greeted by a smiling coach and resentful teammates.

Peter Parker scoring big in a big game.

Norman and Harry United

Norman Osborn has a problem, none of the other test subjects, even the soccer team, can match Peter Parker. What did Peter do at the lab, or what else about him makes the drug work so well on him? Norman approaches Parker after a basketball game, and the kid won't give him the time of day. No one does that to Norman Osborn without consequences.

Norman finally confides all in Harry and enlists his aid in a single cause—hatred of Peter Parker.

ISSUE FOUR — THE WORDS LEFT UNSAID

Spoiled Superstar

Peter finally has a cool life for a teenager. Peter is in all his glory during games. He is fast as lightning, a great ball handler, a huge leaper and can sense every move the other players will make. He plays point guard but never gives up the rock. The coach says Peter should get the other players more involved in the game, so the team can be really great, but Peter ignores him. The team hasn't lost yet, and Peter doesn't really care. For him the games are pure fun—trash talking, fan baiting, point scoring.

Still, after one practice, when a generous St. John's University booster approaches Peter with a briefcase full of cash, he turns it down; somewhere deep inside, he remains Peter Parker.

Peter barely shows up at school, but as long as he makes it on game days, the principal and the coach are happy. They both love him because of the notoriety the basketball program is bringing to them.

Kidnap

Norman's project isn't working so well. The kids develop a serious dependency on Oz and need massive doses. They are also beginning to look creepy.

Norman hires a professional kidnapper named the Sandman to bring Peter to him—by any means.

Peter Moves Out

One night, Peter comes home at 3:00 AM and finds Uncle Ben waiting up for him, with his report card. Ben has never pushed Peter to study, but this kid who never got below a B+ in his life, is now failing four classes. Something is wrong, and Ben wants to talk it through. Peter wants no part of that. They have the second fight in two weeks (and only the second one in their lives). This time Peter doesn't just storm out of the house, he goes up to his room, packs a duffle bag, and heads over to his coach's house.

The Sandman had planned on snatching the powerful youngster in his sleep. Peter's bedroom was on the first floor. The thug wanted to slip in, chloroform the kid, drop him out the window, and carry him into the car. Now, he'd have to do it the hard way. He accosts Peter at knifepoint in a dark alley. Peter easily avoids the knife and flings his duffle bag at the guy. Sandman runs off in defeat.

Peter is a mess by the time he arrives at the coach's house at 5:00 AM, but that's no problem for this coach. With Peter as his ward, the coach will have real credibility when he tells the colleges: hire me and I'll deliver Parker.

Three Missions

Mary Jane: Peter still loves science and still cares for MJ, so he does come to chemistry lab where MJ is his partner. MJ has a turning point where she decides to make a real move for Peter; she gets up the nerve to ask him out. She thinks about Peter's transformation, and while she can't say she's pleased with what he is becoming, she can't argue with the results. She thinks maybe it's time for a change of her own. Perhaps a new haircut, a little bit of rouge, clothes that fit her body a little more closely. She's definitely not ready for the Britney Spears look, and she isn't even sure what it is that she's trying to accomplish, but perhaps it's time to show the world that she can loosen up, too. She spends the day on her new look — and she becomes flat-out beautiful.

Uncle Ben is getting ready to pay his own visit to Peter. Ben and May are at their wits' end. Basically, this 15-year-old boy ran away from home, and he must come back. But they know Peter may not come willingly. They called the coach and the principal, but they want Peter to stay were he is, even if it takes a formal custody proceeding. Should Ben call the police or social services? No, Ben must find his nephew and pull him back by the heartstrings.

Harry Osborn promises Norman that he can lure Peter back to the lab so they can do some real work on him.

So, MJ and Ben and Harry are all are on their way.

MJ will show up first, and that's too bad. Peter Parker had been getting ready for MJ at the coach's apartment. The coach lets the team and cheerleaders party there on the weekends. Nowadays, the boy cleans up real good. He looks so nice to one of the cheerleaders that she makes a move for him. She gives him his first beer, and by the time he's on his second, she's pretty much all over him as MJ walks in the door. MJ splits, despite Peter's protests. Just as Peter decides to go after her, Uncle Ben shows up.

Uncle Ben finds Peter with the empty beer can in his hand. Ben takes the boy aside to ask him to come home. Ben offers to let Peter come and go as he pleases, and to stay out of the way. He just wants him in a better environment. Peter (pumped up by alcohol and freaked by MJ leaving) tells his uncle that he never wants to see him again. Uncle Ben continues to plead with him, saying that he only wants what's right for the boy. Peter gets up into Uncle Ben's face and says to him, "You are not my father. I don't want anything more to do with you." Uncle Ben walks out of the house crestfallen, and Peter immediately regrets getting so rough with the old man. He'll make it up to him some day.

Here's Harry; he's got it figured out. He connects with Parker at the one level he can: wheels. Peter's not old enough to drive yet, and Harry volunteers to drive him and the cheerleader all over town in his new Porsche.

Madison Square Garden

Peter wins a huge wrestling match at Madison Square Garden. But the fake battle did not go according to the script; Spider-Man slams his opponent to the ground—way too hard. The man lies there with three broken ribs and a punctured lung. The crowd thinks this is all part of the show, and they go wild as the paramedics remove the stricken man. Peter is concerned until the promoter slaps him on the back and hands him his biggest purse ever.

On the way out of the Garden, he sees a thief snatch a woman's purse and knock her to the ground. The thief runs right by the kid with the super strength, speed and agility. But the kid doesn't lift a finger. Peter Parker is on top of the world, and he doesn't care about anyone else.

Spider-Sense

Harry talks Peter into coming to his house for a party. Harry is driving, and Peter has no idea that this is a trap.

Suddenly, Peter senses something is wrong. He tells Harry to drive him home, and as they turn the corner onto Aunt May and Uncle Ben's block, they see the house surrounded by police cars. Peter leaves Harry and runs out of the car and into the house. There, he sees his frail aunt in tears. A burglar has killed Uncle Ben. One officer had been alerted to sounds of a struggle by a neighbor and nearly stopped the crime in progress. The cop got a good look at the thief, but couldn't apprehend him. He tries to explain everything to the boy, but Peter can't really listen. He can think of nothing but his last cruel words to his uncle. All those years of kindness and caring had been thrown away in a few months of stupidity. Peter Parker will forever be haunted by the things he never had a chance to say to Uncle Ben.

In his panic, and then in his torment, he doesn't notice immediately that Mary Jane is in the room with the cops and Aunt May. He sees her and falls into her arms, sobbing an apology before bursting into tears.

ISSUE FIVE — WITH GREAT POWER COMES GREAT RESPONSIBILITY

You can go home

Peter Parker moves back in with Aunt May. He can hear his uncle's last words to him, asking him

to come home and begging him to clean up his life. Peter will attend every class and re-dedicate himself to his studies.

Peter knows that Mary Jane is his best friend—perhaps the only real friend—he's ever had. He wants her by his side whenever possible. They go out for long walks, they go to school functions together, and they talk on the phone late at night.

He starts carrying a simple gold chain—the first gift from his father to his mother. He just needs to get the nerve to give it to her.

She enjoys their "good friends" relationship, but would like to make it more serious.

Giving up Wrestling

Daily Bugle headline: Spider-Man—Mysterious Menace. Peter reads the article. The Bugle discovered that Spider-Man has seriously injured an opponent in his last match and finds that the WCW has been giving him illegal cash payments without withholding taxes or even knowing his identity. It urges the police to track down this dangerous villain.

Peter had thought about giving up wrestling after hurting that guy, and this clinched it. But he and Aunt May still need money.

He turns to the classifieds and circles an ad in which Bugle.com is looking for a Webmaster.

Norman hires Kingpin, Harry Mainlines

Norman Osborn is getting nowhere using his son to deliver Peter Parker. Parker continuously rebukes Harry's offers of visits to his father's lab and his son has basically turned into the punk's chauffeur.

In the meantime, Norman continues testing various dosages and venoms out on the teenagers he's captured, and he is getting results, if not necessarily the ones he was looking for. All of the teens show increased muscular strength and several are beginning to show the development of some of Peter Parker's powers. And all of them have gotten a lot meaner—thank goodness for that tranquilizer gun. He's going to have to find lots of teenage "volunteers."

Norman returns to his lab to find Harry with a syringe. Harry has been injecting himself with a mixture of Oz and plant toxins. His first theory was that plant venoms might be more stable than animal venoms. His second theory was that this would please his father. Norman finally gets it. Years of pushing have pushed Harry over the edge. His son's life is in danger; these drugs are too dangerous. They need to learn how to stabilize the chemical reaction, and the secret lies inside Peter Parker's body.

Daily Bugle & Crime Fighting

Peter takes a night job at the Daily Bugle for two reasons. First, his uncle's insurance money isn't going to pay all the bills, and Aunt May can't bring in any money herself in her condition. But equally importantly, the job allows him to monitor the police radio. Disguised as Spider-Man, he crashes in on every crime in progress in his quest to find his uncle's murderer. He also hits on a pretty good scheme to make extra money. He brings along his camera to take shots of the police action so that he can sell them back to the Bugle. (After the damage he did to his opponent in the last match, Peter does not want to go back to wrestling.)

Peter's powers are in full bloom, and he uses them to take down some minor criminals over the course of the book. He builds the web shooters and learns to use them. He also develops the famous Spider-Man battle banter. He turns the trash talking he learned on the basketball court against the bad guys in battles.

Mary Jane Misunderstanding

On one of their long walks, Peter finds the courage to tell Mary Jane that he really cares about her. Unfortunately, he can't really find the words. What he does is pull out the gold chain, tell her what it is and hand it over. Mary Jane is pleased, but overwhelmed. "Peter, I can't accept this, it's part of your family history, you shouldn't give it away."

Peter thinks he went too far. He takes the necklace right back. "Okay, no problem, I mean to me this is just a pretty piece of metal, but I'll hang on to it." And, he changes the subject and gets away.

Missing Teenagers

The Daily Bugle is on to a great new story. Teenagers, mostly street kids and runaways, are disappearing without a trace. The police are baffled, but Jonah Jameson is not. He has the paper run huge headlines—"Mysterious Spider Monster May Be Kidnapping Kids and Feeding on their Blood!"

The Burglar

Spider-Man goes from crime to crime, until finally, in an electronics store not far from Aunt May's house, Spider-Man helps the police capture Uncle Ben's killer.

The killer is identified on the spot by the same cop who had been at the scene of the crime. He is also identified on the spot by Spider-Man, because this burglar who murdered Uncle Ben, was also the purse-snatcher outside of Madison Square Garden. Had Peter reached out to stop that thief, Uncle Ben would be alive today. And, with that realization, comes another: that with great power there must also come great responsibility.

ISSUE SIX — YOUR FRIENDLY NEIGHBORHOOD SPIDER-MAN

Quitting the basketball team

Peter Parker wants to live up to his responsibilities. Unfortunately this means gearing back from big man on campus to science club geek. [This transformation back to wimpy Peter Parker is a crucial part of the Spider-Man saga, and the reader should fully understand and relate to Peter's reasoning].

Peter quits the basketball team (leaving sports stardom behind) because he should continue his father's research. He must spend afternoons in the lab and studying. Now, the basketball players hate him as much as the soccer team does. When the abuse starts up again, Peter doesn't fight back. He asks the principal and coach for help, but they show their true colors and turn their backs on him. Still, Peter doesn't fight back; for one thing, he doesn't feel much physical pain from a teenage kick or punch. Sure it hurts on the inside, but Peter now believes that the best response to a slap in the face may be to turn the other cheek.

Moreover, the Daily Bugle continues to look for Spider-Man. Believing him to be a teenager, they have reporters interviewing high school teachers and kids. The Bugle also has most of the Tri-State Area believing that Spider-Man is a blood-sucking monster and master-criminal to boot. Peter decides that Spider-Man will be well-hidden as Peter Parker—a science nerd getting pushed around by high school punks.

Swinging Nights

Every night and all day Saturday, Peter Parker works at The Daily Bugle.com. He feeds news from the police radio onto the website. When he knows the police need help, he swings into action as Spider-Man.

As your friendly neighborhood Spider-Man, Peter finds a few hours of true happiness every night. He climbs the highest buildings and swings across the NYC skyline. The police work is better sport than a basketball game; he trash talks and webs-up criminals all night long. In fact, the only place Peter Parker can go for release and relief is into his Spider-Man alter ego.

Personal sacrifices

But it's tough to go to school all day, hold down an afternoon job, and save New York from destruction at night. He does want to make time for the two people who matter to him the most: Aunt May (who needs emotional support as much as she needs financial help) and Mary Jane (they are already in love, but not yet in a relationship.) Unfortunately, Peter finds that he constantly sacrifices his personal life to live up to his responsibilities. He constantly frustrates his family and friends and is always in trouble at work and school. So, at night he's a hero, but all day, he's still a zero.

Missing Teenagers

Spider-Man increasingly focuses on the mystery of the missing teenagers. Three more have been pulled from the streets, and people are getting very nervous. Now Harry Osborn, a student at the local high school and son to one of the richest men in New York, has disappeared, and his father has offered a huge reward for his safe return. If kids like Harry Osborn are vulnerable, anyone can be next.

Harry, of course, is hard at work with his father training the teenage team. Father and son are working on the plan to capture Peter. There is quite a bit of urgency here, because they are both afraid that Harry's condition will deteriorate as his dependency on Oz continues to grow.

Mary Jane

Mary Jane is definitely coming out into the world. She's enjoying the increased attention that her new look brings her, even as she cringes at the superficiality of it all.

Peter finally asks MJ out for a real date. He had brought a digital camera on his last Spider-Man jaunt, mounted it on a tripod, and got 100 shots (3 seconds apart) of Spider-Man breaking up a jewelry store robbery in process. Jonah selected one of Spider-Man with his hands full of the stolen jewels. He had of course, been returning them to the police, but the Bugle ran the photo with the headline "Red Menace Caught Red Handed." Oh well, they paid $400, which is $250 for Aunt May, $100 for software, and $50 for dinner and a movie with Mary Jane next Saturday night.

The Trap

By Saturday night Norman Osborn is nearly ready. He has spent weeks adjusting dosages and training his best troops. He doesn't have anyone with all of the skills of Spider-Man, but he does have the numbers. His attempts to lure Spider-Man in have proven futile, so he decides to go out

to get him. If he can capture Peter Parker alive and turn him to his cause, great. But dissecting a dead Parker will be fine as well. In either case, he will have the secret of Spider-Man for his very own soon.

So as it turns out, Peter Parker never solves the case of the missing teens. Instead, the case comes to him. As he's about to leave work on Saturday, Peter hears that six bulked-up, crazed teens are creating a riot downtown. Peter wants to go on his date with MJ and let the police handle the problem but knows that he must fulfill his great responsibilities.

Peter is shocked to see the ringleader. He's bulked up, angry and strange-looking, but he's Harry Osborn. This is the first real super-hero battle of Spidey's career, yet he only has half of his mind and heart in the game because he keeps thinking about MJ alone in the restaurant and that these teens are really victims, not criminals. But he knows that Aunt May could not survive without him, so he forces himself to concentrate.

Each of the teenagers possesses some of his skills, and while none of them are as powerful or agile as he is, together they are a potent force. Spider-Man's superior powers will help him subdue five of the six, but Harry continues to battle. Spidey lures Harry to the top of a building—away from innocent bystanders. But just as he's about to nab Harry, a chopper lands and helps him escape.

Norman and Harry fly back to the lab. If they can close down the operation before the police get there, nobody will really believe "Spider-Man" that Harry Osborn was involved in a riot.

The Morning After

In the aftermath of the battle, the city is in an uproar. As news comes out about the physical modifications that were done to the captured teens, and the Bugle's story puts Spider-Man behind the sordid experiments and nasty riot. The police defend Spidey, but no one can deny that the damage done during his battle is going to stress an already tight municipal budget.

When Peter sees MJ on Sunday morning, the best he can do is deliver a lame excuse for standing her up and try to skulk away. But MJ will not let him go that easily; she knows that something is wrong and discovers that he is covered with bruises. He won't say what actually happened, and she won't let the matter completely drop, but they look into each other's eyes and all the way to each other's hearts, and they kiss for the first time.

The End.

Now that you've savored the original plot synopsis, check out Mark Bagley's initial sketches for the various super-villains who populated the second story arc and beyond.

Enjoy…

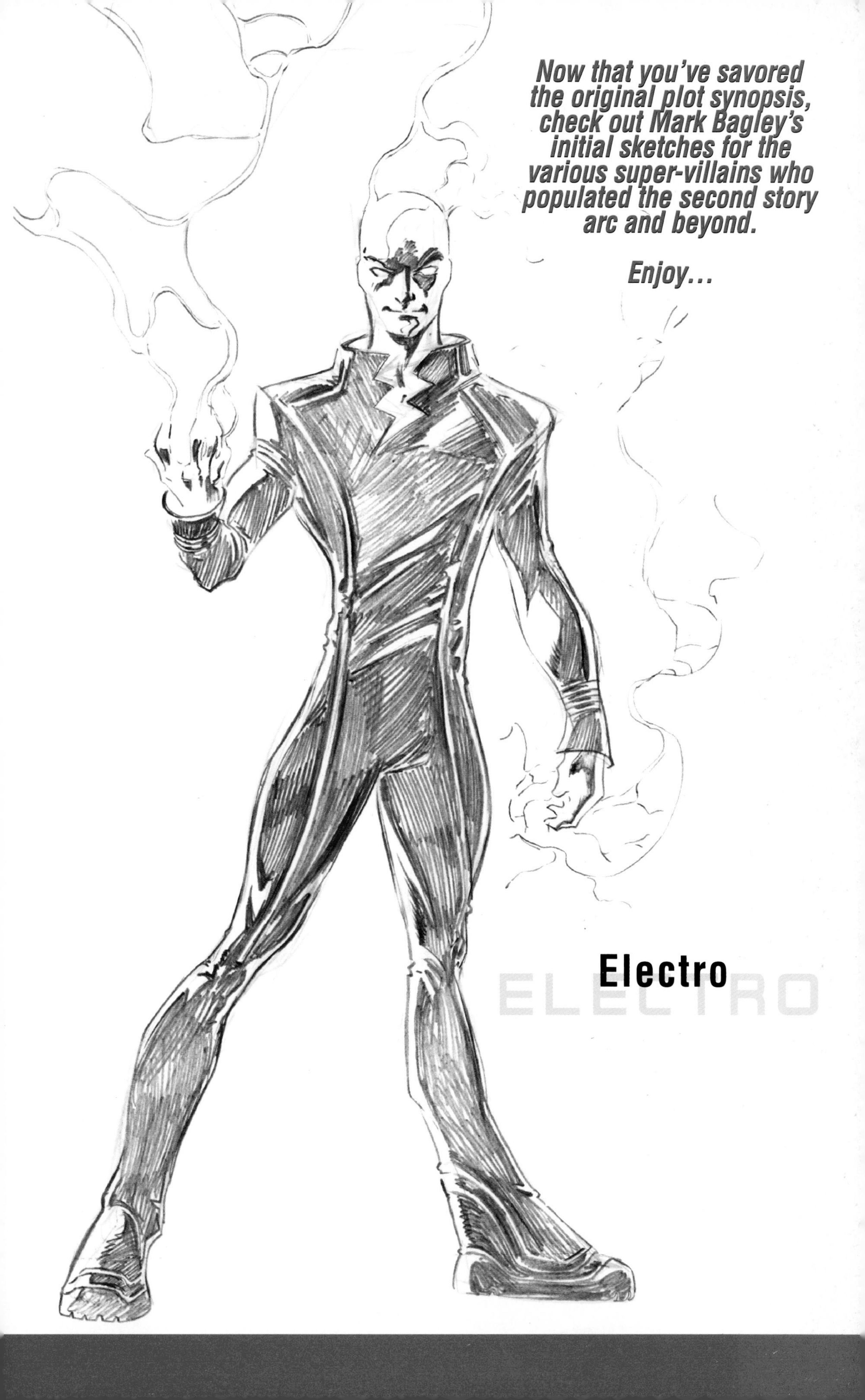

Electro

ELECTRO

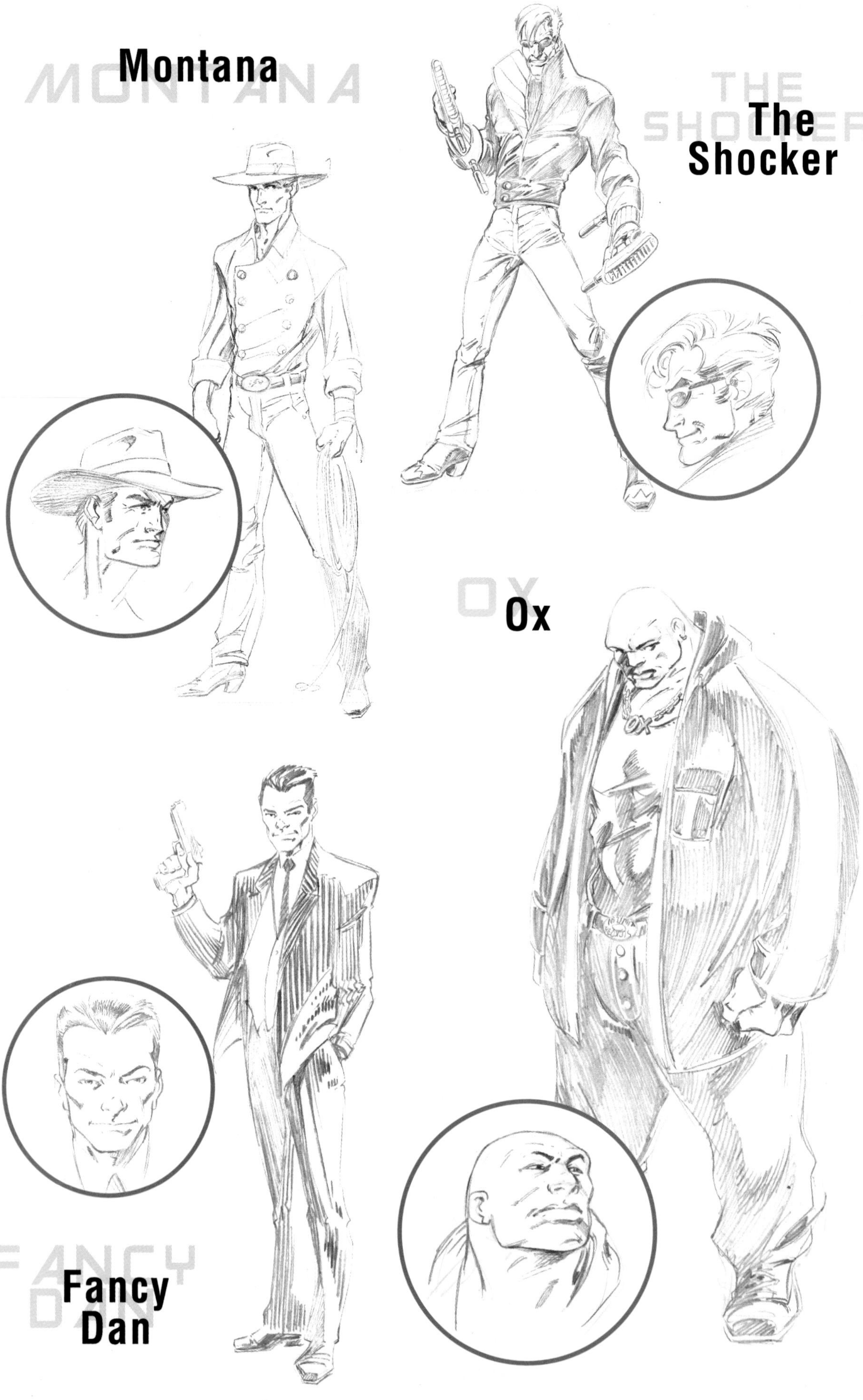
Montana
The Shocker
Ox
Fancy Dan

Kingpin

KINGPIN

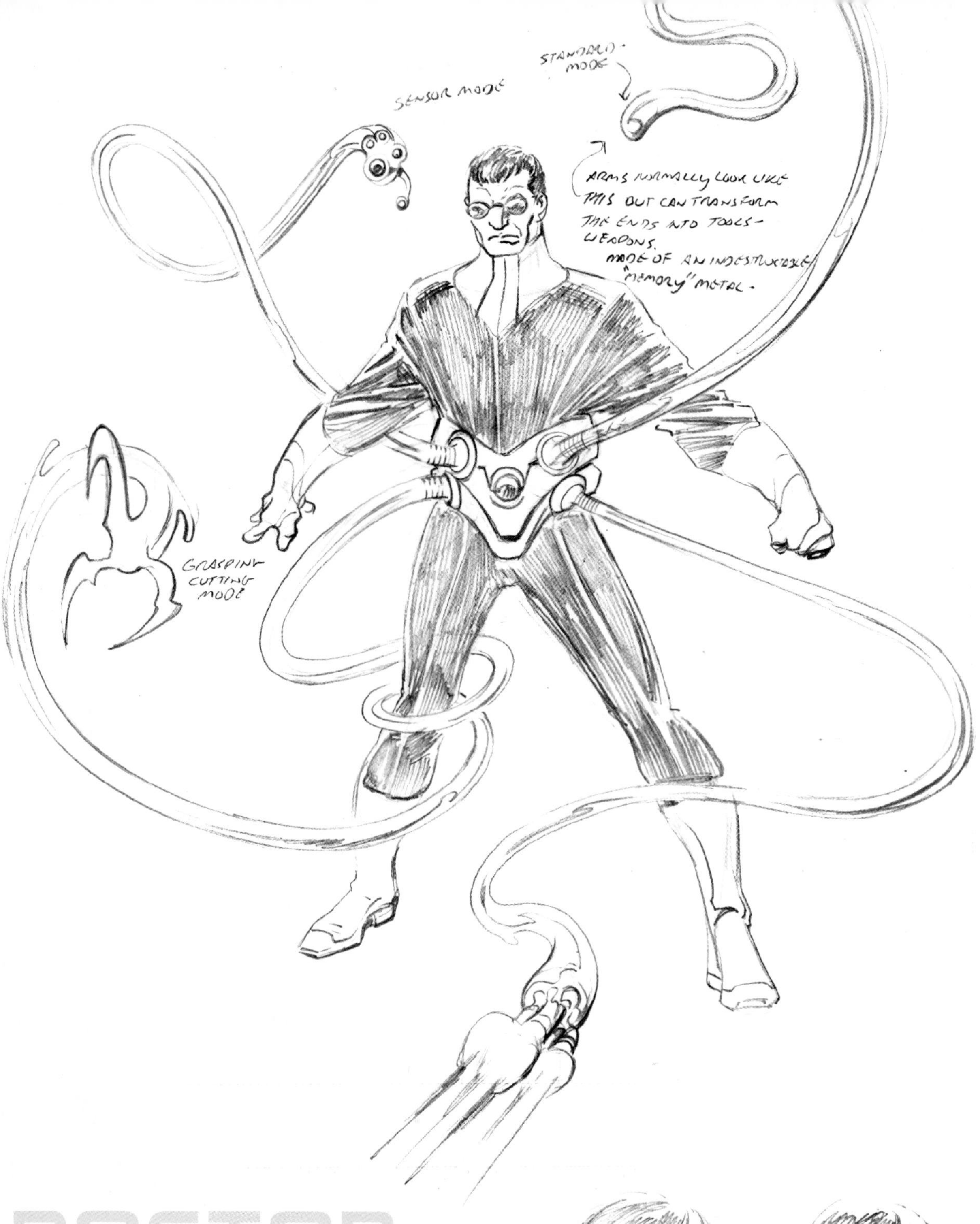
STANDARD-MODE
SENSOR MODE
ARMS NORMALLY LOOK LIKE THIS BUT CAN TRANSFORM THE ENDS INTO TOOLS-WEAPONS.
MADE OF AN INDESTRUCTIBLE "MEMORY" METAL-
GRASPING CUTTING MODE

DOCTOR OCTOPUS

Doctor Octopus

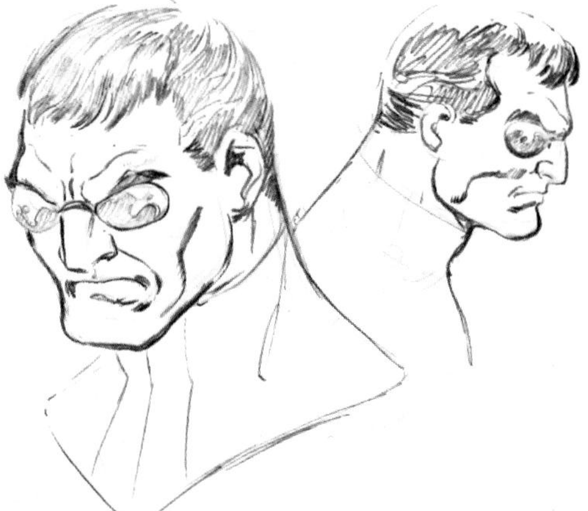

A brief, deleted scene from issue three wherein Peter and Kong converse in the high school gym locker room. Ever the perfectionist, writer Bendis removed the scene and replaced it with a similar one in issue four where it more effectively enhanced the story.

PAGE 14

1- THE MEN'S LOCKER ROOM. PETER IN THE FOREGROUND TYING UP HIS SHOE. HE HAS A LOOK OF CONTENTMENT ON HIS FACE.

KONG WALKING BY IN THE BACKGROUND. HE HAS HIS LETTER JACKET AND HIS BAG. HE IS STOPPING TO ACKNOWLEDGE PETER.

> KONG
> THAT WAS MEAN BALL.

> PETER
> THANKS.

> KONG
> YA REALLY KNOW HOW TO TALK TRASH TOO MAN. THAT'S AN ART ALL IN ITSELF.

> PETER
> YEAH, A REAL ART.

2- KONG IMPRESSED.

> KONG
> DIDN'T KNOW YOU HAD IT IN YOU.

3- PETER KEEPS TYING HIS SHOE.

> PETER
> YOU WERE TO BUSY TAKING MY LUNCH MONEY AWAY FROM ME.

4- KONG LAUGHS TO HIMSELF.

> KONG
> YEAH, THAT WAS FUNNY. WE HAD SOME GOOD TIMES…

5- PETER STANDS AND LOOKS AT HEM LIKE HE IS NUTS.

6- KONG STOPS LAUGHING. REALIZES IT IS ONLY FUNNY TO HIM.

> KONG (CONT'D)
> WELL… I DID.

> BUT ANYWAY, LISTEN MAN, WE'RE TEAMMATES NOW AND I SEEN THAT YOU'VE GROWN UP INTO A NEW KIND OF PARKER.

> I CAN SEE THAT.

AND I'M A BELIEVER IN GIVING PEOPLE A SECOND CHANCE IN LIFE.

PAGE 16

1- PETER STANDS UP TO KONG. KONG IS BEING WARM AND INVITING WITH HIS HAND OUT.

> KONG (CONT'D)
> I MEAN, YOU WOULDN'T BE ABLE TO TELL BY LOOKING AT ME, BUT WHEN I WAS YOUNGER I HAD WHAT SOMEONE MIGHT CALL A BIT OF A WEIGHT PROBLEM.

> PETER
> NO...

> KONG
> YES.

> SO, I'M NOT ABOVE LOOKING AT WHO YOU ARE NOW. AND WHO YOU ARE NOW IS A KICK ASS HOOPSTER.

> FRIENDS?

2- PETER TAKES HIS HAND.

> PETER
> SURE. HEY, YOU GOT ANY MONEY ON YOU? CUZ I-

3- KONG REACHES INTO HIS POCKET.

> KINGPIN
> YEAH, I GOT A FINSKY, I THINK.

4- PETER SNATCHES THE FIVE DOLLAR BILL.

> PETER
> GREAT.

5- KONG LAUGHS AT PETER STROLLING AWAY.

> PETER (CONT'D)
> COUGH UP A HUNDRED AND FORTY MORE AND WE'RE EVEN.

> KONG
> HA HA HA- YOU ARE A MANIAC.

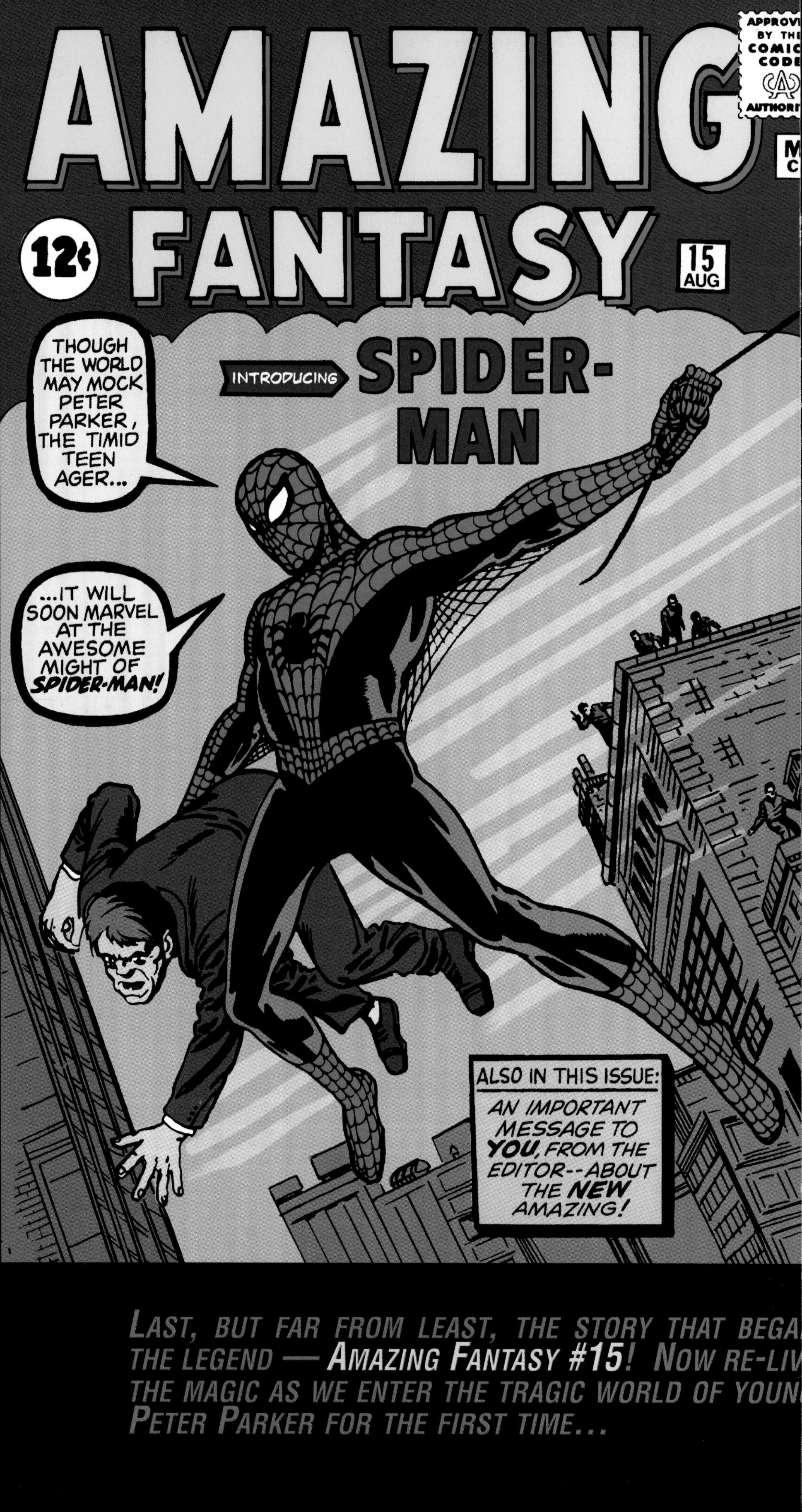
AMAZING
FANTASY
12¢
15 AUG
THOUGH THE WORLD MAY MOCK PETER PARKER, THE TIMID TEEN AGER...
INTRODUCING SPIDER-MAN
...IT WILL SOON MARVEL AT THE AWESOME MIGHT OF SPIDER-MAN!
ALSO IN THIS ISSUE:
AN IMPORTANT MESSAGE TO YOU, FROM THE EDITOR--ABOUT THE NEW AMAZING!

*LAST, BUT FAR FROM LEAST, THE STORY THAT BEGA THE LEGEND — **AMAZING FANTASY #15**! NOW RE-LIV THE MAGIC AS WE ENTER THE TRAGIC WORLD OF YOUN PETER PARKER FOR THE FIRST TIME...*

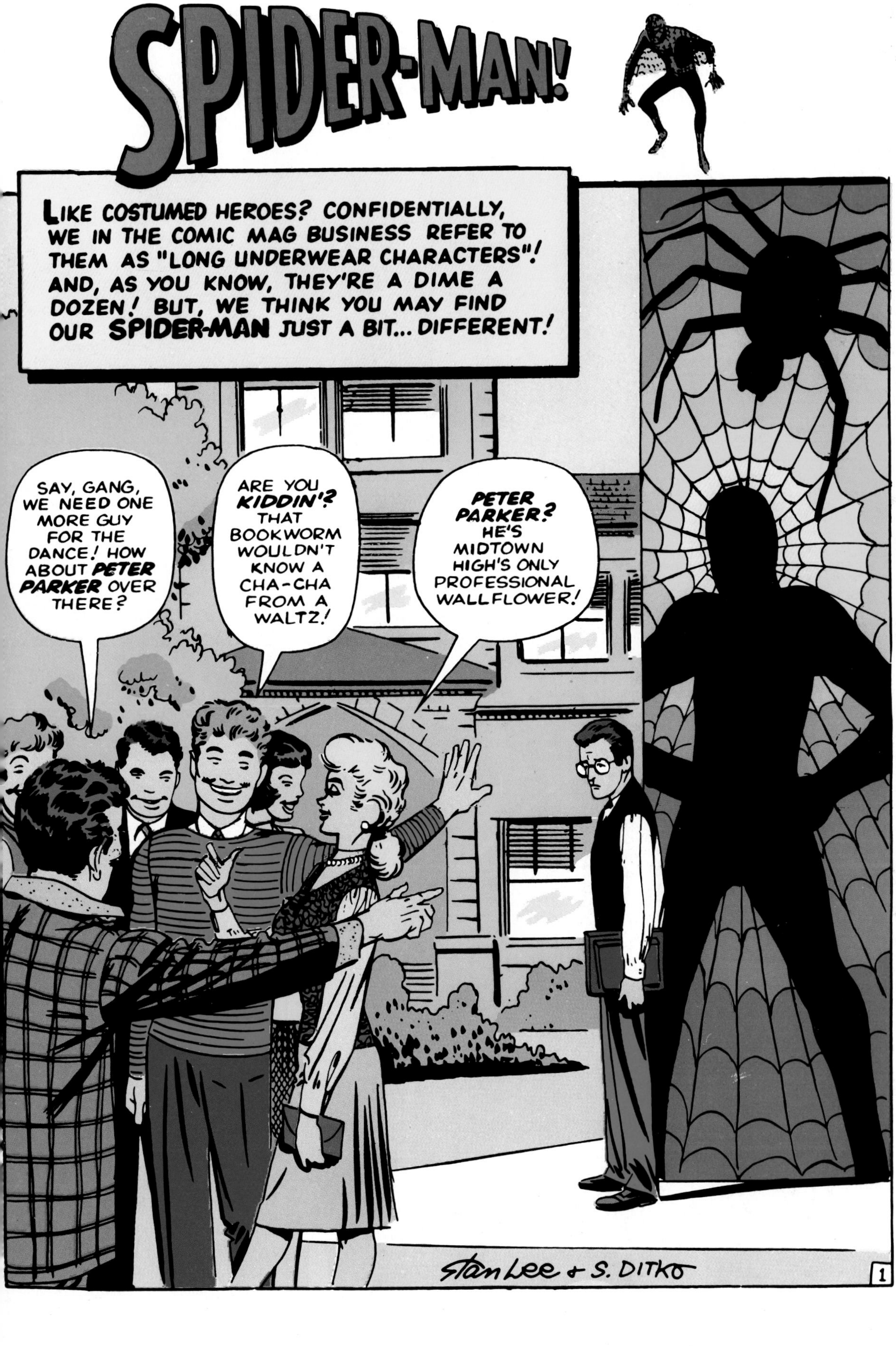
SPIDER-MAN!
LIKE COSTUMED HEROES? CONFIDENTIALLY, WE IN THE COMIC MAG BUSINESS REFER TO THEM AS "LONG UNDERWEAR CHARACTERS"! AND, AS YOU KNOW, THEY'RE A DIME A DOZEN! BUT, WE THINK YOU MAY FIND OUR SPIDER-MAN JUST A BIT... DIFFERENT!
SAY, GANG, WE NEED ONE MORE GUY FOR THE DANCE! HOW ABOUT PETER PARKER OVER THERE?
ARE YOU KIDDIN'? THAT BOOKWORM WOULDN'T KNOW A CHA-CHA FROM A WALTZ!
PETER PARKER? HE'S MIDTOWN HIGH'S ONLY PROFESSIONAL WALLFLOWER!
Stan Lee + S. DITKO
1

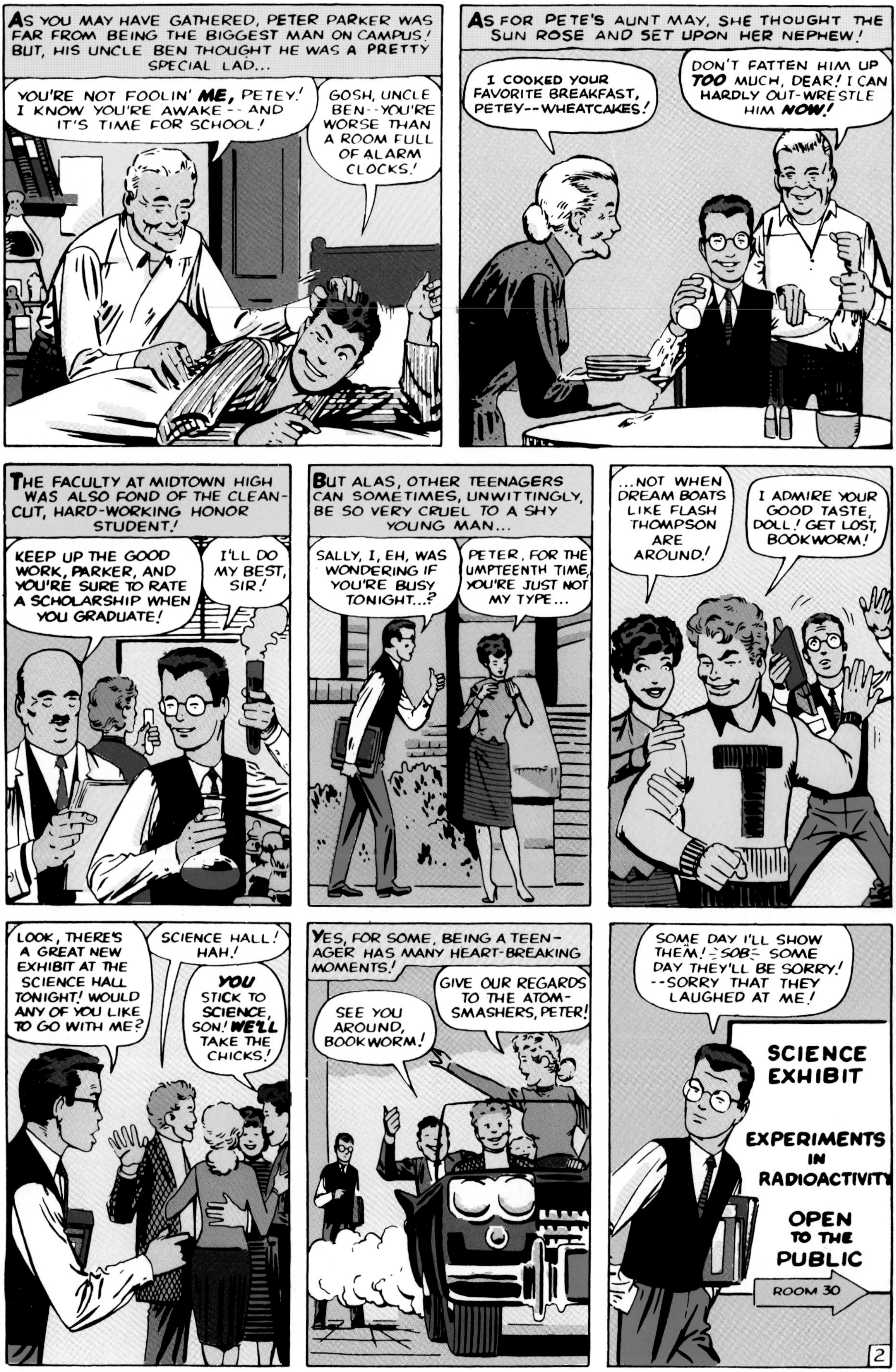
AS YOU MAY HAVE GATHERED, PETER PARKER WAS FAR FROM BEING THE BIGGEST MAN ON CAMPUS! BUT, HIS UNCLE BEN THOUGHT HE WAS A PRETTY SPECIAL LAD...
YOU'RE NOT FOOLIN' ME, PETEY! I KNOW YOU'RE AWAKE--AND IT'S TIME FOR SCHOOL!
GOSH, UNCLE BEN--YOU'RE WORSE THAN A ROOM FULL OF ALARM CLOCKS!
AS FOR PETE'S AUNT MAY, SHE THOUGHT THE SUN ROSE AND SET UPON HER NEPHEW!
I COOKED YOUR FAVORITE BREAKFAST, PETEY--WHEATCAKES!
DON'T FATTEN HIM UP TOO MUCH, DEAR! I CAN HARDLY OUT-WRESTLE HIM NOW!
THE FACULTY AT MIDTOWN HIGH WAS ALSO FOND OF THE CLEAN-CUT, HARD-WORKING HONOR STUDENT!
KEEP UP THE GOOD WORK, PARKER, AND YOU'RE SURE TO RATE A SCHOLARSHIP WHEN YOU GRADUATE!
I'LL DO MY BEST, SIR!
BUT ALAS, OTHER TEENAGERS CAN SOMETIMES, UNWITTINGLY, BE SO VERY CRUEL TO A SHY YOUNG MAN...
SALLY, I, EH, WAS WONDERING IF YOU'RE BUSY TONIGHT...?
PETER, FOR THE UMPTEENTH TIME, YOU'RE JUST NOT MY TYPE...
...NOT WHEN DREAM BOATS LIKE FLASH THOMPSON ARE AROUND!
I ADMIRE YOUR GOOD TASTE, DOLL! GET LOST, BOOKWORM!
LOOK, THERE'S A GREAT NEW EXHIBIT AT THE SCIENCE HALL TONIGHT! WOULD ANY OF YOU LIKE TO GO WITH ME?
SCIENCE HALL! HAH!
YOU STICK TO SCIENCE, SON! WE'LL TAKE THE CHICKS!
YES, FOR SOME, BEING A TEEN-AGER HAS MANY HEART-BREAKING MOMENTS!
SEE YOU AROUND, BOOKWORM!
GIVE OUR REGARDS TO THE ATOM-SMASHERS, PETER!
SOME DAY I'LL SHOW THEM! -SOB- SOME DAY THEY'LL BE SORRY! --SORRY THAT THEY LAUGHED AT ME!
SCIENCE EXHIBIT
EXPERIMENTS IN RADIOACTIVITY
OPEN TO THE PUBLIC
ROOM 30
2

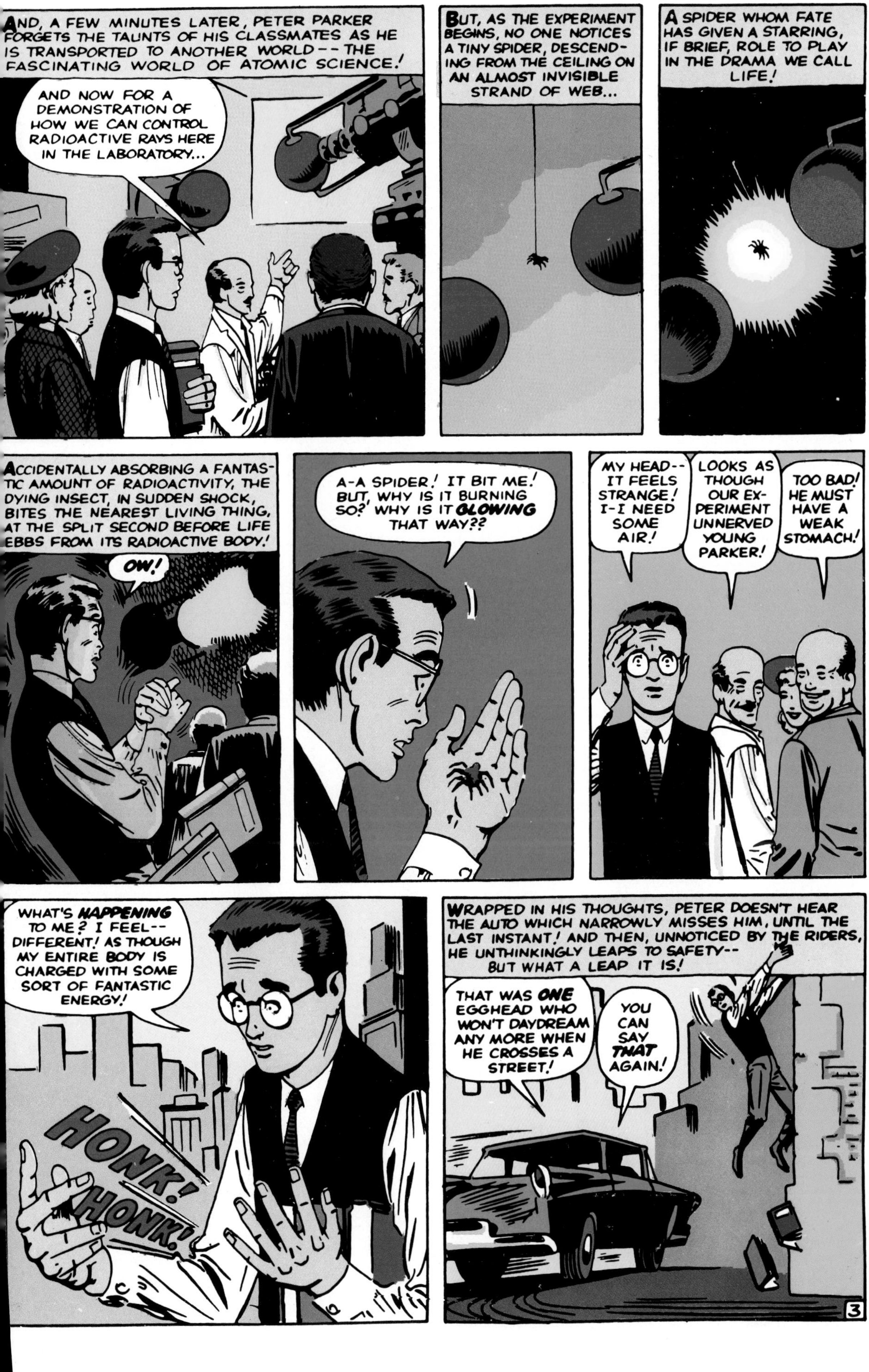
AND, A FEW MINUTES LATER, PETER PARKER FORGETS THE TAUNTS OF HIS CLASSMATES AS HE IS TRANSPORTED TO ANOTHER WORLD -- THE FASCINATING WORLD OF ATOMIC SCIENCE!
AND NOW FOR A DEMONSTRATION OF HOW WE CAN CONTROL RADIOACTIVE RAYS HERE IN THE LABORATORY...
BUT, AS THE EXPERIMENT BEGINS, NO ONE NOTICES A TINY SPIDER, DESCENDING FROM THE CEILING ON AN ALMOST INVISIBLE STRAND OF WEB...
A SPIDER WHOM FATE HAS GIVEN A STARRING, IF BRIEF, ROLE TO PLAY IN THE DRAMA WE CALL LIFE!
ACCIDENTALLY ABSORBING A FANTASTIC AMOUNT OF RADIOACTIVITY, THE DYING INSECT, IN SUDDEN SHOCK, BITES THE NEAREST LIVING THING, AT THE SPLIT SECOND BEFORE LIFE EBBS FROM ITS RADIOACTIVE BODY!
OW!
A-A SPIDER! IT BIT ME! BUT, WHY IS IT BURNING SO? WHY IS IT GLOWING THAT WAY??
MY HEAD-- IT FEELS STRANGE! I-I NEED SOME AIR!
LOOKS AS THOUGH OUR EXPERIMENT UNNERVED YOUNG PARKER!
TOO BAD! HE MUST HAVE A WEAK STOMACH!
WHAT'S HAPPENING TO ME? I FEEL-- DIFFERENT! AS THOUGH MY ENTIRE BODY IS CHARGED WITH SOME SORT OF FANTASTIC ENERGY!
HONK! HONK!
WRAPPED IN HIS THOUGHTS, PETER DOESN'T HEAR THE AUTO WHICH NARROWLY MISSES HIM, UNTIL THE LAST INSTANT! AND THEN, UNNOTICED BY THE RIDERS, HE UNTHINKINGLY LEAPS TO SAFETY-- BUT WHAT A LEAP IT IS!
THAT WAS ONE EGGHEAD WHO WON'T DAYDREAM ANY MORE WHEN HE CROSSES A STREET!
YOU CAN SAY THAT AGAIN!
3

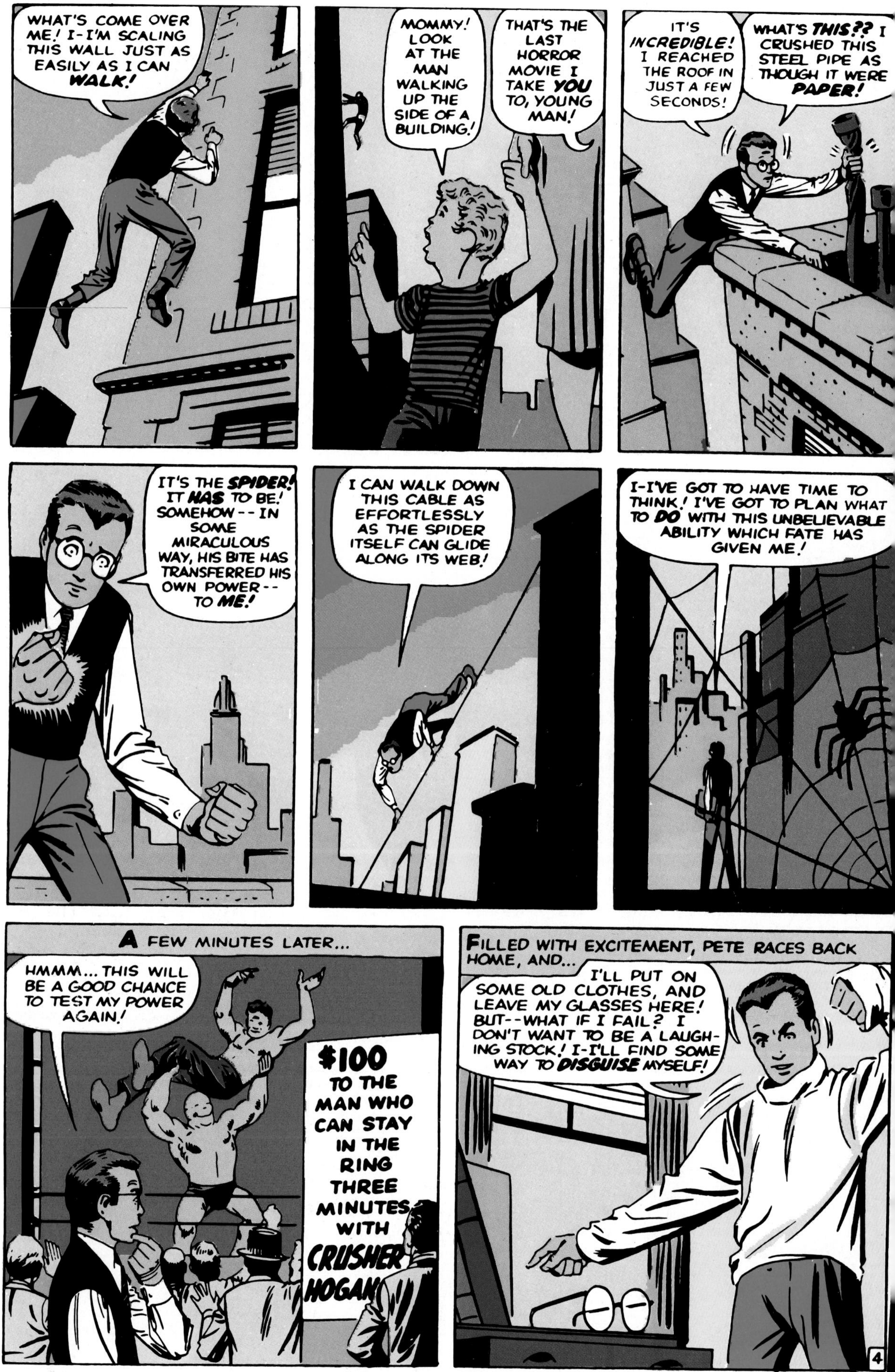
WHAT'S COME OVER ME! I-I'M SCALING THIS WALL JUST AS EASILY AS I CAN WALK!
MOMMY! LOOK AT THE MAN WALKING UP THE SIDE OF A BUILDING!
THAT'S THE LAST HORROR MOVIE I TAKE YOU TO, YOUNG MAN!
IT'S INCREDIBLE! I REACHED THE ROOF IN JUST A FEW SECONDS!
WHAT'S THIS?? I CRUSHED THIS STEEL PIPE AS THOUGH IT WERE PAPER!
IT'S THE SPIDER! IT HAS TO BE! SOMEHOW -- IN SOME MIRACULOUS WAY, HIS BITE HAS TRANSFERRED HIS OWN POWER -- TO ME!
I CAN WALK DOWN THIS CABLE AS EFFORTLESSLY AS THE SPIDER ITSELF CAN GLIDE ALONG ITS WEB!
I-I'VE GOT TO HAVE TIME TO THINK! I'VE GOT TO PLAN WHAT TO DO WITH THIS UNBELIEVABLE ABILITY WHICH FATE HAS GIVEN ME!
A FEW MINUTES LATER...
HMMM... THIS WILL BE A GOOD CHANCE TO TEST MY POWER AGAIN!
$100 TO THE MAN WHO CAN STAY IN THE RING THREE MINUTES WITH CRUSHER HOGAN
FILLED WITH EXCITEMENT, PETE RACES BACK HOME, AND...
I'LL PUT ON SOME OLD CLOTHES, AND LEAVE MY GLASSES HERE! BUT--WHAT IF I FAIL? I DON'T WANT TO BE A LAUGHING STOCK! I-I'LL FIND SOME WAY TO DISGUISE MYSELF!
4

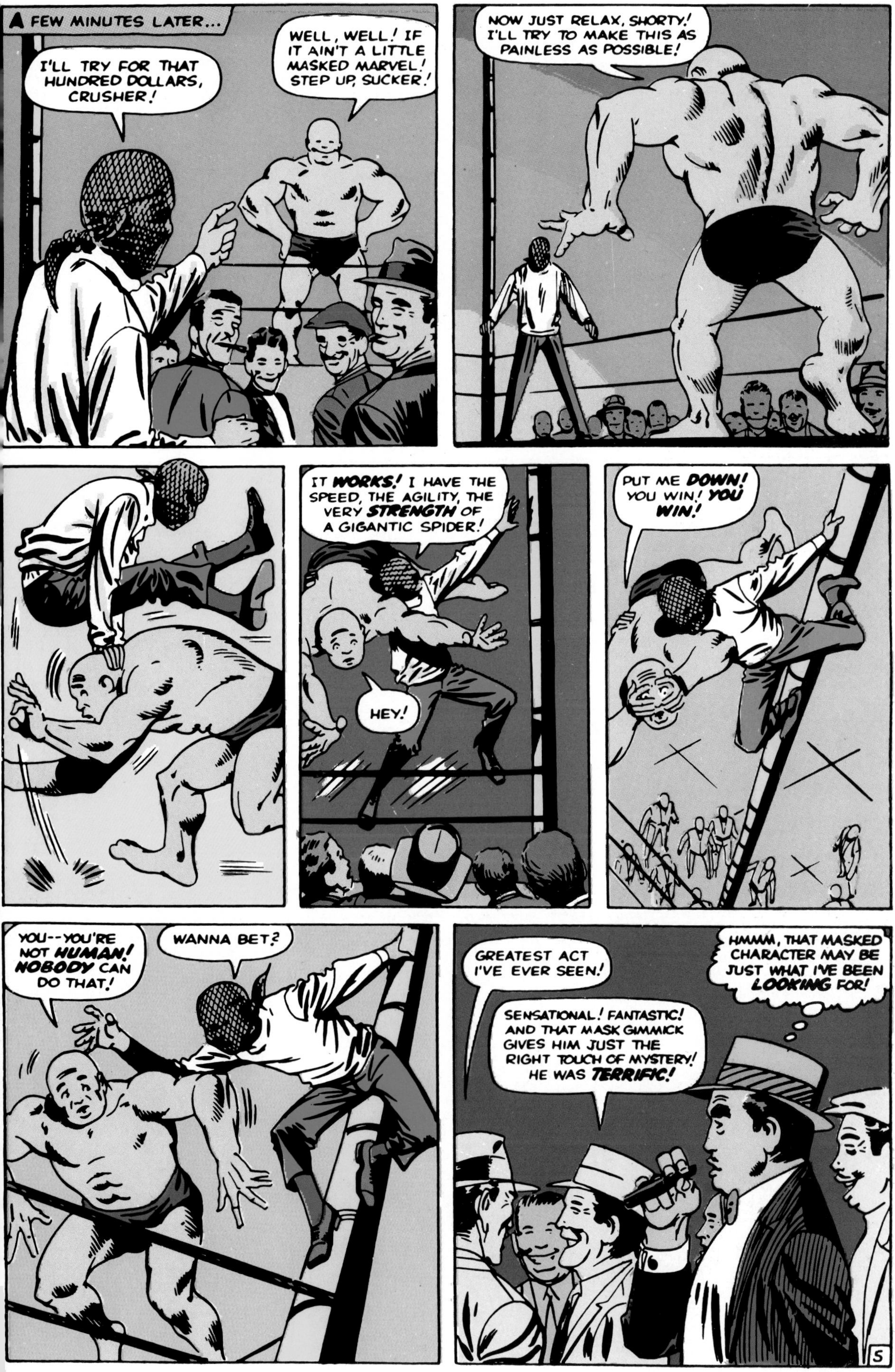
A FEW MINUTES LATER...
I'LL TRY FOR THAT HUNDRED DOLLARS, CRUSHER!
WELL, WELL! IF IT AIN'T A LITTLE MASKED MARVEL! STEP UP, SUCKER!
NOW JUST RELAX, SHORTY! I'LL TRY TO MAKE THIS AS PAINLESS AS POSSIBLE!
IT WORKS! I HAVE THE SPEED, THE AGILITY, THE VERY STRENGTH OF A GIGANTIC SPIDER!
HEY!
PUT ME DOWN! YOU WIN! YOU WIN!
YOU--YOU'RE NOT HUMAN! NOBODY CAN DO THAT!
WANNA BET?
GREATEST ACT I'VE EVER SEEN!
HMMM, THAT MASKED CHARACTER MAY BE JUST WHAT I'VE BEEN LOOKING FOR!
SENSATIONAL! FANTASTIC! AND THAT MASK GIMMICK GIVES HIM JUST THE RIGHT TOUCH OF MYSTERY! HE WAS TERRIFIC!
5

LISTEN, FRIEND, I'M A TV PRODUCER! WITH THAT ACT OF YOURS I CAN MAKE YOU A *FORTUNE!* AND KEEP THE MASK ANGLE -- IT'S GREAT SHOWMANSHIP! HERE'S MY CARD! CALL ME! YOU'D BE A SMASH ON ED SULLIVAN'S SHOW!

THANKS...

LATER, AT HOME AGAIN...

SHOWMANSHIP?? HE HASN'T SEEN *ANYTHING* YET! SINCE I HAVE THE *POWERS* OF A SPIDER, I'LL DESIGN MYSELF A *SPIDER COSTUME!* AND... OH, HI, AUNT MAY!

YOU LOOKED A LITTLE TIRED, PETEY, SO WE BROUGHT YOU SOME CRACKERS AND MILK!

CRACKERS AND MILK! BLESS 'EM -- IF THEY ONLY *KNEW!*

NOW LET'S SEE -- A SPIDER NEEDS A WEB! THIS LITTLE DEVICE SHOULD JUST DO THE TRICK!

I'LL FASTEN ONE TO EACH ARM -- IT'LL OPERATE BY THE SLIGHTEST PRESSURE OF ANY FINGER!

I'LL NEED A NAME -- WELL, GUESS *SPIDER-MAN* IS AS GOOD AS ANY! LOOKS PRETTY GOOD, IF I *DO* SAY SO MYSELF!

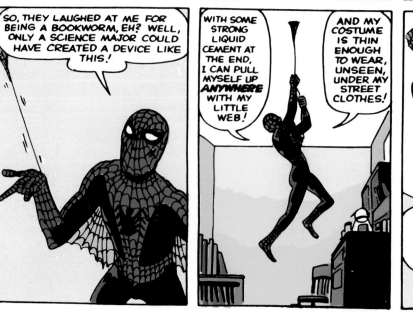

SO, THEY LAUGHED AT ME FOR BEING A BOOKWORM, EH? WELL, ONLY A SCIENCE MAJOR COULD HAVE CREATED A DEVICE LIKE THIS!

WITH SOME STRONG LIQUID CEMENT AT THE END, I CAN PULL MYSELF UP *ANYWHERE* WITH MY LITTLE WEB!

AND MY COSTUME IS THIN ENOUGH TO WEAR, UNSEEN, UNDER MY STREET CLOTHES!

OKAY, WORLD -- BETTER HANG ONTO YOUR HAT! HERE COMES THE *SPIDER-MAN!*

6

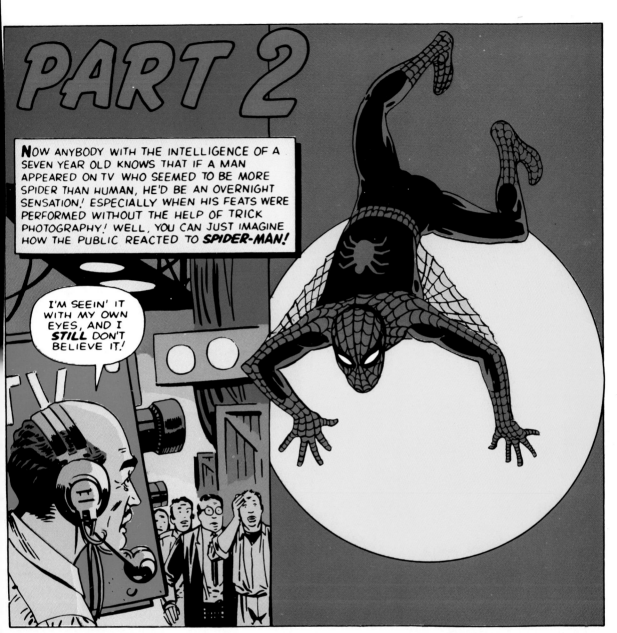

PART 2

NOW ANYBODY WITH THE INTELLIGENCE OF A SEVEN YEAR OLD KNOWS THAT IF A MAN APPEARED ON TV WHO SEEMED TO BE MORE SPIDER THAN HUMAN, HE'D BE AN OVERNIGHT SENSATION! ESPECIALLY WHEN HIS FEATS WERE PERFORMED WITHOUT THE HELP OF TRICK PHOTOGRAPHY! WELL, YOU CAN JUST IMAGINE HOW THE PUBLIC REACTED TO **SPIDER-MAN!**

I'M SEEIN' IT WITH MY OWN EYES, AND I **STILL** DON'T BELIEVE IT.!

SURE THEY LOOK AMAZED, INCREDULOUS, AWESTRICKEN! WOULDN'T **YOU**???

AFTER ALL, WHEN WAS THE LAST TIME **YOU** SAW A MAN WITH HIS OWN FANTASTIC SPIDER WEB???

OKAY, SPIDER-MAN --CUT.! THAT'S ENOUGH.! DON'T SHOW 'EM **TOO MUCH!** LEAVE 'EM BEGGIN' FOR MORE.!

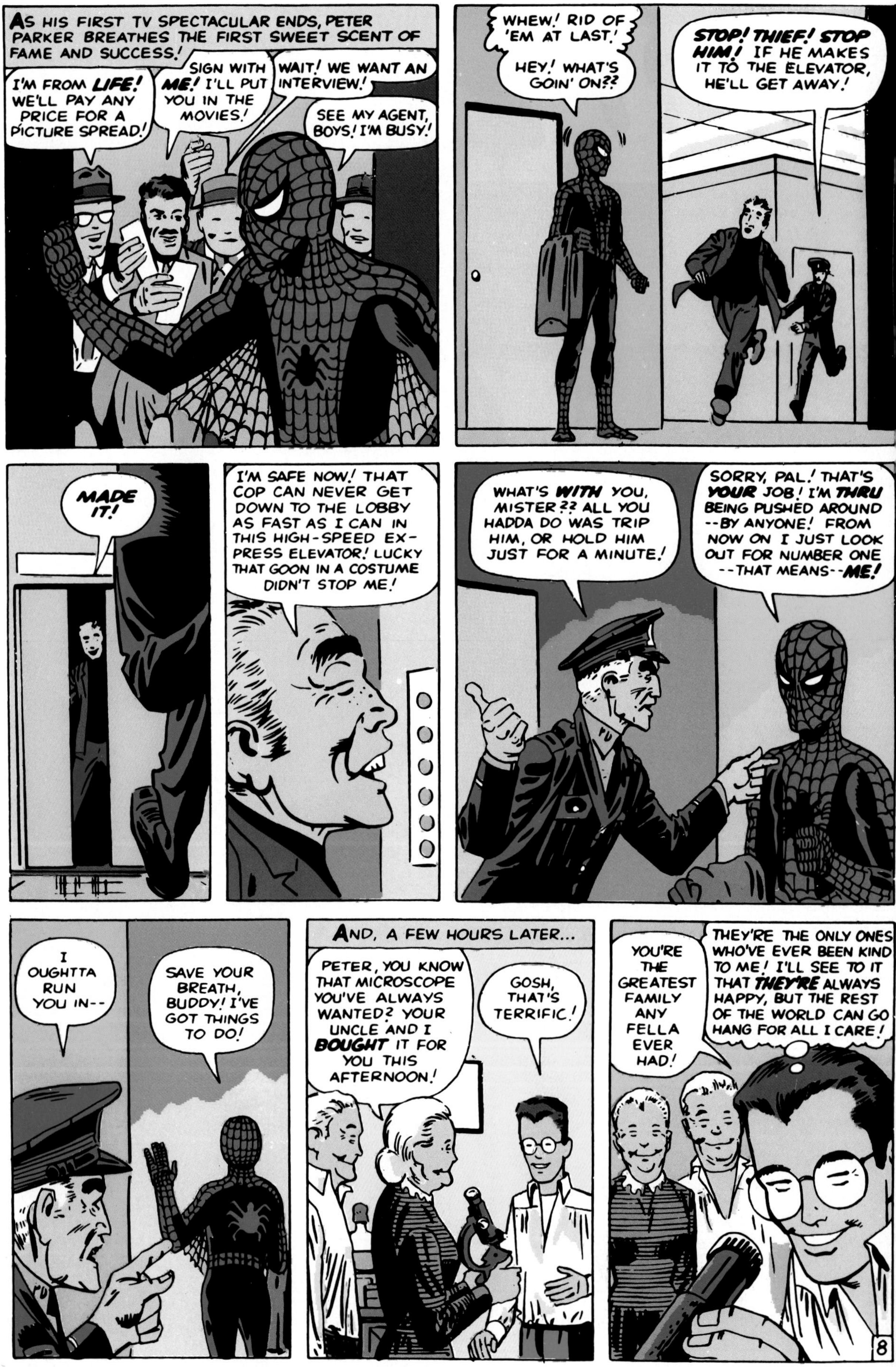
AS HIS FIRST TV SPECTACULAR ENDS, PETER PARKER BREATHES THE FIRST SWEET SCENT OF FAME AND SUCCESS!
I'M FROM LIFE! WE'LL PAY ANY PRICE FOR A PICTURE SPREAD!
SIGN WITH ME! I'LL PUT YOU IN THE MOVIES!
WAIT! WE WANT AN INTERVIEW!
SEE MY AGENT, BOYS! I'M BUSY!
WHEW! RID OF 'EM AT LAST!
HEY! WHAT'S GOIN' ON??
STOP! THIEF! STOP HIM! IF HE MAKES IT TO THE ELEVATOR, HE'LL GET AWAY!
MADE IT!
I'M SAFE NOW! THAT COP CAN NEVER GET DOWN TO THE LOBBY AS FAST AS I CAN IN THIS HIGH-SPEED EX-PRESS ELEVATOR! LUCKY THAT GOON IN A COSTUME DIDN'T STOP ME!
WHAT'S WITH YOU, MISTER?? ALL YOU HADDA DO WAS TRIP HIM, OR HOLD HIM JUST FOR A MINUTE!
SORRY, PAL! THAT'S YOUR JOB! I'M THRU BEING PUSHED AROUND --BY ANYONE! FROM NOW ON I JUST LOOK OUT FOR NUMBER ONE --THAT MEANS--ME!
I OUGHTTA RUN YOU IN--
SAVE YOUR BREATH, BUDDY! I'VE GOT THINGS TO DO!
AND, A FEW HOURS LATER...
PETER, YOU KNOW THAT MICROSCOPE YOU'VE ALWAYS WANTED? YOUR UNCLE AND I BOUGHT IT FOR YOU THIS AFTERNOON!
GOSH, THAT'S TERRIFIC!
YOU'RE THE GREATEST FAMILY ANY FELLA EVER HAD!
THEY'RE THE ONLY ONES WHO'VE EVER BEEN KIND TO ME! I'LL SEE TO IT THAT THEY'RE ALWAYS HAPPY, BUT THE REST OF THE WORLD CAN GO HANG FOR ALL I CARE!
8

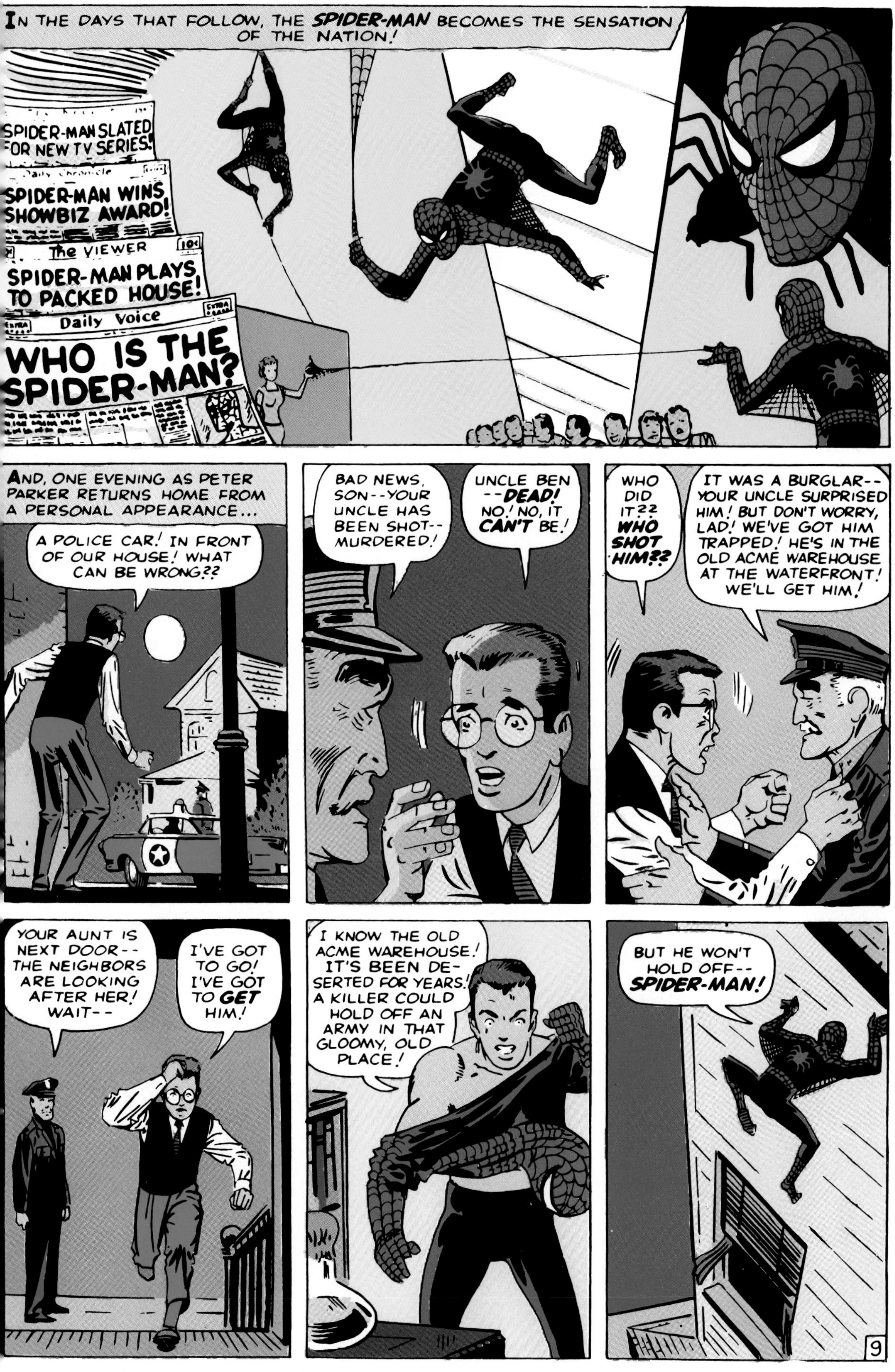
IN THE DAYS THAT FOLLOW, THE SPIDER-MAN BECOMES THE SENSATION OF THE NATION!
SPIDER-MAN SLATED FOR NEW TV SERIES!
Daily Chronicle
SPIDER-MAN WINS SHOWBIZ AWARD!
The VIEWER
10¢
SPIDER-MAN PLAYS TO PACKED HOUSE!
Daily Voice
EXTRA
WHO IS THE SPIDER-MAN?
AND, ONE EVENING AS PETER PARKER RETURNS HOME FROM A PERSONAL APPEARANCE...
A POLICE CAR! IN FRONT OF OUR HOUSE! WHAT CAN BE WRONG??
BAD NEWS, SON--YOUR UNCLE HAS BEEN SHOT--MURDERED!
UNCLE BEN --DEAD! NO! NO, IT CAN'T BE!
WHO DID IT?? WHO SHOT HIM??
IT WAS A BURGLAR--YOUR UNCLE SURPRISED HIM! BUT DON'T WORRY, LAD! WE'VE GOT HIM TRAPPED! HE'S IN THE OLD ACME WAREHOUSE AT THE WATERFRONT! WE'LL GET HIM!
YOUR AUNT IS NEXT DOOR--THE NEIGHBORS ARE LOOKING AFTER HER! WAIT--
I'VE GOT TO GO! I'VE GOT TO GET HIM!
I KNOW THE OLD ACME WAREHOUSE! IT'S BEEN DESERTED FOR YEARS! A KILLER COULD HOLD OFF AN ARMY IN THAT GLOOMY, OLD PLACE!
BUT HE WON'T HOLD OFF--SPIDER-MAN!
9

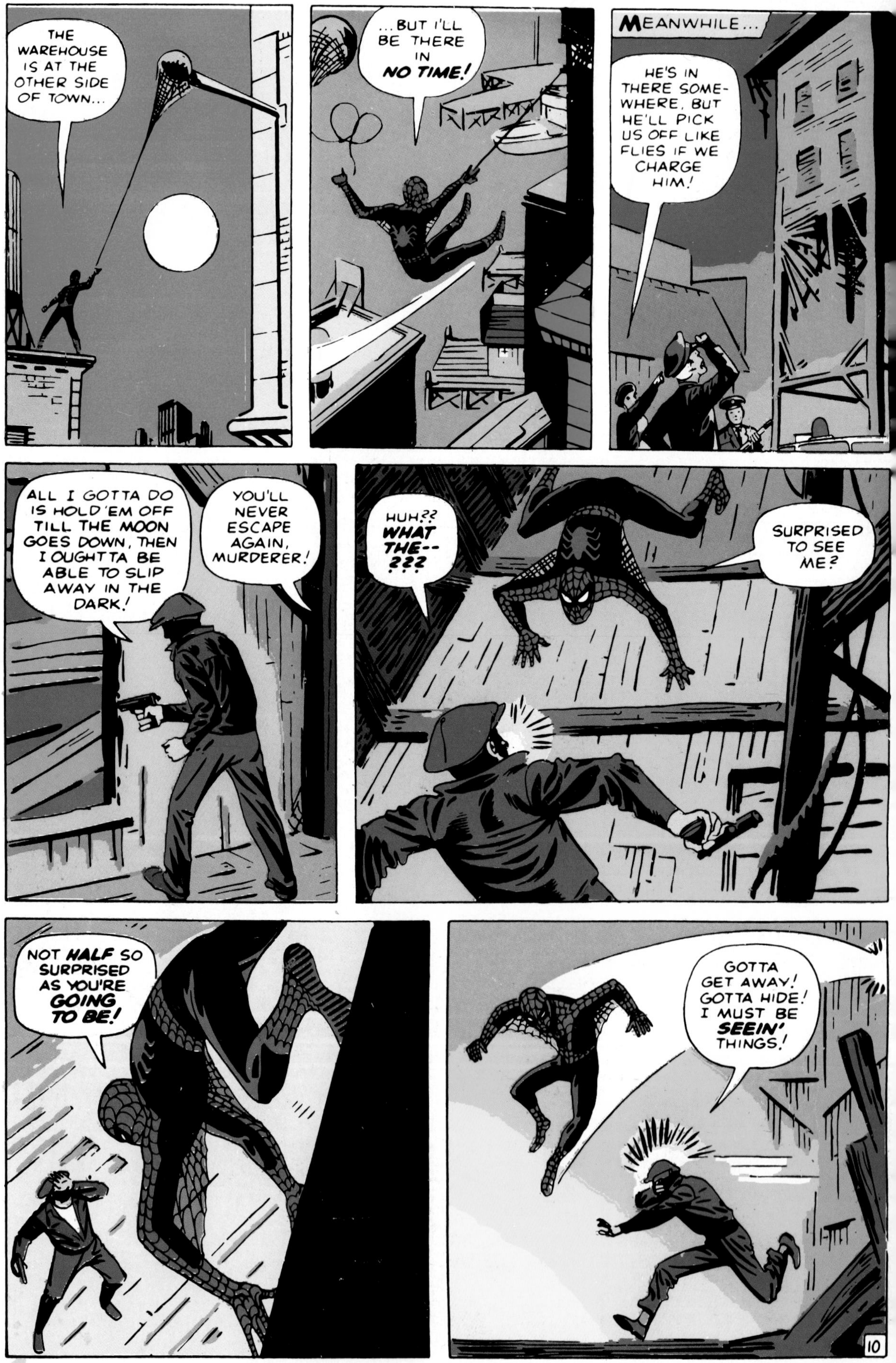
THE WAREHOUSE IS AT THE OTHER SIDE OF TOWN...
...BUT I'LL BE THERE IN NO TIME!
MEANWHILE...
HE'S IN THERE SOMEWHERE, BUT HE'LL PICK US OFF LIKE FLIES IF WE CHARGE HIM!
ALL I GOTTA DO IS HOLD 'EM OFF TILL THE MOON GOES DOWN, THEN I OUGHTTA BE ABLE TO SLIP AWAY IN THE DARK!
YOU'LL NEVER ESCAPE AGAIN, MURDERER!
HUH?? WHAT THE--???
SURPRISED TO SEE ME?
NOT HALF SO SURPRISED AS YOU'RE GOING TO BE!
GOTTA GET AWAY! GOTTA HIDE! I MUST BE SEEIN' THINGS!

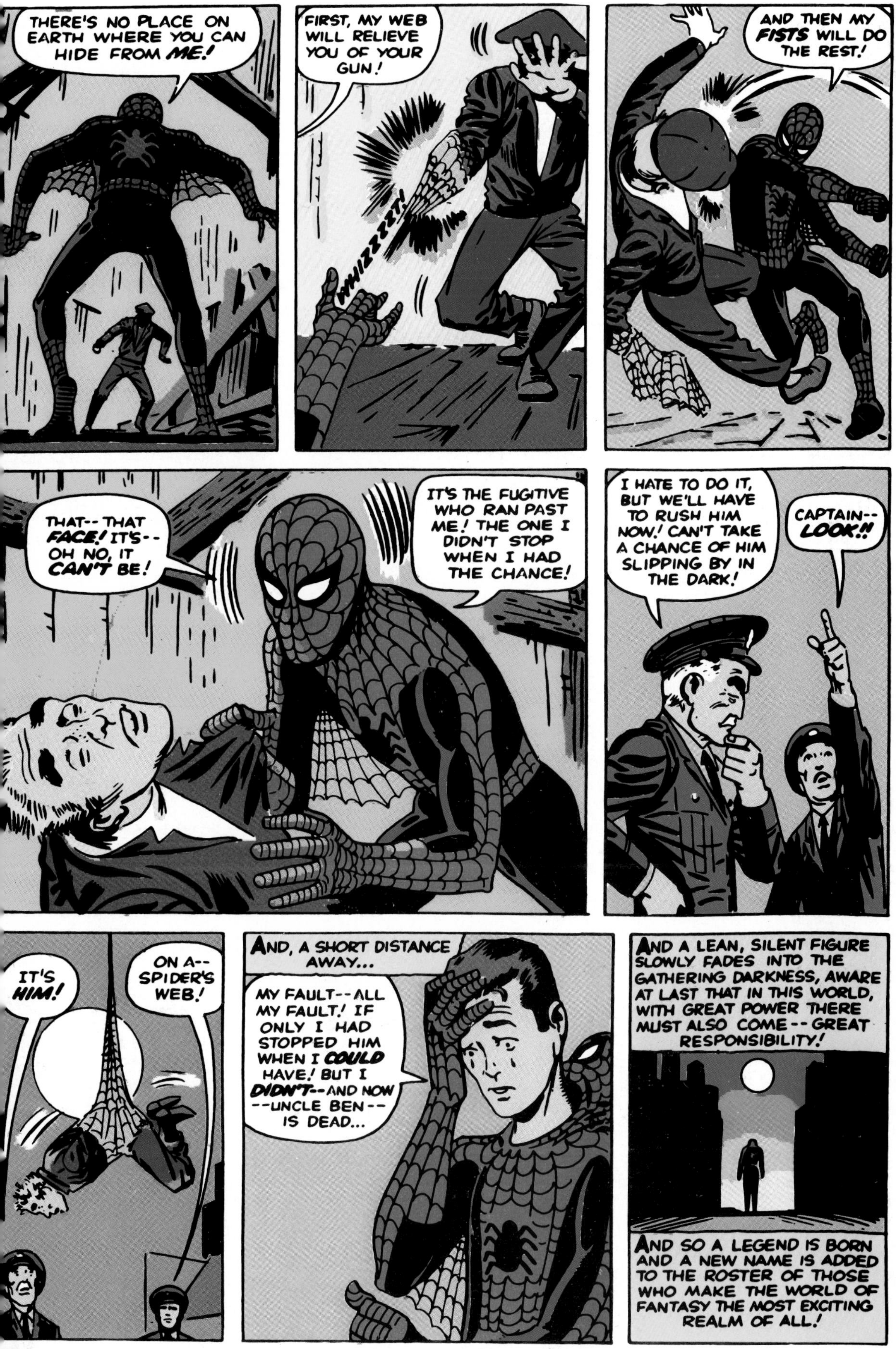
THERE'S NO PLACE ON EARTH WHERE YOU CAN HIDE FROM ME!
FIRST, MY WEB WILL RELIEVE YOU OF YOUR GUN!
WHIZZZZZT!
AND THEN MY FISTS WILL DO THE REST!
THAT--THAT FACE! IT'S--OH NO, IT CAN'T BE!
IT'S THE FUGITIVE WHO RAN PAST ME! THE ONE I DIDN'T STOP WHEN I HAD THE CHANCE!
I HATE TO DO IT, BUT WE'LL HAVE TO RUSH HIM NOW! CAN'T TAKE A CHANCE OF HIM SLIPPING BY IN THE DARK!
CAPTAIN--LOOK!!
IT'S HIM!
ON A--SPIDER'S WEB!
AND, A SHORT DISTANCE AWAY...
MY FAULT--ALL MY FAULT! IF ONLY I HAD STOPPED HIM WHEN I COULD HAVE! BUT I DIDN'T--AND NOW--UNCLE BEN--IS DEAD...
AND A LEAN, SILENT FIGURE SLOWLY FADES INTO THE GATHERING DARKNESS, AWARE AT LAST THAT IN THIS WORLD, WITH GREAT POWER THERE MUST ALSO COME--GREAT RESPONSIBILITY!
AND SO A LEGEND IS BORN AND A NEW NAME IS ADDED TO THE ROSTER OF THOSE WHO MAKE THE WORLD OF FANTASY THE MOST EXCITING REALM OF ALL!

AFTERWORD BY BILL JEMAS

"DADDY, DON'T LET UNCLE BEN DIE. IT'S OK IF HE GETS HURT AND GOES TO THE HOSPITAL, BUT PLEASE DO NOT LET HIM DIE."

That's what my son says to me after he reads issue #4. Unfortunately, by that time issue #5 has been scripted, penciled, inked, half colored, and poor old Ben is pushing up the daisies. Now he's a smart kid, but he's nine, and I can still outsmart him. So I thank him for the input and take him out for ice cream with his little brother.

But then, every day for the next week, I come home to the same thing: "Don't kill Ben" (like it's me with the gun). And, to make it worse, the younger guy – who's six and has the reading thing just about nailed – has made his way through issue #4. Now he joins in with the big guy. They both say Ben ain't dying on their watch. These kids really like Uncle Ben, and they mean business, and a Dad has to know when he's beat. I'm not giving up on Santa till they're 20, but I have no choice other than to turn state's evidence on this one.

"Guys," I say, "Uncle Ben didn't die, because he never lived. We made him up with the rest of this story. We want kids to see what Peter learns the hard way. He is given a wonderful gift – spectacular spider powers beyond his wildest dreams. He could have used those abilities responsibly to do great things for the world, but instead he used them selfishly. And because of that, he lost his best friend, Uncle Ben. See, with great power comes great responsibility."

So the big guy says, "OK about Ben, Dad, but comics are not supposed to be educational." And the little guy pipes up that a spider should bite Flash so he can become Venom.

I am honored to have played a part in the creation of this magical tale. There are so many people that deserve so much credit and so many thanks. Brian is a spectacular writer and has become a real friend. Mark Bagley and Jung Choi, who worked with me on some beautiful Marvel card sets in the early 1990s, have been nothing short of amazing on ULTIMATE SPIDER-MAN. Joe Quesada, Ralph Macchio, and Brian Smith provided wise and wonderful insights. Key contributions in early development came from Bob Harras, Mark Powers, and Lou Aronica. And, as always, we Marvel web-heads tip our hats to Stan Lee and Steve Ditko.

During the past year, our master-inker Art Thibert's father has fallen ill and we dedicated #7 to him.

And now, I'd like a word with my Dad.

The tragedy of Spider-Man is not the death of Uncle Ben – or the unwitting role that poor powerful Peter played in his loss. The ultimate tragedy is that Ben up and died before Peter had the chance to tell him everything that every son should tell his Dad. Pop, I want to dedicate this book -- or at least my share of it – to you, for all you have brought to me, Jane, the boys and our whole family.

BILL JEMAS
PRESIDENT, MARVEL ENTERPRISES
P.S. Hi, Mom!